*The International Library of Sociology*

# COMPARATIVE CRIMINOLOGY
# A TEXT BOOK

*Founded by KARL MANNHEIM*

# The International Library of Sociology

## THE SOCIOLOGY OF LAW AND CRIMINOLOGY
### In 15 Volumes

To

THE STATE UNIVERSITY OF UTRECHT
from one of its
Honorary Doctors of Law
and to its Institute of Criminology
and its Founder and first Director
Professor W. P. J. Pompe

# Contents

CONTENTS

VOLUME TWO

PART FOUR: THE SOCIOLOGY OF CRIME

# Preface

It happened perhaps eleven years ago, not long before my retirement from the teaching of criminology in the University of London. One day, after I had just completed my first lecture of the new session and distributed copies of my, notoriously rather lengthy, reading list for the course, I was approached by a young girl student who, holding her copy in her hand, said in a voice which sounded polite but also rather determined: 'Sir, I am quite willing to read a book on criminology, but it must be only one, in which I can find everything required. Can you recommend such a book?' After some hesitation and with a strong feeling of guilt I replied that I could not comply with her request as there was no such book and she would probably have to read several of the items on my list, whereupon she silently and rather despondently withdrew.

As a university teacher of many years of experience in this field I could of course only too well understand that young people, confronted with ever-growing masses of material on a steadily multiplying number of subjects, were longing for a single, straightforward criminological Bible which could be trusted to relieve them of the need for an unending search in the darker corners of their university libraries. Some of these young beginners may not find it easy to grasp the plain truth that this endless search is a vital part of their academic education and they are inclined to hope for the coming of a 'textbook to end all other books'.

In the present book I have made no attempt to yield to such demands of that little student and others like her. I know that any such undertaking would be bound to fail. In fact, as the reader will see at once, in spite of its considerable length this book deals only with criminology in the narrower sense of the term, i.e., omitting penology. My original agreement with the publishers envisaged the writing of two textbooks, each of medium size, one on criminology and the other on penology, but in the course of my work I came to the conclusion that the real need now was for books which would deal far more fully with these subjects than could be done in two volumes of moderate size. Most American texts used in Britain and many other parts of the globe try to cope in one large volume with both subjects and, usually, in addition with the administration of criminal justice and the police. On a smaller scale and with the omission of these last-mentioned topics this has also been successfully done by my friend and former student Dr. Howard Jones in his *Crime and the Penal System*. In the circumstances, after a lengthy period of hesitation and heartsearching, I decided that instead of trying to copy what had already been well done in this field I should go my own way, i.e., set out to write a textbook on criminology only which would differ from its American and other predecessors in the following ways.

First, it would deal more fully than usual with such fundamental matters as the very concepts of crime and criminology and especially with the highly complex relationship between crime, the criminal law and certain burning moral issues of our time. This I have tried to do in Part One, especially in Chapter 2 of the first volume, which will, I expect, give rise to some controversy.

Secondly, this book would have several chapters on the methods of research used in criminological and penological investigations; chapters which, instead of the brief and scattered observations so far found in textbooks, would present a detailed and coherent picture of the various methods of approach, seen of course from the point of view of the statistical layman. I am fully aware of the many weaknesses and the rather elementary nature of this undertaking, which has been attempted with some diffidence mainly to fill an undeniable gap and *'pour encourager les autres'*. In addition to Part Two (Chapters 3 to 10), which deals exclusively with 'Research and Methodology', more space than customary has been given in several subsequent chapters to critical summaries of important researches carried out in various countries.

Thirdly, while in view of the dominant position held at present by American criminology much of the material presented in some of the sociological chapters of Part Four had to be taken from American sources, this does not apply to the book as a whole. It is the almost exclusive reliance on 'indigenous' material with only very few, not always systematic and well-balanced, glimpses at British and Continental European publications that diminishes the value of American textbooks to non-American readers. As the present writer has repeatedly stressed, especially in his *Group Problems in Crime and Punishment* (Part Three) and his Preface to *Pioneers in Criminology*, our indebtedness to American criminology is immense and lasting, but non-American countries possess not only their own crime problems but also their own criminological literature. No doubt, some of these problems can be brought considerably nearer to a solution or at least to a better understanding with the aid of American theories and experience. Others, however, have to be interpreted more independently and without a wholesale take-over of American ideas. Therefore, a special effort has been made in the present book to use not only British but also Continental criminological literature, especially German and to a smaller extent French and Italian, and occasionally also material neither European nor American. Naturally, limitations of space, language, and of access to the sources often created insurmountable obstacles, and it was for such reasons that the author had to concentrate mainly on those countries with which he is particularly familiar, i.e., Britain and Germany. Moreover, criminological literature has grown so enormously after the last World War that it is clearly impossible nowadays to be fully conversant with more than that of a few countries. It is with such important reservations that the present book is offered as a moderate contribution to international and comparative criminology and as an attempt to bridge some of the gaps between the various ways of approach. I realize that I may not have been very successful in this, but I regard the matter as important enough to justify the choice of the title. Many of us have been rightly impressed by Professor Sheldon Glueck's clarion call at the Hague Congress of 1960 for a 'Comparative Criminology' (now reproduced in *Ventures in Criminology*, Chapter 18). What he had in mind was something more ambitious and comprehensive than the comparative survey here carried out by one single worker: he understood by it the replication of researches 'designed to uncover etiologic *universals* operative as causal agents irrespective of cultural differences among the different countries'. In Professor Glueck's lecture several problems are mentioned as particularly suitable for, and in need of, a comparative approach by means of replication studies, e.g., the age curve of crime, the effect of growing industrialization and mobility, the somatotype study of young delinquents, and others. In the present book an attempt has been made to present some of the comparative material produced by research workers in various countries on a number of such topics, but so far usually without the co-ordinated teamwork and integration of research techniques which Sheldon Glueck had in mind and which is now slowly emerging from the work of the Gluecks, from that of Marshall B. Clinard, from the joint efforts of Marvin E. Wolfgang and Franco Ferracuti, and others. We non-Americans are likely to benefit from these efforts and we should clearly understand that, and why, our attitudes towards American criminology are—perhaps inevitably—ambivalent, i.e., a mixture of admiration, envy, inferiority feelings, criticism, and the unconscious desire to convince ourselves that, given the same opportunities, we could do just as well or possibly even better than our American colleagues. In 1963, the Assistant Director of the National Research and Information Center on Crime and Delinquency in New York, on his return from a study tour to a large number of European countries, reported how often he had been told in the course of his visits that American research workers were regarded as particularly fortunate, having at their disposal such lavish financial and other facilities for their work. While the comparative scarcity of research funds outside the U.S.A. may easily create a justifiable feeling of frustration, it is not the only source of that 'overly pessimistic attitude' encountered by this American observer. After all, any comparison of existing facilities for criminological research has to take into consideration the vastness of the American scene, the number and size of their universities and research organizations, the intensity and practical urgency of their crime problem, and their belief that they have a certain moral responsibility towards other countries, underdeveloped or not, to supply them with useful information. Perhaps equally important as the greater financial support and encouragement enjoyed by American research workers, though probably its natural consequence, is the more systematic nature of their research habits, which has no real counterpart in other countries. Once a plausible hypothesis has been put forward by responsible research workers in U.S.A. it is a matter of course that it should be tested and re-tested and the results be widely and critically discussed and wherever possible applied and applied again to the relevant practical problems. One has only to consider the systematic way in which prediction researches have been followed up in the United States as compared with similar investigations elsewhere. One of the few examples of cross-cultural re-testing of a criminological hypothesis outside the U.S.A. is the recent work on 'delinquent generations'. Now it is perfectly true that some of those carefully nursed problems and hypotheses of recent American criminological research may have hardly been worth the trouble taken with them, but even here one should not ignore the simple fact that the solution of the larger, more important and worthwhile problems can often be achieved, if at all, only by a piecemeal splitting up into smaller and smaller sub-problems. While, therefore, the sub- or sub-sub-problems in hand tend to appear less and less significant and the reports on the research done on them may become duller and duller, they may eventually constitute the basic material on which the structure of a new theory of real value to the progress of criminology can be erected.

In accordance with the existing 'distribution of powers' in our field most American textbooks on criminology, with a few important exceptions, have been written by sociologists, whereas elsewhere they have more often been the work of lawyers. The present writer has occasionally described himself as a cross between a lawyer and a 'sociological criminologist'; he is not a trained psychologist, psychiatrist, biologist, or statistician. From these limitations it follows that in the chapters of this book dealing with the last-mentioned subjects he has had to rely more than otherwise on the work of specialists in those disciplines. While this is a serious drawback, it is one which is shared by practically all other criminological writings. The criminologist who would be equally competent in every sector of his discipline does not yet exist, and most probably he will never exist. Perhaps the future will belong to teams of authors with different backgrounds of training, although this too may have its dangers.

Another problem exists for every writer of a textbook on criminology, whatever may be his credentials, i.e., how much space to give to certain legal aspects which have a close bearing on the subject. Many students of criminology, in Anglo-American countries even the majority, possess no legal training and cannot be expected to devote much time to matters of criminal law and procedure. On the other hand, there are certain criminological issues which cannot be properly treated without at least a modicum of knowledge of the corresponding legal aspects. This applies, for example, to the subject of mental abnormality, the legal implications of which have therefore been briefly discussed in a special Chapter 18; to the various forms of association in crime, where the legal side has at least been touched in Chapter 25. Moreover, as already indicated above, the relationships between the legal and the criminological concepts of crime and between the legal and the moral approach to criminological problems have been dealt with in Part One.

Our treatment of juvenile, including adolescent, delinquency, too, differs from that in most other textbooks, While the great significance of this subject is beyond doubt, the wisdom of separating it from that of adult crime by allocating it to a special section is less certain. The various criminological aspects involved are so closely related to those of their counterparts concerning adult crime that it is thought to be in the interest of the reader to treat both as far as possible together.

When deciding to concentrate in this book on criminology to the exclusion of penology two considerations have been in the mind of the author. First, criminology is not only the logical (though not historical) *prius*, it also provides the essential foundations without which the whole structure of penology would be left floating in mid-air. While this does not mean that each and every step in the field of penal reform should have to wait until all the mysteries of causation have been solved by criminological studies it does mean that the basic features of a future penal system cannot be sensibly mapped

out before agreement has been reached on the nature of the fundamental criminogenic factors in our society, and the responsibility
for them has been clearly established. To many this will seem post-
poning action until doomsday, but no action may occasionally be
better than ill-conceived improvisation. This applies to legislation
as well as to administration. Doctors have, of course, often to treat
patients without being able to make a proper diagnosis of their illness, but this is nothing but a makeshift imposed upon the medical
profession by sheer necessity and should not become the rule. While
the legislator and the practical penologist may find themselves in the
role of the medical practitioner more frequently than they would
wish to, their theoretical advisers should leave nothing undone to
supply them with the essential tools. Here again, however, a word of
caution does not seem to be out of place, especially in view of what
has been said before on the more fortunate position of American
research workers. Nobody who has followed the development of
criminology, as the present writer has, for the past fifty years or so
can deny that its progress has been spectacular. In particular after
the last World War publications, research projects, journals, societies, institutes, as shown in the Appendix, have greatly multiplied
almost everywhere. International, regional, and national congresses
and conferences abound. To a considerable extent, Britain has
participated in all these developments, although compared with the
expansion of similar disciplines criminology here, as in some other
countries, has still remained under a cloud and is still regarded as a
pseudo-science even by many of those who should know better. In
the circumstances it is not surprising that criminology has had its
regrettable share in the exodus of scholars of first-rate ability. However, the material side of scientific work, though of great importance,
is not everything. More and higher grants for research, more Institutes, more senior posts are no doubt highly desirable for the future
development of criminology, but they alone cannot be expected to
solve all existing difficulties. Not long ago an English cancer expert
issued a warning that in his field 'merely extending existing facilities
without rethinking their aim' was likely 'to prove a great waste of
money and a big disappointment' (Professor D. W. Smithers, *The
Times*, 24.11.1964). The position is not likely to be different in the
field of criminology. Here, too, research, in order to be useful, has
not only to tackle the really crucial problems, but it has to do so in
a spirit of resolution and realism. 'Parkinson's law' is lurking in
*every* corner of the vast structure of scientific endeavour.

As to my second consideration, penology, it has been argued not
entirely without reason, is so much in a state of flux at present, and
there is so much uncertainty about the value of each of the existing

methods of treatment, that the time is not yet ripe for an authoritative textbook which could provide the much-needed guidance to the practitioner. Nevertheless, just as the British Government has recently decided that the time is ripe for a 'fundamental review of the whole penal system' this may also be the moment for a comprehensive scholarly survey of the state of our knowledge on penal methods in Britain and abroad. It is my hope that a team of younger research workers may take up the torch and provide such a survey.

Every textbook writer can be expected to make it clear at once for whom his work is intended. In the present case I have in mind readers of widely differing qualifications and expectations. There is in the first place of course the serious research student wishing to familiarize himself with the existing literature and the principal methods of criminological research. I am addressing myself also, however, to the beginner who, bearing in mind what has been written earlier on in this Preface, is willing to devote more than the barest minimum of time and effort to the study of criminology. He may not wish to make full use of the documentation supplied in the Notes, but may prefer his own selection for which the Selected Reading Lists at the end of each volume will, I hope, be of some assistance, and he may also wish to skip the material printed in smaller type.

This book has, however, not been written only for university students and similar categories of predominantly academic users. The need for more than merely superficial information on a branch of knowledge struggling with problems of ever growing seriousness to the whole of modern society will be obvious to many members of legislative bodies, to judges, magistrates, lawyers, psychiatrists and psychologists engaged in work with criminals and juvenile delinquents, to penal administrators, probation officers and other social workers.

A few readers may object to the abundance of Notes, references and cross-references, and also perhaps to occasional repetitions. They should bear in mind that this is intended to be a textbook and a work of reference, and that it is often useful or indeed even essential to be reminded that the same problems may have to be treated from more than one angle. It should also be realized that the structure of the present book, containing as it does a separate methodological Part followed by the Sections dealing with the various 'Factors and Causes' necessitated a certain amount of repetition and cross-references. Moreover, it has been the wish of the author, as far as humanly possible, instead of trying to impose his personal views on the reader, rather to show how far these views were in agreement with those prevailing in the literature. All this requires much space.

I am most grateful to the publishers for having, ungrudgingly, given me all the space required for the purpose, and I wish to express my sincere thanks to them, especially to Mr. Norman Franklin who has been in charge of this publication, for their extraordinary patience and unfailing courtesy. The members of their staff who had to deal with my book have been most helpful, too.

Furthermore, I wish to acknowledge my indebtness to the librarian and staff of the British Library of Political and Economic Science in London, whose willing co-operation has made my task much easier, and to many friends and colleagues who, while watching the all-too-slow progress of my work, have through their interest and encouragement helped me to persist.

To University Secretarial Services and Research Publishers Limited, I am indebted for their valuable typing assistance.

Finally, my wife has, here as with all my previous books, given me her invaluable help and advice during the many years of preparing and writing this book.

HERMANN MANNHEIM

*London, Spring 1965.*

# PART ONE
# Introductory

# Chapter 1

## THE NATURE, SCOPE AND OBJECTS OF CRIMINOLOGY

By tradition, textbook writers are required first of all to define their subjects, but if they follow this tradition they are criticized for ignoring the fact that meaningful definitions cannot be produced without the knowledge which the textbook is expected to supply. In a way, such criticism is justified—our initial definition of 'Criminology', for example, will have to include words such as 'crime' and perhaps also 'punishment' whose real meaning can unfold itself only in the light of the material presented in later sections. It is generally agreed, however, that even with such limitations a preliminary working definition is indispensable as a provisional basis for further discussion.

### I. NATURE AND OBJECTS OF CRIMINOLOGY

Criminology, in the narrower sense in which it is used in this book, means the study of crime. In its wider sense it also includes penology, the study of punishment and of similar methods of dealing with crime, and of the problem of preventing crime by non-punitive measures. Provisionally, we can define crime in legal terms as human behaviour which is punishable by the criminal law. The study of such behaviour can assume three basic forms:

### 1. *The Descriptive Approach*

It can be purely descriptive. Criminology in this sense means the observation and collection of facts about crime and criminals: the various forms of criminal behaviour; how crimes are committed; their frequency in different places and at different times; age, sex and many other characteristics of criminals; and the evolution of a criminal career. This might be called the *phenomenology* or *symptomatology* of crime.

'Description' should, however, not be taken in the narrow sense of

3

the word. Moreover, while it is essential as the first step, while it can furnish indispensable material and build the foundations for further enquiries, it should not remain the *only* object of criminological study. First of all, as will be pointed out in our later sections on methodology, 'facts' cannot be collected at random; they have to be selected on the basis of a scientific hypothesis or of a whole system of hypotheses.[1] The research worker, just as the judge who has to decide a case, finds himself surrounded by myriads of 'facts'. In order to make a reasonable and useful selection of the facts they wish to collect they have to define their objects. For the judge this is done by the formal indictment (the French *acte d'accusation*, the German *Anklageschrift*); for the research worker its place is taken by the hypothesis. Neither the judge nor the research worker can adopt the technique of a small schoolboy who spends a few hours trying to catch 'butterflies' at random. 'Science cannot start with observations, or with the "collection of data", as some students believe. Before we can collect data, our interest in *data of a certain kind* must be aroused; the *problem* always comes first', writes Popper.[2]

Secondly, 'facts' have no meaning without interpretation, evaluation and general understanding, and we may need a considerable knowledge of life in general and experience of certain specific sectors of life to arrive at a correct interpretation of the facts collected by observation. To the man from the moon who knows nothing about the institution of Parliament, or the structure of an orchestra, even the most careful observation of the happenings at a parliamentary session or a concert will convey not the slightest understanding of the real meaning of what is going on there. The fact that two people embrace and kiss each other, or that one of them puts a chain around the other's neck, may mean many different things, and the correct interpretation requires an intimate knowledge of the mores and traditions of a whole civilization.[3] This is what is meant by *verstehen* as opposed to a mere *beschreiben* or even *erklären* in German psychology and sociology. The general significance of this contrast has been explained mainly by Wilhelm Dilthey[4] and Max Weber,[5] and its specific meaning for criminology has been recognized by Franz Exner.[6] Whether it is the assassination of Julius Caesar or the outrages committed by Mau Mau or Eoka, or a complicated business fraud, the criminologist's task is not only to describe and, if possible, to give a reasoned explanation, but also to 'understand'. What such a wider interpretation of the descriptive function of criminology involves will be shown more fully below, especially in Part II.

4

## 2. *The Causal Approach*

(*a*) The approach can also be of a causal nature, i.e. the interpretation of the observed facts can be used to search for the causes of crime, either in general or in individual cases. Having observed, for example, that murder means very often the killing of women by men, or that in an individual case it meant poisoning of a husband by his wife, we wish to discover the causes of these phenomena. This aspect is called the etiology of crime. Whereas in former times it was regarded as the most important function of criminology, the role of causal research has recently become a more controversial issue. 'One can continue to write about "Causation and its place in modern Society" indefinitely, if one fails to notice how rarely the word "cause" appears in the writings of professional scientists', says Stephen Toulmin.[7] And Leslie Wilkins, who is altogether highly critical of the causal approach, writes: '. . . simple models of "cause" and "effect" will not be adequate to explain social phenomena' (p. 133 of his *Social Deviance* referred to below in Chapter 3, Note 2).

Causal research in criminology has, of course, functions different from the criminal lawyer's search for the causal connection between the behaviour of an individual and a specific crime. To obtain a conviction it must be proved that there was a causal nexus between an act (or in certain circumstances, an omission) of the accused and the prohibited result. Needless to say that more than such causal nexus, i.e. in particular *mens rea*, guilt, is usually required to establish criminal responsibility, and as, thanks to this requirement of guilt, unreasonable results can usually be avoided, the criminal law can safely use a very broad conception of causal nexus.[8] It is only in cases of so-called strict responsibility, where no guilt, or only a diluted form of guilt, is required, that the need for a narrower interpretation of 'causal nexus' may arise which tries to distinguish between different kinds of causes (see in particular the theory of 'adequate cause' in German literature).[9]

What interests us here is that whereas the criminal law, in order to establish the criminal responsibility of individuals (or in exceptional cases of a corporation), is concerned with the causal link between the forbidden act (or omission) and the result, the work of the criminologist begins at a later stage, i.e. when that causal link has already been established. For him, the question is not 'Has A committed this crime?' but '*Why* has he committed this crime?' or 'Why do persons of this kind commit crime in general or crimes of this kind?' The answers to such questions may be of considerable practical importance to the criminal court at the sentencing stage, but they will hardly affect the first stage of its work, which is concerned with criminal

5

responsibility. In spite of this difference, certain basic problems of causality are, however, common to both criminal law and criminology, in particular that of how to define 'cause' itself.[10] Criminologists have, not without reason, been chided for employing an unscientific conception of causation,[11] and it is certainly true that more attention has been paid to the matter by criminal lawyers, especially on the Continent, than by criminologists.[12]

(b) What do we mean by 'cause'? Can criminologists, can social scientists in general borrow the concept of cause used by the natural sciences? Although still widely discussed by philosophers and the social sciences, this concept is, according to Bertrand Russell,[13] 'apparently not used in any advanced science', by which he means the natural sciences. One of the reasons may be that 'most empiricists have held that "cause" means nothing but "invariable antecedent"' whereas 'for most philosophers "cause" means something different'. As Russell admits, 'invariable antecedents' are extremely rare, as something may always intervene to prevent the expected result, and it is this possibility that has led physics 'to state its laws in the form of differential equations, which may be regarded as stating what is tending to happen'.[14] There is, however, by no means unanimity even among modern physicists as to the role of causal laws in the natural sciences. While for Max Planck the law of causality was still 'a fundamental hypothesis', to many of his younger colleagues the dependence of statistical laws upon causal laws is no longer an unchallengeable truth, and a statistical law is not necessarily regarded as 'the sign that there is a causal law that has not yet been discovered'.[15]

Popper stresses the difference between the causal explanation of an 'individual or singular specific event' and that of some regularity or law,[16] adding that in the first case causal explanation requires some universal laws, well tested and corroborated, plus the 'specific initial conditions' usually called the 'cause'. In this he follows John Stuart Mill, making it clear, however, that the latter understands by 'cause' both universal laws and singular events. Popper further stresses that while the theoretical sciences (natural or social) are mainly concerned with the discovery and testing of universal laws, the historical sciences are mainly interested in singular events, in 'how and why' questions. Sociology and criminology are interested in both the universal laws and singular events, in other words, they are both nomothetic and idiographic disciplines.[17]

John Stuart Mill distinguishes sufficient and necessary causes. If B invariably follows A whatever else may or may not happen, A would be called a sufficient, but not always a necessary, cause.[18] If, however, B follows A only if A and certain other factors are present, then A is a necessary, but not a sufficient cause. If B invariably follows A without any other factors being required, and A cannot be replaced by any other alternative, then A is both a sufficient and a necessary cause. As pointed out above, the criminal law usually employs the widest possible conception, which is that of the necessary, but not sufficient cause, i.e. 'a man can be said to have caused the *actus reus* of a crime if that *actus* would not have occurred without his participation',[19] although many other factors were also necessary to produce the result. As far as the interpretation of individual cases is concerned, the same conception can be used in criminology, and here it can be done without any of the risks of injustice referred to above. A kills B with a knife, when he meets him in a pub. According to the judgment of the court, this would not have happened but for the presence of the following factors: (*a*) A was drunk; (*b*) he was a man of unstable and irritable temperament and low intelligence; (*c*) B was a Negro and a member of a rival gang; (*d*) A's attention was drawn to his presence by C; (*e*) D gave him a knife; (*f*) E locked the exit through which B was trying to escape, and (*g*) it was an exceptionally hot and sultry day. All or most of these, and many other known and unknown factors, may have been necessary causes; none of them in isolation was a sufficient cause. Obviously, the criminal court will be more or less interested in each of these seven factors to assess the guilt and responsibility of A, C, D and E. The criminologist will concentrate on the effect of alcohol on a person of A's temperament, and on the role played by alcohol, low intelligence and mental instability, gang rivalry, racial enmity and heat on such an individual. In their interpretation of A's actions, both the criminal court and the criminologist will be greatly dependent on the general body of scientific knowledge existing on these subjects. Indeed, the very selection of the five factors, drink, mental instability, gang rivalry, race conflict and heat, out of a multitude of possible explanations has very likely been the result of certain views about factors generally regarded as criminogenic. Every age has its preconceived ideas on the subject which determine at least the initial selection of criminogenic factors. If this kind of preliminary selection is done with an open mind and clearly recognized as merely a beginning, it can do little harm. Surrounded as we are by myriads of potential causes, we have to start somewhere in our unending search for causal explanations. The real danger arises when we are satisfied with our findings and abandon our search at too early a stage. It has occasionally been suggested that in the selection of causal factors criminal courts (and criminologists alike) have so far concentrated mainly on those phenomena which are regarded as capable of being altered more easily than others,[20] or those which are nearer to the prohibited effect, i.e. the crime, to the disadvantage of the more remote ones; and to simpler factors at the expense of more complicated ones. This has not always been so, and in particular under the influence of the anthropological-biological school the emphasis has been on more or less unalterable factors.[21]

(c) What are the consequences to be drawn by criminologists from these philosophical definitions and distinctions?

First of all, there is the very simple but fundamental insight that in criminology there are no causes of crime which are both sufficient and necessary. There are only factors which may be 'necessary' to produce crime in conjunction with other factors. Neither crime in general nor any specific crime can ever be due to one single factor which would invariably produce this result. This means a death blow to all one-factor theories of crime, such as Lombroso's, and leads straight to William Healy's and Cyril Burt's theory of the multiplicity of factors,[22] which might have become a commonplace by now had it not been for the determined opposition of Edwin H. Sutherland and his followers. It is interesting to note that the most influential pronouncement of the basic theories of the Sutherland school, his *Principles of Criminology*,[23] first appeared ten years after Healy's and one year before Burt's classic works. While a discussion of his theory of 'differential association' has to be left for a later stage (Chapter 23), it is here that his views on causation have to find their place. Thanks to the devoted work of some of his former colleagues and students they can now be more clearly seen in their historical evolution.[24]

Sutherland accepted the distinction of necessary and sufficient causes, but being dissatisfied with the multi-factor theory, this 'catalogue of disparate and unco-ordinated "causes"',[25] his ambition was to discover ' "the" sufficient and necessary cause'. He believed he had found it in differential association. No concrete condition, such as being a Negro or a male, can, he stated, be a cause of crime; rather should we try to abstract from the varying concrete conditions factors universally associated with it. The tests he applied to his own theory were very strict, 'the one thing being needed to disprove an hypothesis is a single exception'. Perhaps the best exposition of this rigid theory of causation in criminology has been given by Alfred R. Lindesmith, who rightly argues in its favour that it requires constant testing and reformulation, whereas the 'defeatist' multiple causation theory evades the real issue by admitting exceptions in advance.[26] It is true that the challenge of the Sutherland school has been a valuable stimulus to further thought, but the task which it has set itself has so far proved insoluble. As we can now read in a posthumously published paper, intended for private circulation only and originally entitled 'The Swan Song of Differential Association',[27] after twenty years of

8

unremitting thought Sutherland himself seems to have become sincerely doubtful of the tenability of his single-factor theory. Other factors such as opportunities, intensity of need and available alternatives may, he indicates, play their part in the causation of crime in addition to differential association. This seems to mark the end, so far, of the search for a single cause, and the multiple factor approach, though only 'a makeshift to be tolerated' until something better has been found, now reigns supreme. Its eclectic nature is obvious. The longer the list of potentially causal factors which we have been able to collect in the course of our labours—whether it is Burt's 'more than 170 distinct conditions, every one conducive to childish misconduct',[28] or his 70 major factors, or his 'nine or ten subversive circumstances' operative in the case of each delinquent child, or whether it is Healy's more modest estimate of 3·5 factors per case—the picture seems to become less and less impressive with the growing thoroughness of our search. In the last resort, this was also the essence of Durkheim's criticism of Mill's theory which he regarded as 'a negation of the principle of causality'.[29] *Qui trop embrasse mal étreint*—is this true of the multiple theory of crime causation? Have we made much progress in our efforts first to isolate and then to combine the various causal factors? Perhaps the most conspicuous progress has been the negative one of excluding, by means of statistical techniques, a number of factors previously believed to have high causative value. The position is less satisfactory with regard to the positive side, i.e. obtaining scientifically more valuable evidence of the causative role of certain factors. We are here, at present, concerned not with the actual contents of such factors but with the current views on their causative nature. The customary technique—to be discussed more fully later on—is still to establish statistical correlations and then to assert that they prove cause and effect. It is this critical 'jump' from statistical correlation to causation which has been made hardly less hazardous through the research done in the course of this century. All we can claim is that we have perhaps become better aware of the existence and width of the gap. It would be presumptuous to assume that a master of research techniques such as Burt did not see the problem in all its ramifications when writing his *Young Delinquent*, but he gives at least the impression there that his statistical correlations are sufficient evidence of causal nexus. Writing fifteen years after Burt, McIver produced what is perhaps the clearest discussion of the processes which may gradually lead from mere correlation to the establishment of causal nexus,[30] but while leaving the details for later it should be stressed now that what these processes can achieve is merely to narrow, not to bridge, the gap. Correlations, as McIver says, are signposts, and as such of the greatest practical value,[31] but as far as causation is concerned we cannot argue that whatever the facts may be the signpost must be invariably right.

In *Unraveling Juvenile Delinquency* the Gluecks, consciously or not, have essentially followed McIver's prescriptions and, after throwing out factors showing no significant correlation, concentrate on those 'with probable causal significance'. While stressing that such correlations do not necessarily mean actual functional relationship, they nevertheless eventually produce their 'tentative causal formula or law of juvenile delinquency',[32] and one of these authors has in his otherwise masterly criticism of the theory of differential association only recently expressed his view that factors very frequently associated with delinquency make a 'very excessive' contribution to 'the causal scales'.[33] More cautious is the treatment in their *Physique and Delinquency*,[34] where the authors explain that they use terms such as 'causal' and 'criminogenic' not in the customary sense.

Perhaps the most obvious, but also the most important conclusion from the theory of multiple causation is the need to classify and bring some sort of meaningful order into the apparently chaotic lists of potentially causal factors found to bear a statistically significant correlation to crime. This can be done in a quantitative sense by classifying factors according to the degree of correlation, and, equally indispensable, in a qualitative sense by distinguishing primary and secondary or pre-disposing and precipitating factors and, finally, by attempting to combine various factors according to their nature. This recent search for a synthesis, for combinations, concatenations and permutations, is in fact the concession which the multiple causation theory has inevitably had to make to Sutherland and his followers, and it may eventually bridge the gap between the two extremes. Moreover, the more successful we are in our qualitative approach the more are we likely to 'understand'.[35] In passing, it may also be added that the controversy between the causal and the descriptive approach has, in recent years, become particularly acute in the field of prediction research (see below, Chapter 7).

In his recent book *Social Deviance* (see below, Chapter 3, Note 2) Wilkins has expressed the view that the theory of multiple causation 'can hardly be dignified by the term theory'; it 'does not facilitate the deduction of any hypotheses or practical consequences that are of any help whatsoever' (pp. 36–7). Rightly regarding it with Popper as an essential criterion of any theory that one should be able to disprove it he argues that the multiple causation theory cannot be proved wrong and is therefore no theory but 'at best an anti-theory which proposes that no theory can be formed regarding crime'. He further uses the argument that on the basis of the multiple causation theory crime preventing measures would have to be so all-embracing as to be entirely impracticable (p. 126); moreover, it would be impossible to discover which of the many preventive measures put into operation had been effective (if any). The latter assertion is of course true if all, or several, of these measures would be put into operation at the same time; it is not correct, however, if one is tried out after the other. Moreover, Wilkins's assertion is not an argument against the scientific correctness of the multiple causation theory; it merely shows once more how utterly complicated and confusing the search for the causes of crime still is. Nor does Wilkins show why it should be theoretically impossible to prove that theory to be wrong; all one would have to do is to take one by one the alleged causal factors and prove that, with one exception, they are actually not causal factors, the only exception being of course the factor described by the differential association theory.—To sum up this part of our discussion: Why not admit, first, that the theory of multiple causation is a real theory, but not an ideal one, and that improvements—or if possible refutation—would be highly desirable, and, secondly, that differential association has to take its place side by side, not above, all other theories of criminological causation?

In conclusion, three final points should be made in this preliminary exploration of present-day views on crime causation:

First, as mentioned above, when building up our lists of factors statistically associated with crime and therefore potentially causative, we have to realize that our initial selection of factors for statistical analysis depends on our previous and almost inevitably preconceived notions about potentially causal factors.[36] This means that factors which do not fit into the picture painted by our personal bias will be more easily ignored and given less opportunity for further examination than those which appeal to us in view of our, perhaps unconscious, attitudes, our *Weltanschauung*. As Arnold Rose and others have pointed out, our personal value premises play an important, often even decisive, part in the very selection of our topics for research[37] (see below, Chapter 3).

Second, the question cannot be evaded of whether the time may not have come to discard the search for the causes of crime altogether and to replace the eclectic and to many scholars meaningless theory of multiple causation by some less ambitious but more practical formula such as statistical correlations, 'Decision theory',[38] 'Categoric risks'[39] and the like. In the present writer's view this step would be too radical. The search for causes has been an essential element of the work of social scientists for too long and still possesses an individual appeal too strong to dispense with it at a time when, except for certain limited practical purposes such as prediction techniques, those substitutes have not yet been adequately developed to fill the gap. 'The nature of a phenomenon'—wrote Durkheim sixty years ago[40]—'is much more profoundly got at by knowing its causes than by knowing its characteristics only, even the essential ones.' On the other hand, the practical penologist cannot be expected to wait with his preventive, predictive, protective and curative measures until the causes have been found,[41] just as medical practitioners may have to act before they are able properly to diagnose.[42] Moreover, we have to be aware not only of the difficulty of proving causal nexus but also of its limited practical value for treatment and prevention. An offence may have been due to certain specific and easily discoverable causes, but once it has been committed the latter may have spent their force, and the individual's future behaviour may be dominated by other factors (see below, Chapter 7). This is particularly likely in the case of juveniles whose personalities sometimes undergo rapid changes, and it may considerably affect the prognosis of recidivism.

Third, and arising from this, if statistics cannot prove causal relation, can this be done by the other extreme, the fullest possible individual case study? Or can we perhaps expect 'summit talks' between these two parties to lift the iron curtain still separating causation from correlation? The answer has to wait for the discussion of the various research techniques in Part II.

## 3. *The Normative Approach*

It has already been said elsewhere (*Group Problems*, pp. 261-4) that criminology is both an 'idiographic' discipline studying facts, causes and probabilities in individual cases and a 'nomothetic' discipline aiming at the discovery of universally valid scientific laws and uniformities or trends. The second part of this statement leads, naturally, to an examination of the nature of criminological 'laws' and trends. What is the difference between such 'laws' and mere trends, and between them and 'legal' or 'juridical' laws? Is criminology, in the same sense as jurisprudence, a 'normative' science? Or are we mistaken in assuming that legal laws are 'normative'? Closer scrutiny of the literature shows that not too much should be taken for granted in this field. On the one hand, with regard to the nature of juridical laws, the traditional view that such laws, in particular criminal law, are commands, rules, norms, imperatives, ordering the citizen to act or not to act in a certain way,[43] has been assailed from various quarters in the course of the present century. First, a distinction has often been made between a legal provision such as 'whoever steals will be punished', which, it has been argued, is nothing but a statement of fact, and the 'norm' behind it forbidding such an act (Binding's so-called *Normentheorie*). Secondly, even as far as the legal norm itself is concerned its normative character has often been disputed. Emphasis has been placed upon the 'law shaping force of custom and habit' and the 'normative power of the factual' (Georg Jellinek's *Normative Kraft des Faktischen*),[44] i.e. what has been done over a long period of time will eventually be regarded as lawful. Moreover, important schools of legal philosophy, especially in the United States, such as the positivist and pragmatic schools, and the 'realist' movement, interpret law not as a body of norms but merely as a body of generalized predictions of what the courts will actually do in individual cases brought before them, which makes legal laws less different from the laws of the natural sciences than generally assumed.[45] Our criticism of this view is in brief that, while the function of law as a predictive instrument is of great practical importance, it is in no way incompatible with its equally important normative functions.

On the other hand, the difference between criminological laws, should they actually exist, and the laws of the natural, social and legal sciences is also in need of discussion. If, in opposition to the 'realist' view of law, we believe in the normative character of legal provisions, the contrast between the latter and any other kind of 'law' may seem to be clear. Criminology is not a normative, but a factual discipline. However, as the normative character of juridical laws has been questioned so has the non-normative character of criminology been doubted by other writers. H. Bianchi in particular has recently asserted that, since crime is a normative concept, this 'forces criminology to make a study of norms'[46] and it is therefore a normative discipline. This, however, seems to betray a confusion between the study of norms, which is in itself not normative, and the creation, establishment and use of norms, which characterize a normative discipline. It is a matter of opinion and terminology whether the scope of criminology should be widened so as to include *Kriminalpolitik, politique criminelle*, i.e. the questions of what *ought* to be done to reform the criminal law and the penal system. As the writer has already argued elsewhere[47] it is preferable to treat this as a separate discipline based upon the factual findings of the criminologist and penologist, whereas criminology should remain a non-policy-making discipline, 'piecemeal social engineering' which regards the 'ends' as beyond its province. This does, of course, not prevent the criminologist from advocating a certain measure of legal and administrative penal reform, but he has to do it as a politician or an ordinary citizen and voter rather than in his capacity of criminologist (see also below, Chapter 3, p. 78).

Having defined criminology as a factual, non-normative discipline we now have to examine the existence and nature of criminological 'laws'. Obviously, the position must be essentially the same here as in sociology or psychology. As we have already seen, most of these so-called criminological laws are attempts to formulate either a casual nexus or at least a statistical association between certain factors and crime. Take, for example, Adolphe Quetelet's 'thermic law of delinquency', according to which crimes against the person are more frequent in warm climates and seasons, whereas crimes against property are more prevalent in cold climates and in winter, or Prince Peter Kropotkin's even more ambitious formula using temperature and humidity to predict the exact number of future homicides in a given country,[48] or if we use Popper's way of formulating natural as well as sociological laws,[49] for example, 'You cannot have wars without an aftermath of crime'. It will be clear that Quetelet's thermic law is nothing but the precise formula asserting a high positive correlation between heat and crime against the person and, on the other hand, between a cold temperature and crime against property. In Chapter 11, an attempt will be made to interpret these correlations and to assess their significance, but they are not 'laws', but merely trends which could be manipulated and changed through a suitable administrative machinery.[50] If, for example, the police force were greatly strengthened and unemployment benefits and similar measures increased during the winter months, crime against property might easily become lower than in summer. It may be more difficult to devise effective crime-preventing counter-measures against the criminogenic after-effects of wars, unless we assume that future atomic wars will do their work so thoroughly that nobody will be left to commit crimes. As the whole of our discussion in the present book will show, criminology is not yet able to produce real 'laws'.

## II. THE SCOPE OF CRIMINOLOGY

Should criminology, as suggested by Vouin-Léauté,[51] also include the study of the reaction of society against crime? It might be argued that this belongs, strictly speaking, to the domain of the sociology of the criminal law, but it has to be admitted that the reaction of society against crime is at least as important as the reaction of the state which is the subject-matter of penology. They are both strongly criminogenic forces and should therefore be studied by criminologists.

Even more controversial is the question whether criminology should confine itself to the study of crime in the legal sense or whether it should also cover anti-social behaviour which is legally not treated as a crime. The principal exponent of the broader view is Thorsten Sellin,[52] and it is shared by the present writer.[53] This view has been frequently criticized, among others recently by Vouin-Léauté[54] who argue that as all the more serious anti-social acts are anyhow legally crimes, the principle de minimis non curat praetor should be accepted by criminologists, too, in order to avoid a serious discrepancy between criminal law and criminology. Moreover, they believe that criminology is so much dependent on the machinery of the criminal law to supply it with its material of study that the cases remaining outside that machinery would hardly be worth bothering about. These arguments are hardly valid, first because the present controversy is not concerned with acts which, though crimes, are not dealt with by the organs of the State—that such acts if they can be reached are the legitimate subject of criminological study has never been doubted—but with anti-social behaviour not punishable by the criminal law. Secondly, whether or not the current legal systems of all countries, or at least of the western world, actually cover all those forms of human behaviour which should be dealt with by the criminal law is an assumption which cannot be proved without thorough examinations of the whole field at present left outside. It is the scientific right of the criminologist to carry out such examinations that forms the object of the controversy. Clearly, the wider our concept of crime, the narrower the scope of this controversy; if we use a concept—as Bianchi does[55]—embracing violations not only of legal and social, but also of religious and moral norms, there will be hardly any need to extend the scope of criminology beyond the frontiers of this concept. There is still another point in favour of Sellin's view which seems so far to have escaped notice. Most systems of criminal law recognize —either explicitly as in most continental countries, or implicitly as in Anglo-American law—the principle *nullum crimen sine lege*, which means that behaviour no less blameworthy than behaviour falling under the criminal law can often not be dealt with as crime. In such cases it is for the criminologist, who is not bound by that principle, to supply the factual material required by the legislator to bring about a change in the law.

Even those who, keeping within the limits of the criminal law, prefer the narrower definition of criminology will agree that when studying a certain type of criminal behaviour it is not infrequently advisable to depart from the legal definition. In this way, not only greater uniformity of criminological studies can be achieved in spite of national differences in legal definitions, but the object of such studies can be more easily reached unfettered by perhaps antiquated legal formulations. It was for such reasons that Donald R. Cressey, in his *Other People's Money*, found it necessary to replace the concepts of 'embezzlement', 'forgery' and others, as used in American penal codes by a uniform, more sociological concept of 'criminal violation of financial trust'.[56] Similarly, the criminological study of murder should not follow too slavishly the definition of murder given in this or that particular penal code or statute (see p. 33 below).

Should criminology include the study of the technical processes applied by the police and criminal courts to obtain evidence of the commission of a certain crime by a certain individual or number of individuals, i.e. techniques such as dactyloscopy, photography, toxology, or the application of blood tests, 'lie detectors', hypnosis, narco-analysis? In brief, should it include criminalistics as the study of 'criminal identification'? Or should it be confined to the study of crime in general and of criminals after they have been found guilty or of those whose crimes are not in dispute although there has been no formal finding of guilt? Clearly, we are here concerned with two different aspects of the crime problem, both of equal importance, and no logical reasons can be adduced to exclude criminalistics, the French *Criminalistique*, the German *Kriminalistik*, from the work of the criminologist. To the man-in-the-street, those technical aspects which, all too narrowly, he relates mainly to detective work, or popularly 'Scotland Yard', are the only part of criminology of which he is aware, which he understands and respects. In one country, Austria, the study of criminalistics has for the past sixty years been regarded not only as an integral but even as the most important element of criminology. Hans Gross (1847–1915), first an examining magistrate, later a public prosecutor, a high court judge, and finally a professor of criminal law in various Austrian universities, was the founder of this school. His most important works were his *Handbuch für Untersuchungsrichter als System der Kriminalistik* (1st ed. 1893), later called *Handbuch der Kriminalistik* (8th ed. 1944 ff.) and his *Kriminalpsychologic* (1st ed. 1898, 2nd ed. 1905). In 1921 he founded the first Institute of Criminalistics (the K. K. Kriminalistische Universitätsinstitut) in Graz, and already in 1898 he published his periodical, the *Archiv für Kriminalanthropologic und Kriminalistik* (later called *Archiv für Kriminologie*), of which more than one hundred volumes have so far been published. His work has been continued at the universities of Graz and Vienna by his principal followers, the late Ernst Seelig, Roland Grassberger[57] and others. In Vienna, the University Institute for the Universal Penal Sciences and for Criminalistics was established in 1923, later called University Institute for Criminology. Both Institutes are administered by the faculties of law and political science and include criminalistics in their plans of studies.[58]

In several other countries, in particular Belgium,[59] Brazil,[60] France,[61] Italy,[62] and the United States (mainly in the School of Criminology of the University of California at Berkeley), the study of criminalistics is also to some extent included in the curriculum of the universities. It is different, as a rule, in Great Britain and Western Germany, perhaps not so much for reasons of principle, but because it is felt that this aspect of criminology is better left to the police colleges which possess the technical equipment needed.[63] Special care should of course be taken to uphold full scientific standards in the teaching of these subjects.

Other auxiliary disciplines, such as forensic medicine and the psychology of criminal procedure (judges and witnesses), are also treated in different ways in individual countries.[64]

In the textbooks of criminology, the auxiliary disciplines are, with few exceptions,[65] not included.

As most criminal acts, with the exception of very trivial cases, have to be interpreted in the light of the offender's personality and environment (see below, Part III) criminology has to depend on the findings of many other disciplines, notably anthropology, medicine, psychology, psychiatry, sociology, law, economics and statistics. As history shows, practically all contributions to its development have been made by scholars belonging to one or other of these disciplines, and this will to some extent no doubt also be true in the future. It may, therefore, quite legitimately be asked why it has been regarded as necessary to establish criminology as a new and independent branch of knowledge, and whether its representatives are real 'criminologists' or merely psychologists, sociologists, jurists, and so on, in disguise. The answer to the first question is simple; those other disciplines, important and indispensable as their contributions to the common pool have been, can in fairness be expected to pay only limited attention to the specific problems of crime. The psychology of crime will never form more than one section out of many in the whole of psychology, and the position is the same in other branches of knowledge. As long as the choice of subjects for research and the decisive voice in the preparation of syllabi and timetables for teaching purposes have to be left to the representatives of other disciplines, the field will be covered only partially and in a casual and badly balanced manner, especially as each of these various disciplines is really interested only in those aspects of crime nearest to it. The literature of criminology shows unmistakable traces of this lack of balance. Moreover, the methods of research and the scientific language employed, for example, by psychiatrists differ so greatly from those of sociologists and lawyers that without outside help they may not even fully comprehend each other's work.[66] It is not here suggested that criminologists will ever be able to acquire the all-round training needed to master all those different techniques and languages, nor would they even be wise to indulge in futile attempts to become 'Jacks of all trades'.[67] What they might possibly be capable of achieving is a more comprehensive understanding of the peculiarities and the mental climates of each of those disciplines than possessed by their average representatives, and by doing so they might eventually provide a neutral territory as a meeting place for the exchange of ideas on criminological issues. This is in fact the aim of certain existing organizations, such as the International Society of Criminology.

All this shows that the need for cross-disciplinary teamwork is particularly urgent in criminology.[68] In theory this has become universally accepted; in actual practice it still very often remains a distant ideal to which mere lip-service is paid at inter-disciplinary congresses and conferences.

Even more complicated is the relationship between criminology and the scientific study of the criminal law which, unlike those other disciplines, concentrates exclusively on the subject of crime and its punishment and treatment. In *Group Problems in Crime and Punishment* this relationship and also the line of demarcation between criminology, *Kriminalpolitik*, the sociology of the criminal law and sociological jurisprudence have been discussed at length,[69] and there is no need to go into the matter again. Reference may be made, however, to H. Bianchi's recent attempt to establish criminology as a 'metascience' to the criminal law,[70] i.e. a science of wider scope whose terminology can be used to clarify the conceptions and problems of the latter. Far from being a mere auxiliary to the criminal law it is therefore superior to it. Provided the distinction between criminology and *Kriminalpolitik* (see above) is preserved we can accept Bianchi's view.

One of the many fields where criminology can be used to widen the horizon of the criminal law is the international one. Being less restricted by national boundaries than the law, the criminologist can more easily work within an international framework.

So far the existence of criminology as an independent scientific discipline, with criminologists as its representatives, has been taken for granted. In fact, it has repeatedly been queried not only by outsiders but even by some of the most outstanding workers in this field. In his *General Report on the Sociological Aspects of Criminology* submitted to the Second International Congress of Criminology in Paris, 1950, Thorsten Sellin has coined the often-repeated phrase of criminologists as 'kings without a country', being nothing but sociologists, psychiatrists, jurists, and so on, with the courtesy title of criminologists. Against this, Van Bemmelen has however pointed out that, after all, no branch of science can nowadays thrive without the aid of others and also that criminology possesses a true king in the person of the judge, who decides the individual case.[72] While agreeing with his first argument, we are not convinced by the second. Scientific issues, unlike practical ones, cannot be settled by judicial decisions, which, moreover, can cover only comparatively small sections of the whole field. However, true as Sellin's phrase might have been in the past, criminology has in recent years made considerable progress from colonial to 'dominion' status and further towards complete independence. No longer are we entitled, as Erwin Frey could still do in his remarkable critical survey of the work of the Paris Congress of 1950, to maintain that 'there exists at bottom no direct criminological research . . ., and criminology is in fact nothing but the scientific clearing house between the various other disciplines'.[73] With increasing facilities for criminological teaching and research, the latter can now often be done in the open, without having to use one of the back doors provided by other disciplines. The exceptions are largely due to the prejudices and guilt feelings of society which make it difficult for the average citizen squarely to face the existence of the crime problem within the community and to tackle it in a scientific spirit. However, this, as the whole idea of 'kings without a country', is after all only a passing phase without any future, and the criminologist, to stress his dependence on other disciplines and on public opinion, might rather be compared to the President of the United States. No such metaphors can, of course, decide the real issue whether or not criminology can already claim to be an independent branch of science. This is a difficulty in no way peculiar to it. Sociology, in particular, though slightly more consolidated and powerful, has still to contend with similar scruples. 'Has sociology in fact got a special contribution of its own to make, a body of knowledge, an angle of vision, a discipline and a method, or is it just a hotch-potch of fragments drawn from other fields?' asked T. H. Marshall in 1946.[74] In the case of both disciplines our answer can be re-assuring. On behalf of criminology it can even be claimed that in recent years it has not only been able to embark on research of a cross-disciplinary character making it less dependent on any single one of the participating disciplines, but is also beginning to repay old debts by producing control group material of direct value to the other social sciences. In spite of this on the whole optimistic tone of our discussion we have to admit that, in Great Britain at least, progress towards the formation of an independent profession of criminologists has been very erratic and generally unsatisfactory. As we wrote a few years ago (*Society*, London, 1962, p. 284), it is still 'too dangerous for young men to be branded as narrow specialists in a subject which may well turn out to be a "blind alley". . . . This is most unfortunate. Our discipline is still in too precarious a position to allow itself to become unduly crowded with, and dependent on, birds of passage finding temporary shelter within its territory but constantly longing for a warmer climate.'

The scientific character of criminology has further been doubted because, it has been claimed, the treatment of offenders is an art rather than a science. As pointed out in an earlier publication,[75] this

19

argument is based upon a fallacy. In the treatment of offenders, as in that of physical or mental illnesses, both art and science have to play their part. It would even be mistaken to believe that the theoretical part of criminology is the exclusive domain of science and the practical treatment of offenders that of art. The two elements are inextricably mixed in both fields.

What makes a subject 'scientific' is far from clear and undisputed. Is it, as Malinowski thought, dependent upon 'the existence of general laws, a field for experiment or observation, . . . control of academic discourse by practical application'?[76] Is it the 'systematic collection of related facts' (Cantor)?[77] Is the emphasis on the availability and application of scientific method ('primacy of method') or on the existence of a worthwhile subject in need of independent study ('primacy of subject matter') even if adequate techniques of study are not yet available?[78] Or is it simply the fact 'that it has been . . . accepted into the scientific tradition'?[79] If this scientific tradition should not yet exist in this field, it is for the criminologist to build it up. Even in 1933 it was only with some exaggeration that Michael and Adler, in their devastating criticism of the scientific foundations of criminology, stated an empirical science of criminology to be impossible at the time because of the non-existence of psychology and sociology as empirical disciplines.[80] In the meantime, such a completely negative attitude has become still less justified.

Practical needs are particularly strong in the study of crime and punishment, and it is for this reason that criminology has sometimes been regarded as a technology rather than a scientific discipline. As Sellin has pointed out, there is here a 'clear-cut need for both', the work of the scientist aiming 'at the discovery of constants in the relationships among certain defined facts', and that of the technologist concerned with the 'adaptation of knowledge to the social needs of the moment'.[81] We cannot, however, accept his conclusion that the term 'criminology' should not include these technological aspects. Not only the study of criminalistics in the sense of the Viennese school might well be included but with even greater justification the study of the 'techniques required to apply scientific . . . knowledge to the treatment of criminals or the prevention of crime'. In fact, with the growing interest in more scientific methods now shown by many practical penologists it will often be difficult and invidious to distinguish between the scientific and the technological side of criminology, which latter stands much to gain from the closest contact with the practical application of criminal justice. 'Piecemeal social technology' (Popper)[82] presents the theoretical criminologist with many problems of which he would otherwise be unaware.

Being a non-legal discipline, criminology bears a stronger international flavour than the study of the criminal law which has often, especially in the past, tended to be parochial in its outlook. In the legal sphere, useful work has been done in the past quarter of a century, however, by the International Association of Penal Law and its journal, the *Revue internationale de Droit Pénal*. Criminology, unhampered by the limits of any national legislation, can afford to tackle its problems in a world-wide spirit. Actually, the opportunity has not always been taken, in part because of language difficulties, in part because of the varying nature of the problems concerned and the existing contrasts in approach and outlook. It is symptomatic of recent changes in the right direction that M. Jean Pinatel, the distinguished General Secretary of the International Society of Criminology, has in his text book *Criminologie* (Paris, 1963) deliberately and not without success attempted to give wider scope to international literature than had previously been customary in Continental criminological writings. As will be shown in subsequent chapters, different countries or regions have often been interested in different aspects of crime, have employed different methods of study and produced greatly differing answers. As a consequence, we are not seldom faced with the spectacle of several national or regional disciplines instead of one united body.[83] The work of the two international criminological organizations, the International Society of Criminology, founded before the Second World War, and the International Society of Social Defence, established in 1946, to some extent reflects these differences in emphasis.

# Chapter 2

## CRIME: ITS MEANING IN RELATION TO LAW, RELIGION, CUSTOM AND MORALS

Crime is, first of all, a legal conception, human behaviour punishable under the criminal law. It is, however, much more than only a legal phenomenon. The frontiers of criminology would not be so difficult to define as will have appeared from the previous chapter if there would not be so many doubts as to the meaning of its fundamental concept, crime. It is a dilemma confronting probably all scientific disciplines that they are engaged in an unending search for the definition of their basic concepts. Kant's famous dictum: *Noch suchen die Juristen eine Definition zu ihrem Begriffe vom Recht*[1] (Jurists are still trying to find their definition of 'law'), was, as the context shows, meant neither in a disparaging sense nor as pointing to a weakness peculiar to the science of law. The same lack of clear-cut definition characterizes such other basic concepts as health and disease, or electricity, or society, and it has even been maintained as a general proposition that it is not for the specialist but for the philosopher to provide all such definitions.[2] In this sense, too, criminologists may find their right challenged to be masters in their own house.

It is the object of this chapter to discuss and clarify the concept of crime in its relation to law and other forms of social control of human behaviour.

### I. CRIME AND THE LAW

While the legal definition of crime as something punishable under the criminal law appears from the outside to be more precise, though less informative, than any other definition, closer scrutiny reveals certain weak spots even here.

*1. The legal term 'Crime' is too wide. Should 'Public Welfare Offences' or similar ones be excluded from it and if so what should be the legal consequences?*

(a) First, it has been argued that the notion of crime as covering everything punishable under the criminal law has become too wide, notably in legal systems which, as English law, make but little distinction in principle between serious crimes and petty offences. Felonies, misdemeanours and summary or petty offences, it is true, are distinguished in certain technical, especially procedural, respects, and there is also the division, now generally considered to be of little value, into indictable and non-indictable offences. This, however, does not alter the fact that 'the word "crime" is properly applicable to all these', even where the maximum penalty can be only a fine.[3] In the French and German Penal Codes so far a similar tripartite classification has been used, i.e. *crimes, délits, contraventions,* and *Verbrechen, Vergehen, Übertretungen* respectively, distinguished only according to the severity of the penalties which can be imposed, with the consequence that, apart from the question of punishment, there is very little difference in principle between the most serious and the most trivial violations of the criminal law. The widespread feeling that this lack of adequate differentiation is either unfair to those guilty of petty offences, or weakens the stigma of very serious crimes, has led to a number of attempts to classify violations of the criminal law according to various terminological or material criteria. The following are the most important of them. For crimes committed by juveniles the term 'delinquency' is now generally used to express the feeling among the community that altogether different considerations have to be applied to them than to those applied to adult offenders. The same, though to a lesser degree, is true with regard to 'female delinquency'. Regardless of the age and sex of the offenders and on a wider basis, there has been a tendency in several countries to split off from the main body of 'real' offences certain others mainly introduced into the penal codes in the course of the present century to serve the requirements of the modern industrial mass age and the Welfare State. In so far as the legal-philosophical and legislative-technical details of this development are concerned considerable differences can be noticed between the Anglo-American systems and those of the Continental and non-European countries concerned. It has to be admitted, though, that there is hardly any uniformity even within the latter group.[4] Some of these countries, notably Western Germany, Austria, and a number of Swiss Cantons,[5] Poland, Argentina, and Ethiopia (Code of 1957), possess separate codifications or at least separate statutes dealing with the so-called administrative offences, leaving the latter to the competence of administrative authorities. Other countries, while recognizing that certain categories of minor offences are in need of special treatment by the law, do not go so far as to hand them over to the administration. As an example of the first category, in Western

Germany a statute of the 25th March 1952[6] provides that acts which are punishable only by *Geldbussen*, i.e. non-criminal fines, are called *Ordnungswidrigkeiten* and have to be dealt with by administrative authorities. Their characteristic, it has been stated, is not that they are regarded as less important than criminal offences but that they are essentially different from them, violations not of norms for the protection of the fundamental values of society but of technical provisions useful in the interest of a well-ordered administration.[7] Punishment is therefore not necessarily dependent on guilt (§ 11 of the statute), but no *Geldbusse* can be imposed in case of excusable error (§ 12), and the offender has always the right of appeal to a judge (§ 54). Moreover, the same act may, according to circumstances, especially its gravity, be dealt with either by the ordinary court or by the administrative authority (§ 1). The German system therefore represents a compromise between judicial and administrative criminal justice. In view of the passing of the Act of 1952 the new Western German Draft Penal Code deals only with crimes and misdemeanours, not with contraventions.[8]

(*b*) In Anglo-American law attempts to distinguish a special category of 'strict (or absolute) liability offences' have been made for more than a century.[9] These offences have been largely identified as so-called *public welfare offences*, a name not very happily chosen since, as Glanville Williams has said, all offences are, in a sense, public welfare offences. In recent years the term 'regulatory offences' has therefore often been preferred. Their number and practical importance have immensely increased in recent years with the development of an administration grappling with the complicated problems of the modern mass-age and the Welfare State, their elephantine economy and the corresponding maze of laws and regulations. It has been argued, therefore, that this type of offence cannot be dealt with effectively in accordance with the traditional principles of criminal law and procedure which are still based on the ideas of moral guilt and *in dubio pro reo*. Their mass character, the pettiness of most of them if taken individually, contrasted with their dangerousness to society if considered in their totality, seem to make it impossible to apply to them those standards of thoroughness and fairness which we have come to expect from any civilized system of criminal justice. As Francis A. Allen has put it in a brilliant lecture on 'The Borderland of the Criminal Law':[10] 'It is more than poetic metaphor to suggest that the system of criminal justice may be viewed as a weary Atlas upon whose shoulders we have heaped a crushing burden of responsibilities relating to public policy in its various aspects. This we have done thoughtlessly without inquiring whether the burden can be effectively borne.' On the other hand, to ignore those traditional standards even in a limited field of criminal justice might easily undermine the whole fabric unless certain clearly defined criteria can be established which would show beyond doubt that the offences to which the principle of strict liability applies are different from all others not only in numbers but in fundamental issues. Various criteria have been suggested to distinguish the group of public welfare offences from the rest. First, according to Glanville Williams, they are mainly concerned with sale, possession, master and servant relations and road traffic.[11] There is, however, as Jerome Hall suggests,[12] also a 'great additional miscellany' that can hardly be brought under any classification. In fact, with regard to the characteristic features of this very important branch of legislation no further general formula can probably be used than that they owe their origin to the awakening concern of the modern State for the positive well-being of its members and to its growing realization that this well-being can be jeopardized in many ways not understood by former generations. It was only natural that this discovery should have led to the creation of a multitude of new criminal offences since, old-fashioned and clumsy as it was, the criminal law offered itself as one of the few instruments ready at hand to deal with such an emergency. No other body of systematic legal thinking was available to examine the possibilities of social control through alternative, in particular administrative, techniques. It was one of the principal recommendations in the present writer's *Criminal Justice and Social Reconstruction* that such administrative techniques should, in certain sectors, gradually relieve the criminal law of a burden which had become too heavy for it to be borne unaided.[13] This was argued mainly with reference to forms of anti-social behaviour, such as monopolistic conspiracies, too complex and powerful to be fought with the weapons of the criminal law alone. As we have seen, the corresponding problem arises at the other end of the scale with reference to offences often regarded as too trivial to be the concern of the criminal law, and here, too, it is only natural that attempts should have been made to shift the burden, which is here one of numbers rather than of complexity, on to the administration.

(c) This mass character of public welfare and similar offences, which have become far more frequent than all other offences put together, is another characteristic which, it has been said, justifies the demand for special treatment. The requirement of guilt, even in its milder form of criminal negligence, has often been regarded as obsolete by the legislator or the courts, and, as indicated above, it is here that the danger lies. No doubt, the large numbers of these offences impose a strain on criminal justice which might become intolerable if each case be treated 'according to rule', but from the point of view of the individual defendant any relaxation of standards would be a denial of justice just as a rise in certain other types of offence can be no real justification for the use of stiffer penalties for the sake of deterrence. If it is argued[14] that 'there would be little point in enacting that no one should break the defences against flood, and at the same time excusing anyone who did it innocently', the same argument could with the same justification be used even in cases of homicide. The utmost concession that can be made to ease the burden of the prosecution in certain offences is to shift the onus of proof to the accused, a device frequently used by the legislator.[15]

(d) The 'petty nature of the offences and of the penalties'—usually only fines—which can be imposed for them are usually mentioned as criteria of this category and also as justifying their special treatment. Here it is overlooked that the very fact of having to appear before a criminal court and of a criminal conviction with the acquisition of a criminal record are no mere trifles, and any attempt to treat them as such weakens the authority of the criminal law in the eyes of the public. For such reasons, the suggestion to regard public welfare offences as 'quasi-civil wrongs' or even as civil torts, is no solution as the stigma attached to a conviction would remain. Moreover, the idea that public welfare offences are by their very nature and without exception only trivial is in itself misleading; as in the case of many other offences, especially larceny, the potential harm done by them to society covers the whole scale from the minimum to the maximum.[16]

(e) The distinction of *mala per se* and *mala prohibita*, that 'ancient and revered theory' (Jerome Hall) with its underlying idea that there are certain offences which are at the same time moral wrongs and others which are not, has often been used as the criterion. As will be shown below, attempts to differentiate on such lines have so far failed, and it is inadvisable to try to narrow the scope of the concept of 'crime' by excluding the *mala prohibita*. What could be done is to select a number of minor offences, whether 'public welfare', petty traffic, or similar ones which show, as a rule, the characteristics listed above, and deal with them by way of some non-criminal, administrative procedure, but always leaving open recourse to the courts at the request of the prosecution or of the defendant.

## 2. *Crime and Torts*. Mala in se *and* mala prohibita. *Legal and Sociological Classifications of Crime*

Secondly, the difference between crime and *civil wrongs*, called *torts* in English law, is also far from clear. It is already controversial whether in primitive law such a distinction was known.[17] While Max Weber and many nineteenth-century legal writers denied its existence

26

in primitive systems, more recent anthropological researches seem to have refuted their view. The distinction did exist, though it was one not of substance but merely of emphasis, according to whether it was the public or the private element that predominated.[18] In English law, it has been 'a commonplace for over seven hundred years', but one of procedure only.[19] Blackstone revived the old Roman distinction of *delicta publica* (crimes) and *delicta privata* (torts), or injury done to the community and injury done to individuals. In some ways, this reminds us of the contrast between 'public welfare' and other offences (see § 1 above), with the difference that Roman law and Blackstone regard the *delicta publica* as representing not the fringe, but the very heart of the concept of crime. As in the case of public welfare offences, however, it is now generally agreed that Blackstone's, or indeed any other distinction based on the differences in the contents of the specific act of wrong-doing is bound to fail.[20] The original idea of acts morally wrong *versus* acts merely prohibited by law is here as controversial as elsewhere (below, pp. 39 ff.). Nor would it be entirely correct to say that the commission of a crime, if detected and brought before a criminal court, must invariably lead to punishment—probation and absolute discharge are no penalties—whereas the commission of a civil wrong entails only the payment of damages or restitution—there are 'penal' or 'exemplary' damages in English law. It is true, however, that the latter go to the individual plaintiff, whereas fines imposed for criminal offences go to the State or another public agency. The best distinction so far is that referring to differences in procedure, but even here it is not invariably true that criminal proceedings, as opposed to civil ones, can be started only by the State. Kenny thought the way in which legal proceedings can be terminated, i.e. whether permission of a public authority is required for it, might be the crucial test, but as his editor, following Winfield, has pointed out,[21] this is a vicious circle since the decision as to whether such a permission is required in its turn depends on the question whether the wrong is a crime or only a tort.

To a very considerable extent, crimes and torts overlap, since most serious crimes, such as murder, arson, rape, robbery, are at the same time torts entitling the victim to claim civil damages. How far such damages can be claimed in the course of criminal proceedings varies from one country to another. English law has been comparatively reluctant in this respect,[22] but under the Criminal Justice Act, 1948, s. 11 (2), the court, when making a probation order or an order for conditional discharge, has power to order the offender to pay reasonable damages for injury or compensation for loss caused by him, the latter not exceeding £100 in all in the case of an order made by a court of summary jurisdiction. This reluctance may, to some extent, reflect the historical development from the primitive stage when criminal proceedings were largely left to the initiative of the victim and his family or tribe to the present stage when this power is, on the whole, concentrated in the hands of the State. It is only recently that the part played by the victim of a crime and his interests have been receiving closer attention (see below, Chapter 25), and the proposal has been made that he should in suitable cases even be compensated by the State. This, together with the growing tendency in some countries to put less emphasis than before on the element of moral guilt in crime (below), represents a *rapprochement* between criminal and civil wrongs.

There is not only overlapping between crime and tort in the sense that the same wrong may be both and lead to punishment and to the payment of damages or compensation. In recent times, the idea, already mentioned, that the legislator can and should treat these two concepts as *alternatives*, with administrative action as the third possibility, has been playing an ever-increasing part in public policy. Not only in American anti-monopoly laws, but also in statutes dealing with the wartime black-market the American legislator provided a variety of remedies, and the Office of Price Administration (O.P.A.) in Washington was given authority to decide which of these remedies should be used in an individual case.[23] As a result, mainly for practical reasons of administrative convenience, but also because of the unwieldiness of Federal criminal procedure, less than 6 per cent of all O.P.A. cases were dealt with by way of criminal proceedings, and there was no evidence that those violations which were treated as criminal offences could be clearly distinguished from the rest.[24] Another important factor reducing the proportion of criminal prosecutions as against civil or administrative measures was the feeling of many officials, as well as non-officials, that these black-market offences were not really criminal in character and that the offenders were honest businessmen who had, more by accident than design, had the misfortune of falling foul of an over-strict law. This leads to the controversial question whether in particular 'white collar crime' (see Chapter 21) is crime, even when it is dealt with by non-criminal processes.[25]

It is this latter point, on which there has been a great deal of confused thinking, that concerns us at present, rather than the special problem of 'white collar crime'. The matter is closely connected with the contrast of *mala in se* and *mala prohibita* and also with the idea of 'natural crime', but it has a sociological rather than a moral and legal flavour.

The distinction of *mala in se* and *mala prohibita* has been popular in English law at least since the Middle Ages when it was held that the king, 'though he might deal with merely human laws and the offences created by them (*mala prohibita*) . . . could not deal with the offences created by these higher laws (*mala in se*)'. Coining, for example, belonged to the former, fornication to the latter category.[26] Blackstone taught that there were offences against 'those rights which God and nature have established', as compared with violations of 'laws which enjoin only positive duties and forbid any such things as are not *mala in se* . . . without any intermixture of moral guilt'.[27] It is an idea which, in a way, goes back to Aristotle's of φυςιϰὸν δίϰαιον and νομιϰὸν δίϰαιον or natural law and legal or positive law,[28] and the whole theory of the 'law of nature',[29] i.e. the idea that there is a body of law founded on the nature of man which is independent of time and place and of man-made laws; the idea that there are acts wrong 'by nature' and acts wrong only 'by convention'. This is not the place for any detailed discussion of the many different formulations of the concept of 'law of nature', its great merits and equally considerable dangers. On this see the 'historical sketch' below, pp. 42 ff. In the present connection it has to be stressed, however, that the fundamental object of that concept was not so much to exclude the positive law altogether from the definition of law as to establish the supremacy of the law of nature over the law of the State in cases where the two systems seemed to clash. The object of Blackstone's distinction between *mala per se* and *mala prohibita*, as that of the invention of the more recent category of 'public welfare offences', on the other hand, was not to establish supremacies in cases of conflict between two legal systems, of which one seemed to be superimposed on the other; rather was it to exclude certain offences altogether from the concept of 'crime' or at least from the applicability of certain provisions of the ordinary criminal law, in particular those concerning *mens rea*, or of certain forms of criminal procedure not regarded as suitable for them. The critics of Blackstone, however, have largely used the same argument as employed by the opponents of the natural law school, i.e. that there are no actions criminal in themselves regardless of time and place. While this is perfectly true, it does not entirely dispose of the claim of the natural law school that no such empirical differences can by themselves prove the futility of the search for universally valid formal categories.[30] This is the significance of Stammler's formal concept of 'natural law with varied content'.[31]

The distinction of *mala in se* and *mala prohibita* has recently been revived by the Dutch criminologist H. Bianchi who identifies the latter with his category of 'criminoid' behaviour, which is essentially not criminal, or immoral, but anti-social, 'not usually held blameworthy', a mere non-consideration of the demands of society and of 'living-together', a 'kind of behaviour which testifies to a person's degree of

29

socialization', an indication of a 'dangerous state'.[32] What Bianchi has, apparently, in mind, seems to be more or less identical with the category of 'public welfare offences'. Whether or not they may properly be called 'criminoid', it cannot be admitted that they are usually not blameworthy and that a non-consideration of the demands of 'living-together' is usually a trifling matter.

In connection with Edwin H. Sutherland's discovery of the concept of 'white collar crime' an interesting controversy has arisen between lawyers and sociologists, between what is regarded as the legal and the sociological definition of crime. 'Is "White Collar crime" Crime?' is the title of one of Sutherland's best-known papers.[33] He was surprised to find that only in a very small proportion, 9 per cent of a sample of 547 cases, of violations of anti-trust, patent and similar statutes, the offenders had been punished by criminal courts, whereas the other cases had been dealt with by non-criminal agencies. Could it, in spite of this, still be maintained that all such violations were 'crimes'? His answer is in the affirmative as both legal requirements, the legal provision of a penalty and the socially injurious quality of these acts, were present, and the manner in which they had actually been dealt with by the State was indifferent. With regard to their gravity, such violations, he argues, may vary from *male in se* to mere *mala prohibita*. As mentioned above, a very similar situation was discovered by Marshall B. Clinard in his post-mortem investigation of the wartime activities of the American black-market and the O.P.A., and he follows Sutherland in regarding black-market violations as crimes regardless of the treatment received on the part of the authorities and of the fact that neither public opinion nor the offenders themselves had been willing to regard them as *mala in se*.[34] This view has been criticized from the sociological side because, it is argued, in view of the attitude of the public and the businessmen concerned their violations of the law cannot sociologically be regarded as crimes,[35] and from the legal side because to the lawyer 'only those are criminals who have been adjudicated as such by the courts'.[36] Paul W. Tappan, who has been the principal spokesman of this legalistic view, points out that, although unconvicted offenders are representative of important groups and the criminological study of these groups may be very desirable, these groups are still too vague and ill-defined and merely an expression of the 'desire to discover and study wrongs which are absolute and eternal rather than mere violations of a statutory and case law system which varies in time and place'. Tappan's criticisms are a mixture of truth and error. It is true that the sociological concepts of 'conduct norms' and 'socially injurious' are, in spite of the pioneer work of Sellin[37] and others, still in need of further clarification. It is mistaken, however, to think that sociologists in general here tried to include in their conception of crime mere violations of conduct norms which were not legally punishable. Sutherland in particular, as already stated, requires the legal provision of a penalty for the act, whereas Clinard seems to require merely 'a law outlawing certain behaviour' without making it entirely clear whether this must be a penal law in the strict sense. Our own view may be stated as follows: The whole controversy is partly, though not wholly, terminological, and it is essential to clarify the various issues involved.

Whether or not the *Oxford English Dictionary* is correct in giving the fourteenth century as the date of the earliest reference to the word 'crime'[38]—we might just as well go back to the Merovingian King Chlotar's Edict of 614 in which the term *causae criminales* is used[39]—in any case Bianchi is right when he stresses that 'the objective semantic function of the term "crime" is, as much as the phenomenon itself, independent of any legislative operation...' The term and the phenomenon are evidently pre-legislative. 'They exist independently of and in spite of any legislative use of the terms ... On the contrary, the legislator takes it for granted that the term must have a previous sense'—this against Michael and Adler's 'disreputable sophism' that 'without a criminal code there would be no crime'.[40] And, long before Bianchi, Garofalo had opened his famous discourse on 'natural crime' and the sociological concept of crime (see below, p. 220) with the statement:

'*Le législateur n'a pas créé ce mot; il l'a emprunté au langage populaire; il ne l'a pas même défini, il n'a fait que rassembler un certain nombre d'actions, qui, selon lui, étaient des crimes*'[41] (on this see below, Chapter 12). Sociologists are, therefore, entirely free to use their own conception of crime. It does not necessarily follow, however, that they would always be wise to do so since they have not created the concept either and have so far, on the whole, not been able to define it more clearly than the jurists. What are in fact the reasons for their desire to establish a concept of crime independently of that of the criminal law or even of the civil law concept of wrong?

There are, it is suggested, mainly the following considerations:

There is the perfectly legitimate wish of lawyers and sociologists alike, indeed of everybody interested in the just and fair administration of the law, to know exactly what kind of human conduct has to be brought under the umbrella of the term 'crime' when the application of statutes is in question which attach certain disabilities to the commission of a crime, such as, for example, ineligibility to be admitted as an immigrant or to be naturalized, or of statutes which make a person eligible to be treated as a recidivist,[42] sentenced to preventive detention, corrective training, etc. It is clear, however, that these are matters to be decided in terms of the positive law, i.e. crime can here be only an act regarded as such by the statute concerned. The latter may explicitly exclude certain criminal acts although they are legally crimes, for example those committed by juveniles. Sociological or moral considerations may here be introduced not as part of the conception of crime itself, but by making the operation of the statute dependent on the presence of certain additional requirements, such as 'moral turpitude', or of a penalty of a certain gravity such as imprisonment, thereby excluding minor offences which can be punished only by a fine. Whether or not a specific case of 'white collar crime' is a crime within the meaning of any such statute, thereby making the offender ineligible for immigration, naturalization, etc., or whether a white collar offender is a recidivist in the legal sense can be decided only in accordance with the wording of the statute concerned. In this connection it is interesting to note that those criminal statutes which provide loss of voting and other civil rights usually attach them not to the crime committed, but to the penalty imposed. While this may be regarded as unfair, the degrading character of former penal systems offers an explanation, though not an excuse.[43]

It would be a mistake, however, to push this legalistic view, with Tappan, so far as to maintain that 'only those are criminals who have been adjudicated as such by the courts'.[44] This is true for the application of statutes explicitly requiring a conviction, which most, if not all, the statutes just referred to do. It is not true, however, in any other way, and should in particular not be taken for granted where the question of stigma arises in a general, not legally stereotyped, sense, i.e. as social stigma rather than as legal disability or liability. Here a distinction has to be made between those 'unconvicted offenders' whose guilt has not been established by any legal tribunal and who should, therefore, not be stigmatized as 'criminals' and those who, though found guilty of an offence, have, for a variety of reasons, been dealt with by civil courts or administrative tribunals. It was this second group with which Sutherland was concerned, and seeing that, in the actual practice of the American anti-trust and similar statutes, the great majority of violators were spared a criminal conviction, his feeling of justice revolted against what he regarded as unfair discrimination in favour of the big 'white collar criminal'. An unlawful act, he rightly stated, 'is not defined as criminal by the fact that it is punished, but by the fact that it is punishable'.[45] He did not fail to see that in the case of non-criminal agencies the requirement of *mens rea* and the rules of evidence might be less strict than in criminal courts, but thought this argument could be refuted by referring to recent tendencies in favour of strict liability and the like.[46] It is here, however, that the real dilemma lies. Unless the separation of the criminal law from other branches of the law and unless the whole conception of crime are to be deprived of any meaning and function—a process in any case already too far advanced—criminal justice must preserve the full rigidity of its requirement of *mens rea* and of its rules of evidence. From this, it follows that where the law provides, or could provide, several alternatives of dealing with violators, the criminal law route should be chosen not merely for reasons of social prejudice or administrative convenience, but according to the merits of the individual case, which requires considerations not only of a legal but also of a sociological nature concerning the need to inflict a greater or lesser stigma or no stigma at all. The legalistic view, as represented by Tappan, is unsatisfactory in arguing that punishable acts are crimes only if actually dealt with by a criminal court, but the sociological view, as represented by Sutherland, is also questionable at present in maintaining that punishable acts are always crimes, even if dealt with by non-criminal agencies. What is needed is an injection of sociological thinking into the whole administration of criminal justice to ensure that the present incongruities between stigma and conviction will be reduced to the unavoidable minimum. This is a problem going beyond the scope of those specific phenomena which have given rise to the discussion.

While the divergence of views between criminal law and sociology so far discussed is one concerning the practical application of the former, the definition of crime has also caused difficulties in the field of theoretical criminology. It is not only the sociologist's feeling of justice that has been hurt by the legalistic definition of crime but his scientific conscience, too, has been dissatisfied by the rigid and often out-of-date classifications developed by the criminal law. It was found by Cressey, for example, that the concept of 'embezzlement' in American criminal codes did not cover a sociologically homogeneous form of behaviour, and for purposes of research it had to be replaced by the conception of accepting a position of trust in good faith and afterwards violating that trust by committing crimes such as embezzlement, larceny by bailee, or certain forms of forgery or confidence tricks. This sociological conception of 'criminal violation of financial trust', it was claimed, included all forms of criminal behaviour which are essentially similar from the economic and sociological point of view, but excluded cases essentially different, though covered by the legal terms of embezzlement, forgery, etc. In this way a sound criminological basis could be established for research into the socio-psychological characteristics of criminal violations of financial trust which, nevertheless, to some extent used the traditional legal concepts.[47] Another illustration could be drawn from the term 'manslaughter' which in English law has developed in a purely 'negative way' as being 'a homicide which for one reason or another did not amount to murder . . . even at the present day such is the confusion . . . that it is not possible to give an authoritative definition of manslaughter in plain terms'.[48] The fact that the same term manslaughter covers acts so different in character as voluntary and involuntary killing has particularly added to the present confusion. The scope of the concept of 'murder', too, differs so widely that criminologists might not be blamed for trying to study it as a socio-psychological entity rather than in strictly legal terms.[49] The immense variety of this crime has in fact been one of the arguments against establishing legal 'degrees' of murder: 'legal stereotyping and a doctrinaire approach would destroy the elasticity which today enables not three but many degrees of murder to be recognized', wrote Sir Norwood East.[50] Instead of any possible legal, and inevitably too rigid, classification criminologists rather distinguish murder according to its psychological and sociological features, especially its motives, the age, sex, race, family status and other personal characteristics of the murderer, his relationship to the victim, etc.[51] H. C. Brearley even regards the legal distinction between premeditated murder and impulsive manslaughter as of little sociological significance.[52]

The essential points of this discussion are, first, that the term 'crime' should be used in technical language only with reference to conduct that is legally crime. Secondly, such conduct, if fully proved, is crime regardless of whether it actually leads to a conviction before a criminal court or whether it is dealt with by other agencies or not at all. Thirdly, the decision as to which of the available alternatives is to be used should depend entirely on the merits of the individual case. Lastly, criminology is in no way limited in the scope of its scientific investigation to what is legally crime in a given country at a given time, and it is free to use its own classifications.

## II. THE RELATION OF CRIME TO RELIGION, CUSTOM AND MORALITY

From our premises that the term 'crime' should in technical language be used only with reference to conduct which is legally crime, but that criminology, on the other hand, should be free to pursue its studies unfettered by the legal conception of crime, it follows that criminologists and legal reformers have to be given at least a minimum of extra-legal guidance as to what *should* be treated as crime. It is only in this way that they can be provided with an approximate idea of where to look for potential problems. Otherwise their work would have no proper frame of reference, and they would be left to sail without a compass in an uncharted ocean of questionable 'facts' and untestable hypotheses. The guidance which we require can be obtained only if it is borne in mind that the law is nothing but one system of norms among other systems ordering human thoughts and behaviour, or in psycho-analytical language only one taboo among many. Where the law fails to provide the answer or where the answer it offers seems to be unsatisfactory we have to turn to religion, custom, morality, and other value systems operating in a given culture. This does not imply an undervaluation of the law as such and its relegation to a minor role as compared with those other controlling forces. It does not mean, for example, an uncritical acceptance of the orthodox Marxist view of the law as being a mere 'superstructure' created on a basis of economic factors, a mere 'function of economic processes without any independent existence' and independent history.[53] While fully admitting the strong influence which economic factors, throughout the course of history, have exercised on the contents and administration of the law we cannot ignore the reverse side of the picture: the law in its turn has also often affected the economic system and sometimes it has developed regardless of, or even contrary to, economic trends, which has usually meant that it has fallen behind the realities of economic life.[54] Nor is the position basically different in the non-economic sectors of cultural life: there has been mutual stimulation and cross-fertilization between the law, on the one hand, and religion, custom and social values and convictions, on the other, the law occasionally taking the lead, more often however lagging behind developments in other fields. In the following, the relationship between the criminal law and the most important of those other systems of social control will be briefly surveyed.

## 1. The Relation of Crime to Religion

Can we find in *religious* norms the guidance for which we are searching as to what should be treated as crime? Is crime identical with sin, and should the criminal law be a catalogue of sinful acts? Historically, the nineteenth-century theory of the religious origin of the law (Maine)[55] and the doctrine of crime as a pollution of the community have been abandoned by many modern writers. Diamond has been one of the most outspoken critics of Maine. There are, he writes, no rules in primitive religion for the conduct of man towards man, sanctioned by a regard for the will of supernatural beings, and 'the notion that homicide is wrongful made its appearance in the religion after it had appeared in the law, and it was derived from the legal notion'.[56] Other writers, such as David Daube and G. W. Paton, are more cautious. 'Is it safe', asks Daube, 'to argue that because the devout authors of the Bible see law as part of religion, law must have formed part of religion in the Hebrew State?' but he concludes that neither

35

view can be regarded as safely established.[57] Considering how difficult, and often impossible, it is to distinguish between religious and legal rules this conclusion is not surprising.[58] Regardless of this controversy as to the historical priority of religion or law, however, it is a fact that the norms of the criminal law have not throughout developed on the same lines as those of the main religions. Taking the Ten Commandments as an illustration, it is obvious that some of these have hardly ever been embodied in the provisions of any system of positive criminal law, probably because they are concerned with sentiments and desires rather than with actions or omissions which make them technically unsuitable for the work of the legislator. Modern legal systems have largely taken their cue from the secular conception of the State established after one of the most prolonged and painful struggles in history. Anthropologists, too, have found in primitive societies of today a legal order of some kind which they think was not based on religious beliefs.[59] As far as the problems of western civilization are concerned, all this means, however, only three things: in the first place, the renunciation of the old conception of the ecclesiastical law as being superior to, or taking the place of, secular criminal law, and the abolition of institutions arising from that conception, such as the 'Benefit of Clergy'.[60] Secondly, it means that most modern criminal codes contain provisions protecting not religion or the Churches as such but merely the religious feelings of individual citizens and the peaceful exercise of public or private worship.[61] Thirdly, it means that when trying to answer our question what kind of human conduct should be regarded as criminal we cannot borrow wholesale from the list of acts or omissions treated as sins by the various religions. Already the fact that different religions may have different views in the matter would make this impracticable. The discrepancy between religious principles or, perhaps more accurately, between the doctrines of some of the Churches and the criminal law of many countries has become particularly striking in the case of problems such as birth control, abortion, suicide, artificial insemination, although even here legal progress has often been hampered by ecclesiastical opposition.[62] Regarding homosexuality on the other hand, some of the Churches have recently expressed views more progressive than those still embodied in English criminal law. Regardless, however, of which system happens to be more progressive on a certain topic at a certain time in a certain place, generally speaking it should not be assumed that religious beliefs and values are, or should be, of no significance to the secular legislator, or to the criminologist, even an agnostic one. There are three very strong, though closely inter-related, arguments to the contrary. First, the decline in religious belief is often regarded as a potent cause of crime, and even if this view should be mistaken or at least not provable (see below, Chapter 23) its existence cannot be altogether ignored. Secondly, religion plays an important part in the philosophy and psychology of punishment. Psychoanalysis and Christianity alike, although in different ways, are deeply concerned with the idea of guilt, which in its turn is closely related to the origin and institution of punishment (Chapter 17, below). Thirdly, and arising from this, religion can often play a therapeutic role in the process of punishment and treatment of offenders and in the prevention of crime. The ideas of reparation and confession are essential elements in both religion and penology.[63] In short, as Tappan writes, 'its potential role is tremendous', though the actual fulfilment of this potentiality depends 'on the vitality of a religion in the lives of its professants'.[64] That religion may be an important factor in our dealings with lawbreakers is of course a highly controversial statement and one very difficult to prove or disprove by scientific methods, especially as any case material which might be produced is likely to come from persons rightly regarded as prejudiced. The history of penology knows of tragic mistakes committed by ardent believers in the name of religion, from the persecution of the early Christians to the burning of the witches and the Pennsylvanian system of solitary confinement.[65]

In the light of these considerations it goes without saying that we cannot accept the recent attempt of H. Bianchi to define crime as 'invariably an act against God',[66] even bearing in mind that his conception of crime excludes what he calls 'criminoid' behaviour.

## 2. The Relation of Crime to Custom

We have now to consider how far *custom, mores*, may be able to help the legislator in his search for the material contents of both the positive and the ideal criminal law. What we have in mind is not legal custom, which is itself law—though perhaps a primitive form of it—but social custom, *mœurs, coutumes*, in German *Sitte*. H. Kantorowicz, in his important posthumous work *The Definition of Law*,[67] has given a useful list of such rules of custom which are not law; he distinguishes rules concerning (*a*) good manners (at table, in the street); (*b*) the occasions for and the appropriateness of gifts; (*c*) forms of greetings and styles of address; (*d*) topics of conversation; (*e*) forms of letter-writing; (*f*) court and professional etiquette; (*g*) tact; (*h*) behaviour at ceremonies; (*i*) cleanliness of clothes; (*j*) degree of liberty allowed in social intercourse of the sexes; (*k*) comity of nations, and so on. As he admits, even this lengthy list is not exhaustive. The social class and caste system, for example, is almost exclusively based on custom and only in exceptional cases touched by law.[68] Evidently, many of these rules, in particular those under (*a*), (*b*), (*c*), (*f*), (h), (i), and (j), might in certain circumstances, in a given place and at a given time, become provisions of the criminal law. The rule which tells us not to jump a queue is usually only one of good manners, i.e. mere custom, but in periods of special emergency, for example in wartime, it may become a criminal offence to do so. The liberal distribution of gifts may be something entirely innocuous, but it may also be the subject of an official enquiry (e.g. that of the Lynskey Tribunal in 1949)[69] or even of a criminal charge of corruption. Violations of professional etiquette may be merely frowned upon by other members of the profession, or they may have serious disciplinary consequences or lead to a prison sentence, and similar considerations apply to misbehaviour at ceremonies (blasphemy) and towards the female sex (indecent assault). It would be a fascinating task to try to disentangle the respective contributions of law and custom to the 'American dilemma'[70] and to the treatment of minority groups in general (on the latter see below, Chapter 23), or to that of such social outcasts as ex-prisoners and homosexuals. Our present task is to find the discriminating criteria and to search for the lessons to be learnt from them by the legislator. One of the profoundest legal philosophers of the current century, Gustav Radbruch,[71] thought not only that all attempts to differentiate law and custom had so far been unsuccessful but that their futility could even be proved since these two institutions were so fundamentally different—law meaning cultural norm and value, custom having no relation to either—that no comparison was possible. On the other hand, he regarded custom as a kind of preparatory stage (*Vorschule*) to the law. This is often true, but occasionally the historical development takes the opposite course. As a rule, disabilities, prohibitions, privileges originate in custom (e.g. queueing, segregation), and are subsequently reinforced by the law either because custom proves too weak to achieve its objects without legal backing or because it proves so overwhelmingly strong that the legislator, *nolens volens*, has to yield to it. In the end, he may be able occasionally to abolish a bad custom, but it may also survive legal prohibition (duelling, segregation, customs supporting white collar crime, in some areas even blood-vengeance). Have we to conclude from this that 'custom is king', that 'mores can make anything appear right, even incest and cannibalism and the killing of the old'?[72] It certainly can do so for a period of time, but not for ever.

While these considerations are largely concerned with historical sequence and material strength of custom and law, we have now to turn to similarities and differences. Custom and law, it has been argued, both require only external compliance regardless of motive, which latter is the essential element in the moral sphere (see below, s. 3); and, against Radbruch who stresses the significance of internal compliance in the field of custom, it is true to say that in custom and law the emphasis is more on the external side,[73] though all this is very much a matter of degree. Those who act in accordance with custom will, except perhaps in a totalitarian regime, not be too closely questioned about their inner feelings.

An important difference between law and custom is that the latter is more often limited to certain geographical regions and social classes within the State, whereas the law with minor exceptions (local by-laws, ordinances) tends to be uniform for the whole country. It has also been said that while both law and custom are heteronomous, i.e. receive their norms from outside, only the law has at its disposal an organization to enforce its will. This is not altogether correct in the sense that enforceability is not a universal quality of the law and that, on the other hand, custom is also enforceable, though in a different way. As Max Weber has pointed out, the law can rely on a special staff whose task it is to take action in cases of transgression.[74] Custom possesses no such special staff; it is enforced by public opinion or, perhaps even more frequently, by the belief of the man in the street—however mistaken it may occasionally be—that this is what the majority wants.

Bad customs, for example in the field of racial discrimination, may breed actual crime, but even regardless of such acute potentialities it is the proper task of the criminologist to study them and to examine the case for and against criminal legislation in this field and the possibilities of crime prevention.

## 3. The Relation of Crime to Morality

Important as norms of religion and custom are to the criminal lawyer and criminologist, the problems presented by them are only preludes to those likely to arise from a potential clash between legal and *moral* rules. Here it is that our real battles are waged and only too often lost. Even if we should regard Jerome Hall's claim as slightly exaggerated that the 'moral quality of the criminal law ... is the major issue of our times and permeates all the social disciplines',[75] there still remains ample reason for us to ponder and to worry about the matter, and it hardly needed the recent experience of the Wolfenden Report as a reminder.[76] If it is the business of criminologists to study crime and criminals and their treatment by law and society, the moral problems involved cannot possibly be set aside.

Of what kind are these problems? First and foremost, what is the true relation between the criminal law and the moral law; are they on identical or at least similar lines? Can we look to the moral law as the originator, interpreter, and protector of the criminal law of the State?

Can it be used as a guide by the legislator to use the weapon of the criminal law in order to enforce moral standards? Can we tell the offender, who is often disdainful of the whole machinery of criminal justice and regards his punishment as unfair, that he has broken not merely the law but the moral code, too, and that there is no higher authority left on earth to whom he could appeal? And the judge in sentencing and the penal administrator in carrying out the sentence—should they put into motion the full blast of moral indignation to make the greatest possible impact on the criminal and on the community? Considering that very few of those who are indifferent to religion and even willing to ignore the rules of custom would wish openly to defy the moral code, it might be of the greatest help to the upholders of law and order if the force of morality could be placed at their service without reservations. In fact, there are all too many such reservations.

The problem 'Law and Morality' has been unduly neglected by criminologists (in the narrower sense of the term), especially by those without a legal or philosophical background. Some of them, apparently, believe that it is not their problem at all. Penologists have shown slightly more interest and understanding because it so obviously goes to the roots of penal philosophy. Let us, before going into details, try to define the scope of the matter. All too often it has been regarded as something affecting only the field of legislation, and even here merely the question of whether a specific kind of human behaviour should, or should not, be punished as a crime. It was this aspect which was discussed by the Wolfenden Committee in connection with homosexuality and prostitution, but these two phenomena are by no means the only aspects of criminal legislation where the relationship between law and morals may play an important part. This relationship is of equally crucial importance for such matters as the attitude of the criminal law to birth control, artificial insemination, euthanasia, abortion, suicide, or the limits of the defence of 'superior orders' or of the legal right of an individual to sacrifice other innocent human beings in order to save his own life in a situation of common danger, such as shipwreck (the English *Mignonette* case and the American *Holmes* case).[77] In addition to such subjects, we can say that wherever the criminal law, rightly or wrongly, uses degrading penalties or makes the choice between different penalties, for example between penal servitude and imprisonment, dependent on the moral character of the offender or the moral quality of his offence—the *ehrlose Gesinnung* of the German Criminal Code (§ 20)—considerations of a moral nature become part and parcel of criminal justice. The same applies where the law contains directives for the sentencing policy of the criminal courts to treat certain moral qualities of the

40

offender or of his action, especially his motives, as either aggravating or mitigating circumstances, or where, as for example certain American statutes do, the law makes the deportation of an alien dependent upon his conviction of a crime involving 'moral turpitude'.[78] Even in the absence of any such provisions judges and magistrates are often faced with similar questions within the limits left to their discretion.

As it is sometimes thought that homilies delivered by a judge or magistrate when passing sentence may influence an offender for good it is important to know how far moral exhortations should, as in fact they often are, be included on such occasions. Corresponding problems, only still more intricate and intense, arise for institutional staffs, after-care and probation officers in all their dealings with the offender after he has made his fleeting appearance in court. Twenty-five years ago the present writer was bold enough to assert, in no moralizing spirit: 'Only on a moral basis is it possible successfully to argue with the lawbreaker',[79] a formula now approved by the eminent American authority on criminal law and jurisprudence, Jerome Hall.[80] How far, and in what sense, is this still true in the light of more recent developments? And if it should be true in principle, can it be defended as a practical proposition in cases where the indispensable minimum requisites of such moral arguments may seem to be non-existent? To such questions an answer can be given only on the basis of an analysis of the personal qualities of individual offenders, which no doubt falls within the province of the criminologist.

Clearly, no solution can be attempted without considering at least a few of the milestones in the long history of the subject and of some of its vast literature—a history very closely bound up with that of the movement of 'natural law'.[81] As the present writer has pointed out before, it was the fundamental weakness of the Wolfenden Report, depriving it of much of its persuasive force, that it paid no attention to that history and literature. It is the fundamental idea behind the concept of a natural law that there exists an unwritten legal system, derived from the 'nature of man', side by side with, but independent of, and superior to, the positive law of the State. The natural law is thought to be immutable and eternal, valid regardless of time and place; it is of divine origin and in perfect harmony with nature itself and with justice. While these are the ideas which have given the natural law movement its immense driving force, closer scrutiny reveals many internal differences and sometimes almost imperceptible, but nevertheless profound, changes in its contents. 'The mere fact', writes d'Entrèves, 'that an identical expression recurs in different writers, is no proof of continuity of thought from one to the other. That Cicero and Locke should both have defined natural law in a very similar manner is no evidence of the uninterrupted acceptance of that notion during the eighteen odd centuries which separate them.'[82] In fact, the history of the natural law movement has sometimes been over-simplified and condensed so as to conceal the truth that it presents a united front in its negative rather than in its positive aspects, i.e. in its negation of the monopolistic claims of the law of the State rather than in its own doctrines. Moreover, while its history is of the utmost importance for our present problem, the relationship of law and morals—d'Entrèves calls this the distinguishing mark of natural law history[83]—it also shows that the movement has, at least in its earlier stages, been concerned with the relationship between human and divine laws rather than between human law and morals. It is in particular Erik Wolf[84] who has closely examined the immense variety of possible and actual definitions of natural law and stressed that it has received its substance from the leading cultural values of the age, which may be of an individualistic or of a collective, social, political, economic, scientific, religious, or moral character.

## 4. *Historical Sketch of the Natural Law Movement*

According to the traditional interpretation of the history of the natural law, the problem did not arise in the earlier stages of ancient Greece since no distinction was then made between law, religion and morals; strictly speaking, there was no 'moral-free' sphere, nor could there be any criticism of the positive law on religious or moral grounds—there could be no 'unjust law'. As Welzel pointed out,[85] the idea of a natural law could originate only in a period of crisis, i.e. for Greece in the age of Pericles and the Sophists in the middle of the fifth century B.C. Even to Socrates, who appeared as the great questioner of all things human and divine, justice was, strangely enough, still identical with the rules of the positive law; having to fight against the attempts of some of the Sophists to undermine the force of law altogether, he preferred to be a rebel not against the positive law but merely against what seemed to him its mistaken application by the court.[86] Whether this was the opinion of Plato, too, appears somewhat doubtful, and this not merely in view of the many contrasts between the different periods of his writings. Considering his authoritarian leanings and his pragmatism; his maxim that the end justifies the means and that justice is what is useful to the State; his confession, through his mouthpiece Socrates, that he does not know the true nature of justice and that much further consideration would be needed to understand that nature, we may well be left with the impression that the idea of an eternal law of nature and of the possibility of an 'unjust' positive law was finally dismissed by Plato.[87] There are, however, also certain passages in his *Dialogues* which can be quoted for the contrary view (though not the dictum 'an evil decree cannot be law' in *Minos*, as the latter is a pseudo-Platonic, much later dialogue).[88]

Nor are Aristotle's writings on the subject free of inconsistencies.[89] While his starting point is the belief in the supremacy of the positive law ($\nu \acute{o} \mu o \varsigma$)

over justice (δίκαιον), while his idea of equality means equality according to the positive law, he also feels dissatisfied with the resulting identification of law and justice. He tries to construct a model of an ideal Constitution, but abandons this attempt because of the relative character of an ideal which would be different for different people. Here as in the case of Plato it is sometimes the emphasis on the positive and sometimes the emphasis on the ideal law that has been given pride of place by their various interpreters, but the final impression has usually been one of vacillation and doubt. It was the *Stoa* with its pantheistic and cosmopolitan philosophy (it 'took the step from the Polis to the Cosmopolis', Welzel); with its conception of reason as a universal force dominating the cosmos regardless of sex, nationality or race; its concentration on the internal side of human actions and on the conscience that promised a solution of the problem of natural law at a time of political and religious crises.[90] Obedience to the law of nature, based on reason, becomes a moral duty. Although the Stoics, too, had to make concessions to practical realities, their doctrines inspired the teachings of Cicero, the law of Justinian, and the early Christian thinkers. Previous attempts to fill the formal idea of natural law with contents of an objective character had failed. Aristotle's idea of equality, as part of the natural law, for example, remained sterile as long as no material formula, no yardstick, was provided to say which factors had to be considered and which others to be ignored when deciding whether two cases were in fact 'equal'. The same applies to the famous Roman formula *suum cuique* where it is not clear what this 'suum' is.[91] The Stoics provided an answer by basing the natural law on the moral convictions of the individual,[92] thereby strengthening its popular appeal but sacrificing its claim to objectivity.

Roman law has often been credited with having worked out a conception of natural law clearer than that of the Greek philosophers. Actually, modern historical jurisprudence stresses rather the many contradictions in the writings of classical Roman jurists. There was, it is true, their famous distinction between *jus civile, jus gentium*, and *jus naturale*, but the relationship thought to exist between these three systems is far from clear. To some writers the *jus naturale* is identical with the *jus gentium*, the law of nations, or even with the *jus civile*, to others it is their opposite;[93] and the whole trichotomy is nowadays often regarded as a later invention, although as d'Entrèves suggests it may well express the different stages in the evolution of Roman law. There is, however, unanimity on one important feature: on the fact that in the Roman view the law of nature was not superior to the positive law. If any proof were needed of this, the institution of slavery would provide it. Slavery was regarded as part of the *jus gentium* and therefore positive Roman law, although it was against one of the most fundamental notions of the law of nature, the Stoic ideal of equality of all men. It was under the influence of this ideal, however, that, although the institution itself was retained, at least some important improvements were gradually made in the legal and social position of slaves.[94]

It is this self-abdication of the Roman version of the law of nature that distinguishes it from the early Christian doctrine and medieval Canon law

43

from St. Augustine to St. Thomas Aquinas, nine hundred years later, neither of whom had any doubt that where positive law deviates from the law of nature it has no binding force, it is not *lex legalis* but merely a *legis corruptio*. 'St. Augustine says: "There is no law unless it be just". So the validity of law depends upon its justice. But in human affairs a thing is said to be just when it accords aright with the rule of reason, and . . . the first rule of reason is the natural law' (Thomas).[95] In Canon law the law of nature is derived from reason and from God, it is the source of all moral ideas, too; therefore it must be absolute and binding, and disobedience to unjust law becomes not only a right but also a duty. There are, however, several weak spots in this grandiose structure. First, according to Canon law the rules of natural law are of a very general kind only, such as 'Do the Good and avoid the Evil', and have therefore to be supplemented by the more specific provisions of the positive law of the State. With very few exceptions, all the adherents of the natural law school admit the necessity of such a system of positive law—a fact used by Kelsen and others to justify their rejection of the whole idea of natural law.[96] Secondly, to Thomas even the latter represents only one, not the final, step towards 'eternal blessedness'; and as new developments may require new institutions it is not altogether exempt from the general law that everything is subject to change.[97] Finally, Thomas shares with Plato and Augustine the tendency to ignore the rights of the individual and of minorities such as slaves and heretics.[98]

To Duns Scotus, too, the law of nature is founded on God's will alone, with the reservation that God himself is subject to what is logically possible. Moreover, a point of special importance to the theory of criminal law, there are for him no actions which are good or bad *per se*, and this view was shared by William of Ockham, according to whom acts such as larceny or adultery are not bad in themselves but only because they are prohibited.[99] A fundamental change could occur only at a later stage, in the seventeenth century, when the theological doctrines of natural law were replaced by the secular ones of Thomas Hobbes, Hugo Grotius, Samuel Pufendorf and their successors; when, in the words of Welzel,[100] the place of the theologians was taken by 'politically minded philosophers and philosophizing jurists'.

Whether Hobbes can be regarded as a member of any school of natural law seems to be very doubtful. His scepticism, imbued as it was with the teachings of natural science, was calculated to destroy rather than to rebuild that idea. As according to him man's nature, previously regarded as a positive and constructive force, is thoroughly bad and as good and evil are relative and subjective terms, salvation can come only from the sovereign State and its positive law. The latter can never clash with reason; therefore, it is for the State to decide what the law of nature requires, and the only function of the latter is to furnish the justification for the law of the State, which means 'the negation of natural law by natural law' (Kelsen).[101] The private conscience of the citizen has to be subordinated to the public conscience of the sovereign. Somewhat paradoxically, there remains, it is true, a private sphere where the individual is free to interpret the law of nature for himself, though the boundaries of this sphere are uncertain and the contents of this law of nature very formal only.[102] On no account, however, can a violation of the positive law on the grounds of its divergence from the natural law be justified; the former may be bad, but it can never be 'unjust'. 'Every crime is a sinne', he wrote, 'but not every sinne a crime' (*Leviathan*), which in a way anticipates Georg Jellinek's theory of the law as the ethical minimum (see below).

Hugo Grotius (1583–1645) may not have been the 'founder of the natural law school' (Pufendorf), but his contributions to it have nevertheless been profound. It was he who, in his *De jure Belli ac pacis* (1625)—not for the first time and with cautious reservations—merely as a hypothetical possibility, but nevertheless with tremendous effect, put forward the view that the law of nature would be valid even if there were no God or if he would disinterest himself in human affairs; even God himself cannot change it.[103] This is so because the law of nature consists of eternal truths similar to mathematical principles. In his attempts to work out a detailed system of principles of natural law Grotius was eventually forced, however, to admit that the true quality of human actions was too difficult to determine and could not therefore provide the basis for a right of the citizen to disobey the positive law. In fact, he quotes Sophocles' Antigone: 'You must obey him whom the State has placed in power, in things unjust as well as just.'[104] He had begun by freeing the law of nature from its theological fetters, but he ended by subjecting it to the will of the sovereign State. Nor was he able to work out any new principles of natural law which would have added to Aristotle's formal principle of equality as the essence of justice.[105]

His successor Samuel Pufendorf (1632–94), too, in his *De jure naturae et gentium* (1672) had to admit that the law of nature provided no proof of the goodness or badness of specific forms of human behaviour. He rejected any claim that, for example, adultery or incest or larceny were morally bad *per se* (doctrine of *perseitas*); all one could say was that, for example, monogamy was probably the best way of regulating sexual relations, but even this could not be proved through the doctrines of natural law.[106] The real problem was to discover *why* certain acts were good and others bad. He found the basis of the natural law in the idea of *socialitas*, i.e. the human need to live closely together with other human beings, an idea which he used to develop his social system.[107] Concerning the relationship between natural law and positive law, while rejecting Hobbes' view that the State can do no wrong and his identification of natural law and the law of the State, he nevertheless established at least a presumption in favour of the latter, and the right of resistance to legal injustice was correspondingly restricted.[108]

One of the most important contributions which Pufendorf made to legal philosophy and ethics was to show the different role played by motives and other internal factors in human actions. While before the forum of ethics and theology such internal factors mattered even in acts which were externally irreproachable, the law—including natural law—enquired into the internal side only in the case of an illegal action. If an act was in

45

conformity with the law, its motives were of no interest to the latter. Here, Pufendorf 'anticipated Kant's distinction of legality and morality'.[109]

According to John Locke (1632–1704) resistance to the state is allowed, but only if the latter acts contrary to its own positive law as well as to natural law; the people, however, shall judge whether this has happened.[110] His doctrine of the natural liberty of the individual and the absolute right of the latter to be protected in his life, freedom and property became— together with the teachings of Pufendorf—the philosophical justification of the American Declaration of Independence.[111]

Christian Thomasius (1655–1728) further developed the distinction of law and morality on the lines laid down by his teacher Pufendorf. He tried to separate the law (*iustum*), which imposes only external duties and is based on compulsion, from morality (*honestum*) and mores (*decorum*) which are interested in the internal side of human behaviour. Natural law, using no compulsion and pronouncing recommendations rather than commands, is not really law, it is social ethics. On the other hand, it requires more than does the positive law: while the latter prescribes only that we should not do to others what we do not want others to do to us, the natural law requires that we should do to others what we want them to do to us. Thomasius 'was drawing the moral of two centuries of religious strife and persecution', writes d'Entrèves. 'His theory lays the foundations of the modern, secular, tolerant State. Its novelty, however, is practical rather than theoretical.'[112] But d'Entrèves, while stressing the fact that the difference between law and morality had been recognized long before Thomasius, makes it clear that the practical consequences of that insight, in particular regarding the exclusion of the State from the sphere of conscience, were sharply drawn only by writers such as Pufendorf and Thomasius.

As pointed out by most historians of the law of nature movement, its crucial testing time came towards the end of the eighteenth and the beginning of the nineteenth centuries, under the impact of the teachings of Immanuel Kant, on the one hand, and of the historical law school, on the other. While Kant's (1724–1804) philosophy of law has been called 'a typical application of the natural law doctrine'[113] it has also been regarded as its death-knell. The truth lies between these extreme views. If the doctrine of natural law 'is in fact nothing but an assertion that law is a part of ethics' (d'Entrèves),[114] Kant, whose *Einteilung der Moral* included the whole legal system,[115] might well be regarded as a member of the natural law school. At the same time, however, his emphatic distinction of legality (*Gesetzmässigkeit*), which he defines as the mere conformity of an act with the positive law regardless of its motives, and morality (*Sittlichkeit*), where the idea of a moral duty provides the only valid motive, shows him clearly as a follower of Pufendorf's doctrine (above).[116] Kant's concept of the 'good will' (*der gute Wille*) as the only criterion of a morally good act made it impossible of course to discover any objective basis for the natural law. On the political-practical side, he expressed himself strongly against any attempt to construct a right of resistance to the legislative power of the State.[117]

46

Nevertheless, 'lip-service continued to be paid to the idea of natural law' by great and influential lawyers such as Sir William Blackstone (1723–1780), who could write 'This law of nature being coeval with mankind and dictated by God himself is, of course, superior in obligation to any other' and at the same time maintain the absolute legislative power of Parliament.[118] It was the utilitarian school and the legal positivists and analysts, notably Bentham and Austin, who insisted again on a clear-cut distinction of the law as it is and the law as it ought to be and 'condemned the natural-law thinkers precisely because they had blurred this apparently simple but vital distinction'.[119]

Much more sharply than in Kant occurred the break with the whole conception of natural law in the writings of Hegel (1770–1831). In the first instance, in the period between the publication of Kant's and Hegel's main works, legal philosophy had undergone fundamental changes through the emergence of the powerful school of historical jurisprudence, led by Savigny, which stressed the ever-changing character of law and was averse to any attempt to deduce a universal system of law from reason and the nature of man, instead of studying the historical development and the collective *Volksgeist* (a term translated by d'Entrèves as 'particular genius of each nation').[120] Secondly, largely under the influence of political developments Hegel became the leading protagonist of a deified conception of the State.[121] If 'what is reasonable is real, and what is real is reasonable';[122] if the State is the realization of morality, then there is no room for the dualism of State law and natural law. Nor was there any place in his system for Kant's attempt to found morality on the subjective element of the 'good will'. The emphasis on the importance of the historical change and on the futility of working out any universal laws of reason and of nature was no doubt one of the merits of Hegel's philosophy, but even he could not finally destroy the idea of a law of nature as such.

Perhaps the most famous, though universally criticized, of the twentieth-century theories was Rudolf Stammler's compromising formula of the 'natural law with changing contents' which, while abandoning the hope of deriving any material rules of natural law from human nature and reason, tries to construct a few, supposedly only formal, principles of universal validity as part of the positive law itself. In this Stammler failed, and the prolific discussion provoked by his theory has shown that a purely formal version cannot satisfy the craving of men for some real yardstick of the validity of the positive law.[123]

Summing up the main lessons to be drawn from this age-old and tragic history of the natural law, we might make the following points.

(*a*) There is no single and unchanging concept of natural law. While its underlying idea is the longing of mankind for an absolute yardstick to measure the goodness or badness of human actions and the law of the State and to define their relations to religion and morality, the final lesson is that no such yardstick can be found.

(*b*) Starting from a condition where there was no clear distinction between the religious, the moral and the legal codes, the natural law school, without clearly defining the place of the natural law between these two systems, eventually at least succeeded in establishing certain distinguishing criteria between law and morality. The theological foundation of the natural law was almost entirely abandoned in the course of the seventeenth century.

(c) The natural law school, being incapable of working out any universally valid material criteria of natural law, could not prove in general terms why certain specific acts had to be regarded as bad in themselves (*per se*).

(d) Nor could it develop any universally accepted theory regarding the relationship between natural and positive law; but the latter came more and more to be regarded as indispensable even by adherents of the natural law school. In cases where the two systems clashed the medieval view of the superiority of the natural law was gradually abandoned; nor was any clearly defined right of the individual established to resist the application of 'unjust' positive laws. In the theories of Hobbes and Hegel the defeat of the original concept of natural law reached its climax through the more or less complete fusion of natural law and positive law and the absolute view of the rights of the State. Even the view that chronologically the natural law had emerged before the positive law has been challenged, and it has been suggested that the very existence of the latter may have stimulated criticism and thus led to the idea of a natural law.[124]

(e) In spite of this defeat of the natural law school its basic idea has survived in various shades, as has also the attempt to confine it to certain purely formal principles. It has become clear that we have here to deal with a certain attitude of mind rather than with a clearly definable theory. This is the peculiar strength and the weakness of the natural law, which has emerged from its long and complex history as the moral conscience of the positive law rather than as a second, independent, system of law.

(f) As we have seen, perhaps the greatest achievement of the natural law movement has been that, through the writings of both its adherents and its opponents, it has produced a better understanding of the relationship between law and morality. Let us now reconsider the principal criteria which have emerged in the course of this long discussion.[125]

(g) Going back to Pufendorf, Thomasius and Kant, there is the view that the law is concerned only with *external* conduct, morality only with the *internal* side of our conduct, with our motives and intentions.[126] On the surface, this is clearly unsatisfactory since the law, especially the criminal law, has to an ever-growing extent shown the tendency to pay attention to internal factors. The history of the criminal law is in part the history of this movement to exculpate offenders because of their general incapacity of acting with a 'guilty mind' (young children, low-grade mental defectives, certain categories of insane persons) or because in specific instances they did not act with the kind of intent required by the law (e.g. because of error, compulsion, etc.). The moral quality of the offender's motive, it is true, is generally not considered essential for the question of legal guilt itself, but it is usually taken into account in the choice of the penalty (see above, Note 78). In short, the courts 'are increasingly busy with ascertaining subjective mental states and with adjudging legal effects in accordance with them'.[127] Where, as in the cases of 'strict liability' (see above, p. 24), it is different, we feel that such provisions are not quite appropriate for inclusion in the criminal law, although they may be indispensable to other legal disciplines. If the criminal law would be entirely divorced from internal factors criminology, too, would be in danger of losing two of its most important branches, criminal psychology and forensic psychiatry.

Moreover, even the view that before the forum of morality it is only motive and intention that matter cannot be as fully accepted as it appears from Kant's rigoristic formula that nothing can be called morally good except a good will and an action done from a sense of moral duty. To quote only a few of the many philosophers who have opposed Kant on this point, Sir David Ross thinks that 'our (moral) duty is to do certain things, not to do them from the sense of duty',[128] admitting, however, that 'the moral worth of my doing it depends mainly on the worth of the motive', and Hocking writes: 'It is true that moral problems are matters of conscience and are referred to inner regions of motivation. But what are these hidden motives concerned with if not with decisions regarding behaviour?'[129] And a nineteenth-century legal philosopher, Georg Jellinek, concludes from the historical origin of both law and morality, which he finds in the *mores*, and in accordance with the emphasis he places on the social side of morality, that not only the legal, but also the moral norm requires for its fulfilment an action in accordance with that norm.[130] Another legal philosopher, Gustav Radbruch, distinguishes four different meanings of the contrast 'external-internal':[131] in addition to the one just mentioned, it could, he thinks, also mean that the law is concerned with the value of human actions to the community, and morality with the absolute value, from which it is sometimes concluded that in law there are not only duties but also corresponding rights of other persons whereas in morals there are only duties without corresponding rights.[132] The latter, however, can, as Radbruch and Kantorowicz have shown,[133] hardly be accepted in this generality. 'Mutual promises to be faithful to each other between lovers and friends are usually of a definitely non-legal, purely moral character,

49

but they are felt to be contractually binding, as is shown by the violent reaction when they are broken' (Kantorowicz). More support has been given to a third interpretation of the distinction 'external-internal' as meaning that the law is 'heteronomous', morality 'autonomous'. But as Ginsberg points out, 'even in highly developed forms of morality the rules are in large measure heteronomous, since they come to the individual from the group and are maintained to a great extent by external sanctions'.[134] For this reason, it would be equally misleading to say that the law uses external force to safeguard its rules, whereas morality knows only the persuasive force of our own conscience. Although the law has often to resort to external force, there are legal provisions which dispense with the latter, and it can altogether be maintained that in the last resort the strength of the law, too, has to rest on something else than mere compulsion.[135]

Nevertheless, there is a great deal of truth in the view, which was first adumbrated by the great eighteenth-century teachers of natural law, Pufendorf and Thomasius, and then more clearly stated by Kant that the law 'never *prescribes* internal conduct' (Kantorowicz); it requires mere 'legality', external conformity. If only we conform to the requirements of the law, we are not questioned concerning our motives for doing so, whereas from the point of view of morality our conduct, though lawful, may have to be condemned. Because of our bad motives, Kantorowicz therefore calls this kind of 'legalistic justice' quasi-morality, and it is all, he thinks, that can be achieved by 'social reform, practical politics and the pressure of public opinion', although it may eventually lead to genuine morality (p. 49).

(*h*) Closely related to the points discussed under (*g*) is the generally held view that the criminal law does not, as a rule, prescribe positive action on the part of the citizen at all, but is rather satisfied with something negative, i.e. not to commit murder, rape, etc., whereas morality may well require us to do something to put our moral ideals into action. From this rule, however, there is a growing number of exceptions. It is obvious that the forces behind the development of the Welfare State are to some extent responsible for this trend. If it is an offence, for example, to make use of a vessel which is not seaworthy or a car which is not roadworthy, this means from the practical point of view in the last resort not merely that we should abstain from using such vessels or cars, but also that we should do something to improve their sea- or roadworthiness since mere passivity would lead to economic stagnation and the ultimate breakdown of communal life. Therefore, the shipowner commits a criminal offence if he does not provide his vessel with the lifeboats and other equipment needed for its safety. In other fields, too, the prohibition not to act in a certain way is supplemented by the legal command to do something. In his famous rhetorical question concerning the failure to save another person's life although it could have been done without any personal risk Jeremy Bentham regarded such omissions as clearly deserving legal punishment ('Who is there that in any of these cases would think punishment misapplied?').[136] English law has not yet accepted this view, provided of course that no specific duty to save life (such as, for example, in the case of parents towards their children) exists in which case omissions would be punishable.[137] The German Criminal Code, § 330c, however, establishes such a duty for cases of accidents or general communal danger and punishes contraventions with imprisonment up to one year or a fine, and the German Draft Code of 1962, § 232, proposes the same and points out[138] that the provision marks a break with the older conception of criminal law and means the inclusion within the latter of a sphere previously reserved to morality. The justification for this change is seen in the idea of the growing interdependence of all citizens and their increased responsibilities towards the community. Apart from this comparatively limited subject of mutual assistance in accidents, etc., there are certain instances where English law has provided penalties for mere inaction.[139] There is first the old common law misdemeanour 'misprision of felony', i.e. failure to reveal a felony to the authorities, and there is the case, referred to by Glanville Williams, of s. 22 of the Road Traffic Act, 1930, which punishes the driver of a vehicle for failing to report an accident, but in the latter case the driver is more than simply an onlooker; he has been somehow, though perhaps innocently, involved in the matter. The same applies to the case, also quoted by Williams, of the owner of a car convicted of abetting the driver in driving at dangerous speed although he had done nothing to encourage him. However, even without such doubtful examples there remains enough material to illustrate the growing tendency to punish mere omissions. The well-known legal tag 'Thou shalt not kill, but need not strive officiously to keep alive' is no longer as generally valid as it was in former times.

(*i*) One of the apparently simplest and therefore most popular distinctions has been Georg Jellinek's description of the law as the 'ethical minimum',[140] but it would be correct only if the criminal law would actually penalize all the worst cases of immoral behaviour. If this were so we could say that these cases form the minimum standard expected by the Moral Code, and all the less revolting cases of immorality would be excluded from the scope of the criminal law. However, neither of this is true. Once we realize that there are many cases of misbehaviour which are morally far worse than cases coming under the scope of the criminal law, Jellinek's formula falls to the ground. (It is of course a different matter to say that the ground covered by

51

the criminal law is narrower than that covered by moral rules.) To give only a few illustrations, bigamy is an offence in probably all countries possessing the institution of monogamous marriage, but provided there is no deception of the innocent spouse it is difficult to regard bigamy as morally worse than adultery, which is not punishable in most of those countries; actually adultery may often be far worse morally.[141] Or take the offence of false pretences: it is traditionally limited to false statements on 'existing facts', whereas mere promises for the future are as a rule not punishable, although such promises have occasionally been interpreted as implying a present intention to do something in the future, which would constitute an inner fact.[142] This limitation to false statements concerning the present may be wise jurisprudence, but its moral justification is more than doubtful. In the interesting case *R v. Dent* the Court of Criminal Appeal quashed a conviction on the ground that the accused had made only a promise as to his future conduct, Mr. Justice Devlin (as he then was) reading the judgment of the Court and the Lord Chief Justice addressing the appellant with the words: 'Do not think that we are doing it because we think you are an honest man because we do not.'[143] There is, we might add, of course common agreement that many highly immoral acts are committed every day which cannot, and should not, be legally punishable because of certain intrinsic limitations arising from the nature of law, some of which are mentioned below under (k).

Yet another view holds that law is 'standardized morality'. This is correct in its emphasis on the greater standardization needed by the law as compared with moral rules and on the fact that the latter distinguish more thoroughly between one type of conduct and another and that certain legal distinctions can be explained only by the need of the law to establish hard and fast lines of demarcation which may have no moral justification. The seduction of a girl of slightly over sixteen may be morally far worse in the light of the circumstances of the individual case than the seduction of a girl slightly under that age, but the criminal law treats only the latter as a crime.

(k) Certainty and predictability, 'provability', clarity and precision of definition are also regarded as essential attributes of the criminal law, whereas in the moral sphere, owing to the great individuality of moral decisions and the absence of specially trained legislators and interpreters, these qualities are even more difficult to achieve than in the legal field where, in fact, they are also more an ideal than reality.[144] Predictability, moreover, is a value hardly indispensable in moral decisions.

## 5. *The Present Dispute on Law and Morality*

The discussions of recent years, largely but not exclusively provoked by the Wolfenden Report of 1957, can here be considered only in their briefest outlines. Their main stages have been marked by the publication of a British Academy lecture on 'The Enforcement of Morals', delivered in 1959 by a judge of high repute, Sir Patrick (now Lord) Devlin, criticizing the Wolfenden Report and in its turn criticized by Professor H. L. A. Hart of Oxford in his Stanford University lectures on *Law, Liberty and Morality*, published in 1963, and already before in a B.B.C. broadcast of 1959 on 'Immorality and Treason'. These publications have been widely and thoughtfully reviewed both in Britain and the United States.[145] What are the principal points at issue in this controversy, which are likely to be of more than passing interest to the criminologist? Apart from its failure, already noted, adequately to consider the historical-philosophical literature on the problem the weakness of the Wolfenden Report was that it based its argument too strongly on the difference between crime and sin rather than on that between crime and immorality. 'Unless a deliberate attempt is to be made by society, acting through the agency of the law, to equate the sphere of crime with that of sin, there must remain a realm of private morality and immorality which is, in brief and crude terms, not the law's business' (para. 62).

This sentence can easily be interpreted as meaning complete identification of religious and moral concepts which should no longer be regarded as acceptable ever since Grotius had freed the law of nature of its theological fetters (see above). To base on it the principal, and highly creditable, recommendation of the Report, i.e. that homosexual conduct between consenting adults should no longer be a punishable offence, was a strategic mistake which has weakened the force of the Report. This has recently been admitted by Norman St. John Stevas, M.P., a Catholic lawyer and writer, who also takes issue with the Wolfenden Report on the ground that 'the distinction between crime and sin is not the appropriate one to draw. Sin, as such, is a theological concept.'[146]

Lord Devlin's attitude to this question of law and sin is not very clear, but after some hesitation he, too, reaches the conclusion that, while as a matter of history the moral principles which the law enforces have been derived from Christian teaching (a far too general statement which may be disputed in those very large parts of the world which do not adhere to the Christian religion), 'the law can no longer rely on doctrines in which citizens are entitled to disbelieve. It is necessary therefore to look for some other source' (p. 9).[147] This other source is what he calls 'public morality': 'Every society has a moral structure as well as a political one' (p. 11)—which may be true as an ideal but hardly as present-day reality—and every society has, he thinks, the right to pass judgment on matters of morals and to enforce its judgment by force of law. What, however, is 'public morality'? According to Lord Devlin immorality is 'what every right-minded person is presumed to consider to be immoral', or one can also say, what 'the man on the Clapham omnibus' or 'the man in the jury box' regards as immoral (p. 16). This 'right-minded' or 'reasonable' man is not necessarily identical with the 'rational' man: 'matters of this sort are not determined by rational argument. Every moral judgment, unless it claims a divine source, is simply a feeling that no right-minded man could behave in any other way without admitting that he was doing wrong. It is the power of a common sense and not the power of reason that is behind the judgments of society' (p. 18). Unfortunately, this last sentence is largely true, but such an abdication of reason on the part of society is highly regrettable and dangerous; it deserves no encouragement, and it is surprising that it should here be praised as an ideal state of affairs by a former judge of high authority who has no doubt always tried to base his own judgments not on vague feelings but on clear reasoning. Moreover, we cannot but note the use of an extremely hazy terminology in the formula just quoted, 'what every right-minded person is presumed to consider to be immoral': who decides whether a man is 'right-minded'? Probably the one who agrees with his views. Who 'presumes' that such a person 'considers' certain acts to be immoral? Again, presumably only the one who agrees with the views which that person is 'presumed' to have. This strange reasoning reaches its climax in the sentence: 'If the reasonable man believes that a practice is immoral and believes also—no matter whether the belief is right or wrong, so be it that it is honest and dispassionate—that no right-minded member of his society could think otherwise, then for the purpose of the law it is immoral' (p. 23). Surely, this constitutes a complete self-abdication of reason, law and ethics in favour of the views, however absurd and misguided, of the man whom the author regards as 'reasonable'.

However, we have now to proceed to the next stage of Lord Devlin's argument. According to him, in order to put the machinery of the criminal law into motion it is not enough for his right-minded man to harbour certain feelings; a balance has to be struck between the rights and interests of society and those of the individual. The latter has a *locus standi* too: 'he cannot be expected to surrender to the judgment of society the whole conduct of his life. . . . There must be toleration of the maximum individual freedom that is consistent with the integrity of society', although 'it cannot be said that this is a principle that runs all through the criminal law' (p. 17). Because of this need for toleration it is 'not nearly enough to say that a majority dislike a practice; there must be a real feeling of reprobation. . . . Not everything is to be tolerated. No society can do without intolerance, indignation, and disgust; they are the forces behind the moral law. . . .' After this trumpet-call for moral and legal judgments based on emotions rather than reasoning it comes almost as an anti-climax to be told that 'But before a society can put a practice beyond the limits of tolerance there must be a deliberate judgment that the practice is injurious to society' (p. 18). Moreover, while 'moral standards do not shift', the 'limits of tolerance' shift from generation to generation, and a time may come when the 'swell of indignation may have abated and the law left without the strong backing which it needs. But it is then difficult to alter the law without giving the impression that moral judgment is being weakened. This is now one of the factors that is strongly militating against any alteration to the law of homosexuality' (p. 19). While we can agree with much of this, especially with the emphasis on the need for a 'deliberate judgment that the practice is injurious to society'—this was in fact the *leitmotiv* of our *Criminal Justice* (p. 5)—we believe that not only the limits of tolerance but the underlying moral standards themselves do change. Moreover, while it is certainly a 'good working principle' that in any new matter of morals 'the law should be slow to act' (p. 19), it is difficult to understand the logic of the conclusion drawn by Lord Devlin that because the next generation may feel less indignation in matters of homosexuality, thus leaving the law without moral backing, this should be one of the reasons against changing the present law on the subject. The contrary should be true.

To sum up, the followers of Lord Devlin seem to be left with a criminal law founded not upon reason and a morality founded not on love, forgiveness and justice, but on the combination of three emotions which can scarcely be regarded as highly creditable: intolerance, indignation and disgust. Nor is Lord Devlin's concept of law and morality founded on Durkheim's theory of the 'collective conscience', which he ignores throughout.[148] One cannot help sympathizing with Professor Hart's comment:

If this is what morality is . . . we may well ask what justification there is for taking it, and turning it as such, into criminal law with all the misery which criminal punishment entails. . . . Why should we not summon all the resources of our reason, sympathetic understanding, as well as critical intelligence, and insist that before general moral feeling is turned into criminal law it is submitted to scrutiny of a different kind from Sir Patrick's? Surely, the legislator should ask whether the general morality is based on ignorance, superstition, or misunderstanding. . . . To any theory which, like this one, asserts that the criminal law may be used on the vague ground that the preservation of morality is essential to society and yet omits to stress the need for critical scrutiny, our reply should be: 'Morality, what crimes may be committed in thy name!'[149]

We have in fact already been reminded that 'we once burnt old women because, without giving our reasons, we felt in our hearts that witchcraft was intolerable', and Hitler's philosophy was also one of 'intolerance, indignation and disgust' as the forces behind his brand of the moral law.

Professor Ginsberg, too, though slightly less critical than Hart of Devlin's theory, concludes that the latter 'nowhere explains why he thinks society has the right to inflict pain or suffering on the offender other than that involved in the expression of public disapproval'. He also takes issue with Devlin's view that the value of an investigation such as that by the Wolfenden Committee lies in providing information on the question of how to balance the conflicting claims of society and the individual and how to find out whether a particular practice is regarded by society as sufficiently abhorrent to take penal action. In fact, as Ginsberg rightly remarks, the Wolfenden Report showed no way of how to discover an 'unequivocal public opinion' on the subjects of its enquiry nor, we have to add, did it even try to ascertain the state of such opinion.[150]

Turning now to Professor Hart's own views as far as they are not directly reflected in his criticism of Lord Devlin, he distinguishes four major questions concerning the relations between law and morality, each of them possibly to be sub-divided into several minor ones: First, has law been influenced in its development by morals? Second, has morality been influenced by law? In both cases the answer is 'yes'. Thirdly, is law open to moral criticism? Here, too, the answer is clearly in the affirmative. It is the fourth question, however, that is the real subject of Hart's Stanford lectures; it is the same as that of Lord Devlin's: the legal enforcement of morals. 'Ought immorality as such to be a crime?' Needless to say, Hart comes out strongly against this, taking his illustrative material mainly from the sphere of sexual morality, in particular from the topics of the Wolfenden Report and from the widely discussed case *Shaw* v. *Director of Public Prosecutions*.[151] In the latter, the House of Lords has, in Hart's words, 'fashioned a very formidable weapon for punishing immorality as such' (p. 10) by reviving the old 'exceedingly vague and indeed obscure' common law offence of 'conspiring to corrupt public morals'. In his view, there is a danger that the resuscitation of this antiquated concept might nullify the efforts of modern legislation such as the Obscene Publications Act, 1959, to restrict the powers of the criminal law to intrude into the realm of morals and to prevent the criminal courts from re-establishing themselves as *custodes morum*. Seen in conjunction with Lord Devlin's statement that 'in a number of crimes its function (i.e. that of the criminal law) is simply to enforce a moral principle and nothing else' (p. 9) and his views as to how to ascertain the existence of such principles and their hold on majority opinion, cases such as Shaw's do indeed seem to reveal the presence in the legal thinking of high judicial authorities of a tendency to play the role of sole arbiters in matters of morality, regardless of whether a particular brand of immorality causes real harm to the community.

Hart then goes on (pp. 17–25) to discuss the distinction between 'positive' and 'critical' morality, the former meaning the morality actually accepted by a given social group—this is the morality which Lord Devlin treats as the only one—whereas 'critical' morality embodies the 'general moral principles used in the criticism of actual social institutions including positive morality'. Here it seems we have a crucial distinction in the field of morality parallel to the one between positive law and natural law in the legal field, the natural law movement asking for the credentials of the positive law of the State and 'critical' morality asking for those of the 'positive' morality of society. Against Lord Devlin's thesis that 'society is justified in taking the same steps to preserve its moral code as it does to preserve its government and other essential institutions' (p. 15) Hart argues that this right depends on what sort of society it is and what the steps to be taken are: 'If the society were mainly devoted to the cruel persecution of a racial or religious minority, or if the steps to be taken included hideous tortures, it is arguable that what Lord Devlin terms the "disintegration" of such a society would be morally better than its continued existence, and steps ought not to be taken to preserve it' (p. 19).

Welcome as this restoration of a more critical attitude towards traditional morality is, it does not yet solve all our problems. We have already seen that the natural law school had failed in its prolonged efforts to produce a workable justification for the right of the individual to resist the application of 'unjust' positive laws. Closely allied to this is the corresponding question whether the courts have the right and the duty to treat as not binding statutes which they regard as violating the moral law. The matter assumed an unprecedented topicality and urgency in Germany after the Second World War in relation to laws made under the Nazi regime which were regarded as immoral after its downfall. In his Oliver Wendell Holmes lecture delivered in 1957 at the Harvard Law School, Hart discusses one of these cases, which is typical of many others.[152] In 1944, a German soldier was denounced by his wife, who wanted to get rid of him, for making insulting remarks on Hitler; he was sentenced to death under a Nazi statute, not however executed but sent to the front after a short spell

57

in prison. In 1949 the wife was convicted of the offence of having, through the medium of the criminal courts, unlawfully deprived her husband of his liberty (§ 239 Criminal Code). The statute under which he had been sentenced was declared null and void as being 'contrary to the sound conscience and sense of justice of all decent human beings'. This sentence was representative of many similar ones passed on Nazi informers by German criminal courts at the time. Hart has some doubts as to whether the wife's conviction could be justified in this way; he would have preferred a retrospective law to the same effect; this would, he thinks, 'at least have had the merits of candour'. This is the logical consequence of his general view which is fundamentally in accord with that of the legal positivists and holds that law remains law even if it is evil, but if it is too evil it must not be obeyed. The opposite view, represented, for example, by the Harvard Professor of Jurisprudence Lon L. Fuller in his spirited reply to Hart and also by Gustav Radbruch in his later writings, claims that 'law' which is morally evil is not law at all. As far as the ultimate effect is concerned there is hardly any practical difference between these two points of view as they both agree that in certain extreme cases the law, or alleged 'law', ceases to be binding. They even agree, although for different reasons, that in the informer cases the passing of a retroactive statute might have been preferable to the alternative of leaving the decision to the courts.[153] The present writer shares this latter view, but mainly for the more practical than theoretical reason that if such matters are left to the judges their decisions may differ from court to court, whereas the legislator can achieve uniformity.[154] There is, however, one final point to be added to the Hart-Fuller debate of which these two brilliant exponents of Anglo-American legal philosophy have apparently been unaware: stimulated by the profoundly impressive experience of what Hart calls Gustav Radbruch's 'conversion' (p. 616), under the impact of the spectacle of the Nazi regime, from legal positivism to an attitude much closer to the teachings of the natural law school,[155] they reflect that the strongly positivist leanings of pre-Hitler German legal philosophy had undermined the sensitivity to moral issues and thus contributed to the success of the Nazi movement. Here it seems to have been ignored that already in the years before 1933 strong anti-positivist tendencies had come to the surface not only in parts of German legal literature but even in certain utterances of the Supreme Court of the Reich. Proof of this is, first, the support given in both theory and practice to the concept of *Ubergesetzlicher Notstand*, i.e. the idea that there are cases of acting under duress which, though not explicitly recognized by the positive law as grounds for justification or excuse, have nevertheless to be accepted as exempting the actor from punishment.[156] This was an idea

58

developed not *contra* but merely *praeter legem*, and, being in the interest of the accused, such exemptions were easily reconcilable with the general principles of the criminal law. First formulated as 'professorial' law, the concept soon became judicial law, and after the passing of the present German Draft Code (see Note 156 above) it will be promoted to the dignity of statutory law. It is a concept of great practical significance which tries to provide a legal solution for a wide variety of fundamental moral problems. Its essential features are briefly these: If a person can avert a present danger to his or another person's life, health, honour, liberty, property, etc., only by acting against the law such action is permissible if he has properly balanced the conflicting interests and if, in particular, the interests which he wishes to protect are of considerably higher value on the generally accepted scale of values than the interests he violates. This requires an assessment of conflicting interests and valuations which may force the acting person and, subsequently, the court to make moral judgments of the greatest complexity and responsibility. For a few typical constellations of this kind, such as abortions and operations performed without the patient's consent, the Draft Code provides detailed special regulations (§§ 152–62).[157] Compared with the Draft Code, the detailed analysis of the English case law of duress and necessity given by Glanville Williams (Chapters 17 and 18) shows that in the latter very similar considerations of how to balance the conflicting interests and evils have been used, with the main difference that according to the 'general, but not universal' view duress is not a defence against a charge of murder (see Note 77 above), whereas no general exception has been made for this crime in the Draft Code. Williams rightly concludes his analysis with the words: 'The solution may be that there is no general solution', and even the German formula can provide nothing but the abstract framework, within which the individuals and the courts will have to work out their own solutions as to the morality and legality of each individual case.

The second, far more extreme, illustration of natural law tendencies in recent German legal history occurred in the sphere not of criminal but of civil law when the judges of the Supreme Court in a public statement openly refused to apply a federal statute dealing with certain aspects of the German inflation because the judges regarded the way adopted by that statute as grossly unfair and therefore violating the moral law.[158] This was in the first place of course a striking symptom of the weakness of the Weimar Republic and of the scant respect for it on the part of some sections of the judiciary, but it was also an expression of the trend in favour of the ideas of the natural law school. How deeply the concern for problems of natural law and the relation of law to morality is felt in the present-day German literature on criminal law and legal philosophy is shown in such writings as the programmatical study by Thomas Würtenberger on *Die geistige Situation der deutschen Strafrechtswissenschaft*[159] (The Psychological Situation of the German Science of Criminal Law). While this author is somewhat critical towards the subject of natural law in view of the confusing variety of modern interpretations and opposes any attempts to replace careful legal reasoning on specific problems by premature appeals to natural law ideas, he nevertheless accepts the latter as an 'indispensable element of human existence' to which recourse has to be taken in cases of emergency and of the gravest attacks on human dignity (pp. 20–9), which is a clear reference to the Nazi outrages.

After these excursions into some of the historical, international and political aspects of the matter we now return to our starting point: Of what kind are the lessons to be drawn for our original question of how to argue with the lawbreaker on moral grounds? First, it has clearly emerged that the discussion stimulated by the Wolfenden Report has often been kept within the far too narrow boundaries of sexual morality, and even with the addition of certain border-line problems such as sterilization or artificial insemination by a donor and of such non-sexual matters as mercy-killing (the Liége Thalidomide Trial), abortion and other crimes against the person the discussion is on an inadequate basis. What we are here concerned with is lawbreaking in its entirety, i.e. the whole range of the social and economic problems behind the criminal law to be treated below in Part Four. Is it immoral to steal from the small owner, but moral to do so from a large one? Is the 'white collar criminal' morally in his right because he is backed by his peers and does not regard himself as a criminal? Or, for similar reasons, the traffic offender, who usually has most motorists, i.e. a very large part of the population, on his side? Is it true that '50,000 Frenchmen can do no wrong', and that the majority is morally justified in imposing its will on minority groups by means of violence? How far can a Michael Kohlhaas and the other social rebels go in their search for justice, or the worker who feels that he is denied the status which he thinks he can expect on account of his skill and performance? Have our 'angry young men' the right to break the law made for them by their elders and betters who, they argue, are incapable of understanding their peculiar problems, or have women this right in the interest of their families? Or what should be our moral judgment if in cases of swindling the victim's motives are as immoral as those of the swindler, i.e. if he is out to make high profits, to get rich quick? Should there be a squaring of accounts, with the guilt of the victim attenuating or entirely wiping out that of the offender? And what about the 'criminal from a sense of guilt' (Chapter 17)? With him, it seems, we need hardly argue except to persuade him that he could perhaps get rid of his guilt feeling by means other than crime. But the psychopath (Chapter 15)? Has he no guilt feelings at all, is he not receptive to moral argument?

So far, neither our moral philosophers nor our philosophizing lawyers have given us entirely satisfactory answers to such highly practical questions. Nor can we be expected to supply them here, but the material presented below will perhaps encourage some of those better qualified to try again. In a previous book and in the earlier part of the present chapter we came to the conclusion that there is one moral argument that could possibly be used in our discussion with the law-breaker—an argument in no way new and original, but for the time being apparently the only one at hand: As there is no system of natural law that could successfully compete with the specific provisions of the positive law of the state, the latter has to be obeyed even where in an individual case it seems to be unjust. And—to confine the argument for a moment to some aspects of economic crime—whoever wishes to expropriate the proprietor could do so, if at all, only in the interest of the community as a whole, not in his own selfish interest, and on condition that he does not claim for himself the protection of the same law which he has repudiated by his own action. Even then he has hardly at his disposal the technical means to undertake such a general redistribution of the wealth of the community more fairly than the latter with its greater resources of trained manpower and technical know-how. Therefore, he should better abstain from trying by means of criminal action to reform the world in which he wishes to live. In *Criminal Justice and Social Reconstruction* (especially Chapter 7) we have dealt with these matters at greater length and quoted (p. 107), among other references, what Friedrich Engels wrote in 1844 in his *Condition of the Working Class in England*: 'The workers soon realized that crime did not help matters . . . Besides, theft was the most primitive form of protest. . . . A new form of opposition had to be found . . .', i.e. the political. Since then, political and economic conditions have changed almost out of recognition, and it is more than ever true that breaking the law is, as a rule, not the best way of how to solve problems of inequality. Moreover, and this point will be obvious and accepted even by the least intelligent of the 'rebels', as in the case of Michael Kohlhaas's rebellion the damage done by crime usually falls on the innocent and poor far more than on the guilty ones. For other forms of economic crime, for example, white collar offences, the argument will of course have to be on different lines and probably more sophisticated.

To the general rule there is one exception, which has emerged from our survey of the history of the natural law movement up to the present time: only one, but it is fundamental: Where the State itself is dominated by criminals, where an utterly brutal and callous form of dictatorship leaves no door open for legitimate political opposition, where its so-called law is only a pretence to make their crimes appear outwardly respectable and where its crimes are on a gigantic scale, resistance becomes a moral right and even a duty. This introduces a quantitative element into moral questions, but there often comes a point where quantity turns into quality. It is, moreover, the point where the criminal law merges into the law of revolution. 'The existence of heaven', wrote the historian Friedrich Meinecke,[160] 'made the existence of hell tolerable', which can only mean that with the weakening of religious beliefs the will to resist tyrannical governments on earth has been gaining strength and moral justification. Perhaps we have not, after all, made quite as much progress in our thinking as we often believe since the great Pufendorf wrote, three hundred years ago: 'individuals must endure the misuse of the State's authority as men endure storm and bad weather: they must go into exile themselves rather than expel the ruler; but they may be competent to resist if the worst comes to the worst and the fundamental contract itself is broken'.[161] And his perhaps even greater English contemporary John Locke—as we have seen, they were both born in the same year 1632—proclaimed essentially the same doctrine more cautiously in different words.[162] Long before them, however, another German thinker, Johannes Althusius (1557–1638), to whom Otto Gierke devoted his important monograph,[163] had developed his doctrine of the sovereignty of the people. Even so, the fundamental question of the existence and the scope of the *jus resistendi* and in particular whether such a right should be given to the people themselves or only to Parliament never received a clear and unambiguous answer in the literature of the natural law school. Nor was Luther, whose opposition was largely responsible for the defeat of the German Peasants' Revolt, more helpful in clarifying that doctrine, although he was inclined to affirm the existence of such a right whenever the vital interests of religion were at stake.[164]

The reader, whose patience will by now have become thoroughly exhausted, is likely to ask: 'Well and good, but what have these cogitations of sixteenth- and seventeenth-century philosophers, lawyers and theologians to do with the problem in hand?' Our answer is that all this is vital to our line of argument, and in fact no less so than the corresponding disputes between modern legal philosophers (Devlin–Hart–Fuller–Radbruch). But where, it will be asked, is the criminological significance of our discussion to be found? Is not criminology, as pointed out in Chapter 1, basically a 'fact'-finding, not a normative discipline? Has it not here become too deeply involved in moral disputes? We take the view that we are still keeping within the limits of a discipline which tries to understand the causes of crime and the evolution of a criminal career. If it is true that the criminal from a sense of injustice is an important criminological phenomenon we have to understand the genesis of that sense just as the psycho-analyst keeps within the boundaries of criminology when trying to understand the genesis of the criminal from a sense of guilt. And if it should be said that our explanations are unlikely to cut much ice with the modern criminal, at least with the, still probably not very large, category of the real professional, we might retort that even if this should be true we have still to try to understand him regardless of his understanding of our argument. Moreover, it is our contention that in spite of his far greater sophistication and the vastly expanded range of his technical abilities, experience and know-how, the average lawbreaker of today has not much advanced in his moral and social thinking beyond that of his predecessor of three or four hundred years ago—it is mainly the form in which he expresses his discontent that has changed—and if he claims to have done nothing but defend his human rights against an unjust government and system we may have to reply in terms not very dissimilar from that of the writers of the natural law school. This even more so since at that time there was, at least in some of the countries of Western Europe where they worked, no Parliament worthy of the name; there was no 'Question Time', nor was there an Ombudsman to help to redress well-founded grievances. On the other hand, even Parliament and Ombudsman can only see to it that the existing law is obeyed and faithfully applied; to change it in essential points without a change in government is often impossible. And if 'Robert Allerton' argues that, being less patient than his father, he is not willing to wait a hundred years for changes in the law and social system (Chapter 20, 1 (3)) we can again only point out with Friedrich Engels that crime is only a primitive and purely individual response which cannot solve general social problems. To illustrate some of these points we can perhaps not do better than once more to refer to the famous story of Michael Kohlhaas immortalized by Heinrich von Kleist. Kohlhaas, a horsedealer and smallholder living in the middle of the sixteenth century in Saxony not far from Brandenburg, is introduced by Kleist as 'one of the most honest but at the same time most terrifying men of his time. Until he reached the age of thirty he could be regarded as the model of a good citizen . . . but then his sense of justice made him a robber and murderer.' It so happened that he suffered grievous and entirely unprovoked ill-treatment with humiliation and loss of property through the servants of a nobleman of his district, a member of one of the most distinguished and influential families of the country. As all his efforts to obtain redress by legal means had failed—his petitions were in fact intercepted by relatives of the culprit who held high positions at the court of Saxony; therefore they never reached the tribunal and the prince to whom they were addressed—he disposed of the rest of his property and became a rebel against his sovereign. With the help of a quickly assembled gang he burned towns and villages, killing and robbing the inhabitants. When his rebellion had reached its peak, Martin Luther himself, who lived in the neighbourhood, issued a strongly worded appeal to him to come to his senses, pointing out that whatever injustice might have been done to him by subordinates the sovereign himself had had no part in it; but after hearing from Kohlhaas personally the details of his story he advised the sovereign not only to grant him safe conduct to enable him to bring his case before the competent tribunal but also to pardon him for his rebellion, thereby anticipating the provision made by Pufendorf a century later for cases where 'the worst comes to the worst and the fundamental contract itself is broken'. After a confused period of the usual court intrigues eventually only the first part of Luther's advice was accepted; Kohlhaas was given full and generous compensation for the losses and humiliation he had suffered; his enemy was severely punished, but he himself was executed for his crimes. There is something of the grandeur of Greek tragedy in this ending: having received belated satisfaction for the injustices done to him Kohlhaas willingly, in fact joyfully, accepts the penalty of death for his part in the tragedy—a rare example of successful legal and moral argument with the lawbreaker. There is one feature in this story, however, which somehow seems to detract from the stature of Kohlhaas as the perfect rebel and avenger of injustice: his all too complacent acceptance of the satisfaction offered to him without the slightest desire to understand his case as a mere symptom of the general misrule of class justice—he remains an individualist, without ever becoming a social and political reformer.

The modern state has put an end to rebellion of the Kohlhaas type, but it has not abolished the idea of social rebellion itself, and the criminal from a sense of injustice still remains, though in different forms, a criminological problem more frequent and more important than the psycho-analytical figure of the criminal from a sense of guilt (for example see below, Chapters 16 and 17).

## 6. *Summary and Conclusions*

It might be advisable for us now to look back and retrace at least some of our steps in the second part of this lengthy chapter.

(*a*) Searching for a workable definition of crime we had no doubt that any purely formal definition was inadequate and had to be supplemented by calling to our assistance the other, non-legal, forces of social control of human behaviour. If we think it unsatisfactory merely to say 'crime is what is punishable according to the criminal law', if we wish to enquire 'but *why* is just this kind of behaviour punishable and that one not?', we shall inevitably have to turn to the norms of religion, custom and morality. Thus we found that, while crime was not identical with conduct violating the norms of religion or custom, these two were often closely related to legal norms, either by inspiring the lawmaker or by being in their turn influenced by him (II, 1 and 2).

(b) Of even greater importance and complexity was, we found, the question of the relationship between the legal and the moral codes (II, 3). It is best described as two overlapping circles, with a large sector of each circle common to both, i.e. showing a large field of disapproved human behaviour as being both criminal and a violation of moral norms, but also showing considerable parts as remaining out-

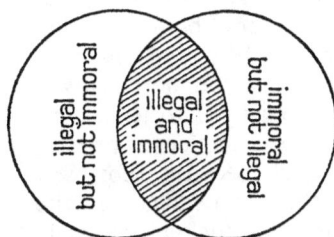

side the field covered by the two circles. In other words, there are many forms of human behaviour which are criminal without being against moral norms and also many forms which violate moral norms without being criminal. Such discrepancies had to be explained by reference to certain intrinsic differences between law and morality, their nature and objects; the law emphasizing more the external, morality more the internal side of human behaviour; the former stressing more the need not to commit disapproved acts than to do something positive, the latter expecting us not only to refrain but also to act; the law requiring of its norms and decisions a certain amount of standardization, precision and predictability, values which are less vital in the field of morality. Notwithstanding all such very important differences, however, it is imperative that law and morality should not be allowed to drift apart too often and too conspicuously, as otherwise the law would lose one of its strongest supports.

(c) These considerations led us first to a historical sketch of the teachings of the natural law school as the movement which, again and again, has tried to uphold the strength of the moral element in the law without, however, arriving at a clear conception of the actual relationship between the two sets of norms. Secondly, they led to a critical analysis of the present dispute on 'law and morality', largely stimulated by the Wolfenden *Report on Homosexuality and Prostitution* and continued in the writings of Lord Devlin, and Professors Hart and Fuller, and previously by Radbruch. Perhaps the most important of the many issues raised in these writings is this: whereas Devlin is content with a generally, i.e. by a vaguely defined majority, accepted brand of 'morality' as the basis for the criminal law, others, in particular Hart, ask for the moral credentials of that brand. Whether morally untenable laws have to be treated as null and void by the courts and citizens or whether they should be formally declared so by retrospective statute is also controversial. More important than this latter controversy, however, is the question of what the individual citizen is entitled to do when faced with an unjust system of law and government and when no court or statute or any other lawful way out is available to help him to get what he regards as his due. It is this situation that lies at the root of both revolution and certain forms of crime, i.e. those committed by criminals from a sense of injustice. With regard to the latter, it does not greatly matter whether the injustice to be averted is actually in existence or whether it is mistakenly felt to exist: 'If men regard situations as real they are real in their consequences' (W. I. Thomas, see also below Chapter 16, text to Note 108). This is the question with which the writers of the natural law school have been concerned for centuries and to which, as we have seen, Pufendorf and others gave the cautious answer that only 'when the worst comes to the worst and the fundamental contract is broken' can a right to revolution and to crime be recognized. Such an answer was in the end accepted by Michael Kohlhaas, but it will be of little comfort to professional criminals of the 'Robert Allerton' type, for whom the ordinary progress of social evolution is all too slow (Chapter 20 below). How large this latter group may be is a matter for speculation, but our discussion below in Chapters 19 ff. will show that it is not likely to be insignificant; moreover, for what it may be lacking in size it makes up in intensity. It is the task of the theoretical criminologist to try to give society an understanding of this human type and it is the task of the practical penologist to make him see that the alternative to what we might, for the sake of brevity, call 'Pufendorf's answer' would be injustice greater than that against which he fights, and that it may even mean utter chaos.

(*d*) So far, the discussions of this chapter have once more confirmed the truth that neither religion nor custom or morals can provide absolutely safe guides in our search for the definition of crime and the appropriate boundaries of the criminal law. This does not mean, however, that our findings have been wholly negative; quite the contrary: We have seen that, with all due reservations, those three great non-legal forces of controlling human behaviour can very often decisively determine not only the contents of criminal legislation but also the ways in which men act and react to the systems of law and society under which they have to live. This applies in particular to the crucial moral issues of our time: moral arguments with the law-breaker, of whatever kind they may be and at whatever level they may be carried on, simply cannot be altogether avoided, and criminal lawyers and judges, criminologists and penologists of all shades have to be aware of this.

Many years ago, in *Criminal Justice and Social Reconstruction* (pp. 5–6) we based our programme for the reform of the criminal law on the view that the guiding light of any such reform had to be the character of crime as *anti-social* (as contrasted to anti-religious or immoral) behaviour: 'no form of human behaviour which is not anti-social should ever be treated as crime. . . . The reverse, however, is far from true. There are very many types of anti-social behaviour which are not, and many others which should not be, crimes', and we went on briefly to explain the reasons for this state of affairs. This formula has been widely accepted, but also occasionally misunderstood. It was never intended as an extremist, 'out-and-out' sociological interpretation, but rather as a warning to the lawgiver not to penalize acts whose anti-social character could not be clearly seen. Our present discussion has a far wider scope, and its implications are in the last resort of a criminological rather than of a legal nature, i.e. we are concerned with the behaviour of actual or potential offenders more than with that of the lawgiver. Even in the present context, however, it is essential that crime should not be produced unnecessarily and artificially by a body of criminal law which interferes with acts not clearly anti-social. It is in this sense that our previous discussion links up with the points made in the present chapter.

# PART TWO
# Research and Methodology

# Chapter 3

## RESEARCH

### I. ITS MEANING AND OBJECTS

Research can be defined as the use of standardized, systematic procedures in the search of knowledge.[1] The accent here is on 'standardized and systematic' as opposed to the casual accumulation of knowledge. The meaning of these adjectives will become clearer when the various methods of research are discussed below. Research has no monopoly in the search for knowledge; the latter may also be acquired by casual methods and by pure chance, but in this case it will usually be less reliable unless the casually acquired knowledge is confirmed by systematic research. Moreover, chance can as a rule lead to important discoveries only where it has been preceded by research as otherwise their significance will hardly be recognized. The role of chance in Sir Alexander Fleming's discovery of penicillin and Roentgen's discovery of the X-rays has often been described.

Although the term 'knowledge' includes far more than purely factual knowledge, research is primarily concerned with the discovery of facts, taken in the broadest sense of the word. If it can also lead to an improved understanding and evaluation of the facts observed all the better. Should it lead to the building up of generalizations, of theories, and to the discovery of scientific 'laws'? What is the relation between research and theory, and what is the place of the hypothesis in research? What are the principal pitfalls in research? These are fundamental questions so far hardly ever discussed in textbooks of criminology, with the partial exception of Vold's *Theoretical Criminology*, which tends, however, to over-estimate the role of a theory in this connection. In his chapter 'Theory as the Basis for Research'[2] he rightly stresses that criminological research has to be based on a theory of criminality and that it can find only what the theory underlying the project 'makes it possible to look for'. The results of research, he writes, may be 'pointless and meaningless' because the underlying theory is inappropriate and non-applicable to the problem in hand.[3] While all this is true, it does not fully explain the role of a theory *vis-à-vis* a specific piece of research, and the theories used by Vold as illustrations tend to be too general and vague to form the basis for research. Theories suitable for research purposes have to be rather narrow and specific in order to be testable. There are of course also what Merton calls 'general sociological orientations',[4] which make it easier for the theorist to formulate his specific hypothesis. These general orientations which often stand behind a specific theory and are not necessarily sociological but may be psychological or biological as well, are themselves not testable and have first to be changed into the smaller coin of a specific theory. We are here using the terms 'specific theory' and 'hypothesis' as interchangeable,[5] and this is what they actually are. No general theory or 'orientation', such as, for example, the concept of anomie, can directly be used for research, and no specific theory should ever pretend to be more than a mere hypothesis, permanently liable to be tested by research.[6] Stephen Toulmin,[7] dealing mainly with the philosophy of the natural sciences, is inclined to reject the view that: '*all* empirical statements are hypotheses, which can, strictly speaking, never be called more than "highly probable" ' . . . For although all the statements we meet in science are such that one can conceive of their being reconsidered in the light of experience (i.e. empirical) only some of them can, in the present sense, be called "hypothetical" ' . . . One can distinguish, in any science, between the problems which are currently under discussion, and those earlier problems whose solutions have to be taken for granted if we are even to state our current problems.' 'Certainly', he writes, 'every statement in a science should conceivably be *capable* of being called in question, and of being shown empirically to be unjustified; for only so can the science be saved from dogmatism. But it is equally important that in any particular investigation many of these propositions should not actually be called in question, for by questioning some we deprive others of their very meaning. It is in this sense that the propositions of an exact science form a hierarchy and are built one upon another . . .' If we try to apply this to criminology, which is of course not an exact science, we might say, for example, that the statement that women are in general less likely to commit crime than men is a proposition which should not be called in question when we undertake to test the hypothesis that prostitution is an explanation for the lower female crime rate, but this immunity of our first proposition can be regarded only as temporary and never as final. There are important types of research which can, or even have to, be done without a hypothesis, i.e. mainly general surveys, for example, of the crime situation in a certain locality, or so-called action-research which has its origin in a general problem and will be discussed below (see Chapter 10). Even here it should not be overlooked, however, that where there is a general problem requiring investigation it can usually form the starting point for the formulation of a number of specific hypotheses. The latter, as a rule, have their origin in a broad and vaguely felt problem.[8]

The testing and retesting of hypotheses is an essential and the most obvious function of research, but not the only one. It helps to re-formulate or radically to change hypotheses and to prepare for the next step in this never-ending process of readjustment which is going on between theory and hypothesis and research and the facts estab-lished by the latter.[9] It is a sign of progress in recent criminological research that it is becoming more and more used to the testing of specific hypotheses.[10]

A hypothesis has to be specific and precise, but otherwise it does not greatly matter how it is formulated, for example whether it asserts the existence of a certain correlation or whether it denies it, or whether we start from the hypothesis that there is a high positive correlation between the rate of crime against property in a certain district on the one hand and urbanism or the proportion of persons living on public assistance on the other, or whether we use the 'null' hypothesis that there is no such correlation.[11] It can safely be left to the research to find out whether the positive or the negative statement is correct. Moreover, a 'wrong' hypothesis can be as useful as a 'right' one.[12] The purpose of the hypothesis is merely to define the scope of the research, not to determine its result. It should, however, try to avoid bias (see II below).

Where does a specific hypothesis have its origin? To this vexed question Aubrey Lewis gives the answer that it 'is arrived at by divers routes, about which on the whole little is known',[13] and we might add that it is usually derived from our study of the relevant literature or from previous research or, as stated before, from a vaguely felt problem, a simple 'hunch'[14] and our experience of life. The latter may have given us the impression, for example, that certain family troubles produce juvenile delinquency.

Criminological research is most frequently concerned with the dis-covery of the causes of crime and the effect of various methods of treatment. Research into the frequency and distribution of crime according to age, sex, area and other social or psychological factors plays also an important role.

## II. DIFFICULTIES AND DANGERS IN CRIMINOLOGICAL RESEARCH

(a) While, as we shall soon see, each of the research techniques discussed below has its specific difficulties and pitfalls, some of the latter are common to most of these techniques and might therefore be mentioned already at this stage. Some of the difficulties can be found in research in other disciplines as well, but a few are peculiar to criminology. Access to research material, for example, may be difficult to obtain in many disciplines, but the fact of penalization makes it almost impossible sometimes to obtain the material required because the fear of punishment and stigmatization deters offenders and others from giving information. This is particularly true of homosexual offences, abortion and all offences with a highly emotional flavour or offences where the police have to rely more than elsewhere on information from the public, but it also applies to the more commonplace types of offences, as the emotions connected with the fact of penalization easily falsify statistical information as well as case study material. Teachers and parents, for example, are notoriously disinclined to give truthful information about the delinquency of juveniles, unless their patience has reached breaking point. Occasionally, criminological research has to be disguised and done, for example, under the cloak of other, less stigmatizing, subjects such as housing, health or education. Access to criminological research material may be particularly difficult, moreover, because so much of it is in the possession of public authorities such as the prison administration or government departments or local authorities administering or controlling institutions for delinquent children. In some countries, including Great Britain and the United States, recent years have, however, seen considerable changes in the attitude of many authorities towards research which have removed some of the previously existing barriers. An outstanding illustration of the progress made is the study of Pentonville Prison in London, where the authors, Terence and Pauline Morris, acknowledge the 'virtually unlimited and hitherto unparalleled facilities for research' given them by the Prison Commission for England and Wales.[15]

As the fact of penalization affects the availability of case material criminological research is to some extent dependent on the contents of the criminal law; if certain penal sanctions are removed from the Statute Book access to relevant material should become easier and vice versa. It has to be borne in mind, however, that although the criminal law is strongly dependent upon public opinion legal changes may not invariably be accompanied by changes in the latter, and potential sources of information may therefore remain closed to research in spite of a relaxation in the law. The question of how far the law affects moral judgments has recently been experimentally studied by Nigel Walker and Michael Argyle (*Brit. J. Crim.*, Oct. 1964).

(*b*) The second difficulty arises from the existence of bias in the person of the research worker. Why should he be biased? Should not his scientific training enable him to recognize and exclude his own bias and to fight it wherever he encounters it in others? Is he not primarily concerned with the objective and dispassionate discovery of facts and facts alone? Moreover, are not his problems often selected for him by others, which should make it still easier for him to preserve an unprejudiced and unemotional attitude towards his work? To such questions the answer has to be 'yes and no'. Right from the beginning it has to be stated that our personalities and our work are dominated by certain values which determine our *Weltanschauung*.[16] We are not here concerned with their origin, we rather accept their existence as a fact from which we try to draw our conclusions, and we have also to accept the likelihood that of some of our values we are not even aware and that in our system of values—if one can here speak of a 'system' at all—conflict may be more conspicuous than consistency. A person who, whether consciously or not, holds certain values is likely to be prejudiced in a certain direction, and this may determine, first of all, the research worker's choice of his problem and his working hypothesis. There are, of course, as already indicated, cases where the choice is made for him, for example, by the foundation financing the research—although this will not often happen nowadays—or by the Government or university department which employs him. In other cases, however, the research worker is rightly left free to select the problem he wishes to study. He will choose one in which he is particularly interested, i.e. which has an emotional meaning to him, whereas other problems and hypotheses may be dismissed out of hand or may even entirely escape his attention. If he decides to work, say, in the field of capital punishment it is likely that he holds already certain views on the matter, and one might even venture to guess that if he works in a country still adhering to the death penalty he is likely to be an abolitionist who wishes to collect evidence in favour of abolition, and vice versa. In other words, the individual in question, before becoming a research worker in criminology or penology, is already a social or penal reformer of some sort, although he may not admit or even not know it. This conforms to the general development of criminology and penology which had their origin not in scientific but in humanitarian ideas.

While it is only right and proper to leave the research worker free to choose his own subject, completely unfettered freedom, too, may have its dangers. It is a common complaint in some disciplines, notably sociology, that too much research is wasted on entirely unimportant subjects, and with some slight exaggeration the sociologist has been called 'a man who spends fifty thousand dollars to find the way to a whorehouse', and 'what is worse is that with a team of collaborators, he then produces a book telling one exactly how it was done'.[17] Let criminologists beware lest they should be accused of telling us even less important things at still greater expense. Research 'should have both direction and purpose',[18] and especially the inexperienced worker has to be given both by his supervisors and the sponsoring bodies.

From the choice of the problem we proceed to that of the research technique to be employed, and here, too, personal bias may be decisive, although we should not forget that this is a choice largely predetermined by the worker's scientific training which, of course, may also depend on his special abilities and inclinations. On this we shall have more to say in Chapter 4.

Once the factual material collected by the research worker has been assembled he is faced with the question of how to present it—a task which almost inevitably means having to cut out masses of material regarded as less important or of doubtful quality. Into this process of selection an element of bias can also easily intrude.

Particular care is needed in the ultimate interpretation, classification and evaluation of the research findings. Statistics as well as case histories are often capable of contradictory interpretations, and unless we are aware of our hidden prejudices we may too rashly and exclusively accept those interpretations which fit in with our preconceived views.

Our research may not only be coloured by the values which we hold but also by our knowledge of criminological theories and literature. Case workers may be tempted to write their case records so as to fit into one of the theories encountered in their studies, not by falsifying the facts but unconsciously giving too much emphasis to some of them at the expense of others; and research workers using such records may uncritically employ them to buttress their own favourite theories.[19] Workers trained at one university department may therefore reach different conclusions from those trained at another.

Accepting the fact that our research may be coloured by our personal bias we have to ask whether anything can be done to counter the dangers threatening the integrity of our work from this quarter. As we cannot rid ourselves of our valuations and prejudices we have to live with them, but we can at least by making our own position clear protect others who may wish to avail themselves of our findings. 'There is no other device for excluding biases in the social sciences than to face the evaluations and to introduce them as explicitly stated, specific, and sufficiently concretized, value premises.'[20] Evidently, this protective device does not go very far as we can make our prejudices clear to others only if we are aware of them ourselves;[21]

76

in some cases others may spot them without our aid, but there will always remain a residuum of undiscovered prejudices.

(c) Criminology and penology are practical disciplines in the sense that they are generally expected to produce results likely to prevent or reduce crime and in particular to provide more effective methods of treatment. This is an important consideration in the choice of subjects for research. Projects which can have some immediate practical usefulness will often be preferred to more theoretical subjects whose practical value appears to be doubtful and in any case remote. Government departments in particular cannot be blamed if they expect something of value to the 'job in hand' to emerge from the research which they instigate and finance, and it can also be argued that 'fundamental knowledge will best be gained not by seeking it directly but as by-products of research which is designed first and only to be useful'.[22] All this is perfectly legitimate as long as it does not lead to a complete monopoly of purely 'practical' exercises. The physicist 'does not scorn to develop theoretical principles which have potential practical value', indeed he rightly assumes that 'all his theoretical findings will have ultimate practical value'.[23] The difference between criminology and certain other branches of the social sciences, for example sociology, is that whereas in the latter 'pure' research has always been given pride of place and applied practical research had to be artificially stimulated, the opposite holds true of criminology and specially penology which have too often been dominated by considerations of a too narrowly practical nature. Informed opinion is beginning to realize, however, that in the case of most criminological research projects, even if their character seems to be pre-eminently practical, no immediate practical results should be expected and research findings may have their value even if they cannot at once be exchanged into the ready cash of legislative or administrative reforms. The working out of a suitable technique for the construction of prediction tables is worth while although because of the inadequacy of the underlying case records, the tables cannot be offered for immediate use in the administration of criminal justice.

All this leads to a consideration of the attitude which the research worker should adopt and the role he should play with regard to his own findings. Clearly, the more he is engaged in research on practical problems the more strongly will he feel the urge to have penal policy shaped in accordance with the results of his research. On the other hand, it is the prevailing view among social scientists that the role of the research worker as such should be limited to the presentation of his findings, and that he has to leave it to others to struggle for their acceptance in the legislative and administrative fields. This does not exclude, however, the possibility of his entering the political arena in his capacity of a citizen who has the same right as everybody else to fight for what he thinks right,[24] and in this fight he may join forces with political parties and propaganda organizations specializing in his subject.[25] Moreover, his role may differ according to the different character of the research projects and findings, which might be divided into three categories: First, those projects which produce results leading straight to the demand for certain action in the field of penal legislation or administration or court practice, for example abolition of capital or corporal punishment or of short prison sentences for certain categories of offenders, or greater use of pre-sentence enquiries. Secondly, findings which draw attention to certain specific social evils—real or alleged—outside the area of criminal justice proper, in the field of techniques of mass communication such as films or television, or of criminogenic business methods such as certain types of hire-purchase agreements. Thirdly, findings which seem to lay bare the criminogenic effect of certain more general aspects of our culture, for example in connection with the concepts of anomie or the 'criminal subculture'. The criminologist *qua* criminologist will be freer to express his views as to what should be done and to fight for their acceptance with regard to the first category than to the second and third categories, for the simple reasons that the two last-mentioned involve problems which are outside his own expert knowledge and that it is even more difficult here to produce convincing evidence than it is with regard to the first category.

The distinction between ends and means, to which Myrdal had given much thought,[26] also plays an important part in this problem. Criminological and especially penological research is usually concerned with questions of means rather than ends. The construction of tables trying to predict the future behaviour of offenders, for example, makes sense only if we expect the courts and penal administrators to react differently according to whether or not a person is likely to offend again and if they wish to adopt measures of crime prevention. If courts and administrators should adhere to a purely retributive policy such prediction tables would serve no purpose. The same applies to the whole of our present reformative efforts within the institutional and non-institutional penal systems of today; they would make no sense if the object were merely retribution. It is for the criminologist to produce evidence regarding the best means of crime prevention if this is what present-day society wants, and it is also his task as a penal historian and philosopher to produce evidence as to whether prevention is preferable to retribution, but to make the final choice between the various possible objects of punishment is not for him but for society through its appropriate organs.

78

## III. THE AGENCIES OF CRIMINOLOGICAL RESEARCH

So far, we have referred to the criminological research worker without enquiring who he is, from where he comes, and how it is made possible for him to do this kind of work. By and large, criminological research has hitherto usually been done in one of the following ways:

(a) by private individuals working alone: for example John Howard, Jeremy Bentham, Henry Mayhew;

(b) by public officials having access to official material, but working in a private capacity, for example A. M. Guerry, Cesare Lombroso, Gabriel Tarde, Cyril Burt;

(c) by public officials working in an official capacity, e.g. Charles Goring, Norwood East;

(d) by university departments or individual teachers, which is the largest category;

(e) by Government departments or special research units, for example in England the Home Office Research Unit established on the financial basis provided by the Criminal Justice Act, 1948 (s.77), which enables the Home Secretary and the Prison Commissioners to spend money on 'research into the causes of delinquency and the treatment of offenders, and matters connected therewith'. Under this provision the *Studies in the Causes of Delinquency and the Treatment of Offenders* are produced and published.[27] As can be seen from the White Paper on *Penal Practice in a Changing Society*,[28] and more recently still from the White Paper on *The War against Crime in England and Wales 1959–1964*,[29] the activities of the Home Office Research Unit cover a very wide range, consisting partly of projects undertaken by the Unit itself and partly of projects wholly or in part financed or otherwise assisted by it. As already indicated, the first category includes mostly studies of a practical penological nature, but it has to be regarded as an important step in the right direction that these practical problems are now examined officially with Government assistance. Many years ago, Professor Thorsten Sellin, referring to the follow-up and prediction studies of the Gluecks, expressed the view that to carry out such research was the duty of properly organized prison and parole departments, and that it should not be left to private organizations to keep the results of penal treatment under review.[30] In some countries this is now the accepted policy. It might be objected, of course, that such work which could lead to highly critical appraisals of the Government agencies involved should better be left to impartial outsiders, but as the latter would in any case be dependent on governmental good will and co-operation

79

their impartiality could always be doubted by sceptics. There are in fact cases on record where strongly critical surveys of the activities of courts or Government departments have been encouraged and their publication sanctioned by those criticized.[31] Even so, it has to be admitted that the most appropriate dividing line between governmental and private research in criminology has still to be worked out. In a penetrating short paper, one of our younger criminologists has recently published a well-balanced critical survey of the present policy of the principal grant-giving bodies in Britain, and we are in full agreement with his view that 'as a matter of principle it seems undesirable for too much power to be concentrated in one body, because there is always a risk of inhibition of creativity and restriction of independence. In the last resort it should always be possible to launch a study which might substantially undermine official policy.'[32] It is only fair to add, however, that a few such studies have actually been financed or at least encouraged by the Home Office in recent years, but it has to be admitted that the crucial test may still have to come.

The emergence of the Home Office Research Unit does not mean that before its establishment no officially sponsored research had been done in Britain. Although such instances have not been numerous, reference can be made to four projects: Charles Goring's *The English Convict* (1919), Grace W. Pailthorpe's *Studies in the Psychology of Delinquency* (1932), Norwood East's *The Adolescent Criminal* (1942), and A. M. Carr-Saunders, Hermann Mannheim and E. C. Rhodes' *The Young Offender* (1944).

Nor does the present easier availability of governmental research grants mean that there is no place any more in this field for the contributions of private foundations. On the contrary, most valuable grants have been made in recent years by the Nuffield Foundation, the Carnegie United Kingdom Trust, the Ford Foundation and others.

Criminological research projects undertaken since 1950 are listed in the section 'Research and Methodology' of the *British Journal of Delinquency* (since 1960 called *The British Journal of Criminology*) and for recent years in the White Papers mentioned before, but neither of these lists can be regarded as complete.[33] A few international compilations are listed in the Appendix.

(*f*) To some extent, Royal Commissions and Departmental or Inter-departmental Committees and more recently the Home Office Advisory Council on the Treatment of Offenders have also to be mentioned as potential research agencies. Some of the more important reports of these bodies up to the year 1939 have been listed elsewhere,[34] and there are also several post-war reports:

*Royal Commission on Justices of the Peace 1946–48*, July 1948, Cmd. 7463;

*Royal Commission on Capital Punishment 1949–53*, September 1953, Cmd. 8932;

*Royal Commission on the law relating to Mental Illness and Mental Deficiency 1954–57*, May 1857, Cmd. 169;

*Committee on Homosexual Offences and Prostitution*, September 1957, Cmd. 247;

*Committee on Children and Young Persons*, October 1960, Cmd. 1191;

*Advisory Council on the Treatment of Offenders on Alternatives to Short Terms of Imprisonment*, 1957;

*On the Treatment of Young Offenders*, 1959;

*On Corporal Punishment, 1960*, Cmd. 1213;

*On Preventive Detention*, 1963.

While much of the material collected by such bodies is of considerable value, their work can, as a rule, not be classified as research in the strict sense of the word. They start not with a hypothesis, but with the terms of reference received from the Government which usually ask not for the establishment of facts and correlations but for an expression of views on certain points of law reform, for example whether capital punishment should be abolished or corporal punishment be reintroduced or the law of homosexual offences and prostitution be amended. The terms of reference prescribed by the Government for these bodies are sometimes not the most suitable ones and may occasionally even try to evade the real issue, as in the case of the Royal Commission on Capital Punishment, which was not asked to deal with the question of abolition. Moreover, their techniques differ from those of the research worker in that they strongly rely on witnesses, individuals or organizations, giving oral or written evidence which is usually a mixture of facts and opinions. Statistics are often collected, but hardly ever on strictly scientific lines, experts may be heard, but they are sometimes allowed to submit masses of ill-assorted material and make biased statements without being required to produce scientifically admissible evidence. In only very exceptional cases has independent research been done or instigated by these Commissions or Committees.[35] An examination of their status and work and of their relationship to the growing body of research seems to be overdue. They are not likely to be completely superseded by research because they are regarded as indispensable mediators between the Government and public opinion as the latter is thought to be more inclined to listen to the views of these Commissions and Committees than to the conclusions of research bodies. Past experience shows, however, that it is usually more the attitude of the Government and Parliament than public opinion—whatever that may mean—which determines the fate of recommendations for changes in law and administration, from whatever quarter they may come.[36] It is true, however, that commissions, etc., consisting partly of interested laymen, may find it easier to reach the ear of the public and of Parliament, and a case can be made out for the existence side by side of Commissions of Enquiry and research provided both sides are aware of their different functions and techniques. An attempt to demonstrate this was made, though rather one-sidedly, in recent research on problems of short-term imprisonment.[37]

A close comparison between the report of the Home Office Advisory Council on the subject and a piece of research, undertaken by a psychologist and financed by the Home Office and the Nuffield Foundation at the request of the present writer, seems to be illuminating. The governmental body obtained written and oral evidence from a large number of official and other organizations and a few individuals, and statistics were supplied by the Home Office Statistical Adviser and the Scottish Home Department; but their report, valuable as it is in many ways, has of necessity remained on the surface. They realize that, in order to reach decisions on the merits or otherwise of short-term imprisonment and the question of its alternatives offenders have to be divided into categories, but these categories are largely based on the nature of the offence committed. When faced with the necessity of classifying according to personal traits of the offenders all they are able to say in the light of the evidence submitted to them is that, apart from the prisoner 'whose offence suggests that *prima facie* prison is unsuitable and useless'—they refer here among others to the fine defaulter and the chronic alcoholic—there is also the prisoner 'convicted of a criminal offence such as larceny, breaking or assault and given without the option of a fine a sentence of imprisonment which, it is said, will neither train nor deter but possibly contaminate him and for which there does not at present exist a suitable or adequate alternative. This is a much more elusive category. It would need the most extensive research to form even a tentative estimate of the numbers it contains. We have, however, formed the opinion that it exists in sufficient numbers to constitute a problem' (para. 8). No attempt is made further to define and sub-divide this category in a manner useful for practical purposes. The research worker, on the other hand, who began his work unaware of the evidence and findings of the Advisory Council, tackled his problem in an entirely different way. Following the suggestion made earlier on by the present writer[38] he interviewed a carefully selected sample of slightly over a hundred short-term prisoners in a London prison, collected further information from their files, and studied their post-release records over a short period to see which of them became recidivists and which did not. This, together with a factorial analysis of the data obtained, enabled him to divide his sample into various categories according to psychological traits for whose treatment he made tentative recommendations indicating which of them he regarded as in need of a prison sentence and which should receive different treatment, the nature of which he outlined. Although, in view of the smallness of the sample and the shortness of the follow-up period and other technical drawbacks, this can be regarded only as a pilot study, it shows at least the direction which further work on the subject should take.

Shortly after the last war the whole question of existing and required facilities for social and economic research in Britain was competently surveyed by two bodies, one of them official and one private.[39] Although many changes and improvements have taken place since these reports were published their comments and recommendations are still of interest, and while criminology had not yet achieved sufficient status at the time to be regarded as worthy of consideration as one of the branches of the social sciences some of the facts collected and views expressed by the two committees are directly applicable to criminological research of today. To mention only a few basic points, we are still trying to clarify the relationship between Government sponsored and university or private research; we are still anxious to define the role of private foundations in the provision of funds and to demonstrate the need for permanent rather than casual financial provision for criminological research. Above all, we are still suffering from a lack of sufficiently trained workers which is at present perhaps a more serious impediment to research than lack of finance.

In 1963, the then Home Secretary set up a 'Committee of Inquiry into Research in the Social Sciences' under the Chairmanship of Lord Heyworth. Its terms of reference are: 'to review the research at present being done in the field of social studies in Government departments, universities, and other institutions, and to advise whether changes are needed in the arrangements for supporting and co-ordinating this research'. It still has to be seen whether criminology will be included in this review, and if so, whether any useful results will be forthcoming. In April 1964, however, another step was taken by the British Government which is likely to give a stronger and more specific stimulus to criminological research: the setting up of a Royal Commission was announced by the Prime Minister with terms of reference which include, among others, the following objects: 'In the light of modern knowledge of crime and its causes and of modern penal practice here and abroad, to re-examine the concepts and purposes which should underlie the punishment and treatment of offenders in England and Wales . . .' (White Paper of 1964, p. 13). The White Paper comments on this that while in 1959 it was, 'by common consent', too early for such a fundamental re-examination, in the light of more recent developments the time for it was now ripe (p. 3). It may be doubted whether this change of attitude on the part of the Government has really been due to such fresh developments or whether it had not become all too obvious in the meantime that the refusal to take the necessary steps already in 1959 had been too timid. In view of what has been said above on Royal Commissions in general there is no need here to stress again that the mere setting up of such a body is no guarantee that the right type of research and of practical reforms will result from it—it all depends on the quality and expert knowledge of its membership and the will and power of the Government to implement the Commission's recommendations. It will also depend on the right choice of subjects and the priority given to each of them: if the Commission should over-concentrate on all the milder and more easily tangible forms of deviant misbehaviour, including juvenile and adolescent delinquency—the then Home Secretary is reported to have already asked for an Interim Report on the latter—at the expense of the really serious problems of the affluent society, including the structure and extent of organized crime (see below, Chapter 25, IV), which are among the strongest factors behind the misbehaviour of the younger generation, it is not likely to reach its objects.

## IV. GENERAL TRENDS IN CRIMINOLOGICAL RESEARCH

Assuming the correctness of our views about the need for a specific hypothesis as the usual, though not always essential, starting point of research we may roughly distinguish the following three stages in the historical development of criminological research over the past two hundred years:[40]

### (a) The Pre-Scientific Stage

Here no hypothesis is formulated and tested, and no attempt is made to tackle the problem in hand without prejudice and to study the facts as they are found. This does not mean that such studies have no value. On the contrary, while most of the magnificent penological literature of the eighteenth and the first half of the nineteenth centuries belong to this category, the humanitarian progress in our penal systems is largely due to examples of this kind. They were highly emotional and biased, in the best sense of the word, but well adapted to the needs of the age and therefore often better able to reach their object than the detached work of the scholar. Even if Bentham's gentle reproach was justified that John Howard, his 'venerable friend', had collected 'a quarry of stones' rather than constructed a house, these stones could at least be used by his successors to demolish and replace the antiquated dungeons of the past. And even for present-day research we have already expressed the view that it can sometimes usefully be done without a hypothesis.

## (b) The Semi-Scientific Stage

Work here starts from a hypothesis which may be explicit or implicit, but it is too wide and ambitious to be amenable to accurate testing. Moreover, no scientifically acceptable techniques of testing are available. Among mid-nineteenth-century penologists Captain Alexander Maconochie, in particular, comes to mind as an outstanding example. His system of marks and progressive stages and his idea of the indeterminate sentence clearly sprang from theories which could be formulated as hypotheses, and he tried to operate and validate them by what would nowadays be called operational techniques of research.[41] Cesare Lombroso, too, had a definite theory of the born criminal, theories of atavism, degeneration, epilepsy, etc., and various hypotheses which he tried to prove by careful observation of the clinical material at his disposal, but his techniques of examination, interpretation and validation were inadequate by present-day standards and his gift of enthusiastic intuition and imagination often got the better of him. Some more detailed criticisms will have to be made below when Lombroso's work will be discussed in Chapter 12.[42] Some of the mid-nineteenth-century European ecologists, such as Guerry (see below, Chapter 23), worked upon 'a series of *ad hoc* hypotheses', but without a 'specific body of theory'.[43]

## (c) The Scientific Stage

To say that all the requirements so far outlined have been fulfilled at this stage would of course be to paint an ideal and entirely unrealistic picture: there would have to be a specific hypothesis originating in a general theory, tested by the correct application of one or several of the universally approved techniques, and the results would be subjected to careful and unprejudiced interpretation and validation. If necessary, the original hypothesis would be modified in the light of the research findings, and the whole process repeated with reference to this new hypothesis. Needless to say, there has never been such a perfect piece of research and we are not likely ever to see it; all we can do is to try in the light of previous experience to avoid the worst blunders.

Our criticism of Lombroso's excessive reliance on intuition[44] is not directed against the use of intuitive methods as such which have not only their legitimate place in criminological research but are often indispensable, especially in the formulation of a new hypothesis and

85

in the interpretation of the findings.[45] It is only the unfettered, uncritical and uncontrolled use of intuitive methods that should be avoided, and 'our intuitions must be tested'.[46]

## V. THE VALUE OF CRIMINOLOGICAL RESEARCH

Already in 1949, the present writer posed, but did not attempt to answer, the question: 'Has the research so far done been of any practical use to anybody . . . or has it simply been so much waste of effort and of paper?'[47] Today, our answer can be confidently given that criminological research had been of practical value in the following directions:

(a) It has destroyed or at least weakened many erroneous beliefs, mainly about alleged causes of crime and the efficiency of various methods of treatment. Illustrations will be given in the course of this book. This does not mean that such beliefs are no longer held anywhere. There are inevitably individuals who do not care to find out whether and why they should change certain strongly held views which have a deep-seated emotional appeal to them, and there are others who stick to their views although on a rational level they are conscious of their unreasonableness. The existence of scientific refutation, however, forces them into a defensive attitude which weakens their position and makes them occasionally more amenable to compromise. This has happened in particular in the struggle for the abolition of capital punishment.[48]

(b) On the more positive side, it has been responsible for a number of improvements in penal treatment needed to fill the gaps left by the disappearance of outmoded methods. Although progress of this kind lies mainly in the penological field, the changes in attitudes thus produced have also affected the causative side by reducing the criminogenic effect of such methods. Moreover, outside the narrow field of the penal system proper the growing insight into the working of the human mind and of social institutions, due not only to sociological and psychological but also to criminological research, has given rise to a less timid and hide-bound approach to the whole problem of crime. The day is perhaps not too distant when criminological research will take its place beside the press and the Royal Commissions and Departmental Committees 'as an equal partner among the public opinion forming bodies'.[49] Moreover, it is playing an increasing part in providing the factual basis for legislation (on 'experimental legislation' see 'experimental methods', Chapter 9, below).

On the other hand, criminologists would do well to take Gunnar Myrdal's[50] warning to heart that social scientists should not claim too much credit for their recent successes which are still greatly over-shadowed by their failures. They should be conscious, in particular, of the crudeness of most of their techniques, statistical and otherwise. To give only two illustrations out of many, it is sometimes pathetic to see how much reliance is placed on information derived from interviews which, at best, can produce a picture of the interviewee only at the moment of the interview without showing anything about the crucial process of his whole development over a period of years. It is equally pathetic to observe how many statistical refinements are wasted on utterly inadequate basic material.

(c) Criminology, for so long the debtor of other disciplines and their scientific discoveries, is now slowly and in a small way assuming the role of creditor as well, mainly through its control group and ecological researches which have provided general information pre-viously not available on non-delinquents and on localities of various characteristics.

# Chapter 4

## METHODOLOGY OF RESEARCH IN GENERAL

### I. PROBLEM VERSUS METHOD

Once the hypothesis to be tested has been formulated, or if in exceptional cases we prefer to proceed without one, we have to decide on the methods to be used for a particular research project. A difference of opinion has arisen between the supporters of 'problem orientation' and those of 'methods orientation'.[1] Is it preferable in research to have a worthwhile subject for investigation, even if it can be studied only by second-rate methods, or to be able to apply first-rate methods to a subject of doubtful significance to the progress of criminology? Which of the two ways of thinking should dominate and which should have to adapt itself to the other? It is tempting enough for the enthusiastic methodologist to vote in favour of the second alternative, and it is here that our remarks on the subjective element in the selection of a suitable subject for research are also applicable (see above, Chapter 3, II(b)). Criminology has been suffering from such an abundance of research on important matters carried out with complete neglect of the most elementary methodological principles[2] that we might well be forgiven for preaching the gospel of the primacy of method. There is much to be said for the view that there should be no research on subjects which cannot be properly tackled with the methods or material at present available. 'Without an awl the cobbler's nobody.' On the other hand, to place all the emphasis on the perfection of methods at the expense of the quality of the subject to be investigated would lead to a mere *l'art pour l'art* mentality and to the building up of a secluded, highly abstract and sophisticated, methodology which would soon lose touch with reality and squander its resources on problems which interest nobody but its own high-priests and their acolytes. What we need is *both* worthwhile subjects and up-to-date methods of investigation, but if we find that with the material and the techniques at present at our disposal we cannot expect to obtain scientifically reliable results we should be self-denying and honest enough to postpone research on the problem in question, however interesting and pressing it may appear. Sometimes this will mean that in the interval we can profitably make arrangements for the training of staff and the collection of better material for future research.[3]

## II. NATURAL OR SOCIAL SCIENCE METHODS IN CRIMINOLOGICAL RESEARCH?

Here we have to face two basic considerations:

(a) Although criminology is a branch of the social sciences, the causes of crime are physical as well as social (see the later chapters). Criminology, not unlike medicine, has its roots in both of these two camps, just as psychiatry, in the words of Aubrey Lewis,[4] is at the same time 'a form of applied social science' and of medicine. Moreover, as has been argued elsewhere,[5] criminology is at the same time a nomothetic discipline, aiming at the discovery of uniformities and general 'laws' in the sense explained in Chapter 1, and an idiographic discipline, concerned with the observation and systematic classification of facts about human behaviour in individual cases.

(b) Being a young discipline, not yet able to work out its own methods, criminology has still largely to use the methods employed by other, more fully developed branches of the natural and social sciences. This poses a serious dilemma because it means that criminology has to rely in part on the methods of the natural and in part on those of the social sciences and because these two are far from being identical. How can this dilemma be solved? Should we simply accept the fact that there is, and will always be, a dualism of methods in criminological research or should we try to overcome this dualism by attempting to reconcile the two methods?

First, are they actually so very different? No doubt, to mention only some of the most striking points, the social sciences are more complex, less accurate and less amenable to experimentation (see below, Chapter 9). The events they study are less likely to be repeatable in exactly the same way; mental factors, which can be ignored in the natural sciences, play a very important role in social causation; and it is also more difficult here to isolate the various causal factors. Moreover, the social researcher cannot 'put himself, as an impartial observer, outside of society'[6] because he is himself part of the society he observes, and inevitably he approves or disapproves much of what he sees, whereas the natural scientist can preserve a neutral attitude. In a way, medicine has to face a similar dilemma as criminology; it is concerned with individuals, but there is a 'social' medicine and, more specifically, a 'social' psychiatry as well. In the latter and in epidemiology, 'the study of the mass aspects of disease',[7] we find the closest parallels to the social science elements in criminology. There can be no doubt that the techniques of research used in the purely medical, psychiatric and in particular psycho-analytic sectors of criminology are different from those in the sociological and statistical ones. Should we conclude from this that, as Aubrey Lewis implies, once we accept the existence of those differences, a 'bewildering zig-zag' is likely to result, making the progress of criminology as of psychiatry 'a little indecisive and wobbly at times'? Or will a synthesis between these opposing disciplines eventually be achieved?[8] It would be claiming too much to say that such a synthesis is already in sight, but there are certain straws in the wind.[9] Even so, the student of criminology has to pay careful attention to the scientific background of the writers whose guidance he seeks because the writings of a natural scientist, his concept of causation, his views on experimentation, etc., may require a different interpretation from those of a sociologist or a lawyer.

### III. THE NEED FOR TEAMWORK[10]

The conception of teamwork implies co-operation, but not necessarily between persons of different qualifications. Co-operation between workers of the same category is more and more needed as the size of research projects extends beyond the powers of one single person. In practice, however, we think of it mainly as co-operation between individuals possessing different abilities or training. From the fact that criminology is dependent upon the contributions of several other disciplines and from the multi-factor theory of crime causation follows the need for research in this field often to be planned and carried out by a team of scholars with widely differing backgrounds and interests. For prediction research at least a statistician and a penologist, for research of an ecological character a sociologist and a psychologist, both with criminological training, are required. The Bristol Social Project employed, at one stage or another, a sociologist, a psychiatric social worker, a group worker, a social worker, and, directing the whole operation, a criminologist with sociological training.[11] The Gluecks had on their staff for *Unraveling Juvenile Delinquency*[12] a large assortment of 'social investigators', psychologists, a 'psychiatrist-physician', two Rorschach Test specialists, physical anthropologists and statisticians, but no sociologist, an omission which has often been criticized.

This teamwork approach, essential as it is, entails considerable expenses and technical and psychological difficulties. First, unless one member of the team is obviously singled out as the leader by age and scientific eminence or has been appointed as such by the directing body, the question of who should lead has to be settled by the team itself, which may easily cause friction. It can be solved according to disciplines only if one of the latter is clearly of outstanding importance to the project. In Child Guidance work the leadership of the psychiatrist has so far usually been taken for granted, but his claims have recently been challenged by psychologists.[13] Secondly, in order to mould into one team workers of different scientific backgrounds, approaching the subject from different angles and accustomed to different research techniques, a great deal of tact and self-denial has to be expected from each member. It is not enough to have representatives of various disciplines employed on a project; there has also to be genuine co-operation and inter-action between them. Moreover, as Norbert Wiener writes in his *Cybernetics*,[14] each member should possess 'a thoroughly sound and trained acquaintance with the fields of his neighbours', and they should all know 'one another's intellectual customs'. This is an ideal often difficult to achieve, among other reasons because for the sake of economy they may have to be appointed for different stages of the project, which in fact often rules out the possibility of real teamwork, or if they are simultaneously employed they may be kept artificially separated because the project director may be afraid that they may influence one another's views and findings. In the project described in *Unraveling Juvenile Delinquency*, the Gluecks felt it necessary to 'curb the curiosity of their team members about the findings of those portions of the study in which they had no part ... we were convinced that the data of each discipline should be gathered independently of all the others, not only to avoid circular reasoning and unconscious bias, but also ultimately to permit proper assessment of the contribution of each avenue of approach to the mosaic of crime causation'.[15] In the light of our previous remarks on the danger of bias in research this is a very serious consideration, but if driven to its logical conclusion it might mean the end of team research as it would rule out any kind of co-operation and discussion between members of a team. In fact, the Gluecks felt obliged to arrange occasional staff conferences with joint discussions.

There are still social scientists who believe in the unique value of individual as opposed to team research,[16] and it has to be admitted that most really great discoveries in the social sciences, including criminology, have so far been due to individuals rather than teams. Psycho-analysts, the most individualistic of all scholars, have been particularly sceptical of teamwork, but it is worthy of note that one of the most distinguished among them, Edward Glover, has at least seriously surveyed and delimited the possibilities and risks of team research on delinquency.[17] The sociologist, on the other hand, is probably the one most sympathetically inclined to the idea of team-work in research, and some of the most penetrating discussions of the subject can be found in John Spencer's report on the Bristol Social Project.[18] From the psychologist's point of view R. G. Andry's chapter in *Criminology in Transition* (1965) is also very valuable.

## IV. THE NEED FOR REPLICATION AND PILOT STUDIES

Replication studies differ from teamwork in that here a project is carried out by the same or other workers as a replica of research already completed; and often it is done independently of the first. They are essential in order to increase the validity and reliability of research findings. Each single research project has to be regarded as one link in a chain of studies which combined are more likely to produce scientifically acceptable evidence than each of them would in isolation. One way of placing the individual project in the right per-spective is to study the literature of the subject and to examine how far the present enquiry, its scope, material, techniques and findings differ from those of its predecessors. This is an essential procedure which the individual research worker can neglect only at his peril—'if it is true that "no man is an island", the same applies, in an increasing measure, to research in general and criminological re-search in particular'.[19] The second, and hitherto less customary, way is the replication study. Such studies should be undertaken in the same country or, as cross-cultural studies, elsewhere to see whether results produced in one country can be confirmed in another country, possibly one with a different culture. Two distinguished American sociologists, Arnold M. Rose in the field of the social sciences in general and Marshall B. Clinard for criminology, have given much thought to this subject,[20] and it also has been deplored by criminolo-gists that consecutive studies on the same subject are so often not comparable because of the use of slightly different terms and tech-niques.[21] Comparability is needed in particular because criminolo-gical researches have, largely for financial reasons, hitherto often been using very small samples, and it has been one of the most common weaknesses to base conclusions on numbers of cases not suf-ficiently representative. On the other hand, Wilkins, *Social Deviance*, p. 155, has forcefully stressed the often superior value of small as against large samples. Moreover, research findings which may have been adequate to confirm a certain hypothesis for the country or culture of their origin are sometimes entirely beside the point else-where in a different social, economic or psychological atmosphere. It is for this reason that American scholars in particular, conscious of the unique features of their own culture, have felt the need to test some of their hypotheses not only within the United States but also abroad in order to make them usable as a basis of a general theory. As Arnold M. Rose has pointed out, replication may mean either the repetition of a study with the same or similar techniques but different material or an effort to test the conclusions of a previous study with different techniques and different material. We are here mainly concerned with the first alternative which seems to be more fruitful for purposes of comparison and testing. It is often difficult, however, to apply the same methods of research with different material and in different surroundings. The research worker is sometimes forced to make concessions to the latter which may involve changes in the procedure as originally planned. Moreover, and this applies not only to cross-cultural but to all replication studies, the problem in question has to be formulated 'in generally meaningful terms' to provide the basis for fruitful replication.[22]

Replication studies are of course possible only if the study in question is actually 'repeatable', which will as a rule be the case if it employs objective rather than subjective criteria. Much depends of course on the question 'repeatable by whom?', i.e. by highly trained or semi- or untrained workers. As the matter is of particular importance to prediction studies it will be further discussed under that heading.

Validation studies are similar to replication studies, but validation can also be sought by means other than replication.[23] It may consist of the application of methods entirely different from those used in the study for which validation is required. As in criminological research validation, too, has mainly been tried for prediction studies the subject will also be further discussed below in connection with them.

*Pilot* studies, too, are of two different kinds. The usual meaning of the term refers to the preliminary stage of a larger project designed to try out the usefulness and accuracy of the methods to be applied to the project as a whole. The idea behind such studies is to spot at an early stage methodological errors or the suitability of the case material, of the area, or the questionnaire, etc., provisionally selected. No large-scale project should be undertaken without such a safety valve.[24]

Occasionally, however, we call a study a pilot study which was originally not intended to be one, because eventually it has been found that to achieve its objects the research should have been undertaken on a larger scale, for example with a larger sample or with a larger number of different groups to be used for the purpose of comparison. Myrdal has strongly criticized such procedures. 'Social scientists', he writes, 'have become accustomed to answer that "very much more detailed factual research is necessary before wise action can be planned upon the basis of scientific knowledge".' This statement, which, with few verbal variations, will be found so often in our literature, is an expression of scientific modesty. But it also expresses 'escape . . . practical action or inaction must be decided from day to day and cannot wait until eventually a lagging social science has collected enough detailed data for shouldering its part of the responsibility . . . [and] even with much more money and exertion spent on research, social science will, in this complicated and rapidly changing world, probably always be able to present this same excuse . . .'[25] There is, as experience shows, much truth in this. Research workers are often perfectionists and also too timid to offer the results of their small-scale studies as reliable foundations for responsible social action possibly determining the fate of many individuals. All too often, however, the fault is not theirs, and their attitude is due to their better insight into the small size and imperfect quality of their material and the doubtful value of existing techniques. The problem of 'subject versus method' may here be relevant (see s. I above).

# Chapter 5

## THE PLACE OF STATISTICS IN CRIMINOLOGICAL RESEARCH I

In this and the following chapters a survey will be given of the functions of the various methods of criminological research. To put it in a nutshell, such research can be done by means of any one of the following methods, either alone or, more usually, in combination:

*Principal methods:* Statistical | Typological | Individual (psychological or psychiatric) Case Study

*Secondary methods:* Sociological (dealing with Institutions, Groups, Areas) | Experimental | Prediction | Operational (action research)

The above scheme is intended to show, first, that the typological method stands between the two extremes of the statistical method, which is only concerned with the mass aspects of crime and punishment, and the case study method, which is solely concerned with the individual case. Secondly, it is intended to show that each of the secondary methods has to make use of one or several of the three principal methods. The sociological method, for example, has to employ either statistical, or typological, or case study methods or all three combined, and the same applies to experimental, prediction and operational methods.

### General and Historical Considerations

The present chapter and Chapter 6 are concerned with the use of statistical methods in criminology.[1] It is not their object to deal with the matter from the point of view of the trained statistician; but merely to explain what kinds of criminal statistics and statistical methods are available or are needed, what has been their historical development, what use can be made of them, and which pitfalls have to be avoided in doing so.

Before going into details, a few remarks will not be out of place on the early beginnings of the scientific study of criminal statistics in the first decades of the nineteenth century, beginnings usually connected with the name of the famous Belgian statistician and Professor of Astronomy in Brussels, Adolphe Quetelet (1796–1874).[2] His main works are: *Sur l'homme et le développement de ses facultés, ou Essai de physique sociale* (Paris 1835, 2 vols.); *Recherches sur le penchant au crime aux différent ages* (1831); *Du système social et des lois qui le régissent* (1848). It was Quetelet who, aided by comprehensive statistical material drawn from French and Belgian sources, pointed out that, as many other social happenings such as marriage, divorce, suicide, birth and death, crime was more than something purely individual, that it was a mass phenomenon, and that the study of crime in the mass, i.e. criminal statistics, could therefore better than any other method lead to the discovery of important regularities and perhaps even social laws. The best-known of his observations was probably his assertion that the volume and kind of crime in a certain country need to remain strikingly constant, and that any fluctuations which may occur over a period of time were comparatively insignificant, provided the basic circumstances, economic, social, political, etc., did not substantially change. This proviso is, of course, of the greatest importance since, at least over longer periods of time, these circumstances will almost invariably undergo marked changes. It is significant that the statistical table first used by Quetelet to prove his thesis was one showing the number of murders committed in France in the years 1826–31, a period of six years only, also showing the weapons employed in these crimes. The figures are indeed fairly constant, varying only from a minimum of 205 in 1830 to a maximum of 266 in 1831 (see the table in Bonger, p. 51), and one wonders how far the revolution of July 1830 may have contributed to the sudden rise between these two years. If Quetelet had known the figures with their striking fluctuations presented in *Social Aspects of Crime in England between the Wars* for Germany (pp. 105–6) and for England (pp. 106–7) and for a later period below in this Chapter (p. 106), he would have rightly concluded that these must have been periods of profound economic, social and political upheavals. It is only in this sense and with such provisos that his famous dictum is correct that crime is *'un budget qu'on paie avec une régularité effrayante. . . . Triste condition de l'espèce humaine. . . . La société renferme en elle les germes de tous les crimes qui vont se commettre, en même temps que les facilités nécessaires à leur développement . . .'*—It is correct only if we bear in mind that other budgets, too, may undergo drastic changes.

Quetelet was not content to collect figures to demonstrate the constancy of crime; he also tried to explain it scientifically. The distinguished Dutch criminologist J. M. van Bemmelen, who has made a special study of Quetelet's ideas, summarizes them roughly as follows (as has also been done briefly by Bonger in his *Introduction to Criminology*): The life of man, as that of all other creatures, is governed by certain laws of nature. This means that when we look at mankind as a whole, the individual faculties of men, physical, mental, social, are distributed in accordance with the law of individual variations as shown in the so-called Gaussian law, i.e. in the form of a bell-shaped curve, the largest numbers, about 70 per cent, are grouped in the middle, with the extremes, being the exceptions from the average, at both ends about 15 per cent each. For example, people with about average intelligence are much more frequent than geniuses or morons (Moroney, p. 110), and the same applies to height, weight and eventually also to what Quetelet, somewhat misleadingly, called the *penchant au crime*, the tendency to commit crime. What he meant was simply the statistical probability that of a given number of individuals in a certain country and at a certain time a certain number would commit a crime of a certain kind; it was likely to be a small minority, whereas the majority would remain law-abiding. Quetelet was conscious of the fact that this was a mere statistical probability, but by calling the *penchant au crime* a 'moral element' he introduced an element of value into it which was out of place.

When thus looking at crime as a mass phenomenon, which particular individual belongs to the criminal minority is of course irrevelant, and it was this consideration which led Quetelet, Bonger and others to the erroneous conclusion that psychological factors did not matter in the explanation of criminal behaviour. It all depends on the particular objectives that we have in mind, whether we happen to be more interested in the mass or in the individual aspects of crime. Quetelet's concept of the *homme moyen* was a useful tool when dealing with the mass aspects, but useless for the study of the individual aspects; it was, as he described it himself, 'a fiction, an imaginary creature to whom everything occurs in accordance with the average results obtained by the society in which he lives' (van Bemmelen, *Journal*, p. 224). In accordance with his general tendency to underestimate the importance of individual characteristics Quetelet's philosophy was rigidly deterministic, and there was no scope in it for the will of the individual.

While Quetelet was the most influential of the social statisticians of the early nineteenth century whose work determined the historical progress of criminological thought for several decades until the coming of the Lombrosian school, he was by no means the only one. Another important figure was his contemporary, the French statistician A. M. Guerry, who was mainly interested in the study of geographical areas of France and who, through the application of the cartographic technique, became the forerunner of the Chicago school of criminal ecology (see below, Chapter 23). His work has been described in some detail in Terence Morris's book *The Criminal Area* (pp. 44–52).

As in other fields of statistics, we can distinguish between officially produced criminal statistics and statistical information produced by private research workers. Although the distinction has become somewhat blurred in recent years through the emergence of a Government agency, the Home Office Research Unit, one of whose tasks it is to supply statistical information in much the same way and of the same quality as done by private workers, it is still useful to distinguish between the statistical material published by the various central and local authorities as a form of primitive accounting of the volume of crime and punishment and statistical research carried out privately. Sorokin's distinction between 'humble or book-keeping' and 'highbrow' statistics[3] or, for that matter, Bowley's distinction between administrative and scientific statistics are, however, no longer identical with that between official and private criminal statistics. The real distinction is now between statistical information presented more or less regularly on a certain minimum of items—usually the work of official agencies—and information collected irregularly on matters not included in the first category, usually but not necessarily by private workers in order to investigate a certain specific problem or to test a specific hypothesis, for example whether it is true that most juvenile delinquents come from 'broken' homes or from the working classes or are of subnormal intelligence. In other words, whereas the ordinary 'book-keeping' statistics are collected and published regardless of whether they are needed to solve a specific problem this is usually not done in the case of the 'scientific' statistics. Even regularity, however, is not invariably a characteristic of official statistics as shown by the very irregularly published reports of the Children's Branch of the Home Office.

## ORDINARY 'BOOK-KEEPING' CRIMINAL STATISTICS

### 1. *Their General Object*

Their general object is as already indicated, to provide the interested Government departments, Parliament, the press and the public with a certain minimum of data concerning three broad categories of facts, i.e. relating to *offence, offender* and methods of *disposal*. This information usually refers to, first, the volume of, and changes in, crimes of various kinds and their local and seasonal distribution; secondly, the age and sex ratio of offenders, their previous convictions, sometimes their economic position, marital status, occupation, domicile, religious denomination and, very rarely, the offender's motive; thirdly, particulars of the sentences imposed or other forms of disposal used by different courts. However, this is only the average picture, and in some countries more, in others less information is actually provided.[4] In the present chapter, the position in Great Britain is described,[5] with only a few sidelights on other countries.

The object of this kind of simple book-keeping—the simplicity of which is in many ways deceptive—is to give the most elementary facts regarding the evolution and present position of crime in the mass, the main characteristics of those who commit it, again in the mass, and of the ways they are dealt with by the organs of the State. How far these objects are actually achieved by official criminal statistics will be discussed below.

Criminal statistics can be based upon the work of the police or on that of the courts. In the first case 'offences known to the police' (Police Statistics), in the second case 'offenders charged' or 'offenders found guilty' by the various courts (Court Statistics) are taken as the basis. The respective advantages and disadvantages of these two types will be discussed below (Chapter 6).

## 2. Historical Sketch of Official Criminal Statistics

Although occasional legislation, or legislative drafts such as the English Penitentiary Bill of 1778, provided for regular statistical returns on certain limited aspects of the matter, for example statistics of prisoners in individual penal institutions,[6] regular and systematic compilations in this field began only in the early nineteenth century with the publication of the first general censuses, which made it possible to relate the crime figures to those of the general population. Statistical material on crimes and penalties, usually from private sources, is of course available for much earlier periods, but it is mostly unreliable and unrelated to population and other social statistics.[7] In Britain the census was first established in 1801, and in the Parliamentary Papers of 1810[7a] we find *A Return of the Number of Persons, Male or Female, Committed to the Several Gaols in England and Wales for Trial at the Different Great Sessions, Assizes and Quarter Sessions. In the Years 1805, 1806, 1807, 1808.* In these returns the numbers are given of those convicted, acquitted or discharged, and also the sentences imposed. In 1805, for example, the totals amounted to 3,267 males and 1,338 females, of whom 1,962 and 768 respectively were convicted, 782 and 310 were acquitted and the others discharged. Death sentences were passed on 314 males and 36 females, of whom 62 males and 6 females were executed. In 146 and 15 cases the death sentences were commuted to transportation for life, whereas 29 and 5 received 14 years' and 434 and 127 7 years' transportation. The remaining offenders received sentences of imprisonment, whipping or fines. Gradually, these official statistics became more elaborate, and the *Report on Committals for the Years 1826-7*, for example, consists already of 18 pages.[8] These committals, divided according to districts, numbered 13,710 in 1820 and 16,147 in 1826, with 107 and 57 executions respectively.

Improvements were not infrequently made, and in 1895 the whole system was drastically revised in accordance with the report of a Departmental Committee published as an Appendix to *Judicial Statistics*, 1893.[9] Among other points this report recommended the complete separation of criminal and civil statistics; the transfer of certain tables from criminal statistics to the *Annual Reports of the Prison Commissioners and Inspectors of Reformatory and Industrial Schools*; the compilation of tables for calendar years instead of following the system used in the police returns which ended on the 29th September of each year; and the report also urged that tables using vague and unscientific terms such as 'suspicious character' or 'known thief' should be altogether abolished. Moreover, it proposed that wherever possible the proportions to population should be given and that much greater attention should be paid to comparisons with foreign criminal statistics. 'In France, Germany and Italy great improvements have in recent years been made in statistical methods, and we think that their annual volumes of judicial statistics should always be carefully studied by the Statistical Branch of the Home Office'; on the other hand, the report gives a warning that the 'extreme elaboration' which distinguished the German and Italian tables should not be imitated. Of considerable interest are the remarks of the report on the contents of the Introduction to the annual volumes. In addition to comparisons with foreign criminal statistics to be undertaken from time to time these Introductions, it was suggested, should contain 'not merely a repetition of what is contained in the tables'. Most readers 'will expect to find results and conclusions . . .' Regarding the arrangements of the tables, the report takes the view that this should not follow the chronological order of criminal proceedings, but the results of judicial proceedings, as the most important and accurate sources, should take precedence over the police returns although the latter are earlier in point of time—a recommendation which was followed for many years. The controversial question of how many details, apart from age and sex as the indispensable minimum, relating to the personal condition of criminals should be included is also discussed at some length. English criminal statistics at the time contained information on the birthplace, but not on the domicile, of criminals and on their occupation or profession. The committee was not in favour of going much beyond this: 'We cannot admit that this class of statistics has the pre-eminent value for the scientific study of crime which appears to be claimed for it.' Such personal data were regarded as interesting, but 'no deductions of practical utility have been obtained from them', and their object is 'mainly speculative'. Nevertheless, the report concludes, 'at some future time . . . a serious attempt should be made to obtain more precise and complete statistics on some of those subjects', but it should be restricted to prisoners (which was only natural at a time when the prison population was much more representative of the criminal population than it is now) and not necessarily presented every year or for the whole country. As items to be treated in this way the report mentions education, marital status, occupation, religion, nationality, domicile.[10] In accordance with the prevailing nineteenth-century tendency the report also recommended the publication of more maps and diagrams showing the regional distribution of crime.

One of the most important innovations made in the *Judicial Statistics* for 1893, published simultaneously with the report of 1895, is a table showing for the first time in detail the number of previous convictions of prisoners. It was found that 45 per cent of them had no such convictions, but it had to be admitted that the records were often too defective to give a reliable picture. An interesting attempt was also made in that volume to assess the effect of previous convictions on the length of sentences.

Among the recommendations of the report of 1893 taken up in subsequent volumes the following may be mentioned.[11]

(a) The Introductions were made more informative by providing material on the geographical distribution of crime (1899 and 1905), on the statistical relation between strikes and increases in crime (1908), on education (1928), on industrial depression (1929), on differences between the North and South of England (1929 and 1930), on the statistical results of different methods of penal treatment (1932 and 1938) and on corporal punishment (1935). Since 1950, a special analysis has annually been provided 'showing for all indictable offences combined the number of different persons in each age group found guilty during the year and the number of additional findings of guilt of indictable offences recorded at the same time as the principal findings of guilt'.[12] This is an important attempt to link the number of offences to that of individual offenders and at the same time to check the efficiency of the police. Moreover, a summary of the

101

statistics of police cautions is now given.[13] The significance of these additions will be discussed below.

(b) As far as the 'Annual Tables' are concerned, it is worth mentioning that the bulk of the prison returns was transferred in 1928 to the *Annual Reports of the Prison Commissioners* and that the *Returns of the Reformatory and Industrial Schools* became, in 1923, part of a special publication, the *Reports of the Children's Branch of the Home Office.* On the other hand, probation statistics began to appear from 1908 as a consequence of the passing of the Probation of Offenders Act, 1907, and figures for sentences of Borstal and Preventive Detention commenced in 1909 after the passing of the Prevention of Crime Act, 1908. Many important tables had to be omitted in 1914 and 1915 because of the war, and while some of them were restored in 1918 or 1919, others re-appeared only several years after the coming of peace or not at all as a result of the economy drive.[14] In 1938, however, new tables were introduced containing more detailed information for the different age groups.

(c) From 1949 on, *Supplementary Statistics relating to Crime and Criminal Proceedings* have been published annually by the Home Office and distributed to a number of libraries, universities and organizations interested in the subject, and copies are also supplied to other organizations or individuals on application. They contain in part information which up to 1938 had been included in the published *Criminal Statistics*, in part they provide additional material. To the first category belong in particular the tables showing age, sex and offence of persons found guilty by magistrates' courts in each police district and by individual Assizes and Quarter Sessions, which makes it possible again to study the geographical distribution of crime. Additional material is provided especially on the numbers of persons found guilty of indictable offences, according to age, showing the numbers of such offences of either the same or other categories previously proved against the offender. In the year 1958, for example, of a total of 66,716 different persons aged 21 and over found guilty of indictable offences at all courts 42,701 had no previous proved indictable offences of the same category and 38,205 no previous proved indictable offences of all categories; 534 and 850 respectively had over 20 such previous offences. Information is also supplied in *Supplementary Statistics* on the numbers of indictable offences taken into consideration by the court when passing sentence and on the numbers of cautions administered by the police.[15] The material is thereby made available which enables some research to be done on such important matters as the extent of recidivism and the effect of the taking into account system and of police cautioning on the real statistical volume of detected crime.

3. *The Present Contents of English Criminal Statistics and Subsidiary Publications*

The following are the most important official publications.

(a) *Criminal Statistics England and Wales. Statistics relating to Crime and Criminal Proceedings.* This is a series published annually as a blue book, usually about six months after the close of the year to which it refers, which by international standards is very quick work. As the sub-title indicates, this publication is primarily concerned with crime and criminal proceedings, whereas data concerning the person of the criminal take second rank. 'Abstracts of Police Returns, which are laid before Parliament in accordance with the requirement of s.14 of the County and Borough Police Act, 1856' are also included. The report consists of an Introductory Note with Appendices; Comparative Tables comparing the figures of police and court statistics, related to the population, for the past thirty years; and of Annual Tables for the year in question.

*The Introduction* provides a short guide through the main body of the volume, summarizes the principal results in the light of previous years, illustrated by a number of graphs, gives percentages not to be found in the main body, highlights certain important findings, and draws attention to the contents of the *Supplementary Statistics*. It also includes an analysis of the number of persons against whom additional findings of guilt were recorded during the year. Very useful are the Appendices to this Note relating the number of persons found guilty of indictable offences to the estimated total number of persons of the same age and sex in the general population and showing, over a period of several years, the numbers of offenders per 100,000 of the population of the same sex in the particular age group, e.g. 2,313 males aged 14 and under 17 found guilty in 1959, as against 1,131 in 1938, per 100,000 of the male population in that age group. Another Appendix contains under 73 headings the 'List of Indictable Offences showing Classification Numbers', i.e. the number under which the offence in question can be found throughout the volume, for example, murder is No. 1, embezzlement No. 37, the various forms of larceny are Nos. 38–49. Occasionally, several offences of a different nature are lumped together under one number, with the consequence that no separate figures are obtainable for each offence, for example, No. 19 'Rape' includes also carnal knowledge of female idiots, lunatics or defectives, and No. 53 'Other Frauds' includes a great variety of fraudulent actions, and No. 49 'Other Simple and Minor Larcenies' a miscellaneous assortment of different kinds of stealing. The offences are further classified under six categories: Class I, Offences against the Person (which includes sex offences); Class II, Offences against

103

Property with Violence; Class III, Offences against Property without Violence; Class IV, Malicious Injuries to Property; Class V, Forgery and Offences against the Currency; Class VI, Other Offences (which is a mixed bag containing such heterogeneous offences as High Treason and other offences against the State, Libel, attempted Suicide and the more serious Motoring Offences). The non-indictable offences are listed under approximately 200 headings in the 'Magistrates' Courts Tables'.

No definition of the term 'indictable' offences is given in the volume. The whole distinction is largely obsolete, and the dividing line changes from time to time. In fact, 'all crimes are indictable unless by statute they are made triable summarily', i.e. without formal indictment. 'There are certain crimes which may only be tried upon indictment, but there is a large number of indictable offences which may, in certain circumstances, be tried summarily. Conversely, there are certain summary offences which may, if the accused so wishes, be tried upon indictment.'[16] A list of indictable offences is given in the Criminal Justice Act, 1925, but there have been several later amendments. The term 'offences' itself is also used very loosely, sometimes as a generic term to cover any kind of contravention of the criminal law, sometimes in a narrower sense so as to exclude the most serious crimes, i.e. meaning misdemeanours, not felonies. In English criminal statistics it is used in the wider sense and the only distinction according to seriousness is that between indictable and non-indictable offences.

*The Comparative Tables* go back over thirty years, showing at a glance the fluctuations of both police and court figures for individual offences per million of population, but as they usually lump together periods of five years important features may remain hidden and, as throughout the volume, the population figures can in the absence of an annual census be only estimated.

*The Annual Tables* now begin with the police returns of indictable offences known to the police with numbers 'cleared up', of persons proceeded against according to sex and the results of proceedings. According to the official definition,[17] 'offences cleared up include those for which a person is arrested or summoned or for which he is cautioned, those taken into consideration by a court when the offender is found guilty on another charge, and certain of those of which a person is known or suspected to be guilty but for which he cannot for some reason be prosecuted (e.g. because he had died)', a definition to which we shall have to return later on. Offences cleared up in this way amounted to 50·1 per cent of the total known to the police in 1938 and to 44·7 per cent in 1959, which figures refer to the whole country, with considerable variations for individual police districts[18] and different categories of offences. In the Metropolitan Police District, the percentage figure of crimes cleared up (for which a definition slightly different from that in *Criminal Statistics* is given) was in 1957 only 30·3 for all indictable offences, and only 20·8 for housebreaking, but 108·3 for manslaughter and infanticide, a figure which seems almost too good to be true and can only be due to the fact that more offences were cleared up than had become known to the police *during the year* in question. In Scotland the percentages of crimes cleared up is slightly lower than in England, but there the term 'crime' is distinguished from 'offences' for which the percentages are much higher.

The police returns give also the numbers of persons proceeded against for non-indictable offences, with results of proceedings. The police returns are followed by tables showing the numbers of persons tried at Assizes and Quarter Sessions, with nature of offence, and results of proceedings according to sex and age and also sex related to offence and length of sentence. The tables for Magistrates' Courts are given for indictable and non-indictable offences and also divided according to sex, age, offence and results of proceedings, and there are special tables for courts of appeal, for probation orders, public prosecutions, Broadmoor patients, legal aid and a few others.

It is thus a special feature of English criminal statistics that they present both police and court statistics, thereby enabling us to compare these two sets of figures, whereas many other countries concentrate on court statistics. Such comparisons, as will be seen later, lead to a number of interesting questions.

(*b*) Second in importance rank the annual *Reports of the Commissioners of Prisons*, also published one year after the period covered. (The Prison Commission has now been abolished, and its functions have been taken over by the Prison Department of the Home Office.) Although their principal interest lies not in the statistical material provided but in their general material on the administration of prisons, borstals and detention centres, they contain many tables of statistical interest on the characteristics of the population of these institutions, e.g. their age in relation to the length of the sentence (not shown in *Criminal Statistics*), on the daily average population of each institution, on the employment of inmates, on expenditure and many more. Together with these publications, the annual *Reports of the Council of the Central After-Care Association* (C.A.C.A.) should be studied, which provide information on the work of the various bodies forming the Association, especially related to recidivism.

(*c*) The annual *Reports of the Commissioner of Police of the Metropolis* provide information for the London area similar to that given in *Criminal Statistics* for the whole country, with special emphasis on

105

matters of interest to the police such as arrests, motoring offences, drunkenness, percentages of offences cleared up.

(d) The, irregularly published, *Reports of the Children's Department, Home Office*, contain statistics on juvenile delinquency, the Approved School population, children in the care of local authorities, juvenile courts and similar matters. The most recent of these reports is the one for the years 1961-3, H.M.S.O., H.C. 155, London, 1964.

There are further several more specialized annual publications such as *Offences relating to Motor Vehicles* and *Offences of Drunkenness* and occasional papers such as *Papers relating to the Large Number of Crimes Accompanied by Violence Occurring in Large Cities* (House of Lords [121], July 1951). Attention may also be briefly drawn to *Criminal Statistics—Scotland*, published annually for the year before that of publication, giving statistics similar to that in *Criminal Statistics England and Wales*, but adapted to the different criminal law and procedure in Scotland and with informative notes on these legal differences in procedure.[19]

4. *Some Figures from 'English Criminal Statistics' and the Other Publications mentioned in Section 3*

To give an idea of the actual volume and development of crime and matters related to it, as reflected in these various publications, the following figures may be quoted:[20]

(a) *Indictable offences known to the police*

| Year | Larceny | Breaking and entering | Frauds and false pretences | Sexual offences | Violence against the person | Total (which also includes receiving and other offences) |
|------|---------|-----------------------|----------------------------|-----------------|-----------------------------|----------------------------------------------------------|
| 1938 | 199,951 | 49,184  | 16,097 | 5,018  | 2,721  | 283,220 |
| 1945 | 323,310 | 108,266 | 13,122 | 8,546  | 4,743  | 478,394 |
| 1952 | 341,512 | 97,941  | 27,230 | 14,967 | 6,997  | 513,559 |
| 1959 | 445,888 | 133,962 | 34,061 | 20,024 | 13,876 | 675,626 |
| 1963 | 635,627 | 219,138 | 45,823 | 20,518 | 20,083 | 978,076 |

Source: *Criminal Statistics England and Wales.*

### (b) Persons found guilty of offences

| Year | Indictable | Non-indictable | (Persons dealt with summarily) |
|---|---|---|---|
| 1938 | 78,463 | Annual averages 1935–39 | 797,026 |
| 1945 | 115,974 | Annual averages 1945–49 | 583,913 |
| 1952 | 131,047 | Annual averages 1950–54 | 731,654 |
| 1959 | 153,190 | Annual averages 1959 | 1,049,946 |
| | | Number of persons found guilty in 1959 | 887,532 |
| 1963 | 211,718 | | 1,107,429 |

Source: *Criminal Statistics England and Wales*, for the years concerned, Introductory Note, Chapter 6.

### (c) Persons found guilty of traffic offences
### (Nos. 122–138 of list of non-indictable offences)

| 1938 | 475,124 | 1959 | 635,366 |
|---|---|---|---|
| 1945 | 148,419 | 1963 | 820,780 |
| 1955 | 407,815 | | |

Source: *Criminal Statistics England and Wales*, for the years concerned, Introductory Note, Chapter 4.

### (d) Persons of different ages found guilty of indictable offences per 100,000 of population of the age or age group

| Age or age group | 1938 | | 1959 | |
|---|---|---|---|---|
| | Males | Females | Males | Females |
| 8 | 220 | 9 | 270 | 15 |
| 9 | 451 | 27 | 635 | 35 |
| 10 | 703 | 37 | 967 | 57 |
| 11 | 931 | 62 | 1,257 | 89 |
| 12 | 1,111 | 66 | 1,539 | 135 |
| 13 | 1,315 | 73 | 2,236 | 218 |
| 14 | 1,141 | 84 | 2,855 | 291 |
| 15 | 1,145 | 97 | 2,025 | 210 |
| 16 | 1,110 | 91 | 2,048 | 220 |
| 17 | 867 | 99 | 2,163 | 224 |
| 18 | 740 | 106 | 2,214 | 231 |
| 19 | 766 | 108 | 1,988 | 194 |
| 20 | 665 | 94 | 1,752 | 156 |
| 21 and under 25 | 559 | 77 | 1,436 | 129 |
| 25 and under 30 | 431 | 62 | 960 | 103 |
| 30 and under 40 | 307 | 61 | 572 | 89 |
| 40 and under 50 | 182 | 50 | 313 | 77 |
| 50 and under 60 | 101 | 30 | 162 | 55 |
| 60 and over | 51 | 10 | 60 | 21 |

Source: *Criminal Statistics England and Wales, 1959*, Introductory Note, Appendix III(a). The corresponding figures for 1962 are given below in Vol. II, p. 679.

(e) Daily average population in prisons and Borstals
(men and women)

| | | | |
|------|--------|------|--------|
| 1938 | 11,086 | 1951 | 20,787 |
| 1940 | 9,377  | 1959 | 25,453 |
| 1962 | 31,063 (incl. Detention Centres) | | |

Source: *Annual Reports of the Prison Commissioners* for the years 1939-41, p. 27, 1959, p. 9, 1962, p. 1.

(f) Indictable offences known to the police, and Persons arrested for all offences in the Metropolitan Police District

| | Ind. offences known to police | Persons arrested for all offences |
|------|--------|--------|
| 1938 | 95,280  | |
| 1955 | 95,262  | 76,416 |
| 1957 | 125,754 | 99,005 |
| 1962 | 214,120 | |

Source: *Reports of the Commissioner of Police of the Metropolis for the years* 1957 and 1962.

Only a few comments are needed at this stage. First, the number of indictable offences known to the police has risen between 1938 and 1959 more than that of persons found guilty of such offences, and the number of persons dealt with for non-indictable offences has risen even less than the corresponding number for indictable offences. Even for traffic offences the rise was not as marked as often believed. When we look at the various groups of indictable offences separately, we find that sexual offences and offences of violence against the person have risen more than the others. Moreover, non-indictable offences do not invariably move in the same direction as indictable offences, which can be seen particularly in the immediate post-war years. The few figures presented under (a) and (b) may already suffice to indicate that conclusions should never be drawn from the figures for all offences taken together as each individual category of offence has its own peculiar trends and problems. As far as the different age groups are concerned, the increase per 100,000 of population of the same age or age group was greatest for males aged 13, 14, 15, 16, 17, 18. The total increase for all ages was only slightly greater for males than females. The total volume of crime, however, was eight to nine times as much for males as for females. In 1938, indictable offences known to the police numbered approximately three and a half times the figure for persons found guilty of such offences, whereas in 1959 the proportion had risen to approximately four and a half.[21] As already

108

mentioned under 3(*a*), the overall percentage of crimes cleared up has slightly fallen in recent years, which may partly explain the changed proportion. Naturally, the proportion of crimes cleared up differs greatly for different categories of offences; in 1950, for example, the ratio of offences cleared up to offences known to the police was 100 for receiving, 93 for frauds and false pretences, 90 for violence against the person, 78 for sexual offences, 54 for robbery, 40 for larceny and 38 for breaking and entering.[22] Most, but not all, of these differences can be explained by the characteristics of each category of offences; the ratio for sexual offences, for example, appears surprisingly high.

Finally, the fluctuations of prison statistics should never be regarded as evidence for corresponding changes in the rate of crime; they reflect the sentencing policy of the courts rather than real movements of crime, and it is very doubtful whether increases in the latter produce, as a rule, a similar increase in prison sentences and vice versa. From 1938 to 1940, for example, there was a slight increase in the number of crimes known to the police, whereas the prison population declined, and its rise between 1940 and 1951 was much more marked than the rise in crime.

### 5. *The Interpretation of Official Criminal Statistics—Difficulties and Pitfalls*[23]

(*a*) *The Dark Figure.* The concepts 'crimes known to the police' and 'crimes cleared up' show already our awareness of one of the most fundamental limitations of crime statistics, the existence of crimes which remain either entirely unknown to the police or are at least not cleared up. This can be explained in various ways: First, the commission of an offence may remain altogether unknown, for example the disappearance of the murdered person may not be noticed, which can easily happen in the case of persons living alone and having no relations, neighbours or friends, or of tramps and vagrants or persons travelling abroad; or a theft may be committed without the owner noticing the loss or a fraud without the victim realizing that he has been cheated; or a child may be sexually assaulted without understanding the nature of the act or informing anybody. Secondly, the death of a person or the disappearance of an article may be noticed but explained in an innocuous way, for example murder may be cleverly disguised as death by accident or suicide. In this connection, special attention has lately been drawn by Havard to the low proportion of autopsies held by coroners in some districts.[24] Thirdly, the commission of an offence may become known to others or at least suspected by them, but the authorities are not informed and no official action is taken. This, too, may happen for a great variety of reasons, such as fear of reprisals or of public disapproval or shame, which latter feeling plays a large part in the case of rape and indecent assault; or to spare children the experience of having to appear in court as witnesss; or to shield the offender, which is often the case with incests or indecent assaults within the family; or because of the feeling that the lenient treatment which the offender is expected to get from the court would not justify the trouble of starting criminal proceedings; or because of disapproval of the law which has been violated, for example against homosexual or betting and gambling offences; or because of a generally anti-social attitude on the part of the person concerned who refuses on principle to co-operate with the authorities; or simply because of indifference and laziness. In an investigation made several years ago in Liverpool of losses incurred in foreign trade the author concluded: 'It is surprising how few of the thefts involving import or export goods appear to be reported to the authorities.' One explanation, he thinks, may be the lapse of time which frequently occurs before the theft is discovered.[25] Observations of this kind may in part help to explain the reluctance of some firms to enter the foreign market at all.

To the category of offences not brought to the notice of the police may be added that of offences classified as 'cleared up' where the offender is regarded as 'known' to the police because he has been charged or at least been suspected, but no prosecution has been possible or no conviction obtained because of insufficient evidence or for other reasons (see the official definition, 3(a) above). The dark figure resulting from these various causes not only explains the discrepancy between the numbers of crimes known to the police and persons found guilty, but must also throw some considerable doubt on the value of any official crime statistics. To deal first with the gap between police figures and court convictions, our immediate reaction to it will be to regard it as a reflection on the efficiency of the police, and to some extent this is correct. There are, however, also certain factors which have to be considered in favour of the police. Offences for which the offender is cautioned by the police, for example, necessarily reduce the number of persons found guilty without reflecting on the efficiency of the police; while such factors should always be considered, their numerical significance should, however, not be overrated.

Apart from such questions concerning the efficiency of the police we have to examine whether the existence of these dark figures of crime completely destroys the value of crime statistics or whether we can draw certain conclusions from the information at our disposal which may allow us at least to speculate as to the real size of the dark figures. Scientific work, after all, is largely an attempt to reduce the extent of the unknown by making the right use of the facts already known. Briefly, the information at our disposal comes mainly from three sources: it is, first, information derived from interviewing selected samples of persons on the number of offences which they had committed without being detected; secondly, information from persons or institutions unconnected with the police and the penal system who are in a position to hear about undetected offences; and, thirdly, information derived from our general knowledge of the nature of the offence concerned and the attitude of persons towards its detection and prosecution. As to the first, the literature on 'hidden delinquency', mostly American, is mainly concerned with juveniles or at least with offences reported by adults as committed in their youth. As the author wrote many years ago, 'when reading the autobiographies of criminals, one is usually struck by the immense number of petty offences they have committed as children before being caught'.[26] According to one of the most widely quoted of these studies, of a group of 337 Texas college students every one had committed, apart from traffic offences, illegal acts for which he could have been charged if they had become known.[27] A Swedish enquiry by Strahl and Nyquist among law students of the University of Uppsala showed that out of 75 male and 21 female students only 2 reported that they had never committed any of the offences listed in the questionnaire, and only about 20 per cent of them stated that at least one of their offences had become known to the police.[28] The questionnaire included various forms of stealing and fraud, drunken driving, etc., and 57·3 per cent of the male and 9·5 per cent of the female students confessed to offences of shoplifting. In an interesting Liverpool study by Mays of 80 boys, members of a club and interviewed by him as youth worker, the majority 'admitted having committed delinquent acts at some time or another during childhood and adolescence', i.e. acts for which they could have been charged.[29] 34 of them had been convicted and another 22 admitted criminal acts, some of them rather serious ones, without having ever appeared in court, one of them having committed as many as 12 undetected offences. One has to bear in mind that, mainly owing to the very low minimum age of criminal responsibility in this country, many people believe that in the case of very young children it is better to do nothing than to bring them before the juvenile court.

A few similar enquiries are concerned with adults, as for example a study by Wallerstein and Wyle which showed that of 1,698 persons in New York City who answered a questionnaire anonymously 91 per cent stated that they had committed crimes after the age of 16.[30]

It may be argued that such enquiries, notably those carried out merely by means of questionnaires, are not convincing as there is no guarantee whatsoever for the accuracy of the answers. There is, however, a certain amount of supporting evidence to be found not only in the above quoted percentages of crimes cleared up by the police, which show a considerable residue of undetected crime, but also evidence from other sources. An attempt was made by the author before the last war to discover the prosecuting policies of a number of large London stores with regard to thefts committed on their premises by their own employees and by strangers, both juveniles and adults. The result showed that these policies varied considerably in every direction, but the general impression was that big firms usually did not prosecute their own employees and that in the case of strangers there was a great variety of systems.[31] Similarly, Sellin found that in Philadelphia shoplifting, unless of a professional character, was rarely reported and that in the year 1933 more such thefts were known to the three large department stores investigated than the total known to the police for the whole of the city.[32]

Another example of an offence where some light on the extent of the dark figure can be thrown by outside agencies is abortion. The Inter-Departmental Committee on the subject, when trying to assess the frequency of this offence,[33] refers to an estimate of the British Medical Association of 1936, according to which from 16 to 20 per cent of all pregnancies ended in abortion. This estimate, which was supported by the records of various hospitals and clinics, led to a total of 110,000 to 150,000 abortions per year, of which about 40 per cent, i.e. 50–70,000, were regarded as criminal. In pre-war Germany the number of criminal abortions was for 1934–36 estimated at 200,000 per year.[34] On the other hand, the highest figure of abortion offences known to the police in England and Wales for the past thirty years was 347 as the annual average for 1940–4, usually the average annual figure is between 100 and 200.

For homosexual offences psycho-analysts and other experts maintain from their clinical observations that, while the number of detected offenders depends to some extent on the activities of the police, it is only a small proportion of cases that is detected.[35] For the most serious crimes, such as murder, we are tempted to minimize the size of the dark figure. 'The murderer', writes Hans von Hentig,[36] 'who, as every mass murderer does for years or even for ever, walks about in our midst without appearing in court and in the statistics, wounds our feeling of self-respect so deeply that we prefer to know nothing about the problem of the "unknown murderer". Police statistics try to comfort us with a rate of 89·3 per cent of cleared up murders, but the facts make us disbelieve this optimism, provided we use the word "cleared up" in its usual meaning.'

How far is it possible, in the light of the material so far presented and of our knowledge of the nature of specific categories of offences and of certain sociological and psychological factors relating to them, to make any positive statements regarding the dark figure of crime? To some extent, this question has already been answered. On the one hand, no such statements can be made regarding crime as such. On the other hand, however, our knowledge of the peculiar character- istics of individual categories of offences, the techniques of detection and the socio-psychological atmosphere surrounding them may en- able us to say that this or that category is likely to have a high or low dark figure. To some slight extent the percentages of crimes cleared up, as quoted above, may also serve as a guide, although the factors which determine the ease of clearing up an offence brought to the notice of the police may not necessarily be identical with the factors material for the question of whether an offence becomes known to the police. Once, for example, the commission of a homosexual offence has become known it is comparatively easy to clear it up—the diffi- culty lies before that stage. Of considerable assistance will be our knowledge of the attitudes of wide circles of the population to the type of offence in question. Abortion offences will, as a rule, only be detected if they result in death; and the reporting of rape will almost entirely depend on the willingness of the assaulted woman to inform others. In any case, it would be grossly misleading to treat the dark figures as representing a fixed proportion of the totals of the offences known in that particular category.[37] For some categories of offences these totals are likely to be higher, for others they are almost certain to be much lower than the dark figure, and the relationship between detected and undetected offences may differ not only according to type of offence, but also according to type of district, character and law-abidingness of population, popularity of local police and many other factors. Our conclusion, therefore, has to be that not much weight can be attached to the crime figures as such, as published in official criminal statistics. For juvenile delinquency, in particular, the author can only reiterate his conviction that 'statistics of juvenile delinquency can do little more than indicate the varying degree of willingness on the part of the public and the police to bring this cate- gory of delinquents before the juvenile courts'.[38] From all this it fol- lows that not too much weight should be attached by press and public to published figures and their movements unless they are carefully inter- preted. In short, it is the business of the police and the man in the street to reduce the size of the dark figures of crime, and it is the task of the criminologist to interpret them in the light of what is known to him.

(b) *Police Statistics and Court Statistics.* The report of 1893 (s. 2 above) regarded court statistics as more reliable than police statistics, and rightly so, but each of the two has its strong and its weak points. Police statistics cover a larger field and give the most comprehensive picture of the crime situation normally available to us, but the methods of recording employed by the various local or county police forces differ greatly and used in former years to be even 'purely discretionary', leading often to striking and unexplainable differences between neighbouring towns or counties. Technical changes in methods of police book-keeping may easily produce striking increases or decreases in police figures without any corresponding changes in the crime situation itself. The classical example is the abolition of the 'Suspected Stolen Book' in the Metropolitan area which resulted in a sudden 'rise' of property offences from 26,000 in 1931 to 83,000 in 1932.[39] Following the recommendations of a Departmental Committee of 1938 on Detective Work and Procedure there has been an improvement and greater uniformity since the last war,[40] but a number of other weaknesses still remain. Police statistics, as a rule, give no details concerning the person of the offender; they have to depend on possibly quite unreliable information from witnesses whose evidence can be evaluated only later in court; from the legal point of view they may classify reported offences differently from the classification ultimately decided by the court.[41] Moreover, police statistics reflect the activities of the police at any given time and place and are, therefore, greatly dependent on the interest taken by the police in a certain type of crime or certain classes of persons as also on the use made by the police of cautioning instead of formal charges, a factor the extent of which can now at least be ascertained from *Criminal Statistics*. The differential rates of arrest have been frequently discussed by American criminologists, and in a famous sociological study of an American community[42] the percentages of arrests are given as ranging from 0·43 for the 'upper-upper' class to 7·80 for the lower-middle class and 64·69 for the 'lower-lower class', the implication being that these wide differences in rates of arrest are not likely to be a true reflection of the actual crime situation. Moreover, the higher 'visibility' of certain minority groups, in particular Negroes, which makes them more liable to arrest and prosecution by the police, has often been commented on.[43]

Court statistics, while giving a more reliable picture not only of the crime but also of certain personal characteristics of the offender, are entirely dependent on the cases brought before the courts by the prosecution. While we can be reasonably sure that a person against whom a finding of guilt has been recorded in the court statistics was actually guilty of the offence there will be many others equally guilty but never appearing in court. Court statistics may be statistics of persons proceeded against (or persons for trial) or of persons found guilty. Both sets of figures are needed, the first because it includes the important categories of persons acquitted or 'charge withdrawn or dismissed', the latter because it contains only cases where the evidence has fully

114

proved that this particular crime was committed by this particular person.

When all is said we have to conclude that both police and court statistics are needed, although for different purposes and each of them with many reservations. Moreover, the existence side by side of statistics of offences and statistics of offenders poses various specific problems. How can these two sets be brought into the most effective relationship, considering that very often one offence does not correspond to one offender and that one offence may be committed by several persons and, vice versa, one person may have committed several offences? With regard to the latter question, 'Surely', wrote the author in 1942, 'neither to society at large nor to the practical penologist can it be indifferent whether 100,000 offences "known to the police" have been committed by 100,000 first offenders or by a small group of perhaps 2,000 habitual law-breakers, each of whom is responsible for an average of fifty offences.'[44] To some extent, this information is now available in the *Introduction to Criminal Statistics* and in *Supplementary Statistics* (2(c) and 3(a) above). From the latter we can discover, for example, that in 1957 6,978 persons were found guilty of shopbreaking and that 10,500 offences against property without violence were recorded against them. While this is interesting it still leaves a number of questions unanswered.

On the question of how many crimes are committed by more than one person no information is at present available, except for some data in the, generally unpublished, *Annual Reports of Local Chief Constables*,[45] which refer to crimes committed by gangs, and except for those rare offences where the police returns show that the number of persons proceeded against was higher than that of crimes known to the police. This will, naturally be the case with offences such as rioting and unlawful assembly (Nos. 64 and 65 of classified list), but even here it does not help us very much to find, for example, that in 1959 crimes of the latter category numbered 8 as against 47 persons proceeded against.

Statistics of recidivism have nothing to do with the relationship between police and court statistics as previous offences committed by an individual may have been recorded as known to the police some years before he was found guilty by a court for his latest offence. *Criminal Statistics* at present gives no information on recidivism, but *Supplementary Statistics* (2(c) above) does and even more so the *Annual Reports of the Prison Commissioners* and of the C.A.C.A. (3(b) above).

(c) *Other Considerations concerning the Interpretation of Criminal Statistics.* So far we have drawn attention to certain weaknesses of the official figures arising from the existence of the 'dark figures' of

115

undetected crime and from other deficiencies of police and court statistics. Now we have to consider various additional factors which may influence the interpretation of these official figures and occasionally even determine on paper the very extent of crime as reflected in *Criminal Statistics*. These factors are the criminal law, the law and practice of criminal procedure and of evidence, public opinion and, strangely enough, the criminal statistics.[46] First, the criminal law: if it is too strict it will often be disregarded by the public, the police and the jury, and the declining crime figures will mistakenly be taken as proof that its rigidity has had the deterrent effect desired; if it is lenient, those concerned may be more willing to co-operate with the law and to prosecute, which may give the impression that its leniency encourages crime; on the other hand, if it is too lenient, a prosecution may no longer appear to be worth while. Secondly, the law and practice of criminal procedure and of evidence: The strictness of certain rules of evidence, for example concerning previous convictions of the accused person, sometimes leads to an acquittal of offenders in spite of their guilt. Moreover, prosecutions by the police instead of being conducted, as abroad and in Scotland, by legally trained public prosecutors may occasionally have the same effect, and the lack of uniformity in prosecutions, due to the absence of a centralized system—the Director of Public Prosecutions intervenes only in serious cases[47]—may falsify the local crime picture, especially for minor offences. Whether lay magistrates are more inclined than professional lawyers to acquit or dismiss a case is impossible to judge on the strength of the available material. Less difficult to assess is the effect of certain changes in criminal procedure such as transfers of jurisdiction for an offence from a jury court to a court of summary jurisdiction where proceedings are less formal and costly. It has repeatedly been observed that as a result of such transfers the number of cases brought before the magistrates' courts greatly exceeded the decline in prosecutions for the offence in question before higher courts.[48]

While the effect of police methods on the official crime figures has already been discussed above, it may be mentioned in passing that the requirements of insurance companies of different kinds may greatly influence these figures by prescribing that police proceedings should be opened before claims can be acknowledged. Similar considerations apply to railway police regulations concerning thefts of goods in transit.[49]

Particularly high is the proportion of thefts of goods in transit which are not recorded in the official *Criminal Statistics*. 'Since the statistics are compiled by the Home Office from information supplied by each Police District there is a distinct possibility that "unplaced" thefts may not be counted at all. This applies particularly to thefts of

116

goods in transit where there is no evidence to show where the thefts took place.'[50]

The influence on the volume of reported crime of public opinion, or rather of the views, attitudes and customs of various classes of the population, is quite immeasurable[51] and probably far exceeds even that of the police. We are not yet in a position, however, to give chapter and verse for this statement. Closely connected with it is the fact that the publication of official statistical figures in the field of crime and the way in which they are used by the press have a considerable effect upon subsequent changes in these figures. If a striking increase in crime of a certain type or in a certain district or for a certain age group is reported public opinion or the press take a special interest in the matter, as a result of which there is often an increase in cases reported to the police and therefore a further rise in official statistics. The figures 'gain momentum as a result of their own dead weight'.[52]

(d) *In Particular: the Relativity of Criminal Statistics and the Possibility of an 'Index of Criminality'*. Each single figure in *Criminal Statistics*, if taken in isolation, is almost meaningless. It conveys very little to us if we find, for example, that the number of murders of persons aged one year and over as known to the police in England and Wales during 1959 was 142 or the number of burglaries 4,627. We cannot even say that this is very much or very little. There is no objective way of defining the 'right' volume of crime of a certain type for a certain time or place. Such figures can acquire significance only if they are compared with others. Only if we know such facts as that the corresponding figures for the period 1930-4 were 103 for murder and 1,596 for burglary or that the number of male persons aged 14 found guilty of ind. offences was 1,141 in 1938 and 2,855 in 1959 per 100,000 of population of that age can our interest be aroused. Comparisons are the essence of criminal statistics and their interpretation, comparisons related to each of the various details published in these volumes: notably time, place, age, sex, type of offence and disposal. The factor perhaps most frequently used for such comparisons is time, but it is here that we have to face almost insuperable difficulties. The period of time used for our comparisons must be neither too short nor too long. If the periods are very short, for example a comparison of the murder rate over a period of three years, differences may mean very little because any changes observed may be due to chance. If we wish to study, for example, the influence of the Homicide Act, 1957, on the rate of murder we have to wait until a period of at least, say, five or ten years has elapsed so that any trends may become clearly marked. On the other hand, if we take very long periods, for example 30 or 50 years, we run the risk that within these years important factors such as the law, criminal

117

procedure, the population of the area, social and economic conditions and—last but not least—the structure of criminal statistics may all have changed so much that it is impossible to say which of these changes might have been responsible for the variations in the crime rate which we wish to explain. This, by the way, is an important consideration whenever changes in the structure of the tables of criminal statistics are contemplated; such changes should be made only when the advantages would greatly outweigh the drawbacks which inevitably arise for statistical research. There is no general rule for the optimum length of the period to be examined, and for each research the problem has to be solved independently in the light of the prevailing circumstances,

In view of the difficulties of interpreting and comparing the figures of criminal statistics criminologists have been trying for years to work out a reliable 'Index of Criminality' which could serve as a basis for further studies. The idea behind such an Index would be to select from the masses of published figures those which are most likely to present a true picture of the extent and movements of criminality in a certain country over a given period. Sellin, who has given much thought to the matter,[53] has established the following criteria to which such an Index would have to conform: it should be based on the rates of a few selected offences which are regarded as particularly dangerous to society, which are subject to public prosecution and where the greatest possible co-operation between the victim and the authorities can be expected. It is clear that such an Index should be formulated not in absolute figures, but related to 100,000 of the population at risk, i.e. preferably of the population liable to criminal prosecution. While an 'Index of Criminality' would have the advantage that it would present in a nutshell everything that is valuable in statistical figures it should not be interpreted as indicating what should be the normal volume of crime at a certain time in a certain place. The combing out of useless and misleading material is not enough to produce a norm.

## 6. *International and Foreign Criminal Statistics*

(a) Comparisons of the kind mentioned in Section 5(d) would seem to be particularly illuminating with regard to foreign criminal statistics, and many attempts have been made in the past to work out the foundation of an international body of criminal statistics which would make comparisons between the crime figures of different countries reliable and meaningful. As has been pointed out by one of the specialists in this field, Ernst Roesner,[54] already in 1838 work of this kind was undertaken by the French statistician Moreau de Jonnès in his *Statistique de la Grande Bretagne et de l'Irlande*, who thereby transferred to the international sphere some of the methods used some time before him by A. M. Guerry for France in his *Essay sur la Statistique morale de la France* (1833). While these studies were of a private character only, semi-official efforts began in 1853 when the first International Statistical Congress in Brussels, at the instigation of Quetelet, discussed the comparability of national criminal statistics. The International Penal and Penitentiary Congresses, too, repeatedly debated the subject;[55] for example, in 1872 in London the question was on the Agenda 'Is it desirable to establish international prison statistics? and if so, how may this be accomplished?' Similarly, the Stockholm Congress of 1878 and the St. Petersburg Congress of 1890 expressed themselves in favour of international penitentiary statistics, but for decades little progress was made even in this relatively limited field in spite of the appointment in 1932 of a mixed commission for the comparative study of criminal statistics which met several times until 1939. This lack of progress is not surprising, bearing in mind that criminal statistics are closely dependent on such national factors as criminal law, criminal procedure, the structure and functions of the prosecuting authorities, the composition of the criminal courts and the co-operation between the authorities and the public. Where even the definitions of murder, manslaughter, robbery, larceny and many other offences differ from country to country it is but little use comparing figures relating to them,[56] and statements of a comparative nature should be made, if at all, only by those who are thoroughly familiar not only with the whole system of law and penal administration but also with the social and economic structure and atmosphere of the countries concerned.

Some of the existing difficulties could possibly be, if not altogether removed, at least reduced if the recommendations adopted by the Conference of the International Statistical Institute[57] would be carried out that every country should include in its official criminal statistics an exposé of its penal legislation and judicial system, an account of the sources and methods used in collecting criminal statistics, and an explanation of the crime classification employed, and if certain general standards would be adopted for the tabulation of convictions according to age, sex, and other characteristics. It is exasperating to see how many unnecessary differences exist at present in the technique of recording simple facts, for example length of sentences.[58] However, even this, useful as it would be, would hardly penetrate beneath the surface of the problems of international criminal statistics.

(*b*) Concerning foreign criminal statistics in general, there are at present bewildering differences not only in the way of recording the same factors, but also in the selection of factors for recording. It is probably only sex and age of offenders that are universally recorded, and next in frequency come previous convictions, sentences received, place of conviction, occupation, residence, marital status. Rarer is the inclusion of data on religion, education, domicile, time and place of offence, economic position of offender, his alcoholic condition and motive.[59] It would be very difficult to draft minimum rules to which every country should be asked to adhere as the basic material may not be available everywhere. Moreover, one has to resist the temptation to ask more than is really needed; the warning given in the report of 1893 (s. 2 above) was not entirely unjustified, although the addition of two or three items to the present English criminal statistics might be welcome. What should be done internationally is to reach an agreement on the selection and tabulation of those comparatively few factors which are regarded not as merely desirable, but as indispensable for each of the countries concerned, with a set of simple rules for tabulation, which would imply that those countries where the basic material required is not yet in existence should take steps to produce it. For certain other factors, the regular collection of which is regarded as not essential, but desirable, the agreement should indicate that information should be collected and published officially at regular intervals for the whole country or in shorter intervals for various selected districts. For the rest, the collection of material should be left to the private research worker (see below, Chapter 6).

(c) A few data concerning some foreign countries:

*France.* French criminal statistics, *Compte général de l'administration de la justice criminelle*, which began in 1825, are usually regarded as the oldest regular official publication commenced after the creation of a census. This is true only if we disregard the *English Parliamentary Papers* of 1810 mentioned above (s. 2). French criminal statistics are combined in one volume with the *Compte général de l'administration de la justice civile et commerciale*; they are court, not police, statistics, distinguish between recidivists and first offenders and give, in addition to the usual data on age, sex, offence and sentence, detailed information on the departments where the offence is committed, on marital status, nationality and 'milieu social', i.e. occupation related to offence. There is a table 'Affaires concernant les Mineurs', which divides juvenile offenders into three groups, under 13, between 13 and 16, and over 16 years of age, showing the penalties and other measures ordered by the court (there are no penalties for those under 13). The French tables give only absolute figures, not related to population.

*Western Germany.* Considerable changes in the previous system were made when the regular publication of criminal statistics was resumed in 1948.[60] The various stages through which the new system

120

had to go until it reached its present form reflect the processes of up-heaval and consolidation experienced in Western Germany after 1945. For example, religion and occupation were excluded, the former be-cause it had been introduced by the Nazi regime in connection with its racial legislation, the latter because the social and economic changes and the immigration from the East had introduced an ele-ment of instability which would have made the collection of reliable data on the occupational structure of the criminal population too hazardous. Data on occupation and marital status do not appear in the published tables, but are collected by the Länder in case they should at some future stage be required to fulfil international obliga-tions. Often data have been collected in view of the likely require-ments of the impending reform of the penal code and also as a conse-quence of amendments made in the old statutory law. The pre-war classification according to the district of the provincial court of appeal has been given up.

The official title of the present publication is *Polizeiliche Kriminal-statistik*, and it is published by the Bundeskriminalamt in Wiesbaden.

*The United States of America.*[61] Considering the enormous extent and high development of criminological studies in the United States we should expect to find there an equally well-developed system of federal and state criminal statistics. The actual position, however, is disappointing; 'criminal statistics in the United States', writes Thor-sten Sellin, one of the foremost authorities on the subject, 'usually fall far short of reaching even modest standards. . . . The problem of achieving *national* criminal statistics in the United States is somewhat like the problem of establishing uniform statistics for Europe. Who is to collect them and by what authority?' In fact, most of the difficulties outlined above which stand in the way of achieving uniform inter-national criminal statistics apply to the internal position in the U.S.A., too. There are now fifty separate states, the Federal Govern-ment, and the District of Columbia, each with its own criminal law, procedure and law enforcement agencies.[62] Attempts to produce nation-wide judicial criminal statistics began in 1931, but were not particularly successful and had to be given up in 1946. More im-portant were the simultaneous efforts of the police organizations regu-larly to collect and publish *Uniform Crime Reports*. In 1930 this work was taken over by the Federal Bureau of Investigation, United States Department of Justice, and it has continued and grown ever since. It depends on the voluntary co-operation of local police departments, but even so according to Sellin in 1950 the departments filing regular statistical reports with the Bureau numbered about 5,300 covering over 72,000,000 inhabitants or nearly 50 per cent of the total popula-tion at the time, and the rate is steadily growing. Their drawbacks are that they are limited to certain serious crimes—homicide, rape, robbery, aggravated assault, burglary, larceny and auto theft—that they unduly favour urban districts and provide inadequate interpretation of their data. A valuable feature is the division into 6 groups according to the size of cities and the classification according to geographical areas such as New England, Middle Atlantic, Pacific, etc.

In addition, there are juvenile court statistics, compiled by the United States Children's Bureau, and prison statistics. Moreover, most of the states and many municipalities and individual courts publish their own statistical accounts, some of which are of high quality, for example in New Jersey, New York, Massachusetts and Pennsylvania, and the city of Philadelphia.

Efforts have been made for some years to work out a Uniform Criminal Statistics Act providing for the establishment of a Federal Bureau of Criminal Statistics and to prevail on the states to adopt it.[63]

# Chapter 6

## THE PLACE OF STATISTICS IN CRIMINOLOGICAL RESEARCH II: RESEARCH STATISTICS

With the growing refinement of official 'book-keeping' statistics the dividing line between them and research statistics in the narrower sense is getting more and more difficult to draw. As we have seen (Chapter 5 under 'General Considerations'), it is no longer identical with the distinction between official and private collection of figures, although this distinction has not become entirely immaterial. Research statistics are, more often than official statistics, concerned with the solution of a specific problem; they are, therefore, but rarely published at regular intervals, and private research workers are more often than officials inclined to draw conclusions from their studies and use them as a basis and justification for critical appraisals of specific conditions and policies. Official statisticians are, naturally, reluctant to do so. This applies not only to regular official publications in the narrower sense, for example *Criminal Statistics for England and Wales*, where any such critical appraisals of, say, the work of the police or the courts would of course be entirely out of place, but also to official research statistics, such as, for example, the Report of the Home Office Research Unit on *Time Spent Awaiting Trial*[1] where certain figures are presented which could well have been used for criticisms of the police and the courts. It could be argued, however, that such criticisms should rather come from non-official quarters.

### I. THE BASIC FORMS OF STATISTICAL RESEARCH IN CRIMINOLOGY

#### 1. *Elementary Forms*

The criminologist who uses statistical techniques often limits himself to the most elementary of such techniques. Much of his work in this field merely consists in drawing fairly obvious, though often useful, conclusions from the published or unpublished official figures. In the

Report of 1893 (see Chapter 5) the view was expressed that the Introductions to *Criminal Statistics* might well provide the reader with 'results and conclusions'. In fact, this is, as a rule, not done, apart from the occasional adding of percentages to the absolute figures presented, which makes it easier for the reader to grasp the significance of the latter and to follow their movements over a period of time. Here, the researcher can do valuable work by further elaborating the picture given in the official volumes, for example by working out the age and sex ratios of crime over a period of years for specific offences and thereby laying the statistical foundations for further research into juvenile and female delinquency (see Chapter 26 below). Or, another important branch of simple statistical research, the crime statistics may be compared with other social statistics, for example the movements of the figures for property offences with national and local unemployment figures,[2] or the rates of juvenile delinquency related to the degree of urbanization.[3] It is of great importance that criminologists should constantly see their crime figures in the light of social, and occasionally also medical, statistics. The simple correlations worked out in this way should, however, not be regarded as showing cause and effect. Statistical correlations, needless to say, can never prove causal nexus, although they may serve as signposts to further research ultimately perhaps leading to causal explanations.[4]

The same simple statistical techniques are also often employed by workers collecting their own basic material in order to supplement the official figures. Such collections are frequently indispensable since official criminal statistics and their various supplements cannot be expected always to provide the material required to solve specific problems, either because the question to be examined, for example age or sex problems of crime, is not adequately treated in those regular publications or because it is entirely outside the scope of present official statistics, as for example, family, occupational, religious, educational or mental factors. In fact, the special collection of statistical material is one of the most common features of criminological research and it leads at once to more complicated matters of statistical technique, even if the ultimate analysis of the collected material should be on simpler lines.

## 2. *The Use of Samples*

Whereas to the user of official statistics his material is given, as a rule, for the whole country as the total volume of crime in general or, less frequently, in a certain area or of criminals of a certain age or sex, to the researcher who wishes to collect his own material the problem of *sampling* is the first to arise with all its pitfalls.[5] It cannot here be treated in an expert manner, but attention has to be drawn to certain difficulties as they have been found in criminological research. Some of these difficulties are especially related to control group research and will therefore be discussed later on.

The use of samples is often indispensable in the study of specific problems. If we wish to examine, for example, the incidence of 'broken homes' or mental defectives among juvenile delinquents or that of alcoholics or middle-class people among adults guilty of homosexual offences we cannot possibly make a study of every juvenile delinquent or every adult convicted of such an offence. Therefore we have to look around for a suitable, i.e. representative, sample, which would truly reflect all the characteristics of the total population we wish to study. Sample surveys are not necessarily to be regarded as makeshifts; they may in fact be more reliable than surveys of the total population from which the sample is drawn.[6]

The first question to be decided by the research worker is usually that of the size of the sample. It will often be decided by considerations of time and money available for the research. Within limits it may be said that the larger the sample the more likely will it be representative of the total population[7] and the more will it be able to withstand the strain of classifications and repeated sub-divisions to which the sample may have to be subjected in the course of the statistical analysis. It is sometimes frustrating to find that no further splitting-up of the sample is possible because the resulting fractions would become too small to be meaningful.

To illustrate some of the points so far made we might refer to the research described in *Prediction Methods in relation to Borstal Training*. The object of the research was to discover criteria facilitating the distinction between Borstal boys who were likey to be successes, i.e. not to recidivate after discharge, and those likely to be failures; and also to work out prediction tables which would present these criteria in statistical form. For this purpose a sample of Borstal boys was required that was representative of the total Borstal population and could be observed over an adequate follow-up period to enable us to distinguish successes from failures. At the crucial period, about 2,000 boys were received into English Borstal Institutions in the course of a year. 'Within the permitted sum allocated for this research project, it was calculated that about 700 cases would be studied.'[8] Thus, approximately one third of the total population could be covered, which was a comparatively large sample. It had now to be decided whether to take a complete intake for a third of a year, or rather to take every third case throughout a year. To exclude seasonal trends the second course was adopted. The cases were taken from registers of admissions kept at the two Reception Centres, but a small number of cases had to be rejected as mentally defective or because they were not properly included. Next, the most suitable period had to be considered. 'It had to be neither

so recent as to allow for no adequate time for testing after discharge nor so
remote as to be directly affected by the Second World War', which made
the years 1946 and 1947 appear to be most suitable. A special pilot study
was made to see whether there were any significant differences between the
second half of 1946 and the first half of 1947, and as no such differences
were found these two periods were finally selected. In the course of collecting these records, however, another significant difference emerged: cases
of boys who had been sent to various prisons in previous years were often
difficult to trace, and 'we found that there was a direct correlation between
the time it took the Home Office staffs to trace the Borstal files and the
proportion of successes in any batch. In total the success rate was 45 per
cent, but in the first 300 files received the success rate was nearly 70 per
cent. In the end we were 56 files short of the complete sample, and a search
by Criminal Record Office revealed that 46 of these 56 cases were failures—
a rate of 82 per cent. We cannot, therefore, regard the sample for which
data were available from Borstal files as strictly representative of the
Borstal intake in the year surveyed. This was a factor underlying and
modifying a large proportion of our analysis', and certain statistical
adjustments had to be made. Moreover, the completeness of the information recorded in the Borstal files differed from Institution to Institution,
and it was found that 'the Institutions which were the better record-
keepers also tended to have better success rates'.

In short, in this research project it could be demonstrated that an
apparently simple process of sampling did not produce an unbiased
sample as certain cases had a better chance than others of being included and were unrepresentative in their rate of success and other
characteristics.

In any case it should be borne in mind that a sample can be
representative only of the total population from which it has been
drawn and not necessarily of other populations.[9] A study based on a
sample taken from the whole population of Borstal boys of a certain
year can be representative only of the total of boys of this particular
vintage, not of Borstal boys in general, still less of delinquents as
such. An exception would have to be made only in the case of
human behaviour which is unmodifiable, but criminology is very
rarely concerned with such behaviour.

To refer to a few comparatively recent sample surveys, Cyril Burt took
'two hundred consecutive cases of juvenile delinquency—all, in fact, for
which I could get complete information for the particular conditions
reviewed'.[10] This is a frequently used technique which may involve the risk
of an unrepresentative selection if the cases for which full records are
available differ from the rest. Maud A. Merrill, in her American post-war
study, used '300 unselected run-of-the-mill cases . . . without reference to
any selective factors';[11] in the English enquiry *Young Offenders* the first
1,000 cases used were brought before the juvenile courts in London after

the 1st October 1938.[12] Gillin, in his study of inmates of the Wisconsin State Prison, distinguished according to the type of offence and of sentence: his study of the life prisoners, a small group, includes the entire prison population of lifers, and the same applied to the sodomists and rapists. Of the property offenders, however, only every third was included for most of the information collected, but for data easily available in the prison records all the offenders were included. Gillin adds: 'thus we were able to determine how representative our smaller sample was at least with respect to these categories'.[13] R. G. Andry, in his study of short-term prisoners,[14] employed a detailed questionnaire, but for reasons of time he used only some of the questions for a sub-sample of the prisoners.

Many other considerations may determine the selection of the sample. If, for example, it is intended to interview not only a group of delinquent and one of non-delinquent boys but also their parents, the choice of boys in an Institution such as an Approved School taking boys from a very large geographical area will, as a rule, be impracticable because it would involve undue expenditure of time and money in visiting the parents. Therefore, the choice of an Institution receiving only juveniles from a limited area may here be preferable.[15]

What has been said about the need for samples of adequate size does not exclude the use of smaller samples for *Pilot Studies*. The latter are often indispensable to check whether the problem in hand can successfully be investigated in the manner and with the kind of material envisaged, and which adjustments will have to be made. Such pilot studies will prevent avoidable mistakes being made on an unnecessarily large scale and at correspondingly high cost. A successful pilot study should, however, not be used as a pretext to abandon the large and more representative one. It sometimes happens, on the other hand, that a study not originally planned as a pilot study has eventually to be treated as such because its size proves inadequate to deal with all the problems which have emerged in the course of the work.[16] Moreover, as Glaser has recently pointed out, 'in many areas the accomplishment of a first research project can only be to determine the nature and dimensions of some problems, and not to provide solutions for the problems. Such knowledge may suggest solutions, but demonstration of the effectiveness of a proposed solution often requires a second research of a totally different sort.'[17]

### 3. *The Use of Case Records in Statistical Research*

Much statistical research in criminology has to be done by using case records, for example of probationers, prisoners, Borstal boys and so on. Here two possibilities arise: either records have to be used which are already in existence, having been written by probation officers, institutional staffs, etc., in the course of their ordinary duties, or the records are produced especially for the purposes of the research. The second alternative is extremely rare, and research workers have, as a rule, to be content with routine records not originally prepared with the objects of the research project in mind. This inevitably leads to many difficulties as the worker will often search in vain in such records for the kind of information he requires, and even where it is available it will often not be recorded in the specific form needed for the research. The matter has been treated at some length in *Prediction Methods in relation to Borstal Training*, from which the following points may be taken:[18] records compiled by different field workers are often written from different viewpoints, giving slightly different meanings to the same terms, introducing the individual bias of the recording officer, especially where an intuitive style of reporting is employed, giving perhaps a very vivid but highly subjective 'pen-picture' of the offender concerned and his environment. The Prediction Study concluded that for statistical purposes data should be recorded in a form which makes them capable of being reduced to numbers on Hollerith or similar cards, and that all the important items should be dealt with, even if the answer is negative or nothing is known about the item in question. Impressionistic, free style recording should not be discouraged, but it should be used only in addition to, not instead of, rigidly objective data and it should be done in a way which makes the meaning clearly understandable to other users of the records. Data for research purposes should be considered separately from data needed for administrative purposes, and a distinction should be made between data which are essential for every case and data which might be recorded only for certain cases. Reliable information is more useful than very detailed information. Continuous collaboration between the administrators in charge of the recording processes and the research workers making use of their records is essential, but obtainable in practice only in exceptional cases.[19]

The lack of information on certain data which the research worker frequently encounters poses for him the problem whether he should simply discard cases with incomplete data or whether he should rather exclude the factors concerned altogether in order to avoid bias.[20] Each of the two methods has its advantages and disadvantages.

The second possibility referred to above, i.e. that the research project is fortunate enough to collect its own records in accordance with its needs, can be found, for example, in the American Cambridge-Somerville Youth Study, where the forms were designed and filled in by the staff of the project.[21]

It is often regarded as a weakness of having to use existing records that they are known by the research worker to refer to individuals who have committed offences, which knowledge may easily create prejudice and falsify the interpretation and evaluation of certain vague concepts such as 'good or bad family relations', 'bad neighbourhood', 'low intelligence', and many others. Wherever technically feasible, those who have to interpret the records should be unaware of the fact that they refer to a delinquent population. In control group studies this can occasionally be done if the records are privately collected for the special purposes of the research. Such cases, however, are very rare.[22]

## 4. *The Dangers of Post-factum Interpretation*

This leads to a problem of more general significance in social research. Merton[23] has drawn attention to the dangers involved in *post-factum* sociological interpretations, arising from the fact that often 'data are collected and only then subjected to interpretative comment'; an interpretation is introduced after the observations have been made instead of the more correct procedure of 'empirical testing of a predesignated hypothesis'. Merton uses as an example the observation that 'the unemployed tend to read fewer books than they did previously'. This can immediately be 'explained' by formulating the hypothesis that unemployment creates anxiety which makes concentrated thought difficult. If it had been observed, on the contrary, that the unemployed tended to read more, another *post-factum* hypothesis would have been ready at hand, i.e. that the unemployed have more leisure. In other words, it is usually not too difficult to produce a hypothesis which supports our observations. There is, however, also the opposite danger not mentioned by Merton that if we start with a 'predesignated hypothesis' this may prejudice our observations.

While the fallacy which Merton has in mind refers to the explanation of observed facts, the danger inherent in the use of existing records of criminal cases lies in the possibility of producing bias not in explaining but in interpreting the facts or in distorting them to fit into the general picture of a delinquent personality. To avoid such bias it has been suggested that criminological research should concentrate not on the collection and interpretation of criminal records but on the life histories of an unselected population, as it has been done in other branches of social research. Reckless, for example, recommends that information should be collected for an unselected group of 'every white boy enrolled in the fifth grade of the schools of a medium sized large city', that this group should be followed up over a number of years and their criminal conduct studied.[24] Similar suggestions were later made by Albert K. Cohen.[25] Such research would require larger numbers and be correspondingly more expensive, but its advantages are obvious. The Cambridge-Somerville Study did not begin with an unselected sample of the general population but with a mixture of ordinary and 'predelinquent' boys. Mays' Liverpool Study, which comes perhaps nearer than any other done, in this country at least, to the recommendation of Reckless and Cohen, used as the starting point an unselected group of members of a certain club and examined their delinquent habits.

We shall still have to return to the subject in connection with follow-up studies which are discussed later.

## II. CONTROL GROUP STUDIES[26]

More refined statistical techniques may be used in control group (also called horizontal) or follow-up (vertical) studies. The idea of the control group is very old in medical and social research and fairly old in criminology. We cannot well make statements on the distinguishing characteristics of criminals unless we know something about non-criminals. Already the report of 1893 on criminal statistics (Chapter 5, I(2) above) stressed:[27] 'The proportion of prisoners possessing any feature or quality is of little value unless it can be compared with the corresponding proportion in the total general population, or in the general population of the same age and sex.' One of the main criticisms directed against Lombroso's theory of the born criminal (see below, Chapter 12) was the lack of an adequate control group.[28] Charles Goring, one of his principal opponents, used control groups, but they were also inadequate. One can safely say that modern criminological research largely depends on suitable control groups. One of the difficulties which in particular earlier criminologists had to face was the absence of reliable statistical information relating to the general population on many of the data on which they wished to base their comparisons. Even now some of these difficulties still remain, although the development of demography and of social statistics in the Census or elsewhere in the past hundred years has been of considerable assistance to criminological research.[29] It is easier now to find comparable statistics for the general population on such matters as unemployment, wages, housing, size of family, education and illiteracy, but criminologists who search for information, say, on the incidence of 'broken homes' or illegitimacy would have no easy task. It was a fortunate coincidence that the family structure and household size for the families of Borstal boys in the Borstal Prediction Study could be compared with the corresponding items in a sample of the general population which happened to be available.[30] Generally speaking, criminologists have to collect their own control samples to compare with their delinquent samples, and the same rules which apply to the selection of the latter also apply to that of the former, but certain additional difficulties may easily arise. First, whereas the records of the delinquent group are usually at the disposal of the researcher or can be collected with the help of the authorities concerned, the collection of corresponding data for a non-delinquent group, for example on family and home, income and similar private matters, often depends on the voluntary co-operation of the individuals concerned and their families. The difficulty does not arise in studies where the control group, as is sometimes the case, also consists of delinquents, but of a different category, for example first offenders who are to be compared with recidivists, mentally normal with psychopathic offenders, psychopaths with and without head injuries, etc. Secondly, especially where the control group consists of non-delinquents, the information available for them is often much less detailed than that for the delinquents as their contacts with the authorities have usually been less close.[31] Thirdly, we have to make sure that our 'non-delinquent' control group cases are really non-delinquents, which is not easy in view of the considerable volume of hidden delinquency. Fourthly, the two groups have to be matched in respect of as many factors as possible (technique of 'holding constant'), with the exception of the delinquency factor and those items the influence of which we wish to examine. It is for the research worker to select these latter items, but he must be careful not to expect his research to shed light on those factors on which the two groups have been matched. Ideally, the process of matching should produce two groups which are not merely approximately similar but as nearly equal as we can expect human beings to be. It is here that most investigations have so far failed. In their painstaking study *Unraveling Juvenile Delinquency*, the Gluecks matched their 500 delinquent boys committed to a State Correctional School in Massachusetts with 500 non-delinquent boys from public schools in Boston.[32] The eventual matching was done by pairs but when in the course of assembling the case material it was discovered that owing to the chosen method of selection the two groups were obviously dissimilar in certain factors which the researchers wished to hold constant suitable adjustments in the process of selecting were made. The matching of individuals on more than a few obvious factors such as sex and age is very difficult and requires a large original sample from which to choose. Even then exact matching on more refined factors can rarely be achieved.[33] 'At times it was like looking for a needle in a haystack to locate a boy meeting all the matching requirements', write the Gluecks. Not only were the losses very considerable—of 315 boys of one school listed for inclusion only 52 were found suitable—but the final result showed a great many dissimilarities between the two groups. As one reviewer wrote:

In spite of the endless care taken to ensure perfect equality of the two groups with regard to the four factors held constant, one gets the impression that, for reasons no doubt beyond the control of the investigators, this object was not completely achieved. Not only do the age composition and the I.Q.s show not inconsiderable differences (pp. 37–8 and Appendix B), the matching of the 'underprivileged neighbourhood' factor did not necessarily mean that the boys came from the same district, but only that they were selected from districts regarded as equally bad (pp. 30–32 and 40). With regard to ethnical origin Appendix B reveals that occasionally a boy of English origin was matched against one of Scottish ancestry, a Rumanian or Turk against a Syrian, a Lithuanian against a Russian, a Swede against a German or Dutch, a Greek against a Hungarian, and so on. All this only serves as just another illustration of the immense difficulties inherent in any such process of individual matching, difficulties to which attention has repeatedly been drawn in recent American sociological literature.[34]

For certain problems control group studies can be undertaken in two different ways, either by asking how many individuals possessing a certain characteristic, for example having no parents living, are present in a delinquent and in a matched non-delinquent group or by asking how many delinquents are present in a group of parentless and a matched group of other juveniles, how many immigrants and how many non-immigrants are delinquents or how many delinquents and how many non-delinquents are immigrants.[35]

When we said before that every research worker is free to select those items which he wishes to examine, this should not be taken to mean that he is equally free in the selection of those factors which he has to hold constant. Bearing in mind that the ultimate object of control group studies is to discover meaningful relations of cause and effect[36] we can leave uncontrolled those factors which can obviously have no effect on the result. Ernest Greenwood,[37] who refers to the need to identify the relevancy of factors 'through insight', concludes that control need not be absolute but only selective. He gives the example of goitre research where the object was to test the hypothesis that water from source X rather than Y was the cause of goitre, and all members of group A were therefore given water X to drink and all members of group B water Y. By chance it was discovered that the former were all Catholics and the latter all Protestants. Even so, it was obviously not necessary in this research to control the factor 'religion' by holding it constant since our insight tells us that it could not possibly affect the outcome. As Greenwood stresses, the research worker needs some preliminary knowledge of the whole field of his research to determine which factors could be left out of consideration altogether and which have to be controlled. Such knowledge may come from the acquaintance with a large material of individual cases which tells him in which direction to look for his problems. There are, however, many less obvious cases where the selection presents difficulties owing to the immense complexity of social data. Failure to control relevant factors, for example social class in research on physique or intelligence in their relation to delinquency, can have disastrous results.

The research worker, while free in the choice of his problems, is under a scientific obligation to make it clear that the exclusion of certain problems from the scope of his investigation is not intended to prejudge their significance. Moreover, it has to be borne in mind that because of the inter-connection which often exists between apparently very different factors the exclusion of some may closely affect other factors which are not excluded from the research. All this throws a heavy responsibility on the research worker. As an illustration the following may be used: Rubin[38] refers to control group research on American prisoners who had mutilated themselves 'in the institutions of certain states in which prison labor is imposed in an especially brutal way'. 'Obviously', he writes, 'such action calls for a study of the prison administration, and especially its methods of prison labor.' Instead, the research concerned itself with the characteristics of the individual prisoners and its findings were, in Rubin's view, totally irrelevant to the real problem. In other words, the institutional factors were held constant and thereby excluded from the investigation. 'The plain word for this', Rubin adds, 'is whitewash.' We agree with this verdict with the reservation that there might well have been two, not one, subjects for research, one into the conditions prevailing in the Institutions concerned and another into the characteristics of the mutilators as compared with those of the non-mutilators. If only the second study was undertaken, it should have been made clear that a crucial aspect of the problem was excluded from the research and the study actually done could not be expected to provide a complete answer.

Perhaps as a result of the criticisms levelled at the weaknesses of certain outstanding control group studies the general standard of control group research has greatly improved in recent years, and as a model of such more refined work William and Joan McCord's book *Origins of Crime* may be quoted (see Note 49). Even so, the story of control group research in criminology is still largely the story of compromise and concessions made to the inevitable weaknesses of this technique and also one of obvious mistakes in applying it.

Gillin,[39] whose controls consisted of the non-criminal brothers of his prisoners group, had to exclude all prisoners who had no criminal brother; if one of the criminal brothers was not available for interview another had to be taken, and as availability for interview often means greater stability there was 'a bias towards stability' in the control group. This factor, availability for interview, often introduces an element of unrepresentativeness into the control group. To choose siblings as controls, as was done by Healy and Bronner,[40] has the advantage of controlling, to some extent, the heredity factor, but it excludes all only children, an important section of the population; it also excludes what may well be the socially worst cases, i.e. those whose siblings are all delinquents, too, and may lead to an over-representation of psychologically disturbed cases.[41]

One of the principal concessions to be made in such studies is the admission that 'non-delinquency' can usually mean only absence of officially known delinquency. Matching with regard to geographical residence often means not the same area but one which to the researcher seems to possess the same characteristics, which leaves a wide field open to discretion. This in particular as we now know that under-privileged areas and even street-blocks which look identical to the superficial observer may actually be very different in their whole atmosphere.[42] This means that advancing sociological and psychological knowledge makes control group research more and more difficult as the scope of what can properly be 'matched' will be more and more reduced.

Particularly serious mistakes were made in older studies comparing the delinquency rates of American immigrants and native-born whites. Such comparisons often neglected important differences in the composition of the two groups: the typical European immigrant was, as a rule, a male adult city dweller and could therefore be compared not with an unselected group of white Americans, but only with a matched group of male adult white American city dwellers. If this was done it was found that the crime rate of the latter was, on the whole, higher than that of the former.[43]

Criminologists may find some comfort in the knowledge that other disciplines, especially medicine, encounter similar difficulties in their controlled researches. 'Without "control" comparisons', writes a well-known epidemiologist,[44] 'unbiased interpretation is impossible. It would be rash to assign significance to a finding that 40 per cent of patients gave a history of nail-biting in youth, without some knowledge of the frequency of such a habit in the population at large from which these patients are drawn. Yet this is a common error in clinical research.' Medical research workers find it easier, however, to use control groups in research on the effect of different methods of treatment, a field where criminologists are still much more restricted. In medicine, objections are less strong to giving experimental treatment to one only of two matched groups (see below, Chapter 9).

It means perhaps stretching the idea of controlled research slightly too far when Cressey calls each of the cases of 'trust-violators' whom he studied, 'his own "control" ' because in each case the psychological position of the violator concerned at the time of the interview when a 'non-shareable problem' was present could be compared with his position at a previous stage when no such problem existed.[45]

It is one of the great merits of criminological control group research that it has collected a considerable amount of information on the characteristics of the non-delinquent population not otherwise available. On the other hand, it has been attacked, and sometimes even totally rejected, not only because of the faults in application to which attention has been drawn above but also because of certain inherent weaknesses. Durkheim did it because he thought it impossible to find properly matched control groups,[46] Stott because neither delinquents nor non-delinquents as such formed homogeneous groups which could be contrasted,[47] an objection which could probably be met by forming smaller comparable sub-groups. By far the strongest criticism is that control group research, by splitting the human personality and its environment into separate factors, particles, atoms, which are made the object of comparisons between the two groups, inevitably loses sight of the personality as a whole. We compare innumerable single characteristics and forget the unity behind them.[48] Moreover, control group techniques are usually static, i.e. they compare human beings and their environments only with respect to a single moment, without giving due consideration to the unending changes which they undergo in the course of their development. These are very real dangers which can be avoided only by combining the control group method with other methods which restore the balance by emphasizing the psychological, individual and dynamic aspects of criminological research. Control group methods have to be supplemented by individual case studies, and by typological and follow-up studies, and if this is properly done the criticism of 'atomization' loses much of its force. There are other, similar, processes used in scientific work, such as, for example, intelligence tests which are full of pitfalls when applied in isolation, but useful in conjunction with other, more individual, psychological methods.

### III. FOLLOW-UP AND OTHER DESCRIPTIVE STUDIES OF CRIMINAL CAREERS[49]

#### 1. General Considerations

These studies are different from control group studies in that they do not compare individual offenders with others, offenders or non-offenders, at a certain stage of their careers. Instead, they examine the evolution of criminal careers over a period of time; they are dynamic, not static. If they concentrate on the details of one individual life they are case history studies, which will be discussed later (Chapter 8); if they are rather interested in the fate of groups of offenders they are follow-up studies in the narrower sense. Often they are used as the basis for prediction research (see below, Chapter 7), but this is not necessarily so. They had their origin in the earlier part of the present century in the desire of penologists to check the results of institutional treatment. How much recidivism was there among offenders discharged from prisons and reformatories, and could one discover its causes? How far was it due to weaknesses in the penal methods applied and how far to other circumstances? This type of research was, therefore, closely connected with the phenomenon of recidivism which was as greatly worrying penal reformers at the turn of the century as it is now. Its value to the understanding of recidivism and of the effect of various treatment methods is, however, only one aspect of the follow-up study; it is equally indispensable to our efforts to understand, if not the causes, at least the evolution of criminal careers. If the latter are studied *en masse* a better appreciation of their structure and of the driving factors behind them can be achieved. While less detailed than individual case histories, such studies can provide valuable insight into the morphology and symptomatology of criminal behaviour. Descriptive studies in this more specific sense are distinct from follow-up studies in not being limited to the after-histories of criminals discharged from penal institutions or from a period of probation and to the study of the effect of such treatment, but rather examining the evolution of criminal careers of large numbers of individuals who may or may not have been subjected to penal treatment. Such descriptive studies are of criminological rather than of penological interest, and they deal with structure and patterns rather than with causes. If they can contribute to our understanding of the etiology of crime all the better, but even if they should not do so they retain their independent value. A beginning was made with such descriptive studies, with special reference to recidivism, at the Third International Congress of Criminology in London, 1955, but it has apparently not been followed up.[50]

## 2. *Follow-up Studies in Particular*

The technique and specific difficulties of follow-up studies have been so fully described in the various publications by the Gluecks (see Note 49) that it is hardly necessary to go into details. Moreover, we are in this chapter concerned with the techniques rather than with the findings of these follow-up studies.

Follow-up studies, as they have been developed mainly by the Gluecks, are greatly superior to the usual brand of official statistics of recidivism as their material is far more detailed. Whereas official statistics give merely the percentage figures of recidivism, sometimes distinguished according to sex, age, offence, and the type of institution from which the offender has been discharged, follow-up studies supplement these scanty data by searching for information not merely on the presence or absence of reconvictions over periods of, say, from five to fifteen years, but also on changes in behaviour of a more subtle kind. 'While the basic aim of the peno-correctional system is to render men less criminalistic than they were before, any programme which relies on something more than just punishment calculated to frighten prisoners into being good citizens when returned to society must be designed to improve skills, means of recreational outlet, habits and attitudes generally.'[51] In a follow-up study of 1,000 persons placed on probation in 1937 in Essex County in the State of New Jersey, the authors examined the outcome over a period of eleven years in terms of personal adjustment in a number of 'basic areas of social life',[52] i.e. the physical, mental, familial and economic areas, and a lengthy list of criteria was drawn up by which adjustment or maladjustment was measured. To provide information of this kind, follow-up studies have to rely largely on sources outside the official records of prisons, probation and after-care officers, which latter can usually offer only a minimum of reliable information on the data required. Even if special investigations are conducted by the authorities concerned, they are, to quote the Gluecks again, 'while doubtless of some value, not likely to be as reliable as those made by neutral, outside investigators who have no special interest to protect, no axe to grind, no apologies to make, and who have achieved a degree of special competence in this type of research'.[53]

Obviously, research of this kind is expensive and time-consuming. It requires a staff of trained investigators and interviewers. Apart from a careful collection and verification of all the facts already known about the individuals concerned, the first task of a follow-up study is to locate the individuals selected for the follow-up. In the first study made by the Gluecks, that of 510 men released from the Massachusetts Reformatory at Concord, whose sentences expired in 1921 and 1922, a five-year post-parole test period was available to judge their success or failure. Over 90 per cent of this group were located at the end of that period, i.e. some eight or ten years after their discharge from the Reformatory, which must be regarded as a very high rate, especially when the great mobility of criminals and the absence of a centralized identification system in the United States are considered.[54] After being traced the men were interviewed by a highly experienced field worker,[55] and the information collected by him was then compared with the documentary material available. In this way a detailed and reliable body of knowledge about most of these 510 men and practically every aspect of their lives at various stages was assembled. Only in 27 cases no subsequent information was obtainable, and 55 men had died in the meantime. It was ascertained that of the men whose post-parole conduct could be ascertained 21·1 per cent had been successes, 16·8 per cent partial and 61·1 per cent total failures, a result totally different from the customary official picture publicized by the authorities at the time, which gave success rates of around 80 per cent. Among other weaknesses, the low standard of parole supervision was commented upon, though the proportion of failures was measurably lower during the parole than during the post-parole period with its total absence of control,[56] and it was stressed by the Gluecks that 'the aim of the criminal law is not merely to prevent offenders from further wrongdoing merely while they are still in the official toils, but to bring about a more or less permanent abandonment of criminal ways'.[57]

This group of ex-inmates of the Concord Reformatory was further followed up for two consecutive periods of five years each, the first of which is described in *Later Criminal Careers* and the second in *Criminal Careers in Retrospect*, so that altogether a follow-up period of at least fifteen years was available after their discharge from the Institution.[58] One of the most important results was the increase in the proportion of non-recidivists from about 20 per cent after the first period to 30 per cent after the second and 41 per cent after the third period. Considerable changes were also observed in the environmental and personal circumstances in the lives of these men, who had meanwhile reached an average age of 40 years. For example, the proportion of men who moved about excessively from one place of residence to another declined from 54 to 41 per cent, and the proportion of unmarried men from 45 to 32 per cent. Particular care was taken to separate the influence of the reformatory and the parole regime from factors independent of them, and the influence of the process of ageing and maturation was discussed in detail,[59] but we are at this stage concerned not with the substance of the findings, but only with the methodology. Corresponding methods were used by the Gluecks in the following-up of the group of one thousand juvenile delinquents appearing in the Boston Juvenile Court and examined in the Clinic of the Judge Baker Foundation during the years 1917–22.[60] Psychiatrists, too, have made follow-up studies to check the reconviction of various types of mentally abnormal offenders (see Gibbens *et al.*, Note 49). These and other similar studies have greatly contributed to our knowledge of the evolution of criminal careers and created a more realistic picture of the success or failure of correctional institutions.

With regard to European investigations, attention should be drawn in particular to the work of Erwin Frey and Walter Piecha (Note 49). While Frey's material consisted of a variety of follow-up material, Piecha made a detailed study of 66 male and 25 female juveniles discharged as 'uneducable' from the *Niedersächsische Landesjugendheim* Göttingen (an institution similar to Approved Schools and Reformatories) in the period 1945–50. His object was to see how far the unfavourable prognosis of being 'uneducable' was justified in the light of the subsequent careers of these young people. Concerning the yardstick of 'success', the criterion of reconviction is rejected as too narrow and replaced by the more comprehensive concepts of *Lebenserfolg* or *Lebensbewährung*, i.e. success in life. The author spent a year and a half in the institution to study conditions there and he was also able to visit most of the individuals in question. His over-all success rate of nearly 30 per cent is relatively high, considering that the case material consisted only of individuals labelled as uneducable. There were considerable differences in the success rates between different socio-psychological types (see below, Chapter 8, under 'Typology') and also between the sexes, but the numbers are too small for any conclusions to be drawn from these figures.

## 3. *Other Descriptive Studies*

Under this heading studies of the evolution of criminal careers may be briefly considered which are not follow-up studies in the specific sense of the term. As already said, such descriptive studies are not necessarily focused on the after-careers of offenders who have undergone one or the other form of correctional treatment, nor are they primarily concerned with the results of the latter. They are rather interested in the mass structure of criminal careers as important elements of social life and try to provide some of the flesh for the bare bones of criminal statistics. How, for example, does organized crime work as reflected in the histories of large numbers of individuals who play some part in such organizations? What is the pattern behind their evolution and their activities? Clearly, material of this kind would eventually form the basis for a typology of crime (on this see below, Chapter 8). Reckless has tried to construct certain patterns of recidivism, distinguishing primary and secondary components.[61] From his list of thirteen of the latter the following may be mentioned: age of onset of recidivism, socio-economic class origins of recidivists, degree of specificity (i.e. whether recidivists as a rule stick to the same type of crime or whether they are promiscuous in their choice of offences), the factor of maturation, prognosis and treatability. He also suggested that the degree of capacity or incapacity of individuals for socialization should be measured on a scale (Harrison G. Gough's 'De scale') which would determine an individual's tendency to delinquency as 'part of his incapacity to play socially acceptable roles in life'. Other points of interest for such descriptive studies are whether criminals as a rule advance from petty to more and more serious offences, whether persons who commit one type of crime, for example against property, are more inclined to become recidivists in this field than persons who commit another type, for example against life or sexual offences; whether members of minority groups in society are more likely to commit offences, and so on. Official criminal statistics can offer very little information on such matters because they are focused on crimes rather than on criminals and the statistical aspects of life histories are entirely outside their field of enquiry. Similarly, what Reckless has called 'categoric risks in crime'[62] requires in addition to the basic data provided by criminal statistics a great deal of supplementary material which can be derived only from large numbers of histories of criminal careers written according to a uniform pattern. Such studies might well be called 'exploratory rather than definitive', they are intended to 'open up ground for more careful investigation' and 'simply record what is observed and without any formal tests of hypothesis'.[63] In other words, such descriptive studies are a stage preliminary to the individual case history proper and to typological research.

# Chapter 7

## PREDICTION STUDIES[1]

### I. THE OBJECTS OF PREDICTION

Prediction, while not the only object of scientific endeavour, is certainly among its most important ones. Without it, no planned human behaviour would be possible. In everyday life, men have to look into the future, trying to assess in advance how their environment and the physical forces on which they depend, how, in particular, their fellow beings are likely to behave in certain circumstances and how they will react to certain changes which may happen at some stage or another. Weather prediction and election polls, being more systematic and better organized and financed than other forms of prediction, have so far been most conspicuous in the public eye, but there have also been well-known prediction studies in the fields of marital adjustment, child development, vocational success and others.

All those concerned with the administration of criminal justice, judges and magistrates, practical and theoretical penologists and penal reformers, have been trying to predict throughout the ages, consciously or unconsciously, but it is only in the course of the present century that their efforts have been subjected to systematic and scientific scrutiny. Before going into details we should be clear in our minds what the philosophical premises of penological prediction studies are and in what directions predictive methods are required in the field of penology. First of all, it has to be stressed that the need for prediction work rests here largely on the assumption that we adhere to a non-retributive penal philosophy of prevention, deterrence and reformation. To some extent, prediction may be involved in a retributive penal system, too, because one of its objects is to create, at least as a by-product, a feeling of satisfaction in the minds of the victims and onlookers of a crime, but the predictive element is far more conspicuous in a system where the practical effect to be achieved by penal measures is deterrence or reformation. Here the objects of predictive efforts are briefly these:

(*a*) The legislator has to consider the kind of penalties and other measures most likely to achieve his aim of preventing or reducing future crime. Is, for example, the death penalty indispensable for murder or will long terms of imprisonment be equally or even more effective? Is probation likely to have a reformative, and at the same time deterrent, effect? Will Borstal training be preferable to a prison sentence for young offenders of a certain type? Predictive assessments of this nature are implied in legislative phraseology such as 'if the court is satisfied . . . that it is expedient for his reformation and the prevention of crime that he should undergo a period of training in a Borstal Institution' (Criminal Justice Act, 1948, s. 20; similarly s. 21(1) for corrective training) or 'that it is expedient for the protection of the public that he should be detained in custody for a substantial time . . .' (s. 21(2) for preventive detention). What the legislator does for offenders in general, the court has to do in relation to individual offenders. Any sentence or similar form of disposal passed by a criminal or juvenile court involves a predictive assessment of its effect on the future behaviour of the offender. Moreover, both legislators and courts have to try to anticipate the likely reaction of the public to their laws and sentences. Will public opinion be content with the abolition of capital punishment or with the de-penalization of homosexual activities or with the further replacement of prison sentences by probation, with a conditional discharge for this or a fine for that particular offender?

(b) Of equal importance is prediction for the penal administrator who has to assess the effect of innumerable decisions concerning the way he carries out the sentences of the courts, and the present tendency to leave more and more discretion in this field to the administration throws an ever growing burden of responsibility on him. Shall he concentrate on maximum security or rather on open institutions? what should be the ratio of staff to inmates? how should he operate his system of classification or his earning scheme? Should he release on licence at the earliest or at the latest possible moment? These and dozens of other decisions left to his discretion and his judgment of the effect of his actions on individual offenders and on society as a whole require a firm factual basis. To some extent, as in the case of legislators, judges and magistrates, this basis will be provided by their own experience.

Personal experience alone, however, may not be enough; it is subjective and varies in extent and quality according to the personality of those who have to make the decision. It is here that scientific methods of prediction enter the scene and offer not to supplant but to supplement the experience of the administrator or judge. Such methods try to provide a broader foundation for his judgment; they may show that certain measures which he is inclined to take are not likely to have the desired effect, and that certain individuals are likely to react differently from what he would expect in the light of his limited experience. The courts, proud of their judicial independence, may not be willing as yet to take advantage of predictive devices, but administrators, being less rigid and hide-bound, have been doing so to an increasing extent. In fact, most prediction studies in criminology have so far been done not for courts, but for administrators anxious to assess the future conduct of offenders to be discharged from penal or reformatory institutions and, occasionally, also of probationers. In exceptional cases, attempts have been made to predict what kind of persons, not yet delinquent, may be expected to become so.

Whereas follow-up studies are essentially backward looking, prediction, by its very nature, looks forward, but as will be pointed out below, it has to use the material supplied by follow-up work.

## II. POSSIBLE MISUNDERSTANDINGS OF PREDICTION RESEARCH

Before going into the details of prediction techniques three possible misunderstandings might usefully be cleared away.[2]

(a) The first is related to the question: what exactly is the object of prediction work? Is it concerned with predicting the future behaviour of individuals or only that of whole groups, of categories of individuals? Are we here trying to predict how John Smith is going to behave after his discharge from Borstal or merely how a group of, say, a hundred ex-Borstal boys, of whom he is one, is likely to behave? The answer depends on the kind of prediction technique used, but before going into the matter we might well ask: for which of these two questions is an answer needed, for John Smith or for his group? Obviously, there are situations where an answer is needed to the first and situations where an answer is needed to the second of our questions. If, for example, the administration simply wishes to know for how many ex-Borstal boys reconvicted within six months after discharge they will be required to provide places in their institutions they are not interested in John Smith's fate as a person; it is not the individual but only the group that matters to them. If, however, and this is the more important aspect of the matter, they wish to know whether John Smith would do better when placed in an open rather than in a closed Borstal or at what stage he can be safely released then they will prefer an individual to a mass prediction. Needless to say, the courts are exclusively concerned with this individual side of the matter. The question has, therefore, to be faced: can prediction techniques forecast the behaviour of an individual? It is this problem which has given rise to many of the criticisms so far made of the technique

143

most frequently used in prediction research, i.e. the statistical. If it should really be true that statistical techniques are useless for the prediction of individual cases this would seriously impair their value. The main argument of the critics rests on the uniqueness of the individual as contrasted with statistics, which are concerned solely with multitudes. Statistical prediction can refer merely to the behaviour of groups of individuals of whom John Smith is only one. If the statistician finds that John belongs to a group with a failure rate of 80 per cent this tells us nothing about his actual performance after discharge as he may belong to the minority of 20 per cent who are destined to succeed, but the mere fact of his being included in a group with a high rate of failure may, it is argued, adversely influence those who have to deal with him; it may be very detrimental to his chances and contribute to his ultimate failure. In such a case we cannot say that the statistical prediction was 'wrong'; it was correct for the group, nor was it false for John Smith since it allowed for a minority of 20 per cent successes without pretending to make any statement about him personally. Nevertheless, it might easily be claimed that actuarial prediction is not only devoid of meaning as far as the individual is concerned, but actually unfair and dangerous to him. In this argumentation truth and falsehood are closely intermixed. It is certainly true that statistical prediction cannot, and does not pretend to, predict directly for the individual case. With individual prediction in this direct sense we shall be dealing below (v). On the other hand, statistical methods, by forcing us to see the individual as a member of a group, may bring to the surface features of his case which might be overlooked when dealing with him in isolation. Surprisingly enough, it has been found that mass prediction often produces better results than individual prediction.[3] Moreover, it may prepare the ground for the latter by offering a preliminary selection of predictive factors for the use of individual prediction (below, s. v). With regard to the danger of unfairly influencing the fate of an individual who belongs to the minority of 'incorrectly' predicted cases this could be a serious matter only if statistical prediction would be treated as absolutely conclusive.

(b) This brings us to the second of the three misapprehensions referred to above, i.e. that the fate of an individual offender should be decided solely on the strength of his classification under one of the statistical categories of success rates. No responsible worker in the field of prediction research has made such claims. Statistical prediction is nothing but one of many tools to be used in conjunction with others such as the personal impression made by the offender on those who have to deal with him, the experience of other cases within the knowledge of the judges, magistrates and administrators, and in suitable cases also the opinion of psychologists and psychiatrists. The statistical classification of an offender as a risk of 80 per cent failure provides nothing more than a warning to all those concerned with the case. As the Gluecks have repeatedly stressed, 'prediction tables should not be used mechanically and as a substitute for clinical judgment', nor, we might add, for any other well-considered judgment. 'They are intended to help him (the clinician, and we might add, the judge, magistrate, administrator and field worker) to see the individual in the perspective of organized experience with hundreds of other boys. . . .'[4] The name 'experience tables' is, therefore, preferable to that of prediction tables.

In addition to such close practical co-operation there is an equal need for constant interchange in the theoretical field between the statistician and the individual predicter to improve the reliability of the prediction tables. In particular those cases where the actual outcome differs from the statistical classification ('over-achievers' and 'under-achievers') should be closely examined to see which individual factors were responsible for the difference.[5]

(c) It is sometimes believed that the predictive factors used in statistical studies are assumed to be causal factors. If, for example, the factor 'poor working habits' is shown to have a high predictive value for future recidivism, does this mean that this factor was necessarily a strong cause of criminal behaviour in the past? If a bad family atmosphere was a causal factor in the past, will it necessarily have a high predictive value for the future? Obviously not, because with growing age the driving forces in an offender's life history may change his character, and what was of causal significance in the earlier stages of his career may not be so later on. Moreover, predictive factors are often rather broad and general and can be related to a variety of causes. On the other hand, it would be difficult to construct a prediction table on the basis of a multi-factor theory of crime causation; both sides have to be kept separate. Prediction tables are not intended to be catalogues of causal factors; they do not attempt to 'explain' and 'understand' criminal behaviour, or to reflect a certain typology (Chapter 8 below), but are merely practical devices to facilitate decision and action ('decision theory'). In so far, their objects are different from and less ambitious than those of the scientific criminologist. This self-imposed limitation does not mean that those engaged in prediction research should discard the idea of causation as a 'completely redundant concept';[6] it is merely unnecessary in this particular context, and even this only up to a point since in our original selection of potentially predictive factors, i.e. at the stage before the tables are constructed, we are consciously or unconsciously guided by certain views on causation.

## III. THE CONSTRUCTION OF PREDICTION TABLES

The technical side of the matter and its historical development have been so often described in detail that only a summary will here have to be given.[7] The basic idea common to all the various systems is to select a sample of case records representative of the type of offender for whom the prediction is to be made, for example Borstal boys, and to abstract from them information on a number of factors—perhaps sixty or a hundred or more—which might have some bearing on their criminal conduct.[8] It is in the selection of these factors that we have to be guided by the results of previous research on causation or otherwise,[9] although we should, of course, not be entirely dependent upon them. The sample is then divided into two groups, those who have been 'successes' and those who have been 'failures' over a period after discharge from the Institution, and only the factors showing the highest correlations with success or failure are used for predicting future conduct.

In the first important prediction study, made by Professor Ernest W. Burgess in Chicago in the nineteen-twenties[10] and, as so many American studies of this kind, concerned with predicting the results of parole, information was extracted on 21 factors for 3,000 men paroled from three Illinois prisons. Each factor was divided into several sub-classes, for example according to types of offences, and it was found that for certain of these sub-classes the rate of parole violation was considerably higher and for others much lower than the overall rate. For example, for those with no previous work record the rate was 44·4 per cent, but for those with a record of regular work only 12·2 per cent. Burgess then proceeded to attribute to each of his 21 factors the same, arbitrary, weight of one point, so that a parolee whose violation rate was below average for, say, ten factors received ten favourable points. The cases were then scored, and a table was constructed for the various score classes showing, for example, a probable violation rate of 1·5 per cent for men with 16 to 21 good points and for men with only 2 to 4 good points a rate of 76 per cent. The principal weaknesses of this technique are that only material contained in the official records was used; that only conduct during the official period of parole was considered; that some of the categories and their sub-classes were over-lapping or too subjective; that no test was made of the reliability of the results; and that the same arbitrary weight of one point was attached to each factor, although some of them were more strongly correlated to the criterion than others. In spite of these weaknesses, the Burgess technique has been widely adopted, in particular in the well-known and influential work of Ohlin, based on his practical experience as research sociologist in the Division of Correction in the State of Illinois. While following Burgess in most points, for example absence of a weighting system and the use of highly subjective terms, he accepted the Glueck technique of using only a small number of factors (12 against 21 of Burgess).[11] An interesting feature of Ohlin's technique is that he includes 'psychiatric prognosis' in his list of predictive factors.

The distinguishing features of the various Glueck studies are the collection of basic information not contained in the official files, the extension of the testing time to periods of up to fifteen years after the completion of parole, the reduction of the predictive factors, finally used, to the five or six showing the highest correlations with the criterion, and the use of statistical techniques to attach different weight to each factor in accordance with the degree of its correlation with the criterion.[12] The scores of these zero order correlations are then added up and may result, for example, in the following table:[13]

| Score | Success % | Partial failure % | Total failure % | Total % |
|---|---|---|---|---|
| 244–295 | 75·0 | 20·0 | 5·0 | 100 |
| 296–345 | 34·6 | 11·5 | 53·9 | 100 |
| 346–395 | 26·2 | 19·1 | 54·7 | 100 |
| 396 and over | 5·7 | 13·7 | 80·6 | 100 |
| Total | 20·0 | 15·6 | 64·4 | 100 |

Whereas most of the Glueck studies try to predict the future conduct of persons already delinquent, in *Unraveling Juvenile Delinquency* an attempt was made to predict the future delinquency of children aged 6 or 7. The great practical significance of this problem of spotting the danger signs at the onset of a criminal career is obvious, but the difficulties are formidable. The Gluecks realized that much of the information collected when the boys were already between 11½ and nearly 17 years old had but little relevance to very young children and they decided to exclude from the predictive instruments constructed for this purpose all the physical and some of the psychological material collected in the course of this particular study. Therefore they utilized for their three tables (*a*) certain family factors, (*b*) character traits, determined by Rorschach tests, and (*c*) personality traits discovered in psychiatric interviews.[14] They found a fairly high rate of agreement between these three tables and concluded that the latter were ready for experimental application. Several validation studies have since been made, and it is claimed that if the three tables had been applied to very young children in around 90 per cent of the cases their future delinquency or non-delinquency would have been correctly predicted.[15] These claims have been strongly questioned by several critics for various reasons, one of them being that the factor 'residence in an under-privileged neighbourhood' had been held constant and thereby excluded from the investigation,[16] and also because the proportion of delinquents in the Glueck sample was naturally far higher than that in the general population, which latter has to be considered when prediction tables are constructed for non-delinquents.[17]

The technique used for the English Borstal Prediction Study, which was based upon a sample of boys admitted between the 1st August 1946 and the 31st July 1947, was similar to that of the Gluecks, introducing, however, certain statistical improvements of which only a few can here be mentioned. It was thought, for example, that the Glueck technique of adding together the percentages for the factors showing the highest zero order correlations was not the most efficient way of dealing with the problem of possible overlaps between the various factors and that at least considerable overlap should be avoided because, where it occurs, the factors concerned taken together do not contribute substantially more to the result than does each factor separately. Moreover, it was decided to use for the construction of the tables only cases where information was available for all the selected factors.[18] Finally, a special effort was made to deal with the vexed problem of the 'centre group of "unpredictables"', i.e. those cases where the probabilities of success or failure are not very different, at least not different enough to justify a reasonably safe prediction.[19] While for the first equation, worked out for the total of cases, only the weightiest factors were used, dominated by the factor 'past criminal record', at a further stage a second equation was worked out for the centre group only which, using factors of a more personal nature such as intelligence and leisure activities, greatly reduced the number of 'unpredictable' cases.

In the Borstal Prediction Study a special effort was made to exclude predictive factors of a strongly subjective flavour, such as some of those used by Burgess and Ohlin, and to some extent also by the Gluecks. 'Statistics cannot deal with "intangibles"',[20] but outside the field of statistical methods there is no objection to the use of subjective terms. For statistical prediction, as here discussed, it is essential that those who will have to use the tables—possibly persons without statistical or other special training—should find them easy to operate. Repeatability is therefore important. The four basic requirements of such predictive work have been summed up as 'simplicity, efficiency, repeatability or reliability and validity'.[21] The inevitable consequence of such austerity is that the tables look distressingly primitive, and it is not surprising that their lack of refinement should fill psychologists and in particular psychiatrists with contempt and many non-statisticians with the feeling that a ridiculous little mouse has been born as a result of a disproportionately large outlay in money and brainpower. This state of affairs can be improved only if it is more generally appreciated that mathematical formulae cannot be expected to look like psycho-analytical case histories and that they are not meant to provide the final answer.

One problem which all predictive efforts have to face is how to make allowance for unforeseeable future developments affecting the lives of the individuals in the sample, including changes in the penal and after-care systems to which they are subjected. In the Borstal Prediction Study some indications have been given of how such changes might be taken care of by a system of continuous sampling.[22]

## IV. VALIDATION OF PREDICTION TABLES[23]

It is generally agreed that no prediction table can be accepted as useful for practical purposes without validation by testing it on a group of cases different from the original one. For the Borstal Prediction Study the whole intake of one of the Reception Centres for the 6 months' period July to December 1948 was used for purposes of validation, making a total of 338 cases. No second equation was attempted for this group because the necessary information was not available, and no prediction was envisaged for the 'unpredictable' centre group. With these limitations, the validation proved satisfactory as far as success or failure within the Borstal system were concerned, but 'continuing validity is not assured because it has been once demonstrated'. In particular, it was stressed that subsequent changes in the Borstal and After-Care systems would necessitate corresponding alterations in the construction of the tables. As already mentioned, there have been several validation studies of the various Glueck tables, but their value has been controversial.

## V. INDIVIDUAL PREDICTION[24]

Without anticipating the general discussion on the individual case history method (Chapter 8) a few remarks should here be added on the problem of predicting from and for the individual case direct which, as has been stressed before, is the essential supplement of statistical prediction. Case studies are not always made for purposes of prediction; often their object is simply to increase our understanding of present human behaviour.

149

The initial stages of individual prediction (also called 'idiographic' prediction) do not greatly differ from those of actuarial prediction. A certain amount of data is needed in both cases, but, whereas for actuarial prediction it is invariably obtained from factual material relating to a group of individuals, in the case of individual prediction it may be obtained from a variety of sources:[25] (a) either from other cases which show a similar 'configuration' of traits or situations, or (b) by 'typological reduction', or (c) by observing certain 'intra-individual' traits and trends of behaviour relating only to the individual for whom the prediction is to be made, i.e. the 'time sequence' of the 'unique' case.

(a): The life-history of the individual concerned is studied and a configuration of his essential traits is constructed for different periods of his life. This is compared with similar configurations obtained for other individuals whose success or failure in the field in question is already known. This, of course, is a combination of individual, typological, and statistical prediction, but whereas the latter is entirely concerned with the group to which the individual belongs we now place the emphasis on the individual case and look at its configuration in the light of other, similar ones.

(b): On the 'typological reduction', which means reducing the number of configurations to a smaller number of types, more will be said below in Chapter 8.

(c): The prediction is made on the basis of the 'time sequence' of the 'unique' case in the absence of corresponding information concerning similar cases. Here, as Stouffer suggests (see Note 1: Horst et al.), it would be essential to observe the behaviour of the individual in the past, his success or failure, under similar circumstances to see whether he was successful in the past in a life configuration similar to that for which the prediction is made. Even here, where the prediction uses, apparently, only material derived from the 'unique' case, Stouffer insists that the final test of accuracy must be a statistical one. Meehl, too, who deals very fairly with the merits and weaknesses of the two competing methods, thinks that the final word has always to rest with the actuary who has to study the ratio of accuracy in the clinician's guesses.[26]

Faced with this unending quarrel between statisticians and clinicians—to attach to them these over-simplifying labels, although many opponents of statistical prediction are not clinicians—we have to stress that both elements are equally indispensable to successful prediction. Individual techniques have the advantage that they are less rigid and that many more factors can be taken into consideration, especially those of a highly subjective nature such as motivation, insight, pathological states. Therefore, they will contribute far more to

150

the understanding of the individual case, although even here successful prediction is not necessarily dependent upon our understanding of
the causes of the individual's behaviour.[27]

In the existing literature cases of strictly individual prediction,
without any statistical ingredients, are rare. Usually the predictions
are made, although for each individual separately, in fact for a group
to which he is assigned, and statistical success rates are eventually
computed for the group and various sub-groups of it. A good example
is offered by a recent, non-criminological, study connected with the
Menninger Foundation in Topeka, Kansas, and fully reported by
Escalona and Heider.[28]

First a study was made in 1947–51 of a group of infants aged 4–32 weeks
(Infancy Study) who were followed up for some years to see how they
would cope with their problems, and a second study (Coping Project) was
made in 1953. Simultaneously with the latter, one of the original investigators who was not connected with the second study was asked to make
predictions of the subsequent developments of 31 of the infants in ignorance of the findings of the Coping Project. These predictions were made
for each individual child separately, using 16 to 55 predictive items for each,
altogether 1,003 items for the 31 cases and for 46 different content areas.
There were marked differences in the success rate of prediction for various
categories of the children, ranging from a maximum of 92 per cent to a
minimum of 33·3 per cent, with a median rate of 66·6 per cent, and the
predicter had to ask what accounted for the fact that predictions for some
children were more successful than for others. A high degree of interdependence of the predictive items used was observed, which meant that
if one prediction for the child concerned was correct most others were also
correct. Although the amount of statistical work was reduced to a minimum, the investigation had to use at least some statistical techniques to
bring order into what might otherwise have been chaos. Moreover, even in
this highly individualized study the danger was noted that the personality
of the child was lost sight of in the mass of single items, and often, even
where the prediction for each item was correct, 'yet the essence of the child
was missed'—'a personality description is in itself an artefact'.[29]

Granting that the two techniques are inextricably interwoven we
have to consider in what way they can be most profitably used side by
side. Some thought has been given to the matter in the Borstal Prediction Study.[30] There it has been pointed out that there is, first, the
general object of lending colour to the abstract statistical tables
through histories of concrete cases; with this we shall deal below in
Chapter 8. Secondly, in the special field of prediction studies the case
study has the function of illustrating the differences behind the various
statistical risk categories; for example how far do cases in the category of 80 per cent probability of success seem different from cases in
the category of 20 per cent? Here, it should be shown how great a

151

variety of cases can be accommodated in the same risk category, one case being a poor risk perhaps because of a bad family background, the other because of certain inherent weaknesses of personality, and so on, all this related to the predictive items used in the tables and with special emphasis on the multiplicity of possible combinations of factors which, taken together, may produce the same statistical result of, say, a failure score of 451 bad points. Moreover, special attention should be paid to atypical cases, especially to 'over- and under-achievers', to discover the reason why they deviate from the majority of cases in their risk category. Such individual case material may occasionally lead to a revision of the statistical tables, when it is found that important predictive factors have not been given adequate attention in the working out of the tables. On the other hand, the latter will often induce the individual predicter to reconsider his personal evaluation of a case, and in this way a continuous process of give and take will be achieved.

## VI. TYPOLOGICAL PREDICTIONS

Typological predictions have also often been attempted, usually on the basis of constitutional or psychological typologies. The distinction between 'corrigible' and 'incorrigible' criminals which played such an important part in the teachings of the Continental crimino-biological school rested on the belief that, in Kretschmer's terminology, offenders of the pyknic type were mostly occasional and corrigible, whereas those belonging to the leptosome and athletic types were mostly habitual and incorrigible.[31] For the details reference may be made to Chapters 8, II, and 13.

# Chapter 8

## INDIVIDUAL CASE STUDIES AND
## TYPOLOGICAL METHODS

### I. INDIVIDUAL CASE STUDIES[1]

1. *General Considerations*

In Chapter 6, III(1), an attempt was made to draw the line of demarcation between, first, follow-up studies, which are mainly interested in the subsequent fate of groups of offenders who have undergone various forms of correctional treatment; secondly, descriptive studies of the evolution of criminal careers, which are also concerned with groups of offenders, but not necessarily in relation to their correctional experiences (of which there may be none); and, thirdly, individual case studies which concentrate on the life of one individual. There is, naturally, a great deal of overlapping between these three categories; the difference in emphasis, however, should be clear. As far as the object of individual case studies is prediction they have been dealt with in Chapter 7, V. Prediction, however, is by no means their only purpose; they are also indispensable to provide the basic material for a better understanding of motivation, causation, and of the place of the criminal in the world surrounding him. In the words of Earnest Hooton,[2] they are 'absolutely essential as the primary sources from which general deductions may be drawn'. He rightly objects, however, to the way in which the case study method has often been exploited, i.e. by producing highly selected and therefore unrepresentative illustrative cases in order to prove a particular point. The highly selective nature of case studies of homosexuals in particular has been stressed by Glover who writes:[3] 'The case-history, valuable as it undoubtedly is, constitutes merely a classroom diagram concerning such cases as have been indiscreet (or compulsive) enough to have brought detection and punishment on themselves or at most have felt that their homosexual organization is a distressing abnormality or handicap calling for treatment.'

Strictly speaking, there are only two legitimate ways of using this technique: either by presenting the detailed and objective history of one individual, or at most a few, regardless of whether or not it supports a specific criminological theory, leaving it to the reader to draw his own conclusions from the facts and interpretations; or by making a statistically representative selection of the available material to illustrate the different types of cases emerging from the general discussion. The second alternative was recommended above (Chapter 7, v) for use in conjunction with statistical prediction, where it was stressed that only through case histories could the deviations from the statistical norm be explained. Moreover, two individuals may fall into the same statistical prediction group and, nevertheless, be different in essential characteristics which can be highlighted only through detailed study of their cases. William Sheldon's, otherwise not very illuminating, 200 short case studies, classified according to his system of somatotypes (see below, Chapter 13, p. 240), is another example of this technique of presenting case material.[4]

Very often, however, we find in criminological literature case histories, frequently taken from newspaper reports, used in a compromise manner standing somewhere between the two extremes, i.e. a number of 'illustrative' or 'typical' case histories are presented which are loosely related to some of the main points made by the author. No objections can be raised against this as it often helps us to a better understanding of those points, provided only not too much is claimed for the typicality and representativeness of the cases. The great danger of this technique is that, if not carefully handled, it may give undue weight to atypical cases without making the reader aware of it. Much will depend on the kind of readership to which the study is addressed.[5] Sometimes these histories are assembled in one special chapter, sometimes they are scattered over the whole book.[6] In Cressey's *Other People's Money*[7] more than 300 case histories of prisoners were obtained, of whom 133 were interviewed at length; for about one half of the latter short histories were presented, specifically related to some of the points made in the book. Where this can be done it greatly assists in our understanding and evaluation of the argument. The techniques used in the Glueck studies vary.[8] In *500 Delinquent Women*, for example, full histories of eleven women are given which, according to the authors, 'exemplify practically all the major problems of individual and social pathology', and various types are described in impressionistic terms, but it is stressed that these histories, while they may suggest hypotheses, can supply 'no reliable estimate of the extent and ramifications of the problems involved in delinquency'. In *One Thousand Juvenile Delinquents* ten histories were given, apparently not selected to illustrate different types or predictive probabilities, but mainly to demonstrate certain weaknesses in court and clinic procedure, which was the main object of that book.[9]

An interesting, entirely impressionistic, technique of using case histories to illustrate specific points has been developed by Hans von Hentig in his brilliant study *Der Gangster* and the several volumes of his series *Zur Psychologie der Einzeldelikte*.[10] From hundreds of cases a composite picture of the American gangster, or of the murderer, swindler, thief or blackmailer, emerges, but although the same individuals appear again and again in different connections no detailed and coherent case histories of them are presented. The information given is second-hand, taken from other books or from newspapers. While this technique has its merits, it should not be used excessively, and its results require careful checking.

Of a different character are those studies where the case history is not merely used to illustrate some of the theoretical points of the authors and to assist in bringing the typology to life but where, on the contrary, the case studies are the real essence of the book, and whatever theoretical argument may be presented is derived from the cases. As we shall see, the latter condition has only rarely been complied with. Such studies have been written mainly by psychotherapists, but also by sociologists. Some of them concentrate on one single case, for example in the U.S.A. Wertham's *Dark Legend* and more recently Helen Parkhurst's *Undertow*, and in Britain Tony Parker's outstanding books *The Courage of his Convictions* and *The Unknown Citizen*; others present a small number of very detailed histories, for example Bettelheim's *Truants from Life* or Karpman's *Case Studies in the Psychopathology of Crime*.[11] Wertham describes it as the object of his fascinating study of a case of matricide to make it useful not only to Gino, the murderer, but to others as well; it was to be 'his own detective case', and the end in view was to uncover the motive of the deed for which the best parallel seemed to be the story of Orestes. He studied reports of other cases of matricide[12] and found some 'startling similarities'. There was a pattern followed by Gino's and other 'typical' cases, which made it possible to recognize six characteristics of the 'Orestes complex' which Wertham decided to call 'Catathymic Crisis',[13] but although he derived some help from the few superficial data available for those other cases his real understanding and diagnosis of Gino's crime came not from any statistical correlations between them but from the intimate study of his 'unique' case.

An interesting discussion of the theory of case histories has been given by Bruno Bettelheim whose book *Truants from Life* contains four very detailed histories of children at the Sonia Shankman Orthogenic School of the University of Chicago.[14] His object was not 'to demonstrate the optimum that can be achieved for very disturbed

155

children' but rather to show on an unselected sample what this school could do 'on the average'. Therefore several histories were needed. On the other hand, a large number of brief accounts, 'so abundant in the clinical literature', would have been too superficial and could not have convinced the critical reader that the author had 'the correct or the only possible interpretation of complex life experiences that extended over or were separated by weeks—or perhaps years'; on the contrary, the author might have included in his narrative 'only those aspects that fitted the points he wanted to make'. A technique standing between these two extremes was therefore required.

## 2. The Different Sources of Case Histories

The most important sources of case histories, as used in criminological research, are the following: interviews, questionnaires, autobiographies, biographies, medical, psychological and psychiatric examinations, photographs,[15] written reports by those in charge of the case, accounts of participant observation and press reports. In actual practice, two or more of these sources are usually combined to form a 'life history'. In this country, the pre-war 'Mass-Observation' movement which, among others, also produced a volume on juvenile delinquency, had somewhat different objects and used different techniques. While for the details the reader has to be referred to the general literature on the subject[16] a few specifically criminological problems may be briefly discussed here.

Perhaps most of our criminological case histories have been reproduced from interviews conducted by research workers otherwise not connected with the case. The great pioneers in the use of personal documents in the study of the individual offender were the psychiatrist William Healy[17] and the sociologist Clifford R. Shaw, and the heyday for this line of approach was in the earlier part of this century. Healy's first major work in this field, *The Individual Delinquent*, published in 1915, was a landmark in criminological research almost comparable in its impact with Lombroso's *L'Uomo delinquente* nearly forty years earlier, but whereas Lombroso's main concern had been to use individual offenders for the construction of types Healy was primarily concerned with the individual as such. This does not mean that he rejected typology; on the contrary, in the part of the book headed 'Cases, Types, Causative Factors' he writes: 'Out of the chaos . . . we rejoice to see strongly marked causal types or classes emerging.' The book is based upon the study of 1,000 recidivists of an average age of 15–16; his case histories, a few hundred of them, are short and scattered through the book to illustrate specific points. Statistical methods are widely used, but 'statistics will never tell the whole story'. In *Delinquents and Criminals*, already published together with his future collaborator of many years, Augusta Bronner, a few 'fair and typical examples of careers' were used from a very extensive material. It can hardly be said that the case histories presented in these two earlier books were in any way remarkable; their merit was mainly that the technique was used at all. In two later collections, however, *New Light on Delinquency* and *The Roots of Crime*, the latter written jointly with the psycho-analyst Franz Alexander, the histories became more detailed and less superficial.

Rather different is the technique used by Clifford Shaw, especially in his two earlier books *The Jack-Roller* and *Natural History of a Delinquent Career*.[18] Stimulated by the example of Thomas and Znaniecki's great documentary study of *The Polish Peasant* (Note 16) and following the tradition of the Chicago school of sociology he concentrated on the life histories of delinquents as told by them in a long series of personal interviews stenographically recorded. Shaw's contact with these delinquents extended over periods as long as six years, in the case of the five 'brothers in crime' even over 16 years. He insisted that these personal stories had to be carefully checked and supplemented by other material such as interviews with relatives and friends and official records. This precaution has often been neglected, and we possess therefore a large number of books written by ex-prisoners or other ex-inmates of correctional institutions which have in no way been verified from other sources. This does not mean that such books are without any merit; even if their 'facts' are often distorted or entirely invented they can give important insights into the writer's attitudes and system of values, and, to quote W. I. Thomas' famous dictum: 'If men define situations as real, they are real in their consequences'. Their usefulness would be greatly enhanced, however, if the points where they deviate from the objective truth would be revealed.

Shaw's last life history study, *Brothers in Crime*, is distinguished, first, by the fact that here the criminal careers of five brothers are described in their similarities and differences and that in spite of existing personality differences these careers are regarded as typical illustrations of the relationship between delinquency and the culture conflicts in poor immigrant families in the United States. In the chapter on 'Personality Traits' contributed by Ernest Burgess the latter concludes that in the case of these brothers social factors were much more important than personality traits and that this seemed to be true of the vast majority of cases of crime and delinquency in American cities.

Sutherland, in his *Professional Thief*,[19] published the story of a representative of this class, called 'Chic Conwell', told in his own words and covering the period 1905–25. Sutherland started from the not improbable hypothesis that the professional thieves form a group which is in no sense pathological but possesses all the characteristics of other groups and that no one belongs to it unless he is recognized as a professional thief by other members of the group. Chic Conwell's story, he believed, served to confirm that hypothesis.

Many shorter extracts from essays written by prisoners have been published by Clemmer and others.[20] While the great merits of these life histories as presented by Thomas–Znaniecki, Shaw and Sutherland have been generally recognized, certain features have not escaped criticism, notably from Herbert Blumer and John Dollard.[21] Both stress the possible lack of representativeness of these histories and also the intrusion into their interpretation of the theories favoured by the editors. Dollard draws up a list of criteria to which every life history should conform and finds that Shaw's Jack Roller does not measure up to some of them. A personal document of this kind, he thinks, should not only reveal the existence of certain attitudes in the subject but also how they were formed; nor should it concentrate too exclusively on social and cultural factors, neglecting the biological ones. The early childhood of Stanley, the 'Jack Roller', he argues, is ignored: he 'simply appears at the age of 4 or 5 years and is taken for granted from then on'. This is an omission not seldom found in case studies, but easily explained by the difficulties encountered by both the subject and the editor in their attempts to unearth the happenings of these earliest years of childhood. Moreover, if sociologists are inclined to give too much prominence to social and cultural influences in their case histories, psycho-analysts may tend to play them down unduly.

In spite of such shortcomings Shaw's life histories are greatly superior to most of the material presented by certain other, less critical writers who, unconsciously, apply their own moral attitudes and the customs and prejudices of the social class to which they belong as yardsticks to measure and condemn the subjects of their histories.

A good example of this is Sir Leo Page's, otherwise in many ways valuable, study *The Young Lag*.[22] Twenty-three men, aged between 20 and 26 and selected by six prison governors 'as likely to become lifelong offenders', were interviewed in prison by the author with their consent once or twice for three hours or more, and their stories were checked by discussing them with the staffs of the prisons and the institutions in which the men had been before. Important aspects were, however, left unverified and, even more important, one hardly ever gets the impression that the stories obtained penetrate beneath the surface. The author, strongly opposed to any scientific interpretation, sociological or psychological, and unable to understand persons belonging to a class very different from his own, had to confess that many of these young men remained to him 'a saddening and baffling problem'. He particulary resented that some of them had told him lies, but it never occurred to him that lying might have been their most natural reaction in the circumstances.

Much better, though also open to criticism on account of its moralizing attitude, is Andreas Bjerre's *The Psychology of Murder*,[23] a study of three serious criminals in prison, on the lines of Adlerian psychology. Their stories are told in detail not by the subjects but by the author. He is at least capable of seeing the psychological problems of these three men and makes a serious attempt to understand their attitudes in the light of his scientific study of human problems, but, as Clifford Shaw took it for granted that these problems were primarily social ones, Bjerre approached his subjects armed with certain views on the psychology of the criminal. In conformity with Adlerian teachings he believed that the principal characteristics of the serious criminal, especially of the murderer, were weakness and self-deception. As a trained student of human behaviour he was aware that this theory may be an undue generalization and he also realized that the long periods of imprisonment which these men had already undergone at the time of the interviews were bound to influence their views on life, but the possibility that his theories may have coloured his accounts of his interviews cannot be excluded. Moreover, he had to admit that his openly expressed moral condemnation of the conduct of his subjects had the effect of making them gradually less frank in their own statements.

There is far less case material on the female side: One of the few pioneer studies in this field, a near-contemporary English counterpart to *500 Delinquent Women* by the Gluecks, is Grace W. Pailthorpe's study, undertaken on behalf of the Medical Research Council.[24] One hundred female prisoners, aged between 16 and 30, were interviewed in prison by the author, a medical psychologist, and invited to tell their stories which were received without any signs of moral condemnation. In contrast to Sir Leo Page's attitude, lying was regarded as a natural reaction. 'Some at first took the investigator for an official or lady-visitor, and it was of psychological interest to note how the story changed after the discovery was made that the investigator was unofficial and not a religious or moral adviser.' Mental tests were given, and the interviews were continued 'until all that was required had been obtained'. In addition, a group of a hundred girls in Preventive and Rescue Homes were also interviewed.

As in the case of prediction for a 'unique case' (see above, Chapter 7, v), attempts have occasionally been made to subject life histories to statistical treatment, for example, by asking several experts to interpret certain features in a number of such histories and to assess the degree of agreement.[25]

A few further remarks are finally needed on one of the most important and numerous categories of human documents in criminology, books written by prisoners or ex-prisoners. They are very uneven in quality; some of them, such as John Bunyan's *Pilgrim's Progress* or Dostoevsky's *Memoirs from a Dead House* or Silvio Pellico's *My Prisons*, are widely acclaimed masterpieces of world literature, others are poor, sensational stuff. Hans von Hentig, to whose excellent section and copious footnotes on the subject special reference should be made,[26] observes that while American and British books of this kind have been written mainly by confidence men, burglars and pickpockets, the Continental literature has been largely produced by political prisoners. This is an interesting reflection on the differences in the political climate. He also remarks that not much has been done in this field by murderers, sex offenders and blackmailers. The explanation may be that, while blackmailers have very little of interest to tell[27]—it is difficult to envisage the 'Memoirs of a Blackmailer'— murderers had in the past their careers too often cut short by execution. Nevertheless, we do possess a number of highly valuable books by murderers written either while awaiting execution or after reprieve, for example David Lamson, *We Who Are About to Die*, Nathan Leopold's *Life Plus 99 Years*, and Chessman's *Cell 2455*.[28] With regard to sex offenders there is at least one group of them, the homosexuals, who have produced a whole literature, though usually not written in prison. In recent years, Peter Wildeblood's *Against the Law*[29] has received much well-deserved attention. Dr. D. J. West's *Homosexuality*[30] contains a list of the better-known works of fiction concerned with the subject, including one of the most famous among them, Genet's *Notre-Dame des Fleurs*.

There can be little doubt that many of these books by prisoners, even the less reliable ones, have provided a useful stimulus for prison reform as they have been widely discussed in the daily press and professional journals and often forced the authorities to examine complaints and to take action.[31]

Fresh ground has recently been broken by William Clifford, Director of Welfare and Principal of the Oppenheimer College of Social Service in Northern Rhodesia, in collecting, by way of personal interview, ten case histories of African recidivist prisoners with the object 'to augment the meagre information which already exists on crime and criminals in Central Africa'. Though only short, these histories give a vivid picture of the lives of these African habitual offenders, their family ties, religious beliefs, attitudes to crime and punishment and many other aspects of crime among Africans in the Northern Rhodesian Copperbelt.[32]

Not only case histories of offenders but also biographies and autobiographies of non-offenders can be of great interest to criminologists. It is as important for our understanding of crime to study the personal documents of persons who, in spite of considerable handicaps and temptations, succeeded in remaining crime free as it is to speculate on the causes of failure in the case of those who succumbed.

## II. THE TYPOLOGICAL METHOD

### 1. *Definition and General Application. What is a Type?*

As the idea of the type can be applied to a heterogeneous variety of phenomena, personal as well as impersonal, its definition has to be general and vague enough to accommodate all potential forms of application. We mean here by 'type' a combination of several factors regarded as characteristic of the phenomenon studied—usually a configuration of more factors than are capable of being easily correlated in statistical work, but considerably fewer than those emerging from the detailed study of one single unit of the phenomenon. There has to be a rational relationship between these individual factors which is capable of giving the impression that they 'belong' together, which may be entirely absent in the case of the factors in a prediction table. Often, though not always, we find a configuration of factors causally inter-related, mutually influencing each other and working in the same direction. From the point of view of multiple causation (see above, Chapter 1) only type-formations can be envisaged in which elements of each stream of causation are represented and combined. In this sense, our typology depends on our general views of crime causation.

The concept of type enables us to describe in a few words complex phenomena for which, without it, we would need many sentences. The phenomenon in question may be a group of persons, but it may also be wars, diseases, areas, communities, democracies, religions or offences. Typologies are unpopular in some scientific quarters, but they are indispensable. The bare bones of statistics are all too often disappointing and apparently meaningless; full case studies, on the other hand, are but rarely available and certainly not feasible for the masses of phenomena in need of scientific understanding. The typological method, standing somewhere between these two extremes, provides a compromise which may be acceptable at least for the initial stages of research and, *faute de mieux*, often perhaps even as the final answer.

The trend towards typological techniques is not confined to scientific research; writers in other fields, too, have noted, and sometimes regretted, its presence. 'Faced with the complexity almost every human being offers', writes André Gide, 'the eye tends inevitably, spontaneously, unconsciously almost, to simplify to some extent. Such is the French novelist's instinctive effort. He singles out the chief elements in a character, tries to discern clear-cut lines in a figure and reproduce the contours unbroken. Whether Balzac or another, no matter: the desire, the need even, for stylization is all-important. . . .

Woe betide the authors whose ideas refuse to be reduced to a formula!'[33] Or, to quote Edwin Muir: 'The type has become the mainstay of the professional novelist, the convenient counter which absolves him from deeper participation in human experience. . . . The whole tendency of our statistical civilization, with its need to enclose people in categories and its ravenous interest in the human machine as a machine, drives the writer to it.'[34] It may be questioned whether typological tendencies were not marked already in Shakespeare, for example, long before the coming of the 'statistical civilization'. C. G. Jung, in his famous book on *Psychological Types*, devotes a special chapter to 'The Problem of Types in Poetry'.[35]

It should not be too rashly assumed, however, that typology is nothing but a necessary evil, something which conveniently reduces the human personality to a mere figure within a larger unit without adding anything to our understanding of its essential characteristics. On the contrary, by searching for more and more refined typologies we may acquire an insight into complicated behavioural trends and reactions which neither the isolated study of individuals nor mere statistical correlations can supply (see also Chapter 7, v). On the other hand, even the creators of modern typologies, such as Kretschmer, did not claim for them anything like finality; the concept of type is for them rather a symbol for the point where a considerable number of important correlations meet—correlations which, as opposed to many statistical correlations, must be capable of being combined in a meaningful way.[36] A typology is usually developed by way of co-operation between intuitive, speculative thought, on the one hand, and the study of a number of individual cases, on the other.[37]

Complications may arise from the fact that cases belonging to the same type may otherwise exhibit different characteristics. Howard Jones,[38] for example, describes one of his types of drinkers as characterized by 'ego need', stressing that the individuals belonging to it differ otherwise in almost every possible way. 'It is in their general conformation that their fundamental identity with each other, as ego-need cases, is to be seen.' The main characteristics of this type are inferiority feeling, sense of inadequacy, insecurity, need to bolster up their ego-feeling by drink, all of which according to Jones provides strong support for the existence of 'ego-need' as a diagnostic category. Clearly, whatever phenomenon we may be concerned with, its various individual units will always differ in many ways and be identical only in a comparatively limited number of factors. Nevertheless, this may be sufficient to form a type, but exactly how many similarities are needed for it in an ocean of dissimilarities nobody can say with any degree of authority.

The comparative rarity of pure types has been stressed by Jung and

Kretschmer. According to Jung, every individual possesses both extravert and introvert traits; it depends only on their relative strength to which type he belongs, and it is the persistence of this relative strength that creates a type.

Eysenck[39] rightly defines a type as a group of correlated traits and a trait as a group of correlated behavioural acts or action tendencies. The difference between type and trait, therefore, lies in 'the greater inclusiveness' of the concept of type. He also refers to type as 'observed constellations or syndromes of traits' and to traits as 'observed constellations of individual action-tendencies'.

In a more recent book (*Crime and Personality*, pp. 8–19) Eysenck has taken up the interesting question of 'generality' versus 'specificity' of human conduct and character traits which was studied forty years ago by Hartshorne and May (*Studies in Deceit*; see also my *Group Problems*, p. 21). We are here concerned with the nature of such criminologically important traits as honesty and dishonesty: is an individual who is likely to be honest in one type of situation also likely to be honest in another, totally different, one? Hartshorne and May were inclined to decide in favour of the 'specificity' of certain character traits such as dishonesty, but of 'generality' of honesty. Eysenck stresses more the generality of conduct with its greater predictability. In this connection he refers to the recent researches of T. C. Willett on traffic offenders who, he found, were much more often than commonly believed also ordinary offenders.[40]

Modern scientific thought on the subject has received its impetus mainly from two different sources: on the one hand, from Max Weber's conception of the 'ideal type', and, on the other, from the growing popularity of empirical, especially biological-constitutional and psychological typologies. Max Weber has tried to explain his concept of the 'ideal type' briefly as follows:[41] An 'ideal picture' of a certain historical phenomenon, an institution such as 'state' or 'church' or 'sect' or 'capitalism', is constructed which excludes all merely casual elements and concentrates on essential characteristics. Although such an 'ideal type' is purely utopian and can never exist in real life it does not describe an ideal in the usual sense of the term, a model of what should be, which does not mean, however, that there has never been a historical relationship between ideal type and ideal. There are ideal types not only of morally and socially desirable but also of highly undesirable phenomena. In Weber's words, there may be an ideal type of brothels as well as religions. Nor is it a picture of the 'average' or a hypothesis, but it should be a guide to the construction of hypotheses. It is the task of scientific research to examine the relationship between the ideal type and reality. For criminological research Weber's concept might be useful in helping to bind statistical and individual techniques together. As Riemer expresses it, the ideal type is 'a construct for the purpose of guiding theoretical speculations and statistical control towards the end of more significant prediction units'. Its usefulness is, however, not limited to prediction research; because it stands between the innumerable varieties of real life and the unique ideal it can promote understanding of the essential characteristics of a phenomenon.

Empirical typologies have been useful as auxiliary techniques in case history studies where the material collected is often so bulky and unwieldy that it can be handled only by way of 'typological reductions' (Stouffer), i.e. the masses of factual material are classified according to similarities and traits, and the emerging configurations are then further reduced until we are left with something which can be presented as a type.[42] In a psychological investigation into the consistency of extravert-introvert tendencies among problem boys, Newcomb used for his observation a form with thirty items which had to be filled in each day over a period of time to discover the extent to which the boys tended to respond consistently. Some of them showed a consistency which justified the construction of certain traits and eventually an attempt was made to combine a number of these traits to form extravert or introvert 'types'. It was found that about one fifth of the boys were consistent in three to five traits, but no boy was consistent in more than five out of eight possible traits, and occasionally consistency occurred in opposite directions, i.e. in the same boy traits of consistent extraversion were found together with traits of consistent introversion. Therefore no types could be demonstrated.[43] Considering the great difficulty of establishing even single traits the obstacles standing in the way of consistent combinations of several traits to form a type or syndrome are often enormous.[44] Very often two types are needed, especially one personality type and one type of environment, to round off the picture and to produce jointly a certain effect.

It should be clearly understood that typological classifications are not necessarily of a causal character. Phenomena belonging to the same type have different causes, and, vice versa, the same cause may produce different types.[45]

## 2. *Typology in Criminological Research: General Considerations*

In criminological research, empirical typologies have been employed in every possible section, biological, psychological-psychiatric, sociological and prognostic. There is, moreover, the problem of classification of offences according to non-legal, criminologically useful typologies. While the details have to be reserved for later chapters, a few illustrations may be useful already now, but it should be understood that in accordance with the general design of this book, we are here concerned with the methods rather than with the contents and results of typological research.

It is notably the biological-anthropological school of criminology that has concentrated on the development of types, mainly constitutional types such as the born, the epileptic, the insane criminal in the writings of Lombroso,[46] and as that school has been more popular on the European Continent than in Anglo-American countries it is there that most research on typological lines has been done. It is only recently that through the work of W. H. Sheldon and the Gluecks attention has been drawn to constitutional types in American criminology.[47] As the Gluecks, whose typology is largely derived from that of Sheldon, have given a detailed description of their procedure, nothing more is needed here than a summary. Their starting point was Sheldon's 88 somato-types which are related to his three, more general, major constitutional components: endomorphy, mesomorphy, and ectomorphy,[48] to which a fourth, 'balanced' category is added in which none of the three components dominates. These four classes are then related by the Gluecks to 67 'traits' and 42 sociocultural factors, selected from the larger numbers used in *Unraveling*, to compare, for example, the influence of certain traits and factors on the constitutional types, and it was found that some of them had a stronger influence on one of these types than on the others and that traits atypical of the bodily type in question were particularly likely to lead to delinquency. The main result of this typological investigation was negative in the sense that from the correlation between bodily types, personality traits and socio-cultural factors no consistent combinations of physique, character, temperament and environment emerged which would have justified the assumption of a 'delinquent personality'. Nevertheless, the authors believe that there is enough evidence to show that different clusters of traits and socio-cultural factors may have a selective effect on the delinquent behaviour of the various bodily types.[49] Whether or not this conclusion is justified, this research is an interesting example of the use of constitutional types to assess the potential effect of the interplay between physique and other factors involved in the causation of delinquency.

The Finnish criminologist Veli Verkkö, trying to explain the high rate of violent crime in his country in its relation to drink, refers to Kretschmer's typology and his contention that individuals of the athletic type display a particularly poor ability to carry liquor, while the leptosome (schizothyme) type is slightly better and the pyknic (cyclothyme) best of all.[50]

In the field of psychological, in particular characterological, and psychiatric typology mention might here be made, in addition to the extravert-introvert dichotomy, of the many different typological systems which dominate the researches on psychopaths. One writer on this subject, E. Kahn, even uses sixteen different types, another, Kurt Schneider, ten. A frequently used classification is that of Sir David Henderson into predominantly aggressive, inadequate and creative psychopaths.[51] Kurt Schneider's classification has, with certain modifications, been used in Erwin Frey's well-known study of the 'early recidivist'.[52]

On the subject of 'character types' Edward Glover has made a number of pertinent observations.[53] 'A useful classification', he writes, 'is one which avoids undue elaboration without being so simplified as to include under any one heading types that cry out for differentiation. This second condition is a stumbling block to most "type" classifications.' He compares Jung's typology of extraverts and introverts with the Freudian of oral, anal and genital characters, later subdivided according to whether any of these three types encountered gratification or frustration. The correlation of character groups with classical forms of mental disorder leads him to a division into hysterical, obsessional, depressive, alcoholic, hypochondriacal, paranoid, schizoid and psychopathic types, plus the addition of a number of 'special' mainly descriptive, not psychiatric types such as the miser, the gambler, the misanthrope, the moaner, the hypocrite, the egoist, etc. Of particular interest to the criminologist are the Freudian type of the 'criminal impelled by unconscious guilt' (see below, Chapter 17, II)[54] and also his classification of three 'libidinal types', the erotic, obsessional, and narcissistic, of which he regarded the latter, if exposed to frustration, as particularly liable to criminality, stressing that mixed types were much more frequent than pure ones.[55]

To this sketch of Freud's and Glover's psycho-analytic typology dozens of others could of course be added which have, directly or indirectly, played their part in criminological literature.[56]

On the sociological side typological systems outside the field of criminology, but with some bearing on it, have been presented, for example, by Riesman and Howard Becker. Riesman's distinction of three main types, the 'tradition-directed', the 'inner-directed' and the 'other-directed' types, with their sub-types and his attempt to link these different types of 'social character' to different types of society, social classes and population growth have become famous and widely accepted as characteristic not only of the American society to which he refers.[57] Howard Becker[58] distinguished the unsocialized, the desocialized or demoralized, the semi-socialized, the transitionally socialized, the uncritically socialized and other types, W. I. Thomas the 'Philistine', the 'Bohemian' and the 'creative' types.[59] By and large we have to agree with Kimball Young[60] that sociologists have not yet done as much work in this field as psychologists.

Criminological typologies, apart from the constitutional and psycho-analytical ones referred to before, have usually, and rightly, tried to combine the psychological and the sociological ways of approach. Clinard, following Lindesmith and Dunham,[61] uses a system based on social processes and behavioural differences, with the 'individual' type at one end and the 'career criminal' at the other. For the former type personality traits and role adjustment difficulties are decisive factors, for the latter attitudinal factors. At the one end he places the insane, the extreme sex deviate and most occasional offenders, at the other we find the organized and the professional types, with habitual petty offenders, white collar criminals and 'ordinary' criminal careers in the middle of the continuum. Clinard's distinguishing characteristics are the 'degree of development of criminal social roles and life organizations', identification with crime, the offender's conception of himself as a criminal, his patterns of association with others and his personality traits. Lindesmith and Dunham explain the 'individualized' criminal as one who is in his criminal activities 'not supported by a culture which prescribes them', whereas the 'social' criminal can rely on a group and a culture, a distinction particularly important for 'white collar criminals' (Chapter 21 below).

Seelig[62] has, more perhaps than any other criminologist, worked out a detailed typology and put it to the practical test by applying it to the population of 292 male prisoners received in the year 1940 at the prison of Graz. Excluding from his scheme etiological and prognostic elements as secondary in comparison with the phenomenological, descriptive, approach, he employs criteria relating to the offence, the offender and the environmental situation. Only through regular combinations of these three elements can, he thinks, types be formed. He distinguishes *Verhaltens- und Seins-typen*, i.e. types where the behaviour (*Verhalten*) of the offender is the essential factor and types where his personality (his *Sein*) matters most, admitting that in actual life both are closely related and that very often conclusions have to be drawn from the behaviour of an individual to his personality.[63] Seelig also underlines the logical difference between types and classes: whereas the latter are mutually exclusive, the former are not, and mixed types are in fact very frequent. Among his sample of 292 prisoners he found, however, 91·7 per cent pure and only 6·8 per cent mixed types, whereas 1·4 per cent were atypical cases, which seems a rather surprising result in view of the general observation that in real life mixed types appear to be at least as frequent as pure ones. Seelig's eight types are the following: (1) professional criminals who avoid work at any price; (2) property offenders lacking the power of resistance; (3) aggressive criminals; (4) sexually uncontrolled criminals; (5) offenders who in a crisis find only a criminal solution (*Krisenverbrecher*); (6) 'primitive-reacting' offenders; (7) offenders who follow their conviction; (8) offenders lacking in social discipline. This scheme, which on the surface seems rather too general and not without gaps, is supplemented by Seelig by detailed descriptions of subtypes and illustrative case material.

In a recent study of the files of 200 persons sentenced to preventive detention as dangerous habitual criminals under § 20a of the German Criminal Code types are distinguished according to the offence, heredity and family, criminal and other social antecedents and personality types. This may usefully be compared with a similar recent study of one hundred English preventive detainees.[64] In the field of juvenile delinquency attempts have repeatedly been made by the authors of typologies to relate their types of offenders to various types of childhood experiences. Jenkins,[65] for example, offers the following hypotheses for further research: (*a*) the aggressive delinquent was usually rejected from birth and has never known a normal child-parent relationship; (*b*) the loyal member of a delinquent gang is more likely to have enjoyed a normal relationship with his parents in early life, but later on lost it owing to lack of interest and control on the part of the parents and turned exclusively to his delinquent peer-group; (*c*) the 'con-man' type has grown up in an atmosphere of parental disharmony where he had to play off one parent against the other. Therefore he has taken to manipulating and exploiting other people.

One of the best known and most influential among these studies is John Bowlby's which was first developed in his analysis of forty-four juvenile thieves, where he writes:[66] 'statistics and conclusions regarding the cause of juvenile delinquency will remain unsatisfactory so long as no attempt is made to classify types of delinquents and to study each type separately'. His character types are the 'normal', the depressed, the circular, the hyperthymic, the affectionless and the schizoid. The case material consists of Child Guidance Clinic cases, i.e. a highly selected sample, of juvenile thieves, compared with the same number of children from the same source who did not steal. The classification is based on certain character disorders, mostly regarded as due to early childhood deprivations.

Parental rejection plays an important part in John Rich's typology of stealing which distinguishes marauding offences, comforting offences, secondary and other offences.[67]

Also based on differences in child-parent relationship, is the typology of D. H. Stott.[68] While disclaiming any intention to produce a typology of persons he believes to have found in his group of 102 Approved School boys five different 'types of reaction or types of behaviour', but he acknowledges the existence of mixed types. His dominant types of reaction are: (a) 'avoidance excitement', leading the boy into delinquent escapades as a means of suppressing an anxiety with regard to his parents which is too strong for him to be faced; (b) feelings of spite, retaliation and resentment against the parents which drive the boy to commit spectacular offences in order to annoy his parents and force them to pay more attention to him ('delinquent attention'); (c) testing out the parents' loyalty by resorting to crime; (d) withdrawal reaction as a result of a final inability to establish affectionate relationships with the parents, leading eventually to misconduct of a sly and callous nature, possibly also to near-psychotic outbreaks of violence; (e) inferiority-compensation.

In sharp contrast to Jenkins, Bowlby, Rich and Stott, Whyte's well-known distinction of the corner boy and the college boy types has its roots not in diversities of family relations, but in the boys' attitudes to their gangs and their social aspirations.[69] Frankenstein stresses the 'configurational' approach in his case studies, trying to show that 'behaviour does not result from the quantitative combination of independently measurable factors but only from a specific causal constellation' and how the same factor may have different consequences, according to the specific constellation in which it operates.[70]

Of considerable practical importance are those typologies, constitutional, psychological or sociological, which try to relate their different types to differences in responses to treatment. The Continental pre-war crimino-biological school, as already mentioned above (Chapter 7, VI), took it almost for granted that criminals of the pyknic type were usually only occasional and corrigible ones, whereas those of the leptosome and, in particular, of the athletic type were mostly habituals and incorrigibles.[71] Post-war writers have become much more cautious in this respect. The Gluecks, in their *Physique and Delinquency*, admit that 'it is a far cry from diagnosis to therapy', although they express the hope that some of their findings might help to establish the vulnerability to delinquency of the various physical types even better than the prediction tables in *Unraveling Juvenile Delinquency*.[72] In some of their other works they have tried to demonstrate the different probabilities of response to various forms of treatment for individuals falling under their different prediction scores,[73] but the sum total of the latter, the 'prediction profile', often consisting of very heterogeneous factors, will usually not amount to a type in the sense outlined at the beginning of this section.

A Borstal Typological Survey was carried out by a Medical Officer,

Dr. Ogden, in Camp Hill Borstal Institution on 250 boys with the support of the Prison Commissioners and the active co-operation of the whole staff.[74] Its main object was the prediction of future conduct, making preventive action possible. Nine types were formed on the basis of certain medical and administrative criteria, to which an unclassified group and one consisting of abnormal individuals were added. Some of the types were: the adolescent immature, the emotionally unstable, the submissive, the shiftless, the egocentric, the aggressive, the hysterical swindler, the unethical. The assessments were checked against reconvictions after a four-year follow-up period, and considerable differences were found to exist not only between some of these types but also between short- and long-term prospects, some types which failed badly and early being particularly good long-term prospects under proper after-care.

Another careful exercise in personality typing in relation to Borstal training has been made by A. G. Rose.[75] He distinguishes the following types: the apparently abnormal, subnormal, normal (sub-divided: weak, strong, immature, mature, well-adjusted) and the unapproachable, and recommends a different emphasis for the training of each of these types. Here again, further progress in this direction would require detailed comparisons of the types and the case material of such research workers as Ogden and Rose.

## 3. Types of Offence and Conclusions

For the typological classification of offences we have, of course, in the first place to rely on the guidance of the criminal law. In those countries which possess Criminal Codes much thought has usually been given to this subject. The most commonly accepted classification is that of offences against the state, against the person, against property and against the public, leaving a miscellaneous group of unclassified offences. As universally admitted, this is still far too general and full of gaps and overlaps, and it has to be supplemented by a lengthy catalogue of individual offences such as murder, manslaughter, theft, embezzlement and so on. Even this is often not sufficient, and the legislator, rather mistakenly, finds it advisable to create sub-types such as theft from dwelling-houses, public buildings, etc., or of electricity, cattle, dogs, etc. The long list of offences in *Criminal Statistics England and Wales* shows how far this tendency to form sub-types has gone. Legal typology of this kind, however, is often rather useless for purposes of criminological research, and occasionally attempts have been made by criminologists to replace it by other, sociologically or psychologically orientated, types. One of the best known of these attempts is that by Cressey[76] to substitute for the many varieties of 'embezzlement' found in American legislations a uniform and more meaningful concept of 'criminal violation of financial trust'. It is particularly difficult to find a criminologically more meaningful typology of murder. The legal concepts have usually been framed in order to distinguish the most serious forms of unlawful killings from the less serious ones. Very few of these distinctions, however, have proved to be workable in practice.[77] This applies especially to the long history of 'degrees of murder', including the English Homicide Act of 1957 with its untenable line of distinctions of capital and non-capital murder. That the various categories of capital murder in that Act, most of them selected rather casually as a compromise between the two opposing views, do not represent types as understood in this chapter requires no further explanation. It can safely be said that as long as the death penalty is preserved no sensible line of demarcation will ever be drawn between cases for which the penalty is to be used and others. Criminologically, murder may be divided according to intent or motive into cases of murder committed for the sake or in the course of robbery or other property offences including arson, those committed for the sake or in the course of rape or other sex offences, murder committed out of revenge or jealousy and with political purposes or motives.[78] It might also be classified according to the role played by the victim. The latter aspect has been stressed in particular by Wolfgang, von Hentig, Gibbs[79] and recently also by T. P. Morris and Blom-Cooper.[80]

There is one offence—at least in those very few countries where it is still an offence—which has not been classified according to types by the legislator: attempted suicide. Durkheim, in his famous study,[81] established three types: egoistic, altruistic and anomic suicide. He did so not on the strength of individual case histories, which he apparently did not possess, but by way of largely statistical research into the different causes of suicide and by defining his types on the strength of his views on causation. 'We shall be able', he writes, 'to determine the social types of suicide by classifying them not directly by their preliminarily described characteristics, but by the causes which produce them . . . In a word, instead of being morphological, our classification will from the start be aetiological. Nor is this a sign of inferiority, for the nature of a phenomenon is much more profoundly got at by knowing its cause than by knowing its characteristics only, even the essential ones.' This method of establishing types differs, therefore, from that adopted by many other writers, such as Jenkins who draws conclusions from types to causes, not vice versa. Against Durkheim's method it can be objected that it is usually even more difficult to establish causes than types and possibly also that the same causes may produce different types.

The offence of shoplifting has been classified according to types as follows: shoplifting by professionals, by general delinquents, by offenders acting under unusual emotional strain, to whom the stolen goods have symbolic or practical value out of proportion to the risks taken, and by 'kleptomaniacs' who steal for the sake of stealing.[82]

## Conclusion

From this survey a somewhat chaotic picture of typologies has emerged. Some of them are constitutionally oriented, others psychiatrically, psychologically or sociologically, again others according to offences, and within each of these groups there are many sub-groups and combinations. The Adlerian typology differs from the Freudian; juvenile delinquents are typed according to dominant personality patterns, childhood experiences and relations to parents, to peer-groups, social aspirations and so forth; murderers according to their objects and motives, relations to victims, etc. However confusing this picture may appear we have to realize that the chaos of existing typologies presents considerable progress if contrasted with the state of affairs which would prevail if there were no typologies at all. What is now needed is an attempt to bring order into this chaos by comparing and correlating these manifold typologies with one another and extracting the common denominators, always bearing in mind that each of the main groups of causal factors has to be represented and that the type of offence committed and the predictive aspect should not be unduly neglected. If this can be achieved it will be found that the typological approach is not only a step in the right direction, but essential for the progress of criminological research.

## Note

After the completion of this chapter an important paper was published by Clarence Schrag[83] who presents a typological scheme which he regards as useful for purposes of prediction and the evaluation of treatment programmes. It is based on the concept of a criminal subculture and, more specifically, on the responses to questionnaire interviews given by inmates of penal institutions (apparently in the state of Washington). It tries to construct four sets of 'role alternatives' commonly recognized by the inmates and related to other aspects of life in a penal community. It was found that these four types—the 'pro-social', anti-social, pseudo-social and asocial, or in characteristic American prison slang the 'square John', the 'right guy', the 'con politician' and the 'outlaw'—were related to certain differences in criminal careers, patterns of offences, institutional adjustment, family and community experiences and attitudes to crime and society. The difference, already referred to above, between typologies and classification schemes, is rightly stressed by Schrag.

Two other American writers, Gibbons and Garrity, have also offered some 'tentative typologies of adult property offenders, along with tentative descriptions of possible causative factors', which have been described as 'a promising framework upon which future investigations may build'.[84]

These and some of the other researches mentioned in the present chapter make the somewhat disparaging reference to typology by Radzinowicz in his *In Search of Criminology*[85] appear to be rather ill-advised.

# Chapter 9

## EXPERIMENTAL METHODS[1]

### I. DEFINITION

In a way, the whole of our penal system is one big experiment because we often call an experiment any kind of social action the ultimate effects of which are uncertain. In this sense, the legal provisions concerning the establishment of detention centres, the setting up of other new types of correctional institutions, the replacement of a prison sentence by a probation order or the earlier release of an offender on licence may be called experiments just as, in Popper's words, a grocer who opens a new shop is conducting a social experiment.[2] This, however, is not the meaning attached to the term in the present chapter, where it is throughout used in the narrower sense of a strictly controlled experiment which it has in the natural sciences and in experimental psychology. The criteria of such an experiment are as follows: It requires, first, two or more contrasting situations which are usually created by the experimenter (artificial or created experiment); in exceptional cases, however, they are already in existence without any interference on his part ('natural' experiment).[3] Greenwood[4] uses as an illustration the experiment which tries to discover the cause of goitre in certain communities by arranging the supply of water as a suspected cause in such a way that community A receives its supply from source X and community B from source Y (see Chapter 6, II, above). If this arrangement had been in existence by chance already before the experiment started no interference with the sources of supply would have been required. Secondly, two groups of people who drink the water have to be formed and carefully matched with regard to any variables which might possibly also be responsible for the causation of the disease such as age, sex, health, food, occupation, etc. The experimenter has now to make sure that group A uses only water from source X and group B only water from source Y, which is usually called the introduction of the stimulus. Thirdly, the incidence of goitre in the two groups has to be examined after a certain time has elapsed. In this example, which is an illustration of the experiment in its narrowest form, the water would be called the independent and the effect, the disease, the dependent variable or the criterion.[5] If this first experiment should be inconclusive, similar arrangements would have to be made with regard to other variables such as certain items of food, but 'the fundamental rule of the experimental method is to vary only one condition at a time' (Chapin). A statistical correlation has been discovered between the prevalence of dental caries in children and the fluoride content of their water supply. A controlled alteration in the fluoride content has produced a reduction in caries, and this experiment, while revealing nothing about the causal mechanism behind it, makes control and prevention possible.[6] As stressed by Greenwood and others, controlled experiments in this strictest sense of the word are rare in the social sciences, and many sociologists believe them even to be almost impossible. Moreover, where no serious attempt is made to control the situation and to keep the influence of variables out which are not the subject of the experiment it would be misleading to use this term at all. As will be pointed out below (IV) attempts have been made to fill the resulting gap by inventing certain 'quasi-experimental' techniques.

## II. EXPERIMENTS IN OTHER DISCIPLINES

The criminologist who wishes to carry out experiments in his sphere of work will naturally look around, however cursorily, to see how this method has so far been applied by other branches of science. There is no need here to underline the vital importance of the experimental method in the natural sciences which owe most of their achievements to it, with the exception of astronomy where experimentation in the strictest sense of the word is not possible. Closely allied to this, general psychology, too, is largely dependent on the experiment, although it has recently been said that 'experimental psychology has not wholly justified the earlier confidence placed in it as a department of science . . . [and] the whole conception of experiment in psychology awaits clarification'.[7] Social psychology has been employing this method perhaps more fruitfully than any other branch of the social sciences, and much of its experimental work is of interest to the criminologist, too.[8] In medicine the position is not very different from that in penology as much of its work is experimental in the general sense of 'trial and error', but dissimilar in that the controlled medical experiment has here become much more willingly accepted by public opinion. Here it is possible to carry out the large-scale infection of volunteers to study, though not to find, the cause of the common cold. In 1955 it was reported that the South East Metropolitan Regional Hospital Board had authorized one of its hospitals to divide a group of one thousand children waiting to have their tonsils removed into two equal samples and to carry the operation out on members of the one sample, not however on the others, in order to study the effect of this differential treatment. While this procedure produced one indignant letter to *The Times*, its justification has apparently not been widely questioned.[9] Members of the medical profession will, however, try to restrict dangerous experiments to themselves and to volunteers aware of the risk,[10] and as far as vivisectional experiments are concerned the medical profession is still under heavy fire.

With regard to sociological experiments reference can here be made to the excellent treatment of the subject by Greenwood and Chapin (Note 1).

## III. THE PRESENT POSITION IN CRIMINOLOGY

Criminology, being methodologically so much dependent on the work of those other disciplines which deal with human beings, shares their disadvantages, but has in addition to suffer certain disabilities peculiar to it. It has in common with them the extreme difficulty of producing two closely matched groups and of excluding changes in factors other than the one which is the subject of the experiment itself. Some of these difficulties, it is true, in particular that of matching, are inherent in any control-group research (see above, Chapter 6), but while the latter—unless combined with a follow-up study—is static, experimental research is dynamic with the additional pitfalls created by perpetual changes in the situations to be controlled. We might perhaps illustrate all this by taking the case of an experiment designed to study the effect of housing conditions on juvenile delinquency: A group of, say, two hundred families living in overcrowded conditions in a bad slum district is taken and divided into two groups, matched for economic conditions, numbers, sex and age of children, health, intelligence and other possibly relevant factors. One of them, the control group, is left in their slum dwellings, the other, the experimental group, chosen at random, is transferred by the housing authority to a new estate. Clearly, through this process of rehousing not only the independent variable, housing, the causal quality of which we wish to examine, but practically the whole conduct of life of these hundred experimental families will be affected: they will have to find new friends and enemies, new outlets for their leisure activities, new schools and clubs, possibly even new jobs; their fares may go up, furniture may be bought, which may upset their budgets, and so on. To control all these factors by correspondingly altering the circumstances of the families in the other group will be impossible. How, then, can we attribute any subsequent changes in the delinquency rates to the changed housing position? As the latter may have upset many other factors, for example the employment position, it might well be these other changes which have produced the changed rate of delinquency. It is certainly true that, as Popper points out,[11] perfect control is very difficult to achieve in the natural sciences, too, but it is even more so in the social sciences, including criminology. We agree with him, however, in our disapproval of the 'historicist' assertion that the experimental method is totally inapplicable to problems of society, although it is very difficult for the social scientist to vary his experimental conditions at will[12] or to secure strictly comparable control groups. Even natural scientists, for example the animal pathologist W. I. B. Beveridge,[13] complain that in certain fields experiments are often vitiated by compromise arrangements and therefore prove nothing. Beveridge also makes the point, which is pertinent to criminological experimentation too, that once 'an alleged remedy is released for use in human medicine, it is almost impossible subsequently to organise an experiment with untreated controls, and so the alleged remedy becomes adopted as a general practice without anyone knowing if it is really of any use at all'.[14] In criminological terms, this means that once a certain method of treating offenders, for example Borstal or Detention Centres or whatever else it may be, has become generally accepted in the mind of the public as the most promising way of dealing with that particular category it is very difficult to carry out real experiments with two matched groups. The idea of justice, meaning above anything else equal treatment of equal cases, clashes directly with the idea of experimentation which requires differential treatment of equal cases.[15] As an alternative, it requires equal treatment of unequal cases, and we shall see that this, too, has been tried experimentally. It is only if the idea of justice should in future become more treatment-orientated than equality-orientated—a process which cannot be carried beyond narrow limits—that it will be more amenable to experimentation. At present we can hardly expect the criminal courts to take an active part in penological experiments by deliberately treating equal cases as unequal or unequal cases as equal, though juvenile courts, whose main object is not justice but welfare (Children and Young Persons Act, 1933, s. 44), may be in a less fettered position. Not surprisingly, therefore, penological experiments have been undertaken so far not by the courts but by the administration and, in particular, by private agencies in charge of institutions for delinquent children. There is, however, a fairly large reservoir of cases where the courts unintentionally treat essentially equal cases in a different way or vice versa (see below, IV).

R. A. Fisher[16] and, following him, Beveridge have pointed out that we should not unnecessarily restrict the scope of our experimentation to changes in one single variable but could well test several of them at the same time. There are, however, practical limits to this procedure in the social sciences. Referring to our example of the rehousing experiment we might possibly include not only the housing factor but also the employment factor deliberately in our experiment, but the resulting picture is likely to be even more confusing. On the other hand, we might try to vary the employment conditions in the control group as well so as to correspond to the changes produced in the experimental group by rehousing and thereby keep the employment factor constant, but in actual life this would probably go beyond the limits of socially permissible and practicable experimentation.

In his study of the adolescent criminal, Sir Norwood East[17] quotes from a lecture by the first Lord Moynihan on 'The Advance of Medicine' the following sentences: 'We train the power of observation in our students; we neglect to teach the value of reason and relevant experiment. We teach the Hippocratic method; we neglect the Galenic. . . .' Sir Norwood adds: 'This investigation of the adolescent offender proceeded inevitably according to the Hippocratic method, for we were unable to control or experiment with the various facts that were collected.' He pleaded, however, as it were, mitigating circumstances by stressing that the Galenic method might well be served by an investigation on Hippocratic lines.

How far has the Galenic method hitherto been followed in criminological research? The list of the relevant projects is very short, and their achievements are extremely modest. It has to be headed by two large-scale projects, both of them American, the Cambridge-Somerville Youth Study[18] and the Highfields Experiment.[19] A detailed critical account of the former has previously been given by the present writer, to which reference can here be made.[20]

The project was initiated and financed by Dr. Richard Clarke Cabot, Professor of Social Ethics and Clinical Medicine at Harvard University, who wished to test the hypothesis that juvenile delinquency could be prevented by giving young boys heading for it the special services of a social worker, a counsellor and friend. 'A boy', he thought, 'should be early supplied with an ideal', for 'what is it that keeps any of us straight unless it is the contagion of the highest personalities we have known?' To carry out his experiment, which was expected to go on for ten years, a number of boys aged between six and twelve from two Massachusetts towns, Cambridge and Somerville, were to be selected by a committee of experts, one half of them to serve on the treatment group (T), the other as the matched control group (C). Of the 2,000 boys originally referred to the committee mostly by their school teachers, 782 were eventually selected; 46 per cent of them were thought to be 'pre-delinquent', 43 per cent 'normal' and 11 per cent were rated as 'zero'. The inclusion of not 'pre-delinquent' boys was regarded as advisable for reasons of public policy to avoid the project being labelled as only concerned with 'bad' boys. Of these 782, only 650 were retained, 325 for each group, including equal proportions of pre-delinquents, normals and zeros, and the matching was done by two psychologists for distribution into two equal groups. The details of the very complicated process of matching are fully described in the Powers–Witmer study, and the final allocation of the boys to the T and C groups was done by flipping coins. The T-boys were then assigned to their counsellors, each of whom was to have about 35 cases, pre-delinquents, normals and zeros, whereas the C-boys were left to their own and the ordinary community resources. The practical work began a few years before World War II and was seriously disrupted by it as many of the counsellors and older boys enlisted. The original plan to retain the close personal relationship between the worker and his boys throughout the experimental period had to be abandoned, and many other changes had to take place. A few hundred boys had to be prematurely 'retired', and when the practical side of the project was terminated in 1945 only 75 boys were left in it. Then the second major stage, that of evaluation, began, and it is greatly to the credit of the scheme that this was done by an outsider, Dr. Helen Witmer, on objective and scientifically sound lines. We are here concerned not with her findings as to the practical value of the help given to the T-boys—there was in fact very little difference between the two groups in the success rates with regard to delinquent behaviour. It is rather our object in this chapter to evaluate the experiment as a case study of the use of the experimental method in criminology, and here it has largely failed. For various reasons it cannot be regarded as a true experimental test of Dr. Cabot's hypothesis. This was in part due to the nature of the hypothesis itself, which was far too ambitious and vague to be amenable to experimental testing. According to the principles of this technique as outlined above, all other variables except the provision of counsellors should have been rigidly controlled to make sure that any subsequent developments in the behaviour of the T-boys were in fact due to no other influences but the work of the counsellors. No such control was attempted, nor was it possible in the circumstances. Moreover, even as far as the experimental stimulus, the help provided by the counsellors, was concerned, it was of a very different kind according to the personality of the individual counsellor and the changing circumstances of the time. The war, in particular, imposed so many alterations in the original design that the scheme as it emerged towards the end of the experimental period had but little in common with the project as planned by Dr. Cabot.

The Highfields Project has as its object to examine whether the long-term institutional treatment of adolescent offenders may in certain cases safely be replaced by probation coupled with short-term institutionalization with 'guided group interaction'.

The work at Highfields, a small Home in the State of New Jersey, begun in 1950, has taken the form of a comparison between the short-term treatment given there for up to four months and the long-term detention at the

State Reformatory at Annandale where the boys are kept for up to eighteen months, with an average stay of one year. This does not mean that the theoretical object of comparing the success rates of these two institutions was the main purpose behind the Highfields Study; as in the case of the Cambridge-Somerville Project it was in the first place established to achieve certain practical ends in helping young people. At the same time, however, it was a controlled penological experiment designed to test the hypothesis that adjustment can be achieved better and more cheaply by short- than by long-term methods of detention.

To obtain two matched groups for purposes of comparison, one group consisting of boys sent to Highfields and another of boys of the same type sent to Annandale, must have presented exceptional difficulties, greater even than those encountered in the Cambridge-Somerville Study. While the latter was an entirely private enterprise and no principles of public policy were involved in deciding which of the boys should receive the benefits of counselling and which of them should not, in the Highfields experiment it was for the courts to choose between the two institutions concerned. To some extent, the co-operation of the judges seems to have been secured, but even so the two groups were hardly comparable. Highfields took boys with no prior institutional experience, whereas Annandale received those with and without it. There is no evidence in the reports of Highfields to show that the judges tried to send the same type of boy to both institutions; on the contrary, it is admitted that committals were carried out on different lines. To counter this, it was claimed that only those Annandale boys were included in the study who would have been sent to Highfields by the courts if it had already been in existence at the time of their court appearance. This, however, meant that the Annandale group came from the 1946-50 vintages, whereas the Highfields boys were from the years 1950-4, a difference which the evaluators regarded as unimportant.[21] However: 'A common fallacy', writes Beveridge, 'is to compare groups separated by time ... Evidence obtained in this way is never conclusive, though it may be usefully suggestive.'[22] There were other differences, too, not the least important among them when conduct after discharge was to be tested, arising from the fact that the Highfields boys were on probation, the Annandale boys however on parole, i.e. subjected to a different kind of supervision and control. Actually, the existence of considerable differences between the two groups has been admitted in the evaluation study.[23] The latter was done with great care and had the advantage over the Cambridge-Somerville Study that it had been planned and arranged right from the beginning and that a scientific Advising Committee, largely composed of outsiders, was established at an early stage.

To sum up, the Highfields experiment, though of great practical value, cannot be said so far to have produced convincing evidence of the superiority of its work over that of the traditional type of long-term institution.

As another example of controlled penological experimentation the California Intensive Parole Supervision Project may be briefly quoted,[24] designed to test whether lengthy periods on parole can be replaced by shorter, but more intensive, supervision.

Whereas in the examples so far given differential treatment is applied to 'equal' cases, now an experiment may be quoted where, in addition to this, identical treatment was applied to different types of cases.

In this experiment,[25] conducted under the auspices of the Social Research Laboratory in the Department of Sociology of the City College of New York, a group of 'problem' and one of normal children from the same schools were mingled in a natural way in recreational activities to see whether this form of non-segregative, but therapeutic treatment would have the same effect on members of the two categories. The problem children included chronic truants and delinquents who had committed arson and theft. There were 155 children in each category, but special treatment was given only to 120 of them. Experimental and control cases were individually matched, problem against problem, non-problem against non-problem, for sex, race, age, general intelligence, educational achievement and mechanical aptitude. To prevent publicity and stigma, the groups were not labelled as therapeutic, and the identity of the problem children was known only to the director of the experiment and his assistant, not however to the group work leaders, who in most cases were unsuccessful in identifying the members of the groups. The result was that 48 per cent of the experimental cases and 24 per cent of the control groups showed improvement in their behaviour. Another result was that the effect of treatment appeared to replace delinquency by causing emotional instability.

In another experiment, 'Reactions of Delinquent and Other Groups to Experimentally Induced Frustration' were tested by Brian Kay.[26] He applied to a group of delinquent and a matched one of reputedly non-delinquent children certain frustration tests and found that members of the control group showed a higher degree of frustration tolerance than the delinquents.

## IV. QUASI-EXPERIMENTS

In view of the great obstacles standing in the way of genuine experimentation in the social sciences there has been a growing inclination on the part of statisticians, sociologists and others to pretend that social experiments can be carried out just as well without any active manipulation and interference on the part of the experimenter. The so-called *ex post facto* experiment can, it is believed, fully take the place of the real, the so-called projected, experiment. The idea behind the former is that just as the natural scientist may find that nature has created for him contrasting conditions which, without any manipulation on his part, enable him to carry out controlled comparisons of the two conditions, so may society occasionally perform the same service for the social scientists. As pointed out above (s. I), in the goitre experiment it might have happened that without the experimenter's manipulation community A already received its water-supply from source X and community B from source Y. Stuart Chapin has referred to the isolated life of the Eskimos as a natural experiment where many factors existing in other communities are absent. In the provinces of law and penology an illustration may be offered by two neighbouring states of the U.S.A., having similar social and economic conditions, but one of them retaining capital punishment which the other has abolished.[27] This appears to be a suitable setting for a study of the effect of capital punishment (see also below, s. v), and may be illuminating, but would it be an experiment in the narrower sense? Another illustration may be taken from the Borstal Prediction Study where the success rates of open and closed Borstal Institutions had to be compared. A real experiment would require that the experimenter would be given authority to select boys with the same characteristics randomly for the two types of institutions. This could not be done at the time, but the conditions were favourable to the carrying out of a 'natural' experiment because to some small extent at least the same types of boy were actually sent to open and closed institutions.[28] It was possible, therefore, without any manipulation on the part of the research workers to examine whether the same type of boy was more successful in an open than in a closed institution. In the case of the housing experiment (see above, s. III) the housing authority might already have done what the experimenter had in mind, i.e. divided the group of slum-dwellers randomly into two matched sub-groups and re-housed the one of them, leaving to the experimenter only the task of trying to exclude disturbing outside influences and to assess the possible delinquency-preventing effect of the rehousing scheme. The arguments for and against such *ex post facto* experiments have been admirably discussed by Ernest Greenwood,[29] and there is hardly anything of importance to be added to his views. The most serious weakness of the *ex post facto* experiment lies in the very fact that the experimenter has no power to supervise and control the allocation of cases to the two groups. In the housing experiment it might well have happened that the housing authority had left those families whom they regarded as hopeless failures in their old slum dwellings and rehoused only the more promising cases. To some slight extent, what Greenwood calls self-selection[30] of cases may occur in real experiments, too, but as he points out it is more likely to occur in *ex post facto* experiments. Another weakness of the latter is that the experimenter is here entirely dependent upon the existence of good records, whereas in real experiments he can delay the beginning until his requirements are met.[31] For these and other reasons the harshness of the criticisms sometimes levelled at *ex post facto* experiments[32] is understandable, but it has to be borne in mind that the use of such experiments may be well justified if only we are aware of their shortcomings; it might be better, however, to avoid using the word 'experiment' in such cases altogether.

## V. EXPERIMENTS IN JURISPRUDENCE

Law and legal theory being very closely related to criminology some consideration should be given to recent literature on 'experimental jurisprudence'. As already indicated at the beginning of this chapter, in a way every new law is an experiment as its impact on the problem which it is supposed to tackle is more often than not mere guesswork. Even if its preparation, statistical and otherwise, should be more thorough than is usually the case,[33] the effect of a specific piece of legislation is, as a rule, far from predictable. Setting aside this popular usage of the concept of legal experiment the question arises whether some of the experimental techniques applied in the natural and social sciences have, perhaps with some modifications, their place in the theory and practice of legislation, too. The matter has recently been discussed by legal writers such as Wolfgang Friedmann,[34] Thomas A. Cowan,[35] and in particular by Frederick Beutel.[36] The latter has tried to show, with a wealth of material, that legislation should proceed on similar lines as experimental natural sciences and that in fact controlled legal experiments are possible. His argument suffers to some extent from a tendency to blur the lines between the 'natural' and *ex post facto* experiment, on the one hand, and the real experiment, on the other, and some of his illustrations have very little to do with the idea of experimentation, unless we regard the terms 'experimental' and 'scientific' as synonymous. He has provided no single example of legislation applied solely to one experimental group but withheld to a matched control group.

His major piece of research, described in great detail, concerns the offence of issuing bad cheques. He compares the state of affairs in his own state, Nebraska, with that of parts of the neighbouring state of Colorado where, he states, the physical and economic conditions are identical with those in Nebraska whereas the legislation differs in that the offence is technically a felony in Nebraska, with very heavy penalties, whereas it is only a misdemeanour in Colorado, with correspondingly milder penalties. The damage done to society, i.e. losses to business and costs of penal administration, was, according to Beutel, smaller in Colorado than in Nebraska, from which he concludes that the milder form of penalties was more effective than the harsher. Such comparisons between different types of legislation existing in similar surroundings, which are frequent in particular with regard to capital punishment laws,[37] come nearest to the idea of 'natural experiment'.

This type of research is sound provided the relevant conditions in the two legislations to be compared are really similar. Such similarity is more likely to be obtained if the legislator would be willing to arrange a real experiment by making statutes applicable only to certain districts, leaving other districts with identical conditions untouched, which is not often likely to happen because it may be against our ideas of justice=equality. It does occasionally happen that for reasons of economy the legislator or the administrator rightly decides to limit the application of certain measures to a few areas before extending them to the whole country. Normally, of course, the areas selected will be those where the need for such new measures is regarded as greatest, which again would make it more difficult to find suitably matched control areas. Possibilities for 'natural' experiments may arise where the administration provides certain types of institutions, such as detention and attendance centres or remand centres, only for part of the country, but here comparisons of results may be difficult because these centres may be available to offenders from other parts of the country as well.

# Chapter 10

## ACTION (OR OPERATIONAL) RESEARCH AND SOCIOLOGICAL METHODS

### I. ACTION (OR OPERATIONAL) RESEARCH[1]

### 1. *Definition*

The terms action research and operational research are sometimes used as synonyms, and for our present purposes their meaning is in fact essentially the same, although the word 'operational' is sometimes used in a wider sense.[2] Sorokin calls it 'the experimental method *par excellence*', but defines it also as 'the substitution of collected opinions for scientific study of the facts', which would give it a meaning entirely different from that of action research.[3] Ferris F. Laune's technique of using the opinion of fellow-prisoners to predict the parolability of inmates might be an example of operational research in Sorokin's sense.[4] The latter term is, however, more often employed by natural scientists, technologists and mathematicians, whereas social scientists are more inclined to refer to action research. It means, first of all, the closest possible connection between theoretical research and practical action; it means research which is not, as other research, interested primarily in the promotion of knowledge but rather in the improvement of social conditions.[5] It is, however, mainly the emphasis that differs from that in other research (see above, Chapter 3). There is no need here for a formal hypothesis to be tested; control groups are usually dispensed with, and the research is not carried out in isolation, but in the closest collaboration with practical people concerned with practical problems. Action research would not simply try to examine, for example, the role of subnormal intelligence in juvenile delinquency by tests and statistical analysis but might open a club for subnormal youngsters in order to help them in their difficulties and at the same time study their delinquent behaviour, relate it to their subnormality and evaluate the work of the club.

Action research and experimental research (in the stricter sense of the word) have in common the fact that they interfere with the natural

185

course of events, but the former is usually uncontrolled and altogether much less rigid than the latter. In the words of Morse and Kimball it is often observational rather than experimental. The two methods overlap to a considerable extent. Experimental research may involve close co-operation with the practical worker, but may also be carried out in isolation. Action research, on the other hand, may or may not be controlled and experimental.[6] Arnold M. Rose regards evaluation and incorporation into action as the two basic principles of action research, but the former is also needed for projects which are not action research. Some diversity of opinion exists with regard to the exact relationship between action and research: should the latter be itself involved in the action or should the research programme rather be 'built into the action project', or, in other words, should research and action be identical or should the latter have some independent status of its own? Spencer prefers the latter alternative. The answer may depend on the nature and scope of the action programme; if it is intended to go on after the research has come to an end it will have to be given an independent status.

Operational research had its origin in the needs of government departments, especially in time of war, and it is this aspect of the matter which is particularly stressed by natural scientists and technologists.[7] It can be equally useful, however, to communities and private agencies.

Projects applying the technique of participant observation (see also below, s. 2) cannot be action research because the participant observer should not intentionally interfere with the lives of the people whom he observes. Whyte, in his well-known study of Cornerville,[8] calls his own occasional and rather ill-fated attempt to do this 'a violation of the cardinal rule of participant observation', and he is right. One cannot have it both ways, being at the same time active and passive, and even if different members of the research team should be allocated to these opposing functions conflict is likely to ensue which may frustrate the object of the research.

## 2. *The Use of Action Research Methods in Criminology*

Opportunities for the application of such methods in criminology offer themselves mainly in the field of prevention. As far as treatment is concerned its direction lies to some extent in the hands of courts where there is only limited or no scope for action research techniques. Penal administrators, however, may occasionally be inclined to offer that close co-operation with research workers which is essential for action research, and this in particular in after-care work and in institutional or other activities with young delinquents. In these fields

186

the action research approach may promise good results, especially as the line of demarcation between preventive and treatment schemes is here difficult to draw.

To give some illustrations, several of the preventive projects in the U.S.A. described in *Preventing Crime*, edited by the Gluecks,[9] and later in *The Problem of Delinquency*[10] and in *The Annals*[11] seem to have been combined with action research of some kind, although the latter aspect was probably far less conspicuous than the practical work. Without a more intimate knowledge of the way in which action and research were combined in each individual project it is impossible to decide whether it can be justly labelled action research. The best-known of American preventive programmes carried out with an eye on research are Clifford Shaw's Chicago Area Project and the Cambridge-Somerville Study, which has already been referred to in Chapter 9. While the Cambridge-Somerville Study was undoubtedly experimental, its status as a piece of action research is also clear. The members of the experimental group were supplied with the services of counsellors who were able, on a small scale, to dispense various social services, although they were not in a position to initiate larger community projects.[12] The group worked together with the other social services in the communities concerned, but its collaboration with the lay members of these communities seemed to have been limited to the parents of the boys.[13]

Community participation on the largest scale, so far, has been the key-note of the Chicago Area Project, initiated in the early nineteen-thirties, with its slogan 'the local neighbourhood can be organized to deal effectively with its own problems'.[14] In this chapter, we are concerned not with the substance of the Project or its results, but only with its methodology as an outstanding case of action research. It was research in that right from its inception it was closely related to a number of investigations, partly of an ecological character on the 'epidemiology' of delinquency areas[15] in large cities and partly of a socio-psychological character such as the individual case studies referred to above (Chapter 8, I, and Note 18), both of which supplied the ideas and the scientific knowledge from which the practical organization of the Project derived its shape and impetus.[16] And it was action in that it tried to put into practice the conviction that preventive work in juvenile delinquency areas has to work through the medium of suitable local people, who were given a specific active role to play in the programme. Under the supervision of the sociologists of the Illinois Institute for Juvenile Research as one of the sponsoring agencies, indigenous residents were employed to assist in the organization of the civic committees established in the various districts of Chicago in the course of two decades; qualified residents were appointed as staff members and 'the autonomy of the neighbourhood group was scrupulously respected'.[17] Reckless quotes the following statement which is a good summing up of this aspect of the Project: 'The primary and distinctive emphasis of the Project is upon the development of the fullest possible neighbourhood participation through active leadership of responsible residents . . . by providing them with facilities and professional guidance in planning *their own* program for the welfare of *their own* children.'[18]

As Kobrin points out, controlled experiments are hardly possible in projects such as the Chicago Area Project because identical areas for control purposes cannot be found and, if they would exist, it would be regarded as unfair to deny them the 'putative benefits' of the Project. Actually the latter difficulty may not always be present as such projects have an entirely unofficial character, which means that considerations of justice=equality do not arise in their full strength, and as the benefits of the Project may not always be recognized as such by the recipients.

In Britain action research on criminological subjects has been rare and small-scale beginnings which might have led to research of this kind have occasionally been abandoned because the funds and time at the disposal of the committee were inadequate.[19] The following post-war projects deserve to be mentioned.

(a) *The London Barge Boys' Club*.[20] It owed its origin to the widespread feeling among London social workers and social scientists that there were large numbers of delinquent or pre-delinquent boys who were not attached to any of the existing clubs or similar youth organization because none of the latter were capable of catering for the specific needs of these boys. They were therefore commonly labelled 'unclubbables', although the fault did not seem to be altogether on their side. A group, consisting of social workers and social scientists, was formed in 1947 to study the problem and after extensive preliminary discussions and case studies an organization was set up which bought and equipped a Thames sailing barge, *Normanhurst*, to be used as the headquarters of a new type of boys' club. It was intended exclusively for 'unclubbable' boys, defined as 'boys who should be in clubs, but are not; should be because otherwise they will be delinquent or unhappy', and no boy was admitted who could have become a member of one of the other clubs in the Wapping district of East London. A warden with quite exceptional qualifications for this kind of job was appointed. Among the first to join was a complete gang, and soon the practical work coupled with research into the activities of this small group could begin with a membership of twenty boys. Its object was, first, to help the boys and, secondly, in doing so to test the hypothesis that most of the so-called 'unclubbables' could actually become socially better adjusted if provided with an organization which would cater for their specific needs. For the details, reference has to be made to the description given by M. L.

Turner, the warden or 'worker' as he preferred to call himself. His book provides a detailed study of the history of this small group. In 1950 it became apparent to him that the experiment was succeeding and, as he had intended 'only to test the theories',[21] he left. Soon after his departure the older members joined a senior mixed club in the neighbourhood, thereby proving the correctness of the original hypothesis.

(b) *The Liverpool Dolphin Club*. This club for boys several years younger than the Barge boys (the minimum age on admission was eight), whose history over the first four years has been described in considerable detail by John B. Mays,[22] was founded in 1953 as 'a research project concerned with discovering new ways of treating juveniles whose delinquency could for the most part be attributed to environmental and social causes, or whose personal problems had not reached an intransigent phase for which the only hope of remedy is some type of institutional treatment or intensive psychotherapy'.[23] The characteristic feature of this club was a combination of individual case work with group work. While the experiment was to some extent inspired by the Cambridge-Somerville Study and while its type of case work was not fundamentally different from that provided by the latter, it differed from it by emphasizing the group work aspect which had been neglected in the American experiment. The primary purpose of the club was 'to see what could be done . . . to immunize children against delinquent infection',[24] which is, characteristically, a medical formula similar to the underlying idea of the Cambridge-Somerville Study. After the first four years a searching evaluation was undertaken, apparently not, however, as in the case of the American model, by an outsider. No control group was used, and the work, valuable as it was, makes no claim, therefore, to constitute a controlled experiment.

(c) *The Bristol Social Project*.[25] This is the most comprehensive and far-reaching piece of action research in the field of criminal sociology so far undertaken in this country. It has been fully described by its director, John C. Spencer, and his associates. Its scope was not limited to one particular club or other social groups; nor was it confined to delinquency problems, although the latter played an important part in it. Its breadth of design is best explained by reference to the proposals formulated by a 'committee of Bristol's leading citizens' as follows:[26] 'to investigate and take part in the life of a developing community in Bristol in an attempt to establish practical means of tackling those stresses and strains which arise in such a community in the form of delinquency and other disturbances. The main emphasis of the Project will be on encouraging local initiative and in getting local residents to take a greater degree of responsibility for their community life.'

Through its attempt to tackle the life of a whole community and to strengthen the sense of responsibility and self-reliance of its residents the Bristol Study has become the English counterpart of Clifford Shaw's Chicago Area Project. Three working-class areas of Bristol were selected for the research, two of them housing estates on the periphery of the city and one an old area in the centre. One had a population of 12,000, the other of 4,000 and the third of 11,000. Two of them possessed already local councils with and through whom the research team could do their work, concentrating mainly on one of the three areas which had a more than average share of 'stresses and strains'. The work took partly the form of local surveys of the existing community organizations and of certain symptoms of social disorganization; partly it consisted in providing new physical amenities such as a playground for children and a meeting place for small groups, and partly in work with such groups. In this last mentioned direction, groups were formed for toddlers, adolescents and mothers. Among the adolescent groups was an exceptionally difficult one consisting of twenty-six boys and girls, called 'Calypsos', most of them anti-social, destructive and disturbed. The most important features of the Project proved to be its work with the mothers (family research) and with the 'Calypsos', who proved to be the Project's biggest challenge and also the one with the greatest bearing on delinquency problems. There were in addition groups for teachers and social workers.

The Project was designed for a period of five years. Several important methodological conclusions emerged from it, for example:

(*aa*) Action research operating in specific local areas of a big city must be integrated to the whole pattern of civic policy prevailing in the centre of the city's local government;

(*bb*) As a starting point for action research the delinquency problem is of doubtful value because of the conflicting emotional attitudes and the stigma to which it gives rise;[27]

(*cc*) The scale of action projects should be small and its work intensive rather than extensive;

(*dd*) The local residents concerned should be sincerely anxious to participate and free to withdraw at any stage;

(*ee*) Action research, having no professional code as yet, has to evolve rules of its own, some of which closely approximate those regulating the relationship between doctor and patient.

Only a few of the substantive findings of the report can here be mentioned. It is stressed that no stereotyped picture of a uniform 'subcultural' area had emerged, and there seemed to be rather a variety of standards existing side by side within the same locality. In its attempt to explain the high rate of juvenile and adolescent delinquency in some new housing estates the Report states that the latter had suffered the worst of both worlds, lacking the amenities of suburbia without the compensating advantages of a really urban environment. With regard to the alternatives open to official housing policy, one of dispersal of difficult tenants is not regarded as practicable in view of the strong tendency of low status families to come to live together in close proximity. The fact of concentration of such families in one area has to be accepted, and to counter the resulting undesirable features such areas should be given priority in the provision of health and welfare services.

## II. SOCIOLOGICAL METHODS

### 1. *General Considerations*

It might be doubtful whether we are really justified in speaking of a separate sociological method in criminological research, bearing in mind that sociology itself does not claim to have evolved a method of its own. A small, though valuable, literature on sociological methods does exist, but as pointed out in one of the best existing surveys of the subject, methodology is usually not 'bound up with sociological problems *per se* . . . Most of its problems are in common to a number of disciplines . . .'[28] Sociological criminology, as biological or psychological criminology, has to make use of the generally available methods such as statistical, typological, case study, predictive, experimental or operational methods, and its distinguishing features can be seen only in its specific objects of study and have to be closely related to them. Even some of the techniques which seem predominantly to belong to the sociological sphere, such as general surveys, have their place in psychiatric research, too, and on the other hand personal interview techniques, though in a form somewhat different from those used by the psychiatrist, are also needed in sociological studies. There is, however, a certain process of interaction between problem and method, and the one influences the other (see above, Chapter 4, s. 1). It is not entirely beside the point, therefore, briefly to consider the main problems of sociological criminology as they affect the methods of research.

These problems are roughly threefold, concerned, first, with social *institutions* such as social class, the family, property, church and State; secondly, with the *interrelation* between *individuals* as such and as members of social *groups* as formed by whole communities, youth organizations, schools, prisons and many more; thirdly, with geographical *areas*. Obviously, there is here a great deal of overlapping, the family, for example, constituting an institution as well as a group, or the community constituting a group as well as a geographical area, and social class being an institution as well as a 'quasi-group' (Chapters 20 and 24 below).

(*a*) Research on the criminological significance of specific institutions has been largely limited to the role of the various kinds of property where the differences between the position of the large and the small property owner have been studied.[29] The technique adopted in this field has usually been that of the interview by outsiders, in exceptional cases such as that of Dr. N. Muller of Amsterdam, examination by a judge professionally concerned with the matter. As there exist competent and detailed descriptions of interview techniques in the social sciences,[30] there is no need here for their description; they are, moreover, better developed in psychology and psychiatry than in sociological research, and the objects of interviewing are somewhat different according to the professional status of the interviewer.[31] Naturally, interviewing techniques will also show considerable differences according to the specific characteristics of the interviewee, and the same applies to questionnaire techniques. Clemmer[32] rightly stresses the incongruity of applying to a primitive prison population the refined distinctions of a psychological questionnaire on moral values or social attitudes.

In crimino-sociological research into property violations the emphasis has usually been on the interviewee's attitudes towards different types of property and his motives for its violation. Cressey, for example, in his study of embezzlers[33] fashioned his interviews in accordance with his hypothesis about the typical characteristics of the violation of financial trust. As this is an offence almost invariably committed by individuals acting in isolation, the research and interview can be confined to the study of individuals as such, whereas in certain types of stealing the individual offender may be greatly influenced by his group, and the research worker would have to pay attention to group attitudes. Interviews limited to individual offenders would therefore hardly be enough to secure a full understanding of the attitudes, values and motives behind the offence.

G. W. Lynch[34] studied the extent of dishonesty in London industries, individual and group reactions to the risks involved in stealing by employees, the psychological effects of depersonalized ownership, the psychological effects of bulk production on concepts of values, etc. He endeavoured to obtain a sample of employees, whose identity was to remain unknown to him apart from the fact that it had to be representative of the employees in that area. Interviewing men and women who appeared to be representative of the sample required and whom he stopped in the streets, he formulated his questions so as to be acceptable to them, for example he asked not whether the interviewee personally used to take from his place of work goods which did not belong to him, but whether he thought that the 'average person' would take them, how often, in what quantities, which risks he would be willing to run, etc. Moreover, words which were likely to give offence, such as 'stealing' had to be replaced by 'taking goods', 'winning', 'fiddling', etc. The answers indicated personal actions and attitudes or those observed by friends and workmates or were of an entirely general nature.

Criminological research into problems of class has, as will be shown below in Chapters 19 ff., been either statistical (for example Preben Wolf in Denmark) or it has taken the form of investigations into the effect on criminal behaviour of specific patterns of living such as 'deferred gratification' (Chapter 20), or of typological studies (Chapters 20 and 22).

(b) The emphasis on techniques trying to integrate the individual into his group is even more strongly expressed in research of the second category, i.e. on the interrelations between individuals and on the relations between individuals and groups. Individual interviewing will often be necessary, but observation, whether or not in the role of a participant observer, or in some cases action research will be equally important. On observational techniques, too, a considerable literature is available,[35] and only a few brief remarks will be required to show how it has been used by criminologists. Generally speaking, the techniques of (participant or simple) observation have to be used in cases where action research is not feasible, because the research workers are not permitted or have not got the resources needed to take an active and constructive part in solving the problems under examination.

Observational techniques, including the participant form, show many variations. The observer may be concealed or he may be known to his object, but his role as an observer may be disguised. Ackoff seems to regard 'disguised' observation as identical with 'participant', but there is no reason for such usage.[36] It is more natural to call participant observer the person who takes an active part in the life of the group which he is observing. This differs from action research in that the participant observer has scrupulously to refrain from any attempt to influence and to change what he observes. In practice, the dividing line may often be difficult to draw, but it has to be done.[37] One of the most interesting examples of participant observation in penological research is that of the prison reformer Thomas Mott Osborne. Anxious to introduce radical changes in American prison administration in the early years of the present century, he entered Auburn prison for a short period in the disguise of a convict, Tom Brown, in order to study the life of the inmates. His identity was known only to the Warden. After leaving the prison, he described his impressions in his famous book *Within Prison Walls*[38] and began his campaign for prison reform, becoming Warden of Auburn and founding his Mutual Welfare League. This shows that Osborne was somehow aware of the need for keeping action separate from participant observation.

Research on the life of a prison community has been more frequently done by means of simple observation plus interviewing and, above all, informal contacts, for example Sykes' work in the Trenton Penitentiary, New Jersey, or that of T. P. and Pauline Morris in Pentonville Prison.[39] In the latter case, some attempts were occasionally made by a member of the team, a psychiatric social worker, to assist individual prisoners to cope with their personal problems, and in the early stages of the research the principal research worker participated actively in the daily work of the inmates of Maidstone Prison, where a preliminary pilot study was made. This did not, however, alter the essential nature of this research. As these authors write (p. 7), 'It must be emphasized that this study has in no way been an example of "action research", that is to say the research workers did not involve themselves deliberately in activities which are an integral part of the prison's life for the purpose of initiating change. Although the aim throughout has been to observe, inevitably there have been situations of involvement . . .'

Interesting attempts have been made in the United States to let prisoners participate in specific research projects, for example by Donald P. Wilson in his much discussed book *My Six Convicts*[40] and by J. Douglas Grant[41] at Camp Elliot in California. The latter stresses that prisoners can make a useful contribution to society by being given some share in research as subjects, participating observers or clerical workers and he also thinks that prison staffs can play a useful role in it. The example of Nathan Leopold is even better known.[42] On the other hand, John James (Note 44 below) has drawn attention to the dangers which might arise from the use of inmate participant observers.

John C. Spencer's and Norval Morris' researches[43] in various English penal institutions were not intended as general surveys of the institutions concerned but as examinations of a specific criminological problem, i.e. military service as cause of crime and the forms and causes of certain types of recidivism respectively, which could best be done in various penal institutions with inmates who, in the case of the first-mentioned research, had experienced a period of military service or, in the case of the second, were recidivists with repeated experiences of institutionalization. It was the problem, not the institution, that represented here the frame of reference.

In a valuable discussion of 'The Application of the Small Group Concept to the Study of the Prison Community',[44] John James suggests that prison administrators should make use of the knowledge of the theory of small groups which has been accumulated in recent years and indicates the kind of information on the group life of prisoners required for the use of the practical administrator. It goes without saying and is apparent from studies such as those of Clemmer, Sykes and Morris, that prominent among the features to be studied is the complex inter-group structure of the prison community, i.e. relations between prisoners, between staff members, and between prisoners and staffs, and that this involves among others the observation of the working of the underground code of inmates as opposed to the official code.

The Nottingham University study of 'Radby',[45] a mining town of slightly over 20,000 inhabitants in the English Midlands, offers a good example of community research in the open, similar to the Bristol Social Project, but not designed as action research. The methods used were mainly interviewing and participant observation in clubs, pubs, dancing classes, community centre and similar places. In order further to facilitate contact a play room for some of the local children was obtained by the female member of the team, but in contrast to Bristol this was not done consciously to improve social conditions but merely to obtain information and to help explaining the worker's frequent presence in one particular street. The male member of the team worked for some time as an unskilled labourer in one of the local factories. For further details on this research see below, Chapter 22, s. 4.

As already indicated, many community studies are at the same time studies of the area over which the community is distributed, and it is often difficult to decide whether the socio-criminological study of the groups within that community or the study of the local distribution of crime within the area is the primary object of the research. In the cases of the Bristol Social Project and of 'Radby' it was obviously the community and group aspect that prevailed, but in many other cases this is doubtful, and where the aspect of local distribution seems to predominate such studies have here been classified as area research.

There are, in addition, studies of delinquency in certain areas which are, however, neither sociological community nor area studies in the true sense, but contain merely statistical information of a local character.

Sociometric techniques have occasionally been employed in criminological research, and it is worth mentioning that Moreno's original work was done in an institution for delinquent girls at Hudson, New York.[46] Such techniques are of value in the study of small groups, clubs, school classes, open and closed institutions, where isolated and frustrated individuals or sub-groups, pre-delinquents and likely absconders, leaders and easily led can be spotted. In this country sociometric studies in the field of delinquency have been made by Piercy, Rose, Grygier and Croft.[47]

(c) As will be explained below (Chapter 23) *Area Studies* have been done since the early decades of the nineteenth century, roughly following the same pattern. The socio-economic characteristics of the area are closely surveyed and related to the distribution and character of crime and delinquency and the offenders in it. The techniques are those of social surveys, often supplemented by detailed statistical analysis and by case material. The literature is very extensive and will be discussed below.

## 2. The Role of the Research Worker

Although the question of what kind of role the research worker should assume in criminological investigations may arise in connection with other techniques, too, in particular in the field of individual case studies, it is perhaps most acute in research of the sociological type. When doing community research in a group setting, whether in a large community of the 'Cornerville', Bristol or 'Radby' type or with gangs or in a prison, the research worker will immediately arouse suspicion, and sooner or later he will have to give reasons for his presence and his activities. Should he tell the truth, the whole truth, or only part of it or should he altogether disguise himself and pretend to be what he is not? The answers given in different projects cover a very wide range from one extreme to the other, according to the circumstances of the research and the personality of the worker. In criminology the dilemma is more acute than elsewhere. Very few communities or other groups, very few prisoners have any particular desire to see their criminal activities closely scrutinized by an outsider without any obvious benefit to themselves, nor are they likely to take kindly to the intruding scientist. The temptation is strong, therefore, to disguise the object of the enquiry and the role played in it by the research worker. Where the latter—as was the case with Clemmer—is at the same time already on the staff of the prison or club, etc., and therefore generally known in that capacity, the solution is comparatively easy, but this does not happen very often. The frankest explanation, and in most cases the only true one, is that the worker wants 'to write a book' about things he observes and that he hopes its publication will help to improve conditions. Whyte started his research at Cornerville introduced by 'Doc', one of the boys there, as 'his friend', but after a while this explanation no longer satisfied their curiosity; he then pretended to study the social history of the place, but soon this, too, was not plausible enough to justify his activities, and people developed the theory that he was writing a book. Eventually, he came to the conclusion that his acceptance in the locality depended far more on the personal relationships he was able to establish than on the explanation he could offer.[48] While this may have been true in Whyte's case it is not likely to apply in general as the possibility of establishing good personal relations may not arise if the observer has no plausible explanation to start with. If the book eventually appears other difficulties are likely to arise. Whyte is one of the very few research workers who, in the Appendix to the second edition, has something to say about the reception of his book by those directly concerned. Apparently very few of them read it at all, and Doc, the man who had helped

196

him most in his research, realizing the embarrassment it might cause, did his best to discourage the others from reading it.

In the case of the Barge Boys' Club, although a book was eventually written on it this was certainly not the main object of the experiment. According to the explanation given by the worker to the club members his object was 'to test his theories' about the true nature of 'unclubbability', and no deception was involved.

Where some form of disguise is regarded as indispensable—and it should be used only where it is really indispensable—it will assume different forms, depending on the nature of the research, the publicity it has already received, and other factors, and it would be unwise to deviate from the truth more than absolutely necessary. If the worker should tell stories which can easily be disproved he would completely spoil his chances of success. In another direction, too, great caution has to be exercised. Most research workers are sincerely convinced that their work will, at least in the long run, help to improve our understanding of the problems involved and the conditions in our society, and it is tempting enough to paint an over-optimistic picture of the likely results when trying to persuade people to give information. The subsequent disappointment may be very severe and breed cynicism and contempt for the whole idea of research. If the research is done under the auspices of a university or similar institution of universally recognized status reference to it will often be enough to dispel suspicion without any exaggerated statements on the immediate practical value of the research. If the worker and those whose co-operation and confidence he tries to gain have something real in common, all the better. When Grygier,[49] after the war, wished to interview and test Polish displaced persons in Germany, some of them former inmates of concentration camps, he told them truthfully that he was himself a displaced Pole, but had been deported 'to another part of the world'. This proved to be effective with groups where Poles were in the majority. Grygier, while making much use of the Rosenzweig Picture Frustration Test, disapproves of the advice given by Rosenzweig that the tester should deliberately mislead his subjects by making false statements on the object of his testing.

One of the most difficult research situations arises in prisons, in particular in maximum security prisons with a hardened recidivist population. Not only may the role of the worker differ in different prisons, but even without that role his behaviour, attitudes and contacts will have to assume a different colour according to the general atmosphere of the place. Spencer, who deals with the problem very fully,[50] points out that at Dartmoor, as contrasted with Maidstone, it was essential for him not to be identified with the disciplinary staff, and as the Prison Chaplain there was universally accepted as a person to whom prisoners could give confidential information without fear of indiscretion he decided to assume the role of a worker who had come to help the Chaplain in the running of his classes. This also gave him the pretext for moving around the prison and helped him to observe the men in a group situation. Terence and Pauline Morris, on the other hand, in their study of Pentonville, made it clear that they were making 'an independent study of the prison to see how it worked, so that we might be able to assist those responsible for making changes. We hoped that it would eventually appear in book form.' Appendix A contains a discussion on the methodological aspects of the research, such as availability of the material, attitudes of staff and prisoners to the research, the role of a woman research worker in a men's prison, and the 'creation of a research role'.[51] It has to be stressed that in the period of approximately ten years which lies between these two researches, people in general have become more research-minded, and even prisoners seem more willing now to accept research workers inside closed institutions.

In researches which take place in the open, such as the Bristol and Nottingham ('Radby') studies, it has still been found advisable not to disclose crime and delinquency as the main objects of study.

# PART THREE
## Factors and Causes Related to Crime

In view of what has been said in Chapter 1 (I, 2(b)) we intend to deal in this part with 'Factors and Causes', a neutral phrase which may mean a real cause here and a mere 'factor' there. To single out for closer attention a large number of such phenomena in their relation to crime is one of the principal objects of criminology. In our methodological chapters the need for such a procedure has become apparent. In researches of a statistical nature and in the building up of official criminal statistics we have to make a preliminary, and often hazardous decision on which of the very many facets potentially connected with crime statistical material should be collected and which statistical facts can safely be ignored as having no conceivable relation to the subject. The same applies to the construction of prediction tables. Nor can those who assemble the information needed for individual case histories indiscriminately write down whatever facts they may be able to gather from records, personal documents, interviews and so on; they have to be selective, and their technique of selection will be determined by certain preconceived ideas about potential relevance, causal or otherwise. Or the action researcher whose object it is to reduce crime by relieving certain 'stresses and strains': he, too, cannot approach his problem with a completely blank mind. In short, whatever method of research is used in criminology it cannot start from nothing.

For the following chapters no originality is claimed regarding the preliminary selection of these factors or for their classification, and we shall be content to follow the traditional lines. It has become customary to divide these factors into three major spheres, the physical-anthropological-biological, the psychological-psychiatric, and the social-economic. Consequently, we shall deal with these three spheres in three sections, each of them divided into a number of chapters. This is in accordance with the theory of multiple causation which, with certain reservations, we have accepted above (Chapter 1, I, 2(c)).

This customary division into three groups of factors or causes is somewhat artificial, however, because of the high degree of overlapping between them. As a distinguished biologist has written,[1] cultural influences on the human organism are so strong and begin so early in life that 'they become incorporated in the tissues of those who have been exposed to such influence'. Cultural factors are not merely 'added to, or superimposed upon, the physical organism', but actually incorporated into it and an inseparable part of it. Equally close is the interrelationship between psychological and social factors. Physical shortcomings may produce psychological handicaps, and the two together may lead to social inabilities. The latter, in their turn, may account for physical neglect, which may complete the vicious circle. For purposes of clearer presentation and in the interest of easier discussion, however, it is advisable to retain the tripartite scheme. The question arises whether the three groups are, generally speaking, of equal significance for the study of crime, whether they stand on the same level or whether certain distinctions have to be made. That such distinctions will be inevitable for each individual case is obvious as the weight of the factors will differ from case to case. From a general point of view, however, only one distinction can be made which follows from our view that the physical-anthropological-biological as well as the social and economic factors can become operative only by going through the 'transformator' of a psychological or psychiatric factor. This might be shown in the following diagram:

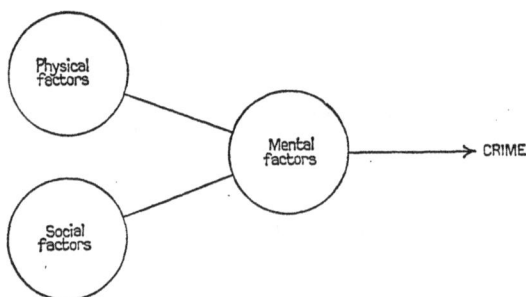

```
   ( Physical
     factors )
               \
                \
                 ( Mental
                   factors ) ───────────→ CRIME
                /
               /
   ( Social
     factors )
```

Only by producing a certain state of mind can any of the other factors lead to crime. This has been well expressed in Bernard Glueck's formula: 'a factor is not a cause unless and until it becomes a motive'.[2] A relationship of this kind does not necessarily mean the invariable pre-eminence of the psychological-psychiatric aspects. The pressure of the other factors may be so overwhelmingly strong in an individual case that the addition of a very small psychological dose may be sufficient to produce crime. It does mean, however, that in the absence of such a dose no crime could happen. On the other hand, a large dose of psychological-psychiatric factors may suffice without the addition of any physical or social factors of a criminogenic nature.

THE PHYSICAL SIDE OF CRIME

# Chapter 11

## PHYSICAL-ANTHROPOLOGICAL-BIOLOGICAL ASPECTS I: GEOGRAPHY AND PHYSICAL HEALTH

The discussion has to be divided into two main aspects: physical factors affecting human environment, from which the individual can escape by changing his environment, and those affecting man himself. The former are the subject of *physical geography*, while the latter belong to human *anthropology* and *biology*. As far as the physical characteristics of delinquents are concerned, it is sometimes overlooked that here, too, we have to deal with two different, though related, problems: first, the question how far the physical health of an individual may be a factor in his criminal behaviour, and, second, whether criminals belong to distinct physical types. It is the first of these questions which will be discussed in the present chapter (ii), whereas the typological problem will be treated in Chapter 12.

### I. PHYSICAL GEOGRAPHY

Physical geography as contrasted with the social aspects of the spatial distribution of the population, or in other words the physical, non-social aspects of biology, has been neglected in modern criminology in spite of various publications on the subject at the beginning of the present century. Older writers had perhaps been inclined to overrate their importance as causes of criminal behaviour, and the present tendency may simply restore the balance. Bonger has briefly reviewed the historical development, from Herodotus via Montesquieu and Quetelet to Roesner.[1] The criminological significance of the physical environment has been studied chiefly with reference to the climate of a country, to the weather and the seasons.[2] Quetelet, Guerry de Champneuf, Lombroso, Ferri, Aschaffenburg and others tried to show statistically that in France, Italy and Germany respectively crimes against the person were more frequent in hot climates and in the summer months, whereas crimes against property prevailed in cold climates and in winter. Lombroso regarded the subject as important enough to devote the first chapter of his *Crime: its Causes and*

*Remedies* to it; he quotes some figures from Guerry and Ferri, adding some of his own, but admits that the statistics do not always seem to be associated with differences in climate. Quetelet even went so far as to deduce from such statistics his 'thermic law of delinquency' (Chapter 1 above), and Prince Peter Kropotkin added to this his even more extravagant formula claiming a fixed correlation between average temperature, the degree of humidity and the volume of crime, especially the number of homicides,[3] a formula which, as Barnes and Teeters point out, is absurd as no allowance is made in it for the size of population of the country concerned. Some of the other statistical material presented in older publications is of a primitive character, too, and open to criticism.[4] As far as international comparisons, in particular, are concerned previous writers have not always been aware of the dangers in comparing homicide rates between countries possessing different legal conceptions of murder and manslaughter and different systems of police and criminal procedure (Chapter 5 above). National comparisons between northern and southern regions of the same country are on safer ground, although even here differences in public attitudes, in police and procedure may play an important part in accounting for variations apparently due to the climate, and the latter, where it influences the activities of offenders, may well have some bearing on those of the forces of law and order, too.

In this country, obviously under the impact of nineteenth-century literature, the Introduction of *Criminal Statistics* of 1893 (see Chapter 5 above) paid special attention to the subject, producing much material to show that crimes against the person were highest in summer and lowest in winter and property crimes had the opposite tendency.[5]

Cyril Burt,[6] in his *Young Delinquent*, criticizes English writers for simply quoting figures from other countries as if they were applicable everywhere regardless of latitude or climate. His own data for juvenile offenders in London show two maxima, June and December, and two minima, February and August, and some small amount of concordance between juvenile delinquency and the length of daylight. He, too, found that offences against the person reached their climax in summer and property offences in winter, but he relates the latter fact to the temptations of Christmas shop windows rather than to the climate. Malicious injury had its maximum in November, which he regards as due to Guy Fawkes day.

For the United States very few studies are available comparing states with different climatic conditions. Dexter made a comparison between New York City and Denver, Colorado,[7] without any conclusive results. He did show, however, that in New York arrests for assaults and battery in the months May to September were much more frequent than in the colder months (in July 24 per cent above, in January 22 per cent below average). Brearley's study of seasonal variations in homicide in South Carolina showed no consistent pattern.[8] He concludes that the months with heavy agricultural work produced less violence than months of leisure, and this regardless of temperature, December and July having the highest figures as months of increased social life and festivities. This he regarded as an illustration of the interrelationship of meteorological and cultural factors.

Wolfgang, in his study of homicide in Philadelphia for the years 1948 to 1952, found no statistically significant differences between hot and cold months, which forced him to reject any hypothesis of a relationship between monthly or seasonal changes and rates of homicide.

One gets the impression that the more recent studies, being less prejudiced and using more refined statistical techniques, fail to corroborate the findings of the more enthusiastic and less critical studies of the nineteenth and early twentieth centuries. This does not necessarily force us completely to deny the influence of climatic conditions on criminal behaviour. The assumption which lay behind the work of those earlier writers that human emotions, sexual or otherwise, are more intense in hot weather and material human needs more acute in a cold climate may well be true. All we can say for the time being is that the expression of such emotions and material needs in criminal acts has not yet been clearly and unequivocally demonstrated in the available statistics. Nor has that assumption been refuted by this negative fact. The reason for this state of affairs may be, as usual, the complexity of the problem and the corresponding difficulty of establishing trends which are not masked by contrary trends:

Not only may the climatic influences be obscured by those of learning but the cultural influences may be so numerous and so powerful as to make the effect of climatic change quite negligible. Climate and geographical location may stimulate physiological functioning and also cultural achievements, provided the culture does not otherwise change and is the same from region to region. But such is never the case. Cultures vary from region to region, and are nearly everywhere in a state of change. Hence the effect of climatic stimulation is small or even infinitesimal compared to the cultural stimulation.[9]

*Mutatis mutandis*, we can agree with this conclusion. As we have seen, the more penetrating studies all show that fluctuations which, superficially, seemed to be due to the climate were in fact more likely to be related to certain cultural events such as Christmas, Guy Fawkes, which happen to occur at certain times of the year and have various complex social and economic repercussions. Strict evidence for this assumption, however, is not available either.

## II. PHYSICAL HEALTH[10]

As already pointed out before, we are in this chapter concerned exclusively with the physical health of delinquents, regardless of whether or not any evidence of ill health, any deviation from what is regarded as 'normal' in this field, may be characteristic of a certain anthropological type.

Evidence on the incidence of ill health among delinquents has been collected partly from statistical samples and partly from individual cases. It is somewhat more plentiful for juveniles than for adults, but there is, regrettably, no routine check of the physical health of every juvenile delinquent appearing before a juvenile court in this country. According to the Children and Young Persons Act, 1933, s. 35(2), it is the duty of the police when bringing a child or young person before the court to notify the local authority, which then has in all cases, except those appearing to be trivial, to make investigations into, among other matters, his health, and the information obtained shall be rendered available to the court. Various studies made of samples of juvenile court cases have shown, however, that medical examinations of physical health are in fact not made as a matter of routine and that the magistrates often rely on the results of out-of-date school medical inspections.[11] Nor does the position appear to be much more favourable in juvenile courts in the United States.[12] On the physical health of offenders above juvenile court age there exists even less general information.

As far as prisoners are concerned, it is provided in the *Statutory Rules for English Prisons* that the Medical Officer has to examine every prisoner on reception, record the state of his health and that he has the care of the physical health of the prisoner throughout his stay in prison.[13] The *Annual Reports of the Prison Commissioners* contain some information on the physical health of the prison population; in the years 1955–9, for example, the daily percentage of prisoners treated in and out of hospitals ranged from 14·6 to 15·6 per cent of the daily population.[14] While this seems to be a fairly high figure, it gives no complete picture of the health of the population, in particular not of the seriousness and length of the illnesses and on the question whether the latter had already existed on reception and at the time of the offence or whether they were contracted subsequently in prison.

In the circumstances we have to rely on whatever scanty information is available from special private investigations into the subject. For juvenile delinquents, what appears to have been the first attempt in Britain to study some physical characteristics of delinquent as compared with non-delinquent children was made in 1883 when a report was published by the Anthropometric Committee of the British Association for the Advancement of Science which had been appointed 'for the purpose of collecting observations on the systematic examination of the height, weight, and other physical characters of the inhabitants of the British Isles'.[15] The approximately 53,000 individuals measured by the Committee included a group of 1,273 boys and 601 girls from Industrial Schools, and comparisons with the general population showed that these delinquent children from Industrial Schools were considerably shorter and lighter in weight than children of the same age in the general population. For children aged 13 years, for example, the following figures were given:

*Average Weight (including clothes) in lb.*

| General Population | Professional Class | Labouring Class | Industrial Schools | |
|---|---|---|---|---|
| | | | Boys | Girls |
| 87·2 | 89·8 | 84·0 | 72·31 | 72·76 |

*Average Height (without shoes) in inches*

| General Population | | Industrial Schools | |
|---|---|---|---|
| Boys | Girls | Boys | Girls |
| 56·91 | 57·77 | 53·23 | 52·98 |

While, on the one hand, the figures for Industrial Schools could at the time be regarded as more representative of juvenile delinquents than Approved School figures would be now, the usefulness of these data suffers from the lack of information how long the children had been in the institution at the time when they were measured.

Soon afterwards a well-known nineteenth-century writer on the subject, the Rev. W. D. Morrison, in his book *Juvenile Offenders*, while complaining about the lack of data, ventured the statement that 'among the many causes which produce a criminal life the physical inferiority of the offender is one of the most important'.[16] More substantial evidence was produced by Cyril Burt, whose chapter on the subject ranks among the best sources of information available.[17] In his samples of delinquent and control cases he found that defective physical conditions were about one and a quarter times as frequent among the former as they were among the latter. Actually, he found an average of 119·3 pathological factors among his delinquent group as against 78·5 among the non-delinquents. With regard to the question of causal nexus he stresses that 'poor health means poor control; and even a temporary physical weakness may be the occasion of a passing criminal lapse', and also that misconduct may appear after the illness has passed, sometimes because of undue pampering while it lasted. 'With most young convalescents, it is character rather than physique that remains permanently enfeebled by the circumstances of their disease'—a good illustration of the truth of our previous remarks on the mental factor as the great 'transformator'. Therefore, he adds, one should not expect too much from a purely medical approach. It is not only true that 'the mere presence in a young thief of a swollen gland or joint does not prove it was the swelling that forced him into theft', but also that the mere removal of a physical defect does not invariably remove its criminogenic effects because in the meantime 'a mental habit may have been formed'. This dependence of the physical factor on the mental transformator does not prove, of course, that the former is of no importance in the chain of causation, and Burt fully endorses the demand that 'every child charged should be carefully examined by an experienced medical practitioner before being brought before the courts'—a demand which, as we have seen, has remained largely unfulfilled in the period of forty years since Burt's book was first published.

Probably under the influence of this study by its eminent psychologist the London County Council produced a full medical account in 1931 on 696 boys and 107 girls admitted to the Ponton-Road Place of Detention.[18] This report showed 'a very marked inferiority in respect of nutritional state and physical make up' when compared with average London children. 22·2 per cent of the Ponton-Road children were estimated to be poorly nourished against the 4·5 per cent of the average London children.

Eilenberg[19] contrasts groups of London Remand Home boys for the years 1935 and 1955 and also compares them with L.C.C. figures for 1954. He concludes that the present higher standard of living in this country has resulted in a generation characterized by an increase in both height and weight and that up to the age of 14 there is little difference in this between the Remand Home boys and those in the general population. There was also noticeable an increased physical well-being and absence of illnesses in the 1955 child compared with the 1930 child.

For Glasgow, Ferguson[20] compared the convictions of a group of 1,349 ordinary boys who had left school in 1947 with those of a group of 489 physically handicapped boys. He found a very slightly higher rate of convictions per head among the latter; only for a few types of physical handicap, those due to injuries and respiratory diseases, the rate was much higher. In the light of his figures his conclusion is hardly justified that 'there seems to be some evidence that poor physique does itself exert an adverse influence on the incidence of juvenile delinquency, particularly where conditions in the home are unsatisfactory'.[21]

With regard to Borstal cases, the present writer found among the files of 606 boys and 411 girls examined before the last war only 37 cases of boys—6·1 per cent—and 14 cases of girls—3·4 per cent—listed as showing 'physical defects and unprepossessing appearance'. The records were, however, rather scanty at the time (the files referred to boys discharged between 1922 and 1936 and to girls discharged between 1916 and 1935), and many cases of this kind may have been overlooked.[22] For a sub-sample of 44 cases of Borstal boys received in 1946-7, whose files were examined in connection with the Borstal Prediction Study,[23] 19 cases were found to be below normal physically and a 'surprisingly high proportion of cases with serious physical defects' was encountered.

The comprehensive investigation made by Norwood East and his associates into the characteristics of 4,000 Borstal boys[24] was handicapped by the lack of an external control group. Therefore, comparisons could be made only within the Borstal sample by distinguishing according to type and frequency of the offences committed. Where, in exceptional cases, comparisons with a corresponding sample of non-criminals were possible, as for height and weight, no significant differences were found.

With regard to adult criminals, Goring's famous investigation,[25] which will be more fully discussed below (Chapter 13), came to the conclusion that the Parkhurst prisoners whom he studied, except for an inferiority in stature and weight, were equal in physique to the general population.

Norval Morris's analysis of his groups of 32 preventive detainees and two hundred and seventy 'confirmed recidivists', studied in English prisons in 1948,[26] includes many details concerning their physical condition. 6 of the 32 he regarded as 'precluded by their physical condition from living for more than a short time outside an institution', while 6 others were seriously hindered by bad health 'from pursuing extra-mural occupations suitable to their mental abilities'. The remaining 20, 'though not necessarily good specimens physically', were at least not in need of frequent medical attention. The average age of this group was 50 years 9 months, with a standard deviation of 8 years 1 month. Of the second group of 270 'confirmed recidivists' the health of 78 is given as fair, of 31 as indifferent and 29 as poor, and 51 were either precluded by bad health from living for more than a short time outside an institution or seriously hindered in pursuing extra-mural occupations in keeping with their mental abilities. The average age of this group when last sentenced was 41 years 6 months, with a standard deviation of 8 years 6 months. The material does not allow any guesses how far these physical abilities had been present at the beginning of the criminal careers of these men, how far they had been responsible for their criminal activities and how far the heavy sentences served had contributed to their physical deterioration. Nor do the case histories add sufficient details on the early condition of these men to permit any guesses in this respect. One has to bear in mind that their criminal histories go back over four decades or more to a time when even less attention than today was paid in court and prison files to the health of offenders.

Approximately ten to twelve years after Norval Morris's observations, Terence and Pauline Morris, in their Pentonville Study, came to the conclusion that the physical health of the prisoners was probably no better and no worse than that of a population of comparable social and economic status outside, whereas the matter was very different for their mental health. At roughly the same time, D. J. West stated that, in his group of Wandsworth prisoners, 'although only a minority were physically afflicted, the incidence of physical illness and handicap was higher than might be expected among a population of working men of similar age', and his interviews gave him the impression that 'an undue proportion of the men were prematurely ageing'. Here again, the position was strikingly more unfavourable with regard to mental health.[27]

In the United States a painstaking enquiry into the subject was conducted by the Gluecks in their *Unraveling Juvenile Delinquency*.[28] In view of the large size of their samples, 500 delinquent and 500 nondelinquent boys, the physical examinations had to be limited to 20–30 minutes per case, and it may be open to doubt whether they could do full justice to all the items mentioned: developmental health history, immunity from contagion, height, weight, dynamometric strength of grip, skeleton and palate, teeth, nose and throat, eyes and ears, heart and lungs, abdomen and genitalia, skin, glands and nervous system. With this important reservation in mind, we note that the findings did not support the view that the health of the delinquents was worse than that of the non-delinquents. Certain minor differences were found, but they are too insignificant to be mentioned. The researchers were asked to consider whether the fact that their delinquents were all selected from inmates of institutions might not have affected their physical condition, but they took the view that the periods of institutionalization had been too short to have any influence.

In an earlier Glueck study *One Thousand Juvenile Delinquents*[29] the percentage of children in poor health had been very high, but as there was no control group no conclusions could be drawn from this. In the follow-up study *Juvenile Delinquents Grown Up*, no difference was found in health between those who had reformed and the recidivists.[30]

The evidence from most other American studies of juvenile delinquency is similarly negative. Typical in this respect are statements by William Healy, the McCords and the Cambridge-Somerville Study.[31]

The authors of the latter stress, in particular, that, as pointed out by Burt long before, the removal of physical handicaps does not necessarily lead to a cessation of delinquent behaviour—a fact which has but little to do with the question of how far such behaviour may have been originally caused or at least precipitated or aggravated by that handicap.

Far more positive is the English study of Pearce[32] who, writing soon after the last war as a psychiatrist with personal experience of several thousands of London juvenile delinquents, endorses the finding of the London County Council's report of twenty years before that the delinquents showed an inferiority both in nutritional state and physical make-up. He disagrees with the conclusion of that report that physical inferiority had little direct bearing on delinquency, but stresses even more its indirect psychological influence and disabilities resulting from absence from school during illness and undue spoiling afterwards.[33]

To sum up: while the statistical evidence of physical ill-health leading to delinquency is, at least for more recent years, not impressive, those with personal knowledge of large numbers of cases are inclined to regard it as an indirectly important factor in the causation of delinquent behaviour. More direct is the effect of certain affections of the brain, such as encephalitis lethargica, which will be discussed in Chapter 14 below.

# Chapter 12

## ANTHROPOLOGICAL-BIOLOGICAL ASPECTS II: THE POSITIVIST SCHOOL

In the present chapter we have to deal not as in the previous one with physical disabilities of any conceivable kind, but with certain types of physical irregularities or stigmata which have been regarded as being characteristic of the criminal. The principal method used by the anthropological-biological school of criminology is the typological one. This school has derived its immense strength largely from the support received through the widespread popular belief that, first, criminals are born, not made, and secondly, that they conform to certain physical characteristics which make them look different and easily distinguishable from ordinary human beings. This belief is strongly reflected not only in popular writings but also in several well-known figures in great works of world literature such as Homer's *Thersites* or Shakespeare's *Richard III* or in part also in *Julius Caesar*:

> Let me have men about me that are fat,
> Sleek-headed men, and such as sleep o' nights;
> Yond Cassius has a lean and hungry look,
> He thinks too much; such men are dangerous.

From here it is only one further step to the conviction expressed in *The Times* of the 11th October 1935: 'The fat, says a judge, do not write anonymous letters . . . It is the lean bodies that sit at writing tables, and bony fingers that dip pens in vitriol and build up bombshells for harmless postmen to deliver.'

### I. THE PHRENOLOGISTS

The scientific study of the matter goes back to the eighteenth and early nineteenth century phrenologists, especially to Franz Joseph Gall (1758–1828), John Gaspar Spurzheim (1776–1832), and the American Charles Caldwell (1772–1853),[1] and to a smaller extent to the physiognomic work of J. K. Lavater (1741–1801). While the impact of the latter, i.e. of the idea that the human physiognomy provides the key to an understanding of the human personality, was insignificant in the field of criminology—Norwood East refers to an English Statute of 1743 which made all persons pretending to have skill in physiognomy liable to be whipped as rogues and vagabonds[2] —phrenology, i.e. the corresponding search for relations between the skull, the brain and social behaviour, aroused somewhat greater interest at least until the middle of the nineteenth century. Gall and his supporters maintained that there was a close correspondence between the exterior shape of the skull, unusual cranial protuberances or other abnormalities of the cranium and the structure of the brain; moreover, the different regions of the latter were related to certain psychological characters, propensities and sentiments, of which phrenologists identified a large number, up to thirty-five. Each of these psychological characters had a specific cerebral organ allocated to it which produced certain abnormalities of the brain causing specific criminal tendencies. This causal nexus was, however, not regarded as inevitable as the so-called lower propensities could well be overcome by the influence of the higher sentiments. This theory led to a number of phrenological studies of the skulls of prisoners, notably in the United States, but any anatomical abnormalities which were discovered might as well have been exhibited by the non-criminal population of which there was no control group. Moreover, as Fink writes, the essential weakness of phrenology was its failure to understand that no single part of the skull and the brain can be held solely responsible for the very complex variations of human behaviour. However, it was the merit of this school, as that of its successor, the anthropological-biological school, that it drew attention to this need for the close examination of individual criminals instead of the vague general theorizing on crime which, with a few exceptions, had monopolized the field up to the beginning of the nineteenth century. In some cases, for example in the Annual Reports of the famous Eastern State Penitentiary of Pennsylvania, phrenological ideas and terms were used for the classification of the prisoners even up to the beginning of the present century.[3] In Europe, the work of the phrenologists was carried on by a number of scholars, especially Lauvergne, Broca, Thomson and others mentioned by Bonger and Wolfgang.[4]

In spite of the stir which the phrenologists and their immediate successors had caused, the immense popularity of the anthropological interpretation of crime was due not so much to them as to Lombroso,[5] whose theories and writings have influenced the course of thinking more deeply than those of any other criminologists.

## II. LOMBROSO'S PERSONALITY AND WORK

Cesare Lombroso was born of Italian-Jewish parents on the 6th November 1835 in Verona, which was at the time still under Austrian rule, and died in 1909.[6] He studied medicine at Pavia and other Italian universities and also at Vienna where he became interested in psychiatry. Philosophically, he was influenced, as Wolfgang writes, 'by the French positivists, the German materialists, and the English evolutionists', and he strongly disagreed with the indeterministic views dominant among contemporary Italian philosophers and jurists. Apart from the phrenologists, Darwin and Comte, as also the French psychiatrists Esquirol and Morel, the German pathologist Virchow and the French anthropologist Broca were among his most important spiritual ancestors.[7] His earliest researches were concerned with cretinism and pellagra, particularly rampant in Italy at the time, and, after becoming an Army physician, he carried out the anthropometric measurement of 3,000 soldiers in order to observe the physical differences existing between the inhabitants of the different regions of Italy. This was followed by work in mental hospitals, leading among other publications to a lecture on *Genio e follia* (1864), a forerunner of one of his best-known later works *L'Uomo di genio* and *Genio e degenerazione* (1897). In 1874 he became a lecturer in legal medicine and public hygiene at the University of Turin, where he later became a professor of psychiatry and of criminal anthropology. In 1880, assisted by his pupils Ferri and Garofalo, he founded the *Archivio di Psichiatria e Anthropologia criminale* and in 1906 the Museum of Criminal Anthropology. In the intervening years he had published many papers on brain pathology and psychiatry, such as the *Antropometria di 400 delinquenti veneti* (1872) and *Affetti e passioni dei delinquenti* (1874).[8] These last papers prepared the ground for his most famous work, *L'Uomo delinquente*, which was first published in 1876 and soon translated into French and German and other languages, but surprisingly enough never into English. In the course of the five Italian editions of this book, covering a period of twenty years, Lombroso expanded it from its original size of 252 pages to a three-volume work of over 1,900 pages (5th ed. 1896–7), modifying and adding continuously under the impact of external criticisms and of the researches of his supporters and his own. In his later work *Le Crime, causes et remèdes* (1899), translated into English as *Crime: its Causes and Remedies*,[9] he once more gave expression to certain changes in his scientific views by underlining the significance of the socio-economic factors, which had been comparatively neglected in most of his previous writings. Together with the husband of one of his daughters, Ferrero, he published a study of *The Female Offender* in 1893, translated into English in 1895.[10] Towards the end of his life he developed an interest in hypnotism and spiritualism, on which he published a book rendered into English as *After Death— What?*[11] The story of his life and work was told by the same daughter Gina after his death.[12]

As far as Lombroso's working techniques are concerned, he firmly believed in the need for first-hand observation and measurement of individual cases instead of philosophical-logical-juridical speculation and abstraction. First through his studies of Italian soldiers and later by examining inmates of Italian prisons he was able to collect a very large body of anthropometric material, some of it relating to the skulls of notorious Italian brigands. Notwithstanding his devotion to facts, however, his style and his basic approach to his problems were often highly intuitive, not to say fanciful. While imagination and inspiration are truly indispensable elements of scientific research, the flashes of insight which they produce have to be rigidly controlled to guard against the danger that unconscious bias may lead to imaginary discoveries not borne out by the facts.[13] Lombroso's scientific method has been characterized by Aschaffenburg, who in spite of many criticisms was favourably disposed towards him, as 'mehr genial schauend als sorgfältig prüfend' (i.e. perceiving with the intuition of genius rather than examining with care).[14] Characteristic of this is his famous description of how he was once standing with the skull of a notorious brigand in his hand and pondering over the problem of crime when suddenly the sun broke through the clouds and the sun-rays fell on the skull. Then, he said, it suddenly dawned on him that this skull and its anatomical structure provided the answer. In contrast to the phrenologists, however, Lombroso did not limit his study of the relation between crime and the human physique to the anatomy of the skull and the brain, but tried to take into consideration the other parts of the body, too. According to him, there exists a distinct anthropological type,[15] the born criminal, *delinquente nato* (a name invented by Ferri), an individual likely, or even bound, to commit crime. This type is characterized by certain malformations of the skeleton and the skull, in particular cranial and facial asymmetry, as well as by other physical stigmata of degeneration: an under- or oversized brain, a receding forehead, high cheek-bones, squinting eyes, bushy and prominent eyebrows, a twisted nose, big ears, a projecting or receding jaw, scanty beard as contrasted with the general hairiness of the body and overdeveloped arms. In addition to these physical stigmata, he noted a lack of moral sense, vanity, cruelty, idleness, the use of a criminal argot, a specific nervous insensibility to pain with contempt of death and suffering, and, finally, an inclination for tattooing which he had first observed among the soldiers. This congenital criminal, this moral imbecile, is an atavistic type, i.e. he represents a reversion to earlier, primitive, human types or even to pre-human ancestors of mankind with cannibalistic instincts. He 'reproduces in his person the ferocious instincts of primitive humanity and the inferior animals', a clear expression of Darwinian ideas. Under the influence of criticisms of this theory Lombroso tried to find a broader basis for it and added to the conception of atavism another explanation, that of epilepsy. While not every epileptic was a born criminal, the latter, according to Lombroso, was always an epileptic. Moreover, this type was an international one, i.e. the Italian born criminal showed the same characteristics as, say, the Chinese or English.

As has already been noted, in the course of his writings Lombroso was quite prepared to compromise on some of his ideas. From the third edition of his *L'Uomo delinquente* on, for example, he restricted the category of the born criminal to about 35 per cent of all criminals, recognizing in addition the existence of the insane and, in particular, the occasional criminal. This latter group, the largest of all, was divided into pseudo-criminals, who commit crimes without evil intent and without seriously harming society; the criminaloids, in whose cases adverse environmental circumstances are mostly to blame, criminals out of passion and, somewhat paradoxically, the habitual criminals who, without showing any of the stigmata, were driven into persistent criminal activities by their upbringing and associations. Another important concession, which greatly facilitated the numerical reduction of the born criminal type to 35 per cent, was Lombroso's insistence that, to fall under this category, an individual had to exhibit at least five of the physical stigmata. It is noteworthy, too, that he opened his late work *Crime: its Causes and Remedies* with the words: 'Every crime has its origin in a multiplicity of causes. . . .'

In making the born criminal, in spite of such reservations, the most important figure in his system Lombroso had powerful allies not only among his predecessors, the phrenologists, but also among his contemporaries. The famous English psychiatrist Henry Maudsley (1835–1918) wrote: 'Of the true thief as of the true poet it may be indeed said that he is born not made.'[16] The question arises: what is here meant by 'true'? In any case Maudsley, too, modified his views with advancing years.[17]

### III. LOMBROSO'S CRITICS AND SUPPORTERS

Criticism of Lombroso's theories began early and became very widespread. His conceptions of atavism and degeneracy as applied to

primitive men were not in keeping with the changing views even of
the immediate post-Darwinian period which did no longer believe in
'evolution along a single line' or expect 'all evolution to be progressive'.[18]

Moreover, 'a psychological and logical analysis of the processes
involved in the thought and behaviour of primitive man as he is
described by modern anthropologists shows that in form or structure
his mentality does not differ radically from that of civilized man'.[19]
As Bertrand Russell writes:[20] ' "Evolution" is a word which is often
used with an ethical flavour, but science is not improved by an ad-
mixture of ethics' and 'the particular motive force which Darwin
suggested, namely the struggle for existence and the survival of the
fittest, is not nearly so popular among biologists as it was fifty years
ago'. In addition, it has been stressed by a writer otherwise not unsympathetic towards Lombroso, Earnest Hooton, that the ideas of
atavism and degeneration do not go well together as the latter is a
concept of pathology, which the former is not.[21] To make matters
worse, Lombroso used the term 'atavism' wrongly. Meaning the re-
appearance in a present-day individual of signs of an earlier trait
which may have remained dormant for many generations, it can be
applied exclusively to hereditary qualities. Lombroso, however, used
that term also to explain certain non-hereditary phenomena such as
the frequency of tattooing, and he seems to have believed in the
possible inheritance of acquired characters.[22]

Apart from criticism of the doubtful quality of some of Lombroso's
most fundamental general conceptions, scepticism regarding the
accuracy of his anthropometric measurements of individual criminals
became also widespread. In the first place, he approached the individual physique not as a dynamic and changing but as a static
phenomenon and was not interested in the observation of morbid
processes.[23] Secondly, he often relied on measurements carried out by
others, of whose techniques he had no first-hand knowledge; thirdly,
in the statistical handling of his material he was not yet able to use the
more advanced methods developed only some decades later by Karl
Pearson at University College, London; and, fourthly—with the
exception of his study of female offenders[24]—he had no control
groups and could not, therefore, prove that the criminals whom he
measured showed physical abnormalities more frequently than non-
criminals. Hooton regards as the most serious objections to Lombroso's claims in the field of craniology the numerical inadequacy and
ethnic and racial heterogeneity of the case material assembled by him
and his students and the absence of any scientific statistical analysis.[25]
He calls the belief that the born criminal presented always the same
anthropological type regardless of ethnic and racial differences

rightly as 'almost too fantastic for serious consideration',[26] and it should indeed be obvious without further evidence that the physical differences between the different races are, generally speaking, far more important than those between criminals and non-criminals of the same race. In spite of such grave shortcomings, however, Hooton maintains that Lombroso's principal ideas, though not proved, have so far not been disproved either.

Outstanding among Lombroso's contemporary critics were A. Lacassagne (1843–1924) who, although a professor of medicine, became the head of the French environmental sociological school of criminology and who coined the famous phrase 'every society gets the criminals it deserves'; the anthropologists L. Manouvrier[27] and Topinard and, in particular, the lawyer and sociologist Gabriel Tarde (1843–1904). In his *La criminalité comparée*[28] Tarde stressed the ever-changing character of crime and the criminal law throughout the ages, the social origins of crime, and the various contradictions in Lombroso's theories. If, for example, one explains crime as atavism one cannot at the same time regard it as a form of insanity which is a product of civilization rather than of savagery. Tarde was interested in the phenomenon of criminal societies such as the Mafia, and in the professional character of crime in general.[29] If one would examine judges, advocates, musicians or labourers in the same way as Lombroso had examined his criminals one might, Tarde suggested, also find born judges, advocates, musicians, etc., among these occupational groups.[30] Lombroso's born criminal was, therefore, perhaps only one professonal type of many. Among other arguments against the anthropological theory of crime he refers to the fact that women, although showing the same stigmata, have a much smaller crime rate than men which, he thought, could not be explained, as Lombroso had suggested in his book *La donna delinquente*, by maintaining that prostitution was the female substitute for crime (on this see Chapter 26 below).[31]

On the other hand, Lombroso was able to build up a very large and powerful following, chiefly in his native country. The most important figures among his friends and students were Ferri and Garofalo.[32]

Enrico Ferri (1856–1929) has rightly been called by Sellin[33] 'one of the most colourful and influential figures in the history of criminology . . . the acknowledged leader of the so-called positive school of criminal science, a highly successful trial lawyer, Member of Parliament, editor of the socialist newspaper *Avanti*, indefatigable public lecturer, university professor, author of highly esteemed scholarly works, founder of a great legal journal, and a tireless polemicist in defence of his ideas'. The principal stages of his development may be sketched as follows: Born of poor parents in the province of

Mantua, he studied law at the University of Bologna. At the end of these studies he wrote a thesis in which he formulated already one of his principal ideas, i.e. that the criminal law should not be based upon free will and moral responsibility, which he regarded as mere fictions.[34] Greatly attracted by Lombroso's *L'Uomo delinquente*, which had appeared a few years earlier, he went to Turin in 1879 to study with the master and to lay the foundations of a lasting, though on his part not entirely uncritical, friendship. Soon, however, he proceeded to Paris where, in an attempt to widen the factual basis of his studies, he embarked on a large-scale analysis of French criminal statistics between 1828 and 1878, in which particular emphasis was placed upon the social factors as the only ones capable of explaining the great increase of crime in France during that period. He was thus able to show that members of the Lombrosian school were not, as commonly believed, exclusively interested in the anthropological side of crime. Ferri, in fact, was a strong advocate of the theory of multiple causation, paying special attention also to such physical factors as race, soil and climate.[35] At the same time, as his examination of several hundred prisoners and a control group of soldiers and his studies of homicide show,[36] he did not neglect his anthropological interests. After several years of teaching at the Universities of Bologna, Siena, Rome and Pisa his academic career suffered a setback when in 1893, because of his socialist activities—he had been a Member of Parliament already for several years—he was deprived of his professorship. It was only in 1906 that he was appointed professor of criminal law in Rome. In the intervening years, he had published, among many other works, his most famous book *Sociologia criminale*.[37] In the legal field he became known as an opponent of the jury, except for political trials, and of the death penalty, and in 1892 he founded a journal which became the centre and mouthpiece of the positive school of criminology, *La scuola positiva*. His influence in Italy and abroad grew steadily, in particular as the result of two brilliantly successful lecture tours to South America in 1908 and 1910. Perhaps nowhere else have his ideas been so enthusiastically acclaimed as in the South American republics, many of whose new Penal Codes purported to be written in accordance with positivist principles, although in some cases mere lip service was paid to them.[38] In Italy, his influence on the reform of the old Penal Code of 1889 was less lasting than originally expected. While a Draft Code published in 1921 was so strongly inspired by him that it became generally known under his name, the final Code of 1930, worked out under the Fascist regime with which, superficially, he had come to terms,[39] shows various important deviations from Ferri's ideas, notably in the field of penalties where the death penalty has been more widely applied in the Code than Ferri could have sincerely approved. A summary of his theories will be given below under IV.

Second in importance among Lombroso's followers ranks Raffaele Garofalo (1852–1934), but the attention paid to his personality and work has never equalled the fascination aroused in wide circles by the other two members of the famous trio. Garofalo, born in Naples, was a lawyer and became a magistrate and professor of criminal law in his native city, but his career lacked the brilliance and the vicissitudes of that of Ferri. Although he produced several books, among them one on reparation for the victims of crime, he has become mainly known through his *Criminologia*, first published in 1885 and usually regarded as the first book to bear this name.[40] Although a leading member of the positivist school, he disagreed in important points with Lombroso and especially with Ferri, whose socialism did not appeal to him, and it has been doubted whether his emphasis on moral conceptions was at all compatible with the main trends of positivist thought. This applies in particular to his theory of 'natural crime' (see Chapter 2 above). With the natural law movement he shared the endeavour to find an extra-legal definition of crime, which he thought should be a sociological one. He realized the impossibility of reaching a material conception of crime which would be valid independent of time and space, but believed that two criteria could be discovered applicable to crime in general: the violation of feelings of pity and probity. One could establish natural crimes by means of the inductive method, 'the only one which the positive school can use'. He explicitly refused to ask whether all that was crime in his age and society had always been so as this would be a childish question. Instead of actions one should analyse sentiments. Although these, too, are changeable, each race possesses, he thought, a nucleus of inborn moral instincts, transmitted by heredity, just as it possesses a physical type. After discussing a number of moral instincts which he regards as fundamental, such as patriotism, religion, honour, shame, he concludes that the idea of crime is associated with actions which are not merely harmful and immoral but violate the fundamental sentiments of pity (crimes of violence) and probity (crimes against property). This, he thinks, is not in violation of the theory of evolution, but his whole line of argument becomes rather tortuous and unconvincing and he has to make a number of exceptions for actions provoked by religious or political commands or social or traditional institutions. Moreover, he writes, if one considers the extreme tolerance usually exercised towards acts of industrial improbity one begins to query the existence of a sentiment of probity in the majority of the population. Mere police contraventions, too, are not crimes, but actions not yet regarded as crimes might acquire this character at a later stage because of the growing refinement of our moral sentiments—a point later to be more fully elaborated by Durkheim. In some of the examples he gave he was right, for example cruelty to animals, and in others, for example exploitation of labour in various forms, he was wrong only because social legislation has stepped in and to some extent taken over the functions of the criminal law. To the criticism that the moral sense cannot be a valid criterion because it, and public opinion with it, are to some considerable extent shaped by the fact and effect of punishment so that it would be a vicious circle to use it as a criterion to decide which acts should be punished he replied that the mere existence of penalties was not enough to give a criminal character to acts otherwise not regarded as such.

As Allen points out,[41] this theory created for Garofalo the formidable task of reconciling the moral concept of crime with the positivist rejection of moral responsibility. Moreover, in spite of important reservations and the concessions which he made to the ever-changing character of crime it was, as Tarde wrote,[42] not easy for an evolutionist 'to attach himself to some fixed point' in the process of evolution. Actually, there is no insurmountable difference in this respect between Garofalo and the evolutionists. Spencer, for example, although an opponent of the idea of a universal moral sense and believing that every society creates for itself the system of morals needed for its survival, thought it possible to reach an 'absolute Ethics' with certain fundamental principles.[43] Ginsberg, too, thinks there is a certain 'relative constancy' in moral rules, and elementary moral duties are widely recognized.[44] The real difficulties arise only when we try to define these duties more specifically and to use them, as Garofalo intended, as the basis for criminal legislation.

It is easy to find the link between Garofalo's legal philosophy and his concept of natural crime, on the one hand, and Lombroso's criminological theory, on the other: the born criminal is an individual particularly lacking in the sentiments of pity and probity.

## IV. THE SYSTEM OF THE POSITIVE SCHOOL

In spite of the considerable differences between the views of its leaders it is possible to sum up the essential features of the positive school.[45] Although it came into being largely in opposition to the classical school it is in fact the first coherent system of criminological thought ever constructed. The classical school, as represented by such great figures as Beccaria, Romilly, Feuerbach and, with many reservations, Bentham, was mainly interested in the reform of criminal law, of criminal procedure and of the system of penalties. It was opposed to the arbitrary and cruel character of the contemporary administration of criminal justice, to the lawmaking powers of the judiciary, to torture, capital punishment and transportation; it favoured equality before the law, trial by jury, fixed penalties and an objective equation between crime and punishment.[46] With the study of the individual offender it was but little concerned, and it did hardly anything to provide the scientific tools for such study; even the very idea of it was premature at the time. The 'statistician-sociologists'— to use Bonger's label—who followed them in the middle of the nineteenth century tried to create a scientific criminology, but only for the study of crime as a mass phenomenon. Jeffery has recently made a strong attack on the positivist school for having shifted the whole trend of scientific criminology from crime to the criminal;[47] but he does not pay sufficient attention to the historical fact that this shifting of the emphasis was nothing but a defensive action against the equally one-sided trends which had made their appearance before. It is our task today to restore the balance between these conflicting schools of thought and action.

The principal views, achievements and weaknesses of the positive school can be summarized as follows, and this summary may be read in conjunction with the present writer's analysis of positivism in the Introduction to *Pioneers in Criminology*. It will be clear that the theoretical system of the positivists is far more comprehensive than their specifically anthropological-biological doctrines and that positivists can be found among criminologists who do not support these doctrines.

In the field of criminology proper, (*a*) the positivists took over Comte's idea of the progress of scientific thought from the theological to the metaphysical stage, and from there to the scientific or positive stage. This implied the complete divorce of science and law from morals; the priority of science; the repudiation of free will and moral responsibility, which latter had to be replaced by the legal and social responsibility of the criminal, as the idea of guilt had to be replaced by that of dangerousness (*pericolosità* and its subjective elements, *temibilità*); (*b*) the attempt of the classical school to construct an equation between crime and punishment had to be replaced by an equation between the individual criminal and his treatment; (*c*) therefore, the individual criminal had to be studied by means of scientific quantitative observation of facts, and the effect of treatment by way of experimentation. The legal nature of the crime committed was comparatively unimportant. The classical school, Ferri wrote,[48] wanted to reduce punishment, the positive school wanted to reduce crime by effective treatment of the offender in accordance with his needs.

In the fields of penology and criminal law, it follows (a) that the moralizing concept of punishment had to be replaced by a morally neutral system of measures of security, protecting society against the criminal, and of reform and rehabilitation. Such measures might, in individual cases, be much more severe than the old-fashioned penalties of the classical school as the limiting principle of the just equation between crime and punishment was no longer valid; (b) that, in particular, the system of penalties fixed by the court had to be replaced by indeterminate sentences, the length of which was to be decided in the course of their application in accordance with the needs of treatment; (c) that, if the idea of replacing the concept of guilt by that of dangerousness is to be taken seriously, measures of security and reform should be applied not only to those who have already committed crime, but also preventively to those whose dangerous state (*état dangereux*) makes it likely that they will do so in future (predelinquents). This—one of the most controversial points in the positive programme—would imply the abandonment of the fundamental principle of the criminal law: no punishment without crime, which would be justified, however, in the eyes of the positivists because of the sharp distinction which they made between the moralizing idea of punishment and morally neutral measures of security and reform. In doing so they initiated the long and drawn-out legislative struggle between the compromising double-track system, which tried to keep penalties and measures of security and reforms side by side (e.g. the previous system of preventive detention in the Prevention of Crime Act, 1908), and the more extreme single-track system, which combines both in a uniform sentence (e.g. the new system of preventive detention and corrective training in the Criminal Justice Act, 1948).[49]

Altogether, notwithstanding certain deep-seated differences between individual members of the positivist school,[50] the main outlines of their programme were distinct enough to enable them to exercise a profound practical influence on the criminological and legislative thought of the late nineteenth and early twentieth centuries. Naturally, a criminological theory based upon the idea of a born criminal, of the strength of hereditary biological factors in crime, is bound to be of a pessimistic, negative character as there seems to be very little that can be constructively done to improve these factors, except perhaps through far-reaching eugenic measures. Nevertheless, Lombroso, especially in his later writings, and his friends tried very hard to devise a system of constructive, in particular preventive, measures. To give a few illustrations: Lombroso's very detailed discussion of the alleged dangers of education, especially in penal institutions,[51] bears no doubt a heavy responsibility for the very slow progress of the educational system in prisons, but in spite of all his misgivings Lombroso was most anxious to explain that he was not against education as such. Whilst 'schools in prison' should be suppressed as only serving to multiply recidivism, children in elementary schools found to exhibit the stigmata of the born criminal should be segregated and given some special training designed to strengthen the inhibitory factors and suppress criminal tendencies. Penalties for children should be milder, and imprisonment should not be used for them. Adult offenders should be isolated in cellular prisons and treated under a graded system (Lombroso favoured the Irish system of Sir Walter Crofton). Deportation should be used for criminals by passion; probation he regarded as the best preventive measure for minor and occasional offenders. On the other hand, adult born criminals should be kept in perpetual confinement already for their first crime, if serious, and so should also be recidivists, although they should be subjected to less severe discipline. For incorrigibles special penal institutions and agricultural colonies should be established where they could live under a comparatively relaxed regime, only exceptionally in cellular confinement, but in strict isolation from the outside world. As already indicated, this opened the way to the subsequent building up of non-punitive preventive detention. The death penalty was to be retained—here Lombroso and Garofalo differed from Ferri—but limited to the most hopeless cases of incorrigibility.

In conclusion, it may be said that the ideas of the positive school contain a mixture of truth and falsehood, of progress and deviation, a fact which fully explains the heat of the controversies to which they have given rise. That an up-to-date scientific discipline has to make full use of the methods of factual observation and experimentation and that they should be applied to the study of the individual criminal is incontestably true. There is no reason, however, why such methods should not equally be applied to the less personal aspects of crime in society, and the positivists, though with less originality, did try to include this, too, in their programme. In both fields, however, their scientific tools were not equal to the task. Moreover, while a purely moralizing view of crime is incompatible with the insights of modern criminology and penology, the complete rejection of moral considerations in the interpretation of crime and the treatment of criminals, as favoured by some positivists, went far beyond the limits of what could be tolerated by public opinion (see also Chapter 2 above). The same is true of the slogan that only the criminal, not the kind and gravity of crime committed should be taken into consideration. Some of their most important practical recommendations, such as the use of entirely indeterminate sentences and the replacement of punishment by measures of security and reform, while following logically from their theoretical promises, have had to be watered down by the legislation of most countries to make them generally acceptable.

# Chapter 13

## POST-LOMBROSIAN DEVELOPMENTS. HEREDITY. TWINS AND GLANDS. THE CRIMINO-BIOLOGICAL SCHOOL

### I. POST-LOMBROSIAN DEVELOPMENTS

In the history of criminology there is hardly any chapter more fascinating and thought-provoking than the twentieth-century developments following the death of Lombroso. As already indicated, the influence of his ideas was very different in different countries.[1] Strongest in Italy and South America, weaker in France and Spain, almost completely absent in Russia. In Germany and Austria, after a great deal of original opposition there was a revival, whereas a different historical process took place somewhat later in the United States.[2] In England the two opposing trends are best represented by Havelock Ellis as leader of the pro-Lombrosian party, Charles Goring as his opponent, with Henry Maudsley standing in the middle. Ellis, while not pretending to produce any original material on the subject, made a conscientious and painstaking attempt 'to present to the English reader a critical summary of the results of the science now commonly called criminal anthropology'. In this he was highly successful. By no means uncritical, he opposed Lombroso's use of the concept of atavism; he stressed that there was no uniform 'school' of criminal anthropology and no real type of born criminal, preferring the phrase 'moral insensibility' of the instinctive and habitual criminal.[3] Much of his material is anecdotal and naïve, but he possessed a fairly comprehensive knowledge of the contemporary literature and presented it well. He protests against the accusatorial Anglo-American system of criminal procedure, which heralds 'the barbaric notion of the duel', and asks that on questions of insanity at least two experts should be heard, appointed by the judge. He adopts Ferri's concept of 'social reaction' in the place of punishment and calls for social reforms instead of mere repression, for education 'in the true sense' and for sterilization of the unfit. Like Ellis, Henry Maudsley (1835–1918), the great psychiatrist, was also strongly influenced by the idea of moral insanity as developed earlier in the nineteenth century by James C. Prichard and others.[4] Without completely subscribing to Lombroso's theories he believed in the existence of individuals who, because of congenital or acquired characteristics, are entirely lacking in the capacity for moral feeling and for comprehending moral ideas. This condition, however, was not, as Lombroso thought, a morbid entity, a distinct disease, but could arise from a variety of causes. Crime and madness were both 'antisocial products of degeneracy', but crime, he wrote later, was not necessarily a symptom of degeneracy. Similarly to Lombroso, however, he linked epilepsy with physical stigmata of degeneration and with crime.[5]

It is interesting to observe that in spite of many differences in criminological outlook the practical reform programmes of Ellis, Maudsley and Goring bear a striking similarity. All three pin their faith in the triad of better education in the moral sense, segregation of the dangerous criminals, and, at least Ellis and Goring, sterilization of the unfit.

Passing now to Charles B. Goring (1870–1919), he was a solitary figure, belonging to no criminological 'school', but devoting his considerable gifts and energies to the one object of testing and refuting the claims made by Lombroso and his followers. A prison medical officer, a physician with an exceptional mastery of statistical and biometrical techniques, he was appointed by the English Prison Commissioners in 1902 to continue and complete the work begun shortly before by his colleague Dr. Griffiths in Parkhurst Prison. He enjoyed the full support of the Government and the advice of Karl Pearson and his staff at University College, London. The resulting book *The English Convict*,[6] remained, with only a few exceptions, practically unchallenged as the refutation of Lombroso for a quarter of a century until strongly attacked by Hooton in 1939. It was based upon a painstaking biometric examination of 3,000 English convicts. Those measurements were compared internally, i.e. by contrasting the data for different offences, and externally—with a motley group of controls: Oxford and Cambridge undergraduates, inmates of a General Hospital, Royal Engineers, etc. He started with the idea that there existed in every person what he called a 'criminal diathesis', a 'hypothetical character of some kind, a constitutional proclivity', an 'inward potentiality' to commit crime, which if Lombroso's theories were correct, should differ according to physical type. He did find certain physical differences, which were partly related to the type of crime committed—thieves and burglars were smaller in stature than other offenders and also than members of his control groups—and partly to the social class to which the offenders belonged. Accordingly, he arranged his material in four social and seven occupational classes. Among his final conclusions are the following: 'When a sample of criminals and a sample of non-criminals are similarly constructed with regard to the proportional numbers of professional men, shop-keepers, labourers, artisans, etc., . . . criminals, on the average, are seen to be 1·7 inches less in stature than the law-abiding population', and a similar inferiority was shown in body weight. In addition, he found criminals, with the possible exception of those convicted of certain kinds of fraud, to be markedly inferior in intelligence: 'In every class and occupation of life it is feeble mind and the inferior forms of physique which tend to be selected for a criminal career' (p. 261). The following dictum has become rather famous, however: 'From a knowledge only of an undergraduate's cephalic measurements, a better judgment could be given as to whether he were studying at an English or Scottish university than a prediction could be made as to whether he would eventually become a university professor or a convicted felon' (p. 145). Although he found insanity and epilepsy to be more frequent in prison than outside the difference was hardly sufficient to support Lombroso's claims. In the controversy 'heredity or environment', however, he was on Lombroso's side, and perhaps even more than the latter he was inclined to underrate environmental influences: 'Crime is only to a trifling extent (if to any) the product of social inequalities, of adverse environment or of other manifestations of . . . the force of circumstances' (p. 371). To support this theory, he uses, among others, the following strange argument: 'The earlier a child commits a criminal offence and is consequently removed from his home, the more a criminal does he become; and, accordingly, we conclude that criminal proclivities are more bred in the home than inoculated there' (p. 368). Apart from the concept of the criminal type, there were indeed many similarities between Goring and the anthropological school against which he fought.

Hooton, notwithstanding his profound admiration for Goring's 'statistical genius', accused him of a strong preconceived emotional bias against Lombroso's work and even of twisting the results of his investigation to make them conform to his bias. Among other grounds for criticism are the unrepresentative nature of Goring's control groups, the reliance upon insignificantly small coefficients of correlation to prove his points, his crude technique of measuring intelligence, his failure to divide his English convicts according to their social origins. According to Hooton Goring left the problem of the physique of the criminal unsolved.

## II. HERIDITY. THE 'CRIMINAL FAMILIES'. TWIN RESEARCH. GLANDS.

### (a) Heredity and the Criminal Families

Before continuing our historical sketch of the aftermath of Lombrosianism it seems advisable to deal more specifically with what was, after all, one of its main features: the part played by heredity in the causation of crime. It was the period around the turn of the century when this question was most heatedly discussed. Lombroso himself devoted to it a chapter of his *Crime: its Causes and Remedies*, in which he presented a collection of vague and questionable statistical data purporting to show the frequency of crime, alcoholism, physical illnesses, insanity, suicide and other undesirable features among the ancestors of criminals. American nineteenth-century literature betrays, according to Fink,[7] a strong belief in the inheritance of crime, but disagreement as to what exactly it is that is inherited and how the transmission takes place: is it crime itself or merely a propensity, a predisposition to it? The latter view prevailed and received strong support eventually through the work of William Healy. Strangely enough, it was in the long run also supported by the publication of several books on the so-called 'criminal families'. The first of them, Richard Dugdale's *The Jukes* (1877),[8] the study of a family with a striking number of criminal or otherwise socially deviant members, has often been misinterpreted as if purporting to prove the hereditarian theory. Actually, as pointed out by Fink, Dugdale was anxious to stress the tentative nature of this work and to do justice to both hereditary and environmental influences. Much later, in 1912, two similar studies of criminal pedigrees were published in the U.S.A.: *The Nam Family* by Estabrook and Davenport and Henry H. Goddard's *The Kallikaks*, and Estabrook also published in 1916 a further follow-up study of the Jukes. They were, however, studies of the heredity of feeble-mindedness rather than of crime, and Goddard in particular queried the direct inheritance of criminal tendencies.[9] Family histories of this type are not convincing evidence because the families selected are entirely unrepresentative and because the material collected is incomplete and not tested in accordance with modern scientific methods. At the crucial time when the founders of these families lived, reliable information on their biological constitution was not available, and the research done at some later period could not satisfactorily fill the original gaps. It is therefore mere guesswork to maintain, as Exner does in spite of his critical attitude towards these researches, that the accumulation of criminality in those families was much too long to be explainable by

229

environmental influence alone.[10] Exner agrees, however, that research into the question of heredity can successfully be done not by singling out individual family pedigrees, but only by the collection of statistical material on large numbers of cases. He quotes several German and Austrian investigations of this kind on the frequency of insanity, psychopathy, drunkenness, and criminality among the parents and other relatives of criminals, which show especially for criminality very high percentage figures for the parents of recidivists. Here again, Exner rightly stresses that such figures alone cannot prove the strength of hereditary factors as the children of criminals are, as a rule, naturally exposed to very unfavourable environmental influences. He also quotes, however, an investigation by Kuttner into the criminality of several hundred children and stepchildren of Bavarian preventive detainees which shows that approximately 50 per cent of these children had been convicted whereas the corresponding figures for the stepchildren were much lower. Exner regards this difference as proving the strength of heredity against environment. This conclusion would be justified only if it would be shown that the stepchildren had been under the influence of their stepfathers for as long as the own children of these detainees; moreover, the frequent antagonism between stepfathers and stepchildren will often militate against a willing acceptance by the latter of the criminal habits of the stepfathers and identification with them.

In England, research into the problem of hereditary criminal tendencies has used statistics rather than selected pedigrees. Cyril Burt[11] found major or minor unfavourable congenital factors more than three times as often recorded among delinquent children than among the controls, and in between one third and rather less than one half of the delinquents some 'deep constitutional failing' seemed to be the primary source of the misconduct. Of the hereditary conditions which he lists most are either physical or 'temperamental (with moral symptoms)', fewer are intellectual. His conclusion is that, while the share of innate conditions in the causation of juvenile delinquency is considerable, it would be a gross distortion to regard every criminal as the helpless victim of his inborn nature—a distortion, we may add, which is nowadays hardly ever encountered among responsible writers.

In the next large-scale English study, East's *Adolescent Criminal*, no attempt was made to determine the relative share of endogenous and external factors, but some figures are given to show the connection between inherited and familial defects and the offences committed. A criminal history of the father was recorded in 9 per 1,000 and of the mother in 3 per 1,000 of the Borstal lads, and from both sides in 1·5 per 1,000, and a family history of sexual immorality, epilepsy and insanity in somewhat higher proportions, but there is no material on the question of hereditary transmission,[12] and in a later work the same writer states explicitly that neither this research nor his other experiences have given him any reason to regard criminality 'as such' as transmissible.[13]

### (b) Twin Research

Of greater interest than the rather obsolete attempts to trace the pedigrees of criminal families are the more recent researches into the criminal behaviour of twins.[14] Their main value lies in the methodological field. If we compare the life histories of criminals with different hereditary endowment and different environment it will be difficult or even impossible to decide how far their criminal behaviour has been due to the one or to the other. If we should be able, however, to eliminate one set of differences by keeping it constant our task would be easier. If, for example, all hereditary differences could be eliminated it would be clear that any contrasts in the criminal behaviour of the individuals concerned must be due to environmental differences, and, on the other hand, if in spite of such differences their criminal behaviour should be identical then the conclusion would seem inevitable that it is heredity that matters in the causation of crime. Nature, by creating the so-called identical, also called uniovular or monozygotic twins, has apparently provided us with favourable conditions for researches where hereditary differences are eliminated. Whereas dizygotic, also called fraternal, binovular or ordinary, twins come from two separate eggs, which have been simultaneously fertilized, and therefore carry separate sets of genes, monozygotic or identical twins, who are always of the same sex, are born as the result of the splitting of one egg after fertilization and carry the same set of genes. Accordingly, it can be assumed that identical twins have the same hereditary endowment and should provide the ideal material for research into crime causation. It was probably Sir Francis Galton who first recognized that there were two kinds of twins and collected data on a large number, one hundred pairs of twins. In the twentieth century twin research has been done in several countries, including the United States, Soviet Russia, Holland, Japan, Germany[15] and in Britain.[16] While much of it has been unconnected with criminology, there have also been a number of investigations of criminal twins. The first and most widely discussed of them is that by the German psychiatrist Johannes Lange, who examined all male inmates of Bavarian prisons who were twins and also such inmates of the German Psychiatric Institute in Munich who were criminals and twins. Wherever possible, the non-institutionalized

231

twin was traced and physically and mentally examined. In this way, he obtained information on 30 pairs of twins. Of them, 13 pairs were monozygotic, and in 10 of these cases the other twin had also been in prison (which is called 'concordant behaviour'), whereas of the 17 dizygotic pairs the other twin had been imprisoned in only 2 cases. From these figures and from the whole life histories of these twins Lange concluded that, as far as crime is concerned, monozygotic twins on the whole react in a similar manner, whereas dizygotic ones often behave differently ('discordant'), although their upbringing and environment had been just as much alike as those of the monozygotic twins. It is surprising how widely these findings, especially in the years following publication, were accepted as convincing proof of the hereditary nature of crime. Eventually, however, the critical voices have prevailed. Among the objections brought forward against Lange are the following: First, the number of his cases was too small for sweeping generalizations; secondly, some of the cases were taken from a psychiatric clinic, presumably showing some mental abnormality, and their criminal behaviour might therefore have been determined more by this abnormality than by heredity; thirdly, most of the identical twins had been brought up in the same environment, which makes it impossible to say with any certainty how far they had both been likewise affected by this environment and also by each other; thus all the more because of their exceptional likeness in appearance the environmental responses to which they are subjected are probably much more similar than in the case of ordinary twins, who can easily be distinguished;[17] fourthly, the similarities in the behaviour of identical twins observed by Lange are often not at all impressive and could easily occur without the existence of identical heredity—especially as Lange took only imprisonment, not criminality as such, as his criterion; fifthly, in view of the difficulties, pointed out by some biologists, of diagnosing identity in twins,[18] Lange's diagnosis, too, may occasionally have been wrong; sixthly, important congenital differences have been reported even in identical twins, for example congenital syphilis is one of them,[19] which shatters the fundamental assumption of equal heredity; seventhly, it has been argued, for example by Reckless, that if heredity were really the determining factor discordant identical twins should be impossible, whereas Lange's figures showed their existence in three out of thirteen cases.

While later investigations, especially the American one/by Rosanoff, have considerably added to the size of Lange's case material and made certain improvements in his methods, some of the criticisms listed above have remained. Ashley Montagu[20] summarizes the five best-known studies as showing together among the identical twins

67·3 per cent concordant and 32·7 per cent discordant behaviour, among the fraternal twins 33·0 per cent concordant and 67·0 per cent discordant behaviour, in other words a considerable minority of discordant cases even among the identical ones. Stumpfl[21] criticizes the superficial way in which Lange dealt with his dizygotic cases and his method of finding concordant behaviour among monozygotic twins in cases where it hardly existed. He estimates that there is discordant behaviour in the latter in 37·40 per cent and in the former in 54·59 per cent, a difference which is far from impressive. He himself tries to give more precise definitions of the concept concordant behaviour by distinguishing degrees of it according to the degree of similarity of criminal activities and in other respects. He stresses that concordant behaviour in identical twins is largely limited to serious criminals with hereditary psychopathic tendencies. For them, he thinks, the hereditary factor is decisive, whereas environmental influences are material only for less serious criminals.[22]

In an investigation of 8 pairs of monozygotic and 16 pairs of dizygotic twins, it was found that only one twin of each pair of monozygotics had committed suicide and that the behaviour of the dizygotics had also been discordant in this respect. It was concluded that suicide could not be simply explained by a certain type of genetic constitution and personality.[23] On the other hand, Kallmann claims not to have found in his researches a single pair of monozygotic twins, reared together or apart, who did not exhibit the same kind of homosexuality, whereas in dizygotics the situation was quite different.[24]

Of an entirely different character is the investigation into behavioural differences of brothers made at the same time by William Healy and Augusta Bronner.[25] Among their material was no pair of identical twins, and the differences in the behaviour of the children from the same families whom they studied—including several pairs of fraternal twins—are entirely traced back to inner stresses in their parental relations from which the delinquent, not however the control cases, suffered. They dismiss Lange's material as proving merely the identical behaviour of mentally abnormal, not of criminal, personalities.

An important contribution to criminological twin research has been made in Japan, where Shûfu Yoshimasu, Professor of Criminal Psychology and Forensic Psychiatry in Tokyo, has published the results of his follow-up studies between 1941 and 1961 of 28 uniovular and 18 binovular pairs.[26] He, too, found far more concordant criminal behaviour in the former than in the latter sample, but it is interesting to note that up to the end of the last war the concordance rates of both groups were much lower than found elsewhere, only 50 per cent for uniovular and 0 per cent for binovular twins. After the war, however, the rates went up to 60·6 per cent and 11·1 per cent respectively, an increase which Yoshimasu relates to the general post-war increase in crime in Japan: if the crime rate for the whole population greatly increases, the likelihood that there will be more crime and therefore concordant criminal behaviour among twins will also increase. Of the other results of this study the observation may be mentioned that most of the criminals among the discordant uniovular twins were first offenders and late starters, whereas almost all the concordant uniovulars committed a crime before the age of 25 and repeated it many times. The author also presents two case histories of uniovular twins separated and brought up in different families soon after birth—thus constituting what he calls, not without justi-fication, the most interesting problem in criminology. In one of these cases the author concludes that both twins, though reared in different families from birth, had 'in the long run the same outcome in criminal career'; one might point out, however, that these twins went to the same elementary school. In the other case, the contrast in social behaviour was profound and could be explained only 'through the striking difference of their environments from the time of birth'. There were also differences in basic personality traits and in health, although both suffered from pulmonary tuberculosis, an illness from which their mother had died when they were 14 years of age. In short, inconclusive as these two case histories are they have the great merit of underlining the immense variety of factors which come together to produce the life history of an individual, a variety which makes the factor 'uni- or bi-ovular' birth almost insignificant as com-pared with the sum total of all the other happenings in human life.

In conclusion it may be said that the view prevailing thirty years ago in many quarters of the convincing nature of the evidence in favour of heredity produced by the twin researchers has been re-placed by sober criticism of their material. They have been able to present only very few cases where, owing to very early separation, environmental influences on identical twins have been so different as to be safely ignored. In fact, most of the twin researchers, notably Lange himself (in spite of the sensational title of his book), and Rosanoff, have frankly admitted that the question 'heredity or en-vironment' is misleading because it over-simplifies a very complex problem. After presenting a model investigation of one pair of iden-tical twins with different life histories Dr. Wheelan concludes by emphasizing 'the difficulties of drawing unequivocal conclusions from twin research'.[27] We are again thrown back to our original question: what is it that can be inherited? Crime as such, it is clear, being not a biological but a legal and social phenomenon, cannot be trans-mitted by heredity, but can character? 'Environment', writes Martin

Turnell in a reference to Stendhal's *Le Rouge et le Noir*,[28] 'does not determine a man's character, but it does determine his fate.' On the other hand, 'characters are not and cannot be inherited in the sense in which inheritance is used by the geneticist,' says Julian Huxley, 'what are inherited are genes, factors, genetic outfit. Any character whatsoever can only be a resultant between genes and environment . . . the old question whether nature or nurture is the more important is meaningless . . .'[29] This being so, it is hardly surprising that Exner, who among modern textbook-writers has paid particular attention to these problems, concludes his discussion with the not very startling statement that there are individuals who become criminals because of their environment and others who do so because of their heredity.[30] Even less enlightening is the treatment of the matter by Olof Kinberg who, in his *Basic Principles of Criminology*, while maintaining that much knowledge has been accumulated on the way that predispositions are transmitted fails to give any further information.[31] Kretschmer stresses the highly complicated ways in which temperamental traits are transmitted from ancestors to descendants.

The practical significance of the whole controversy lies only in part in the differences in treatment proposed by the followers of the opposing camps. It is clear that the environmentalists will put their faith more in the manipulation of the living conditions of the potential or actual criminal, while the believers in hereditary transmission will recommend eugenic programmes. Perhaps more important than this are the dangers of a fatalistic attitude so easily assumed by members of the public who are always ready to regard an offender as incorrigible because 'it is in his blood'.

## (c) *Endocrinology*

Almost simultaneously with Lange's *Crime as Destiny* a book was published in the United States which partly supported and partly contested Lombroso's theories: *The New Criminology* by Schlapp and Smith.[32] In this highly controversial publication it was claimed that individuals suffering from endocrine disturbances were the typical born criminals 'with their destiny largely determined'. It is interesting that the authors used this theory in order to explain what was at that time regarded as an indisputable fact, i.e. the particularly high crime rate among the first American born generation of foreign immigrants: they believed to have found the cause in glandular disturbances of the mothers who, on their voyage and after arrival in the foreign country, had to undergo a period of great physical and mental strain coupled with economic worries and transmitted the resulting glandular imbalance to their next-born children. The difference between this theory and that of Lombroso is that, while emphasizing the overwhelming importance of the inheritance of physical, especially endocrinological factors in the causation of crime, these authors did not regard hereditary endowment as unchangeable. The same immigrant mother might a few years later, with improved living conditions, give birth to a healthy child. This theory offers, therefore, a convenient explanation of the fact that so often only one child of a family becomes a criminal. Moreover, while Lombroso had no medical cure for unfavourable hereditary factors the endocrinologists regard a cure as possible, although some of them are more optimistic than others. Many cases of endocrine disturbances are not due to inheritance at all.[33] Apart from the special case of certain sex offenders, the prevailing view explains the possible connection between glandular imbalance and criminal conduct as an indirect, psychological, one in that the feeling of abnormality and inadequacy caused by disorders of the pituitary or other glands may give rise to aggressiveness and other compensatory emotional reactions leading to crime.[34] Especially in cases of sex offenders hormone treatment is sometimes believed to be successful. In this country it has been cautiously advocated, mainly by Golla and Hodge.[35]

### III. THE MODERN CRIMINO-BIOLOGICAL SCHOOL

This school originated in the nineteen-twenties in Germany, Austria and Italy. Its scientific value has at times greatly suffered from the exaggerated claims made on its behalf by the totalitarian regimes at the time in power in these countries. Its leading ideas and literature can best be studied in the writings of one of its most prominent legal exponents, Eduard Mezger,[36] and of the famous German psychiatrist Ernst Kretschmer. It is the latter in particular who has done the fundamental typological spadework on which the whole structure of that school has been erected. In his book *Körperbau and Charakter* which, slowly expanded over a period of more than thirty years and running into more than twenty editions, has become one of the international classics of psychiatry, he did not at the outset deal with criminological problems, and in the English translation of 1936 there is only one insignificant reference to criminals.[37] In contrast, the most recent German editions contain a full-sized chapter on 'constitution and crime'.[38] Kretschmer's original object was to examine the complex relationships between the various types of physique, character and mental abnormality. He distinguished three major constitutional types which, as he stressed, were not 'ideal types' but empirical ones:

(*a*) the *leptosome* or *asthenic* type, characterized by long and thin limbs, narrow shoulders, lean arms with under-developed muscles and by a tendency to premature ageing. 'In extreme cases,' Kretschmer writes, 'I found men of between 35 and 40 years already quite senile.' While the term leptosome is used for the whole range covered by this type, the term asthenic is reserved for the more extreme cases approaching the morbid. Leptosomes are frigid, reserved, unsociable and cold.

(b) the *athletic* type, roughly the opposite of the first, with strongly developed skeleton and musculature. To describe their temperament, Kretschmer uses the term '*viscös*', which he defines as stable, heavy, not nervous, but occasionally explosive.[39]

(c) the *pyknic* type, small and round, with a pronounced development of the body cavities and a tendency to a distribution of fat around the trunk. They are friendly and sociable.

Mixed types he regarded as very frequent.

In addition, he established a number of so-called 'dysplastic' special types, the members of which differed greatly from any of the three main types and were characterized in particular by certain glandular disturbances.[40]

In working out this typology, which is here only very roughly reproduced, Kretschmer tried to take account of every single feature of the biological personality instead of limiting himself to a comparatively few selected characteristics. He stressed that his three main types were meant to be '*wertfrei*', i.e. neither 'normal' nor 'abnormal' in the usual sense, but normal in that they referred to the most frequently met anthropological phenomena and abnormal in that they reflected certain dispositions towards potential pathological conditions.[41] His next step was to see whether there was a clear relation between these constitutional types and specific forms of mental disease or at least dispositions towards them. His answer was in the affirmative, i.e. he found a strong positive correlation, a biological affinity between leptosomes, athletics and certain dysplastics, on the one hand, and schizophrenia on the other, and also between the pyknic type and manic-depressive, circular forms of insanity. There was very little affinity between the pyknic type and schizophrenia or between the leptosomes and athletics and manic-depressive insanity.[42] Kretschmer quotes statistical material for several thousand cases to prove these correlations, which have by now been commonly accepted.

The scope of Kretschmer's theory is however not limited to the relation between biological constitution and the various forms of mental illness. As already indicated, he regards the two forms of psychosis with which he is mainly concerned only as extreme forms of psychological dispositions, traces of which can also be found in normal individuals. The great masses of normal human beings constitute reservoirs from which these two forms of psychosis are recruited. He calls the members of that large constitutional class who, *if* they should ever become insane, are most likely to develop schizophrenia *schizothymes* and those normal people who, *if* they should become insane, are likely to become manic-depressive *cyclothymes*.[43] And, finally, there is a third pair of types, the *schizoids* and the *cycloids*, consisting of individuals who stand between health and sickness and exhibit the psychological symptoms of the corresponding abnormal types to a slighter degree.[44] Kretschmer offers a wealth of psychological observations and some case material to characterize these two intermediate types. They are sometimes related to the Jungian typology as the schizoids are extreme introverts and the cycloids extreme extraverts.[45]

The final task is now to relate these Kretschmerian types to different forms of criminality. On this, a considerable literature has grown up, mainly in the Continental countries primarily devoted to Kretschmer's typology and the ideas of the crimino-biological school,[46] and Kretschmer himself has now dealt with the matter fairly fully on the basis of material derived from 4,414 cases. He stresses from the outset that the kind and gravity of social failure are no necessary indication of the abnormality of personality structure, which latter has to be measured according to entirely different yardsticks, such as physical constitution and heredity. He also points out that a person may be a serious psychopath 'in the sociological sense' without possessing a seriously morbid constitution and heredity. Legal concepts such as 'murderer' cannot be taken as the starting point for the formation of constitutional and hereditary typology; they cannot show any specific physical characteristics. All we can say in this respect is that certain groups of serious habitual criminals show the signs of serious hereditary degeneration and a higher proportion of dysplastics than the normal population. These dysplastic abnormalities of criminals are, however, not exclusively peculiar to them, but can also be found in mental defectives and serious hereditary illnesses. This higher proportion of dysplastic abnormalities is not to be found among criminals in general, but only among serious habituals—a fact which Kretschmer thinks is difficult to reconcile with Lombroso's doctrine of the accumulation of physical stigmata. Here Kretschmer seems to forget that Lombroso, too, restricted his theory of the stigmata to one type, the born criminal.

The most important points in Kretschmer's system of criminal biology are these: On the whole, criminals show roughly the same proportional distribution of constitutional types as the general population, i.e. approximately 20 per cent pyknics, 40–50 per cent leptosomes and athletics, 5–10 per cent dysplastics, and less than

30 per cent mixed types, except that there are somewhat fewer pyknics among criminals than among the whole population. Pyknics are socially better adaptable, their criminality begins later, and they recidivate much less than the other types. The 'life curve' of criminality of leptosomes has its peak very early, that of pyknics has it very late, between 40 and 50, when that of the leptosomes is already very low. Athletics show a fairly stable degree of criminality up to the age of 55. Regarding the offences committed by members of the different types, the leptosomes are very strongly represented among thieves and swindlers, athletics among offences against the person, sexual and others. Pyknics tend to commit frauds, dysplastics commit sexual offences. Throughout it has to be borne in mind, however, that even if members of different constitutional types commit crimes of the same legal classification, for example murder, the criminological characteristics of that crime would be entirely different in accordance with their different biological and temperamental features.[47] Mezger, while quoting further material in support of Kretschmer's theory, points out[48] that the claims of the crimino-biological school are much more modest than those of Lombroso: one does no longer pretend to be able to predict whether an individual will become a criminal, but only which forms his criminal activities are likely to assume *if* he should become one. The latter question can, he admits, often not be answered on the |strength of the individual's biological constitution regardless of environmental factors. Even with such reservations, however, it can hardly be denied that the work of the Continental boards of crimino-biological investigation, established in the nineteen-twenties in order to draw the practical conclusions from the theoretical studies of this school, placed the emphasis mainly on the biological aspects of crime.[49] The same was true of the Crimino-Biological Society, founded in 1927 by Adolf Lenz in Graz, whose work has, however, in recent years been placed on a more comprehensive basis.[50] One of the most important criticisms voiced against the work of the boards and of the Society was that the theory of the likely incorrigibility of offenders of the leptosome and athletic types was insufficiently supported by the available scientific facts and could easily lead to a sterile and reactionary system of penal administration,[51] a danger which became soon reality under the Nazi regime.

While the crimino-biological school had practically no following in Britain, its ideas aroused much interest in the United States. It is doubtful, though, how far Earnest Hooton[52] was influenced by them as his published work shows no awareness of post-Goring developments. His major opus, *The American Criminal*, of which he could complete only the first volume, has been so widely criticized that it is hardly worth while to summarize it.[53] His principal findings were that criminals were biologically inferior and that their inferiority was largely hereditary.

Far more influential have been the writings of William H. Sheldon, especially his *Varieties of Delinquent Youth*,[54] whose classification and technique of somatotyping have been accepted, among others, by the Gluecks (see below). There exists a clear connection between Sheldon and Kretschmer, the former acknowledging a certain indebtedness to Kretschmer, whose work he studied on the spot, and the latter referring repeatedly and approvingly to Sheldon's typology—if it can be called a typology at all—which, he thinks, has reached essentially similar results from a different methodological angle.[55] Sheldon's main criticism of Kretschmer is that the latter was satisfied with mere verbal descriptions of his somatotypes and disliked the idea of making his descriptions more exact by quantification.

Sheldon's very complicated terminology[56] differs from that of Kretschmer. Instead of leptosomes he speaks of ectomorphs, instead of athletics of mesomorphs, and instead of pyknics of endomorphs. Their physical characteristics are, however, essentially the same as those described by Kretschmer. He uses a statistical technique which enables him to describe the constitution of an individual by using a 3-digit number indicating the strength of each of those three components, with 1 as the minimum and 7 as the maximum. An extreme mesomorph, for example, would be described as 1–7–1, an extreme ectomorph as 1–1–7. The term dysplastic is used differently from Kretschmer to describe disharmonious mixtures of the three components in different parts of the body. Sheldon used his classification for a minute morphological description of two hundred delinquent boys from the Hayden Goodwill Inn, a rehabilitation home in Boston. They showed a preponderance of mesomorphs and very few ectomorphs, with the endomorph type standing between. A previously collected group of 4,000 college boys showed a more balanced distribution between mesomorphs and ectomorphs. Sheldon tries, as Kretschmer did, to relate his somatotypes to temperamental and psychiatric types, for which relationships he has coined several odd-sounding terms. This part of his investigation, too, shows results very similar to those of Kretschmer. His work has been widely criticized, most vehemently by Sutherland who regards it as useless.[57] His technique of somatotyping has, however, been widely accepted by research workers of various disciplines. Especially his careful collection of standardized photographs of each subject in his series has been useful, and he himself described the omission of this technique in Hooton's study as 'criminal' since no measurements and verbal descriptions of physical types could be a substitute for photographs.[58] As far as criminological research is concerned, his influence has been mainly indirect, through the adoption of his basic ideas and typology by the Gluecks.

The Gluecks had made use of Sheldon's somatotypes already in their *Unraveling Juvenile Delinquency*, when each boy in their series was photographed in accordance with Sheldon's technique.[59] Appendix C of that book consists of a very detailed study by a physical anthropologist, Dr. Carl C. Seltzer, of the morphological characteristics of the 500 delinquents and the 500 non-delinquents in the series, showing—as in Sheldon's own work—an excess of mesomorphs and a deficiency of ectomorphs and extreme endomorphs among the delinquents. These findings provide the starting point for the subsequent study *Physique and Delinquency*,[60] not, as the authors are careful to point out, because of any belief in the preponderant criminogenic role of the bodily structure, but only as one of several studies to follow up the results of *Unraveling*. One of these findings was that 60 per cent of the delinquent boys were mesomorphs against only 30 per cent in the control group. It was, however, an isolated discovery not related to the other findings regarding the two groups. An attempt was therefore made in the second study to search for certain syndromes by correlating various other factors to Sheldon's somatotypes. Correlations were worked out between the latter and a selection of sixty-seven traits and forty-two socio-cultural factors to compare the delinquent and non-delinquent groups. The technique used is to show, first, the statistical significance of a trait or factor in the total group of delinquents as compared with the total group of non-delinquents and, secondly, the same for each somatotype separately. The object was to see which trait or factor had a stronger or weaker influence on the delinquency of one somatotype than on that of another. The results are very complicated and not always revealing. Only a minority of the traits and factors thus examined were found to vary in their relationships to the different somatotypes. To give but one example of difference in these relationships, the factors 'broken home' and 'incompatibility of parents' were found to distinguish more sharply between delinquents and non-delinquents of the sensitive ectomorph type than in the other somatotypes. In the view of the authors, the material thus collected seems to explain the higher delinquency potential of the mesomorphs and also which particular traits or factors are likely to make them actual delinquents. On the other hand, unfavourable socio-cultural factors seem to produce delinquency in mesomorphs less often than they do in the other somatotypes. The final conclusion is, however, that there is no specific combination of physique, character and temperament to be found which would determine whether an individual becomes a delinquent.

PSYCHOLOGICAL AND PSYCHIATRIC
ASPECTS OF CRIME

# Chapter 14

## MENTAL DISORDERS I: PSYCHOSES, ALCOHOLISM AND DRUG ADDICTION

When dealing with the psychological and psychiatric aspects of crime it seems advisable to take a course which may seem contrary to common sense and natural expectation, i.e. to begin with the psychiatric, pathological part of the subject and to leave the psychology of the normal lawbreaker to the end. Our justification lies in the regrettable fact that the concept of mental health is so very difficult to define[1] and that it is therefore largely limited to what remains after deducting all those cases where mental ill health is generally assumed. This, as should be stressed already now, does not mean that we regard the pathological section of offenders as numerically stronger than the normal one—the opposite is true. Within the field of the pathological, we shall also deal first with the most seriously abnormal group, that of the psychotics, and proceed from there via the less extreme groups of neurotics and psychopaths to the mental defectives, of whom there are many classes of varying degree of abnormality. This procedure is, of course, again the reverse of the statistical picture since cases of psychosis are very rare among the general population as well as among criminals, whilst neuroses and psychopathic states are more frequent and the great majority of criminals can be regarded as mentally normal.

Our presentation of the subject, which has to be made from the point of view of the interested and, to some extent, informed psychiatric layman, has to overcome certain formidable obstacles arising from the existing lack of a generally accepted terminology and from the innumerable controversies encountered in present psychiatric literature.[2] The Royal Commission on the Law relating to Mental Illness and Mental Deficiency 1954–7, which reported in 1957,[3] and, following its recommendations, the Mental Health Act, 1959, s. 4, have tried to bring order into the existing confusion. The Act, avoiding the discredited word 'insanity', introduces the general term 'mental disorder' to cover 'mental illness, arrested or incomplete development of mind, psychopathic disorder, and any other disorder or disability of mind'. It is clear from the Act and, in particular, from the report of the Royal Commission that the term 'mental illness' is here used in a much narrower sense than 'mental disorder' and that it is largely confined to the various forms of psychosis. It is further clear that the Act upholds the previous distinction between insanity and mental deficiency by defining the latter as a state of 'arrested or incomplete development of mind', whereas it is the characteristic of mental illness (insanity or psychosis) that it occurs in persons 'whose minds have previously functioned normally and have become affected by some disorder, usually in adult life'.[4] It goes without saying that a mentally defective person may also develop a form of mental illness.

We have now to give a brief survey of the various forms of *mental illness* in relation to crime. The classification used is in all essentials similar to that in the well-known psychiatric standard works,[5] but the reader has to bear in mind that there is frequent disagreement between psychiatrists with regard to the details. The essential feature of this classification is the distinction between those forms of psychosis which are of an organic origin and those which are functional, i.e. not due to any physical illness.

## I. ORGANIC PSYCHOSES

For our purposes the most important organic psychoses are the general paralysis of the insane (or dementia paralytica), due to syphilitic infection, encephalitis lethargica, traumatic psychoses caused by accidents, the various forms of intoxication and senile dementia.[6]

(a) *The general paralysis of the insane*[7] is characterized by a progressive deterioration of the whole personality. In its initial stages criminal acts such as thefts, frauds, forgeries, may be committed with astonishing openness and silliness. In a case reported by East the accused had carried away some table knives in the presence of several witnesses; in another case he had smashed a window and waited to be arrested. In the later stages of the illness the patient is usually confined in an institution where his opportunities to commit offences are very limited.

In this as in other forms of psychosis the offences are nearly always committed without accomplices as the psychotic is too deeply withdrawn into his own world to wish to enlist, and too abnormal in his behaviour to attract, associates.

(b) *Traumatic psychoses* due to injuries to the brain caused by accidents, may also produce profound personality changes leading to criminality and/or vagabondage and may make the injured person particularly susceptible to the effect of alcohol.[8] The so-called Korsakoff syndrome may be present in such cases.[9] Patients may easily become excited and prone to crimes of violence. The case has been reported[10] of a child of eight who breaks his skull and receives a serious concussion. The consequence was feeble-mindedness coupled with persistent criminal tendencies, but twenty years later another complete change occurs and his behaviour becomes again normal.

(c) A form of organic psychosis which was particularly frequent among children in this country after the First World War is *encephalitis lethargica*, popularly called sleepy sickness.[11] It is an acute infectious fever producing an inflammation of the brain, usually followed by serious and lasting after-effects and changes in physique, intelligence and character. 'The younger the patient the more likely is it that he will develop disagreeable anomalies of personality.... Many children and adolescents after their acute attack become social problems ...' (Mapother and Lewis).[12] Highly anti-social acts, often of an explosive or sexual nature, may easily happen in the post-encephalitic period.

(d) *Senile dementia*[13] is another organic form of mental illness. East[14] and others distinguish between senile and arteriosclerotic dementia, but the difference is not clear and there is said to be an occasional overlap of symptoms. The impairment of the physical and mental faculties, emotional disturbances and the loss of control over sexual urges, coupled with growing suspicion of other people, may provoke acts of violence or sexual assaults on children. The nature of the crimes committed may vary according to whether the dementia takes a depressive, manic or paranoid form.[15] In a case quoted by East a man of sixty-eight killed his wife under the delusion that she had incestuous relation with her son and was pregnant. Silly acts of petty theft may also occur, as in the case of a company director of means and excellent character who stole three eggs from a shop.[16]

(e) While encephalitis lethargica affects the young and senile dementia the old, *puerperal insanity* is the illness of the pregnant and post-pregnant mother. It is a form of exhaustion psychosis occurring in women in a condition of extreme anxiety due, for example, to the birth of an illegitimate child, economic stress plus physical fatigue.[17] English law has a special provision for such cases, the Infanticide Act, 1938, which provides that when a woman by any wilful act or omission causes the death of her child, being a child under the age of twelve months, but at the time of the act or omission the balance of her mind was disturbed by reason of her not having fully recovered from the effect of giving birth to the child, or by reason of the effect of lactation consequent upon the birth of the child, then she is treated as being guilty not of murder but of infanticide and punishable for manslaughter.[18] Apart from child-killing, other offences, such as theft, may also be committed by women suffering from this form of transitory psychosis.

(*f*) *Epilepsy*, one of the most widely known types of mental disorder, is at the same time among the most difficult ones to grasp, not only for the layman but apparently for the specialist, too.[19] Because of the different forms which it can assume many psychiatrists refer to 'epilepsies' rather than to epilepsy. The attention of criminologists was drawn to it mainly by Lombroso who exaggerated its criminological significance by maintaining that all born criminals were epileptics and that among occasional criminals there was at least one class, the epileptoids, in whom a trace of epilepsy was the origin of their criminal tendencies.[20] Actually, reliable estimates of the frequency of epilepsy among criminals are very difficult to obtain, and most of the more recent ones are very low,[21] partly perhaps because of the great difficulties often encountered in the diagnosis of this illness. The electro-encephalogram (E.E.G.) has somewhat reduced, but by no means resolved these difficulties since 'some persons who are clinically known to be epileptic do not show the characteristic E.E.G. abnormality and its absence does not therefore conclusively disprove the absence of epilepsy'. This was the conclusion of the Royal Commission on Capital Punishment, following the evidence of Dr. Denis Hill.[22] The latter has also stressed that abnormal E.E.G.s are found in only 60–70 per cent of epileptics and that, while the E.E.G. is a most valuable diagnostic aid, taken alone it can provide proof of epilepsy in only 15–20 per cent of all cases.[23] If it is often difficult, therefore, to diagnose epilepsy, evidence that a crime is actually caused by it is sometimes also not easy to obtain.[24] It is commonly believed, however, that epileptics are prone to sudden outbreaks of apparently motiveless violence and to develop strongly anti-social attitudes. In fact, the feeling of the epileptic to be at a permanent disadvantage in his employment and in many other ways, which is likely to have a depressing and irritating effect on him, may be responsible.[25] Apart from this, it is mainly the so-called epileptic equivalents, i.e. states of delirium, unconsciousness and epileptic furor, or post-epileptic automatism, in which crimes are committed. In post-epileptic automatism originally harmless actions may be continued, for example cutting sandwiches, which had begun before the fit, but are now carried on in such a way as to injure other persons.[26]

With the ever-increasing volume of motor traffic the epileptic motorist who endangers the life and health of others is becoming a real problem. Not long ago a man aged 39, charged with causing the death of two others by dangerous driving, was found not guilty at Stafford Assizes because since the age of ten he had been suffering from epilepsy and committed the offence in a state of automatism during an attack of *petit mal* with a total loss of reasoning. It was stated on his behalf that he had never been told by his doctors that he was an epileptic and should not drive. All the court could do was to send a request to the licensing authority that his licence should be withdrawn.[27] This ignorance of the nature of his illness had saved him from punishment. In similar cases of traffic accidents reported by Brousseau in his valuable paper on the subject[28] this excuse was not available. Brousseau also draws attention to the grave danger of acts of violence being committed during the periods of a few hours to two or three days preceding the *paroxysme épileptique* with their profound changes in the temper, character and conduct of the patient.

Sleep-walking and the so-called 'blackout' may also be forms of epileptic automatism.[29]

In the much discussed case of Lees-Smith in 1943, hypoglycaemia (abnormally low blood sugar content) was believed to be an important factor in the killing of his mother by an epileptic. Before the act he had taken four pints of mild beer, but was in no state of drunkenness; the same quantity of water would, it was stated, have had the same effect of producing an abnormal state of mind.[30]

In the state of so-called epileptic Fugue patients may become disorientated, wander about aimlessly for long periods and commit minor offences.

(g) *Intoxication psychosis, especially alcoholic disorders.* As morphinism, cocainism and similar forms of intoxication[31] are not very frequent in this country,[32] we are first concentrating on alcoholism.[33] The part played by alcoholic intoxication as a potential cause of crime has for many years been a favourite subject in criminology, but drink has important social as well as psychological and psychiatric causes and consequences, and only comparatively few cases of alcoholic intoxication lead to a psychosis. It seems to be advisable, however, to deal with the whole subject—including some of its social aspects—briefly in this chapter. There is no suggestion, of course, that drunkenness invariably produces a psychosis, see below (*cc*). The following questions have to be asked: (*aa*) How far is drunkenness itself an offence? (*bb*) How far is it a cause of crime? (*cc*) What is its psychiatric significance? (*dd*) How does the criminal law deal with crimes committed in the various stages of drunkenness? This last question will be dealt with later in Chapter 18 in connection with our discussion of the other legal problems of mental illness.

(*aa*) According to the Licensing Act of 1872, every person found drunk in a highway or other public place, or on licensed premises, is punishable with a fine up to 40*s*. This is the non-indictable offence of so-called simple drunkenness. Moreover, every person guilty while drunk of riotous or disorderly behaviour in a highway or public place, or who is drunk and in charge of any carriage or of a child, etc., is punishable either by a fine of up to 40*s*. or by imprisonment up to one month or, in certain cases, for a longer period. This is the offence of drunkenness with aggravations. Drunkenness as such is, therefore, not an offence. Taken as a whole, the number of such convictions has gone down very markedly in this country in the present century, from an annual average of about 200–220,000 to roughly one quarter.[34] However, there has been a steep upward movement, in the past twenty years, especially among young people, and in 1962 the number was over 80,000, or, according to *The Times* of 9.5.1963, even 92,000, where the results of the Licensing Act of 1961 have been called disastrous. Convictions per 10,000 males aged 14 to 16 in England and Wales increased from 1·5 in 1946 to 4·0 in 1954.[35] Penalties have changed, too. In the *Annual Report of the Prison Commissioners for 1919* we read: 'It is almost inconceivable that fifteen years ago 70,000 persons were committed to prison on a charge of drunkenness . . . The numbers committed last year were actually no more than 671 males and 999 females.' In 1959, 963 persons were committed to prison without the option of a fine. On the sex ratio of convictions and prison sentences something will have to be said later in Chapter 26, II(3).

Local differences in the frequency of these convictions are often very considerable, but it is doubtful how far they are due to real differences in the drunkenness rate and how far merely to different police methods.[36] Apart from this difficulty of making local comparisons, it is certain, however, that the decline in convictions reflects a real fall in drunkenness in this country, due to a great variety of reasons, such as changes in drinking habits brought about by the world wars, by higher social and educational standards reached by the great masses, changes in licensing hours, the higher price of alcoholic drinks, their weaker alcohol content, the habit of drinking in closed clubs, etc., and especially the availability of other media of mass entertainment, such as cinema, radio and television.

(*bb*) Of greater interest than the number of these minor drunkenness offences is the question how far drunkenness has to be regarded as a cause of other, possibly much more serious, offences.[37] The official *Criminal Statistics* gives no information on this subject, although the previous system, under which in the case of several convictions for different offences only the offence was tabulated in our *Criminal Statistics* for which the heaviest punishment was awarded, has now been given up for cases where a person is convicted for an indictable and a non-indictable offence.[38] While this means that the recording of drunkenness offences is now less incomplete than before, even the present system gives no indication of how often drunkenness offences are committed together with other offences—a gap which is filled by the *Licensing Statistics*, Table VI. A mere coincidence of this kind, however, does not imply cause and effect, and it has to be borne in mind that it is not the object of statistical tables to indicate causal relations. The proportion of these other offences is small, between 3 and 5 per cent of drunkenness offences for men and around 2 per cent for women. Most of them are likely to be of a less serious character as in the case of serious crimes there will hardly be a separate charge for drunkenness. Views on the criminogenic effect of drink differ greatly according to time, place and the type of offence. For the various forms of non-indictable assault, for example, the decline from an annual average of 55,000 in 1900–9 to 18,000 in 1938 and about 16,000 in 1962 can be explained by the fall in drunkenness.[39]

Far more complex is the relationship between drink and motoring offences. For the successful execution of payroll, mail or bank robberies and similar carefully planned crimes abstention from alcohol is almost essential, and alcoholic members of the gang will soon be got rid of as unsuitable by their colleagues. Of greater interest in the present connection is the offence of driving under the influence of drink or drug. Convictions for it number about 5,000 per year. Road accidents attributed to drivers under the influence of alcohol are regarded as responsible for about 500 deaths and 2,000–3,000 injuries annually.[40] In the view of an experienced Chief Constable, the task of proving this offence is so difficult that the prospect of a conviction has become too remote to act as a deterrent.[41] In other countries the tests for drunkenness are said to be much stricter,[42] and the penalties more severe. The matter is at present under active consideration in this country.

With regard to homicide, Wolfgang made a detailed study of the relationship between alcohol and his Philadelphia sample, regretting the absence of a record in the police files of the amount of alcohol in the blood, liver, brain or urine of the offender and his victim.[43] The files contained sufficient information, however, to record whether either of them had been drinking directly before the crime and whether the drinking had been excessive and over a prolonged period. He found that in 36 per cent of his 588 cases alcohol had been entirely absent; in 44 per cent it had been present in both the offender and the victim, and in the remaining 20 per cent either in the one or in the other. A number of other correlations were worked out, and a review of the literature is given. The part played by drunkenness of the victim has been frequently discussed by other writers, too.[44]

Dr. Glatt, a psychiatrist specializing in the treatment of alcoholics, has made a study of the relationship between alcoholism and crime in this country.[45] His material shows that, while the great majority of alcoholics do not get into serious conflicts with the law, inebriety by releasing aggressive tendencies is a contributing factor to crime in a substantial minority of cases. This estimate is borne out by a number of studies. In certain other countries, notably Sweden and Finland, the part played by drink is more important. Veli Verkkö (Note 33) has shown that in his country the connection between crimes of violence and alcohol is very close; he concludes: 'a feature of the Finnish national character is the Finn's poor capacity to hold his liquor', trying to explain this characteristic by reference to Kretschmer's theory of the 'viscous' temperament of the athletic type common in Finland.[46]

The criminality of the children of alcoholic parents, too, has often been discussed. Burt found parental alcoholism to be three times as frequent among his delinquents as among his control group, but he rightly stresses that its effect on descendants may be environmental as well as hereditary.[47] In Dr. Young's series of 2,217 consecutive cases of youths aged 16 to 21 in Wormwood Scrubs Prison parental drunkenness occurred only in 4·51 per cent of the cases.[48] Norwood East found little definite evidence in his group of Borstal boys that the offspring of drunkards are themselves predisposed to become alcoholics, but he regards alcoholism as an indication of a psychopathic inheritance.[49] Case histories of notorious criminals often contain references to alcoholism of the father,[50] but most of them are unchecked.

(cc) Passing now to the psychological and psychiatric significance of drink, we have to distinguish between different types of drinking, with very different psychological origins and effects and possibly also different criminological consequences. First, as Exner, Verkkö, Howard Jones and other writers have pointed out and as every traveller in foreign lands can easily discover for himself through personal observation, the consumption of alcohol and alcoholism do not have the same meaning everywhere. 'The alcohol addict in France may be a psychologically more normal person, and the Jew who becomes an alcoholic is likely to be even more deviant than his counterpart in Anglo-Saxon culture' (Jones, p. 155). Secondly, even within the same culture one has to distinguish between the mere drunkard who 'still has the ability to decide for himself at what times he will drink and how much he will take at any particular time' and the true alcoholic addict who has no such freedom of choice any more. According to Howard Jones, there were an estimated number of over 350,000 such addicts in England and Wales in 1961.[51]

From the psychiatric and criminological points of view, three types may have to be distinguished: First, the normal type of drunkenness which occurs from time to time in the average, healthy person and may produce a transitory form of dementia, leading to more or less serious disturbances of the physical and mental capacities of the individual. Crimes of violence, though usually not very serious in character, sexual offences, arson or malicious damage may occasionally be the result. The second, less common but potentially more dangerous, type is the so-called pathological drunkenness occurring in mentally unstable persons, people who have suffered some head injury or heatstroke or who are epileptics or mental defectives, psychopaths or psychotics. Such persons may become violent even under the influence of very small doses of alcohol.[52] The third group is that of chronic alcoholism which may lead to delirium tremens with its hallucinations—there is here an overlap with paranoia (see below)—sleeplessness and over-excitement. 'There is usually a state of extreme terror, and assaults on persons entering the room are not infrequent.'[53] Suspicions of marital infidelity may result in murder or suicide.

## II. FUNCTIONAL PSYCHOSES

The most important forms of functional psychosis are paranoia and paraphrenia, schizophrenia and manic-depressive psychosis.

(a) The characteristics of *paranoia*[54]—in many ways highly controversial—are well systematized and unshakable delusions with little or no visible impairment of other mental functions, and no definite external factor such as alcohol present. The alcoholic psychosis is thereby excluded from this narrow definition which roughly conforms to that given by Emil Kraepelin, the great nineteenth-century psychiatrist on whose researches the original conception of paranoia was mainly based.[55] Other writers have expressed doubts as to whether it is worth while to retain so narrow a syndrome as an independent unit, especially as some of the cases previously regarded as paranoic are now brought under the umbrella of schizophrenia. In forensic psychiatry, however, the concept of paranoia, though usually interpreted in a somewhat broader sense than by the followers of Kraepelin, continues to play an important role, especially in murder cases. In modern writings on the subject the importance of environmental factors in the aetiology of criminal paranoia has been underlined, in particular by Milner who points out that it may sometimes be a reaction to, and indeed the only escape from, an intolerable and seemingly inescapable situation and that the further removed a case of paranoia is from the schizophrenic syndrome the more obvious is the role of such external factors.[56] Among the various forms of paranoia are the persecution and the religious forms, according to the contents of the delusions. The sufferer may imagine himself to be so mercilessly persecuted by his enemies that the only way out is to kill them in self-defence, or he may be so firmly convinced of the misery of this world that it is his religious duty to kill his whole family. In other cases the main feature is extreme quarrelsomeness leading to interminable, costly and hopeless lawsuits, or amorous delusions resulting in very inappropriate attempts at one-sided courtship and love-making.[57] Another well-known symptom complex in paranoid and schizophrenic disorders is morbid jealousy with delusions of marital infidelity, but it may also occur in neurotic, non-psychotic, cases.[58]

Paraphrenia is closely related to paranoia, the difference being that the delusions are less completely systematized and any crimes committed by the paraphrenic may be unplanned sudden reactions to hallucinations.[59]

(b) The characteristic feature of the *manic-depressive psychosis*,[60] a form of affective disorder, is the alternating of moods of elation and excitement (periods of mania) and of depression and melancholia. Each phase may last for days or weeks or even longer, and there may be periods of apparent normality occurring between them. Kretschmer's view that manic-depressives usually belong to the pyknic somatotype and that their criminality is usually less serious has been mentioned before (Chapter 13, III). Crimes, especially of violence, and suicide will occur mainly in the depressive phase, whereas in the manic phase petty stealing, swindling and drunkenness offences are more frequent.[61] Most homicidal attacks are made on members of the sufferer's own family for reasons basically similar to those of the religious paranoiac. In 1941, a professor of linguistics was charged at the Central Criminal Court in London with the murder of his wife and found guilty but insane, suffering from manic-depressive insanity. He had been under the impression that he could no longer cope with his work and rather than expect his wife to face what he thought to be a bleak future he had decided to kill her.[62] Particularly severe attacks of depression and agitation occur in cases of so-called involutional melancholia, especially in women at or after the menopause and, though less often, in men in their fifties.[63] In 1937, a woman of 44 was charged, also at the Central Criminal Court, with the murder of her daughter, aged 15, and found guilty but insane, suffering from involutional melancholia. Because the daughter, who had otherwise done well at school, had failed in an examination owing to ill health, the mother had decided to strangle her.[64] Several other cases of crimes due to depression have been reported by Dr.

251

G. M. Woddis, with special reference to the preventative role of psychiatry and the possibility of predicting the development of homicidal tendencies in such persons.[65] The same author has found among 91 offenders examined by him 14 cases of reactive and 15 cases of endogenous depression, of whom 14 cases were cases of murder.[66]

(c) *Schizophrenia*[67] is generally regarded in forensic psychiatry as the most frequent and important form of functional psychosis.[68] Kraepelin called it *dementia praecox*, regarding its onset in adolescence and its inevitable termination in complete dementia as essential features. Since the writings of E. Bleuler, the Swiss psychiatrist, in the early decades of the present century the term schizophrenia, popularly called split-mindedness, has superseded the older one,[69] but the nature and causes of this illness are still controversial. While Kraepelin, Kretschmer, Lange, Mapother-Lewis and many others stress its constitutional and heredity character,[70] the opposite view of a psychic origin has also strong support. Endocrine disturbances have been held responsible, too. The essential features are a complete withdrawal of the patient's personality into himself ('shut-in' type) with a progressive deterioration and disorder of thought, emotions and conduct, flight into phantasy life, defects of judgment, peculiar mannerisms, delusions and hallucinations. 'Thinking is incoherent, rambling and jumbled. He brings together the most far-fetched topics ... The usual logical sequences are ignored ...'[71] Contact with reality is eventually completely lost. 'Often the patient complains that people work on his mind, hypnotize him, influence him for his own good, set about to drive him mad or ruin him.'[72] In most cases the illness begins between the ages of 15 and 25, but it has been argued, by Stern for example, that phantasy life is a normal feature of the child's life and is therefore recognized as pathological only later in adolescence.

It goes without saying that a mental disorder of this kind makes the patient a potentially dangerous person, and it may in fact lead to almost any crime, notably homicide. Kretschmer's picture of the schizophrenic as belonging usually to the athletic or, more often, to the leptosome types has been mentioned above (Chapter 13, III).

To give a few illustrations, a theological student aged 21 was found guilty but insane on a charge of murdering a pantry boy of 16. He was described as 'intensely and narrowly religious and by nature unsociable and reserved, living in two worlds, one described as a world of phantasy and the other of dissociation'. His attitude at his first interview with the psychiatric expert was described as 'comparable to a child who has been brought in from his solitary play to listen to the polite conversation in a drawing room of grown-ups. He was mildly bored and not in the slightest interested. . . . He played with the idea of dismembering the victim—taking off his arms and legs . . . He still thinks that it could be done without the death of the victim, and he would then keep the trunk and play with it.'

The psychiatric expert found him to be a schizophrenic, and he was sentenced to be detained during His Majesty's pleasure.[73] The same verdict was returned for similar reasons in the case of a soldier of 20 who had killed his father by blowing him up with a land mine which he had placed in his father's invalid chair.[74]

A phenomenon may once more be briefly mentioned here which, although in itself constituting neither a psychosis nor a neurosis, might be a symptom of mental disorder: *amnesia*. It indicates 'an alleged interruption of consciousness, complete or partial, with alleged inability of the accused to recall his actions' during the time when he committed a crime. A psychiatrist, Brian A. O'Connell, in a study of fifty murderers, found that twenty of them had 'claimed at one time or another to have no memory, or at best only the haziest recollection of the actions that had led to their arrest'.[75] He discovered certain differences in personality between the amnesic and the non-amnesic cases, in particular a far higher percentage of dullards and hysterics in the former group; there was however a higher percentage of abnormal E.E.G.s in the non-amnesic group. He concluded that, 'excluding the possible contribution of alcoholic intoxication, amnesia for a criminal act is likely to be of emotional rather than organic origin' and that 'epileptic features seemed to be of little aetiological significance'. Hypoglycaemia, however, is regarded as potentially leading to a state of confusion with subsequent amnesia, and a case of this kind is quoted where a young married man, 'following an enforced starvation of three days, murdered, for no reason, one of his children, with whom he had been on the best of terms. . . . The abnormality of his E.E.G. became more marked as his blood sugar fell and was associated with confusion.' He had no memory of his action, but 'recalled waking up to find himself covered in sweat'.

## NOTE ON DRUG ADDICTION[76]

Similarly to alcoholism, drug addiction is a social as well as a psychological and psychiatric problem, and, as alcoholism, it may lead to psychotic and neurotic disorders or itself be caused by the latter. Therefore, the same difficulties of placing it correctly in a criminological system arise as in the case of alcoholism. As compared with the latter, the extent of drug addiction in Britain is believed to be small, certainly much smaller than in the United States, where it has become one of the major social problems, especially for young people. Whereas the volume of British literature on it is correspondingly inconsiderable, the American output has been huge and is steadily growing. One of the aspects of the matter which has been attracting the special attention of American students in recent years is the question why the position should appear to be so much more favourable in Britain, and to this question Edwin M. Schur in particular has devoted a painstaking study, based on prolonged first-hand observations of the British system of dealing with drug addicts. He finds the answer essentially in the fact that, in contrast to the U.S.A., drug addiction as such is not an offence in Britain; that the addict commits an offence only if he obtains drugs illegally; that there is no compulsory treatment of drug addicts in Britain, and that the Government gives the medical profession 'almost complete professional autonomy in deciding whether an addict needs and should receive drugs for health reasons'. If the doctor regards this as necessary the patient may obtain the prescribed drugs under the National Health Service, which makes it unnecessary for him to pay excessive prices in the black market; therefore, there is but little incentive for the latter to operate extensively in Britain. So far so good, but in this country as in many other countries, there are two sides to the matter: drug addiction as a problem of the individual sufferer and illicit traffic in drugs, but the latter need not always be the supplier for the home market only: it may mainly cater for an international market and therefore have little bearing on the internal position. Whereas drug addiction is a medical and possibly a psychiatric problem, trafficking in drugs is an economic crime, with which we are not primarily concerned in the present chapter. Nevertheless, a few cases may be quoted.

In July, 1962, three Chinese members of the crew of the cruiser H.M.S. *Belfast* were sentenced at the Central Criminal Court in London to terms of imprisonment ranging from 12 months to five years for unlawfully possessing opium and heroin. It was stated that, while the ordinary value of these drugs was £670, their illicit value on the black market was approximately £325,000, the 'biggest single haul of illicit drugs that has ever been made' and far in excess of what could reasonably be sold in Britain. It was clear, therefore, that most of this quantity was destined for abroad, notably for North or South America. (*The Times*, 26.7.1962.)

Five years before, a quantity of Indian hemp, 175 lb in weight, had been seized in the Port of London, valued at £100,000 in the black market and destined to be smoked as 'reefers' in cafés, night clubs, and so on, in London or other places (*The Times*, 15.7.1957). It was stated at the time that of the persons convicted of dealing in Indian hemp seven out of eight were coloured men, mainly West Indians. In

254

their Pentonville study, T. and P. Morris found 13 cases of offences against the Dangerous Drugs Act, 1951, among the prisoners there, all non-white men sentenced for possessing marijuana (p. 59). The total of prosecutions for these offences was 727 in 1962 (*Criminal Statistics England and Wales 1962*, p. 29), but no distinction is here possible according to colour and origin. Modern music club and dance band leaders are said to be particularly prominent among these offenders, but white girls who are friendly with West Indians are also introduced to hemp smoking. The Denning Report[77] contains some references to this. Opium, on the other hand, is said to be largely confined to the Chinese population of London and since the war in particular Liverpool, but even here it is believed to be declining in favour of other pastimes. Recently, a drug drinamyl, popularly known as 'purple heart' tablets, has been named in the House of Commons as being addictive and very widely used among young people in London (*Hansard*, 30.1.1964).

Gasoline smelling among juvenile delinquents in the United States has been the subject of an interesting case study by two American medical experts.[78]

From the sociological side Cloward and Ohlin (Chapter 22, below) have dealt with the problem of drug addiction as a special type of the delinquent subculture, the 'retreatist'. Its characteristic features are cultural and social isolation and exclusion from the dominant streams of society. Feelings of frustration and discontent are particularly noticeable among these addicts, and the high proportion of adolescent Negroes among them is therefore not surprising. While these observations are no doubt correct it is less convincing to treat the drug addicts as a sub-type of the delinquent subculture, on a par with the other types worked out by these authors and responsible for gang formation; and in fact Cloward and Ohlin admit that the ties among addicts are not as close as those uniting members of the other forms of subculture (p. 179).

The psychiatric effect of drug-taking differs greatly according to the type and quantity of the drug and the personality involved. Reckless, after a detailed examination of the available evidence, concludes that one can only assume that there is a strong relation between mental abnormality and drug addiction, but one does not know 'how much connection actually exists' (p. 366).

The criminological significance of drug-taking is twofold: first, law-breaking as a concomitant of the process of obtaining the drug, including the forgery of prescriptions and the stealing of money to purchase the drugs; and, secondly, lawbreaking unconnected with this process but rather a consequence of taking the drug. The first aspect, as already indicated, depends greatly on the state of the law, which is stricter in the U.S.A. than in some other countries. Regarding the second aspect, the evidence is not very impressive. Reckless (p. 356) believes that stealing and drug peddling are the two major realities of the relation between drug addiction and crime and that any other connections are comparatively minor. Bloch and Geis are similarly sceptical, pointing out how difficult it is to determine how much crime the individual would have committed if he had not become a drug addict and that the latter usually do not commit serious crimes of violence (pp. 238 and 356). Valuable as such case studies as that on gasoline smelling are psychologically and psychiatrically, they shed hardly any light on the specifically criminological effect of this phenomenon. Clearly, much more research on the subject will have to be done particularly in this country, before any meaningful statements can be made on the extent and the criminological aspects of drug addiction.

After this note was written, public anxiety over the growing illicit possession of and traffic in 'pep pills' among young persons and in particular over their alleged, though not proved, use to stimulate offences of the 'Clacton' type (Chapter 25 below) reached such dimensions that the Home Secretary felt compelled, in March 1964, to introduce a Bill, the Drugs (Prevention of Misuse) Bill, to make the unauthorized possession of a specified number of these pills or their importation without licence an offence punishable with a fine of up to £200 and/or six months' imprisonment. This Bill would give the police power to deal with these pep pills in a similar way as with heroin, morphine and Indian hemp, and would strengthen the penal element in the English law on drugs. For this reason the Bill has been not unanimously welcomed by doctors and social workers.[79] At the Committee stage of the House of Commons debate on the Bill the Government was criticized for not having sufficiently studied the 'Soho nerve centre' of the 'purple heart' racket, and reference was made to certain clubs which were alleged to be involved in this racket (*Evening Standard*, 9.6.1964).

After this had been written, the Bill became law on the 31.7.64.

# Chapter 15

## MENTAL DISORDERS II:
## NEUROSES AND PSYCHOPATHY.
## MENTAL DEFICIENCY AND ITS OPPOSITE

### I. NEUROSES AND PSYCHOPATHY

### 1. *Neuroses and Psycho-neuroses*

The nature of the difference between psychosis, neurosis and psycho-neurosis is controversial.[1] While some authorities regard it as merely quantitative in the sense that the psychosis represents a more severe form or stage of the neurosis or psycho-neurosis, others make a qualitative distinction: the psychotic, they say, lives in a world of phantasy no longer subject to the ordinary laws of nature and has completely lost contact with reality; the neurotic still lives in the real world but cannot any longer cope with its difficulties. According to this second view, a neurosis may in certain cases be a more serious disturbance of the personality than a psychosis. Whichever view we may prefer, it is generally accepted that in practice the dividing line is often very difficult to draw and that a neurosis or psycho-neurosis may eventually lead to a psychosis, for example a depression to a manic-depressive psychosis.[2] Again, the terms neurosis and psycho-neurosis are often used indiscriminately by psychiatrists, whereas others distinguish between them.[3] The meaning of the distinction is that neuroses can have a somatic origin, psycho-neuroses not. Glover agrees to call certain 'instinctual and affective disturbances of somatic function *organ-neuroses*; so long as it is remembered that they have no psychic *content* and are not therefore psycho-neuroses'.[4] In the following, the term neurosis will be used for the sake of simplicity to cover both categories.

The incidence of the various forms of neurosis in the general population is very high. In a survey, sponsored by the Medical Research Council, on the incidence of neurosis among factory workers it was found that in a sample of over 3,000 male and female workers in engineering factories 10 per cent had suffered from 'definite and disabling neurotic illness and a further 20 per cent from minor forms of neurosis, during the course of six months'.[5] Admittedly, this enquiry was concerned with 'stabilized wartime conditions', but peacetime investigations had shown similar figures.[6] Among delinquents, too, neurosis is far more frequent than psychosis. A survey made of all cases seen at the Institute for the Study and Treatment of Delinquency in London (I.S.T.D.) in the years 1937–41 showed the following significant figures: 2 per cent psychotic, 4½ per cent borderline psychotic, 1 per cent alcoholic, 25 per cent sexual disorders, 29 per cent psycho-neurotic, 5 per cent behaviour problems, 5 per cent cases of organic origin. This excludes 3 per cent mentally defective, 8 per cent borderline mentally defective and 13 per cent psychopathic personality—categories with which we are not concerned at present. For juveniles only, the figures were much higher for psycho-neurosis, 37 per cent, character cases (including behaviour problems) 22 per cent, mentally defectives 5 per cent and borderline mentally defectives 11 per cent.[7] It has to be borne in mind that the cases sent to the I.S.T.D. (now The Portman Clinic) are carefully selected and therefore hardly representative. With the exception of the psychopath, who will be discussed below and who should preferably not be regarded as a neurotic at all, the relationship between neurosis and delinquency is less close than frequently assumed. To some extent it is even believed that this relationship is of an alternative rather than of a cumulative character, i.e. rather than being both neurotic and delinquent people tend to be either the one or the other. 'Neurosis is uncommon in the prison population', writes a prison medical officer of very long experience.[8] The explanation lies in the nature of the neurotic illness, which is rooted in inner conflict. If the individual has, unconsciously, to choose between neurosis and delinquency, his choice may depend on the source of the conflict responsible for his difficulties. If they are rooted in himself, he is likely to develop a neurosis; if, however, they are caused by other people, he is more likely to commit delinquent acts,[9] but he may also take refuge in a neurosis as a defence against his aggressive impulses.[10] The delinquent who is somehow deprived of his delinquent outlets may occasionally develop neurotic symptoms,[11] especially if his victory over his delinquent tendencies was achieved through overgreat self-control.

According to Freudian teachings on which the dominant theory of the neurosis is largely based (see also Chapter 17 below), the latter arise from an unconscious inner conflict between the ego and the instinctive, mainly sexual (in an 'extended sense') desires which have to be repressed because they are incompatible with the demands of the outside world, the ego and especially the super-ego.[12] According to Freud, the Oedipus complex is 'the nuclear complex of the neurosis'.[13] Such conflicts may also exist in the mind of the normal person, but here they are usually suppressed without creating special difficulties. In certain cases, however, the process of repressing them requires an excessive effort and thereby produces an unconscious feeling of guilt and the need for self-punishment, i.e. a neurosis. The neurotic, who is in most cases highly moral, tends to turn against himself to satisfy his need for punishment (see also Chapter 17 below) instead of hurting others. The delinquent, however, 'deals with his guilt by the mechanism of punishing the environment'.[14] 'The delinquent usually does not suffer.'[15] If all this were universally true there could be no neurotic delinquents, whereas their existence is beyond doubt; what is doubtful is merely the size of this group. We may take as an example of neurotic delinquency Franz Alexander's 'neurotic character', an individual who, different from the true neurotic, lives out his impulses which are often asocial, who is active whereas the true neurotic is inactive. Nevertheless, the neurotic character is not a 'real' criminal as at least one part of his personality condemns his anti-social actions. As there is, therefore, a split in his personality the inner conflict characteristic of the true neurotic does exist here as well.[16] Apart from this controversial category, the neurotic character, there are other, though limited, possibilities too of combining neurosis and delinquency.[17] This might be illustrated by briefly reviewing a few of the most important forms of neurosis:

(a) *Anxiety Neurosis and Phobias*.[18] This condition is characterized by a morbid, excessive and largely unjustified fear of dangers from within or without. If associated with a specific object or idea and entirely unjustified it is called phobia. One of the most frequent forms of neurosis, it has very little criminological significance. East gives the example of a young man who embezzles money because he is afraid that he may lose his girl unless he spends more money on her than he can afford. Anxiety may also be a cause of suicide.

(b) *Hysteria.* A term which has different connotations to the layman and the medical expert.[19] The latter distinguishes between conversion hysteria and anxiety hysteria; according to whether the pathogenic energies are discharged 'primarily through somatic or through ideational and affective channels' (Glover). Hysterics may 'almost unwittingly manufacture some situation . . . and enter into it emotionally with a rapidity and fervour impossible for more stable people. Egotism and untruthfulness (pseudologia phantastica) may be pushed to the point of delinquency. The emotional attitude of a hysteric towards other people is often influenced by sexual factors' (Mapother and Lewis). Hysteria is more common in women than in men. Offences such as writing anonymous libellous letters or wrongly accusing men of indecent assaults may be committed by hysterical women.[20]

(c) *Obsessional and Compulsive Neurosis*.[21] One might distinguish between obsessional thoughts, actions, doubts, ruminations and rituals (Glover, *Psycho-Analysis*). Neurotics of this type are seldom aggressive—although they may feel an urge to push another person over a cliff or in front of a train they will but rarely act it out—but many sexual perversions contain obsessive elements, for example exhibitionism, fetishism and also kleptomania and pyromania, both of which will be discussed separately below. Freud was, at one time at least, inclined to regard the neuroses as 'the negative of perversions', but as Schmideberg points out, both neurotic and perverse symptoms have a similar aetiology, although the pervert is more anti-social than the neurotic and normally turns his abnormal urges against others instead of himself.[22] It is certainly true that only a comparatively small proportion of perverts are obsessional neurotics.[23] To take, for example, exhibitionism, one of the most frequent sexual offences, it can be found in persons of very different mental make-up, acting with a great variety of motives, including cases of obsessional neurosis as probably one of the smallest groups.[24] East found only five psycho-neurotics in a series of 150 exhibitionists, and in the East-de Hubert Report it is also stated that very few exhibitionists show symptoms of a long-standing obsessional personality.[25]

Two forms of criminality are often regarded as particularly clear expressions of obsessional-compulsive neurosis: the so-called kleptomania and pyromania. Both terms are ill-chosen because they give the impression of referring to forms of mania in the sense of monomania, i.e. the old idea of a mental illness which affects only one small sector of the mind, leaving the personality as a whole totally unaffected. This would mean that a kleptomaniac is a mentally normal person whose only weakness is an obsessional urge to steal, a pyromaniac the same with a corresponding urge to commit arson, etc. Modern psychiatry has abandoned this idea, realizing that an individual who suffers from obsessional urges of this kind cannot be regarded as 'otherwise normal'. 'All mental symptoms, whether major or minor, always involve the total personality', writes Bowlby.[26] Another misconception encouraged by the term kleptomania is its frequent use to describe any kind of excessive, repetitive and apparently unreasonable stealing, especially from shops. The misuse of the word to provide an easy defence for habitual shoplifters belonging to the middle classes has recently led to a reaction, and the man-in-the-street now believes that the idea of kleptomania is nothing but a trick invented by psychiatrists and defence counsel to provide well-to-do people with an easy excuse. 'What is called pilfering east of

Temple Bar is called kleptomania in the West-end.' The truth lies somewhere between these extremes. Recent investigations into shoplifting, especially by Gibbens,[27] distinguish four overlapping types of shoplifters: (a) the professional who steals, often in collaboration with receivers, in order to sell the goods; (b) the ordinary offender who wants the goods for himself; (c) people, mostly women of good character, who act under an emotional stress, anxiety and depression because the stolen goods, regardless of their practical value, have a symbolic significance for them which forces them to disregard the social risk they run; (d) kleptomaniacs who steal for the sake of stealing in a repetitive, compulsive manner. The act of touching and handling the goods gives them sexual excitement, and it is often committed during or after menstruation or at the onset of the menopause. The thefts are carried out in a clumsy way, sometimes without any attempt at concealment; shining, glittering things are preferred, and they are often hoarded without ever being used. As Gibbens writes, 'There is no doubt that such cases exist, but they are relatively rare.' Fetishism may be connected with, or a preliminary stage to, kleptomania.[28] Glover[29] regards kleptomania as 'essentially obsessional in type', but distinguishes it from 'compulsive delinquencies of a psychopathic type', in which some degree of satisfaction is obtained, whereas in true kleptomania the stealing is often followed by some action of an expiatory nature such as a donation to charity. This requirement, too, shows how restricted the use of the term kleptomania is in modern psychiatric and psycho-analytical literature.

While pyromania also shows obsessive-compulsive features, with a similar background of inner conflict, often of a sexual nature, its object is destruction rather than acquisition, and it occurs more frequently in the younger age groups, notably among adolescent girls.[30] Epileptics seem to be fairly well represented among them,[31] which is not surprising in view of their well-known difficulties (see Chapter 14 above). Young people, deprived of a happy home life and feeling sexually frustrated and generally unhappy, may become obsessed with the urge to set fire to external objects which are to them symbols of a hostile and wicked world only fit to be destroyed and replaced by a better one. A soldier aged 20 was tried in 1939 by Nottinghamshire Assizes on a charge of setting fire to stores at a Royal Ordnance Depot and causing £36,000 of damage because 'he felt that the social system of the country was not as it should be and he decided to register a protest against it'. The police were satisfied that he was not connected with any subversive movement nor influenced by other people.[32] The prison medical officer thought he was a schizophrenic, but the same offence might have been committed by an obsessional-compulsive neurotic.

261

'There is a strong similarity', writes Schmideberg,[33] 'between the arsonist and the sex offender, both etiologically and symptomatically, and in the reaction they elicit from the community, justice, and our law-enforcing agencies.' She stresses in particular the sadistic element in many pathological firesetters and also the absence of any emotion or feeling of guilt relating to the crime. In an older German investigation covering 100 cases Többen[34] found the following main motives of arson: revenge and hatred in 38 cases, alcohol in 6, poverty or greed in 22, homesickness in 7, to cover up other crimes in 4, to get away from a reformatory or from military service in 7, the pleasure of firesetting or naughtiness in 5, motives connected with mental disorder in 11. He refers to an early publication of Karl Jaspers who stresses the importance of loneliness and homesickness in young girls. Loneliness may have similar effects also on individuals who are not so very young any more. A single woman clerk aged 29 was charged with setting fire to the local Church Hall because, as a member of the church council, she was disappointed to hear that the vicar, from whom she had received some pastoral attention because of her loneliness, was moving to another district. Soon afterwards, she set fire to the vicarage to which he had moved (*The Times*, 23.3.1962).

Occasionally, an element of financial gain may be present which, at least to the superficial observer, may be difficult to separate from the deeper, emotional, subconscious ones. On the 15th March 1962, a part-time fireman, aged 32, married with four young children, was sentenced at Winchester Assizes to seven years imprisonment for sixteen crimes of arson. Soon after he had taken up his employment with the fire brigade he caused 'a reign of terror' in his district by starting on an average one fire a week and causing over £27,000 of damage. He was stated to have received nearly £2 a week for turning out and fighting the fires he had raised. He told the police: 'I don't know what I do it for, only that I feel good in uniform and it gives me some sense of importance.' The psychiatric expert thought he could be helped by psychological treatment.[35]

A similar case was reported soon afterwards from Breconshire where a grocer, aged 39, a former leading fireman, was committed for trial to Assizes for setting fire to four buildings. He was alleged to have made a confession, saying: 'After each fire I decided it would be the last, but found myself carrying on again . . . it always seems to be on a sudden impulse.' The offences were stated to have occurred between 24th March and 8th September 1962 (*The Times*, 20.9.1962), i.e. starting approximately a week after the two previously mentioned cases had been reported in the press.

The accused, a married man with four children, who was said to have been very helpful to the police on a number of occasions and had received recommendations from the Chief Constable, asked for five similar cases to be taken into consideration. A medical report stated that he was not insane in the legal sense, but was suffering from an anxiety state, worried over his business and had started the fires to relieve his anxieties. The case was adjourned for a further medical report (*The Times*, 20.11.1962).

Although this brief discussion of a few types of neurosis may have shown that the latter is less important than often believed as a causal factor in delinquency this does not necessarily mean that very few delinquents are neurotics. It does mean, however, that they may have become delinquents for reasons other than their neurosis. In his survey of the Wakefield Prison population, Roper who, as we have seen (Note 8), regards neurosis and criminality as 'in many ways the reverse of each other', notes that 'neurosis in prison consists largely of somatized anxiety and comes out mainly in fear of disease and in exaggerated reaction to simple ailments',[36] i.e. neurosis does exist among prisoners, but it is not necessarily the cause of their delinquency.

## 2. Psychopathy[37]

The term psychopath has changed its meaning many times since it was first introduced, apparently in 1888 by Koch whose 'psychopathic inferiority' was a very broad conception including much of what would now be called neurosis.[38] Historically, its forerunner was Prichard's 'moral insanity', and the description of this condition given by the latter as early as 1834 is still regarded as containing much of the essence of the modern term psychopath.[39] In 1870, Isaac Ray, the great American psychiatrist, quoting Prichard, spoke of moral mania.[40] The main characteristic of this condition was that it was a morbid perversion of feelings, temper, habit and moral disposition without any notable impairment of the intellectual faculties. Apart from this emphasis on moral, as opposed to intellectual, defect there was in the older literature on the subject also a strong tendency to use the term as a convenient pigeon-hole where any form of mental abnormality which did not seem to fall under any other recognized form of mental illness could be accommodated. The modern trend is opposed to this, and psychiatrists have made great—though not always successful—efforts to limit the concept to certain clearly definable types and to underline in particular the differences rather than the similarities between the psychopath and the neurotic.

The emphasis on moral weaknesses led, understandably, to the temptation to over-estimate the closeness of the relationship between psychopathy and crime, in other words to regard, if not every criminal as a psychopath, at least every psychopath as a criminal. Present-day psychiatrists, however, have worked out typologies in which the criminal psychopath is only one of many types of psychopathic personality.[41] Among the most influential of these typologies are those by Kurt Schneider, who has many followers especially on the Continent, and by Sir David Henderson. While Schneider distinguishes ten different types of psychopaths,[42] Henderson is content with three. It should be borne in mind, however, that Schneider's typology is intended as an empirical description of certain combinations of characteristic qualities rather than as a theoretical typology.[43] His definition of psychopaths as abnormal personalities 'who suffer from their abnormality or produce suffering in their environment' has been widely quoted; the two parts of this definition should, however, not be interpreted as being mutually exclusive as it is quite possible for a person to suffer himself and to cause suffering to others. It is one of the merits of Schneider's definition to make it clear that the psychopath is not a person who suffers from an illness called psychopathy, but that the term characterizes the personality as a whole.[44]

Henderson's three types are (a) the predominantly aggressive, (b) the predominantly inadequate, and (c) the predominantly creative. It will be noted that he has no special type of criminal psychopath, but divides the latter between his first two groups. Glover[45] suggests a division into two subgroups, 'a condition of "private" and (in the social sense) "benign" psychopathy in which the condition affects the individual's private life and character and a (again socially speaking) "malignant" or "criminal" psychopathy where the condition gives rise to serious and persistent anti-social manifestations', or 'masochistic' and 'sadistic' psychopathy.

*The Chief Characteristics and Aetiology of the Psychopath.* A recent writer, after surveying two hundred publications on the subject, produced the following list of 'signs attributed to psychopathic syndromes', in order of frequency:[46] (a) affectionlessness or lack of relation to others; (b) disregard of community or group standards with antisocial behaviour on a verbal, acquisitive, personal or sexual plane; (c) apparent absence of guilt feeling and failure to learn by punishment; (d) emotional liability and immaturity, leading to short circuit reactions with immediate pleasure, satisfaction or unpremeditated violence; (e) a lack of foresight; (f) continued sexual experimentation, immaturity or aberration; (g) undue dependence on others.

The element under (a), lack of ability to establish warm personal relations with others, has been underlined perhaps more often than anything else. Another psychiatrist, Anthony Storr, has recently described it well as the inability 'to put himself in other people's shoes and . . . to appreciate their feelings. It is probably our capacity for identification which makes us behave relatively decently. If this is absent we treat people as things rather than as human beings' (*New Statesman*, 27.4.1962, p. 572).

This list, while highlighting the principal characteristics of the psychopath as discussed in the literature, has of course to be interpreted critically, and checked against and supplemented in the light of the results of more detailed studies of the problem such as those by Glover and others. To mention only one recent study, it has been suggested by members of the Eysenck school of psychology, notably by Franks,[47] that extraverts condition very poorly and that, as the psychopath is usually an extravert, he too is unable to condition, to profit from experience, and that this explains his high rate of recidivism. As we shall see below (Chapter 17) this characteristic plays an important part in other studies too.

Barbara Wootton's criticism of the whole concept, while a useful antidote to the enthusiasm of certain over-credulous adherents of modern psychiatry, goes too far in its equally exaggerated scepticism. It culminates in the sentence: 'He [i.e. the psychopath] is, in fact, *par excellence*, and without shame or qualification, the model of the circular process by which mental abnormality is inferred from anti-social behaviour while anti-social behaviour is explained by mental abnormality.'[48] She rightly insists that the mental abnormality of the psychopath should be deducible from criteria other than his anti-social conduct, but she ignores the fact that this very requirement has to some extent been met by modern psychiatric research and she has therefore thrown out the baby with the bathwater. An investigation of a group of 104 prisoners in three London prisons, all of them clinically classified by the prison medical officers as psychopaths, with 61 non-psychopathic controls,[49] for example, has shown that the psychopath can be distinguished from non-psychopaths in many ways quite *apart* from his anti-social tendencies: he shows abnormalities in the electrophysiological, constitutional, and psychological fields which make his criminal behaviour appear 'almost irrelevant. Certainly criminality *per se* seems to add little to our knowledge of this particular form of character disorder': failure to mature and inability to accept authority in any form are the most outstanding characterological qualities emerging from this study,[50] but in addition to them the electrophysiological examination showed a significant positive correlation with abnormality on the part of the psychopaths as compared with the controls. Moreover, capillaroscopy—a newly developed diagnostic procedure—suggested 'developmental anomalies and dysplasias at the morphological level' in 81 per cent of the psychopaths against only 19 per cent of the controls. As part of the clinical study the response of the prisoners to punishment was examined under four headings: (a) punishment accepted and altera- tion of conduct displayed; (b) punishment apparently accepted, but no alteration of conduct; (c) punishment resented but an attempt made to avoid trouble; (d) punishment resented with the response of rebellion and a determination to get even with society. The results showed that 'the majority of the psychopaths fell under the last three categories, whereas the majority of the controls fell under the first category, and this socio-psychological criterion, attitude to punish- ment, agreed with the clinical diagnosis of psychopathy in 89·3 per cent.[51]' This was regarded by the authors as the nearest sociometric method for providing objective confirmation of a clinical impression.[52]

It is this negative response to punishment on the part of the psycho- path—explained by Franks as part of his extraversion and poor ability to condition and learn from experience—that has been selected by the Danish Penal Code of 1930 as the guiding criterion for the choice of treatment on the part of the criminal court. Section 17(1) of the Code provides that, 'if at the time of committing the punishable act the permanent condition of the perpetrator involved defective development, or impairment or disturbance of his mental facilities, including sexual abnormality, of a nature other than indicated in § 16 of this Act (which deals with insanity and pronounced mental deficiency), the court shall decide, on the basis of a medical report and all other available evidence, whether he may be considered susceptible to punishment'.[53] As a definition of psychopathy this is of course just as inadequate as the equally negative formula in s. 4(1) of the English Criminal Justice Act, 1948, but the courts in both Den- mark and England have interpreted it as referring to the various forms of neurosis and psychopathy. A survey published in 1948 by the Danish psychiatrist and Director of the Asylum for Psychopathic Criminals at Herstedvester, Dr. Georg Stürup,[54] shows that § 17 had been applied to considerable numbers of psychopaths. Similarly, Grünhut found in an examination of the manner in which s. 4(1) of the Act of 1948 had been applied,[55] that out of 414 offenders placed on probation with a condition of mental treatment 154 were labelled constitutional and 41 environmental psychopaths. With regard to the criterion of susceptibility to punishment, §§ 17 and 70 of the Danish Penal Code provide, in short, that those who are regarded as possess- ing this susceptibility may be committed to penal institutions, especially to a so-called psychopathics prison, whereas the others may be sent to the asylum at Herstedvester. A great deal of discretion is, however, left to the courts, and susceptibility to punishment is not the only criterion to be considered by them. For this reason and also because of the great difficulty of establishing the presence or absence of the criterion in individual cases the dividing line between the inmates of penal institutions and of Herstedvester is far from clear.[56]

Whereas the Danish Code uses 'susceptibility to punishment' as an important criterion, s. 4 of the Criminal Justice Act, 1948, uses susceptibility to treatment as a requirement for a probation order with condition of mental treatment, and the definition now given in the Mental Health Act, 1959, s. 4(4), does the same: 'In this Act "psychopathic disorder" means a persistent disorder or disability of mind (whether or not including subnormality of intelligence) which results in abnormally aggressive or seriously irresponsible conduct on the part of the patient, and requires or is susceptible to medical treatment.' By stressing the possibility that psychopaths, while not responding constructively to punishment, may be amenable to treatment, modern legislators and psychiatrists show a more positive approach to the problem than some of their predecessors. It is also of special significance in this respect that the Mental Health Act, 1959, provides in s. 4(5) that a person should not be treated as suffering from mental disorder 'by reason only of promiscuity or other immoral conduct'. A provision of this kind was needed in particular because of the experiences met with in the American so-called psychopathic sex offenders laws. While no detailed analysis of this type of legislation can here be given,[57] it has to be said that one of its main weaknesses lies in its failure to provide a reasonably clear definition of the term 'sexual psychopath', in its over-emphasis on the sexual aspects of psychopathy and its tendency to permit danger-ous inroads into the liberty of the individual without providing in exchange scientifically sound measures of treatment. More recent American legislation, for example in California and Maryland, tries to remedy at least some of these defects, and the Maryland Defective Delinquency Law of 1951[58] does no longer single out the sexual psychopath for special treatment, but provides indetermin-ate confinement coupled with treatment for the 'defective' delin-quent whom it defines as 'an individual who, by the demonstra-tion of persistent aggravated anti-social or criminal behaviour, evidences a propensity toward criminal activity, and who is found to have either such intellectual deficiency or emotional unbalance, or both, as to clearly demonstrate an actual danger to society so as to re-quire confinement and treatment under an indeterminate sentence...'

Those responsible for the administration of this Act admit that, although tests for the assessment of the degree of emotional un-balance are available, they are not sufficiently precise to enable them to decide whether an individual is so unbalanced emotionally as to justify the application of the Act, and case histories and clinical impressions will have to supplement the picture. It is clear, however, that it is the object of the Maryland Act to protect society against the dangerous psychopath. The English Mental Health Act of 1959, sects. 60, 65, 66, contains provisions for detention and treatment of psychopaths and other mentally abnormal persons which are not very dissimilar to those of the Maryland Act, and it remains to be seen whether its definitions provide greater protection for the individuals concerned.

All the statutory definitions of psychopathy so far mentioned wisely abstain from including any statements about the *aetiology* of psychopathic disorders. This issue is still much too controversial to be suitable for legislative formulation. Here as in many other fields we can observe a certain difference of views between Continental and Anglo-American writers, the emphasis on constitutional and inherited factors being slightly stronger among the former and that on environmental factors slightly stronger among the latter. On the whole, however, we find here too a growing willingness on both sides to admit the complexity of the interplay of constitution and environment, although most attempts to arrive at a face-saving formula have to be hedged around with many reservations and exceptions from the rule. Lange, for example, writes:

Psychopathies are abnormal permanent states which we regard mostly as inborn. . . . On the other hand there is no doubt that many of these childhood neuroses can be favourably influenced or even cured by changes in the milieu or very simple medical treatment . . . and there are schools of psychotherapy which put the main emphasis regarding the causes of the psychopathies on external influences and experiences. Against this we have to stress that certain forms of psychopathy are definitely hereditary or exist at least as inherited anomalies. . . . We have to assume that, apart from certain permanent psychopathies which are transmitted wholly by heredity . . ., the other psychopathies are again and again revived in the course of inherited transmission by force of the unfortunate coincidence of qualities which are not unfavourable as such but incompatible.[59]

He adds that one occasionally sees the coming into existence of psychopathies which look similar to the inherited ones but are in fact the consequence of serious external damage, for example the injuries due to encephalitis epidemica or other serious brain damage. In his survey of recent research on aetiology Craft[60] notes three general syndromes as emerging from his review: (a) syndromes due predominantly to brain damage; (b) syndromes which are predominantly affectionless, usually due to 'a deprivation of essential parental figures or a lack of training of affective bonds'; (c) syndromes consisting predominantly of emotional immaturity or instability, 'the result of erratic training by antagonistic or variable parent figures'. It is also interesting that, according to the *Report of the Royal Commission on Mental Illness and Mental Deficiency, 1954-7*: 'most of our witnesses who spoke to us about psychopaths emphasized that psychopathy usually seems to have its origins in the social environment in which the patient grew up.'[61]

In accordance with the different emphasis given to constitutional and environmental factors respectively, expert views on the chances of treatment differ. Glover[62] stresses that the previously assumed incorrigibility of the psychopath meant merely incorrigibility by the penal methods then employed, lack of response to punishment, admitting however that 'until comparatively recently the psycho-therapeutic methods employed were not specially designed for the psychopathic criminal; they were methods that had been found use-ful in a number of psycho-pathological states (neuroses, character disorders and sexual disabilities) in which as a rule no special anti-social features are present'. 'The prerequisite of any therapy of the psychopath is a capacity to endure repeated disappointment...' 'The criminal psychopath begins treatment in a state of hostile defence ... he persists in trying to exploit his analyst ... there is in fact no end to the crises ... that the psychopath may engineer ...' In spite of all this, Glover concludes that given the right treatment the criminal psychopath is not so refractory as generally supposed, and this conclusion seems also to be borne out by the results of special treatment centres such as Herstedvester, Utrecht, or Belmont in this country.[63] Eysenck, too, comes to similar results from the entirely different angle of learning theory. As already mentioned above, in his view the psychopath conditions poorly, but 'he does condition'.[64] It is therefore fairly generally agreed that psychopaths usually become socially more or less adjusted by the age of forty or even earlier.[65] In this connection, a follow-up study of the psycho-pathic prisoners in various London prisons, to which reference was made above, is also of interest. It was found that eight years after the original investigation their rate of recidivism was not as high as ex-pected, and while the rate was higher than that of the control cases, 24 per cent of them had only one or no reconvictions. 'Clearly,' the authors conclude, 'the diagnosis of psychopathic personality, even in severe cases, does not inevitably portend as hopeless a prognosis as is usually implied.'[66]

The legal responsibility of neurotic and psychopathic offenders will be discussed below in Chapter 18.

An interesting attempt has recently been made by a prison psycho-logist, Paul de Berker, to contrast the psychopath and the inadequate personality, although the latter, as will be remembered, is one of

Henderson's three types of psychopaths.[67] In de Berker's view the differences are chiefly as follows: While the psychopath shows a certain exuberance and determination in the pursuit of his short-term goals, this is lacking in the inadequate: 'the psychopath has at least invested in himself; the inadequate has invested nothing.' It is this 'lack of drive and general purpose that permeates the whole of the life picture'. He is not a neurotic either, because inner conflict and his response to stress are not, as in the case of the latter, specific, there is 'no symptom-like neurotic pattern', perhaps with one exception: marriage breakdown seems to be a specific symptom amongst inadequate personalities. Considering that prison psychologists and doctors are inclined to regard a very high proportion of prisoners, in particular of preventive detainees and corrective trainees, as falling into this category,[68] the practical significance of this classification is evident. What is not yet clear is, however, how far these inadequate personalities have to be treated as 'abnormal'. This leads to the question of how to define 'normality', which will be discussed below (Chapter 16, II).

## II. MENTAL DEFICIENCY (SUBNORMALITY) AND ITS OPPOSITE[69]

### 1. Definitions

The same question of how to define normality is also at the bottom of the problems of mental deficiency, but with the emphasis on intelligence rather than on character and personality defects. Moreover, while attempts to produce legal definitions of psychopathy and to provide a privileged legal position for it are of very recent date, all this has been done in the case of mental defectives already for many centuries. English legal history of the subject is said to go back to the reign of Edward I, when a distinction was already drawn between the 'born fool' or idiot and the 'lunatick', i.e. a person who 'at birth hath had understanding, but by disease, grief, or other accident, hath lost the use of his reason'.[70] In later centuries, the distinction became blurred and cases of *dementia* ('lunatics') and *amentia* ('idiots') were often dealt with indiscriminately until in the later decades of the last century the special needs of the latter and the existence of various grades of amentia were more clearly recognized by the law. Nor were psychiatrists much more advanced than the lawyers, and it was only in 1838 that the French psychiatrist Esquirol and the American Isaac Ray produced a clear distinction between amentia and dementia.[71] In English law, it was the Idiots Act of 1886 which used the terms 'idiot' and 'lunatic' as mutually exclusive and the Mental Deficiency Act of 1913, based on the *Report of the Royal Commission on the*

*Care and Control of the Feeble-minded of 1908,* defined four classes of defectives, i.e. idiots, imbeciles, feeble-minded persons and moral imbeciles. The amending Act of 1927 re-defined these classes and replaced the term 'moral imbecile' by 'moral defective'. The overall definition of mental defectiveness given in this Act was 'a condition of arrested or incomplete development of mind existing before the age of eighteen years, whether arising from inherent causes or induced by disease or injury'. Therefore, the concept of mental deficiency was no longer exclusively confined to 'born fools'; it also included those whose defect had been caused by disease or injury provided it had happened before the age of eighteen. Nevertheless, it is the prevailing view that 'mental deficiency due solely to postnatal factors . . . is comparatively rare . . . In the majority of cases the chief factor, as a detailed study unquestionably shows, is heredity', which does not, however, necessarily imply that the majority of mental defectives are born of mentally defective parents.[72]

There is no need any more to reproduce here the definitions of the four classes given in the Act of 1927 as the whole Act has been repealed by the Mental Health Act, 1959, which replaces the term mental deficiency altogether by two new terms, 'subnormality' and 'severe subnormality', defined as follows (s. 4): ' "Severe subnormality" means a state of arrested or incomplete development of mind which includes subnormality of intelligence and is of such a nature or degree that the patient is incapable of living an independent life or of guarding himself against serious exploitation, or will be so incapable when of an age to do so.' 'Subnormality' means the same, but with the difference that it 'requires or is susceptible to medical treatment or other special care or training of the patient'. The main innovations are the following: The four terms used in the previous Acts have been abolished as offensive or unnecessary. The former applies in particular to the terms 'idiot' and 'imbecile', the latter— for reasons to be given below—to the term 'moral defective'. The term 'mental defective' itself is no longer used because in the previous legislation it was made to cover mental abnormalities of a range too wide to be brought under the same term. It was argued in the report of the Royal Commission of 1957, for example, that there was far more similarity between some feeble-minded persons and psychopaths than between the former and idiots and imbeciles.[73] Moreover, the new classification, by having only two categories instead of the previous four, is more flexible, the former age limit of eighteen years has been given up as causing unnecessary practical difficulties, and there is now an explicit reference to subnormality of 'intelligence', which was missing in the previous Acts. The reason for its absence was probably the fact that previously mental deficiency included 'moral defectives', defined as 'persons in whose case there exists mental defectiveness coupled with strongly vicious or criminal propensities and who require care, supervision and control for the protection of others'. The definition given in the Act of 1913 referred to 'permanent mental defect' and lack of response to punishment, and there is little doubt that the whole idea goes back to Prichard, Ray and Maudsley, with an additional indebtedness to Lombroso.[74] Among more recent psychiatrists, in particular Mercier and Tredgold favoured the idea of an inborn lack of moral sense, whereas many others maintained that the latter was either acquired through adverse circumstances or due to inferior intelligence. One of the most outspoken critics of the concept, the late prison doctor M. Hamblin Smith, wrote in his *Psychology of the Criminal*:[75]

Is there such a thing as a 'moral sense', apart from the intellect? The author has already stated his view that there is no such sense. What we call our 'moral sense', our ideas of 'right and wrong', seems to him indissolubly bound up with our social judgments, and with the gradual growth of our social relationships. Intelligence and experience (which depends upon intelligence) enter into the problem. . . . Many cases have arisen in which moral imbecility has been advanced as a solution. But, upon investigation, they have all been found to be insane, or to be intellectually defective, or to be the subjects of some mental conflict. . . .

While there is much truth in these statements, especially in their emphasis on the importance of upbringing and other social factors, we now realize that they tend to over-simplify a very complex issue and to identify morality too much with intelligence. In any case, considering the highly controversial nature of such questions as the meaning and origin of moral sense[76] it is clearly improper for the legislator to brand certain individuals as 'moral defectives'. In its practical application, this part of the Acts of 1913 and 1927 was almost useless since medical experts refused or were at least very reluctant to certify a person under it. In an often quoted study by Sir Norwood East a group of 283 convicted defectives were classified as consisting of 33 imbeciles, 244 feeble-minded and 6 moral defectives.[77] The Mental Health Act of 1959 has merely underwritten this development by altogether dropping any reference to morality in its definition of subnormality and leaving it to the expert to deal with cases of apparent 'moral deficiency' either as cases of subnormality or of psychopathic disorder. In the latter case it is at least no longer necessary, as it was under the previous Acts, to prove or at least pretend that the individual concerned was not only morally but also mentally deficient, and psychiatrists who have to diagnose a case of psychopathy can do so without having to commit themselves to any rigid statement regarding 'moral obliquity'.

In spite of the absence of rigid classification in the Mental Health Act of 1959 it is fairly certain that intelligence tests will still play some part in helping to answer the question of whether a particular delinquent has to be classified as 'subnormal' or 'severely subnormal'. Although with the abolition of formal certification and growing scepticism regarding the practical value of such tests the former dependence on them may gradually weaken, the material presented below (2) shows that within limits psychiatrists and psychologists cannot be expected altogether to dispense with the use of intelligence tests and the yardstick of the I.Q. As the Gluecks say, intelligence 'still forms an important part of the protocol'.[78] This is not the place to deal with the concept of intelligence itself or with the various intelligence tests, and reference may be made to the extensive literature on these subjects.[79]

It is mainly in deference to the older criminological literature which was largely dependent on lines of demarcation using intelligence tests and I.Q.s that the following data may be given:

As 'idiots' persons were classified showing a mental age of under 3 years and an I.Q. of under 25; as 'imbeciles' persons of a mental age of 3 and under 6 years and an I.Q. of 25–50; as 'feeble-minded' persons of a mental age of 6 and under 10 years and an I.Q. of 50–70.[80] In addition, there was a category of persons who, though of subnormal intelligence, did not fall under the Mental Deficiency Act: the mentally dull or educationally backward children with an I.Q. of over 70 but below 85; whereas the former term referred to subnormal intelligence, backwardness was an educational concept.[81] As far as the frequency of these different states was concerned, an investigation made for the Committee on Mental Deficiency of 1929 estimated that in every 100 mental defectives there were roughly 5 idiots, 20 imbeciles, and 75 feeble-minded, whereas dullness and backwardness was estimated at about 6 times the size of the feeble-minded group. According to older estimates, still reproduced by Burt in 1955, at least 10 per cent of the London school population were 'educationally backward'.[82]

Mental defectives may, as any other person, become psychotics or they may at least undergo psychotic episodes such as paranoid hallucinations.[83]

## 2. Mental Deficiency (Subnormality) and Crime

This subject can be examined by means of the statistical and of the case study methods. It can be approached from the delinquency and from the mental deficiency angles, i.e. we can ask either how many mental defectives there are among offenders as compared with the non-delinquent population, or we can ask how many delinquents there are among mental defectives. As usual, the first way of approach has been more frequently used than the second.

The history of the subject over the past fifty years shows a steady decline in the belief in the importance of mental deficiency as a causal factor in crime. This belief reached its highest point in the first decades of the present century[84] with the publication of the American psychiatrist H. H. Goddard's book *Feeble-mindedness; its Causes and Consequences* (1914). Goddard, already known to us through his book on the Kallikak family, who introduced the Binet-Simon test to the United States and did much mental testing of delinquent children, claimed to have discovered percentages as high as sixty-six of feeble-minded cases in a sample of juvenile delinquents in the Juvenile Court of Newark, and surveying a number of other studies of inmates of Reformatories he found their percentage ranging from 28 to 89. For adult criminals his estimate was at least 25, but possibly 50, per cent. In most of the studies which he surveyed no tests had been used, nor had Goddard himself any control material for the general population. A few years later Charles Goring, as mentioned above (Chapter 13), giving an estimate of between 10 and 20 per cent mental deficiency among adult criminals, also regarded inferior intelligence as one of the most important characteristics of criminals and destined to replace Lombroso's physical stigmata.[85] He did not use intelligence tests, but relied on the subjective opinion of prison officials. On the other hand, he had at his disposal the estimates of mental deficiency among the general population produced by the Royal Commission of 1908 which believed less than half per cent of the general population of England and Wales to be mentally defective. Among a sample of over 2,000 inmates of local prisons, casual wards and shelters, etc., however, the Commission found more than 10 per cent defectives. These figures are misleading. First, the extent of mental deficiency in the general population is difficult to assess. In a report of the Mental Deficiency Committee of 1929, a slightly higher estimate was made than in 1908, i.e. over 0·6 per cent for urban and over 1 per cent for rural districts as persons requiring the type of care provided by the Mental Deficiency Acts. As pointed out in the Report of the Royal Commission of 1957:[86]

. . . any estimate of the number of persons who may require care from the special mental health services is affected by the extent to which general social conditions, such as full employment and general social welfare services, make it possible for persons suffering from mild degrees of mental disability to manage in the general population without special care, and by the degree of administrative separation or integration of mental health services and other social services which is thought desirable at any period. An estimate made in 1929 might not be equally applicable in 1956.

Similarly open to criticism is the figure of over 10 per cent defectives given in the Report of 1908 as an estimate of mental deficiency among criminals. Their sample did not even distinguish between prisoners and inmates of casual wards, nor are prisoners representative of the criminal population as a whole, but even so the estimate of the Report of 1908 was far lower than that of Goring shortly afterwards. Cyril Burt's figure for his sample of juvenile delinquents was 8 per cent mental defectives as tested with the Binet-Simon test, which was five times as much as among the school population at large. From this he concluded that 'mental defect, beyond all controversy, is a notable factor in the production of crime'.[87]

Norwood East, in his study of Borstal boys, also found the proportion of mental defectives, about 3·5 per cent, 'very much higher than would be expected in a random sample of lads from the general population', but it was lower among the recidivists than among the first offenders, probably, he suggests, because many defectives are placed under control, instead of being brought before a criminal court, after their first offence.[88] Dr. Grace Pailthorpe, who about ten years earlier examined a group of 100 female prisoners aged between 16 and 30 in Holloway Prison, found a much higher proportion, 15 per cent, to be mentally defective and another 21 per cent subnormal.[89]

In his survey of 350 American psychometric studies of the subject Sutherland showed that between 1910 and 1928, if the median study is taken as representative of the period, the proportion of feebleminded persons among delinquents decreased from 50 to 20 per cent.[90] If he had repeated his survey thirty years later, he would have found that, with improved tests, the proportion of marked defective delinquents had further declined. The McCords, for example, in their study of 1959 maintain that their sample of Cambridge-Somerville boys showed no correlation between low intelligence and convictions, but none of the boys of high intelligence had been sent to a penal institution. Superior intelligence, they conclude, might influence judicial policy.[91] Mary Woodward, in a table summarizing a number of American studies between 1931 and 1950, shows that the mean I.Q. had increased from 71 to over 92. From her review of British studies she concludes that, while the average intelligence of detected delinquents in Great Britain is not known, it might well be the same as in U.S.A., i.e. somewhat over 90.[92] This still leaves a difference of nearly 10 points in favour of non-delinquents. To some extent, the more cautious attitude towards mental deficiency as a causal factor in crime may have been due not only to the growing refinement of the techniques of mental testing but also to the increased understanding of the role played in the process of testing by cultural factors associated with both low intelligence and delinquency. Attempts have been made, therefore, to match such cultural factors so as to keep them identical for both groups to be tested, delinquents and non-delinquents. None of these attempts have so far succeeded in eliminating all these cultural differences.[93]

Changing views regarding the intelligence of the general population have also contributed to the present, more favourable, view of the intelligence of criminals. The results of tests applied during the First World War to several millions of American Army recruits may have been primarily responsible for these changes. In earlier enquiries the lower limits of normality seem to have been much too high.[94] These American experiences caused Professor Murchison, who was professionally connected with them, even to proclaim the superior intelligence of the criminal.[95]

Besides the technical weaknesses already mentioned, all these comparisons of the intelligence of criminals and non-criminals which consist of counting the percentages of mental defectives in the two groups, suffer from two major defects: First, there is the unavoidable defect that we can deal with the intelligence of the criminal only if he is detected, and there is a probability that detection is positively correlated with inferior intelligence. In *Prediction Methods in relation to Borstal Training*[96] it was found that the more intelligent Borstal boys—with the exception of the most superior ones—had more crimes taken into account at their request when sentenced, i.e. they had probably been more successful in evading arrest for some time than the duller boys. Criminals who are even more intelligent than those in the higher classes of the Borstal study might have been able to evade detection altogether.

Secondly, as all statements or questions referring to 'the criminal' in general terms are beside the point, it is equally senseless to examine the intelligence of this mysterious figure. The least we can do—inadequate though it is—is to distinguish between the various types of crime. Obviously, there are offences which can be successfully planned and carried through only by individuals possessing certain intellectual abilities. Already Goring[97] gave a list of the various types of crimes committed by his group of convicts together with the percentages of crimes committed by mental defectives. While for all types together this percentage was 14·4, it was 55·2 for setting fire to haystacks, 39·5 for indecent assault, 8·8 for murder, 6·3 for embezzling, 2·3 for coining and 2·1 for fraud. Similar lists could probably be produced from other samples of the criminal population.[98] This does not, of course, exclude the possibility that a mental defective may occasionally commit an apparently clever offence or a person of high intelligence do something stupid. Moreover, success in carrying out an offence should not be confused with intelligence as it may be due to stupidity, daring or the inability to see the dangers in a given situation.

However divergent may be the views on the delinquency of mental defectives, it is beyond doubt that the dull and backward group of subnormals has a far higher delinquency rate than persons of average intelligence.[99]

While the material so far presented has been mainly concerned with the incidence of mental deficiency among criminals, we may now turn to the other way of approach to the problem, i.e. the incidence of criminality among mental defectives. We owe most of our knowledge of this side of the picture to psychiatrists working in institutions for mental defectives. For example Dr. R. G. Blake Marsh, Medical Superintendent, Bromham House Colony near Bedford,[100] looking at the matter from the point of view of a psychiatrist charged with the institutional care of mental defectives, distinguishes sharply between the low-grade and the high-grade defectives. The former, feeling themselves at a disadvantage on account of their low earnings, resort to petty thefts or commit sexual offences against young children as normal girls of their own age will have nothing to do with them. Their offences are spontaneous and but rarely planned, and in institutions, where they find themselves with others of the same disability, they give little trouble and usually do well. It is the high-grade defective inmate who is likely to cause trouble. He commits offences, sometimes with cunning and some evidence of planning, to gain prestige and publicity, and he may also induce others of lower mentality to commit offences for him. Another psychiatrist, Dr. K. O. Milner, Medical Superintendent of the Aston Hall Mental Deficiency Institution, near Derby,[101] stresses the great preponderance of sexual crimes and crimes of violence among mental defectives. He refers to a report of the Board of Control (now dissolved under the Mental Health Act, 1959, s. 2) for 1934–6, according to which 26 per cent of the offences committed by mental defectives were sexual offences, and to an investigation by Norwood East who had found 22·6 per cent of such offences in a sample of 283 mental defectives. From this he concludes that sex offences are nearly ten times as common among defectives as in ordinary criminals, whereas crimes of violence are two or three times as frequent. Sadistic acts, too, are not uncommon among them. Milner also mentions the very high proportion of acts of violence among female patients of institutions for mental defectives, due mainly to the feeling of sexual frustration or homosexual or heterosexual jealousy. A non-psychiatrist, Ferguson, in his study of a sample of 301 mentally handicapped Glasgow boys,[102] also found the proportion of boys convicted and of recidivists far higher among those mentally handicapped than among the other groups he examined, and the proportion of sex offences, although not particularly high in absolute figures, far exceeded that for ordinary school-leavers and physically handicapped boys.

In conclusion we might say that the uncertainty still prevailing in this field is reflected in the fact that one of the most recent students of the subject, Mary Woodward, reaches two slightly contradictory conclusions in her simultaneous publications: on the one hand, that 'low intelligence plays little or no part in delinquency', and on the other that it 'cannot be regarded as an important causal factor' in it.[103] We are inclined to prefer the second formula to the first. Here as in many other fields of criminology there is a danger that insight into the exaggerations and shortcomings of previous generations may lead to errors of the opposite kind: over-estimation of the role of subnormality may be replaced by under-valuation.

Finally, passing to a discussion of the reasons why mental subnormality may be a cause of delinquency we are running the risk of trying to explain a phenomenon whose very existence is still in dispute. It is in fact much easier to find reasons for a likely causal relationship between subnormality and delinquency than to establish the relationship itself. Explanations can be found in the intellectual, in the economic and the emotional spheres. In the intellectual sphere: The mental defective may occasionally not grasp the full significance of his actions. Although he knows that stealing and similarly simple offences are forbidden and punishable by law, he may not understand the legal implications of more sophisticated acts such as forgery, embezzlement, stealing by finding and of sexual misbehaviour. Because of the ease with which defectives can be persuaded to take part in criminal exploits they may be used as tools by older and more experienced persons. Naturally, such considerations will lose in weight for the higher grades of deficiency where their place will be taken by emotional difficulties. 'With sufficient intelligence to realize how far they are left behind, they feel they belong nowhere and to nobody . . . what wonder that at times they become violent . . . or act recklessly so that they may obtain some notice. If not credit why not notoriety?'[104] Mistakes made by parents, who may drive them too hard,[105] or by unsympathetic teachers[106] may make things worse. Unlike the physically handicapped, the mental defective is unable to make up for his defects by his achievements in other spheres. Especially if he is of the self-assertive type, he has to shine somehow, and the only way may be delinquency.[107] If detained in closed institutions, where he may have to mix with low-grade defectives, the borderline case may feel particularly humiliated and frustrated. At least as obvious are the economic causes of misbehaviour. Unless specific protective measures are taken on his behalf, the defective will often be the last to get a job and the first to be sacked. Bearing all this in mind we have to agree with Weber who writes: 'It is indeed remarkable that the association of mental backwardness with delinquency is not more frequent than it is.' In any case, it will greatly depend on the social environment whether a mental defective becomes a delinquent. For females Lombroso's view that prostitution often takes the place of crime can hardly be disputed. Most studies of prostitutes draw attention to the high proportion of defectives and in particular of dull girls among them.[108] In an investigation into the causes of sex-delinquency in girls, Burt gives the following figures for his sample: 12 per cent mentally defective, 27·4 per cent definitely dull and 53·2 per cent educationally backward. Here, as always, we have to bear in mind that the prostitute studied by psychologists and social workers is probably even less representative of the *genus* prostitute than the prisoner or probationer is of the criminal.

## 3. *Genius and Crime*

Having treated mental deficiency at some length we should devote at least a few pages to the opposite side of the matter. By including them in a chapter on 'mental disorders' we do not of course imply that geniuses are always mentally ill. The following text will make this clear. It is only as a deviation from the average mental make-up of human beings that this category can legitimately find its place in the present chapter. 'Genius' is not defined by law, it is no mass phenomenon, nor can it easily be investigated statistically, although this has repeatedly been attempted, by Sir Francis Galton for example.[109] Nevertheless, its relation to crime has attracted the attention of criminologists for a long time and mainly for two reasons: first, the alleged affinity of genius and insanity and, secondly, the belief that men of genius are likely to be anti-social, or at least too individualistic and unconventional to be capable of submitting to society's rules. To define the meaning of genius is no easy task. Rejecting the subjective definition of Lange-Eichbaum[110] as genius being something entirely dependent on the recognition by mankind at large we might perhaps accept Kretschmer's formula, 'the ability to create special values bearing a personal stamp . . . novel ideas and forms of expression and the production of factors which initiate new historical epochs'.[111]

The idea that highly creative and original minds are apt to hover on the verge of insanity is very old, as old perhaps as the idea that the personality finds its external expression in the face and bodily structure of man. Kretschmer[112] quotes Aristotle's statement: 'Famous poets, artists and statesmen frequently suffer from melancholia or madness', and in Shakespeare's *Midsummer Night's Dream*, we read (V i): 'the poet's eye, in a fine frenzy rolling'. These are only expressions of an assumed very general association between the two phenomena. Attempts to explain it in more specific psychiatric terms were made much later, notably by Lombroso, Lange-Eichbaum and Kretschmer. The latter, in his brilliant treatment of the subject, strongly attacks the generally held view that mentally sound individuals are always superior to less normal ones and that it would therefore be disparaging to men of genius to state, as Kretschmer does, that among them mental diseases, and especially psychopathic conditions, are 'decidedly more frequent' than among the general population. While it would be difficult to prove this statistically, the general impression given by the material presented by the above-mentioned writers supports Kretschmer's view. If Tredgold disputes the existence of this relationship he may be too much inclined to identify genius with 'outstanding ability' and to ignore the qualitative difference between these two concepts. From these premises, there is only one further step to the conclusion that there is also an over-average rate of crime among men of genius. Havelock Ellis[113] maintained in his *Study of British Genius* that 'at least 160, or over 16 per cent, of our 975 eminent men were imprisoned, once or oftener, for periods of varying lengths, while many others only escaped imprisonment by voluntary exile', a statement which is of little use without a careful distinction between political and common offences. Among men of genius who committed ordinary crimes the most frequently quoted names are François Villon, Veit Stoss, Benvenuto Cellini, the Borgias and Rousseau. Of Cellini, Jacob Burckhardt has said 'he is a man who can do everything, risks everything, and bears his measure within himself'.[114]

Turning now to the younger age groups, it seems to be generally agreed that there are comparatively few offenders among children of super-normal ability and vice versa. In Cyril Burt's group a high degree of super-normality was 'conspicuously rare'.[115] According to Leta Hollingworth,[116] such children are, as a rule, more stable emotionally, more adaptable and better able to resist temptations than normal or subnormal ones. Any difficulties which they may experience arise when there is too great a disproportion between their superior intelligence and their general level of maturity, their inability to suffer fools gladly, their inner isolation and sexual imbalance.

In his profoundly stimulating discussion of what he calls the 'great character'—a concept which probably differs from that of genius in stressing more the moral than the intellectual superiority of the person—Martin Buber stresses that the great character is not

280

beyond the acceptance of norms, 'no responsible person remains a stranger to norms', but in a reference to Ibsen he adds: 'Today the great characters are still "enemies of the people", they who love their society, yet wish not only to preserve it but to raise it to a higher level.'[117] However, not all men of genius are 'great characters' in Buber's sense. Some of them live in that large territory between good and evil where it often depends only on chance whether or not they stray in that part of it which we call crime. Of Tchaikovsky, for example, Gerald Abraham writes[118] that 'in everyday life . . . he seems never to have shrunk from a convenient lie . . . and it is hardly too much to say that his whole outward life was a façade . . . to give the world a certain impression and conceal his true nature'. There is little doubt that he was a 'creative psychopath' of genius who may have been saved from crime by his good fortune of meeting a woman benefactor whose financial help protected him from the cold blasts of ordinary life.

# Chapter 16

## THE PSYCHOLOGY OF THE NORMAL OFFENDER

### I. HISTORICAL INTRODUCTION

The treatment of this subject has long been suffering from two handicaps: it has been neglected in favour of criminal anthropology and biology, and it has been too much identified with the study of criminal pathology, i.e. of the mentally abnormal offender. It is only from the early decades of the present century on, with the gradual weakening of the influence of the Lombrosian school, with the coming of psycho-analysis and the growing awareness that there is no hard and fast line of demarcation between the normal and the abnormal, that the psychology of the normal offender has come into its own. A brief, but valuable sketch of the history of the subject, to which special reference may here be made, has been given by Bonger.[1] Among the first to collect a volume of case material on the matter was the French lawyer F. G. de Pitaval in his *Causes célèbres et intéressantes* (1734 ff. in 20 volumes), followed by a German work *Der Neue Pitaval* (1842 ff.) and several new editions (1742–95), one of them with a preface by no less a person than Friedrich Schiller, whose intense interest in the subject is well known. The nineteenth century saw the publication of Anselm von Feuerbach's *Merkwürdige Kriminalrechtsfälle* (1808–11) and his *Aktenmässige Darstellung merkwürdiger Verbrechen* (1827–9), as of several other works which had this in common with their famous predecessor that they were collections of interesting criminal cases, especially of sensational trials.[2] While these collections have greatly increased our knowledge of individual crimes and criminals, most of them suffered from the weakness that they concentrated too much on the 'interesting', i.e. the sensational, case to the exclusion of the great masses of ordinary 'run of the mill' cases and that they paid too much attention to criminal trials to the exclusion of crimes not brought before the courts. Moreover, their psychology was often primitive, in accordance with the backward state of the scientific study of psychology at the time when the earlier of these publications appeared. More recent collections, such as the 'Notable

British Trials Series',[3] usually consist of verbatim reproductions of the trial with introductions which often attempt to break through the barriers and formalities of English criminal procedure and to make at least a brief assessment of the psychological and psychiatric factors at work.

Apart from the collections of case histories there are also several theoretical works by criminologists entirely or partly devoted to criminal psychology. While Lombroso produced in this field mostly platitudes and unwarranted generalizations such as remarks on the vanity, cruelty and cowardice of 'the' criminal, Goring tried to measure the association between criminality and certain psychological factors such as temperament, suicidal tendencies, egotism and in particular intellectual inferiority.[4] Of far greater value was the material published in the volumes of Hans Gross' *Archiv für Kriminalanthropologie und Kriminalistik* (since 1898), of Aschaffenburg's *Monatsschrift für Kriminalpsychologie und Strafrechtsreform* (since 1904, now called *Monatsschrift für Kriminologie und Strafrechtsreform*) and of the *Abhandlungen aus dem Gesamtgebiete der Kriminalpsychologie* (published in Heidelberg irregularly since 1912). Although there are several books, especially in German, called *Kriminalpsychologie* or *Psychologie des Verbrechers* (e.g. by Gross, Sommer and Wulffen), Hans W. Gruhle, himself the author of various excellent monographs and articles on the subject, was not altogether wrong when he stated as late as 1933 that a textbook of criminal psychology did not yet exist.[5] It is mainly the immense stimulus received from the work of Freud and his successors that has advanced the study of the subject in the present century. In spite of this and of the existence of a vast literature it is still true to say that we do not yet seem to possess any single publication dealing satisfactorily with the psychology of the 'normal' offender in all its aspects.[6] In fact, most writers still tend to neglect the normal in favour of the abnormal.

Of immeasurable value to the study of criminal psychology have, of course, throughout been the great masterworks of world literature, to think only of Shakespeare, Schiller, Dostoevsky, Balzac (of whom it has been said that only his criminals were really alive), Victor Hugo, Dickens, Stendhal, Gorki, Thomas Mann and many others. This, however, is a subject too vast to be treated within the framework of the present chapter.[7] While the contributions of psychoanalysis will be dealt with separately in Chapter 17, certain other issues will here be treated beforehand.

## II. THE CONCEPT OF NORMALITY

We have repeatedly stressed the difficulty of drawing the line between the mentally normal and the abnormal offender. Moreover, the meaning of *'normality'* has so far remained an open question, and the course hitherto followed has been to deal with the various forms of abnormality first. Normality could then be defined as a condition of mind to which neither of these concepts can be applied, i.e. the normal offender would be one who is neither psychotic nor neurotic or psychopathic or mentally defective. It is only natural that we should be inclined to take this easy course. However, as Barbara Wootton rightly points out,[8] the existing difficulties are not altogether avoided by adopting such a negative formula. Is it impossible to find a positive definition of normality or mental health, or, for that matter, of mental illness? Is there a common element in these terms which goes beyond a mere assortment of negations?[9] Wootton and others have shown the existing confusion. To the many quotations given in her book we would only add Durkheim's famous discussion of the concept of normality.[10] To him, crime itself was 'normal' because a society without it was inconceivable; therefore it was an integral element of every healthy society.[11] This did not mean to him that the individual criminal, too, was necessarily healthy and sane; there was a great difference in this respect, he stressed, between sociological and psychological facts. Durkheim admits, moreover, that an excessive rise in crime would be no longer normal but morbid,[12] an admission which, although it leads to the unanswerable question of what is 'excessive' at a given time and a given place,[13] is nothing but a consequence of the fact that in the sociological field, too, there is an imperceptible transition from the normal to the abnormal. The dilemma remains, though, that, according to Durkheim, on the one hand, the normality of crime has nothing to do with the frequency of its occurrence and, on the other hand, the greater its frequency the more likely is it to be regarded as abnormal.

As far as the individual offender and his mental condition are concerned, the concept of normality will usually be considered in relation to the mental condition of the 'average' person of that particular type, which inevitably introduces the statistical element of frequency.[14] In addition, considerations of 'norm' and of behaviour which is sanctioned and approved cannot be altogether avoided, which introduces the element of value.[15] In fact, much of Wootton's discussion is intended to show that most definitions of mental health are permeated with the value concepts of the writers concerned and that in particular the capacity of adjusting oneself to the values of a

284

given society plays a dominant part in those definitions, 'adjustment to a particular culture or to a particular set of institutions', the ability to achieve such adjustment being regarded as the criterion of mental health and normality.[16] It has to be admitted that the literature on criminal psychology is not free from this kind of reasoning and only in extreme cases, such as Nazism, has the desirability of an adjustment to the existing 'culture' been seriously questioned.[17] With this very important proviso, however, the ability to adjust one's conduct to the standards of the majority cannot be altogether ignored in our definition of normality. If the factor 'majority' is properly underlined, the frequent objection falls to the ground that adjustment may also include compliance with criminal norms.[18] It is true, of course, that, as Fromm points out,[19] this is only one aspect of normality or mental health, i.e. the one seen 'from the standpoint of a functioning society', and that there is also another possible point of view, i.e. the happiness of the individual, which may lead to different results. The Mental Health Act, 1959, uses, as we have seen (Chapter 15, II), the formula 'incapable of living an independent life or of guarding himself against serious exploitation', but this 'independence' of the life of the mentally normal person is obviously not meant to imply being independent of the standards of ordinary society.

Granting that normality is closely connected with adaptability to the requirements of life in society, the further question arises whether the degree of normality necessarily corresponds to the ease and completeness of adaptation and adjustment to these requirements. This is likely to be the case, and the neurotic who has to go through serious inner conflicts to achieve that state of external peace with society is clearly less 'normal' than the philistine to whom adjustment comes naturally without any struggle. From this it follows that for our purposes normality can be defined operationally as a condition of mind where no special efforts, no extraordinary measures of a psychiatric nature are required on the part of the criminal law and the penal system to deal satisfactorily with the case. This implies that the dividing line has to be kept very flexible and that it may have to be moved forward or backward from time to time in accordance with our changing views on the matter,[20] and that it also depends on such factors as age, sex and social class. There is no absolute definition of normality, mental health or illness, 'the "normal" mind . . . is obviously impossible to describe'.[21]

## III. PSYCHOLOGICAL AND SOCIOLOGICAL
### APPROACHES TO THE 'NORMAL' OFFENDER.
### EXTRA-, INTRA-, AND IM-PUNITY

When trying to describe the normal offender and to explain his behaviour we are inevitably driven towards the direction of what used to be that vast no-man's-land between psychology and sociology, now to a large extent occupied by the new discipline of social psychology. Bearing in mind what was said in our 'Preliminary Observations' to Part III, i.e. that a mental element has always to be present in criminal behaviour, we might be tempted to accommodate the whole sociology of crime under the heading of 'criminal psychology', and there is indeed no rigid line of demarcation between the two branches. The differences are merely such of degree and emphasis. If we find the ultimate explanation of a crime predominantly in the environment of the offender the problem will be classified as one for the sociologist; if, on balance, we find it more in the individual himself the matter is one for the psychologist. In the words of Dr. Ernest G. Schachtel, the Rorschach Test expert employed by the Gluecks in *Unraveling*,[22] when trying to decide whether or not a boy was likely to be a delinquent, 'I asked myself whether his character structure, as I saw it on the basis of the Rorschach Test, was of a type likely to resist the inducements toward becoming delinquent offered by poor socio-economic circumstances and by the neighborhood.' Sociology tells us that there are certain factors in the individual's environment which might possibly produce crime. Psychology describes the kind of individual personality likely to incline towards crime if exposed to such a challenge. For example, given a frustrating environment, a 'criminal subculture', or conflicting systems of norms and values as to be described below, it is for the psychologist to say which type of person can be expected to overcome such difficulties and which is likely to be overwhelmed by them.

All this means that a great deal of uncertainty and controversy is unavoidable in determining whether an individual case belongs more to the domain of the psychologist or that of the sociologist, and that in our discussion of criminal psychology and sociology there is bound to occur much overlapping and repetition, but these shortcomings are preferable to the superficial appearance of simplicity and to the drawing of artificial lines of demarcation which have no basis in reality. Moreover, as Glaser has said,[23] 'the "great debates" between sociology and psychology have lost some of their former fervor. The disputes ultimately led to concessions on both sides, or, more accurately, to reformulations on both sides.' It still remains true, however, that there are certain considerable differences in the main interests and outlook of the two disciplines.[24] In a forthcoming book by Franco Ferracuti and Marvin E. Wolfgang on the *Subculture of Violence*, Ch. 1, much valuable material is presented on these and kindred problems concerning the object of full 'integration' between different scientific disciplines, in particular sociology, psychology and biology.

Much of the progress that may have been made in recent decades towards a clearer understanding of the psychological characteristics of normal offenders as compared with non-offenders has been due to better classification, less sweeping generalizations and greater scepticism. Senseless statements such as Lombroso's on the psychology of 'the criminal' have become rarer, although they have by no means altogether disappeared. As an illustration of the growing scepticism, not to say complete despair of the possibility of finding any psychological differences between the personality make-up of offenders and non-offenders, an often-quoted article by Schuessler and Cressey may be referred to.[25] These authors made a survey of all American studies published up to 1950, 113 altogether, in which the personality characteristics of delinquents or criminals and non-delinquents or non-criminals were compared, with the result that, in their view, while in a minority of 42 per cent differences in favour of the latter group had been found, in a majority of 58 per cent of the studies no such differences had emerged. Their conclusion was that from these studies, in view of 'the doubtful validity of many of the obtained differences, as well as the lack of consistency in the combined results', no significant association between criminality and personality elements had emerged. While this conclusion has been unreservedly accepted by Wootton,[26] another sociologist, Marshall B. Clinard,[27] has criticized it for two reasons: first, because personality traits are more likely to be significant for certain types of crime than for crime in general, and, secondly, because the researches included in the survey had been made too early to benefit fully from the just constructed Minnesota Multiphasic Personality Inventory (MMPI). With regard to the first point it has to be noted that Schuessler and Cressey themselves criticize the studies included in their survey for lumping all types of crime together. Moreover, they pay attention to the fact that practically all these studies had been done on prisoners, i.e. an unrepresentative group of offenders, and—closely linked with this—that it could not be stated whether crime had to be regarded as the result of a certain personality trait or whether the latter was itself the product of criminal experience, i.e. whether the trait had already existed at the beginning of a criminal career or had developed only later as the result of imprisonment, etc. In short, what the Schuessler-Cressey survey has been able to demonstrate is not the final impossibility of distinguishing the personality of delinquents and non-delinquents, but merely the inadequacy of the studies surveyed by these writers. This is its significance and its limitation.

In view of Clinard's second criticism the question has to be faced whether the MMPI has, more than other projective tests, succeeded in discriminating between the personality traits of delinquents and non-delinquents. The literature on the application of the MMPI in this field is considerable, and one recent American writer refers already to the 'demonstrated capacity of this instrument to discriminate between delinquents and non-delinquents'.[28] Barbara Wootton is more sceptical,[29] and even some of the principal workers on the MMPI have recently expressed themselves with the greatest possible reserve. Summing up the results of a large piece of research they write:[30]

Surely we cannot say that these data put us far ahead either in prediction or understanding. . . . Although the 550 items of the MMPI are probably adequate to explore the maximum relationships between the personality the children put into the patterns of their answers and their behaviour, it is not likely that the scales of the MMPI, as now used, are developing the maximum relationship. In spite of the great amount known about delinquency, we have no way available to sharpen the test tool . . . The facts suggested by the data are not pretentious. They do seem to provide a foundation for the continuing analysis . . . data not presented here show that these various personality traits have environmental correlates, such as with the broken home, but it is a significant finding that the personalities are also partly independent of obvious environmental influence. . . . We suggest that the adolescent himself is a contributing factor both to his environment and his behavior.

In another recent Minnesota study[31] only those children of a previously tested larger group were included who had achieved 'invalid protocols on the basis of high scores on the L and/or F scales or high scores in the "Cannot say" category'.[32] Subsequent follow-up studies showed that delinquency was most frequent among this 'invalid' group, and the central hypothesis of the study was, therefore, that high scores on these three scales might be useful predictors of delinquency. Generally speaking, it cannot be said, however, that this or any other study using the MMPI has produced a workable synthesis of the delinquent personality as such. Moreover, it has to be borne in mind that the scales of the MMPI have been constructed from abnormal clinical cases and that it is expected to spot juvenile delinquents just because delinquency is believed to exhibit the same symptoms as a neurosis or psychosis.[33] The question arises, therefore, how far the usefulness of the MMPI would be reduced if this belief is disputed as an unwarranted generalization. Special attention has here been given to the MMPI because it is widely regarded as one of the most promising modern projection techniques. A modification of the MMPI has been developed by another American psychologist, Harrison G. Gough, to whose work attention has been drawn by Reckless and Clinard and who claims that his scale provides a reliable measurement of an individual's tendency towards delinquency 'as a part of his incapacity to play socially acceptable roles in life'.[34]

The present writer cannot be expected to pass judgment on the extremely complicated question of the value of projective techniques in general; most readers will be familiar with the negative views expressed by Eysenck which leave no doubt about the wide differences of opinion even among professional psychologists.[35]

The criminologist, looking to the latter for help in his efforts to build up, with the aid of projective tests, an image of the personality of the normal offender will find much interesting material in T. Grygier's brilliant study Oppression.[36] It is the main object of this book 'to examine the changes in the psychological aspect of culture under oppression', and, more specifically, whether there is a positive association between oppression and an extrapunitive attitude and crime and between crime and the tendency to direct aggression outwards. Grygier's main hypothesis was that 'an oppressive environment brings about certain measurable changes in personality'. The method used was an examination of samples of persons, mostly Poles, discharged after the last war from German concentration camps, some of them kept in prison for common offences committed after the liberation, while others were not. Care was taken to match the concentration camp and the offenders' groups by individual pairing, and large numbers of both groups were then given intelligence (Otis) and personality tests, the latter consisting of the Thematic Apperception Test (T.A.T.) and Rosenzweig's Picture-Frustration Study (P-F.S.) The latter was mainly employed to establish the rate of extrapunitive, intrapunitive, and impunitive attitudes, i.e. whether a subject was more inclined to blame aggressively other persons or external objects for his feeling of frustration (extrapunitive), or rather to blame himself (intra- or self-punitive) or to blame nobody (impunitive). As already stated, the hypothesis was that delinquency was associated with extrapunitiveness. No personality questionnaires were used, 'as the weaknesses of this technique were considered too great for it to be practicable', nor were any attitude scales applied because of the difficulty of measuring directly 'anything that is merely potential'.[37] While Grygier is much more favourably inclined towards the Rorschach Test than Eysenck, for example, he did not use it in this study because it 'presents a picture of the total personality', whereas he was interested only in certain aspects of it. Moreover, the T.A.T. seemed more useful when the object was to trace major differences between whole groups of people. 'By using both the P-F.S. and the T.A.T. we could not only measure the tendency to direct aggression in a certain direction, but could also trace the psychological mechanism underlying this tendency' (p. 58).

The material used by Grygier for the P-F.S. tests was limited to 15 Polish delinquents with a background of forced labour in industry or agriculture and a control group of non-delinquent Polish displaced persons with a similar background, matched for sex, citizenship, nationality and religion and coming from similar types of community (p. 124). They were not matched for education, intelligence and age—but it was not considered that this invalidated the results. The statistical data suggested that the delinquents were more extra-punitive than the non-delinquents, i.e. they showed a stronger tendency than the others to perceive ambiguous social situations as frustrating to themselves, with the emphasis on the frustrating obstacle, while minimizing the frustration caused by them to others; they also showed a reluctance to admit guilt and blame themselves. 'They rarely express the impunitive type of optimism, but rather tend to think that something must be done to satisfy their needs' (p. 127). Grygier stresses that there may be nothing wrong or antisocial in certain occasional extrapunitive attitudes; what is symptomatic is rather the persistence of this type of response and the tendency to expect that *all* problems will be solved by somebody else (p. 73). Moreover, he admits that on certain aspects of the extrapunitive character his findings were merely suggestive, not conclusive (p. 132), but he regards them as being in line with observations made in the practical administration of criminal justice. He also found that the rate of extrapunitive responses was higher for those who had undergone particularly severe forms of oppression in concentration camps and that these latter forms had produced a particularly high rate of crime, in fact approximately forty-five times greater than for groups who had experienced less severe forms of oppression (p. 108); in other words, the association between degrees of oppression and the rate of crime was proved.

While the P-F.S. measures 'the more superficial level of action', the T.A.T. is 'considered to reveal a deeper level of personality', the level of phantasy, 'the underlying inhibited tendencies which the subject is not willing to admit, or can not admit because he is unconscious of them'.[38] Only a few more of the complicated findings of the Grygier study can here be mentioned: the delinquents showed more abasement and guilt feelings than the non-delinquents, which 'supports the view that delinquency may be associated with unconscious guilt feelings, although in real conflict situations (or in the quasi-real situations of the P-F.S.) the delinquents deny guilt and accuse others' (p. 203), which shows that the results of the T.A.T., reflecting the unconscious level of personality, may differ from the more superficial picture presented by the P-F.S. 'At the level of action the delinquent is aggressive . . . , but at the level of fantasy he is the victim.'[39] Other findings of the T.A.T. were that the heroes of the delinquents live in a more hostile world than those of the non-delinquents, the delinquents tell more stories about rejection by the mother, and there is less family affiliation among them. They are more pessimistic and regard themselves more often as inadequate. 'Their whole perception appears to be coloured by a feeling of the overwhelming power of an inimical Press.'[40] ' "Normal delinquents" show particularly strong feelings of personal inadequacy', 'the delinquent has a different perception of the world around him and of his own role in this world; that general trend of thought changes his perception of social events in which he is involved and affects his actions' (p. 208). Although these statements are formulated in a general way as if they would apply to all delinquents anywhere they are, as the context shows, meant to apply only to the limited sample used for these tests. In fact, researches such as Grygier's, and those of the Minnesota school, show quite clearly how greatly methods of studying the psychology of the criminal have changed from the rather primitive generalizations of many nineteenth-century criminologists. The change in methods has not necessarily produced a wholesale revolution in our views on the subject; some of the factors now regularly quoted as characteristic of criminals were mentioned already seventy or a hundred years ago, for example frustration and the feeling of being teased and irritated was stressed by Maudsley and the absence of repentance and remorse by Lombroso.[41] What the greater sophistication of modern research techniques has done is rather to produce a picture of the criminal personality far more complex than available before and less suitable for general verdicts.

After making a penetrating survey of some of the modern literature on the subject, Grygier concludes that 'all extrapunitive traits are found by observers among psychopathic and delinquent subjects. . . . Our research gives experimental evidence and a conceptual scheme in support of these observations' (p. 244). He admits, however, that 'delinquents as a class seem to vary among themselves much more than they differ from non-delinquents' (p. 240), and this is a point which has to be stressed above anything else. Present-day research, while rightly trying to discover certain traits common to all criminals, should never ignore the fact that the differences are probably more profound than the similarities. Whether the observer notices more the former or the latter may to some extent depend on his own personality.

Another attempt to compare the psychological characteristics of delinquents and non-delinquents by means of personality tests was made by Dr. Ernest Schachtel, a Rorschach expert, as part of the Glueck study *Unraveling Juvenile Delinquency*. The main differences in character and personality structure found by the application of Rorschach tests were as follows:[42] the delinquent boys were much more assertive, defiant, ambivalent to authority, resentful to others, hostile, suspicious, destructive, impulsive and more extravert; they suffered less from fear of failure and defeat, were less co-operative, less conventional and self-controlled. (Here it may be noted that in about one half of the studies surveyed by Schuessler and Cressey the delinquents were found to be slightly more introverted.) In addition to being given the Rorschach test these boys were also interviewed by a psychiatrist who found the delinquents to differ from the non-delinquents in a number of traits characteristic of the 'dynamics of temperament'.[43] It is stressed by the Gluecks that the Rorschach analyst and the psychiatrist were not given access to each other's findings and that their terminology and even the meaning of the terms employed by them were often so different that comparisons were difficult. Nevertheless, with regard to some traits a high measure of agreement was discovered, for example, where the Rorschach analyst had labelled the delinquents as more 'assertive' and 'defiant', the psychiatrist called them more 'stubborn' than the others.[44]

Only one more of the many comparative findings of *Unraveling* may here be mentioned because it contradicts one of the most common assumptions in criminological literature: the delinquents were found to show a slightly lower incidence of feelings of insecurity and anxiety and of not being loved or wanted.

While, as already mentioned above (Chapter 1, I(2c)), the Gluecks in 1950 still believed that from the wealth of data accumulated in *Unraveling* a tentative causal formula or 'law' seemed to emerge which enabled them to construct not only a physical and socio-cultural but also a psychological picture of delinquents as a mass (p. 281), six years later they had to admit that from the evidence available 'we cannot conclude that there is a "delinquent personality" as a relatively constant and stable combination of physique, character, and temperament'.[45] However, if we compare the picture presented in *Unraveling* with the results of other studies using case material of a different kind we find on balance slightly more agreement than disagreement. Certain features such as aggressiveness or the feeling of personal inadequacy are widely regarded as characteristics of the delinquent personality, whereas on others, such as extraversion or insecurity, the views tend to differ.[46] Even where there is a certain measure of agreement that a given trait is more frequent among the delinquents than the non-delinquents the difference, though perhaps statistically significant, is often still small enough to make us wonder whether it really contributes much to our understanding of the delinquent. Added to this, it is the principal weakness of all such statistical comparisons of individual traits that they ignore the personality as a whole. It may be a matter of some interest to us to know that 80 per cent of a group of offenders were found to be aggressive, inadequate and frustrated against, say, only 60 per cent of a group of non-offenders, but this still does not tell us whether these traits have all been present in 80 or 60 per cent respectively of the individual members of these two groups or whether some of those found to be aggressive were not inadequate and frustrated and vice versa. It is here that the typological studies referred to above (Chapter 8, II(2)), with their attempts to work out configurations of several factors, are of value, and recent research designed to show certain relationships between a variety of phenomena by means of factorial analysis may also be mentioned. Through factorial analysis a large number of variables can be correlated with each other in the expectation that 'from this mass of correlations a few factors can be extracted which are themselves independent of each other . . . and if we are lucky we finish up with an explanation of *why* these variables are correlated with each other'.[47] B. Marcus, psychologist at Wakefield Prison, believes he has extracted in this way a factor which distinguishes, sociologically and psychologically, middle-class criminals, for example false pretenders and homosexuals, from working-class criminals, i.e. mainly thieves and housebreakers. Further research on similar lines may produce further concatenations of psychological traits. The latest volume of the Glueck studies, *Family Environment and Delinquency*, published after the completion of the present chapter,[48] in fact provides many illustrations of the complex ways in which psychological, sociological and biological factors may combine in one individual to produce delinquency. To single out a few of these combinations may give a misleading picture; the reader will have to study the book as a whole to appreciate the extreme complexity of this work and the equally great caution with which—as the authors are fully aware—the results have to be interpreted.[49]

## IV. PSYCHOLOGICAL PROBLEMS OF DIFFERENT TYPES OF CRIME AND CRIMINALS, WITH SPECIAL REFERENCE TO MURDER

To make a complete survey of the psychological factors which might potentially lie behind criminal behaviour a systematic analysis would be needed of the main types of both the human personality and the motives which stimulate it into action and then show which of the psychological features of the personality and which motives have been encountered with particular frequency among criminals. Personality—a term of which Allport listed no fewer than 48 definitions already in 1937[50]—could be defined in this connection with Eysenck as 'the more or less stable and enduring organization of a person: character, temperament, intellect, and physique, which determines his unique adjustment to the environment'.[51] In this chapter we are concerned with character and temperament rather than with intellect and physique. Cattell, whose preliminary definition of personality is simply 'that which determines behaviour in a defined situation', distinguishes dynamic traits concerned with 'motivation, action and purpose', temperamental traits concerned with 'pervasive, unchanging qualities and tempos of our actions', and ability.[52] The studies referred to above under III and in Chapter 8, II, have produced some material on various character and temperamental traits of offenders, but, as already stated, it is far from adequate to give a complete picture, and the psychological study of some of the most common types of offenders is still in its infancy or, possibly, in its early adolescence. Whether the legal typology of offences is the most suitable basis for psychological differentiation may be open to doubt, but it has at least the practical advantage that it offers the easiest access to the case material.

Because of its gravity and the fascination which it invariably exerts, more psychological work has been done on homicide than on any other crime, except sexual offences, and the occasional attempts on the part of legislators to use psychological factors, especially motives, in order to distinguish murder from manslaughter[53] have also helped to swell the volume of literature on the subject. It is not surprising that the legislator, if he wishes to introduce in this field psychological factors other than the usual ones such as intent, negligence, malice, should prefer the distinction according to motives, which can be defined comparatively easily, rather than personality types which are more difficult to describe. It should be remembered, however, that with very few exceptions such as the one just mentioned the motive of a crime is irrelevant to the question of legal responsibility and becomes important only for the sentence and for the criminological understanding of the criminal act.

Out of the literature on motives of murder the following deserve special mention: Wolfgang, von Hentig, Bjerre, F. Tennyson Jesse, Roesner, Brearley, Norwood East, Abrahamsen, Ferracuti and Frederic Wertham, to whose study of a case of matricide attention was drawn above (Chapter 8).[54] In addition, there are the E.E.G. studies (Chapter 15 above), which deal mostly, but not exclusively, with abnormal cases, and a few attempts have also been made to assess the motives of murder statistically.[55] Unfortunately, the concept of motive is not always used in the same sense and occasionally confused with intention or cause in general; nor is the terminology on which the statistics are based always identical. Moreover, the frequency of the various motives depends to some extent on the legal definition of murder to which the statistical figures refer, for example if that definition requires certain motives it is obvious that the latter will appear more frequently here than in legislations which do not distinguish murder from manslaughter according to motive. With these important reservations the following statistical data may be reproduced: For 551 cases of murders committed in England and Wales during the 20 years ending 1905 (*Criminal Statistics for England and Wales, 1905*, p. 52, reproduced in *Report on Capital Punishment, 1953*, p. 329) 'quarrels or violent rage' were regarded as the 'motive or cause' in 68 cases, 'jealousy and intrigues' in 92, 'revenge' in 77, robbery in 50, extreme poverty in 39, sexual passion in 26 cases. For 465 persons charged with murder in 1957–60 Morris and Blom-Cooper give as 'motive or reason', theft in 33, sex in 23, quarrel and/or fight in 87, public brawl in 34, fit of temper/desperation in 33, mental disorder in 105, jealousy, etc., in 54, mercy or despair, etc., in 33, revenge or intrigue, etc., in 18 cases. In the figures for 1955–60 in the Home Office Research Unit report, quarrels or violent rage and jealousy and intrigue account for about one half of the cases, with robbery or financial gain and sex accounting together for about 30 per cent. This shows that the picture has not greatly changed in the past seventy years in this country, the emotional type of murder remaining most prominent. In Germany, where the conception of murder has been, both before and after the legal changes of recent decades, narrower than in English law, and where emotional killings are therefore more likely to be treated as manslaughter, a higher proportion of murder cases is due to economic motives, although this applies, naturally, more to murders of men than to murders of women.[56] In the United States, the picture is not so clear, but Wolfgang's recent figures for Philadelphia show a great preponderance of emotional over economic motives. Finally, in accordance with the Egyptian idea of revenge and retaliation as the basis of justice the motive of murder in Egypt is given in the official statistics as revenge, quarrels and disputes in roughly 50 per cent.[57]

Admittedly, all these attempts to classify the motives of murder statistically are bound to remain on the surface as they are by necessity often based on a superficial knowledge of both external and internal facts. For further knowledge we have to turn to more detailed studies of individual cases which will at once demonstrate the utter complexity of the motives sometimes working together in one single murder case, making any generalization very hazardous. There may be a layer of motives, and the one nearest to the deed may be entirely different from the more remote and actually decisive ones. Murder committed for financial gain may have ulterior sexual or political motives, and what seems to be a sexual murder may in fact have been due to financial considerations. Hentig has stressed the dynamic nature of a motive which may have to pass through many environmental changes and stimuli, some of them reinforcing, others weakening the strength of the motive. In many cases, especially of murder for the sake of robbery, the motive seems entirely inadequate in any rational way to explain the crime; the murderer himself is certainly unable to do so, and we have to search for unconscious motives, which means a psycho-analytic explanation (Chapter 17).[58]

This lack of a rational, adequate motive, which would be clearly understood by judges and the public, explains the not infrequent tendency to speak of a *motiveless* crime. A girl of fifteen is found murdered in the lavatory of a train. She has not been sexually assaulted, nor are any of her belongings missing: consequently, according to the prosecution this was 'apparently a crime without motive' (*The Times*, 15.9.1964). Stafford-Clark and F. H. Taylor, in the paper annexed to the *Minutes of the Royal Commission on Capital Punishment*, 1953 (p. 330), include in one of their five groups of cases of murder with different E.E.G.s those cases 'in which the crimes were apparently motiveless or in which the motive was very slight' and in many of which the E.E.G. was slightly or severely abnormal. We are not here concerned, however, with crimes committed by mentally abnormal persons whose motives are often so remote from the understanding of ordinary persons that their actions seem unmotivated to them. Even here, although we find it impossible to accept Cressey's extreme sociological theory of criminal motivation in its entirety he is right in stating that most behaviour traditionally labelled 'compulsive' is in fact motivated.[59] Of André Gide we are told that the idea of the 'unmotivated crime' committed by a normal person had constantly occupied his mind and that he treated it most thoroughly in his novel *The Vatican Cellars*. Has he succeeded in bringing the problem nearer to a solution? Lafcadio, his hero, pushes a man with whom he was travelling, a complete stranger to him, out of the fast moving train to his death. Certainly, no motive in the traditional sense was present in the case of this murder, and we are rather faced with a crime committed with the motive to kill without any of the traditional motives. What Gide has done in this novel is, therefore, not to demonstrate the possibility of a motiveless crime but to add to the catalogue of traditional motives, and this is essentially what he puts into the mouth of his frustrated novelist, Julius de Baraglioul. 'I don't want a motive for the crime—all I want is an explanation of the criminal. Yes! I mean to lead him into committing a crime gratuitously—into wanting to commit a crime without any motive at all. . . . His very reason for committing the crime is just to commit it without any reason.'[60] But, as Gide tries to show, Lafcadio's motive is also to find out whether he is a man capable of doing this: 'It's not so much about events that I'm curious, as about myself. There's many a man thinks he's capable of anything who draws back when it comes to the point. . . . What a gulf between the imagination and the deed!' (p. 185). In other words, we are here faced with yet another motive which we shall soon meet again in Dostoevsky's Raskolnikov: to prove to himself that he is a man capable of translating his imagination into action. In his interesting article on *Liberté et gratuité du crime dans l'œuvre d'André Gide*[61] the Spanish lawyer and writer Antonio Quintano Ripollès argues that Lafcadio shows the most obvious characteristics of the leptosome type (see above, Chapter 13), i.e. poor physique, coldness and egocentricity. He admits that from Gide's description no evidence emerges of mental disorder; on the contrary, he thinks Gide has proved the possibility of a 'motiveless' crime committed by a sane person. Nevertheless, he suggests that Lafcadio may show symptoms of latent schizophrenia or psychopathy, and the latter concept may indeed offer the most likely interpretation of Lafcadio's behaviour.

Motives can become operative only when they are joined together with a certain personality; a motive that will easily drive this particular person into this particular crime may utterly fail if working on another person. This, too, is demonstrated in Gide's novel. This 'motiveless' murder could be committed only by a man to whom human life had no intrinsic moral value: 'I felt as though I could have clasped the whole of mankind to my heart in my single embrace—or strangle it, for that matter. Human life! What a paltry thing! . . .' (p. 177). One can distinguish between crimes which are an expression of the offender's personality (*persönlichkeits-eigen*) and crimes which seem to be a deviation from it, an 'acting out of character' (*persönlichkeits-fremd*).[62] The same applies to the offender's motives, which may or may not be in line with his personality. If a motive is in harmony with the personality of the actor it need not be particularly strong, whereas if it is entirely out of keeping with the latter it will have to be of great force in order to drive a person into crime. The supreme difficulty which this distinction has to overcome lies in the problem to determine whether an act is 'in harmony' with the personality as a whole and whether it is therefore something easily to be expected of a certain individual. It is here that individual prediction will so often go astray (see Chapter 7 above) and it is here, too, that the idea of the *état dangereux*, so widely discussed in recent decades in Continental criminology, encounters one of its major stumbling blocks.[63] This concept, first formulated by Garofalo, has been defined in different ways; its object is to describe a human condition which justifies the expectation that the individual concerned is likely to commit a crime or crimes because of his biological and psychological characteristics, his *perversité constante*, his inability to adapt himself to his social environment. In the Italian Penal Code of 1930, art. 108, the 'delinquent tendency' is mentioned which is regarded as being caused by the particularly mischievous disposition of the offender, and according to art. 133 the judges, in sentencing the offender, have to consider, among other factors, his motives and character as indices of his capacity for wrongdoing. All this reminds us rather ominously of Lombroso and his followers, but it has to be admitted that modern criminology has taken considerable pains to produce a less biased and unscientific picture of the criminal personality. It has, for example, been shown that there are two different types of *état dangereux*, the permanent condition which the Lombrosians had especially in mind and a merely transitory state of mind through which many delinquents have to pass before they commit the criminal act and during which phase much can be done to divert them from it. As Pinatel rightly says[64] it was this second type which has been greatly clarified through the writings of the late Belgian psychiatrist and criminologist Etienne de Greeff, notably in relation to homicides committed out of jealousy or sexual passion.[65] de Greeff describes in detail the phenomena of what he calls *désengagement* and *révalorisation*, taking place in the case of individuals who have suffered an acute disillusionment and betrayal, feelings which lead to a sudden and complete reversal of all their beliefs and values and are the frequent cause of murder and/or suicide. The road to the final catastrophe may be very short or very long, but if those observers who can foresee the seemingly inevitable outcome are able to secure a postponement of the fatal action with some helpful psychological intervention in the interval, that action may sometimes be averted for good. Although both personality and motive may strongly favour the commission of the crime it also requires a certain atmosphere, a mood, a congenial situation and an opportunity, and once they have passed the crime may appear senseless. Othello might have been an example of this type. In striking contrast to such cases there are those where no outside interference short of physical force is capable of creating an effective diversion because of the principal actor's unbending determination to commit the murder. This is mainly the field of the family tragedy or the homicide committed for political ends or for revenge where, for example, a man sentenced to a long period of imprisonment for a crime of which he regards himself to be innocent kills, after his discharge, the principal witness for the prosecution. Here the hope to be able to take revenge has supported him throughout his years in prison, and no force on earth can make him change his mind once he is free.

With such cases we have already entered the field where a distinction is made between crimes with an intense 'ego involvement' and others where the actor's ego is not deeply involved.[66] Although this is very close to the previously mentioned distinction between *persön-lichkeits-eigen* and *persönlichkeits-fremd*, it is not identical with it. While the latter is concerned with the question of whether a particular deed is in harmony with the total personality of the actor, the former is more specifically interested in the relationship between this personality and the victim or object of the crime. If the murderer wants to kill just this particular person or the thief to possess just this particular picture, book, stamp or piece of jewellery; if the murderer feels that his own life depends on the death of this person and the thief that he cannot exist without this article, which is still missing in his collection, then we would say that his ego is deeply involved in the matter.[67] As already indicated, this is the field of many family tragedies, the long drawn-out blood feuds or political murders. Homicides committed as the seemingly only way out of an impossible marital impasse have repeatedly been studied by psychiatrists and psychologists. In a short, but penetrating, Canadian study by Cormier[68] observations are reported on eight men who had killed their wives or women with whom they had stood in an equivalent relationship. They were seen in prison some years after they had been sentenced to imprisonment either for life or for shorter periods. Although these men were very different in personality, attainment, social position and in many other ways, a 'repetitive pattern' emerged from these studies, and eventually the observing psychiatrist 'began to have the sensation that we were listening to the same story'. There had been strong ties between these men and the women, 'a realization from the start that they were in some way interlocked and that they needed one another not only for their well-being, but for the reverse, because of their problems'. In the course of their relationship, distrust, jealousy, violence, separations and reconciliations occurred, but in spite of a growing awareness of the dangers involved in their living together, a 'kind of foreknowledge that it might end in tragedy', neither party was willing or able to make a final break, until the murder occurs 'at a point of intense emotion and a feeling that to continue is inconceivable and to give up impossible'. It is only after the trial that the men begin to understand why the relationship had broken down and in what way each of the partners had been guilty.[69]

A type of murder which was *persönlichkeits-eigen* and in which the ego was also deeply involved, is the case of 'Gunnarsson' discussed by Bjerre.[70] Here, the crime arose without the clash of two incompatible personalities but in a one-sided fashion, if we accept Bjerre's Adlerian interpretation—entirely out of the various defects in the actor's character, his insecurity, inferiority feeling, fear of life, inner isolation, hatred of other people and dependence on his mother.

The opposite extreme is represented by murders, which occur from time to time, of persons who are complete strangers to the actor and who are killed, not as in the case of Gide's Lafcadio, in order deliberately to demonstrate the characteristics of a 'motiveless' crime, but because the actor has the real urge to kill, to kill *in abstracte*, one might say, while the person of his victim is entirely indifferent and uninteresting to him. A prostitute was murdered in London in this way some years ago, not as usual in such cases for sadistic reasons by mentally abnormal persons or for financial gain by a very ordinary customer, but as the killer explained, because 'she would not be missed'. Here, the crime was probably wholly in line with the total personality structure (*persönlichkeits-eigen*), but there was no 'ego-involvement' in this particular murder; the latter concept is therefore narrower than the former.

The Report of the Warren Commission established in 1964 by President Johnson to investigate the circumstances of the assassination of President Kennedy cautiously concluded that, on the strength of the available evidence, no definite analysis could be made of Oswald's personality and motives. Even so, certain driving forces seem to emerge from the facts assembled by the Commission: resentment of any kind of authority; inability to establish meaningful relationships with other persons; an urge 'to try to find a place in history' (which is reminiscent of the 'destroyer' of the Library of Alexandria??); all this combined with the despair over the failure of his various attempts to achieve his object, with his communist indoctrination and his tendency to use violence (*The Times*, 29.9.1964). One might perhaps argue that such a case, as many other political assassinations, stands somewhere between those crimes which are clearly *persönlichkeits-eigen* with ego-involvement and those where, as in the case of the prostitute, there is no ego-involvement. In the Kennedy murder case the ego of the murderer was deeply involved, and the person of the victim was of the greatest significance to him, but not really as an individual but merely as the highest representative of authority (on political crimes see also below, Chapter 21, 1).

The so-called 'short-circuit' actions (*Kurzschluss-Handlungen*) will usually, but not always, be out of harmony with the total personality. This name has been given to crimes where an intensely emotional situation suddenly triggers off an impulsive action, usually homicide.[71] Here, the intense stimulus due to an unexpected, highly affective, external event, such as the discovery of marital infidelity, an insulting word, the unforeseen resistance of the victim of robbery or rape, easily releases acts such as murder by shooting, stabbing or strangling. Lenz describes such cases as reactions to an overwhelmingly strong outside stimulus where the impact of the latter does not 'run through' the whole of the personality, but shows its effect immediately in impulsive action. He mentions as illustrations the 'smash ups' in prisons with furious attacks on officers and furniture and also family murders, which latter may however be of a very different kind.[72]

As an example of a 'short-circuit' murder the case of a man of 21 may be quoted who stabbed to death a 'complete stranger' for, as the prosecution thought, no apparent motive. He gave himself up to the police, stating: 'There was an argument because he bumped into me. I lost my temper and let fly at him with my knife.' According to the psychiatric evidence he had been rejected for the Army because of 'anti-social trends of long standing'. Moreover, the accused had stated that the murdered man had called him a name inferring that he was illegitimate, and to him 'the word was like a spark to gunpowder'.[73] He was sentenced to death, as this happened several years before the Homicide Act of 1957.

Or, another, more recent, case:[74]

While two brothers were watching television a dispute arose between them over whether the dining room door should be shut or open. A scuffle arose, in the course of which the elder brother, aged 16, stabbed and killed the younger, aged 14. He was said to be a well-behaved boy who had never shown any violent temper, and the prison medical officer expressed the view that he was suffering from some emotional immaturity which would probably right itself in the future; there was no need for special treatment. The boy was placed on probation for manslaughter.

Cyril Burt,[75] discussing a similar case, uses it to stress the importance of deep unconscious motives and suspects that 'some long-drawn-out situation has been secretly playing on his (the offender's) deeper emotions, until at last the exasperation has grown too great for his powers to control. In short . . . to understand such exceptional actions, we have to assume, not an exceptional class of persons, but merely the persistence of rough, irrational and emotional springs of action which come into play when, not the person, but his situation becomes exceptional. . . .' Of course, in the above case of the two brothers this does not apply as the situation was hardly exceptional.

Lange[76] draws attention to the close relationship of these short-circuit actions and those committed by schizophrenics and people suffering from chorea.

In the famous case of Albert Camus' *Outsider* (*L'Etranger*) there was the factor of sultry, oppressive heat that provided an additional stimulus to the actor's feeling of intense anxiety as to whether the Arab would attack him with his knife. 'A few hundred miles farther south', writes Cyril Connolly,[77] 'and a touch of the sun would have been readily recognized, no doubt, as a cause for acquittal in the case of a white man accused of murdering a native' (this was written in 1946). Here, the hero, Meursault, shows none of the conventional emotions throughout the whole narrative, neither before or after the shooting incident, nor during or after the trial, until right at the end he explodes. The same impassivity, though in entirely different circumstances, we find in Adolf Eichmann who, however, defended himself to the best of his ability at the trial, whereas Meursault showed no interest in his fate.

The *crime passionnel* has been brilliantly discussed by Marc Ancel[78] from the point of view of the criminologically oriented lawyer and mainly, though not exclusively, within the framework of French law and court practice. Ancel, speaking of the 'new conception of *crimes passionnels* emerging in modern penal legislation', points out that these crimes may be of a very different character psychologically and committed with very different motives, often 'a curious mixture of cupidity, egoism and a warped sense of justice', but likewise the result of violent emotions which paralyse all the forces of self-control. As he rightly says, all this is increasingly taken into account in modern criminal legislation and court practice (see also Chapter 18 below), but, on the other hand, French juries who used to be over-lenient in such cases have of late adopted a sterner attitude. In English law and practice, as the Brighton homicide and other cases show, the opposite trend has become apparent.

The number of homicides committed in Britain between 1957 and 1960 in a 'fit of sudden temper or desperation' has been estimated at 33.[79]

The close connection between murder and suicide, so often stressed in criminological literature, offers very valuable insights into the psychology of the murderer. While it is a wild exaggeration to regard every homicide as a veiled form of suicide there is no doubt that in many cases, especially those with strong ego-involvement, either the homicide is followed by suicide, or at least attempted suicide, or stands psychologically in the place of the latter.[80] In England and Wales between 1955 and 1960, murderers committed suicide in about 20–27 per cent (men who had killed women over 16) and 8–15 per cent (women who had killed men over 16).[81] The fundamental psychological drive is here aggression which is sometimes turned against other persons and sometimes against the individual himself, but in the former case, too, it may happen that this aggression seems only to the superficial observer to be turned against somebody else; indirectly and on a deeper level it is meant to be directed against the actor himself. In the widely discussed Loeb-Leopold case of 1924, according to Abrahamsen[82] the killing of the boy at least for Loeb was 'a psychic killing of himself' and an expression of his desire for punishment. Others are more inclined to think it was done 'for a kick' or to carry out the 'perfect' crime which would defy detection.

On the other hand, a suicide may in fact be nothing but the 'introjected' killing of another person.[83] Here again, however, we enter the realm of psycho-analytical explanations. Where the homicide does not stand in the place of suicide but is combined with it, often as a so-called suicide-pact, the circumstances and motives may show a considerable variety. Where the suicide remains at the stage of attempt intricate questions may arise for the criminal law and its reform,[84] but more because of the difficulty of proving the seriousness of the attempt than because of the other psychological problems involved (the latter have been psycho-analytically explored by Ernest Jones and others).[85]

When all is said about the psychology of murder and the murderer one will have to agree with the Report of the Royal Commission of 1953, referring to their sample of fifty cases (Appendix 4), that this crime 'may be human and understandable, calling more for pity than for censure, or brutal and callous to an almost unbelievable degree. . . . The motives . . . show some of the basest and some of the better emotions of mankind, cupidity, revenge, lust, jealousy, anger, fear, pity, despair, duty, self-righteousness, political fanaticism, or there may be no intelligible motive at all.'[86]

For many crimes other than homicide the range of personality factors, motives, psychological situations, emotions, sentiments, attitudes, drives, etc., which may be regarded as connected with criminal behaviour, is not much less wide. In view of the somewhat uncertain state of modern psychological terminology it is not easy to find generally accepted descriptions of the psychological factors involved. McDougall[87] distinguished between a sentiment which he described as 'an enduring structure within the total structure of the mind or mental organization', and an emotion which was 'a passing phase or, more strictly, an aspect of a phase of mental process'. Nowadays one is more inclined to speak of attitudes than of sentiments. To W. I. Thomas[88] the terms temperament and character were merely concepts to express the fact that 'there are always a few organized groups of attitudes in a personality which play a predominant part in its activity . . .'

V. VARIOUS SPECIFIC PERSONALITY TRAITS: IN PARTICULAR: INADEQUACY AND IMMATURITY. THE FRUSTRATION-AGGRESSION THEORY. THE 'FOUR WISHES'. THE SENSE OF INJUSTICE. THE 'EXTRAORDINARY MAN'. RATIONALIZATION

In addition to the material already presented in this chapter, attention may also be drawn to the following:

As already mentioned (Chapter 15) the 'inadequate' personality of many criminals is an experience which impresses in particular psychologists working in prisons. In Dr. Roper's masterly analysis of 1,100 inmates of Wakefield Prison 1948-9 (all 'stars' with a sentence of at least one year) 51 per cent were classified as inadequate, meaning a 'rather vague and ineffective personality'.[89] Obviously, this is not much different from what Bjerre regards as 'the determining factor in all crime', i.e. weakness or general unfitness, to which he adds self-deception, escape from the realities of life.[90] Moreover, at the end of Chapter 15, I (2), the view of de Berker was mentioned that a large percentage of 'normal' prisoners fall under the category of 'inadequate' personality, and to some extent this was confirmed by Grygier's T.A.T. research.

Roper also stresses the *immaturity* of most criminals. He estimates that in addition to the 'inadequates' another 20 per cent of his sample, schizoids, hysteroids and aggressives, had to be regarded as 'immature' personalities, making a total of 71 per cent. He even suggests that immaturity and criminality may be much the same thing and that, as we all start as immature beings, criminality may be the 'natural' condition of man. 'Crime', he writes, 'is essentially the solution of personal problems at childlike level of conduct either because basic attitudes have never developed beyond that level or because there has been regression to childish attitudes as a result of frustration.'[91] In this, without mentioning Freud, he refers of course to essentially psycho-analytical ideas; see for example Glover's dictum: 'judged by adult social standards the normal baby is for all practical purposes a born criminal'.[92] While this theory, apart from its intrinsic merits, is well in keeping with the statistical age curve of crime (below, Chapter 26) it cannot explain the behaviour of the minority of late starters,[93] whose problems are often quite different from those of the bulk of criminal cases.

An interesting attempt has been made by the Gluecks to work out a theory of *maturation* and to explain why the factor of ageing plays such an important role in the reformative process. Among those who continued their criminal careers after what was regarded as the crucial age of 35 there was, in addition to several unfavourable environ-

mental factors, a markedly higher proportion of 'emotionally unstable' persons.[94] For them, the passage of time which socializes the
environmentally conditioned offender, only tends to aggravate their
maladjustment. The Gluecks suggested the establishment of a 'maturation quotient' (M.Q.) to measure the degree of deviation from the
maturation norm.[95] In their subsequent publications, however, the
matter has not been taken up again.

While, as mentioned above, the Gluecks, in *Unraveling*, did not find
that the delinquents in their sample felt more insecure than the non-
delinquents, the feeling of insecurity has been regarded by other
writers as an important factor in the interpretation of delinquency.
T. R. Fyvel, for example, entitles a book, to be discussed further
below, *The Insecure Offenders*.[96]

The *frustration-aggression theory*, too, has a wide following,
especially since its comprehensive treatment by Dollard.[97] In his very
influential book the assumption is used as the point of departure
that aggression is always a consequence of frustration, although
frustrating situations do not inevitably produce overt aggression.
After briefly discussing the place of the frustration-aggression thesis
in the Freudian and Marxist systems he surveys in his criminological
chapter a large number of factors, such as economic conditions,
occupation, physique, age, sex, in their relation to frustration and the
anticipation of punishment (in its widest sense). His assumption here
is that criminals show 'higher-than-average frustration and lower-
than-average anticipation of punishment', i.e. they are more easily
frustrated and less easily deterred by the expectancy of punishment.
Frustration is of course the all-pervading feeling in our western
civilization at present,[98] but criminals suffer even more from it than
others. Grygier's research has produced some further evidence to
support the frustration-aggression hypothesis. Roper, too, writes:
'crime starts, as I have seen it, as a reaction to frustration . . .' but he
admits that 'special determinants are usually necessary before a
frustration reaction will take the form of crime'. In fact, we might
perhaps say, frustration, especially repeated and prolonged frustration, will express itself somehow, very probably in an anti-social feeling which may take the form of aggression in its widest sense, for example in strikes, 'working to rule', unkindnesses and discourtesies of
all sorts, chicane and so on. If other essential personal and environmental conditions are present it may take the form of crime. For
children Brian Kay found that delinquents and neurotics had a lower
frustration tolerance than the members of his control group, but that
it varied according to frequency, intensity and type of frustration.[99]
An impressive illustration of the psychological effects of persistent
and complete frustration in a primitive setting is given in one of

Maxim Gorki's *Short Stories* in the following dialogue between two Russian peasants of the Tsarist epoch:[100]

'You may have many reasons for it, but it's not your wife's temper that causes you to treat her so unwisely. The cause is your own unenlightened condition.' 'That's just so,' exclaimed Yakoff—'We do indeed live in darkness as black as pitch'—'The conditions of your life irritate you, and your wife has to suffer from it. . . . She is always there ready to your hand, she can't get away from you.' Thereupon Yakoff turns to the other man and says: 'Stop! You beat your wife also, don't you?' 'I'm not saying I don't, because I do. How can I help it? I can't beat the wall with my fists when I feel I must beat something.' 'That's just how I feel,' says Yakoff.

*Mutatis mutandis*, this will go a long way to explain seemingly senseless or psychotic acts of violence.

In his long experience as a prison medical officer Roper found that the anti-social reaction caused by frustration, unless stopped at once by the 'crisis of discovery', might take ten or twenty years to 'burn itself out'—which is probably only another name for the maturation concept of the Gluecks—'partly because crime can be made profitable, and partly because the original frustration situation, if unresolved, is apt to become worse as disgrace and punishment accumulate'. Each of these two considerations helps to explain the making of a persistent criminal career, the one of a successful, the other of an unsuccessful one.

As frustration is largely due to social and economic conditions more will have to be said on it below (Chapters 19 ff.).

In the field of juvenile delinquency it may be useful to classify the various potential sources of frustration by adopting W. I. Thomas's list of the 'four wishes', which if remaining unsatisfied easily lead to anti-social conduct. Although Thomas changed his classification many times,[101] the following four wishes seem to have remained essential components: the desire for security (conflicting with it), for new experience, for response and for recognition. Other psychologically important classifications of the various types of juvenile delinquency have been mentioned above in Chapter 8 (text to Notes 46–7). In popular language, they can perhaps be summed up as follows. Why does a child steal? Because he wants (*a*) to use the article for his own enjoyment, which seems the most 'normal' case; or (*b*) because he wants to hoard it, which betrays some complications; or (*c*) because he wants to give it away to buy with it love, security, response, recognition; or (*d*) for the thrill of stealing (new experience); or (*e*) because he wishes to test somebody's affection, notably that of his parents (Stott's 'delinquency attention'); or (*f*) because he has given up hope and only wishes to spite and hurt (see also Stott). A subsidiary of (*f*) may be the wish to be removed from home (also Stott). While no list of this kind can be exhaustive, this one seems to contain most of the essential possibilities.

This scheme is, however, applicable not only to juveniles. Adults, too, are liable to similar emotions. Their need for recognition, for example, may be responsible for economic offences committed to 'buy' status. While more on this will have to be said below (Chapter 20) as an illustration the following case may here be quoted:

A single woman aged 53, with many previous convictions, had been discharged from prison in 1955 and settled down in a village in South England where she led a blameless life for about five years, attaining a position of trust in the community and becoming a parish councillor and president of the local women's institute. She then began to give expensive parties, to arrange flower shows, etc., for which the money had to be obtained by false pretences. The defence pleaded that she had not acted for personal gain and that there was 'absolutely no motive' for her offences. She was sentenced to 21 months' imprisonment. There was of course a strong motive present, the need for social recognition and rehabilitation, particularly active in a person with her criminal background.

As a more specific form of frustration the *sense of injustice* has to be especially mentioned. As Freud has said, 'the first requisite of culture is justice',[102] and if the individual's sense of justice is outraged his feeling of frustration may drive him to particularly violent acts of aggression. The present writer has in previous publications referred to famous instances of this type of criminal in world literature, such as Karl Moor in Schiller's *The Robbers* and Michael Kohlhaas in Heinrich von Kleist's great novel[103] (above, Chapter 2 at the end). Etienne de Greeff made a special study of this psychological factor, *le sentiment d'injustice subie*, which he regards of supreme importance for the understanding of normal as well as of mentally disordered criminals.[104] According to him, nobody acts in matters of any importance without having first established an at least preliminary harmony with his own conscience, and it is through the medium of his feeling of unjust treatment, be it actually suffered or only imagined, that the criminal brings his action into harmony with his own moral code. Normally, de Greeff thinks, which is probably too sweeping a generalization, no case can be found where the criminal has acted without this mechanism of justifying his conduct through his sense of having suffered some injustice. He links this with the human tendency to suspect an evil intent behind every unhappy experience, and here his reasoning is reminiscent of the discovery of modern anthropology that primitive man tries to explain all happenings, especially those painful to himself, as the result of the sinister machinations of evil spirits.[105] All this shows that what de Greeff had in mind is a somewhat wider concept of injustice than the usual one; almost any kind of unpleasant experience coming from whatever source. His criminal suffering from a sense of injustice resembles the one who tries to rationalize his motives so as to make them acceptable to himself and others (see also below, p. 310).

Rosenzweig and Grygier's extrapunitive type 'aggressively attributes his frustration to other persons or objects', whereas we are here concerned only with cases where the criminal has experienced some specific treatment which he regards as unjust, be it from a court or other official source, or from an employer or teacher or similar authoritative figure. Naturally, the penal system and the criminal courts are particularly conspicuous and frequent sources of this feeling of injustice. Especially the very harsh sentences imposed in former days even for minor offences, the inequality of sentences or sentences on mere suspicion as being a 'suspected person', coupled with the rigours of imprisonment and the inadequacy of the aftercare services, have been major factors in the growing rate of recidivism. Recidivists sentenced to long terms of preventive detention for comparatively minor offences often fail to understand the reasoning behind the system; others sentenced to corrective training who fail to receive the 'training' to which they think they are entitled—all these easily develop a deep-rooted grudge against society and its representatives.[106]

A distinction not apparent in de Greeff's discussion but important for our purposes is that between the sense of injustice (a) as the original factor in the commission of a crime; (b) as something conveniently exploited to fortify an already existing criminal intent; and (c) as an instrument to justify the crime afterwards.[107] Probably in the majority of cases the sense of injustice is nothing very real, but merely a pretence which, in the course of time, may of course become something very real and the criminal's only support. Let us never forget W. I. Thomas's famous doctrine: 'If men define situations as real, they are real in their consequences,'[108] i.e. men act as if they were real.

A factor which detracts somewhat from the moral value of the sense of injustice as a point in favour of the criminal, is the experience of certain investigators that prisoners are in no way sympathetic towards their fellow prisoners. There is but little loyalty between thieves. This has been stressed by Donald Clemmer in his *Prison Community*[109] and in the Californian study of the *Authoritarian Personality*.[110] The latter, which presents the results of questionnaire research on a sample of 110 inmates of San Quentin Prison, concludes that criminals are not to be regarded as genuine rebels with a feeling of real sympathy for the underdog; on the contrary, they are unable to identify with other outcasts and try to make 'moralistic distinctions' between themselves and their fellow prisoners, each inmate tending to be 'an island in itself'. We may not be prepared to accept the San Quentin example as wholly representative of the prison population, still less of the criminal as such. The picture may get somewhat blurred if we consider such special cases as the code of honour which binds the prisoner population together and, if violated, provokes the most violent reactions against informers,[111] or loyalty among members of a gang of adolescents. As will be pointed out below, teenager delinquency is actuated not so much by a feeling of injustice experienced in individual cases, done to and by specific individuals or agencies, as by a general sense of disillusionment directed against society as a whole. This and the whole problem of sociological interpretation of the rebel will be treated below in Chapters 20 ff.

Inadequacy and immaturity are basically negative phenomena, leading mostly to offences of the 'drifting' type, asocial rather than anti-social. Frustration with its potential sequel, aggression and the feeling of injustice, occupy the middle range, i.e. a person smarting under a feeling of frustration or injustice may drift into petty crime or he may indulge in serious acts of violence. The latter are even more likely as the outcome of jealousy.[112] There is a certain psychological affinity between the sense of injustice and jealousy as in both cases the individual feels aggrieved because he cannot get or loses something which he thinks he has a right to possess.[113] Therefore, he sometimes not only kills but also mutilates and dismembers his victim so that nobody else should 'possess' her.[114] André Gide contrasts the behaviour of Othello with that of some of Dostoevsky's jealous characters, in most of whom he thinks the feeling of suffering is stronger than the urge to take violent action, nor is it accompanied by hatred of the rival—on the contrary there may even be some sort of affection for him.[115] McDougall[116] quotes Tolstoy's *Kreutzer Sonata* as a study in jealousy where the anger of the jealous husband turns not against the person of the intruder but against the beloved object. However, the matter is not so clear as McDougall seems to assume. In the first place, it is very doubtful here—and this is one of the crucial issues of that great novel—whether Pozdnishev had ever really loved his wife; according to his own story he did not. And, secondly, as the reader of that terrific murder scene will immediately notice, he might have killed the lover if the latter had not managed to escape and if—to mix a comic element with the general horror—Pozdnishev had not felt that 'it was comic to rush after my wife's lover in my stocking feet, and I wanted to be terrifying and not comic'. In short, there are no fixed rules to decide who will be the victim in such cases; it all depends on chance and on the character of the principal actors and their relations to one another.

Glover confirms the view that the feeling of jealousy is stronger in homosexual than in heterosexual relationships.[117]

Perhaps the most strongly anti-social emotions are lust for power, be it political or economic power, covetousness, greed and vanity. In *War and Crime*[118] attention has been drawn to criminal types of this kind, to a Horatio Bottomley, a Kreuger, in the world of big business, or in the realm of world literature to Ibsen's John Gabriel Borkman, and in that of world politics to a Hitler. Dostoevsky's Raskolnikov commits his murder not, as Gide's Lafcadio did, in order to experience a 'motiveless' murder and to find out whether he was capable of performing it, but to demonstrate the right of an 'extraordinary' man to commit any crime he liked. However, another, psycho-analytical, interpretation—more fully to be discussed below in Chapter 17 II(*b*) —regards Raskolnikov as a severe neurotic with a profound feeling of guilt who kills in order to be punished.[119]

To Colin Wilson,[120] Raskolnikov is a perfect example of the 'outsider' who 'hates his own weakness, he hates human weakness and misery' and thinks that in order to overcome it he has to 'arouse his will to some important purpose, to find *a definite act*', a 'gesture of defiance' which would 'give his future life a settled purpose'. Why did he fail? Wilson rejects the moral explanation that 'our neighbour is more precious than any abstract notion', but is not his own explanation that Raskolnikov is 'over-sensitive and over-estimates his own callousness' in the last resort also a moral one?

An important motivational technique employed to overcome the individual's inner resistance to the commission of crime is *rationalization* (also implied in de Greeff's interpretation of the sense of injustice). As its significance has been stressed by sociologists and psychoanalysts alike it might be mentioned in the present, more neutral, chapter instead of the next, to which it really belongs as a technique of unconscious concealment.[121] Not only criminal acts are rationalized but many others as well. Of one of the leading British politicians of our time it has been said: 'He has the gift—which Gladstone had and Macmillan had to a certain extent—of making a decision for political purposes and then believing in it, with sincerity and even with passion' (*Evening Standard*, 15.2.1962). In short, rationalization is 'constantly employed to cover the minor and major conflicts of everyday life' and has to be distinguished from deliberate lying (Glover). It may appear as a *post facto* justification of behaviour which the actor feels to be wrong, but it may also play its part before the commission of a forbidden act, in which latter case it has some motivational force. Cressey[122] has shown how this technique has worked in a number of cases of trust violation (embezzlers) studied by him. He regards it as an illustration of Sutherland's theory of differential association since it is only through frequent contacts with a culture which justifies trust violation that the would-be offender can acquire the most useful set

310

of rationalizations. It does not seem necessary, however, to resort to Sutherland's theory; rationalization can operate independently of it. As indicated above, the sense of injustice may be closely related to it, and while it may in some cases be caused or at least strengthened by a comparison of the offender's experiences with those of others, it may also come into existence as the result of highly individual disappointments.

*Imitation*, which, although different from rationalization, has certain features in common with it, will be treated in Chapters 20 and 23 as it bears a particularly strong sociological connotation.

# Chapter 17

## THE CONTRIBUTIONS OF PSYCHO-ANALYSIS.[1] FREUD, ADLER, JUNG

### I. BASIC IDEAS OF PSYCHO-ANALYSIS

Considering the vastness and complexity of psycho-analytical literature, it is clear that no complete and original account can here be
given of even the essential features of this branch of psychology as
represented mainly by Sigmund Freud (1856–1939), but a brief summary will be presented as an introduction to the assessment of the
specifically criminological contributions of psycho-analysis. Details
and changes which the system has undergone in the course of its
development will largely have to be ignored, and the same applies
even to essential features such as the theory of dreams, or the mechanism of transference, or the whole question of treatment, which have
no direct bearing on criminological problems. Nor can any critical
evaluation of the whole doctrine be attempted as it would go far
beyond the scope of this book and the author would not be qualified
to undertake it. All that has to be said here by way of introduction is
that in the present writer's view some of the many aspects of psycho-
analytical thought are of the greatest value to the understanding of
crime and punishment, while others can be accepted only with important reservations or not at all.

(a) Probably the best known of these basic ideas is the emphasis
placed on the part played in our mental processes by the *Unconscious*,
the 'submerged, invisible part of the iceberg' which forms the largest,
and in many ways most powerful, sector of our mind.[2] It is distinct
from the 'pre-conscious' which, although unconscious now, can be
recalled to consciousness. The unconscious contains 'our instinctive
urges and our repressed memories', originating to a considerable part
from traumatic experiences in early childhood, some of which may
have been suffered consciously, whereas others had remained unconscious. This means that in our thoughts, emotions and actions we
are governed by forces which are largely hidden and can be brought
to our knowledge, if at all, only through a special technique called
psycho-analysis.

(b) Considerably later than this fundamental, though not altogether original, emphasis on the significance and dynamic power of the unconscious, came the comprehensive Freudian picture of the personality structure as being divided into three layers, the *Ego*, the *Super-Ego*, and the *Id*. In this system of 'mental topography' (Foulkes) the *Id*, so called because of its impersonal, primitive, 'unorganized' quality, represents the lowest level, the 'inherited reservoir of drastic, instinctual demands', illogical and immoral, subject only to the 'Pleasure Principle', seeking immediate gratification of those demands and standing 'at the border between the somatic and the psychic . . . it supplies both the ego and the super-ego with the energies with which they operate. It is permanently unconscious' (Glover, *Psycho-Analysis*, p. 64).

The *Ego* is the largely conscious part of the human personality, but it has also a deeper, unconscious part. It does not yet exist in early childhood; the infant possesses no conscious personality, but slowly an awareness of itself is developed. Gradually, the ego becomes stronger and modifies and controls, at least to some extent, the instinctual and anti-social urges of the id. Although not sharply distinguished from the latter, the ego strives to be moral and to conform to the demands of the external world and the 'Reality Principle', which latter is supposed to govern the mature, adult person.

Finally, the *Super-Ego*, which corresponds essentially to the traditional idea of the conscience. It, too, is largely an unconscious agency. 'Conscious conscience is not the main regulator of moral and ethical behaviour. Morality and social behaviour depend primarily on the smooth operation of unconscious codes, which have been laid down during the process of upbringing.'[3] This super-ego, according to Freudian doctrine, has various sources. Flugel,[4] for example, distinguishes four of them, the most obvious of which is derived from 'the process of "introjection" or incorporation into one's own mind of the precepts and moral attitudes of others, particularly of one's parents or of other persons *in loco parentis* in one's youth'. This is also brought out in Freud's own definition, quoted by Flugel, of the ego-ideal or super-ego as 'the representative of our relation to our parents. When we were little children we knew these higher natures, we admired them and feared them; and later we took them into ourselves' (*The Ego and the Id*). In short, the basis of the super-ego is the internalized authority of the father or father-substitute. The super-ego is, however, as Flugel points out, 'no direct copy of the moral standards of the community'; it often tends to be more severe because the child, frustrated by external circumstances and too weak to turn its aggression outwards, but also because the frustrating agents are often the parents whom he loves, has to turn its aggression against the self, so that 'the inward recoiling aggression also becomes attached to the super-ego'. 'The conscience thus contains a double dose of aggression, the aggression of the father and that towards the father' (Ginsberg, who criticizes the too exclusive concentration of Freud's doctrine on the negative, repressive side of moral life).[5] Therefore, the super-ego may become hyper-moral and tyrannical towards the ego. This and the attempts of the super-ego to control the aggressive tendencies of the ego create conflict and a sense of guilt.

Foulkes compares these three layers of the human personality to another trio: criminal–society–judge, the ordinary citizen standing between the first and the third.

From this very brief and superficial outline of the role played by the three sectors of the personality it follows that the ego is exposed to attacks from two hostile and incompatible powers, the instinctual urges of the id and the 'censorship' exercised by the super-ego. Naturally the ego tries to compromise between the two by shaping the wishes of the id so as to make them more acceptable to the super-ego, which is done by a process of *sublimation*. In the normal person some sort of sublimation will, possibly after many failures, be achieved and with it a more or less satisfactory conciliation of the two opposing forces leading to relative stability within the individual. The little boy learns in time, for example, that instead of hurting other children or pulling off spiders' legs he might better take his toys to pieces and put them together again. 'The instinct has been diverted from its original aim—inflicting pain—to a new social aim, investigation and construction.'[6] In those, very frequent, cases, however, where sublimation is impossible its place has to be taken by forcible *repression*, i.e. the aggressive or otherwise undesirable instincts are not constructively resolved, but pushed back into the unconscious where they have to remain until they break through whenever the opportunity arises. This process of repression prevents those undesirable tendencies from becoming conscious, but it may shape the future development of the personality. If, for example, the first sexual desires of the child are too forcibly repressed this may establish a general pattern of sexual repression for the rest of its life. What kind of instinctual wishes we have to repress depends largely on the kind of culture in which we live.

The struggle between the repressing and the repressed forces leads to the so-called *reaction-formation*. 'In general, reaction-formations are directed against infantile pregenital forms of love and hate. They are built up from about the age of two onwards ... [and] constitute some of the most permanent and recognizable features of normal character, and, when they are excessive, a number of pathological character traits. Excessive scrupulosity, for example, is a typical response of the obsessional character.'[7] Exaggerated prudery as a defence against sexual urges and exaggerated brusqueness as a defence against shyness and inferiority feelings are some of the classical examples of reaction-formation.[8]

(c) The two great drives which dominate the personality are self-preservation and procreation (subsequently replaced in Freud's writings by the Life and Death instincts, Eros and Thanatos). While the first requires hardly any explanation, the second, which is identical with the Freudian concepts of *libido* and *sex*, has been the subject of much doubt and misinterpretation. Although Freud did not hold that sex was the only instinct that mattered, his extremely wide conception of the term which was in no way restricted to the genitals was bound to cause misunderstanding and dislike. We are here only concerned with the great emphasis placed by psycho-analysts on the sex-instinct as dominating human life from earliest childhood and with the resulting doctrine that infantile sexuality consists of three components or zones which, although all of them exist from birth, exercise their primacy during different phases of the child's development: first, the *oral* or suckling phase, followed by an *anal* phase, and, lastly, the *phallic* or *genital* phase.[9] There is much overlapping between the three, but generally speaking each of them has its proper time, and the way in which a child passes through them, i.e. with or without difficulties, profoundly influences its adult behaviour. If, for example, the individual experiences too much satisfaction or frustration at any one of these stages he will turn from the point of frustration to that of satisfaction, and if the latter occurred in childhood he will as an adult go back to the sexual impressions of his childhood (*fixation*).[10] Fixation, thus, is one aspect of the more general phenomenon of *regression*, the falling back upon earlier and more primitive stages in human development when greater happiness had been experienced. This process is regarded as the cause of neurosis and of sexual perversions. The latter are 'indications of conflict over earlier (infantile) forms of sexuality' (Glover, p. 35).

The period between infantile and pubertal forms of sexuality is called the *latency* period, characterized by a comparative quietening down of the sexual urges.

Another important concept is that of *identification*, which can be 'good' or 'bad', according to its objects. If the boy sublimates his feelings of hatred towards his father by trying to identify himself with the latter and to accept him as his model, or if he identifies himself with his mother by trying to comply with her reasonable wishes, this would be all to the good.

(d) So far, no reference has been made to one of the best-known concepts of Freudian theory, the *Oedipus complex*. This complex, called after the King of Thebes in Sophocles' tragedy who killed his father and married his mother without identifying them as such, develops according to Freud at the time of the phallic or genital phase, roughly at the age of three, as the wish to have sexual relations with the parent of the opposite sex accompanied by a feeling of hatred and rebellion against the parent of the same sex. (In the Greek legend Freud saw 'childhood experience reproduced in the guise of adult dramatic action'.) For the boy this incestuous complex is normally resolved by the processes of identification and sublimation, but also by the castration complex and the resulting castration fear,[11] whereas for the girl its place is taken by the Electra complex, also derived from the Greek legend (Electra contributing to the murder of her mother Clytemnestra who had killed her husband Agamemnon).[12] The Oedipus complex will normally die down roughly at the age of four or five and, as Freud expressed it, its heir will be the super-ego and the conscience,[13] but on the other hand the Oedipus complex is also the 'nuclear complex of the neuroses'.[14] As usual in psycho-analytical literature, the details of all these processes are extremely complicated and controversial, but in spite of this Foulkes probably expresses the view prevailing among psycho-analysts that the Oedipus complex is no peculiarity of neurotics but 'universal and inevitable . . . a phase of crucial importance in the life of the individual', and that 'all the deeper conflicts which arise in later life can be traced back to it'.[15]

Not surprisingly, our inborn feelings of aggression and hatred and our incestuous desires create an intense sense of *guilt*. The latter is described as some sort of fear or anxiety, mainly due to the Oedipus complex, to the eventual internalization of the child's primitive impulses and the inevitable deviation from the moral standards of conduct expected by the super-ego.[16] This feeling of guilt, which exists in greatly differing strength in different individuals, is one of the fundamental concepts in the psycho-analytical interpretation of crime (see below).

Another conception of criminological significance arising from psycho-analytical theory is that of *ambivalence*. The feelings of love and hatred existing in the child towards its parents and other persons alternate so often and so rapidly as to create a 'permanent mixed attitude' of simultaneous opposing feelings towards the same object, i.e. ambivalence.[17]

The concepts of *displacement* and *symbolism* are also to be mentioned. Displacement, closely related to transference and symbolism, means the 'unconscious transfer of an interest from an earlier and more primitive object to a later substitute'; it can be a socializing process, but can also be the opposite if, for example, 'hostility is transferred from infantile objects to persons or institutions in the present day'.[18]

Symbolism is a 'primitive thought-system' in which an idea becomes the substitute for another, unconscious, one. Symbols represent mainly the love and hate relations of the child to its parents and consist of objects somehow related to the genitals, such as a dagger or knife and the serpent as representing the male and a house or bag as representing the female genitals.[19] Money or sweets are symbols of love. One object or person stands for another object or person, which latter have to be excluded from the conscious mind. 'The symbol is one of the means whereby forbidden wishes from the unconscious id are allowed to manifest themselves in disguised form in consciousness.'[20] 'Although the number of symbols runs into thousands', writes Glover,[21] 'the unconscious ideas represented in symbols are confined to a small number of primitive interests concerning the subject's own body, family figures and the phenomena of birth, sexuality and death. By far the greatest number are sexual. . . . Contrary to the views held by Jung, the symbol is regarded not as a concrete representation of an abstract idea but as a concrete representation of a more inaccessible idea, i.e. the snake represents the phallus, not just power, virility or sexuality.'

Finally, there is the mechanism of *projection*.[22] This is an unconscious process intended to enable the individual 'to identify pleasure with the self and unpleasure with the non-self'; it is therefore 'a manifestation of Freud's pleasure-principle' (Flugel). In other words, the child, and the adult as well, projects his painful experiences and aggressive desires on to other persons who become the bogies, a process which may lead to phobias, i.e. morbid fears of objects, persons or situations. Projection is one of the methods by which guilt can be diverted from ourselves to somebody else, the scapegoat. Flugel[23] has given a particularly clear analysis of this phenomenon which, with the institution of 'vicarious punishment', presents, as he says, one of the constantly recurring themes in human history. The projection of guilt on to another human group has become a convenient way of dealing with our own aggression or other anti-social instincts.

## II. THE BEARING OF PSYCHO-ANALYTICAL THEORY ON CRIMINOLOGY

Even these few remarks will be sufficient to illustrate the implications of psycho-analytical theory for the understanding of crime and punishment.

(*a*) Above all, it has to be stressed that to the orthodox psychoanalyst man is by nature anti-social. 'Judged by adult social standards the normal baby is for all practical purposes a born criminal.'[24] This makes it necessary from the beginning to enquire into the relationship of Freud to *Lombroso*. One fundamental difference obviously lies in the fact that to Freud all human beings alike enter life with immoral and anti-social instincts, whereas Lombroso distinguishes between the born criminal type and the rest of mankind. The third view, forcibly expressed by Martin Buber, is that 'man is not good, man is not evil. He is, in a pre-eminent sense, good and evil together.'[25] Moreover, Lombroso, at least in his earlier writings, attaches the greatest importance to inborn hereditary, or at least congenital, factors, whereas Freud recognizes the import of external experiences. Not that he ignored the force of the individual's biological and inherited endowment—far from it.[26] It was even one of the major sources of disagreement between Freud and some of the 'Neo-Freudians' whether, as he believed, 'personality is based on biological drives mainly sexual in nature which, rooted in the body with its unalterable hereditary constitution pass inexorably through certain stages of development during the first five years and then cease to develop but continue to influence behaviour throughout life',[27] or whether, as in particular his American successors maintained, the human personality is largely shaped by its social environment. 'We have reason to believe that the extent to which an individual is able to sublimate instinctive urges is dependent on constitutional, that is, inherited factors', writes the Freudian Kate Friedlander.[28] But, contrary to Lombroso, Freud, although he, too, took a too static view of society, was at least fully aware of the developmental factors in human personality, distinguishing them from the constitutional and environmental ones.[29] In addition to the succession of the oral, anal and genital phases already referred to above there is his distinction of three stages of psycho-sexual development: the Infancy period, lasting to the age of approximately five, i.e. to the dying down of the Oedipus complex, the Latency period up to the age of twelve and the Pubertal period to about eighteen. It is also interesting to note that psycho-analysts regard Lombroso's attempt to draw a hard-and-fast line of distinction between the criminal and the non-criminal as 'a narcissistic wish of the scholar to separate himself and his fellows from the criminal'.[30] On the other hand, Freud's interest in evolution brings him in some respects near to the ideas of the Lombrosian school. In his view, the unconscious psychic life of the child seems to recapitulate the evolution of the species. As in the development of the child it became necessary to suppress primitive and even cannibalistic urges, the same happened in the development of civilization as a whole. Especially the anthropologically trained psycho-analysts, Róheim and others, have tried to amalgamate their findings relating to primitive societies with Freudian theories on the development of the individual.[31] Freud himself was profoundly interested in anthropology, but in a way entirely different from Lombroso. While the latter concentrated on the anthropometric measurements of individual criminals in order to demonstrate their atavistic physical characteristics (Chapter 12 above), Freud studied the evolution of the human race to explain such phenomena as totem and taboo, the origin of social institutions, and, what is of special interest to criminal lawyers and criminologists, the sociological and psychological factors behind such crimes as parricide and behind the prohibition of incest. In his books *Totem and Taboo*[32] and *Group Psychology and Analysis of the Ego*[33] Freud, who was sceptical of the existence of a 'herd instinct',[34] tried to explain the origin of human group formation by going back to Darwin's 'primal horde', held together by the absolute power of the tyrannical father. When the sons finally rose in revolt against him and his monopoly over all the females of the horde he was killed, but this first case of parricide led to the creation of the 'two fundamental taboos of totemism out of the sense of guilt of the sons', i.e. murder of the father and incest. The sons—an illustration of their ambivalent attitude to the father, mixed of love and hatred—denounced the fruits of their deed by denying themselves the liberated women. In this way the first two crimes known to mankind were established which the community as such recognized and which forced it to take penal action. In this connection the famous controversy about the explanation of the incest taboo deserves to be mentioned, where we find Sir James Frazer and Freud on one side and Westermarck and Havelock Ellis on the other.[35] They were all interested in the question: Why do we punish incest? Is it because sexual intercourse between near blood relations is, either through instinct or through the fact of joint upbringing in the same household, something so disgusting to the normal person that he demands heavy punishment for it? Or is it because incest is so tempting to us that such punishment is needed as a deterrent? Whereas Westermarck and Ellis preferred the first alternative, Frazer and Freud came down decisively in favour of the second.[36] In their view, the essential object of the criminal law is not merely to make a solemn declaration of those actions of which the community profoundly disapproves, but to reinforce our fight against the strongest temptations in ourselves. 'Every prohibition must conceal a desire' (Freud).

Frazer argued that, far from there being a natural aversion to incest there was rather a natural instinct in its favour, and Freud reinforced his argument by making use of psycho-analytic experience and doctrine which, in his view, proved that the first sexual impulses of children were of an incestuous nature. Obviously, this controversy concerns not only those interested in the *raison d'être* behind our criminal laws, but also criminologists trying to discover the mainspring of criminal behaviour, and psycho-analysis has greatly contributed to the understanding of this problem.

All this has, of course, only a very tenuous connection with our original question of how Freud's theories are related to those of Lombroso. It shows, however, how very different was the use made by these two men of their anthropological studies.

(b) The psycho-analytic *classification*[37] of the criminal population does not basically deviate from others, and often one gets the impression that it is the scientific jargon rather than the substance that makes it sound different from the rest. The usual distinction is made of neurotic, psychotic, physically handicapped, intoxicated, normal and accidental criminals, but the numerical distribution between the various categories is different from the usual one and the interpretation is in accordance with psycho-analytical theories. With regard to the *neurotic* criminal it has to be borne in mind that the Freudian explanation of the origin of the neurosis as an unresolved conflict, on a sexual basis, between the three layers of the personality (see also Chapter 15, I) is still predominant and that psycho-analysts have shown a far greater interest in specifically criminological problems than their principal opponents, for example those of the Eysenckian school. Not surprisingly, this psycho-analytical theory of neurosis attributes to the latter a more important role in the understanding of criminal behaviour than do the followers of other psychological schools, whether they may be Jungian, Eysenckians, etc. While enough has been said in the present chapter and in Chapter 15 on the general subject of neurosis and crime, some further attention has still to be paid to what is perhaps the most fascinating and valuable of Freud's discoveries in our field, the *criminal from a sense of guilt*. He is the opposite extreme to the criminal from a sense of injustice who also may or may not be a neurotic (Chapter 16, v). Whereas the latter suffers from a real or imaginary wrong done to him or others, this Freudian figure is troubled by something he has, or believes he has, done himself, or would have liked to do. As we have seen, this feeling of guilt is attributed by Freudians mainly to the Oedipus complex and the infantile sexual urges related to it. This feeling of guilt, of course, has, as psycho-analysts admit, not been altogether invented by them out of nothing. 'All religion', writes Ernest Jones,[38] 'is founded on the idea of sin, i.e. the sense of guilt at not reaching a prescribed standard', adding however, 'The precise relation of the sin of religion to the psycho-analytical conception of feeling of guilt is too delicate a question for the answer to be given in a word.' In any case, it seems to be clear that the origins of sin in the religious sense are different from those responsible for the feeling of guilt of psycho-analysis. However, as Flugel, summarizing an article by a German theologian, points out,[39] both Christianity and psycho-analysis aim at reducing the sense of guilt, and in both there is a tendency 'to look upon suffering as a punishment for infringing the commands of some stern authority (God and the super-ego respectively)'. In both cases this stern, punishing authority is later replaced by a milder father figure and finally by the moral autonomy of the individual, although as Flugel hints Christianity and, we might add, psycho-analysis too have failed to eliminate altogether 'internal guilt and external aggression'.

According to psycho-analytical theory this feeling of guilt even positively stimulates the commission of crime, because the individual suffering from an excessive and intolerable sense of guilt looks at punishment as a possible relief. He unconsciously wants to be punished because in this way he hopes to atone not only for his new crime but also for his forbidden desires of the earlier past. His actual transgressions are usually of a comparatively minor nature: in any case, his super-ego regards them as less serious than his unconscious wishes. He feels, therefore, that the punishment he receives from the court is too severe, and a surplus remains which can be used to pay for those desires. As Alexander writes,[40] this is a mechanism betraying a primitive theory of justice, but 'latent in the depths of the personality'. It is the theory that any crime can be paid off by punishment or other suffering. Even in the normal criminal it very often leads to recidivism, in particular where in his view the penalty undergone by him has been too severe for the crime actually committed; in the criminal from a sense of guilt it is still more likely to do so because of the psychic relief which the punishment gives him. In a very interesting discourse, Flugel has linked the psycho-analytical concepts of feeling of guilt and consequent need for punishment to the old Greek idea of *Hubris* which, he thinks, has greatly retarded human progress throughout the ages.[41] Pioneers in any field have usually been accused of Hubris, and they and their achievements have been sacrificed in order to forestall divine punishment. 'It is only in so far as this fear of Hubris is diminished that rapid human progress becomes possible.' Flugel calls this fear the *Polycrates complex*, after the tyrant of Samos mentioned by Herodotus whose story is the subject of Schiller's famous poem *Der Ring des Polycrates*. While there is some truth in Flugel's interpretation of the fear of Hubris as a progress blocking force, the latter may, however, also act as a necessary and socially welcome brake which prevents the all-too-reckless exploitation of individual success to the detriment of society at large. Occasionally, this feeling of guilt may operate neither as a progress blocking force nor as a brake, but may be used as a protection against the envy of others. The Swiss psychiatrist André Repond has told the story of highly successful fathers who exploit the criminal activities of their sons to arouse pity for themselves by exhibiting their family misfortunes quite openly and, protected by the sympathetic feelings of the public, continue their own doubtful business practices.[42]

From the Freudian theory of guilt we can draw the following conclusions: First, the normal order of cause and effect between crime and guilt becomes reversed in such cases: instead of the usual sequel of events, i.e. (a) various causal factors leading to crime, (b) guilt, (c) punishment, we find: (a) guilt feelings, (b) crime, (c) punishment, (d) crime, (e) punishment, and so on, the feeling of guilt taking the place of other causal factors. Secondly, the commission of crime can lead to punishment and psychic relief only if the crime is detected. This explains why such criminals so often commit their crimes in a manner designed to lead to discovery and why they frequently show a distinct craving to make a confession, even a wrong one. This craving has been made the subject of a brilliant book by one of the ablest Freudians, Theodor Reik,[43] who, among other points, draws attention to the many indirect ways, for example by apparent slips of the tongue, in which the offender gives his secret away. A classic illustration of the unconscious urge to confess has been given by Dostoevsky in his *Crime and Punishment* to which we referred earlier on as an example of the man who commits murder because he feels himself a superman above the rules of common morality (Chapter 16, v). Raskolnikov's behaviour shows, however, that this feeling was probably only superficial, whereas the deeper, unconscious roots of his crime were his feeling of guilt and desire for punishment.[44] Perhaps the most important sections of that great novel are those which describe the many devious ways by which Raskolnikov's urge for self-betrayal expressed itself, leading to his final open confession and gladly accepted punishment. This urge to confess and to beg for forgiveness is often regarded as a peculiarly Russian characteristic which played its part in some of the notorious political trials of the Stalin regime.[45]

On the other hand, if the feeling of guilt and the desire for punishment are too strong, the offender will not confess since he does not want to be relieved of his guilt in this simple way which may lead to an undesirable mitigation of his punishment. In most cases it is clear, however, that the criminal from a sense of guilt cannot be deterred by punishment. On the contrary, punishment and pain of any kind, for example, in physical illness, may become positively attractive and satisfy latent masochistic tendencies.[46] In psycho-analytical literature cases have been reported of such offenders whose conduct was clearly designed to bring them into conflict with the criminal law, for example the case of 'Bruno' in Alexander and Staub's book, some of the cases in Alexander and Healy's *Roots of Crime*, and the case of 'Dorothy' reported by Hedwig Schwarz (see Note 1). How frequent this type of offender is cannot be ascertained statistically. Sceptics will be inclined to suspect that the sense of guilt and the wish to be punished have been read into the case history by the analyst. Occasionally, this may have happened, but in fairness it has to be stressed that even hard-boiled prison doctors have told the writer of cases where they could find no other explanation of the prisoner's conduct than the psycho-analytical one.

Moreover, it has to be borne in mind that at least some psycho-analysts are conscious that neither the feeling of guilt nor any other of their explanations are in themselves sufficient to serve as causal factors. In particular, Alexander and Healy[47] have been careful to stress the 'interplay of social and psychological factors' and certain features of American life, such as 'the heroic exhibitionist evaluation of criminal deeds' and the adoration of material success as criminogenic phenomena leading to 'over-compensatory reactions' on the part of the unsuccessful. In doing so they express views reminiscent of Adler on the psychological ((d) below) and Merton on the sociological side (see Chapter 22).

Observers are unanimous in ascribing to sex offenders, especially to homosexuals, a particularly intense feeling of guilt.[48] Among white-collar criminals, on the other hand, it is usually regarded as completely lacking, but the absence of adequate case studies may have helped to establish this view.

In his later writings, in particular in *Civilization and its Discontents,*[49] Freud placed the whole phenomenon on a broader basis than the Oedipus complex by explaining guilt as 'the expression of the conflict of ambivalence, the eternal struggle between Eros and the destructive or death instinct', a conflict which arises first within the family, later in wider forms of communal life. The sense of guilt, he writes, is 'the most important problem in the evolution of culture . . . the price of progress in civilization is paid in forfeiting happiness through the heightening of the sense of guilt'. He refers to Goethe's *Lied des Harfners*:

> *Ihr lasst den Armen schuldig werden*
> *Dann überlässt ihr ihn der Pein;*
> *Denn alle Schuld rächt sich auf Erden.*

To existentialist philosophy, too, guilt is a basic problem, but here it arises from man's responsibility for his actions. Existentialists do not accept Freud's theory of the unconscious and of the origin of guilt. To them, the sense of guilt of certain individuals stems not so much from specific acts or omissions as from a much more instinctive sense of badness or worthlessness which attacks their 'very right to be in any respect'.[50] The psychiatrist R. D. Laing, in his case history of 'Peter', relates the latter's guilt feeling to 'being in the world' and 'occupying space' although his parents had not wanted him.[51]

Another potential relationship between guilt and repeated crime may arise from the sense of shame originating from a previous crime. Shame, it is true, normally 'reinforces guilt in the control of non-conformity',[52] but occasionally, just as guilt itself, if it is too strong and threatens to undermine the essential self-respect of the personality, it may also work in the opposite direction. The offender may try to get rid of his feeling of shame by reassuring himself that what he has actually done is not evil, and in order to persuade himself and others that he is right, he commits other crimes which he tries to justify in the same way.

Resuming our description of the psycho-analytical classification of criminals we now pass on to the *normal* criminal. He is naturally much less interesting to psycho-analysts than his neurotic counterpart, and reference is usually made to him only to make it clear how uncertain the line of demarcation is between the two categories. To the psycho-analyst the main criterion of the normal criminal is that his super-ego is criminal, too: there is consequently no friction between it and the other sectors of the personality. Their whole personality identifies itself with the crime, which is of course only a different way of saying that the normal criminal, through his upbringing and environment, has been so thoroughly conditioned to a life of crime that he regards it as natural and has no qualms about it. This definition of 'normality' differs from that adopted in Chapter 16 above, where reference was made to Emanuel Miller's 'operational standard of the normal person as one who is able to meet the requirements of social life without anxiety or a tendency to withdraw . . . and meet fearlessly the inevitable obstacles of life'.[53]

Alexander and Staub include in this category not only many habitual criminals but also persistent minor offenders of the beggar and vagabond type, but in addition they mention as a borderline type the 'genuine' criminal who is socially altogether unadapted and whom they describe in a way reminiscent of Lombroso's born criminal.

While there is nothing worth mentioning in the psycho-analytic description of the physically handicapped and the alcoholic type of criminal, psycho-analysis has made an important contribution to our understanding of the *accidental or occasional* type of offence, and especially of offences due to negligence. This type of offence is subdivided into what Freud called the *Fehlleistungen*, usually translated as 'faulty acts', and the situational offence. With the first Freud dealt in two of his most widely known books, his *Psychopathology of Everyday Life*[54] and his *Introductory Lectures in Psycho-analysis*, Part I.[55] His basic idea was that such 'faulty acts', for example the forgetting of names or words, mistakes in speech, reading or writing, and similar lapses such as the losing or misplacing of articles, are not mere accidents but have a deeper meaning. He formulated the following 'principle': 'Certain inadequacies of our psychic capacities ... and certain performances which are apparently unintentional prove to be well motivated when subjected to the psycho-analytic investigation and are determined through the consciousness of unknown motives.'[56] Although some of Freud's explanations of such faulty acts may seem rather far-fetched and although, apart from their obvious forensic implications,[57] he pays hardly any attention to the criminological significance of his discovery its importance for the understanding of offences due to negligence is very considerable. Already in my *Criminal Justice and Social Reconstruction* (p. 57) I wrote: 'it [i.e. English criminal law] has not yet grasped the profundity of the revolution which Freudian psychology has brought about in our interpretation of the idea of "negligence". Formerly a Cinderella of the criminal law, negligence has become one of its pivotal conceptions which modern legislative technique can no longer afford to neglect. . . . The reckless motorist is only the most frequent and most familiar representative of that new type of offender.' In the intervening years legislators have been trying, no doubt unconsciously, to draw certain practical conclusions from Freud's discovery of the symptomatic character of offences due to negligence, for example, by stiffening the penalties for careless driving, but the old idea that no 'real' guilt or blame attaches to such acts, which are seemingly unconnected with the personality, still lingers on in the unconscious minds of legislators, magistrates and juries alike (see also below, Chapter 21). It is, however, not only the careless motorist whose behaviour can be explained in the psycho-analytical way. The girl who is unconsciously jealous of her baby sister and, in spite of her ostensible love and care for her, lets her fall to the ground three times and nearly kills her, is another example of negligence deeply rooted in the unconscious.

The psycho-analytic explanation of the 'situational' type of occasional offender is that here the feeling of justice has been so badly hurt as to make the power of a usually well-functioning super-ego inoperative. On this type enough has been said above in Chapter 16 in non-psycho-analytical terms.

(c) For all types of criminals, the emphasis on unconscious motivation means that the teachings of psycho-analysis make us less disinclined to believe the offender when he tells us that he does not know himself 'why he did it'. When pressed for an explanation he often produces something which, although it may sound quite plausible, is nothing but a rationalization which occurs to him after the event. In a different field, too, we have been told that certain politicians 'possess the gift of making a decision for political purposes and then believing in it with sincerity and even with passion' (above, p. 310).[58]

This sceptical attitude which we owe to psycho-analysis will not only make us less angry with the offender but also more willing to search for his real motives which may be entirely different from the conscious ones. Without it we are in danger of repeating in another sphere the mistake made by medieval judges who insisted on a confession because they were sure that the accused person must have been the guilty one. In a similar way we are tempted to believe that the guilty person, because he had committed the crime, must know his motives. Moreover, the sceptical attitude which we owe to psychoanalysis—regardless of whether or not we accept its other teachings—will further help us to understand that the real motives of a crime may not only be different from the apparent ones but may even be of a character far removed from that of the crime. If in former times it was taken for granted that theft, robbery or any other economic crime must have been committed for economic reasons we now realize that the reasons may have been sexual or political. There is no inherent homogeneity between the type of crime and its motives. Kleptomania, which has already been discussed before (Chapter 15, I, 1(c)), is the best known, but not the only example of this kind.

All this is closely related to the psycho-analytical theory of *Symbolism* (see s. 1 above). Since according to it every object, every action and every person may have an unconscious symbolic value and stand for something else, this may fundamentally affect the real meaning of a crime as well. The object stolen may represent love, and the person injured may represent another person who somehow reminds the offender of the one he actually wishes to hurt. As most examples of this kind are generally known only a few typical ones may here be mentioned. Alexander and Staub[59] tell the case of a girl who stole a cheap edition of Goethe's *Faust*, worthless pictures representing a mother and child and some dresses which she could not wear. Her explanation that she hoped to become an actress and make use of the things stolen was brushed aside by the authors in favour of the psychoanalytical one that the *Faust* represented for her masculinity, the pictures stood for motherhood and the theft of dresses was an act of revenge against her mother who had neglected her. In short, all her thefts had the object of undoing the wrongs which she believed life had inflicted on her. Or there is Glover's case[60] of the girl who, shortly after the birth of a brother, began to steal cucumbers and later on pencils; these symbolic actions represented 'the desire to deprive the rival of his sexual organ and . . . to compensate herself for what she took to be a sign of girlish inferiority'. Glover adds further details to defend himself against the 'considerable scepticism among lay readers' which, he admits, would be only natural. Hedwig Schwarz's Dorothy (Note 1 above) stole always from a woman, and 'almost invariably a woman in a superior or enviable position (mother figure)', i.e. all her thefts were unconsciously directed against her mother although the actual victims were other female persons. Articles of clothing are symbols of something with which to 'cover up', and hiding clothing becomes an irresistible urge in certain persons. Abrahamsen[61] regards robbery in certain cases 'psychiatrically speaking' as a symbolic expression of rape.

Of special interest is the application of symbolism to *political crimes*. Its starting point is the equation of the State with the father figure; hatred of the latter, therefore, develops into political rebellion in later life. 'There can be little doubt', writes Flugel in an earlier book,[62] 'that much of the general resistance to ... authority that may be exhibited by certain individuals, or at times by whole sections of a community ... derives its motive power from a persistence in the Unconscious of parent hatred.' The political offender, it has been said, builds up a political theory that would enable him to give vent to his father-hatred without feeling guilty. It has also been suggested that displaced father-hatred may often be responsible for strikes as the tyranny of the father is, or used to be in the past, particularly oppressive among the working classes. John Gunther, in *Inside Europe*,[63] refers to the work of another Freudian, Wilhelm Stekel, according to whom 'an attentat is a displacement of a small personal conflict into the life of nations'. 'Perhaps Booth was beaten by a drunken father. So Lincoln died. Perhaps Princip had an unhappy childhood. So the World War came.' While this referred to the First World War, the explorers of Hitler's childhood may be able to draw similar conclusions for the second one. Generally speaking, however, it has to be stressed that, while the revolutionary actions of certain individuals may occasionally be explainable in psycho-analytical terms, political mass movements cannot easily be reduced to this individualistic level. Max Eastman has tried to give a probably over-simplified answer to such attempts from the Marxian point of view: 'Doctors are ... petty bourgeois, and these Freudian doctors are driven on, in their attempts to explain away revolution, by unconscious motives of mass loyalty and pecuniary self-defence.'[64] While this answer is obviously not quite convincing, it seems clear that psycho-analysis has here arrived at a point where it is in danger of over-reaching itself and of ignoring some of the real driving forces in history. Psycho-analysts may retort, however, that their explanation refers merely to the individual side of the problem and does not pretend to deal with its mass-aspects, perhaps also that the distinction between predisposing and precipitating factors of crime, which they frequently stress,[65] may here be applied in a way different from the usual one, treating the mass aspects as predisposing and the individual ones as precipitating factors.

The abortive attempt made in 1936 by a man called MacMahon upon the life of King Edward VIII has been quoted by Bowlby as an example of the ambivalent love-hate mechanism noticeable in some political as well as in non-political crimes.[66] MacMahon's attitude, it is pointed out, was 'a perfect compromise between attacking and protecting' the king. Before the attempt he phoned the police and warned them that an attack would be made, and his attempt consisted not in shooting but in throwing a revolver at the king. Similarly, according to Bowlby, the man who later actually murdered President Doumer of France gave himself up to a policeman and told him that he was going to shoot the president, but the policeman did not take this seriously.

In this connection a case may be mentioned with which the present writer had to deal as a judge. A young man who often quarrelled with his father one day accompanied his friend, a soldier, to the barracks. On leaving he took his friend's service revolver with him, and after wandering aimlessly about for a few days he went to a pawnshop and pawned the revolver, but left the money behind. At his trial he told the court that he had stolen the revolver to commit suicide, but his courage had failed him. The pawnbroker reported that he had made a very distressed and confused impression. The psycho-analyst called by the defence took the view that the prisoner had committed the theft because he identified the State with his father and had taken the revolver as an unconscious act of revenge on the latter. However, in this case the explanation offered by the prisoner may have been the correct one, and it was quite in accordance with the distress he had shown at the pawnshop.

Occasionally the analogy father–state has been extended to explain the great masses of offences against big impersonal bodies within the State, such as nationalized industries, insurance companies, large department stores, etc., and in some cases there may indeed be a feeling of displaced authority-hatred behind such acts. More convincing, however, is the reference to the belief, so frequent among ordinary people, that there is nothing dishonest in robbing or cheating these overgrown bodies because they can afford such small losses and because they rob or cheat you as well.[67]

While we are here not concerned with the psycho-analytical treatment of criminals, a few points have to be made in passing. First, from what has so far been said, it will have become clear that the psycho-analytical interpretation of crime is of great practical relevance to penologists. It has sometimes been asserted that psychoanalysis wants altogether to 'abolish' such concepts as guilt and responsibility, and the institution of punishment. It is true that, while the idea of guilt plays a dominant part in the Freudian system, the scope of free will is considerably limited in it, but, as Ginsberg has said,[68] the object of psycho-analytical treatment being to enable the patient to face realities and to become a responsible person such treatment would be futile if it is assumed at the outset that he could not be helped to help himself. In the case of the girl who stole *Faust*, etc., quoted above from Alexander and Staub, Ginsberg rightly argues that her treatment consisted in bringing her unconscious motives to light and helping her to seek her gratifications in real life instead of living on the 'substitute gratifications of a neurotic'. Likewise, the institution of punishment has not been eliminated by psycho-analysis, but what the latter has done is to produce a far better understanding of the motives behind the penal system and, even more important, behind our own need for self-punishment and the use of scapegoats. It has also shown how very difficult it is to use punishment in the right way, i.e. without creating that sense of injustice and of having 'paid' for one's crimes which we have already diagnosed as one of the strongest incentives to recidivism.

While this is not the place to deal with the many serious obstacles which stand in the way of applying psycho-analytical techniques to the treatment of offenders, one or two points may be briefly made in conclusion. First, some analysts, especially Melitta Schmideberg,[69] have claimed good results for shorter periods of treatment than usually required, which would make the application of such techniques within the penal system at least a practical possibility. Secondly, psycho-analytical methods should never be applied to find out whether a certain crime has been committed by a certain person; they should never play the role of the detective. This was made clear approximately thirty-five or forty years ago on the occasion of the famous Halsmann murder trial in Austria.

(*d*) Of the many followers of Freud who later parted company with him and founded their own schools or at least systems, Adler and Jung have to be briefly mentioned as the psychologists whose writings had probably the strongest impact, second to Freud's own, on criminological thought.

Alfred Adler (1870–1937) became famous as the founder of the school of individual psychology and as the inventor of the inferiority complex.[70] Whereas Freud's system is mainly based on the idea of sex (in its broadest sense), that of Adler rests on the 'will to power', the original sense of inferiority and the consequent struggle for superiority, and it has therefore been compared to the power-philosophy of Friedrich Nietzsche, with which it has otherwise not much in common. While Nietzsche is mainly attracted by the strong superman, Adler rather concentrates on human weakness. When the individual becomes aware of his frailty he tries to compensate for it, and these attempts often lead to over-compensation, i.e. to excesses in the direction opposite to the one where the inferiority is most conspicuous. Demosthenes, the stammerer, by devoting all his energy to the fight against this handicap, becomes a great orator; Beethoven, overcoming his growing deafness, rises to the greatest heights as a composer; but these are very rare exceptions. As Wexberg says, the 'law of compensation' has been recognized in nature for many years, and it is of course closely related to Freud's concept of sublimation.

This concept of the inferiority complex has become one of the most convenient devices for the interpretation of human behaviour, especially as it is a complex which can be attributed to practically everyone. Inferiority is a relative concept, and there will be a sector in the life of every individual when he is, or at least feels, inferior to others, be it his age, sex, physique, intelligence, race, social class or education. Naturally, if an inferiority is shared with very many other persons, its effect will be less harmful than if it is peculiar to only a few. This should apply, for example, to the Freudian penis-envy of the female sex, if one should be permitted to transfer psycho-analytical doctrines to Adlerian concepts. The object of psychological treatment should be, according to Adler, to discover the patient's 'style of life', his specific pattern of compensatory drives.

On this basis, it is easy to understand the practical significance of Adler's teachings in the field of criminology. An inferiority complex can lead to the commission of crime because this is one of the best ways of drawing attention to oneself, of becoming the centre of interest and thereby compensating for one's inferiority. For many people this may be their only chance in life of standing in the limelight which they so fervently desire to bolster up their self-esteem. In the modern machine-age, the feeling of inferiority is, as Adler rightly stressed, deepened by the soulless and mechanical techniques employed in industrial work, which leave very little freedom of self-expression and individual pride in the product of one's labours.

In addition to the sense of weakness and inferiority which to Adler were the main characteristics of the criminal, he found in him a conspicuous lack of co-operation,[71] which he traced back to an unhappy childhood. He particularly mentioned the feeling of frustration aroused in a first-born child who, after the birth of the younger ones, imagines himself to be deprived of his parents' love and attention.

To quote but a few case histories where, apart from Bjerre's murder cases, Adlerian concepts have been used as an explanation, East and Hubert[72] tell the story of a youth, disabled through long illness, who murdered a girl who 'did not refuse him intercourse, but made it clear to him that it would be unwelcome'. They regard the killing as, in Adlerian terminology, 'the masculine protest' of a person unable to accept further evidence of failure and due to an inferiority feeling rather than to sexual excitement.

Or, in a probation record we find the story of a girl of fifteen, born between her mother's two marriages, who tries to make up for her inferior status in the family by committing incest with her three half-brothers.

The general impression left by Adler's writings is that, while his emphasis on inferiority, weakness and lack of co-operation with others has been of considerable value to our understanding of crime, he is inclined to over-simplify matters and to generalize too readily. In contrast to psycho-analytical theory which often strikes the outsider as over-sophisticated and artificially complicated, Adler's opposition tended to 'throw out much of the rich insight into the complexities of mental life that psycho-analysis had won'.[73] As Erich Fromm writes,[74] Adler sees only the rational side of the psychological phenomena he describes, he 'cannot see beyond purposeful and rational determinations of human behaviour', whereas—one might add—Freud concentrated perhaps too much on the irrational side. Nevertheless, Adler's greater willingness to acknowledge the important role of social factors in the causation of crime makes it sometimes easier for sociologists to reach a common basis with the Adlerian than with the orthodox Freudian school. On the whole, however, again apart from a few exceptions such as Bjerre (Chapter 8, I, above) and frequent references in case histories to some of his concepts, Adler's influence on modern criminology has not been significant.

Carl Gustav Jung (1875–1960) and his system of analytical psychology play an important role in the history of criminology mainly through his theory of psychological types and his concepts introvert and extravert, both of which have been mentioned above (Chapters 8, II, and 16).[75] Even after his defection Jung's theories had many points in common with those of Freud, but the points of difference are very numerous and significant. Only very few of them can here be mentioned. Like Adler he disapproved of what he regarded as Freud's excessive emphasis on the sexual instinct, but unlike Adler he regarded it as a mistake to assume 'the continuous operation of a single instinct, as though it were a chemical constituent, always there and always of the same quantity. . . . If that were the case, certainly man would be sexual, as Freud says he is, and intent upon power, as Adler describes him . . . we can easily reconcile Freud with Adler when we consider the psyche not as a rigid and unalterable system.'[76] Consequently, he thought that for purposes of treatment, too, Freudian and Adlerian techniques could be reconciled: 'In the neurosis of a youthful introvert the psychological theory of Adler seldom fails, and in the treatment of the young extravert it is always advisable, indispensable indeed, to take full account of the Freudian standpoint.'[77] Such and similar remarks, however, should not be taken as indicating his agreement with Freud and Adler on other fundamental issues. As Brown writes, 'like Adler, Jung is more concerned with future goals than past history, and he sees the present situation as the key to neurosis',[78] which is in direct opposition to Freud's theory of the latter. He uses the concept of inferiority, but qualifies this by saying that 'to have complexes (a term also introduced by Jung) does not necessarily indicate inferiority'.[79]

The theory that there is 'a continuance from extraversion to introversion on which all human beings could be placed' was not discovered by Jung—according to Eysenck[80] these terms go even back as far as the sixteenth century—but he popularized it and drew important clinical conclusions from it which have recently become the starting point for a number of investigations into the psychological basis of recidivism. One of these conclusions was that hysteric conditions are more likely to develop in extraverts than in introverts, whereas for anxiety states and obsessive-compulsive neuroses the opposite is true. Moreover, according to Eysenck, the introversion-extraversion continuance is one of the basic dimensions of the personality, and, developing Pavlovian ideas, he has hypothesized that extraverts, including in particular psychopaths, are more difficult to condition than introverts and therefore more likely to become recidivists. Reviewing the literature on the subject with special reference to the problems of psychopathy and recidivism, Franks[81] has concluded that there are two kinds of recidivists: first, the introverted ones who can easily be conditioned, but whose environment is so anti-social that their ease in conditioning makes them relapse again and again; and, secondly, the extraverted ones, mostly psychopaths, who are unable to learn the norms of conduct prevailing in their, perhaps socially favourable, environment. In other words, ease of conditioning had the same bad effect on the first group as difficulty in conditioning on the second. Further research done on the subject by Bartholomew has failed to substantiate this hypothesis.[82] Moreover, Alan Little[83] applied the Short Maudsley Personality Inventory to 290 Borstal boys in three institutions receiving boys of various degrees of criminality to test Eysenck's theory as expanded by Franks; none of the predictions based upon this theory could be confirmed, nor was any relationship found between the extraversion and neuroticism scores of the boys and their probability of recidivism as measured by the Mannheim-Wilkins recidivism rates for the different institutions. Little leaves it open, however, whether the Eysenck theory might be useful for adult recidivists. In his latest book *Crime and Personality*[84] Eysenck admits that the evidence for his conditioning theory has not yet been adequately tested and is anyhow not intended to apply indiscriminately to all criminals. For his theory of the extravert character of most reci- divists, however, there exists in his view already more evidence, and in this he is probably justified.

It is not without interest to remember that a typically extravert psychopath, Neville Heath, wrote on the eve of his execution in 1946 to his former Approved School headmaster, Mr. C. A. Joyce: 'It is a great pity I did not remember the many lessons I learnt there, but un- fortunately my memory has always been abominably short, and I have usually paid dearly for it. However, all that is my fault and my fault alone.'[85]

Whereas Jung's fundamental concepts of extravert-introvert have thus been taken up and used by present-day psychological research workers, the same cannot be said of Freudian theories. On the con- trary, it is here that the contrasts and controversies between psychi- atric and psychological methods show themselves more strongly than anywhere else.[86]

# Chapter 18

## THE CRIMINAL LAW AND THE MENTALLY ABNORMAL OFFENDER[1]

It is a debatable point whether, and to what extent, purely legal matters should be included in a book on criminology. Certainly, their treatment should not be too detailed, but an outline of the manner in which the criminal law deals with mentally abnormal offenders would seem to be not out of place.

### I. GENERAL AND HISTORICAL REFLECTIONS

### 1. *The Relationship between Criminal Law and Psychiatry*

On general grounds it would have to be expected that the legal treatment of mentally abnormal offenders should provide a fertile soil for clashes between law and psychiatry. If we look at it from an abstract and dogmatic point of view we have to admit the existence of the following contrasts:

(*a*) The law is concerned with the well-being and protection of society rather than with those of the individual, whose treatment and care are the main interest of the psychiatrist. It is only in recent times that the administration of criminal justice has accepted the reformation and rehabilitation of the offender as one of its objects, but even nowadays they are hardly accepted as equals with deterrence and retribution, which in their turn are tolerated only as perhaps necessary evils by the psychiatrist. The very conception of 'success' has a different colour to each of these two disciplines; to the law it means absence of reconvictions, to the psychiatrist cure of the particular abnormality which he is called upon to diagnose and treat. On the other hand, the criminal law is primarily concerned with one particular action of an individual and widens its interest only at the sentencing stage so as to permit a consideration of the offender's motive and whole personality, whereas the latter is from beginning to end the crucial problem for the psychiatrist.[2]

(*b*) The criminal law is a normative discipline; it contains norms of

334

conduct to be complied with in the interest of society. Psychiatry, as any other branch of medicine, does not evaluate; its norms of conduct are practical rather than moral ones, and it issues only prescriptions which have to be carried out by the patient for his own sake.

(c) The criminal law requires clear-cut terms which provide the individual citizen with well-defined directions; otherwise its effect becomes unpredictable and it cannot act as a deterrent. (That this is only an ideal but rarely realized in legislative practice has been pointed out elsewhere.)[3]

Therefore, the criminal law, even at the risk of being unjust in an individual case, has to use standardized concepts, since only they can, it is believed, ensure certainty and predictability of judicial decisions. Important legal distinctions will, for example, depend on the chronological age of the offender which may in fact be much less important than his mental and emotional age (see above, Chapter 2).

The psychiatrist, on the other hand, delights in the twilight of an often ambiguous terminology and classification, and he tries to base his decisions entirely on the special characteristics of the individual case, although in actual practice he may not always stick to this principle.

(d) The criminal law, as law in general, is a conservative force. As a distinguished American jurist writes, 'the function of the criminal law . . . is not to anticipate but to reflect and implement the consensus already achieved in the community'.[4] While this was written with special reference to offences against property in the United States and in opposition to the present writer's views as expressed in *Criminal Justice and Social Reconstruction*, it reflects the still prevailing general view of lawyers anywhere. Psychiatry, as a much younger discipline and as one which, not unlike criminology, has often been forced into ideological and practical conflict with legal dogmatism, has fewer vested interests and can, therefore, move more freely.

(e) It has often been maintained that the criminal law is based on the dogma of indeterminism, whereas the psychiatrist is wholly opposed to it, and that the law assumes our full responsibility for all our actions, whereas the psychiatrist denies it altogether. Without going here into the ancient problem of free will it can be said that neither of these two extreme positions has many followers any more nowadays. Concessions have been made from both sides. Naturally, the extent of these concessions differs greatly in accordance with the particular brand of criminal law and of psychiatry with which we are concerned, and we may even find lawyers who are more uncompromising determinists than many psychiatrists, and vice versa. While freedom of will was one of the fundamental principles of the classical school of criminal law,[5] it was completely denied by the positivists, notably by Ferri, whose obsession with his fight against any assumption of moral responsibility for criminal acts had gained him the nickname of 'freewill Ferri'.[6] In the half-century or more which has elapsed since these controversies were at their height much water has been poured on to the fire from both sides. Jerome Hall, otherwise a bitter opponent of positivism, admits that while 'some degree of autonomy' is necessary if we have to evaluate human conduct, determinism is an equally necessary postulate for the psychiatrist who wishes to understand rather than evaluate such conduct.[7] Psychoanalytical discoveries, it is true, have, perhaps more than anything else, contributed to a further weakening of our belief in free will by demonstrating that apparently casual and accidental actions were in fact clearly determined, but even Freud was occasionally forced to admit that there were certain limits to his psychic determinism and that, if we follow the development of an individual case from the beginning, instead of tracing it backwards, we may have to admit that there is 'no longer the impression of an inevitable sequence of events which could not be otherwise determined. We notice at once that there might have been another result, and that we might have been just as well able to understand and explain the latter.'[8] This is a reflection which reminds us of what was said in Chapter 7, v, on the difficulties standing in the way of predicting for the individual case.

(*f*) In the field of criminal procedure the conflict between law and psychiatry centres mainly on the position of the expert witness and of he jury. Lawyers, especially in Britain, are inclined to place too much faith in the latter and to make inadequate and often inapt use of the former by putting him into a procedural strait-jacket which makes it often impossible for him to apply his knowledge to the fullest advantage. Naturally, the psychiatric expert has more than any other to suffer from this handicap.[9] He should at least be given the right first of all to present his views fully and coherently, instead of being forced to take part in a play of questions and answers which is often nonsensical and occasionally even designed not to elicit but to hide the truth and to make the expert appear ridiculous in the eyes of the jury. Having presented his views, he should of course be subjected to examination and cross-examination. Giving fuller scope to the psychiatric expert does not mean, however, that he should be allowed to decide the case, nor does he wish to be given this responsibility. It is a distortion of the truth to maintain that psychiatrists as a body are anxious to take the place of judge and jury. Even the treatment tribunals which have been established in different parts of the U.S.A. are bodies composed of penological rather than psychiatric experts.[10]

## 2. The Existing Possibilities

We are now in a position to appreciate that the problems under discussion can be approached from two different angles. From an extreme psychiatric view one might argue that every person who is mentally disordered, or at least every psychotic, should be exempt from responsibility and punishment by the criminal law. In support of this one would have to maintain that neither the concepts of guilt and responsibility nor any of the various objects of punishment apply to mentally disordered lawbreakers. They cannot be deterred by it because they do not react to punishment in the ordinary and generally expected manner; nor can they be reformed by the measures at the disposal of the criminal law; nor does the community, including the victim, insist on punishing them for the sake of retribution. This extreme position, which would make the psychiatric expert the final arbiter in the matter, is, however, taken only by a minority of psychiatrists, whereas most of them—including, as we have seen, many psycho-analysts—would not go so far as completely to deny guilt and responsibility of the mentally abnormal offender nor his potential responsiveness to penal measures; rather would they wish to distinguish according to individual personality and symptoms, and to the extent and seriousness of the disorder.

The lawyer, on the other hand, will argue that the criminal responsibility of a lawbreaker is, after all, a legal problem, and that it is primarily a matter for the law to decide who should be held responsible and how the offender should be punished. While this, too, leads to a distinction according to the nature and seriousness of the abnormality it inevitably makes the proportion of cases in which responsibility is entirely or in part denied smaller than it would be from the psychiatric angle. Lawyers are often prone to assume that even mentally disordered persons can be deterred by punishment and open to educative measures in the same way as normal individuals. Moreover, they are very reluctant to forgo the deterrent effect which, they believe, the punishment of offenders must have on the community at large. The history of the criminal law in most civilized countries shows, however, a continuous inclination to depart from the orthodox legal point of view in favour of greater concessions to psychiatry.

## 3. Historical Developments

The history of the subject forms an important part of the general evolution of the criminal law from its primitive stage, when punishment was imposed for the commission of a criminal act regardless of the mental condition of the actor, to the present age which regards the internal side of a crime as of an importance equal to the external facts. This evolution, tardy and often interrupted by periods of regression, forms one of the truly significant achievements of the human mind. To it we owe the more humane treatment of juvenile lawbreakers and the admission of such legal defences as mistake of fact or duress, and the working out of an elaborate doctrine of *mens rea*.

With regard to the special problem of mental abnormality, the change was very slow and, here as elsewhere, it was brought about at first not so much by considering each individual case on its merits but by exempting from punishment certain standardized situations as such. Moreover, anthropologists have shown that among primitive peoples mental disorder is ascribed not to deficiencies or changes within the individual personality but rather to external causes.[11] This is in conformity with the general refusal of primitives to think in terms of natural causes and with their habit of substituting for them explanations derived from their belief in witchcraft and a system of taboos. Mental illness, as any other disease, is therefore regarded as the work of evil spirits or as retribution for, perhaps unconsciously committed, crimes against divinity. Nowhere has this been more cogently demonstrated, with a wealth of material from anthropological sources, than in Kelsen's *Society and Nature*.[12] In spite of this basically different approach, primitive communities do recognize that mentally ill lawbreakers should not be treated in the same way as normal persons, and their behaviour is often tolerated unless it oversteps the limits of possible toleration.[13] In Ashanti law, for example, a madman was not executed, but was chained to a tree to prevent further crimes, and it was left to his relatives to feed him and keep him alive. At a later period, however, the defence of insanity was abolished because mental illness was no longer regarded as completely and necessarily excluding understanding.[14] Roman law was among the first to admit that *furiosus non intelligit quid agit*, therefore he cannot act with *mens rea*. English law, it is stated, even in its harshest days, recognized insanity as a possible defence, 'but only insanity of a particular and appropriate kind will produce exemption' (Kenny-Turner with reference to a source dated 1313).[15] In the old laws of Iceland and Norway the insane wrongdoer was punished with outlawry, just as the normal one.[16] In the German regional statutes (*Volksrechte*) of the eleventh and twelfth centuries madness, whatever the degree, was not admitted as a mitigating factor in cases of homicide unless the guilty person had clearly demonstrated his madness by inflicting grievous injuries on himself at the time of the murder; and whatever minor concessions were made in the direction towards a more 'guilt-orientated' criminal law were mainly due to the influence of the Church. For Bracton it was only the raving type of madman who was excused; the melancholic type was discovered much later. Even as late as 1724 in the often quoted English case *R. v. Arnold* (16 St. Tr. 695) Tracey, J., instructed the jury that unless a man 'is totally deprived of his understanding and reasoning and does not know what he is doing, any more than an infant, or a wild beast, he was to be punished as any sane person'.[17] At the beginning of the nineteenth century, through the case *R. v. Hadfield* in 1800 (27 St. Tr. 1281), this 'wild beast' test was, however, abandoned in favour of a more progressive attitude. Hadfield,[18] who had sustained very serious head injuries in war, suffered from the delusion that the world was coming to an end and that he had been destined by God to sacrifice himself to save mankind. Not wishing to commit suicide he decided to shoot King George III in order to be hanged (homicide, as we have seen above, not infrequently being an alternative to suicide). He was acquitted on the ground of insanity although neither the wild beast test nor the subsequent M'Naghten Rules would have supported this decision, and in fact when the famous case arose which led to the formulation of these Rules in 1843 English law reverted to far greater rigidity. A man called Daniel M'Naghten had killed a Mr. Drummond, private secretary to the then Prime Minister, Sir Robert Peel, mistaking him for the latter. He suffered from a form of paranoia which made him feel that he was being persecuted by enemies, of whom Peel was one, and he had to kill him in self-defence (4 St. Tr. N.S. 847).[19] He was acquitted, as Hadfield and others had been before him, but this acquittal aroused so much dissatisfaction, shared in particular by Queen Victoria, that after a debate in the House of Lords certain abstract questions on the law concerning insane offenders were submitted by the Lords to the High Court judges—a somewhat unusual procedure considering that it is normally not the function of judges to answer abstract questions of law. The judges, however, complied and gave full written replies, the context of which is through constant application by the courts over a hundred and twenty years still regarded as binding and enforced not only in Great Britain and most parts of the Commonwealth but also in most states of the U.S.A. In some states of Australia and in fourteen states of the U.S.A. they have been modified by the addition of the so-called test of irresistible impulse.[20]

## 4. *The Present English Law: The M'Naghten Rules*

There is no need here to reproduce the full text of these Rules[21] as they are not all of equal significance nowadays. Their essence is the so-called 'right and wrong test', contained in the judges' answers II and III:

to establish a defence on the ground of insanity it must be clearly proved that, at the time of committing the act the accused was labouring under such a defect of reason, from disease of the mind, as not to know the nature and quality of the act he was doing, or, if he did know it, that he did not know he was doing what was wrong.

For a detailed analysis and criticism of these Rules the reader has to be referred to the literature quoted in Notes 2, 19 and 20. Here only the following points may be made: The 'right and wrong' test concerns itself too exclusively with the rational elements of knowledge, neglecting the equally important element of will and emotion and the unconsciousness. To the psychiatrist this test means very little, and a trial and cross-examination limited to it force him to deal with, to him at least, immaterial aspects at the expense of far more essential features of the case.

It is also open to doubt and in fact controversial whether the words 'quality' and 'wrong' refer to the moral or merely to the legal side of the act. While English courts prefer the second interpretation,[22] which is unfavourable to the accused, the High Court of Australia has adopted the first and decided that the criminal liability of the accused 'depends on his ability to reason about the wrongness of his act with a moderate degree of sense and composure'.[23] Moreover, the Rules deal only with the more extreme cases of insanity, excluding the less obvious ones, in particular the 'non-sane non-insane' cases. It has often been maintained by supporters of the Rules that English judges and juries tend to interpret them very broadly and that therefore no injustice is actually done. While this may be true in quite a number of cases it is, as among others the evidence submitted to the Royal Commission of 1953 shows, certainly not true in general. Clear-cut cases of schizophrenia, general paralysis of the insane, paranoia and of similar forms of psychosis will always stand a good chance of being somehow covered by the Rules. What, however, may happen to the others, which probably form a considerable majority? The British Medical Association, in their evidence before the Commission:

gave the following examples of abnormal mental states in which, although the prisoner knew the nature and wrongfulness of his act, responsibility for the crime of murder might in their view be either absent or diminished as a result of emotional disorder.[24]

(a) aggressive psychopathic states;
(b) states associated with organic damage to the brain (epilepsy, epidemic encephalitis, etc.);
(c) depressive states with desire for self-destruction or self-punishment;
(d) early schizophrenia;
(e) paranoia and paraphrenia.

Ignoring for the moment the categories (a) and (c), this list shows

340

that in the view of the British Medical Association certain cases of psychosis are in danger of being left outside the scope of the Rules, even if the latter are fairly liberally interpreted. The paranoiac who kills his wife and children in obedience to what he believes to be a command from God to relieve them from their earthly sufferings and who is firmly convinced that his action, though illegal, was in accordance with his religious and moral duties, is still not entirely out of danger of being convicted of murder. With regard to epilepsy the Royal Commission merely recommended that in murder cases where the offender could not be held to be wholly irresponsible on the ground of insanity the question whether the death penalty should be carried out should be approached 'with the presumption that, if not the epilepsy itself, then the underlying abnormality of the brain may have provided a link in the chain of reaction which led to the crime' (p. 276, also pp. 134–5). The problem of murder committed by psychopaths was also treated by way of a recommendation that, although not amounting to insanity, this form of mental abnormality should be given due weight in deciding whether the death penalty should be carried out (p. 276). All this makes it clear that the Rules exclude the less obvious cases of insanity as well as the 'non-sane non-insane' groups. Controversial is the position of the mental defective who is not at the same time insane according to the narrower interpretation of the M'Naghten Rules. The high-grade mental defective Straffen was found guilty of murder and sentenced to death, though later reprieved. This case gives rise to a number of interesting legal, psychiatric and criminological problems.[25]

Other weaknesses of the Rules are that they place the onus of proof on the defence[26] and that, by restricting their application to the jury courts, they sanction a dual system of justice. Because they are unduly narrow they hand the final decision over to the Home Secretary and his advisers who are thereby established as the supreme arbiters, which gives the court proceedings an air of unreality.

In the circumstances, it is only natural that there should have been frequent attempts to make the Rules less rigid and extend them beyond their present narrow limits, for example by adding the defence of *irresistible impulse* and making special provision for the 'non-sane non-insane' groups. The objection can be raised against the first-mentioned defence that it is often impossible for an expert to state whether an impulse is 'irresistible'[27] and, in the words of the Royal Commission, it 'carries the implication that . . . [the crime] must have been suddenly and impulsively committed after a sharp internal conflict', which is not true, for example, in cases of melancholia where the act may be coolly and carefully prepared, but nevertheless bear all the marks of insanity. The Commission therefore preferred the phrase that the accused 'did not know that it was wrong or was incapable of preventing himself from committing it', which would bring English law closer to most Continental Codes using the formula 'inability to recognize the wrongness of his action or to act in accordance with his insight'.[28] In any case, as Norval Morris points out, in view of the narrow interpretation of the words 'nature and quality' and 'wrong' by the English courts the need for the statutory adoption of a formula of this kind is greater than in countries where, as in Australia, these words receive a more liberal interpretation. Moreover, the Privy Council in the recent Australian case *South Australia v. Brown* agrees with the High Court of Australia that 'irresistible impulse' can be a symptom of 'M'Naghten insanity' (Morris 291), but how tortuous and artificial is the Council's whole reasoning!

Among the many other proposals for the legislative reform of the Rules the following deserve special mention. The Royal Commission of 1953 recommended in the first place to abrogate the Rules altogether and to leave the jury free to determine whether the accused was suffering from disease of the mind (or mental deficiency) to such a degree that he ought not to be held responsible. Failing this, they recommended the formula quoted above in the place of the test of irresistible impulse (paras. 317 and 333). The first recommendation cannot be approved as it would leave the jury without any guidance and result in haphazard and amateurish verdicts; the second would mean an improvement of the present position, but might not go far enough. The emphasis on the inability of the offender to control himself or to prevent himself from committing the act may also, if pronounced publicly at the trial, have an undesirable effect on the offender's future conduct.[29] The formula used by the Danish Criminal Code of 1930, arts. 17 and 70: 'persons unable to be influenced by ordinary punishment' and therefore to be subjected to other measures, might perhaps avoid these dangers. In the U.S.A. two other solutions have been tried out in a small area outside that following the M'Naghten Rules: The New Hampshire Rule, adopted in that state already in 1870, and the Durham Rule, in force in the District of Columbia since 1954.[30] The former, which has repeatedly been revised, was the model for the recommendation of the Royal Commission to leave the issue to the jury whether the accused suffered from a mental disease which had taken away his capacity to form a criminal intent. The Durham Rule, so called after the case *Durham v. United States*, [1954] 214 F. 2d 862 of the Court of Appeal for the District of Columbia, states that an accused is not criminally responsible 'if his unlawful act was the product of mental disease or mental defect', therefore called the 'product-rule'. Finally, the American Law Institute's Draft No. 7 of a Model Code proposes a formula which is in essence a return to the

European Codes referred to above, excluding, however, the psychopath. This is not the appropriate place for a detailed discussion of the merits or otherwise of these various American attempts to solve the legislative problem, and the author can only reiterate his view that more important than an ideal formula, which is in any case out of reach, is 'the harmonious co-operation between well-trained lawyers and psychiatrists, each of them willing to listen to reason and to play his own part instead of trespassing on the field of the other'.[31] And of perhaps equal importance is the manner in which the onus of proof of insanity is distributed since in a high proportion of cases the crucial issue remains in doubt. It is an anomaly contrary to the general principles of the criminal procedure to throw the burden of proof, as the M'Naghten Rules do, entirely on the defence.

If an accused person is found by the jury to be falling under the M'Naghten Rules their 'special' verdict under the Trial of Lunatics Act, 1883, s. 2(1), is 'guilty of the act or omission charged against him, but insane at the time', with the consequence that under the Criminal Lunatics Act, 1800, the court has to order the prisoner to be detained during His (or Her) Majesty's pleasure. Detention now takes place in a special institution at Broadmoor in Berkshire (established in 1863), which under the Criminal Justice Act, 1948, s. 62, was transferred from the prison authorities to the Board of Control and is now, as the latter was dissolved by the Mental Health Act, 1959, s. 2, under the Ministry of Health. The inmates, called at first 'criminal lunatics', later under the Criminal Justice Act, 1948, s. 62, promoted to 'Broadmoor patients', are now, as the Mental Health Act, 1959, repeals that section, simply patients detained under H.M.'s pleasure. Instead of Broadmoor, mental hospitals provided by the National Health Service may be used for less dangerous persons. For mental defectives the Rampton or the Moss Side State Institutions are available.

Of greater practical importance than the legal technicalities arising from the M'Naghten Rules is the right of the Home Secretary under the Criminal Lunatics Act, 1884, s. 2, even in cases where the jury has found the prisoner to be outside the Rules and he has been convicted and sentenced in the ordinary way, to order an enquiry into his mental condition.[32] The Act, though establishing certain technical differentiations between prisoners under sentence of death and others, applies to both categories, and in both cases the Home Secretary has to appoint experts who are not bound in their judgment to apply the M'Naghten Rules with their narrow definition of insanity and their wrong distribution of the burden of proof. If as a result of this statutory enquiry the prisoner is found insane he is removed to Broadmoor 'until further signification of Her Majesty's pleasure' and if he had been under sentence of death the latter is 'respited'. The same applies if the prisoner was actually sane at the time of the crime and the trial, but became insane afterwards.

According to statistics published in the Report of the Royal Commission (p. 311) the number of persons found guilty but insane in proceedings for murder in England and Wales during 1900–49 was 798, that of persons convicted and sentenced to death 1,210, and that of persons certified insane after medical enquiry 48. The number of those death sentences 'respited and commuted to penal servitude for life wholly or partly on grounds of mental condition' after medical enquiry was 37 and without medical enquiry 40. Detention in Broadmoor, if not actually for life, is often for a very long time. As the then Superintendent of Broadmoor told the Royal Commission of 1953, 'as a rule, if a man does not get out within 10 years, he probably does not get out at all'.[33] When the present writer visited it in 1947 he was told that in most cases of homicide the minimum period was 6 years. *Criminal Statistics for England and Wales* provides annual tables of receptions and discharges (at present Tables XIXA and B and XX). On the 31st October 1960 there were 114 male and 50 female patients in Broadmoor who had been detained for 20 years and over (*Criminal Statistics for 1960*, Table XX).

## 5. *The Post-M'Naghten Law*

The impact of the shortcomings of the M'Naghten Rules has in recent years also been greatly reduced in England by two important statutes, the Homicide Act, 1957, and the Mental Health Act, 1959. It is their special merit that they deal with cases of the 'non-sane non-insane' category and of mental deficiency in a more progressive way than do the Rules for cases of insanity.[34] Under the Homicide Act, 1957, s. 2, 'where a person kills or is a party to the killing of another, he shall not be convicted of murder if he was suffering from such abnormality of mind (whether arising from a condition of arrested or retarded development of mind or any inherent causes or induced by disease or injury) as substantially impaired his mental responsibility for his acts and omissions in doing or being a party to the killing'; instead he is liable to be convicted of manslaughter, but the burden of proof is on the defence. This section introduces the legal concept, for a fairly long period already familiar to Continental and Scottish law, of diminished responsibility, and thereby remedies the rigid attitude of the M'Naghten Rules according to which an offender could only be either completely sane or completely insane. Attempts to let the 'knowledge of right and wrong' test enter by the backdoor have been unsuccessful so far. Unfortunately in the last resort the section is unsatisfactory, however, in containing no provisions for psychiatric treatment, except for the facilities already existing for offenders sentenced in the ordinary way to imprisonment, Borstal, etc., or placed on probation. In actual court practice, until 1961, most of those so far found guilty of manslaughter under s. 2, i.e. 45 out of 85, have been sentenced to fixed terms of imprisonment ranging from one to ten years, another 5 to more than 10 years, while 30 received life sentences and 5 were placed on probation with a condition of mental treatment under Criminal Justice Act, 1948, s. 4.[35] It has to be borne in mind that a life sentence is in fact an indeterminate sentence which has to be reviewed periodically and enables the Home Secretary to release a prisoner when he is regarded as a fit person to return to society; it is more elastic, therefore, than a fixed prison term. Apart from this advantage, however, it is equally lacking in treatment facilities. It is somewhat paradoxical that while those found insane under the Rules should be sent to Broadmoor where they can receive appropriate treatment, those found to be of diminished responsibility should often receive nothing but ordinary imprisonment. The position is likely to improve, however, as soon as the new 'psychiatric prison', to be known as H.M. Prison Grendon (in Buckinghamshire), but often referred to as the East-Hubert Institution, will be fully available.[36] This is a maximum security prison for up to 350 inmates to be divided into groups 'to facilitate treatment according to their attitudes and needs'.[37]

Concerning the special care of criminal psychopaths, the courts have recently resisted attempts to exclude them altogether from the operation of s. 2 and rejected the argument that the latter referred only to 'abnormality of the mind', not to emotional abnormalities of the personality. It can be regarded as established, therefore, that a psychopath may, in appropriate cases, be brought under the scope of s. 2.[38] The question when this should be done is, naturally, one of the most difficult ones to confront the criminal courts and the psychiatric experts.

In one of the most recent cases of this kind, *R. v. McCrorey* (*The Times*, 31.7.1962), diminished responsibility was assumed and a life sentence imposed in a case where a psychopath had killed a woman in the furtherance of theft. The psychiatric experts had testified that if the killing had been done on the spur of the moment by a man taken by surprise it was likely that the prisoner had acted in a state of substantial impairment of his faculties, whereas if the killing had been premeditated this would lead to the opposite conclusion. So far, it cannot be said that a clear line of policy has emerged from the literature or from court decisions. One thing is certain, however, i.e. that the problem can be brought nearer to a solution not by adopting the superficially perhaps plausible view of Lady Wootton that the more horrible the crime the more likely a finding of diminished responsibility, but only by further research as indicated above (Chapter 15).

The weaknesses of the present system are still further aggravated by the principle of English criminal procedure that insanity and diminished responsibility are defences which have to be raised by the accused in person or on his behalf with his consent, and that they cannot be raised at all if the accused pleads innocence, especially mistaken identity. The latter point was recently discussed in connection with the Hanratty trial. Here after the prisoner's execution a psychiatrist pointed out that, although the case had shown various circumstances which strongly indicated abnormality of mind, none of those defences could be raised in court because the accused had to the last maintained that he had not been the killer.[39] This attitude of the law is unreasonable; it is difficult to understand why the defence should not have the right to argue that the accused was innocent of the act, but if the court should regard him as guilty of the facts of the offence, the plea would be changed to one of insanity or diminished responsibility.[40]

The value of the contribution made by the Mental Health Act, 1959, is that it has not only given new statutory definitions of mental disorder and for the first time attempted a definition of psychopathy (Chapter 15, above), but that it has also made court decisions and administrative action in such cases more flexible. Under s. 60 the court has discretionary power in all criminal cases except capital murder to authorize the admission of the offender to and his detention in a mental hospital or place him under guardianship, provided the mental disorder is of a nature or degree which warrants such a decision.[41] As rightly stressed by Edwards against Wootton, the Act of 1959, differently from the Homicide Act, is concerned not with the question of criminal responsibility but only with that of treatment; it does not, therefore, eliminate responsibility.

The Act empowers the criminal courts if a person is convicted of any offence except a capital or a very trivial one and they are satisfied on the written or oral evidence of two medical practitioners

(1) that the offender is suffering from mental illness, psychopathic disorder, subnormality or severe subnormality; and
(2) that the mental disorder is of a nature or degree which warrants the detention of the patient in a hospital for medical treatment, or the reception of a patient to guardianship under this Act; and the court is of opinion, having regard to all the circumstances including the nature of the offence and the character and antecedents of the offender, and to the available methods of dealing with him, that the

most suitable method of disposing of the case is by means of an order under this section,

by order to authorize his admission to and detention in a specified hospital or place him under the guardianship of a local health authority or of a person approved by the latter (s. 60). Where a hospital order is made by a court of assize or quarter sessions, and it appears to the court, having regard to the nature of the offence, the antecedents of the offender and the risk of his committing further offences if set at large, that it is necessary for the protection of the public so to do, the court may further order that the offender shall be subject to certain special restrictions, either without limit of time or during a specified period (s. 65(1)). The nature of these restrictions is defined in s. 65 (3); they are related mainly to the duration of the detention, leave of absence, transfer, discharge, and recall, and give very extensive powers to the Home Secretary in all these matters. There are also provisions giving the Home Secretary power to transfer to specified hospitals persons already serving sentences of imprisonment and falling under the categories defined in s. 60 (sects. 72–75), and in such cases he may also impose restrictions of the kind defined in s. 65 (s. 74).

Without going too much into the details of the highly complicated provisions of the Act the following few observations may be made. First, as already stated, s. 60 does not apply to capital murder, where, therefore, the M'Naghten Rules still apply. Moreover, it is left entirely to the discretion of the courts whether in cases falling under s. 60 they wish to make a hospital or guardianship order or whether they prefer to impose, for example, an ordinary prison sentence, and for this reason the powers given in s. 72 to the Home Secretary are of great practical importance. Furthermore, even if an order is made by a court of assize or quarter sessions there has first to be a conviction, although the offender may be insane. Magistrates' courts may make an order without convicting (s. 60 (2)). In spite of certain defects, it is clear, however, that the Mental Health Act provides a procedure far superior to that of the M'Naghten Rules and that its definition of the various forms of mental disorder makes it much easier to conform with modern psychiatric ideas. It is still too early to state how far the courts are, and shall be, ready to exercise their powers under the Act. According to *Criminal Statistics for 1960*, Table XIXB, which covers only a very short period, 50 persons were detained in psychiatric hospitals under restriction orders, but the kind of restriction is not specified. For 1961 (Tables XIX and XX) the number of restriction orders has already risen to 153, and some information is given on the duration of the restriction: 86 were without limit of time, ten for 10 years or more, and the remainder for shorter periods. For 1962 the figures were slightly lower. To give two illustrations from newspaper reports, in the case of a man aged 30 convicted of manslaughter a 40-year restriction order was made, in the case of another, aged 23, sentenced to two years' imprisonment for causing grievous bodily harm, the Court of Criminal Appeal substituted for it a restriction order for three years as the offender had possibly been suffering from an epileptic attack.[42]

There are some special provisions for psychopathic and subnormal persons. While such patients, if not found guilty of an offence, can be detained in hospital or kept under guardianship beyond the age of 25 only if they are found to be dangerous to others or themselves (s. 44), this does not apply to them if they fall under s. 60 (see s. 63 (31)).

An order committing the offender to hospital cannot be combined with imprisonment, detention, a fine or probation, nor shall it be made for the purpose of punishing him, but only for treatment and the safety of society.[43] As Glanville Williams points out, offenders are more likely to have confidence in the disciplinary powers of the judges under the new procedure than in those of the Home Secretary's unknown advisers under the Criminal Lunatics Act, 1884. It has to be borne in mind, however, that within the limits imposed by a judicial restricting order the Home Secretary's powers are still very wide indeed.

.For reasons of space, such special points of procedure as insanity on arraignment or during trial ('unfit to plead') are not dealt with in this chapter, and the reader is referred to the detailed discussion by Glanville Williams, *op. cit.*, 2nd ed. (§ 143). Attention should be drawn, however, to the particularly interesting case *R. v. Podola* (autumn 1959), in which, it is believed, the plea of unfitness to plead on the ground of amnesia was for the first time raised in England. In spite of the extreme thoroughness in which the matter was treated by the courts, this case has led to some just criticisms of the manner such pleas are handled at present in English law (see also p. 253 above).[44]

### 6. *The Law Concerning Offences committed in a State of Drunkenness*[45]

Such offenders have for a long time presented the criminal law with particularly difficult problems. On the one hand, it can be argued that drunkenness might well produce an abnormal condition of mind which should be legally treated in the same way as any other form of mental disorder. On the other hand, the fact that drunkenness is usually self-induced cannot be entirely ignored. (That 'involuntary' drunkenness, occurring for example when a person does not know that he is drinking a heavily intoxicating beverage, is a complete defence is beyond dispute.) While the first argument may in certain cases lead to a denial of criminal responsibility, the second serves as a warning not to be over-generous with such exceptions. This explains the dilemma confronting the law and the criminal courts. Glanville Williams opens his admirable discussion of the matter with the statement that 'there is, in general, no special law on the subject of drunkenness', but is immediately forced to admit a number of significant exceptions to this rule.

If we apply the existing law to the three categories outlined above in Chapter 14, p. 250, the result would be as follows:

(a) The 'normal' drunkenness occurring in an otherwise mentally sane person and being so heavy as to produce a state of mind which amounts to temporary insanity is no defence in law, unless—and this is a very important proviso—it 'negatives' the specific intent or knowledge required for the crime in question or, where not intent but recklessness is required, it negatives the necessary foresight of the likely consequences. For example, if the offender is so drunk as not to realize that he is killing another person he is not guilty of murder, though he may be guilty of manslaughter. Under the Homicide Act, 1957, his responsibility may be regarded as 'diminished', although there has been some doubt as to whether drunkenness can be brought under s. 2(1) of the Act.[46] Or, somebody who hits his victim with a stick may because of his drunkenness, be found not guilty of causing grievous bodily harm, but only of the less serious offence of common assault if he did not have the intent needed for the former, but only that needed for the latter offence. Or a person who, in his drunkenness, walks off with another person's umbrella probably does so without the intent to deprive the owner permanently of his property. Killing in the course of rape, however, has been treated as murder in the famous case of Beard, [1920] A.C. 479 because the intent required to commit rape could not be negatived by drunkenness. Apart from such special cases, ordinary drunkenness, which 'merely removed the brakes' (Goodhart), is no defence. It may, however, affect the penalty. While the Italian Penal Code of 1930, § 92, provides that ordinary drunkenness is not to be treated as a mitigating circumstance, elsewhere the matter is usually left to the discretion of the courts,[47] which means that personal inclinations and prejudices may occasionally decide. Against undue leniency it may be argued that offenders may intentionally get drunk before committing a crime (the *actio libera in causa* of Continental legal doctrine), but such cases are not very frequent (the Gallagher case discussed by Goodhart may be one as the offender had told the police: 'I made up my mind to kill her about a fortnight or three weeks ago').

(b) The pathological drunkenness occurring in mentally unstable or abnormal persons, often caused by very small quantities of alcohol.

In such cases where the two factors of mental abnormality and drunkenness are combined there will usually be no difficulty either in finding the accused 'guilty but insane' or of diminished responsibility or in non-capital offences of imposing a comparatively lenient penalty or making an order under the Mental Health Act. The latter may be advisable particularly in cases where there is need for prolonged medical treatment.

(c) Chronic alcoholism may lead to pathological changes in the brain affecting the whole personality. The result may be delirium tremens and an alcoholic psychosis, and in epileptics a seizure. There is no reason why insanity produced by chronic alcoholism should be excluded from the M'Naghten Rules or the appropriate provisions of the Homicide Act and Mental Health Act.

The real problem in many cases of categories (b) and (c) is not the question of punishment but that of treatment. The regrettable failure of the Inebriates legislation of the last century has not yet led to a more resolute tackling of the institutional side of the matter, although a number of voluntary inebriates' homes are available.[48]

For cases of category (a), where the drunkenness is of such a kind as to provide a defence against charges of manslaughter, wounding, etc., some Continental legislations have provided a new and, it seems, satisfactory solution. The Danish Penal Code of 1930, art. 138, and the German Penal Code, § 330a, have established a special offence of committing a crime while in a condition of wilfully or negligently induced drunkenness excluding normal responsibility for the crime. In other words, while the offender cannot be punished for the crime he happens to commit in such a condition he can be punished for this special offence; the penalty is normally milder than the one which would be imposed if criminal responsibility had not been excluded.[49] These provisions do not apply to cases of *an actio libera in causa*, where the offender got drunk with the intent to commit the crime under the protection of drunkenness; here he may in clear cases be punished for the crime actually committed, unless it seems doubtful whether it was really the outcome of that intent or rather the result of a mere inner resolve to commit it.

# Selected Reading Lists*

Most of the abbreviations in the following Selected Reading Lists and Notes in Vols. I and II are taken from *Excerpta Medica*, 'List of Journals abstracted', 1964, Excerpta Medica Foundation, Amsterdam–New York–London–Milan–Tokyo, with grateful acknowledgments for their permission.

## CHAPTER 1

H. Mannheim, *Group Problems in Crime and Punishment*, London, 1955, Ch. 12.

Karl R. Popper, *The Poverty of Historicism*, London, 1957.

L. Susan Stebbing, *Philosophy and the Physicist*, Harmondsworth, 1944, Ch. 9.

*The Sutherland Papers*, ed. by Albert Cohen, Alfred Lindesmith, and Karl Schuessler, Bloomington, 1956, Part 1.

(On causality): Karl R. Popper, *The Logic of Scientific Discovery*, 1959, pp. 59 ff. and *passim*.

R. M. McIver, *Social Causation*, Boston, 1940.

Sheldon and Eleanor Glueck, *Ventures in Criminology*, London, 1964, Ch. 16.

Arnold M. Rose, *Theory and Method in the Social Sciences*, Minneapolis, 1954.

Hermann Mannheim and Leslie Wilkins, *Prediction Methods in relation to Borstal Training*, H.M.S.O., London, 1955.

W. Friedmann, *Legal Theory*, 3rd ed., London, 1953.

*Pioneers of Criminology*, ed. by H. Mannheim, London, 1960, Ch. 11.

UNESCO, *The University Teaching of Social Sciences: Criminology*, Paris, 1957.

## CHAPTER 2

Kenny's *Outlines of Criminal Law*, an entirely new ed. by J. W. Cecil Turner, Cambridge, 1952.

---

* The publications have been listed here neither in alphabetical order nor according to their importance or date of publication, but in the order in which they appear in the Notes. As the general textbooks of criminology have been listed separately in the Appendix they are not here included. There is inevitably some overlapping, and consequently some publications appear in several lists. Only English language publications have here been included, and the accessibility of the material has also been a consideration.

351

Glanville Williams, *Criminal Law: The General Part*, London, 1953, Ch. 7.
Jerome Hall, *General Principles of Criminal Law*, Minneapolis, 1947, Ch. 10.
Jerome Hall, *Studies in Jurisprudence and Criminal Theory*, New York, 1958.
H. Mannheim, *The Dilemma of Penal Reform*, London, 1939, Ch. 4.
H. Mannheim, *Criminal Justice and Social Reconstruction*, London, 1946.
Morris Ginsberg, *Essays in Sociology and Social Philosophy*, London, 1956.
Thorsten Sellin, *Culture Conflict and Crime*, New York, 1938.
E. Bodenheimer, *Jurisprudence*, New York and London, 1940.
B. Malinowski, *Crime and Custom in Savage Society*, London, 1932.
H. Kantorowicz, *The Definition of Law*, Cambridge, 1958, Ch. 5.
A. P. d'Entrèves, *Natural Law*, London, 4th imp., 1957.
Hans Kelsen, *What is Justice?*, Berkeley and Los Angeles, 1957.
H. L. A. Hart, *Law, Liberty and Morality*, London, Oxford Univ. Press, 1963.
Lon L. Fuller, *The Morality of Law*, New Haven, 1964.
Glanville Williams, *Sanctity of Life and the Criminal Law*, London, 1957.
Norman St. John Stevas, *Life, Death, and the Law*, London, 1961.

CHAPTER 3

Robert K. Merton, *Social Theory and Social Structure*, Glencoe, Ill., 1957.
Gunnar Myrdal, *Value in Social Theory*, London, 1958.
Leslie Wilkins, *Social Deviance*, London, 1964.
Claire Selltiz *et al.*, *Research Methods in Social Relations*, London, 1959.
Arnold M. Rose, *Theory and Method in the Social Sciences*, Minneapolis, 1954.
Hermann Mannheim, Foreword to R. G. Andry, *The Short-Term Prisoner*, Library of Criminology, London, 1963.
Stephen Toulmin, *The Philosophy of Science*, London, 1953.

On the methodology of social research in general see Karl R. Popper, *The Logic of Scientific Discovery*, London, 1959.

CHAPTER 4

Arnold M. Rose, *Theory and Method in the Social Sciences*, Minneapolis, 1954.
H. Bianchi, *Position and Subject-Matter of Criminology*, Amsterdam, 1956.
Morris Ginsberg, 'Social Change', *Brit. J. Sociol.*, Vol. 9, No. 3, 1958.
Wilson Gee, *Social Science Research Methods*, New York, 1950.
Edward Glover, *The Roots of Crime*, London, 1960, Sect. 6, 272 ff.
John C. Spencer, *Stress and Release in an Urban Estate. A Study in Action Research*, London, 1964.
Marshall B. Clinard, 'Research Frontiers in Criminology', *Brit. J. Delinq.*, Vol. 7, No. 2, 1956.
Sheldon and Eleanor Glueck, *Ventures in Criminology*, London, International Library of Criminology, Vol. 9, 1964, Ch. 19.
Hermann Mannheim, *Group Problems in Crime and Punishment*, Ch. 6.
Barbara Wootton, *Social Science and Social Pathology*, London, 1959, Ch. 3.

352

SELECTED READING LISTS

CHAPTER 5

Thorsten Sellin and Marvin E. Wolfgang, *The Measurement of Delinquency*, New York, London, Sydney, 1964.
J. M. van Bemmelen, 'The Constancy of Crime', *Brit. J. Delinq.*, Vol. 2, No. 3, 1952.
Hermann Mannheim, *Social Aspects of Crime in England between the Wars*, London, 1940, Part 1.
M. Grünhut, 'Statistics in Criminology', *J. roy. statist. Soc.*, Vol. 114, Part 2, 1952.
Barbara Wootton, *Social Science and Social Pathology*, London, 1959, Ch. 1.
Lord Pakenham, *Causes of Crime*, London, 1958.
Mabel Elliott, *Crime in Modern Society*, 1952.
Ronald H. Beattie, 'The Sources of Criminal Statistics', *Ann. Amer. Acad. Polit. Soc. Sci.*, Vol. 217, 1941.
Gunnar Fredriksson, *Kriminal-Statistiken och Kriminologien*, Stockholm. Göteborg-Uppsala, with English summary 1962 (to be published in an Eng. translation in the International Library of Criminology, London).

CHAPTER 6

H. Mannheim, *Social Aspects of Crime*, London, 1940, Ch. 5.
M. Grünhut, *Juvenile Offenders before the Courts*, Oxford, 1956.
M. J. Moroney, *Facts from Figures*, Harmondsworth, 1951.
C. A. Moser, *Survey Methods in Social Investigation*, London, 1958.
H. Mannheim and T. Wilkins, *Prediction Methods in relation to Borstal Training*, London, 1955.
(On Control Groups): E. Greenwood, *Experimental Sociology*, 5th imp., New York, 1949, Ch. 6.
Claire Selltiz et al., *Research Methods in Social Relations*, London, 1959.
Sheldon and Eleanor Glueck, *Unraveling Juvenile Delinquency*, New York, 1950.
Sol Rubin, *Crime and Juvenile Delinquency*, 2nd ed., New York, 1961, Ch. 1.
William McCord and Joan McCord et al., *Origins of Crime*, New York, 1959.
(On Follow-up Studies): Sheldon and Eleanor Glueck, *After-Conduct of Discharged Offenders*, London, 1945; the same: *500 Criminal Careers*, New York, 1930.
Jay Rumney and Joseph P. Murphy, *Probation and Social Adjustment*, New Brunswick, 1952.
Walter C. Reckless and C. H. Andersen, *Summary of Proceedings of the Third International Congress of Criminology London 1955*, London, 1957.
A. G. Rose, *Five Hundred Borstal Boys*, Oxford, 1954.

CHAPTER 7

H. Mannheim and Leslie Wilkins, *Prediction Methods in relation to Borstal Training*. London, 1955, 2nd imp. 1965.

Lloyd E. Ohlin, *Selection for Parole*, New York, 1951.
Paul Horst *et al.*, *The Prediction of Personal Adjustment*, Soc. Sci. Res. Counc. Bull. No. 48, New York, 1941.
*Brit. J. Delinq.*, Vol. 6, No. 2, Sept. 1955: Special Number on Prediction and Recidivism.
S. and E. Glueck, *Predicting Delinquency and Crime*, Cambridge, Mass., 1959.
S. and E. Glueck, *Ventures in Criminology*, London, 1964.
Sol Rubin, *Crime and Juvenile Delinquency*, 2nd ed., New York, 1961, Part 6.
Paul E. Meehl, *Clinical v. Statistical Prediction*, Minnesota and London, 2nd imp. 1956.

## CHAPTER 8

(On Individual Case Studies): John Madge, *The Tools of Social Science*, London, 1953, Chs. 2 and 4.
Gordon W. Allport, *The Use of Personal Documents in Psychological Science*, Soc. Sci. Res. Counc. Bull. 49, New York, 1942.
Claire Selltiz *et al.*, *Research Methods in Social Relations*, Chs. 6–9.
Frederic Wertham, *Dark Legend: A Study in Murder*, London, 1947.
William Healy and Augusta Bronner, *New Light on Delinquency*, New Haven, 1936.
Franz Alexander and William Healy, *The Roots of Crime*, New York, 1935.
Clifford R. Shaw, *The Natural History of a Delinquent Career*, Chicago, 1930.
Clifford R. Shaw *et al.*, *Brothers in Crime*, Chicago, 1938.
E. H. Sutherland, *The Professional Thief*, Chicago, 1937.
Grace W. Pailthorpe, *Studies in the Psychology of Delinquency*, London, H.M.S.O., 1932.
Nathan Leopold, *Life plus 99 Years*, London, 1958.
William Clifford, *Profiles in Crime*, Lusaka, 1964.
(On Typological Methods): C. G. Jung, *Psychological Types*, London, 1923.
Ernst Kretschmer, *Physique and Character*, London, 1925.
H. J. Eysenck, *The Structure of Human Personality*, 2nd ed., London, 1960.
Jack B. Gibbs, 'Needed: Analytical Typologies in Criminology', *Southwestern Social Science Quarterly*, Vol. 40, March 1960.
William H. Sheldon, *Varieties of Delinquent Youths*, New York, 1949.
S. and E. Glueck, *Physique and Delinquency*, New York, 1956.
S. and E. Glueck, 'Varieties of Delinquent Types', *Brit. J. Crim.*, Vol. 5, Nos. 4 and 5, 1965.
T. C. N. Gibbens, *Psychiatric Studies of Borstal Lads*, London, 1963.
R. S. Taylor, 'The Habitual Criminal', *Brit. J. Crim.*, Vol. 1, No. 1, July 1960.
John Bowlby, 'Forty-four Juvenile Thieves', *Int. J. Psycho-Anal.*, Vol. 25, 1944.
D. A. Ogden, 'A Borstal Typological Survey (Camp Hill)', *Brit. J. Delinq.*, Vol. 5, No. 2, Oct. 1954.

A. G. Rose, *500 Borstal Boys*, Oxford, 1954, Ch. 7.
D. H. Stott, *Delinquency and Human Nature*, Dunfermline, 1950, esp. Ch. 14.
Marvin E. Wolfgang, *Patterns in Criminal Homicide*, Philadelphia, 1958, esp. Ch. 10.

## CHAPTER 9

Ernest Greenwood, *Experimental Sociology*, New York, 1945, 5th imp., 1949.
Stuart Chapin, *Experimental Designs in Sociological Research*, 2nd ed., New York, 1956.
John Madge, *The Tools of Social Science*, London, 1953, Ch. 5.
W. I. B. Beveridge, *The Art of Scientific Investigation*, London, 1950, Ch. 2.
Edwin Powers and Helen Witmer, *An Experiment in the Prevention of Delinquency*, New York, 1951.
H. Ashley Weeks *et al.*, *Youthful Offenders at Highfields*, Ann Arbor, Michigan, 1958.
Lloyd McCorkle *et al.*, *The Highfields Story*, New York, 1958.
Hermann Mannheim, *Group Problems in Crime and Punishment*, London, 1955, Ch. 6, III.
Brian Kay, 'Reactions of Delinquents and Other Groups to Experimentally Induced Frustration', *Brit. J. Delinq.*, Vol. 4, No. 4, April 1954.
Frederick K. Beutel, *Some Potentialities of Experimental Jurisprudence*, Lincoln, Nebraska, 1957.
(On experiments see also Karl R. Popper, *The Logic of Scientific Discovery*, pp. 106 ff. and 207 fn.)

## CHAPTER 10

(On Action or Operational Research): John C. Spencer, *Stress and Release in an Urban Estate. A Study in Action Research*, London, 1964.
Arnold M. Rose, *Theory and Method in the Social Sciences*, Minneapolis, 1954, Ch. 8.
Claire Selltiz *et al.*, *Research Methods in Social Relations*, Ch. 13.
Sheldon Glueck, *The Problem of Delinquency*, Boston, 1959, Sects. 174-186.
Solomon Kobrin, 'The Chicago Area Project, a 25-year Assessment', *Ann. Amer. Acad. Polit. Soc. Sci.*, Vol. 322, March 1959.
M. L. Turner, *Ship without Sails*, London, 1953.
John B. Mays, *On the Threshold of Delinquency*, Liverpool, 1959.
(On Sociological Methods): John C. McKinney, in *Modern Sociological Theory*, ed. by Howard Becker and Alvin Boskoff, New York, 1957.
George A. Lundberg, *Social Research*, 2nd ed., London–New York, Toronto, 1942.
Donald Clemmer, *The Prison Community*, Boston, 1940.
Donald R. Cressey, *Other People's Money*, Glencoe, Illinois, 1953.
John C. Spencer, *Crime and the Services*, London, 1954.
Norval Morris, *The Habitual Criminal*, London, 1951.

John James, 'The Application of the Small Group Concept to the Study of the Prison Community', *Brit. J. Delinq.*, Vol. 5, No. 4, April 1955.

*The Social Background of Delinquency*, Univ. of Nottingham, Rockefeller Research 1952–54 (unpublished).

Gordon Rose, 'Sociometric Analysis and Observation in a Borstal Institution', *Brit. J. Delinq.*, Vol. 6, Nos. 3 and 4.

Terence and Pauline Morris, *Pentonville*, London, 1963.

## CHAPTER 11

(On Physical Geography): W. A. Bonger, *An Introduction to Criminology*, London, 1936, Sect. 20.

Joseph Cohen, 'The Geography of Crime', *Ann. Amer. Acad. Pol. Soc. Sci.*, Vol. 217, Sept. 1941.

(On Physical Health): Sir Cyril Burt, *The Young Delinquent*, 4th ed., 1944, Ch. 6.

T. Ferguson, *The Young Delinquent in his Social Setting*, Oxford, 1952, Ch. 3.

M. D. Eilenberg, 'Remand Boys 1930 to 1955', *Brit. J. Crim.*, Vol. 2, No. 2, Oct. 1961.

Terence and Pauline Morris, *Pentonville*, London, 1963, Ch. 9.

Sheldon and Eleanor Glueck, *Physique and Delinquency*, New York and London, 1956.

T. C. N. Gibbens, *Psychiatric Studies of Borstal Lads*, Oxford, 1963, Ch. 9.

## CHAPTER 12

(On the Phrenological School): Arthur E. Fink, *Causes of Crime*, Philadelphia, 1938, Ch. 1.

W. Norwood East, *Society and the Criminal*, London, H.M.S.O., 1949, Ch. 7.

(On Lombroso and his School): Marvin E. Wolfgang in *Pioneers in Criminology*, ed. by H. Mannheim, London, 1960, Ch. 9.

Hermann Mannheim, *Group Problems in Crime and Punishment*, London, 1955, Ch. 4.

T. Sellin, in *Pioneers in Criminology*, Ch. 13, and Francis Allen, *ibid.*, Ch. 10.

## CHAPTER 13

(On Post-Lombrosian Developments in general): Hermann Mannheim, Introduction to *Pioneers in Criminology*.

Edwin D. Driver, in *Pioneers in Criminology*, Ch. 17.

(On Heredity and Crime): Arthur E. Fink, *Causes of Crime*, Philadelphia, 1938, Ch. 7.

Cyril Burt, *The Young Delinquent*, 4th ed., 1944, Chs. 2 and 14.

(On Twin Research): H. H. Newman, *Twins and Super-Twins*, London, 1942.

Johannes Lange, *Crime as Destiny*, London, 1931.
Ashley Montagu, 'The Biologist looks at Crime', *Ann. Amer. Acad. Polit. Soc. Sci.*, Vol. 217, Sept. 1941.
William Healy and Augusta Bronner, *New Light on Delinquency*, New Haven, 1936.
Lorna Whelan, 'Aggressive Psychopathy in One of a Pair of Uniovular Twins', *Brit. J. Delinq.*, Vol. 2, No. 2, Oct. 1951.
(On the Crimino-biological School): Ernst Kretschmer, *Physique and Character*, trans. by Sprott, London, 1936.
Hermann Mannheim, *Group Problems in Crime and Punishment*, London, 1955, pp. 75 ff.
William H. Sheldon, *Varieties of Delinquent Youth*, New York, 1949.
T. C. N. Gibbens, *Psychiatric Studies of Borstal Lads*, Oxford, 1963, Ch. 14 (on somato-typing).

CHAPTER 14

Barbara Wootton, *Social Science and Social Pathology*, London, 1959, Ch. 7.
Michael Hakeem, 'A Critique of the Psychiatric Approach to Crime and Correction in "Crime and Correction" ', *Law and Contemporary Problems*, Vol. 23, No. 4, 1958.
Edward Mapother and Aubrey Lewis, 'Psychological Medicine' in F. W. Price, *Textbook of the Practice of Medicine*, 5th ed., 1937.
Sir D. K. Henderson and R. D. Gillespie, *A Textbook of Psychiatry*, 8th ed., 1960.
David Stafford-Clark, *Psychiatry To-day*, 1st ed., 1952.
East and de Hubert, *Psychological Treatment of Crime*, H.M.S.O., 1939.
W. Norwood East, *Introduction to Forensic Psychiatry in the Criminal Courts*, London, 1927; the same, *Society and the Criminal*, London, H.M.S.O., 1949.
Angus MacNiven, in *Mental Abnormality and Crime*, London, 1944.
A. M. Lorentz de Haas, 'Epilepsy and Criminality', *Brit. J. Crim.*, Vol. 3, No. 3, 1963.
(On Alcoholism): H. Mannheim, *Social Aspects of Crime*, London, 1940, Ch. 6.
G. M. Scott, in *Mental Abnormality and Crime*, London, 1944, Ch. 8.
Howard Jones, *Alcoholic Addiction*, London, 1963.
M. M. Glatt, 'Alcoholism, Crime and Juvenile Delinquency', *The Brit. J. Delinq.*, Vol. 9, No. 2, 1958.
(On Schizophrenia): Don D. Jackson (ed.), *The Etiology of Schizophrenia*, New York, 1962.
(On Drug Addiction): Alfred R. Lindesmith, *Opiate Addiction*, Bloomington, 1952.
Edwin M. Schur, *Narcotic Addiction in Britain and America*, Bloomington, Indiana, London, 1964; the same, 'British Narcotics Policies', *J. crim. Law Criminol. Police Sci.*, Vol. 51, No. 6, 1961.

CHAPTER 15

(On Neuroses): Kate Friedlander, *The Psycho-analytical Approach to Juvenile Delinquency*, 1st ed., London, 1947.

Edward Glover, *The Roots of Crime*, London, 1960.

Franz Alexander and Hugo Staub, *The Criminal, the Judge, and the Public*, London, 1931.

Gillespie and MacCalman, in *Mental Abnormality and Crime*, London, 1944.

Edward Mapother and Aubrey Lewis, 'Psychological Medicine' in F. W. Price, *Textbook of the Practice of Medicine*, 5th ed., 1937.

Sigmund Freud, *Collected Papers*, Vol. 5, 1950.

David T. Maclay, *Brit. J. Delinq.*, Vol. 3, No. 1, July 1952.

T. C. N. Gibbens and Joyce Prince, *Shoplifting*, London, 1962.

Melitta Schmideberg, 'Pathological Firesetters', *J. crim. Law Criminol. Police Sci.*, Vol. 44, No. 1, 1953.

(On Psychopathy): D. K. Henderson, *Psychopathic States*, New York, 1939.

*Brit. J. Delinq.*, Vol. 2, No. 2, October 1951: special number on Psychopathy.

Edward Glover, *The Roots of Crime*, London, 1960, Sect. 4.

Michael Craft, *Brit. J. Crim.*, Vol. 1, No. 3, January 1961.

William and Joan McCord, *Psychopathy and Delinquency*, New York and London, 1956.

T. C. N. Gibbens, D. A. Pond, and D. Stafford-Clark, *J. Ment. Sci.*, Vol. 105, No. 438, January 1959.

(On Mental Deficiency): A. F. Tredgold, *Mental Deficiency*, 9th ed., London, 1956.

Mary Woodward, *Low Intelligence and Crime*, London, I.S.T.D., 1955.

Cyril Burt, *The Young Delinquent*, 4th ed., London, 1944, Ch. 7.

Hilda Weber, 'The Borderline Defective Delinquent', *Brit. J. Delinq.*, Vol. 3, No. 3, January 1953.

K. O. Milner, 'Delinquent Types of Mentally Defective Persons', *J. Ment. Sci.*, Vol. 95, No. 401, Oct. 1949.

(On Genius): Ernst Kretschmer, *Psychology of Men of Genius*, London, 1931.

W. Lange-Eichbaum, *The Problem of Genius*, London, 1931.

Leta S. Hollingworth, *Children above 160 I.Q.*, New York, 1942.

CHAPTER 16

David Abrahamsen, *The Psychology of Crime*, London and New York, 1961.

Barbara Wootton, *Social Science and Social Pathology*, London, 1959.

Emanuel Miller, *Brit. J. Delinq.*, Vol. 10, No. 3, January 1960.

Karl F. Schuessler and Donald R. Cressey, 'Personality Characteristics of Criminals', *Amer. J. Sociol.*, Vol. 50, March 1950.

Tadeusz Grygier, *Oppression*, London, 1954.

S. and E. Glueck, *Unraveling Juvenile Delinquency*, New York, 1950, Ch. 18.

H. J. Eysenck, *The Structure of Human Personality*, London and New York, 1953.

SELECTED READING LISTS

Marvin E. Wolfgang, *Patterns of Homicide*, Philadelphia, 1959, Ch. 10.
W. Norwood East, *Society and the Criminal*, London, 1949, Ch. 17.
Franco Ferracuti, 'The Psychology of the Criminal Homicide', *Rev. Jur. Univ. Puerto Rico*, Vol. 32, No. 4, 1963.
Jackson Toby, 'Criminal Motivation', *Brit. J. Crim.*, Vol. 2, No. 4, April 1962.
Leonard Berkowitz, *Aggression: A Social Psychological Analysis*, New York, 1962.
Andreas Bjerre, *The Psychology of Murder*, London, 1927.

CHAPTER 17

Sigmund Freud, *Collected Papers*, Vol. 4, London, 1925.
Edward Glover, *Psycho-Analysis*, 2nd ed., London, 1949; the same, *Roots of Crime*, London, 1960.
Franz Alexander and William Healy, *The Roots of Crime*, New York, 1935.
Franz Alexander and Hugo Staub, *The Criminal, the Judge, and the Public*, New York, 1931.
S. H. Foulkes, *Psycho-Analysis and Crime*, Cambridge and Toronto, 1944.
Kate Friedlander, *The Psycho-Analytical Approach to Juvenile Delinquency*, 1st ed., London, 1947.
Robert M. Lindner, *Rebel without a Cause*, New York, 1944.
G. W. Elles, 'The Closed Circuit', *Brit. J. Crim.*, Vol. 2, No. 1, July 1961.
J. A. C. Brown, *Freud and the Post-Freudians*, Harmondsworth, 1961.

CHAPTER 18

Glanville Williams, *Criminal Law: The General Part*, 2nd ed., London, 1961, Ch. 10.
Sheldon Glueck, *Law and Psychiatry: Cold War or Entente Cordiale?* Baltimore, 1962, and London, 1963.
Hermann Mannheim, *Brit. J. Crim.*, Vol. 1, No. 3, January 1961.
Henry Weihofen, *The Urge to Punish*, London, 1957.
Jerome Hall, *Studies in Jurisprudence and Criminal Theory*, New York, 1958, Ch. 15.
G. W. Keeton, *Guilty but Insane*, London, 1961.
Barbara Wootton, *Crime and the Criminal Law*, London, 1963.
Hermann Mannheim, *Group Problems in Crime and Punishment*, London, 1955, Ch. 13.

# Notes

## CHAPTER 1

[1] H. Mannheim, 'Uber einige neuere Entwicklungstendenzen in der Kriminologischen Forschung', *Mschr. Kriminol. Strafrechtsreform*, Vol. 40, Feb. 1957, reproduced in *Deutsche Strafrechtsreform in englischer Sicht*, München-Berlin, 1960, Ch. 4.

[2] Karl R. Popper, *The Poverty of Historicism*, London, 1957, pp. 121, 134.

[3] See H. Mannheim, 'Beiträge zur Lehre von der Revision', *Abhandlungen aus der Berliner Juristischen Fakultät*, Vol. 3, Berlin, 1925, pp. 51 ff., 41 ff., where a detailed discussion of the discussion of the definition of *Tatsache* (fact) is given.

[4] Wilhelm Dilthey, 'Ideen über eine beschreibende und zerglicdernde Psychologie 1894', *Gesammelte Schriften*, Vol. 5, Leipzig-Berlin, 1924, pp. 139 ff., esp. p. 172; H. A. Hodges, *The Philosophy of Wilhelm Dilthey*, London, 1952, Ch. 5.

[5] Max Weber 'Über einige Kategorien der verstehenden Soziologie, 1913', *Gesammelte Aufsätze zur Wisenschaftslehre*, Tübingen, 1922, pp. 403 ff.; see also Popper, *op. cit.*, pp. 20 ff., who regards this view as 'very closely related to historicism, although it is not invariably combined with it'. McIver, Foreword to B. Lander, *Towards an Understanding of Juvenile Delinquency*, New York, 1954, p.viii, writes 'the end of science is comprehension ... to comprehend human relations is to make them understandable in the light of human responses to conditions'.

[6] Franz Exner, *Kriminologie*, esp. 3rd ed., Berlin-Göttingen-Heidelberg, 1949, p. 6.

[7] Stephen Toulmin, *The Philosophy of Science*, London, 1953, p. 10.

[8] Glanville L. Williams, *Criminal Law: The General Part*, London, 1953, Chs. 4–7.

[9] See the most recent discussions in the *Leipziger Kommentar* on the German Penal Code, Berlin, 1956, pp. 19–30.

[10] Kenny's *Outlines of Criminal Law*. An entirely new edition by T. W. Cecil Turner, Cambridge, 1952. The problem of causality, previously rather neglected by English and American writers on criminal law, has been very fully discussed in Continental literature. This previous deficiency of Anglo-American legal literature has, however, recently been made good by several important publications, especially H. L. A. Hart and A. M. Honoré, *Causation in the Law*, London, 1959; Gerhard O. W. Mueller, 'Causing Criminal Harm' in *Essays in Criminal Science*, ed. by him, London–Hackensack, 1961, Ch. 7; Jerome Hall, *Studies in Jurisprudence and Criminal Theory*, New York, 1958, Ch. 10.

[11] Peter Lejins, *Soc. Forces*, Vol. 29, No. 3, March 1951.

[12] There are a few notable exceptions: Walter C. Reckless, *Criminal Behavior*, New York, 1940, p. 2, and Ch. 9; the same, *The Crime Problem*, 2nd ed., New York, 1955, esp. Ch. 5; Paul W. Tappan, *Juvenile Delinquency*, New York-Toronto-London, 1949, pp. 55 ff.; Sheldon and Eleanor Glueck, *Unraveling Juvenile Delinquency*, New York, 1950, pp. 4, 281; Franz Exner, *op. cit.*, p. 9; Ernst Seelig, *Lehrbuch der Kriminologie*, 1st ed., Graz, 1951, pp. 4, 118.

[13] Bertrand Russell, *Human Knowledge, Its Scope and Limits*, London, 1948, p. 471; also Sir A. S. Eddington, *The Nature of the Physical World*, Cambridge, 1927, pp. 297-8: 'the great laws hitherto accepted as causal appear on minute examination to be of statistical character'.

[14] Bertrand Russell, *op. cit.*, pp. 332 ff.

[15] The text is largely based upon the admirable discussion in the late Professor L. Susan Stebbing's *Philosophy and the Physicists*, Harmondsworth, 1944, Ch. 9. See also John O. Wisdom, *Causation and the Foundation of Science*, Paris, 1946, according to whom 'natural laws are causal laws, scientific laws apparently are not' (p. 7), but the 'concept of scientific laws presupposes that of causation' (p. 20).

[16] K. Popper, *op. cit.*, pp. 122 ff., 143 ff.

[17] H. Mannheim, *Group Problems in Crime and Punishment*, London, 1955, pp. 261-3, with bibliog.

[18] Karl Britton, *John Stuart Mill*, Harmondsworth, 1953, pp. 152 ff.

[19] Kenny-Turner, *op. cit.*, § 13.

[20] So Lejins, *loc. cit.*; see also Lewis S. Feuer, 'Symposium on Causality in the Social Sciences', *J. Philos.* Vol. 51, No. 23, 11.11.1954, pp. 681-94.

[21] See below, Chs. 12/13.

[22] Sir Cyril Burt, *The Young Delinquent*, London, 1st ed., 1925, 4th ed. 1948, p. 599; William Healy, *The Individual Delinquent*, Boston, 1914.

[23] Edwin H. Sutherland, *Principles of Criminology*, 1st ed., Philadelphia, 1927; 5th ed. edited by D. R. Cressey, London, 1955.

[24] See *The Sutherland Papers*, ed. by Albert Cohen, Alfred Lindesmith, and Karl Schuessler, Bloomington, 1956.

[25] Editorial Note in *The Sutherland Papers*, p. 6, see also pp. 19, 31.

[26] Alfred R. Lindesmith, *Opiate Addiction*, Bloomington, 1947, pp. 17-20.

[27] Edwin H. Sutherland, *op. cit.*, pp. 30 ff.

[28] Cyril Burt, *op. cit.*, pp. 600 ff. The same impression is given by Burt's more recent discussion in *The Subnormal Mind*, 3rd ed., London, 1955, p. 163.

[29] Emile Durkheim, *Les Règles de la méthode sociologique*, pp. 125 ff., Eng. ed., Chicago, 1938, pp. 126 ff.

[30] R. M. McIver, *Social Causation*, Boston, 1940.

[31] See also my paper 'Why Delinquency?', reproduced in *Group Problems in Crime and Punishment*, London, 1955, p. 134.

[32] Sheldon and Eleanor Glueck, *Unraveling Juvenile Delinquency*, pp. 272, 281.

[33] Sheldon Glueck, 'Theory and Fact in Criminology', *Brit. J. Delinq.*, Vol. 7, No. 2, Oct. 1956, p. 106, now reproduced in Sheldon and Eleanor Glueck, *Ventures in Criminology*, London, 1964, Ch. 16, on p. 257. In his General Report to the Third International Congress of Criminology, 1955, too, he writes that statistical correlation indicates 'a high probability of a functional relationship . . . even though one cannot as yet trace the specific and subtle links in the chain of causation', see *Summary of the Congress*, London, 1957, p. 163.

[34] Sheldon and Eleanor Glueck, *Physique and Delinquency*, New York, 1956, pp. 40, 43.

[35] Max Weber, *op. cit.*, pp. 412-13.

[36] See W. I. Thomas in *Social Behavior and Personality*, ed. by Edmund H. Volkart, New York, 1951, p. 66.

[37] Arnold M. Rose, *Theory and Method in the Social Sciences*, Minneapolis, 1954, p. 165, and the Review in *Brit. J. Delinq.* Vol. 7, No. 2., Oct. 1956, p. 154; Walter A. Reckless, *Criminal Behavior*, p. 176.

[38] Hermann Mannheim and Leslie T. Wilkins, *Prediction Methods in relation to Borstal Training*, H.M.S.O., London, 1955, pp. 40, 43-5, 217.

[39] Walter A. Reckless, *The Crime Problem*, 2nd ed., New York, 1955, Ch. 3.

[40] Emile Durkheim, *Suicide*, Eng. trans. George Simpson, London, 1952, p. 147.

[41] No more than this has been maintained in Mannheim–Wilkins, *op. cit.*, p. 216, where it is stated: 'research on decisions rather than on finding out things (particularly "causes") is certainly likely to take us much further much faster. . . . Indeed "cause" is an unnecessary concept in the whole *of this part, at least*, of the criminological field' (italics mine).

[42] The medical analogy has been stressed by Dr. R. C. Cabot, as quoted by Edwin Powers and Helen Witmer, *Prevention of Delinquency, The Cambridge-Somerville Youth Study*, New York, 1951, p. 112.

[43] The literature on this subject is enormous. Only a few references can here be given. See, e.g., W. Friedmann, *Legal Theory*, 3rd ed., London, 1953, pp. 192, 196 ff., also 112 ff. on Kelsen and 151 ff. on Austin.

[44] Edgar Bodenheimer, *Jurisprudence*, New York–London, 1940, pp. 208 ff.

[45] See the excellent discussion on 'The Concepts of Juridical and Scientific Law' by Morris Ginsberg in *Reason and Unreason in Society*, London, 1947, Ch. 12; also Bodenheimer, *op. cit.*, pp. 310 ff.

[46] H. Bianchi, *Position and Subject-matter of Criminology*, Amsterdam, 1956, p. 121.

[47] See H. Mannheim, *Group Problems in Crime and Punishment*, London, 1955, pp. 271 ff., also Popper, *op. cit.*, p. 64.

[48] Quoted from Bernaldo de Quiros, *Modern Theories of Criminality*, Boston, 1911.

[49] Karl R. Popper, *op. cit.*, p. 61.

[50] On the difference between laws and trends see Popper, *op. cit.*, pp. 115, 128.

[51] Robert Vouin and Jacques Léauté, *Droit pénal et criminologie*, Paris, 1956, pp. 22, 57.

[52] Thorsten Sellin, *Culture Conflict and Crime*, Soc. Sci. Res. Counc. Bull. 41, New York, 1938, pp. 19 ff., 30 ff.

[53] See *Group Problems*, pp. 136, 262.

[54] Vouin-Léauté, *op. cit.*, pp. 34 ff.

[55] H. Bianchi, *op. cit.*, p. 110.

[56] Donald R. Cressey, *Other People's Money*, Glencoe, Ill., 1953, pp. 19 ff.

[57] See on Hans Gross, esp. Roland Grassberger, *J. crim. Law Criminol. Police Sci.*, Vol. 47, No. 4., Nov.–Dec., 1956, pp. 397 ff. (reproduced in *Pioneers of Criminology*, ed. by H. Mannheim, London, 1960, Ch. 11); Ernst Seelig, *Lehrbuch der Kriminologie*, 1st ed., Graz, 1951, pp. 27 ff., 1952 ff. English translations of Hans Gross's principal works are available.

[58] See the details given by R. Grassberger in *The University Teaching of Social Sciences: Criminology*, Paris, UNESCO, 1957, p. 62. On the Vienna Institute see the details given by W. Gleispach in *Z. ges. Strafrechtwiss.*, Vol. 49, 1929, pp. 586 ff.

[59] UNESCO Report, pp. 70 ff.

[60] *Ibid.*, p. 84.

[61] *Ibid.*, pp. 93 ff. According to Vouin-Léauté, *op. cit.*, p. 21, 'Criminalistics should remain outside Criminology'.

[62] UNESCO Report, pp. 102, 105.

[63] *Ibid.*, p. 131 for Great Britain.

[64] *Ibid.*, pp. 37, 39.

[65] One of the exceptions is Barnes and Teeters, *New Horizons in Criminology*, New York, 1943, where 'scientific methods of detecting and apprehending criminals' are very briefly treated.

[66] See also Thorsten Sellin, 'L'Etude sociologique de la Criminalité', General

Report to the Second International Congress on Criminology, *Proceedings*, Vol. 5, Paris, 1953, p. 113 (also published in English in *J. crim. Law Criminol.*, Vol. 41, 1950).

[67] So rightly H. Bianchi, *op. cit.*, p. 208.

[68] On teamwork in criminology see below, Ch. 4, s. 3.

[69] Hermann Mannheim, *Group Problems*, Ch. 12.

[70] H. Bianchi, *op. cit.*, pp. 16 ff.

[71] Thorsten Sellin, *op. cit.*

[72] T. M. Van Bemmelen, *Juridical Rev.*, Vol. 63, No. 1., April 1951, pp. 24 ff.

[73] Erwin Frey, 'Kriminologie: Programm und Wirklichkeit', *Schweiz. Z. Strafrecht*, Vol. 66, 1951, p. 67.

[74] T. H. Marshall, *Sociology at the Crossroads*, London, 1947, p. 10. See also David Lockwood, *Brit. J. Sociol.*, Vol. 7, No. 2, June 1956, p. 142.

[75] Hermann Mannheim, *Group Problems in Crime and Punishment*, pp. 155-6. See also Max Weber, 'Wissenschaft als Beruf', *Ges. Aufsätze zur Wissenschaftslehre*, pp. 531-2.

[76] Bronislaw Malinowski, *A Scientific Theory of Culture*, New Haven, 1944, pp. 8-11.

[77] Nathaniel Cantor, *Crime and Society*, New York, 1939, p. 10.

[78] Arnold M. Rose, *Theory and Method in the Social Sciences*, Minneapolis, 1954, pp. 246-7.

[79] W. B. Gallie, *Brit. J. Phil. Sci.*, Vol. 8, No. 30, Aug. 1957, pp. 118, 126. See now also L. T. Wilkins, *Social Deviance* (Ch. 3, note 2 below), pp. 1-2.

[80] Jerome Michael and Mortimer J. Adler, *Crime, Law and Social Science*, London, 1933, p. 85.

[81] Thorsten Sellin, *Culture Conflict and Crime*, New York, 1938, p. 3.

[82] Karl R. Popper, *The Poverty of Historicism*, p. 59.

[83] See *Group Problems in Crime and Punishment*, pp. 209-10.

## CHAPTER 2

[1] Immanuel Kant, *Kritik der reinen Vernuft*, Cassirer ed., Vol. 3, p. 495.

[2] See, e.g., Julius Binder, *Philosophie des Rechts*, Berlin, 1925, p. 213.

[3] Kenny's *Outlines of Criminal Law*, an entirely new ed. by J. W. Cecil Turner, Cambridge, 1952; Glanville Williams, 'The Definition of Crime' in *Current Legal Problems*, London, 1955, p. 111.

[4] See the full details in *Materialien zur Strafrechtsreform*, Vol. 1, 1954, pp. 11 ff., and Vol. 2, 1955, pp. 499 ff., and for the legal-philosophical basis of this development Erik Wolf in *Festgabe für R. von Frank*, Tübingen, 1930, Vol. 2, pp. 516 ff.

[5] On the historical development of Swiss legislation on this point see the detailed account of Jean Graven, 'La Classification des Infractions du Code Pénal et ses Effets', *Revue pénale Suisse*, Vol. 73, 1958, pp. 3 ff. Graven was also the redactor of the Ethiopian Penal Code of 1957.

[6] *Gesetz über die Ordnungswidrigkeiten*. For details see the Commentary by H. E. Rotberg, Berlin, 1952, and on the wider theoretical and practical significance of this Act especially the important lecture by H. H. Jescheck in *Juristen Zeitung*, No. 15-16, 14 August 1959.

[7] Rotberg, *op. cit.*, p. 24.

[8] *Entwurf des Allgemeinen Teils eines Strafgesetzbuchs*, Bonn, 1958, 'Begründung', p. 5. The same applies to the Draft Code of 1962; see pp. 98, 121.

[9] For the following text see the illuminating discussions by Jerome Hall, *General Principles of Criminal Law*, Minneapolis, 1947, Ch. 10, and Glanville

Williams, *Criminal Law: The General Part*, London, 1953, Ch. 7. Important also F. B. Sayre, 'Public Welfare Offences', *Columbia Law Rev.*, Vol. 33, 1933, pp. 55 ff., and more recently Colin Howard, *Strict Responsibility*, London, 1954; the same in Norval Morris and Colin Howard, *Studies in Criminal Law*, London, 1964, Ch. 6; James E. Starrs, 'The Regulatory Offence in Historical Perspective', in *Essays in Criminal Science*, ed. by Gerhard O. W. Mueller, London–South Hackensack, 1961, Ch. 9.

[10] Francis A. Allen, 'The Borderland of the Criminal Law: Problems of "Socializing" Criminal Justice', *Soc. Serv. Rev.*, Vol. 32, No. 2, June 1958, pp. 107 ff.

[11] Glanville Williams, *op. cit.*, p. 240.

[12] Jerome Hall, *op. cit.*, p. 285.

[13] Hermann Mannheim, *Criminal Justice and Social Reconstruction*, 2nd imp., London, 1949, pp. 127, 169 ff., 196 ff. and *passim*.

[14] A. L. Goodhart in an Editorial Note, *Law Quart. Rev.*, Vol. 74, July 1958, pp. 342–3, supporting a judgment of the Court of Criminal Appeal in *R. v. St. Margaret's Trust Ltd.*, [1958] 1 W.L.R. 522.

[15] On this see Jerome Hall, *General Principles*, p. 310; Glanville Williams, *Criminal Law*, p. 707. For traffic offences in particular such measures have frequently been suggested to make the police and the courts better equipped to deal with this mass problem of our time; see, e.g., the important essay by Erwin R. Frey, 'Reobjektivierung des Strafrechts im Zeitalter der Technik', in *Die Rechtsordnung im technischen Zeitalter*, Zurich, 1961, which, although based on Swiss law and traffic conditions, is of general interest too.

[16] So rightly Erik Wolf, *loc. cit.*, p. 581.

[17] A. S. Diamond, *Primitive Law*, London, 1935, pp. 277 ff., believes it to have been universal.

[18] See in particular the material quoted by Gerhard O. W. Mueller, 'Tort, Crime and the Primitive', *J. crim. Law Criminol. Police Sci.*, Vol. 46, No. 3, 1955, pp. 303–332.

[19] Theodore F. T. Plucknett, *A Concise History of the Common Law*, 5th ed., London, 1956, p. 421.

[20] For criticisms of Blackstone, see Kenny, *Outlines of Criminal Law*, 1952 ed., App. I, pp. 531 ff; Jerome Hall, *General Principles*, Ch. 7, pp. 188 ff. On the differences between civil and criminal law see also Richard C. Donnelly *et al.*, *Criminal Law*, Glencoe Free Press, New York, 1962, Ch. II, Part 1, and on the 'Requisites of a Crime', Part 4.

[21] P. H. Winfield, *The Province of the Law of Tort*, Cambridge, 1931, pp. 196–8; Turner in Kenny, *op. cit.*, p. 547.

[22] See Stephan Schäfer, *Restitution to Victims of Crime*, London, 1960.

[23] On the following see the detailed account by Marshall B. Clinard, *The Black Market*, New York, 1952, Ch. 9.

[24] Clinard, *op. cit.*, pp. 234, 238.

[25] See Clinard, *op. cit.*, pp. 227 ff.

[26] Sir William Holdsworth, *History of English Law*, Vol. 6, 3rd ed., London, 1922–23, p. 218; also Vol. 2, 3rd ed., 1923, p. 444.

[27] Sir William Blackstone, *Commentaries on the Laws of England*, Vol. I, p. 53. Against him J. W. C. Turner in Kenny, *Outlines*, 1952 ed., p. 22, and in *The Modern Approach to Criminal Law*, London, 1945, pp. 220 ff., 240.

[28] On this see Julius Binder, *Philosophie des Rechts*, pp. 753 ff.

[29] On the history of the Law of Nature, see below, notes 81 ff.

[30] See Gustav Radbruch, *Rechtsphilosophie*, 4th ed., Stuttgart, 1950, ed. by Erik Wolf, p. 107.

[31] Morris Ginsberg, *Essays in Sociology and Social Philosophy*, Vol. 1: 'On the Diversity of Morals', London, 1956, p. 115, and on Stammler in general Vol. 2, Ch. 11.

[32] H. Bianchi, *Position and Subject-Matter of Criminology*, Amsterdam, 1956, Ch. 17.

[33] *Amer. sociol. Rev.*, Vol. 10, 1945, pp. 132 ff.; reprinted in *The Sutherland Papers*, ed. by Albert Cohen, Alfred Lindesmith, Karl Schuessler, Bloomington, 1956, and also in an expanded version as Ch. 3 of Sutherland's book *White-Collar Crime*, New York, 1949.

[34] Clinard, *op. cit.*, p. 236, and the whole of Ch. 9; also his *Sociology of Deviant Behavior*, New York, 1957, pp. 159 ff.

[35] Ernest W. Burgess, *Amer. J. Sociol.*, Vol. 56, 1950, pp. 32–3.

[36] Paul W. Tappan, *Amer. sociol. Rev.*, Vol. 12, 1947, pp. 98 ff.; *Federal Probation*, Vol. 11, 1947, p. 44.

[37] Thorsten Sellin, *Culture Conflict and Crime*, New York, 1938, pp. 25 ff.

[38] This is accepted by Kenny, *Outlines*, 1952 ed., p. 2.

[39] Julius Goebel, *Felony and Misdemeanor*, New York, 1937, pp. 146 ff.

[40] H. Bianchi, *op. cit.*, pp. 95 ff.

[41] R. Garofalo, *La Criminologie*, 2nd French ed., Paris, 1890, p. 2.

[42] For a general survey of provisions dealing with recidivism, see *Summary of Proceedings*, Third International Congress on Criminology, 1955, London, 1957, General Reports, Section 1, by Norval Morris and Roland Grassberger.

[43] On the whole subject, see H. Mannheim, *The Dilemma of Penal Reform*, London, 1939, Ch. 4, esp. p. 117. On the present French law see Vouin-Léauté, *op. cit.*, pp. 585 ff.

[44] Tappan, *Amer. sociol. Rev.*, Vol. 12, p. 100.

[45] Sutherland, *White-Collar Crime*, p. 35.

[46] *Ibid.*, p. 40.

[47] For further details see Donald R. Cressey, *Other People's Money*, Glencoe, Ill., 1953, Introduction.

[48] Kenny, *Outlines of Criminal Law*, 1952 ed., § 129.

[49] See, e.g., Andreas Bjerre, *The Psychology of Murder*, Eng. trans. London, 1927; John Lewis Gillin, *The Wisconsin Prisoner*, Madison, 1946; Hans v. Hentig, *Zur Psychologie der Einzeldelikte* II: *Der Mord*, Tübingen, 1956; Veli Verkkö, *Homicides and Suicides in Finland and their Dependence on National Character*, Copenhagen, 1951; Austin L. Porterfield and Robert H. Talbert, *Mid-Century Crime in our Culture*, Fort Worth, 1954; Marshall B. Clinard, *Sociology of Deviant Behavior*, New York, 1957, pp. 210 ff. Also see below, Ch. 16.

[50] Sir Norwood East, *Society and the Criminal*, London, 1949, p. 254. See also *Report of the Royal Commission on Capital Punishment*, Cmd. 8932, paras. 498 ff.

[51] Ernst Roesner, *Z. ges. Strafrechtswiss.*, Vol. 56, 1936, pp. 336 ff.

[52] H. C. Brearley, *Homicide in the United States*, Chapel Hill, 1932, p. 64.

[53] See E. Bodenheimer, *Jurisprudence*, p. 216; G. Radbruch, *Rechtsphilosophie*, 4th ed., pp. 111, 185. Both writers stress that even Marxism was eventually forced to accept the independence of cultural and especially legal forms (Radbruch). On this subject, see more fully below, Ch. 20.

[54] Hermann Mannheim, *Criminal Justice and Social Reconstruction*, Sections 3, 4; the same, *The Dilemma of Penal Reform*, London, 1939, esp. Parts 1 and 2.

[55] Sir Henry Sumner Maine, *Ancient Law*, London, 1861.

[56] Diamond, *Primitive Law*, pp. 49, 124, 153, 164. William Seagle, *In Quest of Law*, New York, 1941, p. 125, agrees with him and regards Maine's view as representative of the Victorian age.

[57] David Daube, *Studies in Biblical Law*, Cambridge, 1947, Ch. 1; G. W. Paton, *Textbook of Jurisprudence*, Oxford, 1946, p. 44.

[58] 'There is probably no subject in the world about which opinions differ so much as the nature of religion', writes Sir James Fraser, 'Magic and Religion', Ch. 4 of the *Golden Bough*, The Thinker's Library ed., Vol. 100, p. 81. See also K. N. Llewellyn and E. Adamson Hoebel, *The Cheyenne Way*, Norman, Okla., 1941, pp. 55 ff., 132 ff.; Joachim Wach, *Sociology of Religion*, London, 1944, pp. 290 ff.

[59] See, e.g., Bronislaw Malinowski, *Crime and Custom in Savage Society*, London, 1932, p. 51.

[60] On the Benefit of Clergy, see the references in Hermann Mannheim, *Criminal Justice and Social Reconstruction*, p. 94, fn. 2.

[61] See, e.g., the following Criminal Codes: German, §§ 166; Italian, arts. 402 ff.; Swiss, art. 261; Danish, arts. 139–40. In England, the law of blasphemy is part of the law of criminal libel: Rupert Cross and T. Asterley Jones, *An Introduction to Criminal Law*, London, 1948, p. 253. The Soviet Criminal Code penalizes 'any interference with the celebration of any religions, in so far as such rite does not disturb public order and is not accompanied by any attempt to encroach on the rights of any citizen' (art. 127).

[62] For details see Hermann Mannheim, *Criminal Justice and Social Reconstruction*, Ch. 2–5; Glanville Williams, *The Sanctity of Life and the Criminal Law*, London, 1957.

[63] See in particular J. C. Flugel, *Man, Morals and Society*, London, 1945, Ch. 17: 'The Problem of Religion', esp. pp. 271 ff., 146 ff., 164 ff.

[64] Paul W. Tappan, *Juvenile Delinquency*, New York, 1949, p. 514. See also Arthur Kielholz, in *Die Prophylaxe des Verbrechens*, ed. by Heinrich Meng, Basel, 1948, pp. 360 ff. For one of the best discussions on the place of religion in the treatment of juvenile delinquents see W. David Wills, *The Barns Experiment*, London, 1945, Ch. 8.

[65] On the Pennsylvanian system see Negley K. Teeters, *They Were in Prison*, Chicago, 1937; Harry Elmer Barnes and Negley K. Teeters, *New Horizons in Criminology*, New York, 1943, Ch. 23.

[66] H. Bianchi, *Position and Subject-Matter of Criminology*, pp. 110, 128. Against the identification of crime and sin also Sir Walter Moberly, *Responsibility*, Oxford, 1950, p. 36.

[67] H. Kantorowicz, *The Definition of Law*, ed. by A. H. Campbell, with an Introduction by A. L. Goodhart, Cambridge, 1958, Ch. 5, p. 52.

[68] William F. Ogburn and Meyer F. Nimkoff, *A Handbook of Sociology*, London, 1947, pp. 215 ff.

[69] See the details in *Group Problems in Crime and Punishment*, pp. 276 ff.

[70] Gunnar Myrdal *et al.*, *An American Dilemma*, New York; also his *Value in Social Theory*, ed. by Paul Streeten, London, 1958, pp. 78, 99, 139, 180.

[71] Gustav Radbruch, *op. cit.*, pp. 142 ff.

[72] Ogburn-Nimkoff, *op. cit.*, p. 33.

[73] Kantorowicz, *op. cit.*, p. 54.

[74] On Max Weber's view see, e.g., Max Rheinstein in his and E. Shils's Introduction to Max Weber on *Law in Economics and Society*, Cambridge, Mass., 1954, p. lxvii.

[75] Jerome Hall, *Studies in Jurisprudence and Criminal Theory*, New York, 1958, p. 244.

[76] See *Report of the Committee on Homosexual Offences and Prostitution*, H.M.S.O., Cmd. 247, London, 1957, pp. 9, 80; and my contribution to *Law and Opinion in England in the Twentieth Century*, ed. by M. Ginsberg, London, 1959, pp. 274–5.

[77] On these cases see Glanville Williams, *Criminal Law: General Principles*, p. 176; Edmond Cahn, *The Moral Decision*, pp. 61 ff.

[78] On legislation explicitly introducing moral factors and considerations into the process of sentencing see my lecture 'Some Aspects of Judicial Sentencing Policy', *Yale Law J.*, Vol. 67, No. 6, May 1958, esp. p. 963, and on 'moral turpitude' Edmond Cahn, *op. cit.*, p. 166.

[79] *The Dilemma of Penal Reform*, London, 1939, p. 21.

[80] Jerome Hall, 'The Purpose of a System for the Administration of Criminal Justice'. Lecture delivered 9.10.1963, Georgetown University Law Centre, Washington, D.C., p. 17, fn. 41.

[81] The literature on natural law is immense, and any selection is bound to be arbitrary. In addition to the books referred to below (n. 125), which deal more specifically with the relation of law to morality, the following may be mentioned: As an admirable introduction to the subject, with excellent bibliographical notes, A. P. d'Entrèves, *Natural Law. An Introduction to Legal Philosophy*, 4th imp., London, 1957. Also Otto Gierke, *Natural Law and the Theory of Society*, trans. with an Introduction by Ernest Barker, 2 vols., Cambridge, 1934; Gierke, *Johannes Althusius*, 3rd ed., Breslau, 1913; W. Friedmann, *Legal Theory*, 4th ed., London, 1960; Erik Wolf, *Das Problem der Naturrechtslehre*, Karlsruhe, 1955; Hans Welzel, *Naturrecht und materielle Gerechtigkeit*, Göttingen, 1951; Julius Binder, *Philosophie des Rechts*, Berlin, 1925, pp. 751 ff.; Roscoe Pound, *Law and Morals*, 2nd ed., Chapel Hill, 1926; Edgar Bodenheimer, *Jurisprudence*, New York–London, 1940, Part 2, esp. pp. 73, 103, 156; Hans Kelsen, *What is Justice?*, Berkeley and Los Angeles, 1957, pp. 139 ff.; Carlo Antoni, *From History to Sociology*, trans. from the Italian, Detroit, 1959. Thomas Würtenberger, *Archiv für Rechts und Sozialphilosophie*, Vol. 41, No. 1, 1954, pp. 58–87, gives an account of German contributions since 1948 to the history of natural law.

[82] d'Entrèves, *op. cit.*, p. 9.

[83] *Ibid.*, p. 80.

[84] Erik Wolf (*op. cit.* at note 81), p. 87.

[85] Hans Welzel (*op. cit.* at note 81), p. 9.

[86] *Ibid.*, p. 21.

[87] This is the impression given by Hans Kelsen, *What is Justice?*, Ch. 3.

[88] See Jerome Hall, *Studies* (cited at note 75), Ch. 3, esp. pp. 74 ff.; Welzel, *op. cit.*, p. 21.

[89] On Aristotle's views on natural law see Kelsen, *op. cit.*, Ch. 4; Welzel, Ch. 5.

[90] On the Stoa see Bodenheimer, *op. cit.*, pp. 107 ff.; Welzel, *op. cit.*, Ch. 6; Friedmann, *op. cit.*, p. 22.

[91] Wolf, *op. cit.*, p. 89.

[92] Welzel, *op. cit.*, p. 47.

[93] Bodenheimer, *op. cit.*, p. 111; d'Entrèves, *op. cit.*, p. 22.

[94] Bodenheimer, *op. cit.*, p. 113; d'Entrèves, *op. cit.*, p. 22.

[95] This quotation from St. Thomas's *Summa Theologica* is taken from d'Entrèves, *op. cit.*, p. 43. On St. Thomas see also Welzel, *op. cit.*, Part 2, Ch. 2, and Norman St. John Stevas, *Life, Death, and the Law*, London, 1961, pp. 19–22.

[96] Kelsen, *op. cit.*, p. 142; Bodenheimer, *op. cit.*, p. 124.

[97] d'Entrèves, *op. cit.*, pp. 43, 45.

[98] Welzel, *op. cit.*, pp. 65–6.

[99] *Ibid.*, pp. 76, 83.

[100] *Ibid.*, p. 108.

[101] On Hobbes see Kelsen, *op. cit.*, pp. 142 ff.; Welzel, *op. cit.*, p. 112; Wolf, *op. cit.*, p. 100.

[102] See Howard Warrender, *The Political Philosophy of Hobbes*, Oxford, 1957, esp. pp. 322 ff.

[103] d'Entrèves, *op. cit.*, pp. 52, 70; Welzel, *op. cit.*, p. 130.

[104] Kelsen, *op. cit.*, p. 148; Welzel, *op. cit.*, p. 133.

[105] Welzel, *op. cit.*, p. 144.

[106] *Ibid.*, p. 152.

[107] Wolf, *op. cit.*, p. 64; Welzel, *op. cit.*, p. 154.

[108] Kelsen, *op. cit.*, pp. 148–9.

[109] Welzel, *op. cit.*, p. 161.

[110] Kelsen, *op. cit.*, pp. 149–50.

[111] Friedmann, *op. cit.*, p. 42.

[112] d'Entrèves, *op. cit.*, p. 87; Welzel, *op. cit.*, p. 162; Wolf, *op. cit.*, p. 65.

[113] Kelsen, *op. cit.*, p. 150.

[114] d'Entrèves, *op. cit.*, p. 103. On p. 93, however, he warns us 'not to speak of natural law as a confusion between law and morals'.

[115] Kant, *Einteilung der Rechtslehre, Immanuel Kant's Werke*, Berlin, Vol. 7, p. 44.

[116] Kant, *Einleitung in die Metaphysik der Sitten, Werke*, Berlin, Vol. 7, pp. 19 ff.

[117] Kelsen, *op. cit.*, p. 150.

[118] Friedmann, *Legal Theory*, p. 50.

[119] H. L. A. Hart, 'Positivism and the Separation of Law and Morals', *Harv. Law Rev.*, Vol. 71, No. 4, Feb. 1958, pp. 593 ff.

[120] Friedmann, *op. cit.*, pp. 119 ff.; d'Entrèves, *op. cit.*, p. 98.

[121] Welzel, *op. cit.*, p. 177, points out that Hegel's state was not merely organized power, but a spiritual force.

[122] Hegel, *Rechtsphilosophie, Vorrede*, p. 33, *Sämtliche Werke*, ed. Hermann Glockner, Stuttgart, 1928, Vol. 7.

[123] See Friedmann, *op. cit.*, pp. 87 ff. For more general criticisms of Stammler see Ginsberg, *Reason and Unreason in Society*, Ch. 11; Max Weber, *Gesammelte Aufsätze zur Wissenschaftslehre*, pp. 291 ff. More specifically on his theory of natural law: Max Ernst Mayer, *Rechtsphilosophie*, Berlin, 1922, pp. 20–1.

[124] See, e.g., Jerome Hall, *Studies in Jurisprudence and Criminal Theory*, pp. 28–9.

[125] For the following text see, in addition to the literature in notes 81 ff., H. Kantorowicz, *The Definition of Law*, pp. 41 ff.; M. Ginsberg, *Essays in Sociology and Social Philosophy*, Vol. 2, pp. 16 ff.; Edmond Cahn, *The Moral Decision*, pp. 38 ff.; A. L. Goodhart, *The Nature of Law and Morals*, London, 1955; Sir Patrick Devlin, *The Enforcement of Morals*, Oxford, 1959; H. L. A. Hart, *Law, Liberty and Morality*, Oxford, 1963; Lon L. Fuller, 'Positivism and Fidelity to Law—A Reply to Professor Hart', *Harv. Law Rev.*, Vol. 71, No. 4, Feb. 1958, pp. 630–72; M. Ginsberg's review of Hart in *Brit. J. Crim.*, Vol. 4, No. 3., Jan. 1964, pp. 283–90; Kurt Baier, *The Moral Point of View*, Ithaca, 1958. Now Devlin, *The Enforcement of Morals*, Oxford, 1965.

[126] See the literature quoted by Bodenheimer, *op. cit.*, pp. 73, 158 ff.

[127] Cahn, *op. cit.*, p. 45.

[128] Sir David Ross, *Foundations of Ethics*, London, 1939, p. 122.

[129] William Ernest Hocking, 'Ways of Thinking about Rights', in *Law. A Century of Progress, 1835–1935, Contributions in Celebration of the 100th Anniversary of the Founding of the School of Law of New York University*, Vol. 2, 1937, pp. 242 ff.

[130] Georg Jellinek, *Die sozialethische Bedeutung von Recht, Unrecht, Strafe*, 1878, p. 49.

[131] G. Radbruch, *Grundzüge der Rechtsphilosophie*, 1st ed., 1914, p. 43 ff.

[132] This is the view of Leon Petrazycki, *Law and Morality*, Eng. trans., London–Cambridge, Mass., 1955.

[133] H. Kantorowicz, *The Definition of Law*, p. 51.

[134] M. Ginsberg, *op. cit.*, p. 16.

[135] In his discussion of this point Kelsen, *op. cit.*, p. 236, seems to over-estimate the role of compulsion in the law.

[136] See my *Dilemma of Penal Reform*, p. 24.

[137] See Glanville Williams, *op. cit.*, § 69. The German Draft Code of 1962, § 13, tries to define the conditions required for the punishment of omissions and deals very fully with the theory of the matter, pp. 124-6. One of the difficulties is to decide whether omissions should be treated exactly like the corresponding commissions or whether they should be punished as special offences.

[138] Draft Code 1962, p. 396.

[139] Glanville Williams, *op. cit.*, §§ 56, 69.

[140] Jellinek (*op. cit.* at note 130), p. 42.

[141] Hart, *Law, Liberty and Morality*, pp. 38-43.

[142] Kenny-Turner, *op. cit.*, p. 346, and for the German law the commentary by Dreher, note Ac to § 263.

[143] *The Times*, 5.7.1955. Goodhart's view that 'English Law and the moral law are rarely in conflict' (p. 37) is perhaps slightly over-optimistic.

[144] See *Criminal Justice and Social Reconstruction*, Ch. 10, III.

[145] See, e.g., Morris Ginsberg, *Brit. J. Crim.*, Vol. 4, No. 3, Jan. 1964, pp. 284-90; Robert S. Summers, *N.Y. Univ. Law Rev.*, Vol. 38, Dec. 1963, pp. 1201-13.

[146] Norman St. John Stevas, *op. cit.*, p. 35; also in *The Times*, 24.3.1961.

[147] As our historical survey of the development of the natural law has shown, Lord Devlin is not quite correct in thinking that 'up till a century or so ago no one thought it worth distinguishing between religion and morals' (p. 12).

[148] On Durkheim see Walter A. Lunden in *Pioneers of Criminology*, Ch. 14, and briefly my *Dilemma*, pp. 213 ff.

[149] *The Listener*, 30.7.1959, p. 163.

[150] See my article in *Law and Opinion* (*op. cit.* above at note 76), p. 273.

[151] [1961] 2 A.E.R. 446; [1962] A.C. 223.

[152] *Harv. Law Rev.*, Vol. 71, pp. 618-19.

[153] Fuller, *op. cit.*, p. 661.

[154] Wolfgang Friedmann, *Legal Theory*, 4th ed., London, 1960, p. 313, is also inclined to regard the conflict between Hart and Fuller as 'perhaps more verbal than real'.

[155] Compare Radbruch's *Grundzüge der Rechtsphilosophie*, 1st ed., 1914, p. 170, and 4th ed. 1950, p. 336.

[156] This concept has now been incorporated, and thereby deprived of its former status as being *praeter legem*, in the German Draft Code of 1962; see §§ 39, 40, and pp. 158-62 and for the present German law the commentary by Dreher, note 7 to § 54. For English law see Glanville Williams, *op. cit.*, Ch. 18.

[157] See *The Acquittals at Liège*. An account of the trial and correspondence reprinted from *The Times*, London, 1962. Moreover see my *Criminal Justice and Social Reconstruction*, pp. 13-17, and now the admirable discussion by Prof. Jean Graven, 'Le Procès de l'Euthanasie', *Revue pénale Suisse*, Vol. 80, Nos. 2 et 3, 1964, pp. 121-258.

[158] See the statement of the judges of the former Supreme Court of the Reich, published in *Juristische Wochenschrift*, 1924, p. 90, and the famous comment on it by Prof. James Goldschmidt of Berlin University on pp. 245-7: *Gesetzesdämmerung?*

[159] Karlsruhe, 1957, Ch. 2, with many further references.

[160] *Die Idee der Staatsraison*, Munich–Berlin, 1924, p. 532.

[161] See Otto von Gierke, *Natural Law and the Theory of Society* (*op. cit.* above at note 81), Vol. 2, p. 337.

[162] John Locke, *Two Treatises on Government*, ed. by Morley, 1884, Book 2, Ch. 19, §§ 221–2; Bodenheimer, *Jurisprudence*, p. 144. Sir Ernest Barker, in his *Notes to Gierke*, Vol. 2, p. 349, corrects the latter and states Locke's position as follows: 'Locke is arguing that if a controversy arises between the prince and some of the people on a matter on which law is silent or doubtful, the proper umpire is the body of the people who have given him his power as a trust and can therefore decide upon his use or abuse of that power. If the prince, however, declines that way of determination "the appeal then lies nowhere but to Heaven", i.e. the case is carried in the last resort to the divine ordeal of battle in civil war.' On the whole problem of the *jus resistendi* see the German monograph by Kurt Wolzendorff, *Staatsrecht und Naturrecht in der Lehre vom Widerstandsrecht des Volkes, etc.*, Breslau, 1916.

[163] Otto von Gierke, *Johannes Althusius*, 3rd ed., Breslau, 1913, pp. 145 ff.

[164] *Ibid.*, pp. 149, fn. 80 and 308.

CHAPTER 3

[1] Ernest Greenwood, 'Social Work Research: A Decade of Reappraisal', *Soc. Serv. Rev.*, Vol. 31, No. 3, Sept. 1957, p. 312.

[2] George B. Vold, *Theoretical Criminology*, New York, 1958, Ch. 14, p. 265, Ch. 16, p. 310; Marshall B. Clinard, *Sociology of Deviant Behavior*, New York, 1957, pp. 54 ff., also refers to methodological problems. In German: Armand Mergen, *Methodik kriminalbiologischer Untersuchungen*, Stuttgart, 1953; *ibid.*, *Die Wissenschaft vom Verbrechen*, Part IV: 'Die Methoden', Hamburg, Kriminalistik, 1961.

Leslie T. Wilkins's important new book *Social Deviance*, London, 1964, arrived too late to be fully considered. Its scope is far wider than criminology, and it 'attempts to draw together the needs of social action and the techniques of social research, and to define some of the basic problems of social policy.' He also tries to develop a general, value-free, theory of deviance and to measure the degree of the latter. Moreover, he offers some observations on the definition of science and the scientific approach; on pure and applied research, on the need for 'research into research' and on the relationship between science and ethics, and on the technique of matching.

[3] Vold, *op. cit.*, p. 274.

[4] Robert K. Merton, *Social Theory and Social Structure* (revised and enlarged ed.), Glencoe, Ill., 1957, pp. 87–8.

[5] R. B. Braithwaite, *Scientific Explanation*, Cambridge, 1955, p. 22, gives a somewhat different definition.

[6] See the excellent discussion by Gunnar Myrdal, *Value in Social Theory*, London, 1958, pp. 232 ff.

[7] Stephen Toulmin, *The Philosophy of Science*, London, 1953, pp. 80–1. The view that research can begin without a hypothesis is also expressed in Claire Selltiz, Marie Jahoda, Morton Deutsch and Stuart W. Cook, *Research Methods in Social Relations*, London, 1959, p. 35. There are excellent sections in this book on the formulation of a hypothesis and on research and theory.

[8] J. P. Martin, *Social Aspects of Prescribing*, London, 1957, p. 141, states that as the correlations he was able to calculate in order to substantiate his hypotheses were relatively low he had to adopt 'an approach rather different from the tradi-

tional scientific method of verifying specific hypotheses. It was not that we had no hypotheses nor that the correlations discovered were without significance, rather it was that individually they did not tell us very much. Our approach was to collect as much information as possible that had any conceivable relevance whatsoever. Once this was assembled it was subjected to a series of statistical analyses in an attempt to discover the nature of the influences underlying the behaviour in which we were interested. The specific hypotheses, in fact, gave way to a more generalized assumption that a consistent pattern of influences existed and underlay this behaviour. It became our prime concern to discover the nature of this pattern . . .'.

[9] Merton, *op. cit.*, p. 12, also p. 225: 'there is two-way traffic between social theory and empirical research'; also Myrdal, *op. cit.*, p. 233.

[10] See, e.g., Clinard, 'A Cross-cultural Replication of the relation of Urbanism to Criminal Behavior', *Amer. Sociol. Rev.*, Vol. 25, No. 2, April 1960, pp. 253 ff.; *ibid.* in Burgess and Bogue, *Contributions to Urban Sociology*, Chicago, 1964, pp. 541-58; Robert G. Andry, *Delinquency and Parental Pathology*, London, 1960, pp. 17, and *passim*.

[11] On 'null hypothesis' see M. J. Moroney, *Facts from Figures*, Harmondsworth, 1951, p. 217.

[12] Aubrey Lewis, 'Between Guesswork and Certainty in Psychiatry', *The Lancet*, 25.1.1958 and 1.2.1958, with interesting historical material on the subject in general. Also Morris R. Cohen and Ernest Nagel, *An Introduction to Logic and Scientific Method*, London, 1934, p. 208, who quote De Morgan's dictum: 'Wrong hypotheses, rightly worked, have produced more useful results than unguided observation.'

[13] *Loc. cit.*

[14] In his valuable discussion of some of these points Gordon Trasler, *The Explanation of Criminality*, London, 1962, p. 15, rightly says 'hunches are not theories', but they can well become the source of a hypothesis and a theory.

[15] Terence and Pauline Morris, *Pentonville*, London, 1963, p. 13.

[16] On the following text see in particular Gunnar Myrdal, *op. cit.*, esp. Ch. 5 and pp. 128 ff., and in *The American Dilemma*, New York–London, 1944. Arnold M. Rose, *Theory and Method in the Social Sciences*, Minneapolis, 1954, esp. Section 2, and Rose, 'Sociology and the Study of Values', *Brit. J. Sociol.*, Vol. 7, No. 1, March 1956, pp. 1–17, are also indispensable contributions to these problems. See, moreover, Hermann Mannheim, *Deutsche Strafrechtsreform in englischer Sicht*, München, 1960, pp. 113 ff., and *Brit. J. Delinq.*, Vol. 7, No. 2, Oct. 1956, pp. 154 ff.; and G. D. H. Cole, *Brit. J. Sociol.*, Vol. 8, No. 2, June 1957, p. 161.

[17] Donald G. MacRae, 'Between Science and the Arts', *Twentieth Century*, May 1960, p. 435.

[18] *The Times*, 6.6.1960, in a leader on 'Research without Direction'.

[19] See also John Madge, *The Tools of Social Science*, London, 1953, p. 102, fn. 1.

[20] Myrdal, *op. cit.*, p. 132. See also Rose, *Theory and Method*, pp. 163 ff.

[21] In so far the criticism of James Vander Zanden, *Soc. Forces*, Vol. 39, No. 2, Dec. 1960, pp. 192-3, is justified.

[22] Hermann Mannheim and Leslie T. Wilkins, *Prediction Methods in relation to Borstal Training*, H.M.S.O., London, 1955, pp. 217, 223.

[23] Rose, *Theory and Method*, pp. 154 ff.; also Karl R. Popper, *The Poverty of Historicism*, London, 1957, pp. 55 ff.

[24] See Hermann Mannheim, *Group Problems in Crime and Punishment*, London, 1955, pp. 273, 277.

[25] On the work of the Howard League for Penal Reform and other 'pressure groups' see A. Gordon Rose, *The Struggle for Penal Reform*, London, 1961.

[26] Myrdal, *op. cit.*, pp. 48 ff., 206 ff.

[27] No. 1: Hermann Mannheim and Leslie T. Wilkins, *Prediction Methods in relation to Borstal Training*, H.M.S.O., London, 1955; No. 2: Evelyn Gibson, *Time Spent Awaiting Trial*, H.M.S.O., London, 1960; No. 3: Leslie T. Wilkins, *Delinquent Generations*, London, 1960; No. 4: *Murder*, H.M.S.O., London, 1961; No. 5: W. H. Hammond and Edna Chayen, *Persistent Criminals*, H.M.S.O., London, 1963.

[28] London, H.M.S.O., 1959, Cmd. 645, App. B.

[29] London, H.M.S.O., Cmd. 2296, April 1964, Apps. A, B.

[30] Thorsten Sellin, *J. crim. Law Criminol.*, Vol. 35, No. 4, Nov.–Dec. 1944, p. 224.

[31] E.g. Alfred J. Kahn, *A Court for Children*, New York, 1953; Sheldon and Eleanor Glueck, *One Thousand Juvenile Delinquents*, Cambridge, Mass., 1934.

[32] John P. Martin, 'On Beginning Criminological Research', *Cambridge Opinion: Criminology*, Autumn 1960, pp. 35 ff.

[33] There is in fact a regrettable omission in the White Paper of 1964 in that the important study by T. P. and P. Morris on Pentonville is not included. Moreover, the publications in App. B. under Nos. 2, 5 and 6 are listed as 'Library of Criminology' (L.S.E.) whereas that 'Library' is in fact published under the auspices not of the London School of Economics but of the Institute for the Study and Treatment of Delinquency (I.S.T.D.).

[34] Hermann Mannheim, *Social Aspects of Crime in England between the Wars*, London, 1940, pp. 16 ff.; and on juvenile delinquency, Ch. 1 of *Young Offenders*, Cambridge, 1944.

[35] See Hermann Mannheim, *Social Aspects*, p. 20, and *Group Problems in Crime and Punishment*, pp. 235 ff. See also O. R. McGregor, *Divorce in England*, London, 1957, pp. 177–8, for some strong criticisms of the work of the Royal Commission on Divorce; A. G. Rose, *Five Hundred Borstal Boys*, Oxford, 1954, p. 173.

[36] See Hermann Mannheim in *Law and Opinion*, London, 1959, pp. 264 ff., 272–3.

[37] See the *Report on Alternatives to Short Terms of Imprisonment 1957*, on the one hand, and Robert G. Andry, *The Short-Term Prisoner*, London, 1963, with my Introduction, on the other.

[38] *Group Problems*, pp. 253–4.

[39] *Report of the Committee on the Provision for Social and Economic Research*—so-called Clapham Report, H.M.S.O., London, 1946, Cmd. 6868, and Social and Economic Research and Government Departments, Nat. Inst. of Economic and Social Research, London, 1947.

[40] The substance of the following text has been taken from Hermann Mannheim, *Deutsche Strafrechtsreform in englischer Sicht* (cited at note 16 above), pp. 115 ff.

[41] On Maconochie see John Vincent Barry, *Alexander Maconochie of Norfolk Island*, Melbourne, 1958, esp. Chs. 5, 9; also in *Pioneers in Criminology*, ed. by Hermann Mannheim, London, 1960, Ch. 4; Max Grünhut, *Penal Reform*, Oxford, 1948, pp. 78 ff.

[42] On Lombroso see Marvin E. Wolfgang, Ch. 9 in *Pioneers in Criminology*, esp. pp. 182 ff., and on Lombroso's methods of research, pp. 193 ff.

[43] Terence Morris, *The Criminal Area*, London, 1957, p. 42.

[44] See also Hermann Mannheim, *Group Problems in Crime and Punishment*, p. 72.

[45] See Mannheim and Wilkins, *op. cit.*, pp. 37–8.

[46] Wilson Gee, *Social Science Research Methods*, New York, 1950, p. 158.

[47] 'Why Delinquency? The Limits of Present Knowledge', reprinted in *Group Problems*, p. 138. For a spirited discussion of the value of criminological research from the lawyer's point of view see Norval Morris and Cynthia Turner, 'The Lawyer and Criminological Research', *Virginia Law Rev.*, Vol. 44, No. 2, 1958, pp. 163-83.

[48] See *Law and Opinion in England in the Twentieth Century*, pp. 278-9.

[49] *Ibid.*, p. 285.

[50] Gunnar Myrdal, *op. cit.*, p. 28.

## CHAPTER 4

[1] For the following text see the excellent discussions in Arnold M. Rose, *op. cit.*, Ch. 14, and H. Bianchi, *Position and Subject-Matter of Criminology*, Amsterdam, 1956, pp. 8 ff.

[2] See Hermann Mannheim, *Group Problems*, Ch. 6; Barbara Wootton, *Social Science and Social Pathology*, London, 1959, Chs. 3-6, 10, 11.

[3] This is the method adopted in the Borstal Prediction Study; see Mannheim and Wilkins (*op. cit.*, Ch. 3, note 27), pp. 214 ff., 58 ff., 175, 209. There it is stressed that the prediction tables so far constructed were not suitable for immediate practical application and recommendations were made for the improvement of the methods of recording.

[4] Aubrey Lewis, *loc. cit.*, p. 18.

[5] *Group Problems*, p. 263.

[6] Allyn A. Young, quoted from Wilson Gee, *Social Science Research Methods*, New York, 1950, p. 133. On the whole problem see Morris Ginsberg, 'Social Change', *Brit. J. Sociol.*, Vol. 9, No. 3, Sept. 1958, pp. 205 ff.

[7] This definition by Major Greenwood is quoted by D. D. Reid, 'Epidemiological Methods in the Study of Mental Disorders', W.H.O., Geneva, 1960, p. 8. See also Michael Shepherd, 'The Epidemiology of Neurosis', *Int. J. soc. Psychiat.*, Vol. 5, No. 4, Spring 1960, p. 276.

[8] Thomas Würtenberger, *Die geistige Situation der deutschen Strafrechtswissenschaft*, Karlsruhe, 1957, pp. 44-5.

[9] Karl L. Popper, *The Poverty of Historicism*, pp. 130 ff., stresses the 'unity of method' in spite of all those differences, and Ginsberg, *loc. cit.*, p. 220, also acknowledges a fundamental similarity. Moreover see now Wilkins, *Social Deviance*, p. 113.

[10] Hermann Mannheim, 'Teamwork in the Administration of Criminal Justice', *Proc. Canad. Congress Correct.*, Montreal, 1957, pp. 241 ff., reprinted in the (Indian) *J. correct. Wk*, 6th issue, 1959, pp. 1 ff., is mainly concerned with teamwork in correctional practice.

[11] See John C. Spencer, *Stress and Release in an Urban Estate: A Study in Action Research*, London, 1964.

[12] Sheldon and Eleanor Glueck, *Unraveling Juvenile Delinquency*, New York, 1950, p. viii.

[13] See my Teamwork lecture (cited at note 10), p. 7.

[14] Norbert Wiener, *Cybernetics*, New York, 1948, p. 9.

[15] *Unraveling Juvenile Delinquency*, pp. 25-6. On similar dangers of bias see my lecture on Teamwork, p. 8.

[16] On this see, e.g., Wilson Gee (*op. cit.* at note 6), pp. 361 ff.

[17] Edward Glover, *The Roots of Crime*, London, 1960, Section 6, pp. 272 ff.

[18] John C. Spencer, *op. cit.*, Part 1, pp. 61 ff., Part III, pp. 288 ff.

[19] See my review of the Cambridge Study on 'Sex Offences', *Brit. J. Delinq.*, Vol. 9, No. 1, July 1959, p. 70.

[20] See especially the illuminating discussion by Arnold M. Rose, *op. cit.*, pp. 262 ff., where a list of replicated studies is given; also Marshall B. Clinard, 'Research Frontiers in Criminology', *Brit. J. Delinq.*, Vol. 7, No. 2, Oct. 1956, pp. 113 ff.; *ibid.*, 'A Cross-cultural Replication of the Relation of Urbanism to Criminal Behavior', *Amer. Sociol. Rev.*, Vol. 25, No. 2, April 1960, pp. 253 ff. The importance of the matter has also been stressed by Sheldon Glueck, 'Wanted: A Comparative Criminology', *Ventures in Criminology* (cited at Ch. 7, note 2), Ch. 19. On the difficulties of retesting a particular hypothesis see Ronald L. Akers, 'Socio-Economic Status and Delinquent Behavior: A Retest', *J. Res. Crime Delinq.*, Vol. 1, No. 1, Jan. 1964, pp. 38-46.

[21] Hermann Mannheim, *Group Problems*, p. 135; Barbara Wootton, *Social Science and Social Pathology*, London, 1959, Ch. 3, 10.

[22] Selltiz *et al.* (*op. cit.* at Ch. 3, note 7), p. 46.

[23] *Ibid.*, pp. 311 ff., and *passim*.

[24] For examples of such pilot studies see Mannheim and Wilkins, *op. cit.*, p. 53, IV, 5.

[25] Myrdal, *op. cit.*, pp. 132-3.

## CHAPTER 5

[1] Thorsten Sellin and Marvin E. Wolfgang's book *The Measurement of Delinquency*, New York-London-Sydney, 1964, was published too late to be fully considered. Its main object is the construction of 'an index of delinquency that rests on juvenile offences against criminal law but is not dependent on the specific labels given by the law to such offences'. Its significance is, however, wider than the mere construction of such an index, and it has to be regarded as one of the most important modern contributions to the statistical study of crime in general. Similar considerations apply to the Swedish study by Gunnar Fredriksson, *Kriminalstatistiken och Kriminologien*, Stockholm, 1962, which will soon appear in an Eng. trans. in The International Library of Criminology, London.

[2] On Quetelet see J. M. van Bemmelen, *Criminologie*, 3rd ed., Zwolle, 1952, pp. 46 ff., 226 ff.; also, 'The Constancy of Crime,' *Brit. J. Delinq.*, Vol. 2, No. 3, Jan. 1952, pp. 208-28; W. A. Bonger, *An Introduction to Criminology*, London, 1936, pp. 50-3, 121-6; E. Roesner in *Handwörterbuch der Kriminologie*, Vol. 2, Berlin-Leipzig, 1933, pp. 28-9; M. Halbwachs, *La théorie de l'homme moyen*, Paris, 1913; T. P. Morris, *The Criminal Area*, London, 1958, p. 51; Jean Pinatel, *Criminologie*, Paris, 1963, pp. 81-2. On the Gaussian Law M. J. Moroney, *Facts from Figures*, Harmondsworth, 1951, pp. 108 ff., 57.

[3] Pitirim Sorokin, *Fads and Foibles in Modern Sociology and Related Sciences*, Chicago, 1956, pp. 139 ff.

[4] Perhaps the best international survey of the contents of official criminal statistics is given by Ernst Roesner in *Handwörterbuch der Kriminologie* (cited at note 2), Vol. 2, pp. 48-9; but some details have changed in the meantime.

[5] A detailed critical analysis of the structure, interpretation and contents of English criminal statistics has been given in the present writer's *Social Aspects of Crime in England between the Wars*, London, 1940, Part 1. In the following text the most important changes are mentioned which have occurred since that book was published.

[6] M. Grünhut, 'Statistics in Criminology', *J. roy. statist. Soc.*, Series A (general), Vol. 114, Part 2, 1951, pp. 139 ff.

[7] Some material of this kind may be found in Hans von Hentig, 'Kriminalstatistische Daten aus früheren Jahrhunderten', *Schweiz. Z. Strafrecht*, Vol. 72, No. 3, 1957, pp. 276 ff. See also Gustav Radbruch and Heinrich Gwinner,

*Geschichte des Verbrechens*, Stuttgart, 1951, p. 7, who stress that in the absence of reliable statistical data the history of crime has to be written with the assistance of other contemporary sources. Thorsten Sellin, 'Two Myths in the History of Capital Punishment', *J. crim. Law Criminol. Police Sci.*, Vol. 50, No. 2, July-August 1959, pp. 114 ff., shows how these two myths, one of them the widespread belief that there were 72,000 hangings in England during the reign of Henry VIII, had originated and quotes, among other critical voices, James Fitzjames Stephens' statement that it was difficult to discover how Tudor justice worked in practice as 'no statistics as to either convictions or executions were kept then, or till long afterwards' and all that was available were 'a few vague generalities, with here and there a piece of positive evidence'.

[7a] *Accounts and Papers*, Session 23.1—21.6.1810, Vol. 14, pp. 549 ff.

[8] *Accounts and Papers*, 1826-7, Vol. 19, pp. 183 ff.: 'Committals. Summary Statements of the Number of Persons charged with Criminal Offences who were Committed to the Different Gaols in England and Wales, 28.3.1827.'

[9] *Judicial Statistics—England and Wales*, 1893, Part I, 'Criminal Statistics'; 'Statistics relating to Criminal Proceedings, Police, Coroners, Prisons, Reformatory and Industrial Schools, and Criminal Lunatics for the year 1893', *Accounts and Papers*, 1895, Vol. 108, pp. 1 ff.

[10] Similar recommendations were made in the excellent Memorandum by Sir John Macdonell which was appended to the report.

[11] For the following see *Social Aspects of Crime*, pp. 90 ff.

[12] See, e.g., *Introduction to Criminal Statistics*, 1959, paras. 7, 15-18. On the system used up to 1938 see *Social Aspects of Crime*, pp. 32-3.

[13] *Introduction*, paras. 7, 48.

[14] The resulting gaps are discussed in *Social Aspects of Crime*, pp. 94 ff.

[15] The *Supplementary Statistics* go a long way, therefore, towards fulfilling the requirements postulated by the present writer in *Social Aspects of Crime*, pp. 30, 33, 44-5, 74 ff.

[16] Rupert Cross and P. Asterley Jones, *An Introduction to Criminal Law*, London, 1948, art. 10.

[17] *Criminal Statistics—England and Wales*, 1959, p. viii.

[18] See also Lord Pakenham, *Causes of Crime*, London, 1958, p. 25.

[19] Comparisons between English and Scottish crime figures may be found in T. S. Lodge, *Brit. J. Delinq.*, Vol. 7, 1956, pp. 50 ff.; A. M. Struthers, *Measuring Bad Behaviour*, N.C.S.S., London, 1950.

[20] By permission of the Comptroller of H.M.S.O.

[21] On developments before 1938 see the detailed discussion *Social Aspects of Crime*, pp. 40-6.

[22] See T. S. Lodge, *J. roy. statist. Soc.*, Series A (General), Vol. 116, Part 3, 1953, p. 287.

[23] See the details in *Social Aspects of Crime*, Ch. 3.

[24] See in particular on cases of homicide J. D. J. Havard, *The Detection of Secret Homicide*, London, 1960, and on the general problem Bernd Wehner, 'Die Latenz der Straftaten (Die nicht entdeckte Kriminalität)', *Schriftenreihe des Bundeskriminalamtes*, Wiesbaden, 1957, with literature and case material. Also Hans von Hentig, *Crime: Causes and Conditions*, New York, 1947, pp. 58 ff., and in particular Hentig, *Der Mord*, Tübingen, 1956, pp. 19 ff., and *Diebstahl, Einbruch, Raub*, Tübingen, 1956, pp. 18 ff.

[25] H. Silcock, *The Increase in Crimes of Theft 1938-1947*, Liverpool, 1949, p. 27.

[26] *Social Aspects of Crime*, p. 8.

[27] Austin L. Porterfield, *Youth in Trouble*, Fort Worth, 1946, pp. 32-5. Other

American investigations are reported in Marshall B. Clinard, *Sociology of Deviant Behavior*, New York, 1957, p. 165.

[28] See Ola Nyquist, *Juvenile Justice*, London, 1960, pp. 107–8, who also draws attention to a similar Norwegian study.

[29] John B. Mays, *Growing up in the City*, Liverpool, 1954, pp. 76 ff., 32.

[30] James S. Wallerstein and Clement J. Wyle, 'Our Law-abiding Law-breakers', *Probation*, March–April, 1947, pp. 102 ff., quoted from Clinard, *op. cit.*, p. 165.

[31] *Social Aspects of Crime*, pp. 82 ff.

[32] Thorsten Sellin, *Crime in the Depression*, Soc. Sci. Res. Counc. Bull. 27, 1937, p. 69. See also T. C. N. Gibbens, *Thefts from Department Stores*, General Report for the Fourth International Criminological Congress, The Hague, 1960, and C. N. Peijster, *Preparatory Paper for the Congress*.

[33] H.M.S.O., 1939, Ch. 2.

[34] Wehner (*op. cit.* at note 24), p. 37.

[35] Edward Glover, *The Roots of Crime*, London, 1960, p. 204 fn.

[36] Hentig, *Der Mord*, p. 19.

[37] See also T. S. Lodge (*op. cit.* at note 22), p. 491; Thorsten Sellin, *J. crim. Law Criminol.*, Vol. 22, 1931, pp. 335 ff., and *Law Quart. Rev.*, Vol. 67, 1951, p. 489; Georg von Mayr, *Statistik und Cesellschaftslehre*, Vol. 3, 1917, Tübingen, pp. 414 ff. The most recent discussions of the representative character of the 'dark figure' are to be found in Sellin and Wolfgang (*op. cit.* above, note 1), Ch. 8, and more briefly in Wilkins, *Social Deviance*, pp. 140 ff.

[38] *Social Aspects of Crime*, p. 80.

[39] See the discussion in *Social Aspects of Crime*, pp. 35 ff. with bibliog.

[40] See Lodge, *loc. cit.*, p. 288.

[41] *Social Aspects of Crime*, p. 72.

[42] W. Lloyd Warner and Paul S. Lunt, quoted from Barnes and Teeters, *New Horizons in Criminology*, 1st ed., New York, 1943, p. 86. See also Walter C. Reckless, *The Crime Problem*, 2nd ed., New York, 1955, pp. 28 ff.

[43] Marshall B. Clinard, *Deviant Social Behavior*, pp. 23–4; William M. Kephart, 'Negro Visibility', *Amer. Sociol. Rev.*, Vol. 19, No. 4, Aug. 1954, pp. 462 ff. For Liverpool see John B. Mays, *Growing up in the City*, App. B: A Study of a Police Division.

[44] Reprinted in *Group Problems in Crime and Punishment*, p. 102.

[45] *Social Aspects of Crime*, p. 32.

[46] The following text follows closely the more detailed discussion in *Social Aspects of Crime*, p. 48 ff.

[47] According to *Criminal Statistics 1959*, Table 16, the total of prosecutions undertaken by his office in that year was 1,698.

[48] *Social Aspects of Crime*, pp. 63 ff., where the effect of other procedural changes on the figures in criminal statistics is also discussed.

[49] See H. Silcock (*op. cit.* at note 25).

[50] *Ibid.*, p. 21.

[51] On public opinion in general see the references in *Law and Opinion*, pp. 264 ff.

[52] *Social Aspects of Crime*, p. 79.

[53] Thorsten Sellin, *J. crim. Law Criminol.*, Vol. 22, 1931, pp. 335 ff.

[54] *Handwörterbuch der Kriminologie*, Vol. 2, pp. 50 ff.

[55] See Negley Teeters, *Deliberations of the International Penal and Penitentiary Congresses*, Philadelphia (no date).

[56] *Social Aspects of Crime*, p. 48.

[57] 'Directives pour l'élaboration des statistiques criminelles dans les divers pays', *Bulletin de l'Institut International de Statistique*, Vol. 29, No. 3 (Session d'Athènes 1936), The Hague, 1937. See also 'United Nations Survey of Social

Statistics', *Statistical Papers*, Series K, No. 1, Dec. 1954, Ch. 17, and *Transactions of the Third International Congress of Criminology*, London, 1955, published 1957, Conclusions of s. 1, p. 218 (the committee which was recommended in the Resolution has not been formed). An international group of experts, convened by United Nations in 1950, requested the Secretary General to prepare a manual which would establish minimum standards for national criminal statistics and determine the ultimate practicability of international statistics on homicide, aggravated assault, robbery and burglary.

[58] See my article on 'Sentencing' in *Law and Contemporary Problems, Symposium on Sentencing*, Summer 1958, pp. 557 ff.

[59] See the table in Ernst Roesner, *Handwörterbuch der Kriminologie*, Vol. 2, pp. 48–9.

[60] See the detailed account by Hans Bartz in *Mschr. Kriminol. Strafrechtsreform*, Vol. 40, Nos. 1–2, Feb. 1957, pp. 22 ff., on which the following text is largely based.

[61] Principal literature on American Criminal Statistics: Thorsten Sellin, 'The Uniform Criminal Statistics Act', *J. crim. Law Criminol.*, Vol. 40, No. 6, March–April 1950, pp. 679 ff.; also, *Status and Prospects of Criminal Statistics in the United States*, Stockholm, 1949, pp. 290 ff.; Ronald H. Beattie, 'The Sources of Criminal Statistics', *Ann. Amer. Acad. Polit. Soc. Sci.*, Vol. 217, Sept. 1941, pp. 19 ff.; Emil Frankel, *Encyclopedia of Criminology*, ed. by Vernon C. Branham and Samuel B. Kutash, New York, 1949, pp. 478 ff.; National Commission on Law Observance and Enforcement (so-called Wickersham Commission), *Report on Criminal Statistics*, Washington, D.C., 1931; Mabel A. Elliott, *Crime in Modern Society*, 1952, pp. 49 ff.

[62] On a smaller scale, similar problems exist in other Federal States, e.g. in Switzerland.

[63] See, e.g., the draft published by Sellin in the article quoted in note 61 and John G. Yeager, 'Criminal and Correctional Statistics in Pennsylvania', *Prison J.*, Vol. 40, No. 2., pp. 63 ff.

## CHAPTER 6

[1] See Ch. 3, note 27.

[2] This was done in *Social Aspects of Crime*, Ch. 5. See also M. Grünhut, *Juvenile Offenders before the Courts*, Oxford, 1956, p. 47, and the material quoted in Thorsten Sellin, *Crime in the Depression*, Ch. 3.

[3] E. C. Rhodes, *J. roy. statist. Soc.*, Vol. 52, Part 3, 1939, pp. 384 ff.; briefly also A. M. Carr-Saunders, Hermann Mannheim, and E. C. Rhodes, *Young Offenders*, Cambridge, 1944, pp. 48 ff.

[4] See the references in *Group Problems in Crime and Punishment*, pp. 118, 134; also Mannheim and Wilkins, *Prediction Methods in relation to Borstal Training*, pp. 59, 79 and *passim*.

[5] On the subject of sampling see the textbooks on statistics. In addition reference may be made to John Madge, *op. cit.*, pp. 205 ff., Selltiz *et al.*, *op. cit.*, App. B; M. J. Moroney, *Facts from Figures*, Harmondsworth, 1951, pp. 120, 173 ff.; C. A. Moser, *Survey Methods in Social Investigation*, London, 1959; Yon Poh Seng, 'Historical Survey of the Development of Sampling Theories and Practice', *J. roy statist. Soc.*, Series A, Vol. 110, No. 4, Part 2, 1951, pp. 214 ff.

[6] See Madge, *op. cit.*, p. 207 fn.; Selltiz, *op. cit.*, p. 514, and now also Wilkins, *Social Deviance*, p. 155.

[7] Selltiz, *op. cit.*, p. 422, fn. 18; Madge, *op. cit.*, p. 213; A. G. Rose, *Five Hundred Borstal Boys*, Oxford, 1954, p. 170.

[8] Mannheim and Wilkins, *op. cit.*, p. 52.

[9] Arnold M. Rose, *op. cit.*, p. 258.

[10] Cyril Burt, *The Young Delinquent*, 4th ed., London, 1944, p. 12.

[11] Maud A. Merrill, *Problems of Child Delinquency*, London, 1947, p. 15.

[12] A. M. Carr-Saunders, Hermann Mannheim, E. C. Rhodes, *Young Offenders*, p. 55.

[13] John Lewis Gillin, *The Wisconsin Prisoner*, Madison, 1947, pp. 4-5.

[14] R. G. Andry, *The Short-term Prisoner*, London, 1961.

[15] See. e.g., Andry, *Delinquency and Parental Pathology*, London, 1960, p. 10. D. H. Stott, *Delinquency and Human Nature*, Dunfermline, 1950, was able to visit the parents of his group of Approved School Boys.

[16] E.g. Andry, *Delinquency and Parental Pathology*, p. 129. On Pilot studies in general see Russell L. Ackoff, *The Design of Social Research*, Chicago, 1953, pp. 336 ff.

[17] Daniel Glaser, *Prison J.*, Vol. 40, No. 2, Autumn 1960, p. 61.

[18] See *Prediction Methods in relation to Borstal Training*, pp. 54-62, 214-16. Also John Madge, *op. cit.*, p. 101. On the use of existing records see also Selltiz *et al.*, *op. cit.*, pp. 316 ff.

[19] The need for continuous discussions between academic researchers and the leading correctional officials on research plans, policies and progress is also stressed by Glaser, *op. cit.*, p. 52.

[20] *Prediction Methods in relation to Borstal Training*, p. 56.

[21] Edwin Powers and Helen Witmer, *An Experiment in the Prevention of Delinquency. The Cambridge-Somerville Youth Study*, New York, 1951, Ch. 4.

[22] Examples are the Cambridge-Somerville Study and its follow-up by the McCords. See William and Joan McCord with Irving Kenneth Zola, *Origins of Crime*, New York, 1959, pp. vii, 17, 62, 167. According to these writers, the basic information for their work was collected before the onset of criminality.

[23] Robert K. Merton, *Social Theory and Social Structure*, 2nd ed., pp. 93-5, 99.

[24] Walter C. Reckless, *The Etiology of Delinquent and Criminal Behavior*, Soc. Sci. Res. Counc. Bull. 50, 1943, pp. 81-2.

[25] Albert K. Cohen, *Delinquent Boys*, Glencoe, Ill., 1955, p. 170.

[26] For the following text see *Group Problems in Crime and Punishment*, pp. 120 ff., 147 ff., and for more general discussions of the problems involved Ernest Greenwood, *Experimental Sociology*, 5th imp., New York, 1949, esp. p. 23 and Ch. 6: *The Technique of Control in Experimental Sociology*, and Selltiz *et al.*, *op. cit.*, pp. 98 ff.

[27] Report 1893, p. 42.

[28] Marvin E. Wolfgang, chapter on Lombroso in Hermann Mannheim (ed.), *Pioneers in Criminology*, London, 1960, p. 200.

[29] For a brief international account see the UNO Survey of Social Statistics (cited above at Ch. 5, note 57).

[30] See *Prediction Methods in relation to Borstal Training*, pp. 84 ff.

[31] For an example of this see Christian Debuyst, *Criminels et valeurs vécues*, Louvain-Paris, 1960.

[32] The details of this process are described in *Unraveling Juvenile Delinquency* (cited above at Ch. 4, note 12), pp. 33-9.

[33] Selltiz, *op. cit.*, p. 105.

[34] From my 'Critical Notice', *Brit. J. Delinq.*, Vol. 2, No. 3, Jan. 1952, p. 260. On the difficulties of matching now also Wilkins, *Social Deviance*, App. II.

[35] See also Greenwood, *op. cit.*, p. 24.

[36] This is true in spite of what has been said earlier on the place of causal research in criminology.

[37] *Experimental Sociology*, pp. 73 ff.

[38] Sol Rubin, *Crime and Juvenile Delinquency*, New York, 1958, 2nd ed., 1961, p. 23 ff.

[39] J. L. Gillin (*op. cit.* at note 13), pp. 19 ff.

[40] William Healy and Augusta Bronner, *New Light on Delinquency*, New Haven, 1936. Siri Naess, 'Mother–Child Separation and Delinquency', *Brit. J. Delinq.*, Vol. 10, No. 1, July 1959, p. 32, excludes boys who had no brothers born between 1939 and 1947.

[41] Sybil Clement Brown in a review of Healy-Bronner in the *Howard J.*, 1937, p. 392.

[42] On this see esp. the well-known Nottingham University Study 'The Social Background of Delinquency', ed. by W. J. H. Sprott (1954, not published).

[43] Among others, see H. C. Brearley, *Homicide in the United States*, Chapel Hill, 1932, p. 41; Donald R. Taft, *Criminology*, 3rd ed., New York, 1956, pp. 154 ff.; Mabel A. Elliott, *Crime in Modern Society*, New York, 1952, pp. 289 ff.

[44] D. D. Reid, *Epidemiological Methods in the Study of Mental Disorder*, WHO, Geneva, 1960, p. 50, with further illustrations. The history of cancer research is also relevant.

[45] Donald R. Cressey, *Other People's Money*, Glencoe, Ill., 1953, p. 70.

[46] Emile Durkheim, *Les Règles de la Méthode sociologique*, 11th ed., p. 129.

[47] D. H. Stott, *op. cit.*, p. 416.

[48] This is the essence of some of the criticisms of modern criminology by G. Th. Kempe, *Vers une criminologie mieux fondée* in *Une nouvelle Ecole de Science criminelle—l'Ecole d'Utrecht*, presentée par Jacques Léauté, Paris, 1959, esp. pp. 83 ff. See also my *Group Problems*, p. 122, and my review of Kempe, *Brit. J. Crim.*, Vol. 1, No. 3, Jan. 1961, pp. 281 ff.

[49] On the subject see the following literature: Sheldon and Eleanor Glueck, *After-Conduct of Discharged Offenders*, London, 1945; the same, *Five Hundred Criminal Careers*, New York, 1930; the same, *Later Criminal Careers*, New York, 1937; the same, *Criminal Careers in Retrospect*, New York, 1943; the same, *Five Hundred Delinquent Women*, New York, 1934; the same, *One Thousand Juvenile Delinquents*, Cambridge, Mass., 1934; the same, *Juvenile Delinquents Grown Up*, New York, 1940; the same, 'Follow-up Studies', in *Encyclopedia of Criminology*, pp. 167 ff.; the same, *Unraveling Juvenile Delinquency*, New York, 1950, Ch. 20; the same, *Predicting Delinquency and Crime*, Cambridge, Mass., 1959 (with Supplementary Bibliography, 1955–58); Mannheim and Wilkins, *Prediction Methods in relation to Borstal Training*, H.M.S.O., 1955 (with Bibliography up to 1955); A. G. Rose, *Five Hundred Borstal Boys*, Oxford, 1954; the same, 'Follow-up and/or Prediction?' *Brit. J. Delinq.*, Vol. 7, No. 3, April 1957, pp. 309 ff.; Erwin Frey, *Der Frühkriminelle Rückfallsverbrecher*, Basel, 1951, and my review of it reproduced in *Group Problems*, pp. 139 ff.; Edwin Powers and Helen Witmer, *An Experiment in the Prevention of Delinquency. The Cambridge-Somerville Youth Study*; T. C. N. Gibbens, D. A. Pond, and D. Stafford-Clark, 'Follow-up Study of Criminal Psychopaths', *Brit. J. Delinq.*, Vol. 6, No. 2, Sept. 1955, pp. 126 ff.; William and Joan McCord, *The Origins of Crime*, New York, 1959; Jay Rumney and Joseph P. Murphy, *Probation and Social Adjustment*, New Brunswick, 1952; Walter Piecha, *Die Lebensbewährung der als 'unerziehbar' entlassenen Fürsorgezöglinge*, Göttingen, 1959.

[50] See the General Reports by Walter C. Reckless and C. H. Andersen in the *Summary of Proceedings of the Congress*, London, 1957, pp. 88 ff., 100 ff.

[51] Sheldon and Eleanor Glueck, *After-Conduct of Discharged Prisoners*, p. 22.

[52] Rumney and Murphy, *op. cit.*, pp. 12, 84 ff.

[53] Sheldon and Eleanor Glueck, *op. cit.*, pp. 2–3. See also Ch. 3 under III above.

[54] *Five Hundred Criminal Careers*, pp. 7–8, 89 ff.

[55] Sheldon and Eleanor Glueck, *op. cit.*, pp. 101 ff.
[56] For other findings reference may be made to the summary in *Five Hundred Criminal Careers*, pp. 306 ff., and to *After-Conduct of Discharged Prisoners*, pp. 23 ff.
[57] *After-Conduct*, p. 21.
[58] For the detailed findings reference is made to these two books and the summary in *After-Conduct*, pp. 31 ff.
[59] On maturation see, e.g., *Later Criminal Careers*, pp. 105 ff.; *After-Conduct*, pp. 80 ff.; *Juvenile Delinquents Grown Up*, pp. 90 ff., 267 ff.
[60] See *One Thousand Juvenile Delinquents* and *Juvenile Delinquents Grown Up*.
[61] Walter C. Reckless, *Summary of Proceedings*, Third International Congress of Criminology, 1955, London, 1957, p. 94.
[62] *The Crime Problem*, 2nd ed., 1955, Ch. 3.
[63] Thomas C. McCormick and Roy G. Francis, *Methods of Research in the Behavioral Sciences*, New York, 1958, pp. 24 ff.


CHAPTER 7

[1] See the literature to Ch. 6, note 49, and in addition: Paul Horst, Paul Wallin, Louis Guttmann et al., *The Prediction of Personal Adjustment*, Soc. Sci. Res. Counc. Bull. 48, New York, 1941; Sibylle Escalona and Grace Moore Heider, *Prediction and Outcome. A Study in Child Development*, London, 1959; Lloyd E. Ohlin, *Selection for Parole: A Manual of Parole Prediction*, New York, 1951; Walter F. Dearborn and John W. M. Rothney, *Predicting the Child's Development*, Cambridge, Mass., 1941; Samuel A. Stouffer et al., *Measurement and Prediction*, Princeton, 1950; *Brit. J. Delinq.*, Vol. 6, No. 2, Sept. 1955: Special Number on Prediction and Recidivism. From it: D. R. L. Morrison, 'Prediction Research'; Edward Glover, 'Prognosis or Prediction'. Also A. Walters, 'A Note on Statistical Methods of Predicting Delinquency', *Brit. J. Delinq.*, Vol. 6, No. 4, April 1956, pp. 297 ff.; George Benson, 'Prediction Methods and Young Prisoners', *Brit. J. Delinq.*, Vol. 9, No. 3, Jan. 1959, pp. 192 ff.; D. H. Stott, 'The Prediction of Delinquency from Non-delinquent Behaviour', *Brit. J. Delinq.*, Vol. 10, No. 3, Jan. 1960, pp. 195 ff.; Bernard C. Kirby, 'Parole Prediction Using Multiple Correlation', *Amer. J. Sociol.*, Vol. 49, May 1954, pp. 539 ff.; Hermann Mannheim, *Deutsche Strafrechtsreform in englischer Sicht*, München–Berlin, 1960, pp. 33 ff., 123–7; Wolf Middendorff, 'Die Prognose im Strafrecht und in der Kriminologie', *Z. ges. Strafrechtswiss.*, Vol. 72, Nos. 1–2, pp. 108 ff.; Friedrich Geerds, 'Zur kriminellen Prognose', *Mschr. Kriminol. Strafrechtsreform*, Vol. 43, Nos. 3–4, Oct. 1960, pp. 92 ff.; Fritz Meyer, *Der kriminologische Wert von Prognosetafeln, ibid.*, 1959, pp. 214 ff.; Helga Daniela Spieler, *Die vorbeugende Verwahrung*, Bonn, 1960.
[2] For the following text see in particular Mannheim and Wilkins, *op. cit.*, pp. 41 ff.; S. and E. Glueck, *Predicting Delinquency and Crime*, pp. 144 ff.; *Summ. Proc. Third Int. Congress Criminol.*, London, 1955, published 1957, pp. 18, 155 ff. Manuel Lopez-Rey in *Essays in Criminal Science*, ed. by Gerhard O. W. Mueller, London, 1959, pp. 16 ff., repeats most of the usual misconceptions. On this see Mannheim, *Brit. J. Crim.*, Vol. 3, No. 1, July 1962, pp. 94–5, and Wilkins, *ibid.*, Vol. 4, No. 1, July 1963, pp. 74–6. Most of the scattered recent papers by the Gluecks on prediction and other subjects have now been republished with a complete bibliog. of their writings as *Ventures in Criminology*, London, 1964.
[3] See Theodore R. Sarbin in Arthur H. Brayfield (ed.), *Readings in Modern Methods of Counselling*, New York, 1950, pp. 83 ff.; Mannheim and Wilkins, *op. cit.*, pp. 57, 248 ff.

[4] *Unraveling Juvenile Delinquency*, p. 269.

[5] Mannheim and Wilkins, *op. cit.*, p. 174.

[6] See Wilkins, *Brit. J. Delinq.*, Vol. 6, No. 2, p. 83; against him see the other contributions to the Symposium.

[7] See the various writings of the Gluecks and Mannheim-Wilkins, Chs. 4-6 and the historical sketch in Ch. 1.

[8] For the Borstal Prediction Study see the list of factors in App. 1.

[9] See also Ohlin, *op. cit.*, p. 48.

[10] Bruce, Burgess and Harno, *The Working of the Indeterminate Sentence Law and the Parole System in Illinois*, 1928.

[11] Ohlin, *op. cit.*, pp. 51 ff.

[12] See, e.g., *Predicting Delinquency and Crime*, p. 25.

[13] Taken from *After-Conduct of Discharged Offenders*, p. 67.

[14] *Unraveling Juvenile Delinquency*, Ch. 20.

[15] *Ibid.*, Ch. 10, and *J. crim. Law Criminol. Police Sci.*, Vol. 51, No. 3, Sept.-Oct. 1960, pp. 303 ff., and now the Gluecks in *Brit. J. Crim.* Vol. 4, No. 3, Jan. 1964.

[16] Rubin, *Crime and Delinquency*, pp. 225 ff.

[17] A. Walters, *Brit. J. Delinq.*, Vol. 6, No. 4, April 1956, pp. 297 ff.; D. H. Stott, *The Prediction of Delinquency from Non-Delinquent Behaviour*, Vol. 10, No. 3, Jan. 1960, pp. 195 ff.

[18] *Prediction Methods in relation to Borstal Training*, pp. 143 ff.

[19] *Ibid.*, pp. 153 ff. (the reference under VI. 62 should be to Table 81, not 86).

[20] *Ibid.*, pp. 39, 56 ff.

[21] *Ibid.*, pp. 137 ff.

[22] *Ibid.*, p. 219 ff.

[23] *Ibid.*, Ch. 7; S. and E. Glueck, *Predicting Delinquency and Crime*, pp. 47-60, 126-36.

[24] See, in particular, Horst *et al.*, *op. cit.*, pp. 26 ff., 99, 117, 181-249; Mannheim and Wilkins, *op. cit.*, Ch. 8; Stouffer *et al.*, *op. cit.*, pp. 573 ff.; Escalona and Heider, *op. cit.*; Gordon W. Allport, *The Use of Personal Documents in Psychological Science*, Soc. Sci. Res. Counc. Bull. 49, 1942, pp. 148, 154 ff.; Paul E. Meehl, *Clinical versus Statistical Prediction*, Minneapolis, 1954; John D. Benjamin in *Dynamic Psychopathology in Childhood*, by Lucie Jessner and Eleanor Pavenstedt, New York-London, 1959, Ch. 2; T. R. Sarbin, 'A Contribution to the Study in Actuarial and Individual Methods of Prediction', *Amer. J. Sociol.*, Vol. 48, 1943-5, pp. 593 ff.

[25] For the following text see Horst *et al.*, *op. cit.*, pp. 209 ff., 240 ff.; Allport, *op. cit.*, pp. 154 ff.

[26] Mechl, *op. cit.*, p. 137.

[27] This is also admitted by Allport, *op. cit.*, p. 149.

[28] Note 1 above.

[29] Escalona and Heider, *op. cit.*, pp. 107 ff.

[30] *Op. cit.*, Ch. 8, esp. pp. 173 ff.

[31] See *Group Problems in Crime and Punishment*, p. 79.

## CHAPTER 8

[1] On the general principles of individual case studies in criminology see, e.g., Walter C. Reckless, *Criminal Behavior*, London, 1940, pp. 173 ff.; Sheldon Glueck, *The Problem of Delinquency*, Boston, 1959, pp. 237 ff.; Howard Jones, *Crime and the Penal System*, London, 1956, pp. 18 ff.; Arthur Evans Wood, 'Difficulties of Statistical Interpretation of Case Records of Delinquency', *Amer.*

*J. Sociol.*, Vol. 39, 1933-4, pp. 204 ff. On life histories in social science John Madge, *The Tools of Social Science*, London, 1953, pp. 81 ff.; Cavan, Hauser and Stouffer, 'Note on the Statistical Treatment of Life-History Material', *Soc. Forces*, Vol. 9, 1930, pp. 200 ff.

[2] Earnest Albert Hooton, *The American Criminal*, Cambridge, Mass., 1939, 16.

[3] Edward Glover, *The Roots of Crime*, London, 1960, p. 390.

[4] William H. Sheldon, *Varieties of Delinquent Youth*, New York, 1949.

[5] So rightly Thomas C. McCormick and Roy G. Francis, *Methods of Research in the Behavioral Sciences*, New York, 1958, p. 28.

[6] As examples of this technique the following may be quoted out of many: Cyril Burt, *The Young Delinquent*, 4th ed., London, 1944; S. and E. Glueck, *Five Hundred Criminal Careers*, New York, 1930; D. J. West, *Homosexuality*, London, 1955; Howard Jones, *Reluctant Rebels*, London, 1960; Kate Friedlander, *The Psycho-analytical Approach to Juvenile Delinquency*, 1st ed., London, 1947; Norval Morris, *The Habitual Criminal*, London, 1951.

[7] Donald R. Cressey, *Other People's Money*, Glencoe, Ill., 1953.

[8] For a few details see the Borstal Prediction Study, pp. 173-4.

[9] *One Thousand Juvenile Delinquents*, p. 191.

[10] See the titles quoted in my review, *Brit. J. Delinq.*, Vol. 10, No. 2, Oct. 1959, p. 154.

[11] Frederic Wertham, *Dark Legend: A Study in Murder*, London, 1947; Bruno Bettelheim, *Truants from Life*, Glencoe, Ill., 1955; Helen Parkhurst, *Undertow*, New York, 1959, Eng. ed., London, 1964; Tony Parker and Robert Allerton, *The Courage of his Convictions*, London, 1962; Tony Parker, *The Unknown Citizen*, 1963, and on the latter my Critical Notice *Brit. J. Crim.*, Vol. 4, No. 4, April 1964, pp. 395-9; Ben Karpman, *Case Studies in the Psychopathology of Crime*, Vol. 2, Washington, 1944. For psycho-analytical, non-criminal, case studies see Freud's *Collected Papers*, Vol. 3, London, 1925.

[12] For the description of one case of matricide and patricide see Kenneth H. Raizen, *Brit. J. Delinq.*, Vol. 10, No. 4, April 1960. See also Freud's famous essay 'Dostoevsky and Parricide', in his *Collected Papers*, Vol. 5, London, 1950, pp. 222 ff.

[13] Wertham, *op. cit.*, pp. 15, 95 ff.

[14] Bettelheim, *op. cit.*, pp. 4 ff., 473 ff. ('On writing case histories').

[15] Sheldon (*op. cit.* at note 4 above), p. 752, thinks that no amount of measurement and description can be a substitute for photographs.

[16] Horst *et al.* (*op. cit.* above at note 1, Ch. 7), pp. 187 ff.; John Madge, *The Tools of Social Science*, pp. 81 ff., Ch. 4; Selltiz *et al.* (*op. cit.* above at note 7, Ch. 3), esp. Chs. 6-9; Gordon W. Allport (*op. cit.* above at note 24, Ch. 7), Part 2; 'Social Behavior and Personality': Contributions of W. I. Thomas to *Theory and Social Research*, ed. by Edmund H. Volkart, New York, Soc. Sci. Res Counc., 1951, pp. 297 ff., 145 ff.; W. I. Thomas and F. Znaniecki, *The Polish Peasant in Europe and America*, Boston, 1918-20; Gardner Murphy, L. B. Murphy and Theodore M. Newcomb, *Experimental Social Psychology*, New York-London, 1937, pp. 838 ff.; A. Vexliard, *Le Clochard*, Bruges, 1957; Christian Debuyst, *Criminels et valeurs vécues*, Louvain-Paris, 1960.

[17] William Healy, *The Individual Delinquent*, Boston, 1916; William Healy and Augusta F. Bronner, *Delinquents and Criminals. Their Making and Unmaking*, New York, 1926; the same, *New Light on Delinquency*, New Haven, 1936; Franz Alexander and William Healy, *The Roots of Crime*, New York, 1935 (psycho-analytical).

[18] Clifford R. Shaw, *The Jack-Roller*, Chicago, 1930; *The Natural History of a*

*Delinquent Career*, Chicago, 1931; Shaw *et al.*, *Brothers in Crime*, Chicago, 1938.
[19] *The Professional Thief, by a Professional Thief.* Annotated and interpreted by E. H. Sutherland, Chicago, 1937.
[20] Donald Clemmer, *The Prison Community*, Boston, 1940.
[21] On Thomas and Znaniecki see Herbert Blumer, *Critiques of Research in the Social Sciences*, Vol. 1, Soc. Sci. Res. Counc. Bull. 44, 1939; on Shaw's *Jack-Roller* see John Dollard, *Criteria for the Life History*, New Haven, 1935.
[22] Sir Leo Page, *The Young Lag*, London, 1950.
[23] The German original *Zur Psychologie des Mordes* was published in Heidelberg, 1925, the Eng. trans. *The Psychology of Murder,* London, 1927.
[24] *Studies in the Psychology of Delinquency*, H.M.S.O., London, 1932 (reprinted 1934). It is strange that Barbara Wootton who complains so strongly about the neglect of the female delinquent in criminological literature (see Ch. 26 below) does not even mention Dr. Pailthorpe's work.
[25] Cavan, Hauser and Stouffer, *Soc. Forces*, Vol. 9, 1930, pp. 200 ff.
[26] Hans von Hentig, *Crime: Causes and Conditions*, New York–London, 1947, pp. 82 ff.
[27] This does not imply that the crime of blackmail itself is of no interest. v. Hentig has in fact written a fascinating book on it: *Die Erpressung*, Tübingen, 1959.
[28] David Lamson, *We Who Are about to Die,* New York, 1935; Nathan Leopold, *Life plus Ninety-nine Years*, London, 1958; Caryl Chessman, *Cell 2455 Death Row*, London, 1956. On the Chessman case see T. A. Joyce, *The Right to Life*, London, 1962, Ch. 1.
[29] First published London, 1935; Harmondsworth, 1957.
[30] D. J. West, *Homosexuality*, London, 1955, pp. 136–7. On Genet see John Croft, *Brit. J. Delinq.*, Vol. 6, No. 3, Jan. 1956, pp. 236 ff.
[31] The volumes of the *Howard Journal* contain informative reviews of most of these books, and some of the more recent ones are listed in D. L. Howard, *The English Prison*, London, 1960, pp. 164–5, to which may be added Mark Benney's *Low Company*, London, 1936, and Brendan Behan's *Borstal Boy*, London, 1958.
[32] W. Clifford, *Profiles in Crime*, Soc. Wel. Res. Mono. No. 3, published by the Ministry of Housing and Social Development, Northern Rhodesia, 1964.
[33] André Gide, *Dostoevsky*, 2nd ed., London, pp. 107, 119.
[34] Edwin Muir in *The Observer* of 13.5.1951.
[35] C. G. Jung, *Psychological Types*, Eng. trans., London, 1923, Ch. 5. Jung defines a type rather narrowly as 'a characteristic model of a general attitude occurring in many individual forms', adding 'in so far as such an attitude is habitual . . . I speak of a psychological type' (p. 612).
[36] On this see in particular Johannes Hirschmann in *Kriminalbiologische Gegenwartsfragen* (cited at note 47 below), pp. 23 ff., 28.
[37] McCormick and Francis (*op. cit* at note 5 above), p. 26.
[38] Howard Jones, *Alcoholic Addiction*, London, 1963, p. 53.
[39] H. J. Eysenck, *The Structure of Human Personality*, 2nd ed., London–New York, 1960, pp. 10 ff.; *Dimensions of Personality*, London, 1947, pp. 25 ff.; *Crime and Personality*, London, 1964, p. 31.
[40] T. C. Willett, *Criminal on the Road*, London, 1964.
[41] See, e.g., Max Weber, *Gesammelte Aufsätze zur Wissenschafts-Lehre*, Tübingen, 1922, pp. 190 ff.; also Max Rheinstein in his and E. Shils's edition of *Max Weber on Law in Economy and Society*, Cambridge, Mass., 1954, p. xxxvii; Carlo Antoni, *Vom Historizismus zur Soziologie*, 1951, pp. 235 ff.; Morris Ginsberg, *Evolution and Progress*, London, 1961, p. 263; W. J. H. Sprott, *Sociology*,

London, 1956, pp. 37–8. Svend Riemer in Walter C. Reckless, *Etiology of Delinquent and Criminal Behavior*, pp. 138 ff.

[42] Allport, *op. cit.*, p. 146; Paul Wallin in Horst *et al.*, *op. cit.*, pp. 215 ff.

[43] Murphy and Newcomb (*op. cit.* at note 16), pp. 274 ff.

[44] These difficulties are also stressed by W. I. Thomas (*op. cit.* at note 16), pp. 148 ff., 159 ff.

[45] As Howard Jones, *Alcoholic Addiction*, Ch. 7, points out, the type of drinker characterized by maternal dependence may arise out of a great variety of situations, e.g., over-protective or over-domineering maternal attitudes.

[46] On the older literature see, e.g., Arthur Fink, *Causes of Crime*, Philadelphia, 1938; on Lombroso Marvin E. Wolfgang in *Pioneers of Criminology*, ed. by Hermann Mannheim, London, 1960, Ch. 9; on the more recent literature S. and E. Glueck, *Physique and Delinquency*, New York, 1956, pp. 15 ff.

[47] Some of the principal publications on typological research in criminology are: W. A. Willemse, *Constitution Types in Delinquency*, London, 1932; William H. Sheldon, *Varieties of Delinquent Youths*, New York, 1949; S. and E. Glueck (*op. cit.* at note 46; Franz Exner, *Kriminologie*, 3rd ed., Berlin 1949, pp. 203 ff.; Ernst Kretschmer, *Physique and Character*, Eng. trans. by Sprott, London, 1925; in German under the title *Körperbau und Character*, 21st/22nd ed., Hamburg, 1955; Ernst Seelig, *Lehrbuch der Kriminologie*, Graz, 1950; Seelig and Weindler, *Die Typen der Kriminellen*, Munich, 1949; *Kriminalbiologische Gegenwartsfragen*, No. 2, Stuttgart, 1955 (esp. the chapters by Hirschmann and Seelig); René Resten, *Caractérologie du Criminel*, Paris, 1959; on the typology of Borstal boys: D. A. Ogden, 'A Borstal Typological Survey', *Brit. J. Delinq.*, Vol. 5, No. 2, Oct. 1954, pp. 99 ff., and *Annual Report of the Prison Commissioners for 1949*, p. 68; A. G. Rose, *Five Hundred Borstal Boys*, Ch. 7; Peter Scott in *The Roots of Crime*, ed. by Norwood East, London, 1954, Ch. 3; Jack P. Gibbs, 'Needed: Analytical Typologies in Criminology', *Southwest. Soc. Sci. Quart.*, Vol. 40, No. 4, March 1960, pp. 321 ff.

[48] *Physique and Delinquency*, pp. 7 ff.; and also *Unraveling Juvenile Delinquency*, pp. 192 ff. For Sheldon's definition of the 'somato-type' see his *Varieties of Delinquent Youths*, p. 14.

[49] *Op. cit.*, p. 250.

[50] Veli Verkkö, *Homicides and Suicides in Finland and their Dependence on National Character*, Copenhagen, 1951, pp. 87, 142.

[51] See Edward Glover, *The Roots of Crime*, London, 1960, s. 4, esp. pp. 120 ff.; Milton Gurwitz, 'Developments in the Concept of Psychopathic Personality 1900–1950', *Brit. J. Delinq.*, Vol. 2, No. 2, Oct. 1951, pp. 88 ff.; Michael Craft, *Brit. J. Delinq.*, Vol. 2, No. 2, Oct. 1951, pp. 88 ff.; Michael Craft, *Brit. J. Crim.*, Vol. 1, No. 3, pp. 237 ff., both with extensive bibliographies. Craft concludes that three general syndromes emerge from his review of the literature: syndromes due predominantly to brain damage, syndromes which are predominantly affectionless, and syndromes consisting predominantly of emotional immaturity or instability. On Schneider's typology see his classic work *Die psychopathischen Persönlichkeiten*, 9th ed., Vienna, 1950.

[52] Erwin Frey, *Der frühkriminelle Rückfallsverbrecher*, Basel, 1951, pp. 116 ff. On this see *Group Problems*, p. 143.

[53] Edward Glover, *Freud or Jung*, London, 1950, pp. 90 ff.

[54] See, e.g., his *Collected Papers*, Vol. 4, pp. 342 ff.

[55] *Collected Papers*, Vol. 5, pp. 247 ff.

[56] See, e.g., F. Alexander and H. Staub, *The Criminal, The Judge and The Public*, New York, 1931, pp. 145 ff.; Kate Friedländer, *The Psychoanalytical Approach to Juvenile Delinquency*.

[57] David Riesman, Nathan Glazer and Reuel Denney, *The Lonely Crowd*, New Haven, 1950.

[58] Howard Becker, *Through Values to Social Interpretation*, Chapel Hill, 1950, pp. 79 ff.

[59] See Volkart, *op. cit.*, pp. 126, 159.

[60] Kimball Young, *Handbook of Social Psychology*, 2nd ed., London, 1957, pp. 153 ff.

[61] Marshall B. Clinard, *Sociology of Deviant Behavior*, New York, 1957, p. 201; also in *Sociology Today*, New York, 1953, p. 521; Lindesmith and Dunham, 'Some Principles of Criminal Typology', *Soc. Forces*, Vol. 19, March 1941, pp. 307 ff.

[62] See literature cited in note 47.

[63] This is also stressed by Mezger in *Kriminalbiologische Gegenwartsfragen* (cited at note 47), p. 4.

[64] Joachim Hellmer, *Mschr. Kriminol. Strafrechtsreform*, Vol. 43, Nov. 1960, pp. 136 ff.; R. S. Taylor, 'The Habitual Criminal', *Brit. J. Crim.*, Vol. 1, No. 1, July 1960, pp. 21 ff.

[65] Richard L. Jenkins in Reckless, *Etiology of Delinquent and Criminal Behavior*, pp. 144 ff. See also Jenkins and Hewitt, *Amer. J. Orthopsychiat.*, Vol. 14, 1944, pp. 84-9.

[66] John Bowlby, 'Forty-four Juvenile Thieves: their Characters and Home-Life', *Int. J. Psycho-Anal.*, Vol. 25, Parts 1-4, 1944, pp. 6 ff.

[67] John Rich, 'Types of Stealing', *The Lancet*, 21.4.1956, pp. 496 ff.

[68] D. H. Stott, *Delinquency and Human Nature*, Dunfermline, 1950, esp. pp. 328 ff.

[69] William Foote Whyte, *Street Corner Society*, 2nd ed., Chicago, 1955.

[70] Carl Frankenstein, 'The Configurational Approach to Causation in the Study of Juvenile Delinquents', *Arch. crim. Psychodyn.*, 1957, pp. 572 ff.

[71] See *Group Problems*, p. 79.

[72] *Unraveling Juvenile Delinquency*, pp. 264, 258.

[73] See, e.g., their *Predicting Delinquency and Crime*, p. 100 ff.

[74] D. A. Ogden, *Brit. J. Delinq.*, Vol. 5, No. 2, Oct. 1954, pp. 99 ff.

[75] A. G. Rose, *op. cit.*, Ch. 7. For a typology of 'uneducable' inmates of a correctional institution in Germany see Walter Piecha, *Die Lebensbewährung der als 'unerziehbar' entlassenen Fürsorgezöglinge*, Göttingen, 1959, pp. 39 ff.

[76] Donald R. Cressey, *Other People's Money*, Glencoe, Ill., 1953, pp. 19 ff.

[77] On this see the *Report of the Royal Commission on Capital Punishment*, Cmd. 8932, 1953-55, pp. 167 ff.; *Group Problems*, pp. 229 ff.; and Marvin E. Wolfgang, *Patterns in Criminal Homicide*, Philadelphia, 1958.

[78] Wolfgang, *op. cit.*, Ch. 10.

[79] *Ibid.*, Parts 2, 3; von Hentig, *The Criminal and his Victim*, New Haven, 1948; Jack P. Gibbs (*op. cit.* at note 31).

[80] T. P. Morris and Louis Blom-Cooper, *A Calendar of Murder*, London, 1964.

[81] Emile Durkheim, *Suicide*, Eng. trans. ed. by George Simpson, London, 1952, pp. 146-7.

[82] T. C. N. Gibbens, *Thefts from Departmental Stores*, General Report to Fourth International Congress of Criminology, The Hague, 1960, and Gibbens and Prince, *Shoplifting*, London, 1962.

[83] Clarence Schrag, 'A Preliminary Criminal Typology', *Pacific Sociol. Rev.*, Vol. 4, No. 1, Spring 1961, with many references to literature. The same issue contains two other papers on typology.

[84] Don C. Gibbons and Donald L. Garrity, 'Definition and Analysis of Certain Criminal Types', *Amer. J. crim. Law Criminol. Police Sci.*, Vol. 53, No. 1, March

1962, pp. 27–35, and the criticism by Julian B. Roebuck, in the same Journal Vol. 54, No. 4, Dec. 1963, pp. 476–8.

[85] Leon Radzinowicz, *In Search of Criminology*, London, 1961, p. 38.

CHAPTER 9

[1] The general literature on social experiments is fairly comprehensive. The following books are of special importance: Ernest Greenwood, *Experimental Sociology*, New York, 1945, with excellent bibliography; Arnold M. Rose (*op. cit.* above at Ch. 3, note 16), Chs. 14, 16; F. Stuart Chapin, *Experimental Designs in Sociological Reseach*, 2nd ed., New York, 1956; John Madge (*op. cit.* above at Ch. 3, note 19), Ch. 5; Murphy, Gardner, Newcomb, *Experimental Psychology*; Selltiz *et al.* (*op. cit.* above at Ch. 3, note 7), pp. 94 ff.; Gee (*op. cit.* at Ch. 3, note 46), Ch. 11; *Handbook of Research Methods in Child Development*, ed. by Paul H. Mussen, New York–London, 1960; George A. Lundberg, *Social Research*, 2nd ed., New York, 1942, pp. 54 ff. On experiments in general: R. A. Fisher, *The Design of Experiments*, 4th ed., Edinburgh, 1947.

[2] Karl R. Popper, *The Poverty of Historicism*, London, 1957, p. 86.

[3] On natural experiments see Greenwood, *op. cit.*, pp. 10, 25 and *passim*; Selltiz *et al.*, *op. cit.*, p. 92; Madge, *op. cit.*, p. 279 (on Moreno).

[4] Greenwood, *op. cit.*, pp. 22 ff.

[5] Selltiz *et al.*, *op. cit.*, p. 20; *Handbook of Research Methods*, p. 140.

[6] Sir Charles Goodeve, *Proc. First Int. Conf. Operat. Res.*, Oxford, 1957, Engl. Univ. Press Ltd., London, pp. 13 ff.

[7] O. L. Zangwill in *The New Outline of Modern Knowledge*, ed. by Alan Pryce-Jones, London, 1956, pp. 182–3.

[8] The best survey is given in Murphy and Newcomb, *op. cit.*

[9] See *The Times* of 26.4, 7.6, and 16.6.1955.

[10] On the position in psychiatry and epidemiology see Reid (*op. cit.* at Ch. 4, note 7), p. 14. See also A. V. Hill, *The Ethical Dilemma of Science*, Oxford, 1960, pp. 27 ff.

[11] Popper, *op. cit.*, p. 93.

[12] *Ibid.*, p. 96.

[13] See W. I. B. Beveridge, *The Art of Scientific Investigation*, London, 1950, p. 17. The whole of Ch. 2, on 'Experimentation', is worth studying.

[14] *Ibid.*, p. 18.

[15] See already my *Group Problems in Crime and Punishment*, p. 128. Norval Morris and Cynthia Turner, 'The Lawyer and Criminological Research', *Virginian Law Review*, Vol. 44, No. 2, 1958, pp. 178 ff., are strongly in favour of judicial experiments as 'a heroic measure to bring knowledge into the chaos of our correctional methods'.

[16] R. A. Fisher, *The Design of Experiments*.

[17] W. Norwood East, *The Adolescent Criminal*, London, 1942, pp. 6–7.

[18] Edwin Powers and Helen Witmer, *An Experiment in the Prevention of Delinquency: The Cambridge-Somerville Youth Study*, New York, 1951.

[19] H. Ashley Weeks *et al.*, *Youthful Offenders at Highfields*, Ann Arbor, 1958; Lloyd McCorkle *et al.*, *The Highfields Story*, New York, 1958. See the review of these two books by T. P. Morris, *Brit. J. Crim.*, Vol. I, No. 1, July 1960, pp. 80 ff., and briefly my *Group Problems*, pp. 217–19.

[20] *Group Problems*, pp. 146 ff.

[21] Weeks *et al.*, *op. cit.*, p. 140.

[22] Beveridge, *op. cit.*, p. 19.

[23] See also Morris, *loc. cit.*, p. 81.
[24] *Group Problems*, p. 219; *Brit. J. Delinq.*, Vol. 5, pp. 67–8.
[25] Harry Manuel Shulman, 'Delinquency Treatment in the Controlled Activity Group', *Amer. Sociol. Rev.*, Vol. 10, 1945, pp. 405 ff.
[26] Brian Kay, *Brit. J. Delinq.*, Vol. 4, No. 4, April 1954, pp. 245 ff.
[27] See *Report of Royal Commission on Capital Punishment*, 1953, pp. 365 ff.
[28] Mannheim and Wilkins, *op. cit.*, pp. 111–12, 122.
[29] Greenwood, *op. cit.*, *passim*, esp. Chs. 4 and 8.
[30] *Ibid.*, pp. 97 ff., 126 ff.
[31] *Ibid.*, p. 135.
[32] See, e.g., Howard Becker, *Through Values to Social Interpretation*, pp. 102 ff.
[33] 'Even in the second half of the twentieth century, the statistical basis of major legislation can be extraordinarily primitive', wrote *The Times* on 22.12.1960.
[34] Wolfgang Friedmann, *Legal Theory*, 4th ed., 1960.
[35] Thomas A. Cowan, 'Experience and Experiment', *Philosophy and Science*, Vol. 26, No. 2, April 1959, pp. 77 ff.; *Archiv für Rechts- und Sozialphilosophie*, Vol. 44, No. 4, 1958, pp. 465 ff.
[36] Frederick K. Beutel, *Some Potentialities of Experimental Jurisprudence as a new Branch of Social Science*, Lincoln, Nebraska, 1957.
[37] See for a recent example the *Massachusetts Report of the Special Commission, established for the Purpose of Investigating and Studying the Abolition of Death Penalty in Capital Cases*, Boston, No. 2575, 30.12.1958.

CHAPTER 10

[1] The first part of this chapter is particularly indebted to John C. Spencer's report on the Bristol Social Project, the first volume of which has now been published under the title *Stress and Release in an Urban Estate. A Study in Action Research*, London, 1964. In addition, the following may be consulted: Philip M. Morse and George E. Kimball, *Methods of Operations Research*, New York–London, 1951; *Proc. Second Int. Conf. Operat. Res.*, 1960, ed. by J. Banbury and J. Maitland, London, 1961; Arnold M. Rose, *Theory and Method in the Social Sciences*, Ch. 8; Selltiz *et al.*, *op. cit.*, Ch. 13; John Madge, *op. cit.*, pp. 46 ff., 136; John B. Mays, *On the Threshold of Delinquency*, Liverpool, 1959, esp. pp. 22 ff.
[2] Hornell Hart, *Amer. Soc. Rev.*, Vol. 18, 1953, pp. 612 ff., lists four definitions of 'operational', of which only one is 'action' research. According to John C. McKinney in *Modern Sociological Theory*, ed. by Howard Becker and Alvin Boskoff, New York, 1957, p. 207, the doctrine of 'operationalism' was established in physics by Bridgeman in 1927 and taken over by some of the 'more pragmatically inclined' sociologists, such as Lundberg, in the thirties. It means that concepts are nothing more than sets of operations, e.g. 'intelligence is what intelligence tests test', which would imply that there are as many kinds of intelligence as tests. The operational definition of justice, we might add, is 'what is done by the courts in their administration of the law' which is in fact the view of the legal pragmatists. As McKinney writes, this would make any systematic theory impossible. In the following text the term 'operational' is not used in this purely pragmatic sense. A less extreme definition is also given by P. M. S. Blackett who writes (*Operat. Res. Quart.*, Vol. 1, No. 1, March 1950, p. 3): 'the element of relative novelty lies . . . in the comparative freedom of the investigators to seek out their own problems and in the direct relation of the work to the possibilities of executive action'. He also quotes the following definition: 'A scientific method for providing executives with a quantitative basis for decisions'.

[3] Pitirim A. Sorokin, *Facts and Foibles in Modern Sociology and Related Sciences*, Chicago, 1956, Ch. 3, 'The Illusion of Operationalism'.

[4] Ferris F. Laune, 'Predicting Criminality', *Northw. Univ. Stud. Soc. Sci.*, No. 1, Chicago, 1936.

[5] Michael Argyle, *The Scientific Study of Social Behaviour*, London, 1957, p. 13, is for this reason perhaps unduly critical of action research.

[6] Rose, *op. cit.*, p. 169, seems to regard the two methods as identical.

[7] E.g. Morse and Kimball, *op. cit.*, p. 1.

[8] William Foote Whyte, *Street Corner Society*, 2nd ed., Chicago, 1955, pp. 309 ff., 325, 335-6.

[9] *Preventing Crime*. A Symposium ed. by Sheldon and Eleanor Glueck, New York-London, 1936. See, e.g., p. 53 on the research connected with one of these projects.

[10] *The Problem of Delinquency*, ed. by Sheldon Glueck, Boston, 1959, esp. §§ 174-86.

[11] 'Prevention of Juvenile Delinquency', *Ann. Amer. Acad. Polit. Soc. Sci.*, Vol. 322, March 1960. See, e.g., the description of the research for the Boston Delinquency Project by Walter N. Miller, pp. 99 ff., and the contribution by Eva Rosenfeld, pp. 136 ff.

[12] Powers and Witmer (*op. cit.* at Ch. 9, note 18), pp. 99, 154, and Chs. 8, 9, 23.

[13] *Ibid.*, pp. 106 ff., 118, 147 ff.

[14] The literature on the Chicago Area Project will be quoted at Chapter 23, note 1.

[15] See the excellent assessment of the Project by one closely connected with it: Solomon Kobrin, 'The Chicago Area Project—A 25-year Assessment', *Ann. Amer. Acad.* (see note 11), pp. 19 ff.

[16] As Taft writes, the Project was 'an experiment to test the soundness of principles derived from the research which preceded it' and it was also 'a continuation of that research', Donald R. Taft, *Criminology*, 3rd ed., New York, 1956, p. 716.

[17] Kobrin, *op. cit.*, p. 25.

[18] Clifford R. Shaw and Jesse A. Jacobs, quoted by Walter Reckless, *The Crime Problem*, 2nd ed., New York, 1955, p. 69.

[19] See, e.g., M. L. Turner and J. C. Spencer in *Spontaneous Youth Groups*, ed. by P. H. K. Kuenstler, London, 1955, pp. 52 ff.

[20] M. L. Turner, *Ship without Sails*, London, 1953.

[21] *Op. cit.*, p. 131.

[22] John B. Mays, *On the Threshold of Delinquency*, Liverpool, 1959. See also the Review by Herschel Prins, *Brit. J. Crim.*, Vol. 1, No. 1, July 1960, p. 84.

[23] *Op. cit.*, p. 9.

[24] *Op. cit.*, p. 29.

[25] John C. Spencer *et al.* (*op. cit.* at note 1).

[26] Spencer, *op. cit.*, p. 3.

[27] For similar reasons the Cambridge-Somerville Study had to include non pre-delinquent children in its programme (see Ch. 9 under III).

[28] John C. McKinney in *Modern Sociological Theory*, p. 185. Other useful works on sociological methods, in addition to those by Merton, Selltiz *et al.*, and Madge, Rose, Sorokin, Gee, and Greenwood, are Stuart A. Rice (ed.), *Methods in Social Science*, New York, 1931; George A. Lundberg, *Social Research*, 2nd ed., London-New York-Toronto, 1942; R. M. MacIver, *Social Causation*, Boston, 1942; L. L. Bernard, *The Fields and Methods of Sociology*, 2nd ed., New York, 1934 (with a short chapter by Sellin on Criminology); and S. and B. Webb, *Methods of Social Study*, London, 1932. On the use of sociological methods in criminology see my *Group Problems in Crime and Punishment*, Ch. 1, and

my *Deutsche Strafrechtsreform in englisher Sicht*, München–Berlin, 1960, pp. 128 ff.

[29] See *Criminal Justice and Social Reconstruction*, Chs. 6, 7, esp. pp. 103 ff.; *Group Problems*, Ch. 2(i); W. J. H. Sprott, 'Psychology and the Moral Problems of our Time', *Philosophy*, July 1948; J. A. Waites, *Brit. J. Psychol.* (Gen. Sect.), Sept. 1945.

[30] E.g. Madge, *op. cit.*, Ch. 4; Selltiz, *op. cit.*, Ch. 7 and App. C.

[31] *Group Problems*, p. 10.

[32] Donald Clemmer, *The Prison Community*, Boston, 1940, p. 322, which also contains many valuable remarks on interviewing in criminological research.

[33] Donald R. Cressey, *Other People's Money*, Glencoe, Ill., 1953, pp. 23 ff.

[34] G. W. Lynch, 'An Estimate of the Extent of Larceny in Industry', unpublished London M.Sc.(Econ.) thesis, 1954.

[35] E.g. Selltiz, *op. cit.*, Ch. 6; Madge, *op. cit.*, p. 130.

[36] Russell L. Ackoff, *The Design of Social Research*, Chicago, 1953, p. 292.

[37] See note 8 above.

[38] *Within Prison Walls*, New York, 1914.

[39] Gresham M. Sykes, *The Society of Captives*, Princeton, 1958, App. A; Terence and Pauline Morris, *Pentonville*, London, 1963.

[40] Donald P. Wilson, *My Six Convicts*, New York, 1951.

[41] J. Douglas Grant, *Brit. J. Delinq.*, Vol. 7, No. 4, April 1957, pp. 301 ff.

[42] Nathan Leopold (*op. cit.* at Ch. 8, note 28).

[43] John C. Spencer, *Crime and the Services*, London, 1954; Norval Morris, *The Habitual Criminal*, London, 1951.

[44] John James, *Brit. J. Delinq.*, Vol. 5, No. 4, April 1955, pp. 269 ff.

[45] 'The Social Background of Delinquency', University of Nottingham, Rockefeller research 1952–4, Director: Prof. W. J. H. Sprott (unpublished, privately circulated). See note in *Brit. J. Delinq.*, Vol. 5, April 1955, p. 307, and T. P. Morris, *The Criminal Area*, London, 1957, p. 104.

[46] Ludwig Moreno, *Who shall survive?*, Nerv. Ment. Dis. Monogr., Ser., No. 58, Washington, 1954.

[47] E. F. Piercy, 'Boys' Clubs and their Social Patterns', *Brit. J. Delinq.*, Vol. 2, No. 3, 1952, pp. 229 ff.; Gordon Rose, *Sociometric Analysis and Observation in a Borstal Institution, ib.*, Vol. 6, No. 4, April 1956, pp. 285 ff.; the same, *ib.*, Vol. 6, No. 3, Jan. 1956, pp. 202 ff.; J. Croft and T. Grygier, 'Sociometric Study of Truancy and Delinquency in a Secondary School', *Human Relations*, Vol. 9, 1956, pp. 439–66.

[48] Whyte (*op. cit.* at note 8), p. 300.

[49] Tadeusz Grygier, *Oppression. A Study in Social and Criminal Psychology*, London, 1954, pp. 87 ff.

[50] Spencer (*op. cit.* at note 43), pp. 274 ff.

[51] Terence and Pauline Morris, *Pentonville*, p. 9, and App. A.

## PRELIMINARY OBSERVATIONS TO PART THREE

[1] M. F. Ashley Montagu, 'The Biologist looks at Crime', *Ann. Amer. Acad. Polit. Soc. Sci.*, Vol. 217, Sept. 1941, p. 46. See also Marshall B. Clinard, *Sociology of Deviant Behaviour*, New York, 1957, p. 32.

[2] Quoted from S. and E. Glueck, *Physique and Delinquency*, New York, 1956, p. 16. On the inter-relationships between psychiatric and social factors see now also T. C. N. Gibbens, *Psychiatric Studies of Borstal Lads*, Inst. Psychiat.

Maudsley Mono. No. 11, London, 1963. This important work should also be consulted in connection with the subjects of Chapters 11-15.

CHAPTER 11

[1] W. A. Bonger, *An Introduction to Criminology*, transl. from the Dutch by Emil van Loo, London, 1936, pp. 106 ff. See also the revised Dutch ed. by G. Th. Kempe, Haarlem, 1954, pp. 135 ff.

[2] Esp. Ernst Roesner in *Handwörterbuch der Kriminologie*, Berlin-Leipzig, 1933, pp. 688 ff., with full bibliography; Joseph Cohen, 'The Geography of Crime', *Ann. Amer. Acad. Polit. Soc. Sci.*, Vol. 217, Sept. 1941, pp. 29 ff.; Barnes and Teeters, *New Horizons in Criminology*, New York, 1943, pp. 132 ff.; H. C. Brearley, *Homicide in the United States*, Chapel Hill, 1932, Ch. 9; Marvin E. Wolfgang, *Patterns in Criminal Homicide*, Philadelphia, 1958, Ch. 6; Edwin Dexter, *Weather Influences*, New York, 1904; Franz Exner, *Kriminologie*, 3rd ed., Berlin-Göttingen-Heidelberg, 1949, pp. 56 ff.; J. M. van Bemmelen, *Criminologie*, 3rd ed., Zwolle, 1952, pp. 101 ff.; Howard Jones, *Crime and the Penal System*, London, 1956, pp. 112-13.

[3] Quoted by Cohen, *op. cit.*, p. 31.

[4] See, e.g., Wolfgang, *op. cit.*, p. 98, and Cohen, *op. cit.*, p. 31, on Dexter.

[5] Introduction, pp. 92 ff.

[6] Cyril Burt, *The Young Delinquent*, 4th ed., 1944, pp. 161 ff.

[7] See the full account by Brearley, *op. cit.*, pp. 168 ff.

[8] *Ibid.*, p. 177.

[9] William F. Ogburn and Meyer F. Nimkoff, *A Handbook of Sociology*, 4th ed., London, 1960, pp. 73-4.

[10] Useful comparative material for the general population is contained in W. J. Martin, *The Physique of Young Adult Males*, H.M.S.O., 1949 (Medical Research Council Memorandum, No. 20).

[11] See Hermann Mannheim, *Juvenile Delinquency in an English Middletown*, London, 1948, pp. 50, 110.

[12] Teeters and Reinemann, *The Challenge of Delinquency*, New York, 1950, p. 268.

[13] For the details see Lionel Fox, *The English Prison and Borstal Systems*, London, 1952, Ch. 14.

[14] *Annual Report for 1959*, H.M.S.O., London, 1960, p. 101.

[15] British Association for the Advancement of Science, *Annual Report 1833*, pp. 253 ff. See also A. M. Carr-Saunders, Hermann Mannheim, E. C. Rhodes, *Young Offenders*, Cambridge, 1944, pp. 8-9.

[16] W. D. Morrison, *Juvenile Offenders*, London, 1895, p. 102.

[17] Cyril Burt, *op. cit.*, Ch. 6.

[18] *L.C.C. School Medical Officer*, Vol. 3, Part 2, 1930, published May 1931, pp. 76 ff. The investigation was carried out by Dr. Verner Wiley. See also *Young Offenders*, pp. 23-5, for further details.

[19] M. D. Eilenberg, *Brit. J. Crim.*, Vol. 2, No. 2, Oct. 1961, pp. 116-18.

[20] T. Ferguson, *The Young Delinquent in his Social Setting*, Oxford, 1952, Ch. 3.

[21] *Ibid.*, p. 116.

[22] Hermann Mannheim, *Social Aspects of Crime in England between the Wars*, 1940, pp. 250 ff., 262.

[23] Hermann Mannheim and Leslie T. Wilkins, *Prediction Methods in relation to Borstal Training*, p. 209.

390

[24] Norwood East *et al.*, *The Adolescent Criminal*, London, 1942, pp. 175 ff., 186 ff.; also *This Society and the Individual*, Ch. 6, pp. 87 ff.

[25] Charles Goring, *The English Convict*, H.M.S.O., London, 1913, pp. 200-1.

[26] Norval Morris, *The Habitual Criminal*, London, 1951, pp. 310, 354.

[27] Terence and Pauline Morris, *Pentonville*, Ch. 9; D. J. West, *The Habitual Prisoner*, p. 51.

[28] S. and E. Glueck, *Unraveling Juvenile Delinquency*, pp. 55-6, and Ch. 14.

[29] See Ch. 6, note 49 above.

[30] *Juvenile Delinquents Grown Up*, pp. 109, 179, 182, 194.

[31] William Healy, *Mental Conflicts and Misconduct*, Boston, 1936, p. 321; William and Joan McCord with Irving Kenneth Zola, *Origins of Crime*, New York, 1959, p. 66; Powers and Witmer (*op. cit.* at Ch. 9, note 18), pp. 45 ff.

[32] J. D. W. Pearce, *Juvenile Delinquency*, London, 1952, pp. 34 ff.

[33] See also the case history in Maud A. Merrill, *Problems of Child Delinquency*, London, 1947, p. 200.

## CHAPTER 12

[1] On the history of phrenology see Arthur E. Fink, *Causes of Crime*, Philadelphia, 1938, Ch. 1; also Bonger, *An Introduction to Criminology* (cited at Ch. 11, note 1), pp. 44-6; W. Norwood East, *Medical Aspects of Crime*, London, 1936, Ch. 7; George B. Vold, *Theoretical Criminology*, New York, 1958, pp. 44-9. Fink is mainly concerned with the influence on phrenology on American criminology. The following text is largely based upon his work.

[2] W. Norwood East, *Society and the Criminal*, H.M.S.O., London, 1949, p. 70.

[3] Fink, *op. cit.*, pp. 152 ff.; Vold, *op. cit.*

[4] Bonger, *op. cit.*, p. 78; Wolfgang in *Pioneers in Criminology*, pp. 180-1.

[5] The literature on Lombroso and his school is immense. Only the following references can here be given: Marvin A. Wolfgang in *Pioneers in Crimonology*, ed. by Hermann Mannheim, London, 1960, Ch. 9 (with extensive bibliog.), to which the following text is particularly indebted; Hermann Mannheim, *Group Problems in Crime and Punishment*, Ch. 4: 'Lombroso and his Place in Modern Criminology'; W. Norwood East, *op. cit.*, Ch. 6; M. F. Ashley Montagu, 'The Biologist looks at Crime', *Ann. Amer. Acad. Polit. Soc. Sci.*, Vol. 217, Sept. 1941, pp. 46 ff.; Vold (*op. cit.* at note 1); A. E. Hooton, *The American Criminal*, Cambridge, Mass., 1939; Gustav Aschaffenburg, *Crime and its Repression*, Amer. ed., Boston, 1913; the same in *Handwörterbuch der Kriminologie*, Berlin, 1933, Vol. 1, pp. 825 ff.; Edmund Mezger, *Kriminalpolitik*, 1st ed., Stuttgart, 1934.

[6] There are differences of opinion regarding date and place of Lombroso's birth; see Wolfgang, *op. cit.*, p. 169, fn. 2. Vold, p. 28, gives Venice as his place of birth.

[7] Many details on the various scientific influences which helped to shape Lombroso's basic ideas are given by Wolfgang, *op. cit.*, pp. 177 ff. Hooton, *op. cit.*, p. 17, disputes the widely held view that Lombroso's theories had something in common with those of the phrenologists.

[8] See the details given by Wolfgang, *op. cit.*, pp. 171 ff.

[9] Cesare Lombroso, *Crime: Its Causes and Remedies*, Boston, 1913.

[10] Cesare Lombroso and Guglielmo Ferrero, *The Female Offender*, London, 1895.

[11] Cesare Lombroso, *After Death—What?* Boston, 1909.

[12] Gina Lombroso-Ferrero, *Cesare Lombroso*, 2nd ed., Bologna, 1921.

[13] Austin L. Porterfield, *Creative Factors in Scientific Research*, Durham,

N.C., 1941, esp. Parts 2 and 3, has made a special study of this problem. Also Sorokin, *Facts and Foibles*.

[14] *Handwörterbuch der Kriminologie*, Vol. 1, p. 834.

[15] Havelock Ellis, *The Criminal*, London-New York, 1st ed., 1890, 4th ed. 1910, stresses that Lombroso himself did not regard the 'born criminal' as a real type, but 'emphatically asserted that all that can be asserted is a greater frequency of anomalies' (4th ed., p. 58).

[16] Henry Maudsley, *Insanity and Crime*, London, 1964, p. 29.

[17] See Peter Scott in *Pioneers in Criminology*, Ch. 8.

[18] Morris Ginsberg, *Reason and Unreason in Society*, London, 1947, p. 31. Also Karl Popper, *The Poverty of Historicism*, pp. 127, fn. 1, 108, fn. 1.

[19] Ginsberg, *Evolution and Progress*, London, 1961, p. 245.

[20] Bertrand Russell, *Human Knowledge*, London, 1948, pp. 45, 48.

[21] Hooton, *op. cit.*, p. 11.

[22] See Karl Murchison, *Criminal Intelligence*, Worcester, Mass., 1926, p. 28. Against the lamarckian view of such inheritance see Julian Huxley, *Evolution*, London, 1942, pp. 457 ff., and on atavism and degeneration, pp. 20, 567.

[23] Wolfgang, *op. cit.*, p. 194, quoting Kurella, p. 136.

[24] *Ibid.*, p. 202.

[25] Hooton, *op. cit.*, p. 13.

[26] *Ibid.*, p. 15.

[27] On Lacassagne and Manouvrier see Bonger, *Introduction*, pp. 78 ff.

[28] Gabriel Tarde, *La criminalité comparée*, 1st ed. Paris, 1886, 2nd ed., 1890, Ch. 1.

[29] *Op. cit.*, pp. 40 ff. See also Walter Lunden in *Pioneers in Criminology*, Ch. 10.

[30] Tarde, *op. cit.*, p. 52.

[31] *Op. cit.*, 2nd ed., p. 49, fn. 1.

[32] On Ferri see Thorsten Sellin, *Pioneers*, Ch. 13; on Garofalo Francis A. Allen, *Pioneers*, Ch. 10. The following text is greatly indebted to these two articles.

[33] *Pioneers*, p. 277.

[34] Published in 1878 in an enlarged form as *La negazione de libero arbitrio e la teórica dell' imputabilita*.

[35] Sellin, *op. cit.*, p. 283.

[36] *Ibid.*, pp. 285-7.

[37] The 3rd ed., the first to bear this title, was published in 1892, the 5th and last after his death in 1929-30. A full American translation of the 4th ed. appeared in 1917 as *Criminal Sociology*, Boston. The English edition of 1896 is greatly abridged.

[38] See *Pioneers*, pp. 21-2.

[39] *Ibid.*, p. 293.

[40] The American edition was published in 1914 in Boston in the Modern Criminal Science Series where also works by Lombroso and Ferri appeared (see *Pioneers*, p. ix).

[41] Allen, *Pioneers*, p. 268.

[42] Gabriel Tarde, *Penal Philosophy*, Eng. trans. Boston, 1912, p. 72.

[43] See Morris Ginsberg, *On the Diversity of Morals*, London, 1956, p. 99.

[44] *Reason and Unreason in Society*, London, 1947, p. 320.

[45] See my Introduction to *Pioneers in Criminology*, pp. 9 ff., 14 ff.

[46] See the chapters on Beccaria, Bentham, and Maconochie in *Pioneers*.

[47] Clarence Ray Jeffery in *Pioneers*, Ch. 19.

[48] Enrico Ferri, *The Positive School of Criminology*, 1901, Eng. ed., Chicago, 1908, pp. 9, 23, 96.

[49] For the details see Max Grünhut, *Penal Reform*, Oxford, 1948, pp. 391 ff., and in particular Norval Morris, *The Habitual Criminal*, London, 1951, pp. 201 ff., and *passim*.

[50] See *Pioneers*, pp. 23 ff.

[51] Lombroso, *Crime: Its Causes and Remedies*, pp. 114 ff., and the whole of Ch. 6.

## CHAPTER 13

[1] See my Introduction to *Pioneers in Criminology*, pp. 17-23, and Wolfgang, *op. cit.*

[2] On U.S.A. see Arthur E. Fink, *op. cit.*, Chs. 5, 6.

[3] See note 15 to Ch. 12.

[4] On Prichard and his successors see Fink, *op. cit.*, Ch. 3.

[5] See Peter Scott in *Pioneers in Criminology*, Ch. 8, and Maurice Parmelee's Introduction to the English version of Lombroso's *Crime: Its Causes and Remedies*, p. xxi.

[6] H.M.S.O., London, 1913. There exists an abridged edition of 1919. On Goring see Edwin D. Driver in *Pioneers*, Ch. 17, the critical Summary in Walter C. Reckless, *Criminal Behavior*, New York-London, 1940, pp. 170-3, and the full-scale criticism by Earnest A. Hooton, *The American Criminal*, Cambridge, Mass., 1939, pp. 18-31.

[7] Fink, *op. cit.*, Ch. 7, p. 176.

[8] New York, 1877. On it see Fink, *op. cit.*, Ch. 8; Barnes and Teeters, *New Horizons in Criminology*, 1st ed., New York, 1943, pp. 175-6.

[9] Henry H. Goddard, *The Kallikak Family*, New York, 1912; see Fink, *op. cit.*, p. 220, Barnes-Teeters, *op. cit.*, pp. 176 ff.

[10] Franz Exner, *Kriminologie*, 3rd ed., Hamburg, 1949, p. 114.

[11] *The Young Delinquent*, pp. 49 ff., 602 ff.

[12] W. Norwood East, *op. cit.*, pp. 37 ff.

[13] Sir Norwood East, *Society and the Criminal*, H.M.S.O., London, 1949, p. 85.

[14] From the extensive literature the following may be quoted: Johannes Lange, *Verbrechen als Schicksal*, Leipzig, 1929, Eng. trans. by Charlotte Haldane, as *Crime and Destiny*, New York, 1930, London, 1931; Friedrich Stumpfl, *Die Ursprünge des Verbrechens*, Leipzig, 1936; A. J. Rosanoff and others, *J. crim. Law Criminol.*, Vol. 24, 1934, pp. 923 ff.; H. H. Newman, *Twins and Super-Twins*, London, 1942; the same, *Evolution, Genetics and Eugenics*, Chicago, 1930; Walter C. Reckless, *Criminal Behavior*, pp. 185 ff.; R. S. Woodworth, *Heredity and Environment*, New York, Soc. Sci. Res. Counc., 1941.

[15] On Russian twin research see S. G. Levit in *Character and Personality*, Vol. 3, No. 3, March 1935, pp. 188 ff.

[16] James Shields, *Monozygotic Twins*, London, 1962, has hardly anything of criminological interest.

[17] Exner, *Kriminologie*, 3rd ed., p. 125, thinks this argument can be neither proved nor disproved. Newman, however, in *Twins and Super-Twins*, p. 123, regards this as the only serious criticism of the twin method of studying crime causation; here, he thinks, we encounter a 'lack of control features' in Nature's scientific experiments as we can hardly assume that the social environment of ordinary twins will be as similar as that of identical ones. Cases have been reported where identical twins were made to share automatically all the punishments at school incurred by either of them because the masters could not distinguish them; see Beveridge, *Changes in Family Life*, 1932, p. 59.

[18] See H. H. Newman, *Evolution, Genetics and Eugenics*, p. 535, who even

speaks of 'reasoning in a vicious circle with a vengeance', i.e. if two twins correspond to our preconceived ideas of identical twins we classify them as such. In his *Twins and Super-Twins*, Ch. 7, however, he is confident that safe distinctions can be made.

[19] Lionel Penrose, *Mental Defect*, London, 1933, p. 23. Ernst Kretschmer, *Körperbau und Charakter*, 21st/22nd ed., Hamburg, 1955, pp. 157 ff., quotes cases of identical twins with entirely opposite temperamental personalities.

[20] *Ann. Amer. Acad. Polit. Soc. Sci.*, Vol. 217, Sept. 1941, p. 53.

[21] Stumpfl, *op. cit.*, pp. 21-2.

[22] *Ibid.*, pp. 159-60, 171 ff.

[23] Abstract from a study by F. J. Kallmann *et al.*, in the *Eugenics Review*, Oct. 1950, p. 173.

[24] Quoted from M. Guttmacher, *Sex Offences*, 1951, p. 38.

[25] *New Light on Delinquency*, New Haven, 1936.

[26] Shūfu Yoshimasu, 'The Criminological Significance of the Family in the Light of the Study of Criminal Twins', *Acta Criminologiae et Medicinae legalis Japonica*, Vol 27, No. 4, 1961, pp. 117-41.

[27] Lorna Whelan, *Brit. J. Delinq.*, Vol. 2, No. 2, Oct. 1951, pp. 130 ff.

[28] Martin Turnell, *The Novel in France*, London, 1950, p. 146.

[29] Julian Huxley, *The Uniqueness of Man*, London, 1931, p. 42.

[30] Exner, *op. cit.*, p. 133.

[31] Olof Kinberg, revised French ed. of the English original, Copenhagen, 1935, under the title *Les Problèmes fondamentaux de la Criminologie*, Paris, 1960, p. 239.

[32] Max Schlapp and E. H. Smith, *The New Criminology*, New York, 1928. For other discussions of the effect of the glands on crime see Montagu, *op. cit.*, p. 55, Reckless, *op. cit.*, pp. 197 ff., and on endocrinology in general R. G. Hoskins, *The Tides of Life*, London, 1933, and his *Endocrinology*, London, 1941; V. H. Mottram, *The Physical Basis of Personality*, Harmondsworth, 1944.

[33] Mottram, *op. cit.*, p. 61.

[34] Mottram, *op. cit.*, p. 57; Gordon-Harris-Rees, *Introduction to Psychological Medicine*, London, 1936, p. 197; Hoskins, *The Tides of Life*, p. 165; William Wolf, 'The Role of the Endocrine Glands', *J. clin. Psychopath*, Jan. 1946, p. 540.

[35] See F. L. Golla and S. Hodge, *The Lancet*, 2, 1949, pp. 1006-7; also P. A. H. Baan in *Beiträge zur Sexualforschung*, Vol. 2, Stuttgart, 1952, p. 33; Käte Friedländer, *The Psychoanalytical Approach to Juvenile Delinquency*, London, 1947, p. 155; David Abrahamsōn, *The Psychology of Crime*, New York, 1961, p. 234, recommends the matter for special investigation by a Research Institute.

[36] Eduard Mezger, *Kriminalpolitik auf kriminologischer Grundlage*, 1st ed., Stuttgart, 1934, with comprehensive bibliographical notes.

[37] *Physique and Character*, trans. by Sprott, London, 1936. A detailed analysis of Kretschmer's theory and its practical application has now been given in German by the Spanish lawyer and theologian Carlos Maria de Landecho, S.J., *Körperbau, Charakter und Kriminalität*, Bonn, 1964 (*Kriminologische Untersuchungen*, No. 13, editors H. von Weber and Thomas Würtenberger).

[38] See, e.g., the 21st/22nd ed. of 1955 (cited at note 19).

[39] pp. 237 ff.

[40] pp. 77 ff.

[41] See 21st/22nd ed., p. 31.

[42] *Op. cit.*, pp. 38 ff.

[43] pp. 218 ff.

[44] pp. 163, 179.

[45] See, e.g., H. T. P. Young, *J. ment. Sci.*, May 1937, p. 282.

[46] See my *Group Problems in Crime and Punishment*, pp. 78–80; Mezger, *op. cit.*, pp. 95 ff.

[47] pp. 350 ff.

[48] Mezger, *op. cit.*, p. 103.

[49] On the work of these boards see Mezger, *op. cit.*, pp. 111 ff.; Ernst Seelig, *Kriminologie*, Graz, 1951, pp. 276 ff.

[50] See *Kriminalbiologische Gegenwartsfragen*, No. 2, 1955; No. 4, 1960, Stuttgart, with several important contributions.

[51] Such criticisms were expressed early by Rudolf Sieverts, *Mschr. Kriminalpsychologie/Strafrechtsreform*, Vol. 23, 1932, pp. 588 ff. Mezger's reply, *op. cit.*, pp. 128 ff., is hardly convincing.

[52] See note 6 above. A popular edition was simultaneously published under the title *Crime and the Man*, Cambridge, Mass., 1939.

[53] A good summary is given by Richard M. Snodgrasse, *J. crim. Law Criminol. Police Sci.*, Vol. 42, No. 1, May–June 1951, pp. 20 ff. See also my review in the *Law Quart.*, July 1941, Vol. 57, pp. 435 ff. A rather inconclusive attempt to apply Sheldon's somatotypes to a group of hospital patients was made by Leopold Ballak and Robert R. Holt, *Amer. J. Psychiat.*, Vol. 104, No. 11, May 1948, pp. 713 ff.

[54] New York, 1949.

[55] Kretschmer, *op. cit.*, 21st/22nd ed., pp. 19 ff., 242.

[56] On this see the summary by Snodgrasse (cited at note 53), pp. 29 ff.

[57] Edwin H. Sutherland, *Amer. Sociol. Rev.*, Vol. 18, 1951, pp. 142 ff., reproduced in *The Sutherland Papers*, 1956, pp. 279 ff.

[58] Sheldon, *Varieties of Delinquent Youth*, p. 752. F. D. Klingender, 'A Victorian Rogues' Gallery', in *Pilot Papers*, ed. by Charles Madge, Vol. 1, No. 1, Jan. 1946, pp. 55 ff., reproduces a large number of photographs taken by Mr. William Garbutt, a former deputy governor of Derby Gaol in the middle of the last century.

[59] *Unraveling*, p. 55, and Ch. 15.

[60] Sheldon and Eleanor Glueck, *Physique and Delinquency*, New York, 1956. See my review in *Int. J. soc. Psychiat.*, Vol. 3, pp. 72–5, from which some of the following text is taken and to which reference may be made.

## CHAPTER 14

[1] On this see Barbara Wootton, *Social Science and Social Pathology*, London, 1959, Ch. 7.

[2] The existing chaos has been described in detail by Michael Hakeem, 'A Critique of the Psychiatric Approach to Crime and Correction', in *Crime and Correction, Law and Contemporary Problems*, Vol. 23, No. 4, Autumn 1958, pp. 650 ff.

[3] May 1957, Cmd. 169, pp. 24–7, 46 ff., where the complicated historical development is described.

[4] *Report of Royal Commission on the Law relating to Mental Illness and Mental Deficiency*, 1954–7, p. 25.

[5] See, e.g., Edward Mapother and Aubrey Lewis, 'Psychological Medicine' in F. W. Price, *Textbook of the Practice of Medicine*, 5th ed., London, 1937, pp. 1798 ff.; also David Stafford-Clark, *Psychiatry Today*, Harmondsworth, 1952, pp. 82 ff. Sir D. K. Henderson and R. D. Gillespie, *A Textbook of Psychiatry*, 8th ed., London, 1960, pp. 20 ff., reproduce the British and American and also their own systems of classification. East and de Hubert, *Psychological Treatment of Crime*, H.M.S.O., 1939, pp. 5–6, use the scheme of the Prison Commission.

[6] On the criminological issues involved see W. Norwood East, *Introduction to Forensic Psychiatry in the Criminal Courts*, London, 1927; the same, *Medical Aspects of Crime*, London, 1939; the same, *Society and the Criminal*, H.M.S.O., London, 1949; Friedrich Leppmann, *Forensische Psychiatrie*, and Hans Gruhle, 'Geisteskranke Verbrecher und verbrecherische Geisteskranke', *Handwörterbuch der Kriminologie*, Vol. 1, 1932, pp. 456 ff., 559 ff.

[7] Angus MacNiven in *Mental Abnormality and Crime*, London, 1944, pp. 40 ff.

[8] Leppmann, *op. cit.*, p. 462, and the case briefly reported in my *Group Problems*, pp. 293-4.

[9] Henderson-Gillespie, *op. cit.*, p. 527.

[10] *Mschr. Kriminalbiologie*, 1939, pp. 89 ff.

[11] See Cyril Burt, *The Young Delinquent*, pp. 269 ff.; Mapother and Lewis, *op. cit.*, pp. 1826 ff.; F. C. Shrubsall, *J. med. Psychol.*, Vol. 7, 1927, pp. 210 ff.; Lionel Penrose, *Mental Defect*, pp. 116, 177.

[12] See the case described by East and de Hubert (*op. cit.* at note 5), p. 118, No. 60.

[13] Mapother and Lewis, *op. cit.*, pp. 1819 ff.; East, *Introduction to Forensic Psychiatry*, pp. 217 ff.

[14] East, *Crime, Senescence and Senility*, in *Society and the Criminal*, p. 65.

[15] Mapother and Lewis, *op. cit.*, p. 1820.

[16] *The Times*, 3.9.1938.

[17] J. C. M. Matheson, *Medico-legal Rev.*, Vol. 9, Part 3, July 1941; W. S. Craig and Beaton, *Psychological Medicine*, 4th ed., 1926, p. 232.

[18] See D. Seaborne Davies in *The Modern Approach to Criminal Law*, London, 1945, Ch. 17.

[19] Of the very extensive literature the following may be quoted: A. M. Lorentz de Haas, 'Epilepsy and Criminality', *Brit. J. Crim.*, Vol. 3, No. 3, Jan. 1963, pp. 248-56; Cyril Burt, *op. cit.*, pp. 269 ff.; MacNiven (*op. cit.* at note 7), p. 46 ff.; East, *Introduction*, pp. 282, 299; Tylor Fox in R. G. Gordon (ed.), *Survey of Child Psychiatry*, London, 1939, pp. 10, 48 ff.; D. K. Henderson, *Psychopathic States*, New York, 1939, pp. 71 ff.; Matheson and Hill, *Medico-legal Rev.*, Oct.-Dec. 1943, pp. 173 ff.

[20] Wolfgang, in *Pioneers*, pp. 188-9.

[21] See, e.g., East, *The Adolescent Criminal*, pp. 229 ff.; MacNiven, *op. cit.*, p. 48; Burt, *op. cit.*, pp. 268-9, who found only 1 per cent of his cases suffering from grand mal and another 3 per cent as being suspected epileptics. In 1946, out of a total prison population of nearly 15,000, only 62 were considered by the medical officers to be undoubted epileptics; see *Report of Prison Commissioners for 1946*, pp. 66-7, where post-war changes in the treatment of epileptic prisoners are also described. Gibbens and Prince, *Shoplifting*, 1962, p. 64, found only 3 cases of epileptics in their sample, and there was no connection between the offence and a fit.

[22] *Report of 1953*, p. 134, fn. 3; Denis Hill, *Minutes of Evidence*, No. 13, pp. 297 ff.

[23] *Medico-legal Rev.*, 1943, pp. 173 ff.

[24] See esp. de Haas, *op. cit.*, p. 255.

[25] Fox, *op. cit.*, note 19, p. 52.

[26] East, *Introduction*, pp. 281-2; Fox, *op. cit.*, p. 48.

[27] *The Times*, 15.12.1961.

[28] A. Brousseau, 'L'Etat dangereux dans les Epilepsies', in *Le Problème de l'Etat dangereux*, Deuxième Cours International de Criminologie, organisé par la Société Internationale de Criminologie, Paris, 1953, pp. 206 ff.

[29] See Glanville Williams in *Essays in Criminal Science*, ed. by G. O. W.

Mueller, Ch. 12, and in *Criminal Law, General Part*, 2nd ed., 1961, § 156. Also Rupert Cross, *The Listener*, 7.12.1961, p. 967.
[30] On hypoglycaemia see W. Lindesay Neustatter, *Psychological Disorder and Crime*, London, 1953, pp. 169, 192–4; Glanville Williams in *Essays*, p. 352, and *General Part*, § 157; David Abrahamsen, *Psychology of Crime*, p. 219; T. C. N. Gibbens and Joyce Prince, *op. cit.*, p. 77; Brian A. O'Connell, 'Amnesia and Homicide', *Brit. J. Delinq.*, Vol. 10, No. 7, April 1960, pp. 269–70; Sanford J. Fox, 'Delinquency and Biology', *Univ. Miami Law Rev.*, Vol. 16, 1961, pp. 65 ff.
[31] Mapother and Lewis, *op. cit.*, pp. 1833–5; MacNiven, *op. cit.*, p. 43.
[32] Edwin M. Schur, *J. crim. Law Criminol. Police Sci.*, Vol. 51, No. 6, 1961, p. 623. On American law and practice see M. Ploscowe in *Essays in Criminal Science*, ed. by G. O. W. Mueller, London–South Hackensack, N.J., 1961, Ch. 13.
[33] The literature is very large. The following may be mentioned: W. Norwood East, *Society and the Criminal*, Ch. 18; G. M. Scott in *Mental Abnormality and Crime*, Ch. 8; Mapother and Lewis, *op. cit.*, pp. 1830 ff.; on the social aspects Veli Verkkö, *Homicides and Suicides in Finland and their Dependence on National Character*, Copenhagen, 1951, esp. Chs. 8 to 10; Hermann Mannheim, *Social Aspects of Crime in England*, London, 1940, Ch. 6; Exner, *Kriminologie*, 3rd ed., pp. 197 ff.; Donald R. Taft, *Criminology*, 3rd ed., New York, 1956, Ch. 16. On the drink problem in general see Marshall B. Clinard, *The Sociology of Deviant Behavior*, 1957, Ch. 11; Mabel A. Elliott and Francis E. Merrill, *Social Disorganization*, 4th ed., New York, 1961, Ch. 7; Howard Jones, *Alcoholic Addiction*, London, 1943, with extensive bibliog.
[34] See Table XXVII in *Social Aspects*, p. 165.
[35] *Social Problems of Post War Youth*, London, Economic Research Council, Jan. 1956, p. 11.
[36] See my *Social Aspects of Crime*, pp. 169 ff.; *New Survey of London Life and Labour*, Vol. 9, London, 1935, Ch. 9. In 1960, the number of persons prosecuted for drunkenness offences in Liverpool was still more than twice as much as that in Manchester with its larger population.
[37] On this see *Social Aspects*, pp. 175 ff.; Veli Verkkö, *op. cit.*; Marvin E. Wolfgang, *Patterns in Criminal Homicide*, 1958, Ch. 8.
[38] See, e.g., note 6 in *Criminal Statistics for 1959*, p. vii.
[39] A diagram in *Handwörterbuch der Kriminologie*, Vol. 2, 1936, p. 1108, shows the parallel movements of beer consumption and certain crimes of violence in Germany between 1882 and 1931. Such parallel movements have, however, not been found everywhere; for Greece, e.g., the parallelism has been disputed by Gardikas, *Mschr. Kriminologie*, 1935, p. 465.
[40] See the *Observer* of 6.10.1959, referring to a report by the Medical Research Council on the effect of small doses of alcohol on driving.
[41] *The Times* of 7.10.1959.
[42] See an article 'Drinking and Driving' in *The Magistrate* of Nov. 1957, where the view is expressed that 'there is an alcoholic factor in about 40,000 annual road accidents and in 50 per cent of accidents occurring after 10 p.m.'
[43] Marvin E. Wolfgang, *Patterns in Criminal Homicide*, Ch. 8.
[44] See, e.g., Hans v. Hentig, *The Criminal and his Victim*, pp. 156 ff., 412; Margery Fry *et al.*, *Howard J.*, 1938, p. 14; Clifford Shaw, *The Jack-Roller*. Also see below, Ch. 25: Victimology.
[45] M. M. Glatt, *Brit. J. Delinq.*, Vol. 9, No. 2, Oct. 1958, pp. 84 ff.
[46] Veli Verkkö, *op. cit.*, pp. 83, 87 ff.
[47] Burt, *op. cit.*, p. 99. See also the Gluecks, *Unraveling*, pp. 95, 98, 110; Glatt, *op. cit.*, pp. 88 ff.

⁴⁸ Dr. H. T. P. Young, *Brit. J. Inebriety*, Vol. 35, Jan. 1938, pp. 93 ff.

⁴⁹ East, *The Adolescent Criminal*, pp. 55 ff.

⁵⁰ E.g., George Godwin, *Peter Kürten*, London, 1938, p. 26.

⁵¹ Howard Jones in *New Society*, No. 25, 21.3.1963, p. 16.

⁵² See Scott, *op. cit.*, p. 168; East, *Introduction to Forensic Psychiatry*; Mapother and Lewis, *op. cit.*, p. 1830. Also the case reported in *Group Problems*, pp. 293–4.

⁵³ Scott, *op. cit.*, p. 170; Mapother and Lewis, *op. cit.*, p. 1830; East, *op. cit.*, p. 260.

⁵⁴ Mapother and Lewis, *op. cit.*, p. 1869; MacNiven, *op. cit.*, pp. 26 ff.; K. O. Milner, *J. ment. Sci.*, Vol. 95, No. 398, Jan. 1949, pp. 124–32; Henderson and Gillespie, *op. cit.*, Ch. 11; East, *Introduction*, pp. 193 ff.

⁵⁵ See Johannes Lange, *Lehrbuch der Psychiatrie*, 2nd ed., Leipzig, 1936, p. 228.

⁵⁶ Milner, *loc. cit.*; also MacNiven, *op. cit.*, p. 27.

⁵⁷ Illustrative cases are given by East, *op. cit.*

⁵⁸ On morbid jealousy see the valuable discussion, with many case histories, by Michael Shepherd, *J. Ment. Sci.*, Vol. 107, No. 449, July 1961, pp. 687 ff.

⁵⁹ East, *op. cit.*, p. 193; MacNiven, *op. cit.*, p. 34, Henderson–Gillespie, *op. cit.*, p. 345, regard the term paraphrenia as useless.

⁶⁰ Mapother and Lewis, *op. cit.*, pp. 1844 ff.; MacNiven, *op. cit.* pp. 9 ff.; East, *Introduction*, pp. 315 ff.; East and de Hubert, *Report on the Psychological Treatment of Crime* (cited at note 5), p. 30; Stafford-Clark, *op. cit.*, pp. 97 ff.

⁶¹ See the list in East, *op. cit.*, p. 317.

⁶² *The Times* of 11.2.1941.

⁶³ Mapother and Lewis, *op. cit.*, p. 1845; Stafford-Clark, *op. cit.*, p. 98. See also Chapter 26 below, text to note 41.

⁶⁴ *The Times* of 15.12.1937. See also the case described by MacNiven, *op. cit.*, p. 17.

⁶⁵ G. M. Woddis, 'Depression and Crime', *Brit. J. Delinq.*, Vol. 8, No. 2, Oct. 1957, pp. 85–94.

⁶⁶ *Ibid.*, 'Clinical Psychiatry and Crime', *Brit. J. Crim.*, Vol. 4, No. 5, July 1964, pp. 443–60.

⁶⁷ The literature of schizophrenia is immense. See McNiven, *op. cit.*, pp. 18 ff.; Mapother and Lewis, *op. cit.*, pp. 1856 ff.; Stafford-Clark, *op. cit.*, pp. 56, 100 ff.; Lange, *op. cit.*, pp. 164 ff.; Edward S. Stern, 'The Aetiology and Mechanism of Dementia Praecox', *Brit. J. med. Psychol.*, Vol. 19, Part 1, 1941; East, *Introduction*, pp. 164 ff.; H. Warren Dunham, *Amer. Sociol. Rev.*, Vol. 4, 1939, pp. 352 ff.; several articles in *J. ment. Sci.*, Vol. 80, Jan. 1935; Gregory Zilboorg, *Amer. J. Psychiat.*, Vol. 113, No. 6, pp. 519 ff.; R. O. Laing, *Int. J. soc. Psychiat.*, Summer 1964, pp. 184–93; Don D. Jackson (ed.), *The Etiology of Schizophrenia*, New York, 1962.

⁶⁸ In a broadcast of 1958 the late Prof. Alexander Kennedy stated that 'of the 150,000 patients in the mental hospitals of this country at the moment more than three-quarters are schizophrenics of one kind or another'; *The Listener*, 13.2.1958, p. 277: 'The Unsolved Problem of Schizophrenia'.

⁶⁹ On Bleuler see, e.g., Gregory Zilboorg and G. W. Henry, *History of Medical Psychology*, New York, 1941, pp. 501–2.

⁷⁰ Kennedy, too, giving the history of two identical twins, stresses the hereditary side, but also the possibility of treatment in certain cases.

⁷¹ Mapother and Lewis, *op. cit.*, p. 1859.

⁷² *Ibid.*, p. 1861.

⁷³ *The Times* of 7.4 and 8.4.1938.

⁷⁴ *Ibid.*, 5.11.1943.

[75] Brian A. O'Connell, 'Amnesia and Homicide' (cited at note 30 above where other literature on hypoglycaemia is also quoted).

[76] Literature on Drug Addiction: Alfred R. Lindesmith, *Opiate Addiction*, Bloomington, 1952; Edwin M. Schur, *Narcotic Addiction in Britain and America*, Bloomington–London, 1964; the same, 'British Narcotics Policies', *J. crim. Law Criminol. Police Sci.*, Vol. 51, No. 6, March–April 1961, pp. 619–29; Morris Ploscowe, 'Methods of Treatment of Drug Addiction', in *Essays in Criminal Science*, ed. by Gerhard O. W. Mueller, London–South Hackensack, 1961; Fritz A. Freyhan (ed.), *Drug Addiction, A Symposium*, New York, 1963; David Sternberg, 'Synanon House', *J. crim. Law Criminol. Police Sci.*, Vol. 54, No. 4, Dec. 1963; Walter C. Reckless, *The Crime Problem*, 2nd ed., Ch. 16; Herbert A. Bloch and Gilbert Geis, *Man, Crime and Society*, New York, 1962, pp. 236–40, 355–61; Richard A. Cloward and Lloyd E. Ohlin, *Delinquency and Opportunity*, London, 1961, pp. 25–7, 89, 178–86; Isidor Chein *et al.*, *Narcotics, Delinquency and Social Policy*, London, 1964, published in the U.S.A. as *The Road to H.*

[77] Lord Denning's Report, H.M.S.O., London, 1963, pp. 8, 19.

[78] G. E. Voegele and H. J. Dietze, 'Addiction to Gasoline Smelling in Juvenile Delinquents', *Brit. J. Crim.*, Vol. 4, No. 1, July 1963, pp. 43–60.

[79] See, e.g., *The Times*, 31.3., 1.4., 20.4., and 1.5.1964. One London doctor stated at an inquest that in the past year she had treated 70 Canadian drug addicts, some of whom had come to Britain mainly to get drugs, some of which they sold on the black market. On prescription the cost was about 15s. per 100, whereas on the black market it was £1 for four to six pills.

## CHAPTER 15

[1] Aubrey Lewis writes (*The Lancet*, 15.8.1942, pp. 175 ff.): 'The common distinction between neurosis and insanity is at bottom so arbitrary and vague, except for legal and administrative purposes, that many cases fall equally well into either category.'

[2] See, e.g., Stafford-Clark, *Psychiatry Today*, p. 92; Freud, *Collected Papers*, Vol. 2, pp. 250 ff., 277 ff., Vol. 5, pp. 202–3; John Bowlby, *Personality and Mental Illness*, London, 1940, pp. 127 ff.

[3] Edward Glover, *Psycho-analysis*, 2nd ed., London, 1949, p. 130.

[4] *Op. cit.*, p. 173.

[5] Russell Fraser, *The Incidence of Neurosis among Factory Workers*, H.M.S.O., London, 1947, p. 4.

[6] *Op. cit.*, p. 6.

[7] Edward Glover, *The Roots of Crime*, London, 1960, pp. 90–1.

[8] W. F. Roper, *Brit. J. Delinq.*, Vol. I, p. 23.

[9] For other explanations of the 'choice' see Friedländer (*op. cit.* below at note 12), p. 116.

[10] David Abrahamsen, *The Psychology of Crime*, New York, 1960, p. 127.

[11] Healy and Bronner, *New Light on Delinquency*, 1936, p. 194.

[12] See, e.g., Freud, *Collected Papers*, Vol. 5, p. 84, and often; Käte Friedländer, *The Psychoanalytical Approach to Juvenile Delinquency*, London, 1947, pp. 116 ff.

[13] Glover, *Psychoanalysis*, p. 147.

[14] Glover, *The Roots of Crime*, p. 302.

[15] Friedländer, *op. cit.*, p. 223.

[16] Franz Alexander and Hugo Staub, *Der Verbrecher und seine Richter*, Vienna, 1929, pp. 68–9 (Eng. ed., *The Criminal, The Judge, and The Public*, London, 1931); critical E. Glover, *The Roots of Crime*, p. 135.

[17] Some of the cases referred to by Melitta Schmideberg, *Brit. J. Delinq.*, Vol. 4, No. 4, April 1954, pp. 272 ff., are probably neurotics.

[18] Gillespie and MacCalman in *Mental Abnormality and Crime*, pp. 73, 127; Stafford-Clark, *op. cit.*, pp. 93 ff.; Mapother and Lewis, *op. cit.*, pp. 1878-9; Norwood East, *Society and the Criminal*, p. 232; Glover, *Psycho-Analysis*, pp. 47, 149 ff., and *passim*.

[19] Gillespie, *op. cit.*, p. 74; Mapother and Lewis, *op. cit.*, pp. 1870 ff.; Stafford-Clark, *op. cit.*, pp. 113 ff.; Glover, *Psycho-Analysis*, pp. 140 ff.

[20] East in *Mental Abnormality and Crime*, p. 189.

[21] Stafford-Clark, *op. cit.*, 110 ff.; Mapother and Lewis, *op. cit.*, pp. 1879 ff.; Glover, *The Roots of Crime*, pp. 184 ff.; Glover, *Psycho-Analysis*, pp. 157 ff.

[22] Melitta Schmideberg, *Brit. J. Delinq.*, Vol. 7, No. 1, July 1956, pp. 44 ff. Also Glover, *Psycho-Analysis*, p. 254.

[23] Mapother and Lewis, *op. cit.*, p. 1882. Friedländer, *op. cit.*, p. 161, also admits the possibility of a combination of perversion and neurosis.

[24] See David T. Maclay, *Brit. J. Delinq.*, Vol. 3, No. 1, July 1952, p. 34 ff.; Glover, *Roots of Crime*, p. 387.

[25] *Report on The Psychological Treatment of Crime*, 1939, p. 108.

[26] John Bowlby, *Personality and Mental Illness*, p. 4.

[27] T. C. N. Gibbens, *Theft from Department Stores*, General Report to the Fourth International Criminological Congress, The Hague, 1960, and more detailed the same in *Shoplifting* by Gibbens and Joyce Prince, an I.S.T.D. Publication, London, 1962. For a valuable German discussion of the subject see Werner F. J. Krause, 'Ladendiebstahl und Zurechnungsfähigkeit' (Shoplifting and Responsibility), *Mschr. Kriminol. Strafrechtsreform*, Vol. 46, No. 2, April 1963, pp. 49-73. For Belgium Chr. Debuyst, G. Lejour, and A. Racine, *Petits voleurs de grands magasins*, Bruxelles, Centre d'Etude de la délinquance juvenile, 1960. On kleptomania in the case of children, Cyril Burt, *The Young Delinquent*, pp. 585 ff.

[28] Emanuel Miller, *Brit. J. Delinq.*, Vol. 10, No. 3, 1960, p. 170.

[29] *Psycho-Analysis*, pp. 163, 275. Abrahamsen (*op. cit.* above at note 10) regards the kleptomaniac and pyromaniac as prototypes of the obsessive-compulsive offender. W. Lindesay Neustatter, *Psychological Disorder and Crime*, London, 1953, p. 48, doubts whether kleptomania is an obsessive-compulsive state as the clear-cut repetitiveness of thought and action characteristic of it is, he thinks, absent.

[30] Helen Yarnell, *Amer. J. Orthopsychiat.*, April 1940, pp. 272 ff.; Ernst Seelig, *Kriminologie*, pp. 106-7.

[31] J. Clarke, *Brit. J. Crim.*, Vol. 3, No. 2, Oct. 1962, p. 156.

[32] *The Times*, 27.6.1939.

[33] Melitta Schmideberg, 'Pathological Firesetters', *J. crim. Law Criminol. Police Sci.*, Vol. 44, No. 1, May-June, 1953, pp. 30 ff.

[34] Heinrich Többen, *Beiträge zur Psychologie und Psychopathologie der Brandstifter*, Berlin, 1917, pp. 54, 85 ff.

[35] *The Times*, 16.3.1962.

[36] Roper, *Brit. J. Delinq.*, Vol. 1, No. 4, April, 1951, p. 261.

[37] The following is a selection from an enormous literature (most of the publications included here contain full bibliographies): D. K. Henderson, *Psychopathic States*, New York, 1939; H. Cleckley, *The Mask of Sanity*, St. Louis, 1941; *Brit. J. Delinq.*, Vol. 2, No. 2, October 1951 (Special Number): 'Papers on Psychopathy'; Edward Glover, *The Roots of Crime*, Section 4; Norwood East, *Society and The Criminal*, Chs. 8, 14; Michael Craft, *Brit. J. Crim.*, Vol. I, No. 3, Jan. 1961, pp. 237 ff.; Abrahamsen (*op. cit.* above at note 10), pp. 134 ff.; C. M. Franks, *Brit. J. Delinq.*, Vol. 6, No. 3, Jan. 1956, pp. 192 ff.; D. K. Henderson in *Mental*

*Abnormality and Crime*, Ch. 5; Barbara Wootton, *Social Science and Social Pathology*, Ch. 8; William and Joan McCord, *Psychopathy and Delinquency*, New York–London, 1951; *Report of the Royal Commission on Capital Punishment*, 1953, pp. 135 ff.; Peter Scott, *Howard J.*, Vol. 10, No. 1, 1958, pp. 6 ff.; Seymour Parker, *Brit. J. Delinq.*, Vol. 7, No. 4, April 1957, pp. 285–300.

[38] Milton Gurwitz in 'Papers on Psychopathy' (see note 37), p. 88, where a historical survey of developments since 1900 is given.

[39] See, Glover, *op. cit.*, p. 120; Sir David Henderson, *Brit. J. Delinq.*, Vol. 6, No. 1, July 1955, pp. 5 ff.; East, *op. cit.*, p. 128.

[40] Winfred Overholser, in *Pioneers in Criminology*, p. 120.

[41] A short survey of the most important classifications is given by Gurwitz, *loc. cit.*

[42] Schneider's famous book, *Die psychopathischen Persönlichkeiten*, which has gone through many editions, has only very belatedly been translated into English: *Psychopathic Personalities*, London, 1958, which may account for its neglect in this country. On Schneider's typology much of Erwin Frey's *Der Frühkriminelle Rückfallsverbrecher*, Basel, 1951, is based; see esp. pp. 116 ff., also my *Group Problems*, p. 143, Exner, *Kriminologie*, 3rd ed., pp. 185 ff., and Mezger and Leferenz in *Kriminalbiologische Gegenwartsfragen*, Heft 2, Stuttgart, 1955, pp. 6–7, 13 ff.

[43] See Mezger, *loc. cit.*, Exner, *op. cit.*, and Gurwitz, *loc. cit.*, p. 91.

[44] Leferenz, *loc. cit.*, p. 16.

[45] *The Roots of Crime*, pp. 122–3.

[46] Michael Craft (*loc. cit.* above at note 37). See also the description given by witnesses to the Royal Commission in the *Report on Mental Illness and Mental Deficiency*, 1954–7, pp. 52 ff.

[47] C. M. Franks, *Brit. J. Delinq.*, Vol. 6, No. 3., Jan. 1956, p. 192 ff.

[48] Wootton (*op. cit.* at note 37), p. 250.

[49] D. Stafford-Clark, Desmond Pond, and J. W. Lovett Doust, *Brit. J. Delinq.*, Vol. 2, No. 2, 'Papers on Psychopathy', pp. 117 ff.

[50] *loc. cit.*, p. 126.

[51] This part of the investigation has been criticized by William and Joan McCord (*op. cit.* above at note 37), p. 46, on the ground that the selection of prisoners had been made on the basis of Henderson's definition which includes lack of responsiveness to treatment, but they admit that this was not the only important result of the research.

[52] In other studies attention is drawn to the close relationship between the aggressive psychopath and epilepsy, which is also a feature independent of anti-social conduct. See, e.g., the references given by Wheelan, *Brit. J. Delinq.*, Vol. 2, No. 2, p. 141.

[53] See the English translation, Copenhagen, 1958.

[54] Georg Stürup, 'Treatment of Criminal Psychopaths', *Acta psychiat. neurol.*, 1948, pp. 21 ff.

[55] Max Grünhut, *Probation and Mental Treatment*, London, 1963, p. 24.

[56] See Stürup, *loc. cit.* and in *Acta Psychiat. neurol.*, 1946, pp. 781 ff.

[57] See my *Group Problems*, pp. 205 ff., with further references.

[58] See Boslow *et al.*, *Brit. J. Delinq.*, Vol. 10, No. 1, July 1959, pp. 5 ff., and the Editorial, p. 1. See, e.g., the survey of literature in William and Joan McCord, *op. cit.*, Ch. 4.

[59] Johannes Lange, *Kurzgefasstes Lehrbuch der Psychiatrie*, 2nd ed., Leipzig, 1936, p. 210 (my translation).

[60] Craft (*loc. cit.* above at note 37), pp. 243–4

[61] Report 1957, p. 57.

⁶² *The Roots of Crime*, pp. 148 ff.

⁶³ On some of the institutions see T. C. N. Gibbens, 'Papers on Psychopathy' (see note 37), pp. 103 ff.; W. J. Gray, *Howard J.*, Vol. 10, No. 2, 1959, pp. 96 ff.

⁶⁴ H. J. Eysenck, 'Learning Theory and Behaviour Therapy', *J. ment. Sci.*, Vol. 105, No. 438, Jan. 1959, pp. 61 ff. and elsewhere.

⁶⁵ Eysenck, *loc. cit.*, p. 64; Glover, *op. cit.*, p. 161; André Repond in *Die Prophylaxe des Verbrechens*, ed. by Heinrich Meng, Basel, 1948, p. 2. Repond presents a particularly interesting collection of cases of young thieves and swindlers, many of them psychopaths, and shows how, in addition to the usual characteristics of the criminal psychopath, their behaviour had to be explained as a reaction to their domineering fathers and as an inheritance of traits which were also present in the latter, but had there been sublimated and adapted to the requirements of society. See also p. 321.

⁶⁶ T. C. N. Gibbens, D. A. Pond and D. Stafford-Clark, *J. ment. Sci.*, Vol. 105, No. 438, Jan. 1959, pp. 108 ff.

⁶⁷ P. de Berker, *Brit. J. Crim.*, Vol. 1, No. 1, July, 1960, pp. 6 ff.

⁶⁸ In the *Report of the Prison Commissioners for 1956*, p. 166, the proportion of 'inadequate or ineffectual personalities' among preventive detainees is estimated at probably 80 per cent. Roper (*loc. cit.* at note 36), p. 265, regards half the population of his Wakefield prison survey as inadequate. See also the *Report of the Prison Commissioners for 1946*, p. 64.

⁶⁹ Literature on Mental Deficiency and Crime: A. F. Tredgold, *Mental Deficiency*, 5th ed. 1929, 9th ed. 1956, London; L. S. Penrose, *Mental Defect*, London, 1953; Cyril Burt, *The Subnormal Mind*, 3rd ed., London, 1955; the same, *The Young Delinquent*, Ch. 7; E. O. Lewis in *Mental Abnormality and Crime*, Ch. 4; Mary Woodward, *Low Intelligence and Crime*, London, I.S.T.D., 1955 (with bibliog.), also in *Brit. J. Delinq.*, Vol. 5, No. 4, April 1955, pp. 281 ff.; Mapother and Lewis, *op. cit.*, pp. 1839 ff.; Howard Jones, *op. cit.*, pp. 29–33; *Report of the Departmental Committee on Sterilisation*, H.M.S.O., Cmd. 4485, 1934; *Report of Royal Commission on Mental Illness and Mental Deficiency* (see above, note 46); Hilda Weber, 'The Borderline Defective Delinquent', *Brit. J. Delinq.*, Vol. 3, No. 3, Jan. 1953, pp. 173 ff.; B. Marcus, *ibid.*, Vol. 6, No. 2, Sept. 1955, pp. 147 ff.; John E. Tong and G. W. Mackay, *ibid.*, Vol. 9, No. 4, April 1959, pp. 276 ff.; Erik Goldkuhl, *Psychische Insuffizienzzustände bei Oligophrenien leichteren Grades*, Copenhagen, 1938; of the large amount of American literature only the following can here be mentioned: H. H. Goddard, *Feeble-mindedness: its Causes and Consequences*, New York, 1914; Carl Murchison, *Criminal Intelligence*, Worcester, Mass., 1926; S. H. Tulchin, *Intelligence and Crime*, Chicago, 1939; E. H. Sutherland, in *Social Attitudes*, ed. by Kimball Young, New York, 1931, reprinted in *The Sutherland Papers*, Bloomington, 1956, pp. 308 ff.

⁷⁰ Burt, *The Subnormal Mind*, p. 63; Penrose, *op. cit.*, p. 8; on these historical developments, esp. Report of Royal Commission 1957, pp. 44–6.

⁷¹ See Fink, *Causes of Crime*, p. 211.

⁷² Burt, *The Subnormal Mind*, p. 79. See also *Report on Sterilisation*, Ch. 2.

⁷³ Report of the Royal Commission 1957, p. 60.

⁷⁴ See *Pioneers in Criminology*, pp. 119, 149, 187; Burt, *The Young Delinquent*, pp. 35 ff.; *The Subnormal Mind*, p. 68.

⁷⁵ 1st ed., London, 1922, pp. 153 ff.

⁷⁶ See, e.g., Morris Ginsberg, *On the Diversity of Morals*, London, 1956, Ch. 7 and *passim*; *Reason and Unreason in Society*, 1947, pp. 18 ff.; J. C. Flugel, *Man, Morals and Society*, London, 1945, pp. 200–1; Burt, *The Subnormal Mind*, p. 69.

⁷⁷ E. O. Lewis in *Mental Abnormality and Crime*, p. 98.

⁷⁸ *Unraveling Juvenile Delinquency*, p. 14.

[79] Apart from the well-known textbooks of psychology and the books by Burt quoted above, see H. J. Eysenck's *Uses and Abuses of Psychology*, Harmondsworth, 1953, and *Sense and Nonsense in Psychology*, Harmondsworth, 1957; D. R. Price-Williams, *Introductory Psychology*, London, 1958, Ch. 6, and in particular Cyril Burt, *Intelligence and Fertility*, London, 1946, appendix on the Meaning of Intelligence. .

[80] Slightly different, E. O. Lewis, *loc. cit.*, p. 98.

[81] Burt, *The Subnormal Mind*, p. 179.

[82] Mapother and Lewis, *op. cit.*, p. 1842.

[83] Burt, *op. cit.*, p. 119.

[84] On the history in U.S.A. and on other American studies see Arthur E. Fink, *Causes of Crime*, Ch. 10.

[85] Charles Goring, *The English Convict*, London, 1919, pp. 179, 184, 247.

[86] Cmd. 169, p. 310.

[87] Burt, *The Young Delinquent*, p. 300.

[88] East, *The Adolescent Criminal*, p. 234.

[89] Grace W. Pailthorpe, *Studies in the Psychology of Delinquency*, H.M.S.O., London, 1932, p. 16; Woodward, *loc. cit.*

[90] Sutherland (*op. cit.* at note 69), p. 309.

[91] William and Joan McCord, *Origins of Crime*, 1959, pp. 64-6.

[92] Woodward, *Brit. J. Delinq.*, pp. 285-6 (see above, note 69).

[93] *Ibid.*, pp. 287 ff.

[94] Morris Ginsberg, *Studies in Sociology.*, London 1932, p. 148.

[95] Murchison (*op. cit.* at note 69).

[96] Mannheim and Wilkins, *Prediction Methods in relation to Borstal Training*, pp. 81, 98-9.

[97] *The English Convict*, pp. 256-7.

[98] See also Sutherland, *loc. cit.*, p. 324. In the Cambridge Survey of sex offenders, only 3 in 100 of those convicted were mentally defective; *Sexual Offences, English Studies in Criminal Science*, London, 1957, p. 128.

[99] Cyril Burt, *The Young Delinquent*, p. 321.

[100] *Annual Report of the Mental Hospitals Association for 1945.*

[101] K. O. Milner, 'Delinquent Types of Mentally Defective Persons', *J. ment. Sci.*, Vol. 95, No. 401, Oct. 1949, pp. 842 ff.

[102] T. Ferguson, *The Young Delinquent in his Social Setting*, London, 1952, Chs. 4, 6.

[103] Mary Woodward (*loc. cit.* at note 69), under 'Summary and Conclusions'.

[104] Hilda Weber (*loc. cit.* at note 69), p. 174.

[105] See, e.g., the Borstal case in my *Social Aspects of Crime*, p. 316, No. 102.

[106] See the case in Weber, *loc. cit.*, p. 177. She also presents several other cases to show the special importance of sympathetic handling for borderline defectives.

[107] See Berry in R. G. Gordon (ed.), *Survey of Child Psychiatry*, London, 1939, pp. 100 ff.

[108] Glover, *Roots of Crime*, p. 252.

[109] See Lewis M. Terman, *Psychological Approaches to the Biography of Genius*, London, 1947, p. 4, where he criticizes certain studies inspired by Galton as 'stereotyped along statistical lines'. See, moreover, Wolfgang in *Pioneers in Criminology*, p. 198, on Lombroso's *L'Uomo di genio* and W. Lange-Eichbaum, *The Problem of Genius*, translated from the German by Eden and Cedar Paul, London, 1931.

[110] *Op. cit.*, p. x.

[111] Ernst Kretschmer, *Textbook of Medical Psychology*, Eng. trans. by E. B. Strauss, London, 1934, p. 160.

[112] Ernst Kretschmer, *Psychology of Men of Genius*, trans. by R. B. Cattell, London, 1931, pp. 3 ff.

[113] *A Study of British Genius*, London, 1922.

[114] Burckhardt, *Kultur der Renaissance*, Vol. 2, Ch. 5. On Villon, see, e.g., Henry T. F. Rhodes, *Genius and Criminals*, London, 1932, pp. 65 ff. Rhodes's view that 'the genius and the criminal type are fundamentally one and the same thing' (p. 37) is clearly unjustified. Criminals, as a rule, are not creative, men of genius usually are.

[115] *The Young Delinquent*, p. 354.

[116] Leta S. Hollingworth, *Children above 180 I.Q.*, New York, 1942, pp. 254 ff.

[117] Martin Buber, *Between Man and Man*, Paperback ed., London, 1961, pp. 143 ff. (first published London, 1947).

[118] Gerald Abraham, *Tchaikovsky*, London 1944, p. 11.

## CHAPTER 16

[1] W. A. Bonger, *An Introduction to Criminology*, London, 1936, Ch. 8.

[2] See the titles given by Paul English in the *Handwörterbuch der Kriminologie*, Vol. 2, 1934, pp. 301 ff.

[3] London-Edinburgh-Glasgow.

[4] Driver in *Pioneers in Criminology*, p. 341.

[5] Article 'Kriminalpsychologie' in *Handwörterbuch der Kriminologie*, Vol. 1, p. 914.

[6] One of the most recent attempts in this field is David Abrahamsen, *The Psychology of Crime*, London-New York, 1961.

[7] See, e.g., Gerhard Ledig, *Philosophie der Strafe bei Dante und Dostojewski*, Weimar, 1935; Thomas Würtenberger, *Die deutsche Kriminalerzählung*, Erlangen, 1941, with bibliogr.; Hermann Mannheim, 'Rechtsgefühl und Dichtung', *Z.f. Rechtsphilosophie*, Vol. 3, 1920, pp. 251 ff.; on Victor Hugo: Paul Savey-Casard, 'Le Crime dans l'œuvre de Victor Hugo', *Études internationales de Psycho-Sociologie criminelle*, No. 3, Jan.-March, 1957, pp. 16-21; on Dickens: Philip Collins, *Dickens and Crime*, Cambridge Studies in Criminology, Vol. 17, 1962. On Dostoievsky see the literature quoted at the end of the Chapter.

[8] *Social Science and Social Pathology*, pp. 221 ff.

[9] Naturally, the term 'mental disease' and corresponding terms in other languages are commonly used in Criminal Codes, e.g., in § 51 of the German Criminal Code and §§ 24, 25 of the German Draft Code of 1960. This has been criticized, e.g., by the German psychologist Thomae on account of the impossibility of defining the concept of disease (*Krankheit*); see *Mschr. Kriminol, Strafrechtsreform*, August 1961, pp. 117 ff.

[10] Emile Durkheim, *Les règles de la methode sociologique*, 11th ed. Paris, 1950, p. viii and Chs. 3 and 4.

[11] *Op. cit.*, pp. 64 ff.

[12] *Op. cit.*, p. 75, fn. 1, and *Suicide* (Eng. trans., London, 1952), p. 363.

[13] See, however, the illuminating discussion by J. G. Peristiany in his Introduction to Durkheim's *Sociology and Philosophy*, London, 1953, pp. x, xvii ff.: 'The phenomena and the rate of their occurrence are healthy and normal when they reflect conditions of existence which are associated with the average society of this type'.

[14] Against this standard Norwood East, *Society and The Criminal*, p. 232.

[15] For Durkheim, see Peristiany, p. xx.

[16] Wootton, *op. cit.*, p. 218.

[17] The danger that social workers might too easily expect 'the whole process of

social adjustment to come from the client' has been mentioned in my lecture on 'The Unified Approach to the Administration of Criminal Justice', *Proc. Canad. Congress Correct., 1957*, p. 260.

[18] Ginsberg, *Essays in Sociology and Social Philosophy*, Vol. 1, p. 70 ff.

[19] Erich Fromm, *The Fear of Freedom*, London, 1942, p. 118.

[20] See also Emanuel Miller, *Brit. J. Delinq.*, Vol. 10, No. 3, Jan. 1960, p. 168, who refers to an 'operational standard of the normal person' and to Nietzsche's dictum 'What appears as health in one person might appear as contrary to health in another' (p. 165).

[21] Sir Maurice Craig and Thomas Beaton, *Psychological Medicine*, 4th ed., London, 1926, pp. 64–5. See also David Abrahamsen, *The Psychology of Crime*, New York, 1960, p. 209.

[22] *Unraveling Juvenile Delinquency*, p. 216.

[23] Daniel Glaser, in 'Crime and Correction', *Law and Contemporary Problems*, Vol. 23, No. 4, Autumn 1958, p. 687.

[24] On this see Arnold M. Rose, *Theory and Method in the Social Sciences*, 1954, Ch. 12.

[25] Karl F. Schuessler and Donald R. Cressey, 'Personality Characteristics of Criminals', *Amer. J. Sociol.*, Vol. 50, March 1950, pp. 476 ff.

[26] Wootton, *op. cit.*, p. 301.

[27] Marshall B. Clinard, *Sociology of Deviant Behavior*, New York, 1957, p. 206.

[28] Morris G. Caldwell, 'Personality Trends in the Youthful Male Offender', *J. crim. Law Criminol. Police Sci.*, Vol. 49, No. 5, Jan.-Feb. 1959, pp. 405 ff. with bibliog.

[29] Wootton, *op. cit.*, pp. 181, 196.

[30] Hathaway, Monachesi and Young, *J. crim. Law Criminol. Police Sci.*, Vol. 50, No. 5, Jan.-Feb. 1960, pp. 439–40.

[31] Clara Kanun and Elio D. Monachesi, in the same Journal, Vol. 50, No. 6, March-April 1960, pp. 525 ff.

[32] The L scale or score of the MMPI 'consists of a series of items indicating whether the subject falsified his score by consistently choosing responses which place him in a socially approved position', whereas big F scores 'may indicate that the subject was either careless in responding and/or did not comprehend the meaning of the items', Monachesi, *J. crim. Law Criminol. Police Sci.*, Vol. 41, No. 2, July-August 1950, p. 168.

[33] Starke R. Hathaway and Elio D. Monachesi (ed.) *Analysing and Predicting Juvenile Delinquency with the M M P I*, Minneapolis, 1953, p. 9.

[34] Walter C. Reckless in *Summ. Proc. Third Int. Congress Criminol.*, London, 1957, pp. 95–6; Marshall B. Clinard, *Sociology of Deviant Behavior*, pp. 206–7; Harrison G. Gough and Donald R. Peterson, *J. cons. Psychol.*, Vol. 16, April 1952, pp. 207 ff.

[35] H. J. Eysenck, *Sense and Nonsense in Psychology*, Ch. 5, esp. pp. 218 ff.

[36] Tadeusz Grygier, *Oppression*, London, 1954 (with extensive bibliog.).

[37] Grygier, *op. cit.*, pp. 48, 52 ff.

[38] *Ibid.*, p. 189, quoting H. A. Murray, *Thematic-Apperception Test Manual*, Cambridge, Mass., 1943.

[39] *Op. cit.*, p. 207.

[40] The term 'Press' (in T.A.T. literature) 'designates a directional tendency in an object ... or situation which is perceived as able to harm or benefit the subject', Grygier, pp. 79–80. It usually implies the existence of a hero, p. 81.

[41] See *Pioneers in Criminology*: Peter Scott, p. 152, on Maudsley, and Wolfgang, p. 187, on Lombroso.

42 *Unraveling Juvenile Delinquency*, Ch. 18 with Summary, p. 240.

43 *Ibid.*, Ch. 19 with Summary, p. 251.

44 *Ibid.*, pp. 221–2, 275.

45 *Physique and Delinquency*, New York, 1956, p. 269.

46 See, e.g., Grygier, *op. cit.*, pp. 12–13, on the one hand, and *Unraveling*, p. 275, on the other.

47 B. Marcus, 'A Dimensional Study of a Prison Population', *Brit. J. Crim.*, Vol. 1, No. 2, Oct. 1960, pp. 130 ff.

48 London, 1962.

49 See my review in the *Int. J. soc. Psychiat.*, Vol. 8, No. 4, Autumn 1962, pp. 309–11.

50 G. W. Allport, *Personality*, New York, 1937; see also D. R. Price-Williams, *Introductory Psychology*, London, 1958, p. 149.

51 H. J. Eysenck, *The Structure of Human Personality*, London–New York, 1953, p. 2.

52 Raymond Cattell, *An Introduction to Personality Study*, London, 1950, pp. 21, 222.

53 See in particular § 211 of the West German Penal Code as amended in 1941 where 'murderous lust, satisfaction of sexual lust, greed or other mean motives' are enumerated as criteria of murder (similarly § 135 of the West German Draft Code of 1960). In the English Homicide Act, 1957, certain motives such as the commission of theft or the avoidance of arrest are also mentioned as characteristics of capital murder.

54 Marvin E. Wolfgang, *Patterns of Homicide*, Ch. 10; H. von Hentig, *Zur Psychologie der Einzeldelikte*, Vol. 2: *Der Mord*, Tübingen, 1956, esp. Chs. 3, 5; Andreas Bjerre, *The Psychology of Murder*, Eng. trans., London, 1927; F. Tennyson Jesse, *Murder and its Motives*, London, 1924; Ernst Roesner, *Z. ges. Strafrechtwiss.*, Vol. 56, 1936, pp. 336 ff.; Norwood East, *Society and the Criminal*, 1949, Ch. 17; H. C. Brearley, *Homicide in the United States*, 1932; David Abrahamsen, *Crime and the Human Mind*, New York, 1944; Franco Ferracuti, 'La personalità dell'omicida', *Quad. Criminol. clin.*, Oct.-Dec. 1961 (with an excellent bibliog.), now also in English: 'The Psychology of the Criminal Homicide', *Rev. Jur. Univ. Puerto Rico*, Vol. 32, No. 4, 1963; also Wolf Middendorff, *Soziologie des Verbrechens*, Düsseldorf–Köln, 1959, pp. 165 ff.

55 See *Murder: A Home Office Research Unit Report*, H.M.S.O., London, 1961, pp. 23, 32 ff.; Terence Morris and Louis Blom-Cooper, 'Murder in Microcosm', the *Observer*, London, 1961, pp. 8 ff.; Royal Commission on Capital Punishment, 1953, p. 329.

56 Roesner, *op. cit.*, p. 339; Ernst Gennat, *Handwörterbuch der Kriminologie*, Vol. 2, p. 197; *Deutsche Kriminalstatistik für das Jahr 1931*, Berlin, 1934, p. 35.

57 From an unpublished London Ph.D. Thesis by Hassan El-Saaty, 'Juvenile Delinquency in Egypt', 1946, pp. 122–3.

58 On 'criminal motivation' see now Jackson Toby, *Brit. J. Crim.*, Vol. 2, No. 4, April 1962, pp. 317–36, and on motivation in general, R. S. Peters, *The Concept of Motivation*, London, 1960.

59 Donald Cressey, 'The Differential Association Theory and Compulsive Crimes', *J. crim. Law Criminol. Police Sci.*, Vol. 45, No. 1, May-June, 1954, pp. 29 ff. (now Ch. 6 of his *Crime, Delinquency and Differential Association*, The Hague, 1964).

60 Paperback ed., Harmondsworth, pp. 195–6, trans. by Dorothy Bussy.

61 *Rev. int. Criminol. Police tech.*, Vol. 11, No. 4, Oct.-Dec. 1957, pp. 246–54.

62 Norwood East, *Society and the Criminal*, pp. 273 ff., gives a few brief case

histories to illustrate this distinction. Ernst Seelig, *Schuld, Lüge, Sexualität*, Stuttgart, 1955, pp. 46 ff. and 86, presents a detailed critical analysis of the distinction, especially of its implications for problems of guilt and sentencing. He doubts whether it is generally true that crimes which are *'persönlichkeits-fremd'* deserve to be treated more leniently than those which are *'persönlichkeits-eigen'*.

[63] On this see in particular 'Le Problème de l'Etat dangereux', Deuxième Cours International de Criminologie organisé par la Société Internationale de Criminologie, Paris, 1953.

[64] See Jean Pinatel, *La Criminologie*, Paris, 1960, pp. 130 ff.

[65] Etienne de Greeff, *Introduction à la Criminologie*, Vol. 1, Bruxelles, 2nd ed. 1946, pp. 310 ff.; *Le Problème de L'Etat dangereux*, pp. 194 ff.

[66] On this distinction see, e.g., Irwin August Berg and Vernon Fox, *J. Soc. Psychol.* August 1947, pp. 109 ff.

[67] The case described by Robert M. Lindner, *Rebel without a Cause*, New York, 1944, p. 215, of the boy who wanted to kill his father, but as the latter was needed to support the family killed a stranger instead and was quite content, is probably exceptional, but this boy was a psychopath.

[68] Bruno M. Cormier, 'Psychodynamics of Homicide committed in a Marital Relationship', paper read at the Third World Congress of Psychiatry, Montreal, June 1961.

[69] J. L. Gillin, *The Wisconsin Prisoner*, Madison, 1946, p. 70, concludes from his American material that marital disharmony is a potential cause of murder only for persons whose emotional stability is greatly below the average.

[70] Andreas Bjerre, *The Psychology of Murder*, Ch. 2.

[71] See, e.g., Norwood East, *Society and the Criminal*, p. 275; v. Hentig, *Der Mord*, p. 211; Lenz, *Handwörterbuch der Kriminologie*, Vol. 2, p. 266. Glover's 'trigger impulse' has probably a similar meaning, see *Brit. J. Crim.*, Vol. 3, No. 1, July 1962, p. 68, fn. 4.

[72] See, e.g., the Case of Angerstein recounted by Paul Reiwald, *Society and its Criminals*, Eng. trans. by T. E. James, London, 1949, pp. 27 ff. The constant interplay between situation and personality is also stressed by Stephan Quensel, *Sozialpsychologische Aspekte der Kriminologie*, No. 1 of the new series '*Kriminologie. Abhandlungen über abwegiges Sozialverhalten'*, ed. by Thomas Würtenberger, Stuttgart, 1964, Ch. 5, who (p. 82) presents an interesting illustration from Jean Genet's *Notre Dame des Fleurs*.

[73] *The Times*, 4.6.1952.

[74] *Ibid.*, 9.1.1962.

[75] Introduction to Foulkes, *Psycho-Analysis and Crime* (cited below at Ch. 17, note 1), p. 3.

[76] Johannes Lange, *Lehrbuch der Psychiatrie*, Leipzig, 1936, p. 169.

[77] Introduction to *The Outsider*, Eng. ed. London, 1946, p. 10.

[78] Marc Ancel, *Law Quart. Rev.*, Vol. 73, Jan. 1957, pp. 36-47.

[79] Morris and Blom-Cooper, *loc. cit.*, p. 9.

[80] On the history of this problem see Veli Verkkö, *Homicides and Suicides in Finland*, Ch. 15.

[81] *Murder: A Home Office Research Unit Report*, p. 23.

[82] David Abrahamsen, *The Psychology of Crime*, New York, 1960, p. 200. On the Leopold-Loeb case see also Nathan Leopold's book, *Life plus 99 Years*, London, 1960, and the review by T. P. Morris in *Brit. J. Delinq.*, Vol. 9, No. 4, p. 303.

[83] Alexander and Staub (see below, Ch. 17, note 1), German ed., p. 104, with reference to Freud.

[84] The Royal Commission on Capital Punishment, 1953, recommended no

change in the present law according to which the survivor of a suicide pact is guilty of murder; Report, pp. 63, 275.

[85] Ernest Jones, *Essays in Applied Psycho-Analysis*, London, 1923, Chs. 2, 3.

[86] Report, p. 6.

[87] William McDougall, *An Introduction to Social Psychology*, 29th ed., London, 1948, pp. 435 ff.

[88] See *Social Behavior and Personality*, ed. by Edmund H. Volkart, New York, 1951, esp. Ch. 9.

[89] W. F. Roper, *Brit. J. Delinq.*, Vol. 1, No. 4, April 1951, pp. 243 ff., 265.

[90] Bjerre, *op. cit.*, pp. 4 ff.

[91] Roper, *loc. cit.*, Vol. 1, No. 1, p. 18.

[92] Edward Glover, *The Roots of Crime*, p. 8.

[93] See Wootton, *Social Science and Social Pathology*, pp. 159 ff., and her references.

[94] S. and E. Glueck, *Later Criminal Careers*, New York, 1937, pp. 120, 205.

[95] *Juvenile Delinquents Grown Up*, New York, 1940, p. 270.

[96] London, 1961.

[97] John Dollard *et al.*, *Frustration and Aggression*, New Haven, 1939, esp. Ch. 6. On the subject of aggression and crime, see also Leonard Berkowitz, *Aggression: A Social Psychological Analysis*, New York, 1962; Arnold Buss, *The Psychology of Aggression*, New York, 1961.

[98] Not only at present! H. V. Morton, *A Traveller in Rome*, London, 1957, p. 121, refers to the writings of the great Russian historian Rostovtzeff who early in this century mentions the 'disenchantment' which afflicts our civilization, the feeling that the future is not worth while.

[99] Brian Kay, 'Reactions to Experimentally Induced Frustration', *Brit. J. Delinq.*, Vol. 4, No. 4, April, 1954, pp. 245 ff. See also Maud A. Merrill, *Problems of Child Delinquency*, Boston–London, 1947, p. 188.

[100] Quoted from Margaret Kornitzer, *The Modern Woman and Herself*, London, 1932, p. 45.

[101] See Volkart (*op. cit.* at note 88), Ch. 8.

[102] Sigmund Freud, *Civilization and its Discontents*, London, 1939, p. 59.

[103] See my *War and Crime*, London, 1941, p. 56, and my article 'Rechtsgefühl und Dichtung' (cited at note 7), p. 279.

[104] Etienne de Greeff, *Introduction à la Criminologie*, Vol. 1, 2nd ed., Bruxelles, 1946, pp. 258 ff.

[105] On this see in particular Hans Kelsen, *Society and Nature*, London, 1946, Part I.

[106] This has again been confirmed by recent research such as T. P. and Pauline Morris' study of Pentonville.

[107] Edmond N. Cahn, *The Sense of Injustice*, New York, 1949, deals with the subject in another sense, especially with our feeling of sympathy with those who have suffered from actual injustice.

[108] See Volkart (*op. cit.* at note 88), pp. 5, 14.

[109] Donald Clemmer, *The Prison Community*, Boston, 1940, p. 147.

[110] *The Authoritarian Personality* by T. W. Adorno *et al.*, New York, 1940, Ch. 21.

[111] Gresham M. Sykes, *The Society of Captives*, Princeton, 1958, Ch. 5.

[112] On jealousy in the psychotic person see Ch. 14, II.

[113] See de Greeff (*op. cit.* at note 104), p. 267. On jealousy murders see also E. Seelig, *Kriminologie*, pp. 100–1.

[114] David Abrahamsen, *Crime and the Human Mind*, New York, 1944, pp. 162 ff.; the same, *The Psychology of Crime*, p. 197.

[115] André Gide, *Dostoevsky*, Eng. ed., London, 1949, pp. 111–12.

[116] McDougall (*op. cit.* at note 87), p. 120.

[117] Edward Glover, *The Roots of Crime*, p. 210.

[118] *War and Crime*, pp. 41 ff.

[119] Abrahamsen, *op. cit.*, p. 155.

[120] Colin Wilson, *The Outsider*, London, 1956, pp. 163 ff., 250.

[121] Edward Glover, *Psycho-Analysis*, pp. 87–8.

[122] Donald R. Cressey, *Other People's Money*, Glencoe, Ill., 1953, esp. Chs. 4. 5.

## CHAPTER 17

[1] *A Selection of basic publications on Psycho-Analysis and Crime*: August Aichhorn, *Wayward Youth*, revised Eng. ed., London, 1951; Franz Alexander and William Healy, *Roots of Crime*, New York, 1935; Franz Alexander and Hugo Staub, *Der Verbrecher und seine Richter*, Wien, 1929, Eng. trans., *The Criminal, The Judge and the Public*, New York, 1931; Franz Alexander, 'The Development of the Ego-Psychology', in Sandor Lorand, ed., *Psycho-Analysis Today*, London, 1948; J. C. Flugel, *Man, Morals and Society*, London, 1945 (also in a paperback ed.); S. H. Foulkes *Psycho-Analysis and Crime*, English Studies in Crim. Science, Cambridge, and *Canadian Bar Rev.*, Toronto, 1944; *Psycho-analysis and Social Science*, ed. by Hendrik M. Ruitenbeek, New York, 1962 (esp. chapters by Lasswell and Erikson); Sigmund Freud, 'Some Character-Types met with in Psycho-Analytical Work', *Collected Papers*, Vol. 4, pp. 318 ff., London, 1925 (first published in German in 1915). Freud's other contributions to the subject are too numerous and scattered to be mentioned here. A useful bibliography of his writings and of other publications on psycho-analysis can be found in the Appendix to Walter Hollitscher, *Sigmund Freud: An Introduction*, London, 1947. Kate Friedlander, *The Psycho-analytical Approach to Juvenile Delinquency*, London, 1947; Edward Glover, *Psycho-Analysis*, 2nd ed., London, 1949; the same, *The Roots of Crime*, London, 1960; William Healy, Augusta Bronner, and A. M. Bowers, *The Structure and Meaning of Psycho-Analysis*, New York, 1930; A. C. MacIntyre, *The Unconscious*, London, 1961; Paul Reiwald, *Society and its Criminals*, London, 1949; *Proc. Second Int. Congress Criminol.*, Vol. 3, Paris, 1952, pp. 133–92, contributions by various authors; *Searchlights on Delinquency*, dedicated to August Aichhorn, London, 1949. On the further development of Freud's theories see J. A. C. Brown, *Freud and the Post-Freudians*, Harmondsworth, 1961; Martin Birnbach, *Neo-Freudian Social Philosophy*, Stanford, California, 1961.

Critical of certain aspects of psycho-analytical theory Morris Ginsberg, *Essays in Sociology and Social Philosophy*, Vol. 1, Ch. 5, Vol. 2, pp. 24, 190. Critical also William Sheldon, *Varieties of Delinquent Youth*, New York, 1949, Ch. 6, pp. 854 ff.; H. J. Eysenck, *Uses and Abuses of Psychology*, Harmondsworth, 1953, Ch. 12.

Detailed psycho-analytical case histories of delinquents are given, e.g., by Ben Karpman, *Case Studies in the Psychopathology of Crime*, Washington, Vol. 1, 1935, Vol, 2, 1944; Hedwig Schwarz, 'Dorothy: The Psycho-Analysis of a Case of Stealing', *Brit. J. Delinq.*, Vol. 1, July 1950, pp. 29 ff.; Werner O. Lippmann, 'Psychoanalytic Study of a Thief', *Arch. crim. Psychodyn.*, Vol. 2, No. 4, 1957, pp. 782 ff.; Robert M. Lindner, *Rebel Without a Cause*; Frederic Wertham, *Dark Legend*; Bruno Bettelheim, *Truants from Life*, Part 5 (Harry); G. W. Elles, 'The Closed Circuit', *Brit. J. Crim.*, Vol. 2, No. 1, July 1961, pp. 23 ff.; Ethel Perry, *The Psycho-Analysis of a Delinquent*, ed. by Melitta Schmideberg and Marjorie E. Franklin, London, 1946; David Forsyth, *The Case of a Middle-aged Embezzler*,

I.S.T.D. Publication, London, 1938; Karl Abraham, *Geschichte eines Hochstaplers*, Imago, Vol. 10, 1924.
Most textbooks of criminology treat the subject of psycho-analysis very briefly or ignore it altogether. An exception is Clinard's *Sociology of Deviant Behavior*, pp. 125 ff., which of course deals not merely with criminology. See also the brief treatment by Vold, *Theoretical Criminology*, pp. 114 ff.
On the legal side see Helen Silving, 'Psychoanalysis and the Criminal Law', *J. crim. Law Criminol. Police Sci.*, Vol. 51, No. 1, May-June 1960.

[2] Hollitscher, *op. cit.*, pp. 9 ff.; MacIntyre, *op. cit.*

[3] Glover, *Roots of Crime*, p. 12.

[4] Flugel, *op. cit.*, Chs. 3, 6, 7.

[5] Ginsberg, *op. cit.*, Vol. 1, p. 58.

[6] Friedlander, *op. cit.*, pp. 31-2.

[7] Glover, *Psycho-Analysis*, p. 73.

[8] Flugel, *op. cit.*, p. 69.

[9] See, e.g., Glover, *op. cit.*, p. 35; Friedlander, *op. cit.*, pp. 17 ff.; Hollitscher, *op. cit.*, pp. 30 ff.; Brown, *op. cit.*, pp. 20 ff.

[10] Glover, *op. cit.*, p. 82; Friedlander, *op. cit.*, p. 33.

[11] Hollitscher, *op. cit.*, p. 35.

[12] Brown, *op. cit.*, p. 25.

[13] Gregory Zilboorg, art. 'Psychoanalysis and Criminology', in the *Encycl. of Criminol.*, New York, 1949, p. 403, complains that the Super-Ego has too often been confused with the conscience, but fails to make the difference clear.

[14] On all this, see Glover, *op. cit.*, pp. 36, 145; Friedlander, *op. cit.*, p. 42; Flugel, *op. cit.*, p. 106; Brown, *op. cit.*, p. 24; on the Oedipus complex and homosexuality, Glover, *Roots of Crime*, p. 222.

[15] Foulkes, *op. cit.*, p. 21.

[16] Glover, *Psycho-Analysis*, pp. 23, 27, 49; Friedlander, *op. cit.*, p. 48; Flugel, *op. cit.*, pp. 143 ff.

[17] Glover, *op. cit.*, p. 43.

[18] Glover, *Roots of Crime*, p. 13, and more detailed in *Psycho-Analysis*, p. 74. On the theory of symbolism see also Ernest Jones, *Papers on Psycho-Analysis*, 3rd ed., London, 1923, Ch. 8.

[19] Glover, *Psycho-Analysis*, p. 114.

[20] Brown, *op. cit.*, p. 108.

[21] Glover, *Freud or Jung*, London, 1950, p. 42.

[22] Flugel, *op. cit.*, pp. 111 ff., 164 ff., 209 ff.; Glover, *Psycho-Analysis*, pp. 80 ff.

[23] Flugel, *op. cit.*, Ch. 12, See also Reiwald, *op. cit.*, pp. 91 ff.

[24] Glover, *Roots of Crime*, p. 8.

[25] Martin Buber, *Between Man and Man*, London, 1947, Paperback ed. London, 1961, p. 103.

[26] See, e.g., Flugel, *op. cit.*, p. 192; Brown, *op. cit.*, pp. 11 ff., 130.

[27] Brown, *op. cit.*, p. 12.

[28] Friedlander, *op. cit.*, pp. 103-4.

[29] Glover, *Roots of Crime*, p. 133.

[30] Alexander and Staub, *op. cit.*, German ed. p. 25.

[31] Flugel, *op. cit.*, p. 113, and Brown, *op. cit.*, 109 ff.

[32] First published in German in 1912, Eng. translation, Harmondsworth, 1938, pp. 217 ff.

[33] 2nd German ed. 1923, in English 1922, Ch. 10.

[34] See, e.g., Ginsberg, *Essays in Sociology and Social Philosophy*, Vol. 1, p. 301.

[35] See Freud, *Totem and Taboo*, pp. 189 ff. On the incest taboo see also Talcott Parsons, *Brit. J. Sociol.*, Vol. 5, No. 2, June 1954, p. 101, and the references to the

literature in my *Criminal Justice and Social Reconstruction*, p. 77, fn. 2; also Brenda Seligman, *Brit. J. Psychol.*, Vol. 22, 1932, pp. 250 ff.

[36] Freud, *Totem and Taboo*, Paperback ed., pp. 189 ff., 35 ff., p. 116.

[37] See, e.g., Alexander and Staub, *op. cit.*, at the end of their Part I.

[38] Jones in Lorand, *op. cit.*, pp. 322–3. On the problem of guilt in general see now John G. McKenzie, *Guilt*, London, 1962.

[39] Flugel, *op. cit.*, p. 272.

[40] Franz Alexander, *The Medical Value of Psycho-Analysis*, London, 1932, p. 108.

[41] Flugel, *op. cit.*, pp. 151 ff. On the idea of retribution in Greek religion see Hans Kelsen, *Society and Nature*, London, 1946, Ch. 4.

[42] Repond in Heinrich Meng (ed.), *Die Prophylaxe des Verbrechens*, Basel, 1948, p. 4. See also above p. 402, note 65.

[43] Theodor Reik, *Strafbedürfnis und Geständniszwang*, Vienna, 1925; also *The Unknown Murderer*, London, 1936, and Reiwald, *op. cit.*, *passim*.

[44] David Abrahamsen, *The Psychology of Crime*, pp. 186–7, and earlier in his *Crime and the Human Mind*, p. 155.

[45] See, e.g., Sir John Maynard, *The Russian Peasant*, London, 1947, pp. 193, 267–70.

[46] The literature on sadism and masochism is very large; see, e.g., Flugel, Ch. 8; Glover, *Roots of Crime*, p. 180 and *passim*.

[47] Glover, *Roots of Crime*, Ch. 10.

[48] *Roots of Crime*, Ch. 5., Fitch, *Brit. J. Crim.*, Vol. 3, No. 1, July 1962 p. 29.

[49] *Civilization and its Discontents*, Eng. trans. London, 1939, pp. 105 ff.

[50] See, e.g., Maurice Cranston, *Sartre*, Edinburgh–London, 1962, pp. 17–18 50, 74.

[51] R. D. Laing, *The Divided Self*, London, 1961, pp. 131, 141, 171.

[52] See Jackson Toby, 'Criminal Motivation', *Brit. J. Crim.*, Vol. 2, No. 4, April 1962, p. 324.

[53] Emanuel Miller, *Brit. J. Delinq.*, Vol. 10, No. 3, Jan. 1960, p. 168.

[54] First published in German and English in 1914, Paperback ed. Harmondsworth, 1938.

[55] First published in German in 1917, Eng. ed., London, 1922.

[56] *Psychopathology of Every-day Life*, Paperback ed., p. 174. On these 'symptomatic acts' see also Glover, *Psycho-Analysis*, pp. 117 ff.

[57] See, e.g., *Psychopathology*, Paperback ed., pp. 102, 191, fn. 1.

[58] *Evening Standard*, 15.2.1962, p. 8.

[59] *Op. cit.*, German ed. p. 65. For another case of symbolic stealing see Hans Zullinger, *Brit. J. Delinq.*, Vol. 1, No. 3, Jan. 1951, pp. 198–204.

[60] *The Roots of Crime*, p. 14.

[61] David Abrahamsen, *Who are the Guilty?*, London, 1954, p. 174.

[62] *The Psycho-Analytical Study of the Family*, London, 1921, pp. 119–20.

[63] *Inside Europe*, London, p. 380.

[64] *Marxism: is it a Science?* London, 1941, p. 108.

[65] E.g., Glover, *Roots of Crime*, pp. 85 ff., 304.

[66] Bowlby in E. Durbin and C. Catlin, *War and Democracy*, London, 1938.

[67] See *Criminal Justice and Social Reconstruction*, pp. 109 ff.

[68] Ginsberg (*op. cit.* at note 1), Vol. 1, pp. 82–3.

[69] Melitta Schmideberg, *Short-Analytical Therapy in The Nervous Child*, ed. by Ernest Harms, 1950, and *Amer. J. Orthopsychiat.*, Vol. 23, No. 1, Jan. 1953, pp. 13 ff. See also Glover, *Roots of Crime*, pp. 52, 107, on the techniques applied at the Portman Clinic (I.S.T.D.), London.

[70] On Alfred Adler see Hertha Orgler, *Alfred Adler, The Man and his Work*, 3rd rev. ed., London, 1963; Brown, *op. cit.*, pp. 38–41; Flugel, *op. cit.*, pp. 45 ff., and *A Hundred Years of Psychology 1833–1933*, 2nd ed., London, 1951, pp. 294 ff.; Lewis Way, *Alfred Adler*; Erwin Wexberg, *Individual Psychology*, Eng. trans. by W. Beran Wolfe, London, 1929. Of the many books by Adler only the following can be mentioned: *What Life Should Mean to You*, London, 1932; *The Practice and Theory of Individual Psychology*, Eng. trans., by P. Radin, London, 1924; *Social Interest*, London, 1938.

[71] *What Life Should Mean to You*, pp. 201, 205–6.

[72] *The Psychological Treatment of Crime*, London, 1939, p. 13.

[73] Flugel, *A Hundred Years of Psychology*, Ch. 9.

[74] Fromm, *The Fear of Freedom*, p. 129.

[75] Most of Jung's works have been published in English translations in the International Library of Psychology, Psychiatry and Scientific Method, London, in addition to his *Psychological Types*, e.g., his *Contributions to Analytical Psychology*, 1928; *Modern Man in Search of a Soul*, 1933, Eng. trans. London, 1947 (Paperback ed. 1961); *Essays on Contemporary Events*, 1948. Books on Jung: Jolan Jacobi, *The Psychology of C. G. Jung*, London, 1942, trans. by K. W. Bash; Frieda Fordham, *An Introduction to Jung's Psychology* (Paperback ed.). Highly critical Edward Glover, *Freud or Jung*, London, 1950. See also Brown, *op. cit.*, pp. 42 ff.

[76] *Contributions*, p. 344.

[77] *Two Essays on Analytical Psychology*, London, 1928, p. 62.

[78] Brown, *op. cit.*, p. 49.

[79] *Modern Man in Search of a Soul*, p. 91.

[80] Eysenck, *Sense and Nonsense in Psychology*, Paperback ed., pp. 256–7.

[81] C. M. Franks, *Brit. J. Delinq.*, Vol. 6, No. 3, Jan. 1956, pp. 192 ff.

[82] Allen A. Bartholomew, *ibid.*, Vol. 10, No. 2, Oct. 1959, pp. 120 ff. Already before the War, a prison medical officer, Dr. H. T. P. Young, *J. ment. Sci.*, May 1937, pp. 268 ff., had made an assessment of the distribution of extraversion and introversion among a group of 1,000 young offenders aged 16 to 21 in Wormwood Scrubs Prison, with the result that 130 were classified as extraverts, 344 as introverts, whereas the remaining 526 had to be placed at some indefinite point between them. Young was aware of the fact that these two terms did not necessarily describe permanent states, but that conditions varied from time to time in the life of an individual.

[83] Alan Little, *Brit. J. Crim.*, Vol. 4, No. 2, Oct. 1963, pp. 152–63.

[84] H. J. Eysenck, *Crime and Personality*, London, 1964, p. 122.

[85] Quoted by Dr. J. A. Waycott, in the *Magistrate*, Nov. 1960, p. 128. On the Heath case see also Macdonald/Critchley, *Med. legal J.*, Vol. 26, I, 1958, 14–24.

[86] See, e.g., Gardner Lindzey, *Assessment of Human Motives*, New York, 1958; E. R. Hilgard in *Psychoanalysis as Science*, ed. by E. Pumpian-Mindlin; Gordon Trasler, *The Explanation of Criminality*, London, 1962, pp. 32 ff.

## CHAPTER 18

[1] From the vast literature only the following can be quoted here:

(a) *General*

Glanville Williams, *Criminal Law: The General Part*, 2nd ed., London, 1961, Ch. 10 (particularly detailed and valuable); *Report of the Royal Commission on Capital Punishment*, 1953, Chs. 4–6; Hermann Mannheim, 'The Criminal Law and Mentally Abnormal Offenders', *Brit. J. Crim.*, Vol. 1, No. 3, Jan. 1961, pp. 203 ff.

(Hague Congress lecture); Sheldon Glueck, *Mental Disorder and the Criminal Law*, Boston, 1925; the same, *Law and Psychiatry: Cold War or Entente Cordiale?*, Baltimore, 1962, and London, 1963; Jerome Hall, *Studies in Jurisprudence and Criminal Theory*, New York, 1958, Ch. 15; Philip Q. Roche, *The Criminal Mind*, New York, 1958; Henry Weihofen, *The Urge to Punish*, London, 1957; Barbara Wootton, *Crime and the Criminal Law*, London, 1963 (15th Hamlyn Lecture).

(b) *Historical*

Sir William Holdsworth, *History of English Law*, Vol. 3, 3rd ed., London, 1923, pp. 372 ff., Vol. 8, 1925, pp. 439 ff.; Sir James Fitzjames Stephen, *A History of the Criminal Law of England*, 3 vols., London, 1883. Very brief on the historical side the *Report of the Royal Commission on Capital Punishment*, 1953, p. 397.

(c) *Comparative*

American: *American Law Institute Tentative Draft Model Penal Code*, No. 4, Philadelphia, 1955; Jerome Hall, *op. cit.;* John Reid, *Yale Law J.*, Vol. 69, No. 3, Jan. 1960.

French: *Les délinquents anormaux mentaux. Ouvrage publié sous la direction de Georges Levasseur. Introduction comparative de Marc Ancel*, Paris, 1959.

German: H. H. Heldmann in *Materialien zur Strafrechtsreform*, Vol. 2, *Allgemeiner Teil*, Bonn, 1954, pp. 345–65; *Entwurf des Allgemeinen Teils eines Strafgesetzbuchs mit Begründung*, Bonn, 1958.

In general: H. Mannheim, *Group Problems*, Ch. 13; the same, *Brit. J. Crim.* (cited under (a) above); *Vergleichende Darstellung des Deutschen und Ausländischen Strafrechts*, Berlin, Allgemeiner Teil, 1908, Vol. I, pp. 1 ff. (Kahl), Vol. 5, pp. 1 ff. (v. Lilienthal).

[2] Modern criminal law does no longer 'virtually disregard the criminal', as Ben Karpman asserts, *J. crim. Law Criminol. Police Sci.*, Vol. 48, No. 2, July-August 1957, pp. 164 ff.

[3] H. Mannheim, *Criminal Justice*, pp. 202 ff.

[4] Francis A. Allen, *Ann. Amer. Acad. Polit. Soc. Sci.*, Vol. 339, Jan. 1962, p. 76.

[5] For the following see *Pioneers in Criminology*, Index under 'Free Will'.

[6] Sellin in *Pioneers*, p. 279.

[7] Hall, *op. cit.*, p. 271.

[8] Quoted from D. Stafford-Clark, *Psychiatry Today*, p. 289. Glover, *Freud or Jung*, p. 193, too, thinks that even if the amount of 'freed-will' is only marginal, 'it at any rate allows man the freedom to decide to continue the struggle'. See on Freud's psychic determinism Brown, *op. cit.*, pp. 3–4, and Ginsberg (*op. cit.*, at Ch. 17, note 68); on determinism in history Isaiah Berlin, *Historical Inevitability*, London, 1954; on the penological side of the problem Barbara Wootton, *Social Science and Social Pathology*, pp. 245 ff.

[9] On all this see my *Criminal Justice and Social Reconstruction* (Index under 'Experts') and *Group Problems*, pp. 298–9.

[10] On treatment tribunals see *Criminal Justice*, pp. 228 ff., also my *Dilemma of Penal Reform*, London, 1939, pp. 201 ff.

[11] B. J. F. Laubscher, *Sex, Custom and Psychopathology*, London, 1937, contains an excellent chapter on mental disorder among natives.

[12] London, 1946.

[13] See, e.g., Laubscher, *op. cit.*, p. 226.

[14] E. Adamson Hoebel, *The Law of Primitive Man*, Cambridge, Mass., 1954, pp. 237–8.

[15] Kenny-Turner, *Outlines of Criminal Law*, 16th ed., Cambridge, 1952, p. 68.

[16] Rudolf His, *Deutsches Strafrecht bis zur Carolina*, Berlin, 1928, p. 8.

[17] Kenny-Turner, *op. cit.*, p. 68.

[18] See Glanville Williams, *op. cit.*, p. 328; Weihofen, *op. cit.*, p. 175.

[19] On this case and the Rules see, e.g., Royal Commission, p. 79; Williams, *op. cit.*, p. 291; Kenny-Turner, *op. cit.*, p. 68; Roche, *op. cit.*, p. 90; Weihofen, *op. cit.*, Ch. 2; Mannheim, *op. cit.*, p. 209.

[20] On Australia see in particular Norval Morris in *Essays in Criminal Science*, ed. by Gerhard O. W. Mueller, London, 1961, Ch. 10; also, *Med. J. Austr.*, 8.3.1958; J. E. Hall Williams, *Brit. J. Delinq.*, Vol. 5, No. 1, July 1954, pp. 72 ff.

[21] The full text can be found in Appendix 8(a) of the *Report of the Royal Commission on Capital Punishment, 1953*, and in App. A of the *Report of the Committee on Insanity and Crime* (Lord Atkin Report), Cmd. 2005, 1924. Summaries are given by Kenny-Turner, *op. cit.*, p. 69, and Williams, *op. cit.*,

[22] *R. v. Windle*, [1952] 36 Cr. App. R. 85.

[23] *Stapleton v. The Queen*, [1952] 86 C.L.R. 358; Norval Morris, *op. cit.*, p. 283.

[24] *Report of Royal Commission*, p. 88.

[25] See Straffen case, [1952] 36 Crim. App. R. 132; *Report of Royal Commission*, pp. 84, 119, 265; Norval Morris (*op. cit.* at note 14), p. 279; *The Trial of John Thomas Straffen*, ed. by Letitia Fairfield and Eric P. Fullbrook, Notable British Trial Series, London, 1954; *Brit. J. Delinq.*, Vol. 5, No. 4, April 1955, pp. 303–9.

[26] On this see *Group Problems*, p. 297, and Glanville Williams, *Criminal Law*, §§ 102, 224–5, also his contribution to *Essays in Criminal Science*, pp. 348–50.

[27] That the question whether an impulse was 'irresistible' is not always unanswerable is shown by Karl Jaspers in the examples given in his *Allgemeine Psychopathologie*, 4th ed., Berlin–Heidelberg, 1946, p. 98. In one of his cases a schizophrenic (non-criminal) patient reports that one day he was suddenly seized with an overwhelming and to him inexplicable impulse to jump, fully clothed, into a river, and he became aware of the folly of his action only when he was already in the water.

[28] *Report of Royal Commission*, pp. 110, 276; Morris, *op. cit.*, p. 286–98; Mannheim, *op. cit.*, pp. 212–13.

[29] See my Hague lecture (cited at note 1(a)), p. 214.

[30] *Ibid.*, p. 215.

[31] *Ibid.*, p. 216.

[32] *Report of Royal Commission*, p. 157; Glanville Williams, *op. cit.*, General Part, sect. 92.

[33] *Minutes of Evidence*, p. 360, Q. 4388. On life in Broadmoor see C. H. Rolph, *New Statesman*, 24.2.1951.

[34] See on the Homicide Act Glanville Williams, *Howard J.*, Vol. 10, No. 4, 1961; J. E. Hall Williams, *Mod. Law Rev.*, July 1957, pp. 381 ff.; J. Ll. J. Edwards, *Brit. J. Delinq.*, Vol. 8, No. 1, July 1957, pp. 49 ff.; and more recently on diminished responsibility under the Homicide Act and the Mental Health Act, Edwards, *Essays in Criminal Science*, Ch. 11; Glanville Williams in *Medicine, Science and Law*, Vol. 1, No. 1, Oct. 1960; T. P. Morris and Louis Blom-Cooper, 'Murder in Microcosm', *Observer*, 1961, p. 11; W. Lindesay Neustatter, *Medico-Legal J.*, 1960, pp. 92 ff. See, e.g., the decision of the Judicial Committee of the Privy Council in Rose v. The Queen, *The Times*, 6.3.1961.

[35] T. P. Morris and L. Blom-Cooper, *op. cit.*, p. 11. On the practical results of sect. 4 see Max Grünhut, *Probation and Mental Treatment*, London, 1963.

[36] See *Prison Commissioners' Annual Report* for 1960, p. 75; and for 1962, pp. 59–60.

[37] A. W. Peterson, *Brit. J. Crim.*, Vol. 1, No. 4, April 1961, p. 315. The 'three primary tasks' of Grendon have now been described officially as being '(a) the

investigation and treatment of mental disorders generally recognised as responsive to treatment in suitable cases; (b) the investigation of offenders whose offences in themselves suggest mental morbidity; (c) and exploration of the problems of dealing with the psychopath' (*Report of the Commissioners of Prisons, 1962*, pp. 59–60). See also the paper by Dr H. K. Snell, Director of Prison Medical Services, in the *Medico-Legal J.*, Vol. 31, Part 4, 1963, pp. 175 ff., with discussion.

[38] Edwards, *op. cit.*, pp. 320–1; Glanville Williams, *op. cit.*, *General Part* 2nd ed., §§ 173–7.

[40] It has recently been suggested that this course could have been followed even under the present law: *Brit. J. Crim.*, Vol. 4, No. 4, April 1964, pp. 415–6.

[41] On the impact of the Act of 1959 on English criminal law see Edwards, *Essays*, pp. 327 ff.

[42] *The Times*, 31.10.1961.

[43] Glanville Williams, *op. cit.*, *General Part*, 2nd ed., § 152.

[44] On this case see G. W. Keeton, *Guilty but Insane*, London, 1961, Ch. 4; Rupert Furneaux, *Guenther Podola*, London, 1961; C. D. L. Clark, *Brit. J. Delinq.*, Vol. 10, No. 4, April 1960, pp. 302–4, and the full reports in *The Times*, 15, 16, 21.10.1959.

[45] Glanville Williams, *op. cit.*, §§ 178–83; my *Group Problems*, pp. 292–9; A. L. Goodhart, *The Listener*, 28.12.1961, mainly on the case *Attorney General for Northern Ireland v. Gallagher*, [1961] 3 W.L.R. 619.

[46] Edwards, *op. cit.*, pp. 323–4.

[47] *Group Problems*, pp. 292–3.

[48] See G. M. Scott in *Mental Abnormality and Crime*, p. 175; Williams, *op. cit.*, § 179; my *Social Aspects of Crime*, p. 184.

[49] See *Group Problems*, pp. 297–9. Williams, too, seems to favour this solution.

# Index of Subjects

*Note:* As many of the subjects listed here are further discussed in Vol. II, the complete Index for Vols. I and II, printed at the end of Vol. II, should also be consulted.

# Index of Names

See also Note to Subject Index (p. i)

For Product Safety Concerns and Information please contact our EU
representative  GPSR@taylorandfrancis.com
Taylor & Francis Verlag GmbH, Kaufingerstraße 24, 80331 München, Germany

www.ingramcontent.com/pod-product-compliance
Lightning Source LLC
Chambersburg PA
CBHW050556270326
41926CB00012B/2080